College
Reading and
Study Skills

College Reading and Study Skills

FIFTH EDITION

Kathleen T. McWhorter
Niagara County Community College

■ HarperCollins*Publishers*

Sponsoring Editor: Jane Kinney
Development Editor: Hope Rajala
Project Editor: Ellen MacElree
Assistant Art Director: Dorothy Bungert
Cover Design: Nadia Furlan-Lorbek
Cover Photo: Nadia Furlan-Lorbek
Production Administrator: Paula Keller
Compositor: Ruttle, Shaw & Wetherill, Inc.
Printer and Binder: Courier Kendallville, Inc.
Cover Printer: The Lehigh Press, Inc.

College Reading and Study Skills, **Fifth Edition**

Copyright © 1992 by Kathleen T. McWhorter

Library of Congress Cataloging-in-Publication Data

McWhorter, Kathleen T.
    College reading and study skills / Kathleen T. McWhorter. — 5th ed.
        p.   cm.
    Includes bibliographical references (p.   ) and index.
    ISBN 0-673-46442-3
    1. Reading (Higher education)   2. Study, Method of.   I. Title.
    LB2395.3.M386   1992
    428.4'071'1—dc20
                                                          91-19788
                                                          CIP

91 92 93 94 9 8 7 6 5 4 3 2 1

For Thomas, Brette, and Terrence

Contents

PART THREE
Understanding Content 119

22 Skimming and Scanning   401

Preface

Beginning college students require a foundation in reading and study skills that will enable them to handle college-level work. *College Reading and Study Skills,* fifth edition, presents the basic techniques for reading comprehension and efficiency, study, notetaking, written assignments and research papers, and taking exams. The reading and study skills I have chosen to present are those most vital to students' success in college. Each unit teaches skills that are immediately usable—all have clear and direct application to students' course work.

More than twenty-five years of teaching reading and study courses in two- and four-year colleges have demonstrated to me the need for a text that covers both reading and study skills and provides for both instruction and application. This book was written to meet those needs.

Reading and study skills are inseparable. A student must develop skill in each area in order to handle college work successfully. With this goal in mind, I have tried to provide complete coverage of both skills throughout and to show their relationship and interdependency. In doing so, my emphasis has been on direct instruction. My central aim is to teach reading and study through a "how-to" approach.

CONTENT OVERVIEW

The units of the text are interchangeable, enabling the instructor to adapt the material to a variety of instructional sequences:

> PART ONE provides an introduction to the college experience and presents skills, habits, and attitudes that contribute to college success. Topics include active learning, demands and expectations of college, time management, coping with stress, and organizational skills. This section also establishes the theoretical framework of the text by discussing the learning and memory processes and the principles on which many of the skills presented throughout the text are based.
>
> PART TWO encourages students to approach reading and learning as active processes involving planning and preparation, information processing, and evaluation and application. Students analyze their learning style and use knowledge about their style to select appropriate reading and learning strategies. Other topics include monitoring concentration, prereading and predicting, defining purposes for reading, and comprehension monitoring.
>
> PART THREE focuses on the development of comprehension skills. Sentence and paragraph structure are described and recognition of thought patterns introduced. Strategies for reading graphics and technical material are presented.

PART FOUR teaches skills that enable students to learn from text: how to underline and mark a textbook, how to organize a system of study for various academic disciplines, and how to organize information using outlining, summarizing, and mapping. Methods of learning through writing—paraphrasing, self-testing, and keeping a learning journal—are described.

PART FIVE helps students improve their ability to perform in the classroom by describing how to take notes in lectures, how to prepare for and take exams, how to participate in class activities and projects, and how to prepare written class assignments and research papers.

PART SIX focuses on improving vocabulary. Skills include contextual aids and structural analysis.

PART SEVEN discusses reading efficiency, reading flexibility, and skimming and scanning. The chapters emphasize the adjustment of rate to suit purpose, desired level of comprehension, and the nature of the material.

SPECIAL FEATURES

The following features enhance the text's effectiveness and directly contribute to student success:

☐ Each technique is explained in clear, direct language. Explanation of each new technique is followed by exercises illustrating the use of that technique and allowing the student to test its effectiveness. Exercises often quote excerpts from a wide range of college texts, providing realistic examples of college textbook reading.

☐ Two sample textbook chapters are included in the appendixes. Portions of the sample chapters are used throughout the book enabling the student to practice skills with actual textbook material. Other exercises require the student to apply each skill in his or her own course work. The sample textbook chapters described above provide an essential link, or intermediate step, between in-chapter practice and independent application of new techniques. These chapters were selected to be representative of college textbook reading assignments.

☐ The text approaches both reading and study as active processes in which the student assesses the task, selects appropriate strategies, monitors his or her performance, and takes any necessary actions to modify and improve it.

☐ Reading as a cognitive process is emphasized. Applying the findings from the research areas of metacognition and prose structure analysis, students are encouraged to approach reading as an active mental process of selecting, processing, and organizing information to be learned.

☐ The text emphasizes the necessity of adapting skills and techniques to suit the characteristics and requirements of specific academic disciplines, as well as accommodating the student's particular learning style.

☐ A partial Answer Key is included to make the text adaptable to self-instruction and to provide immediate feedback for students as they work through the practice exercises.

☐ An Instructor's Manual gives the instructor a detailed description of the text and specific suggestions for classroom use.

□ Chapter review quizzes, a complete answer key, and a set of overhead projection materials to enhance and supplement classroom instruction are contained in the Instructor's Manual.

□ Interactive computer software accompanies the text and provides the student with opportunities to apply specific strategies and receive immediate feedback on their success.

CHANGES IN THE FIFTH EDITION

The fifth edition of this text includes changes and additions that reflect current emphases and directions in research on adult learning processes.

The increasing diversity of the college population calls for a recognition and analysis of individual student learning characteristics. Chapter 4 introduces the concept of learning style and includes a Learning Style Questionnaire that enables the student to assess their relative strengths and weaknesses in five modalities: auditory-visual, applied-conceptual, spatial-verbal, social-independent, and creative-pragmatic. Students are shown how to improve their learning effectiveness by capitalizing on strengths and compensating for limitations. The section emphasizes that each student's learning style is unique and, consequently, each student must adapt reading and learning strategies to suit his or her particular learning characteristics.

Because students are confronted with more technical or specialized reading material than ever before, a new chapter on reading graphics and technical material has been added. It presents strategies for reading various types of graphics—tables, bar graphs, linear graphs, pie charts, organizational charts, flow charts, pictograms, diagrams, photographs, and maps. Characteristics of technical writing are discussed and strategies for reading and studying technical material are demonstated.

Writing as a means of learning, rather than a mode of communication, is a recent emphasis in college-adult learning. A new chapter section has been added that discusses writing as a means of facilitating learning. Three strategies are discussed: paraphrasing, writing and answering self-test questions, and keeping a learning journal. Students are encouraged to use writing to clarify difficult ideas, provoke thought, and sort, organize, and evaluate ideas and learning strategies.

Part Two of the text, "Strategies for Active Learning," was revised to include a three-stage metacognitive model of active reading and learning: planning and preparation, processing, and evaluation and application. Students are encouraged to activate prior knowledge, preread, make predictions, define their purposes, and select appropriate reading strategies prior to reading. As part of the processing stage, students are shown how to strengthen their comprehension, monitor that comprehension, select what to learn, and organize information. The final stage encourages students to assess the effectiveness of their learning, revise and modify, apply and integrate course content. This model emphasizes reading and learning as active processes in which the student interacts and reacts to the text and focuses on metacognitive strategies—the student's awareness of individual cognitive functioning.

The chapter on the SQ3R method, a classic reading-learning system that has been included in the text since its first edition, has been updated in light of recent research findings and to achieve consistency with the metacognitive model of reading and learning described above. The original SQ3R System is presented, then students are shown how to revise and modify the system to include additional strategies and to make it compatible with their own learning styles.

Other changes in the text include: (1) the addition of cognitive maps to describe each organizational pattern presented in Chapter 9, (2) expansion of the section on stress management to include a Stress Audit, (3) a new condensed section on textbook learning features, (4) new material on anticipating and making predictions about content and structure prior to and during reading, and (5) a new section on selecting reading and learning strategies by considering characteristics of the learner, text characteristics, instructor advice and expectations, and expected follow-up activities.

ACKNOWLEDGMENTS

In preparing this edition, I appreciate the excellent ideas, suggestions, and advice provided by my reviewers: Raymond DeLeon, California State (Long Beach); Susan Martin, University of South Florida; Jane Ochrymowycz, St. Mary's College—Winona, MN; Ilene Rutan, Brookdale Community College; Karen Spring, Edmonds Community College; Cathy Stafford, Grand Canyon University; Mary Ann Wissmueller, Milwaukee Area Technical College. I am particularly indebted to Hope Rajala, my developmental editor, for her patience, advice, and guidance, and to Jane Kinney for her support of this project.

K.T.M.

College
Reading and
Study Skills

PART ONE

Succeeding in College

Many students find their first few weeks in college a confusing and frustrating period. Even excellent students who achieved high grades in high school discover that college is a difficult and challenging experience.

Getting started in college may be difficult for you because it is a completely new situation. The physical surroundings are new and it is easy to feel lost. Many times, too, you don't have many friends with whom to share experiences and ask questions. Also, college classes are conducted differently from high school classes. Your professors may not act like high school teachers, and they may seem to expect different things from you. Finally, you find that you have not only a lot more work and responsibility, but also a lot more freedom. You find that the amount of reading, writing, and studying required is much greater than you expected, and you realize you have a lot of choices and decisions to make. You choose your own courses, your own time schedule, and even whether or not to attend class.

The purpose of Part One is to give you some tips on how to minimize the frustration and confusion that most students experience as they begin college. This part includes specific suggestions that will help you start your courses in an effective and organized way.

Each chapter discusses particular aspects of getting started in college. Chapter 1 offers many specific suggestions on how to approach college learning and study and how to get organized to become a successful student. You will also learn how to get information, how to become familiar with policies and procedures that affect you, how to get help with problems, how to take advantage of services available on campus, and how to manage stress. Chapter 2 is concerned with time efficiency and is designed to help you handle the extra demands of the heavy work load required in most of your courses. Chapter 3 identifies the ability to learn as the key to academic success, describes how learning occurs, and presents the basic principles of learning. It also explains how these principles are behind many of the techniques presented throughout this text.

1

How to Succeed

Use this chapter to:
1. *Learn what is expected of you in college.*
2. *Become an active learner.*
3. *Get off to the right start.*
4. *Learn about campus facilities and resources.*

To be successful in a new part-time job, you must learn quickly what the job involves and how to perform specific tasks. You are expected to be organized and to work effectively and efficiently. You must also become familiar with other personnel and with the facilities in which you will be working. You must learn where items are kept and how to get things done. Similarly, as you begin college, you must learn what is expected of you and how to accomplish it. College is a new experience, and to be successful you must learn what it involves and what is expected of you. Learning through reading and studying is your primary task, and you must learn to handle this task efficiently. It is also important that you get started in an organized manner, thereby making the learning easier and more effective. Finally, you must become familiar with the facilities and resources available on your campus.

COLLEGE: NEW DEMANDS AND EXPECTATIONS

College is a unique learning experience. Whether you have just completed high school or are returning to college with a variety of work experience or family responsibilities, you will face new demands and expectations in college. The following sections describe these demands and discuss how to cope with each.

Set Your Own Operating Rules

College is very different from your other educational experiences and from jobs you may have held because there are few clear limits, rules, or controls. There are no defined work hours. Except for scheduled classes, your time is your own. Often there are no penalties for missing classes or failing to complete assignments. You do what you want, when you want, if you want to at all. For many students, this new freedom requires some adjustment. Some students feel they should spend all their free time studying; others put off study or never quite find the right time for it.

One of the best ways to handle this freedom is to establish your own set of operating rules. For example, you might decide to attend all classes, regardless of whether attendance is taken. Here are other examples of rules successful students have set for themselves.

Study at least three hours each day or evening.
Start studying for a major examination at least a week before the exam.
Complete all homework assignments regardless of whether you get credit for them.
Make review a part of each study session.
Read all assigned chapters before the class in which they were discussed.

Write your rules on paper and post them above your desk as a constant reminder. Consider these as goals and work toward accomplishing each.

EXERCISE 1 _____

Directions: *Analyze the assignments and requirements of each of the courses you are taking this semester. Make a list of five to ten operating rules you intend to follow this term or semester. Include at least one rule that applies to each of your courses. Monitor the effectiveness of these rules during the next two weeks and make any needed changes.*

Make enough time for study.

_____

_____

Take Responsibility for Your Own Learning

In college, learning is mainly up to you. Instructors function as guides. They define and explain what is to be learned, but you do the learning. Class time is far shorter than in high school; time is often insufficient to provide numerous drills, practices, and reviews of factual course content. Instead, college class time is used primarily to introduce content that is to be learned and to discuss ideas. Instructors expect you to learn the material and to be prepared to discuss it in class. *When, where,* and *how* you learn are your decisions. This text will help you in making these decisions: Throughout you will be presented with numerous learning strategies and how to apply them.

Focus on Concepts: Each course you take will seem to have an endless amount of facts, statistics, dates, definitions, formulas, rules, and principles to learn. It is easy to become convinced that these are enough to learn and to become a robot learner—memorizing facts from texts and lectures, then recalling them on exams and quizzes. Actually, factual information is only a starting point, a base from which to approach the real content of a course. Most college instructors expect you to go beyond facts to analysis: to consider what the collection of facts and details *means.* Many students "can't see the forest for the trees"; they get caught up in specifics and fail to see the larger, more important concepts. Be sure to keep these questions in mind as you read and study:

Why do I need to know this?
Why is this important?
What principle or trend does this illustrate?
How can I use this information?
How does this fit with other course content?

Focus on Ideas, Not Right Answers: Through previous schooling, many students have come to expect their answers to be either right or wrong. They assume that learning is limited to a collection of facts and that their mastery of the course is measured by the number of right answers they have learned. When faced with an essay question such as the following, they become distraught:

Defend or criticize the arguments that are offered in favor of capital punishment. Refer to any readings that you have completed.

There is no one right answer: You can either defend the arguments or criticize them. The instructor who asks this question expects you to think and to provide a reasoned, logical, consistent response using information acquired through your reading. Here are a few more examples of questions for which there are no single correct answers.

Do animals think?
Would you be willing to reduce your standard of living by 15 percent if the United States could thereby eliminate poverty? Defend your response.
Imagine a society in which everyone has exactly the same income. You are the manager of an industrial plant. What plans, policies, or programs would you implement that would motivate your employees to work?

Evaluate New Ideas: Throughout college you will continually meet new ideas; you will agree with some and disagree with others. Don't make the mistake of accepting or rejecting a new idea, however, until you have really explored it and have considered its assumptions and implications. Ask questions such as:

What evidence is available in support of this idea?
What opposing evidence is available?
How does my personal experience relate to this idea?
What additional information do I need in order to make a decision?

BECOMING AN ACTIVE LEARNER

A freshman who had always thought of himself as a B student was getting low Cs and Ds in his business course. The instructor gave weekly quizzes; each was a practical problem to solve. Each week the student memorized his lecture notes and carefully reread each assigned chapter in his textbook. When he spoke with his instructor about his low grades, the instructor told him his study methods were not effective and that he needed to

TABLE 1-1   Characteristics of Passive and Active Learners

	Passive Learners	*Active Learners*
Class lectures	Write down what the instuctor says	Decide what is important to write down
Textbook assignments	Read	Read, think, ask questions, try to connect ideas
Studying	Reread	Make outlines and study sheets, predict exam questions, look for trends and patterns
Writing class assignments	Only follow the professor's instructions	Try to disover the significance of the assignment, look for the principles and concepts it illustrates
Writing term papers	Do only what is expected to get a good grade	Try to expand their knowledge and experience with a topic and connect it to the course objective or content

become more active and involved with the subject matter. Memorizing and rereading are passive, inactive approaches. Instead the instructor suggested that he think about content, ask questions, anticipate practical applications, solve potential problems, and draw connections between ideas.

Active Versus Passive Learning   *not way involvement*

active Participation

How did you learn to ride a bike, play racquetball, or change a tire? In each case you learned by doing, by active participation. College learning requires similar active involvement and participation. Active learning, then, is expected in most college courses and can often make the difference between earning barely average grades and top grades. Table 1-1 lists common college learning situations and shows the difference between active and passive learning.

The examples in Table 1-1 show that passive learners do not carry the learning process far enough. They do not go beyond what instructors tell them to do. They fail to think about, organize, and react to course content.

Throughout the remainder of this text you will learn strategies for becoming a more active learner and active reader. You will see that reading and learning is an ongoing decision-making process. You must analyze the task at hand, select appropriate reading and learning strategies, carry them out, and assess their effectiveness.

Active Learning Strategies

When you study, you should be thinking and reacting to the material in front of you. This is how you make it happen.

1. Ask questions about what you are reading. You will find that this helps to focus your attention and improve your concentration.
2. Discover the purpose behind assignments. Why might a sociology assignment require you to spend an hour at the monkey house of the local zoo, for example?
3. Try to see how each assignment fits with the rest of the course. For instance, why does a section titled "Amortization" belong in a business mathematics textbook chapter titled "Business and Consumer Loans"?
4. Relate what you are learning to what you already know from the course and from your background knowledge and personal experience. Connect a law in physics with how your car brakes work, for example.
5. Think of examples or situations in which you can apply the information.

EXERCISE 2 ———————————————

Directions: *Review each of the following learning situations. Answer each question by suggesting active learning approaches.*

1. Having a graded exam returned to you by your history professor. How could you use this as a learning device?

   How history reflect our living today.

2. Being assigned "Letter from Birmingham Jail" by Martin Luther King, Jr., for your English composition class. What questions would you try to answer as you read?

   How, where, when happen

3. Completing a biology lab. How would you prepare for it?

   write down all the term and study

4. Reading an article in *Newsweek* on crime in major U.S. cities assigned by your sociology instructor. How would you record important ideas?

   reason + result

GETTING STARTED

Many college students begin their first semester feeling rushed and confused. Being a successful student requires careful planning and organization. Here are some suggestions that will help make your first term or semester less hectic and get you off to a good start in college.

Attend Information and Orientation Sessions

If the college offers any orientation activities, such as campus tours, a get-acquainted-with-the-college workshop, or a back-to-school social event, try to attend. The activity will give you a chance to meet faculty and students and pick up useful information about the college.

Get Your Life Organized

Arrange your housing, transportation, finances, and part-time job schedule as soon as possible. Unless these are settled and organized, you will find it difficult to concentrate on your courses. Problems with any of these can disrupt your life and take valuable time to solve once you are involved with the semester.

Attend the First Class

Attending the first class of a course is crucial to surviving in that course. Attend it at all costs, even if you are late. Many students think that nothing is taught the first day. They may be correct in that the instructor does not present the first lecture, but they fail to realize that something much more important occurs. It is during the first meeting that the instructor introduces the course, discusses its organization, and explains requirements (tests, exams, papers).

Get to Know Someone in Each Class

During the first week, try to get to know someone in each of your classes. You will find it helpful to have someone to talk to, and you will feel you are part of the class. In case you miss a class, you will have someone from whom you can get the assignment and borrow notes. Also, this person may be able to explain ideas or assignments that are unclear, or you may be able to study with him or her.

Purchase Your Textbooks

As soon as possible after the instructor assigns the text, go to the bookstore and buy it. Do this even if you do not have an assignment to complete right away. Then you'll have the book and can begin an assignment as soon as it is given.

Get Materials for Each Course Organized

You should have a notebook for each class—either spiral bound or loose leaf. You will use it to take lecture notes and to record outlines or summary-study sheets you might prepare from the text or lecture. Be sure to keep the instructor's course outline, or syllabus, as well as the course assignment and/or requirements sheets in a place where you can readily refer to them. The syllabus is particularly useful because it specifies course objectives and provides an overall picture of the course. Also, date and organize day-to-day class handouts; these are important when studying and reviewing for an exam. Be sure to organize and date all of your class homework assignments and to keep returned quizzes, exams, and written assignments.

Organize an Assignment Notebook or Pocket Calendar

College instructors frequently give long-term assignments and announce dates for papers, assignments, and exams much in advance. They frequently do not feel it is their responsibility to remind students as the dates approach. Consequently, you will need to develop some system for keeping track of what assignments need to be done and when each is due.

Many students keep small notebooks in which they record all their assignments as they are given. If you keep one, you can see at a glance what particular assignments, tests, and quizzes are coming up. Crossing assignments off as they are completed will give you a sense of accomplishment and help you feel you are getting things done. Other students use a pocket calendar and record due dates in the appropriate date blocks. Most useful are the monthly calendars that display a full month on one page. These allow you to see upcoming due dates easily without flipping pages. Both assignment notebooks and pocket calendars will eliminate the problem many students experience—realizing at the last moment that an assignment is due and then frantically trying to meet the deadline.

Learn the Early Warning Signals of Academic Difficulty

Because some instructors give only two or three exams per semester, you cannot rely solely on exam grades to determine if you are doing well in each of your courses. Here are a few questions that will tell you whether you are on the right track in a course:

1. Are you getting behind on assignments?
2. Do you feel lost or confused about the course?
3. Have you missed several classes already?
4. Do you have to force yourself to go to class?

If you answer yes to one or more of these questions, you may be heading for academic difficulty. Take action as soon as possible by talking to your instructor to find out how you can catch up.

Get to Know Your Adviser

Most colleges assign each student an adviser to help the student plan his or her academic program. Your adviser can help you with more than just selecting courses and being certain you meet curriculum requirements for graduation. He or she can tell you whom to see to solve a particular problem, give you advice on how to handle certain courses, and provide a perspective on jobs within his or her field or refer you to someone who has more information. Many advisers consider it the student's responsibility to read the college catalog, so before you make an appointment with your adviser, be sure that you are familiar with the information the catalog contains.

Attend Classes Regularly

Instructors vary in their attendance policy. Some require regular attendance and penalize students who exceed a specified number of absences. Others do not have a specific limit on absences and leave it to students' discretion whether or not to attend class. You should not assume that regular attendance is not important just because an instructor does not require it. Classes provide new information, interpretation, and discussion of information presented in the text, as well as vital synthesis, review, and repetition necessary for learning. Studies have indicated that successful students attend class regularly, while unsuccessful students do not.

Get to Know Your Instructors

It is important for you and your instructors to get to know each other. You will find that your instructors are better able to help you if they know something about your background, your career goals, or your special difficulties with the course. You can get to know an instructor by stopping to ask a question after class or by talking with him or her during office hours.

Use Instructors' Office Hours

Each college instructor usually posts a list of several hours per week during which he or she will be available in his or her office to meet individually with students. It is usually not necessary to make an appointment to see an instructor during these times, but if you feel uncomfortable just walking in, you might mention to the instructor after class that you'd like to talk with him or her during office hours.

You can talk with the instructor during office hours about anything related to the course—how you are doing, trouble you are having with the course, difficulty you have encountered with a particular assignment—or to get further information or explanation about a topic.

Make Good Impressions

Based on how you act and react (how much you participate in class, how alert and interested you seem, how serious you are about learning), your instructors will form lasting impressions of you. They are naturally more willing to help a serious, conscientious student than one who seems not to care about learning.

Keep Up with Daily Assignments

Because many instructors do not check or require you to complete assignments as they are given, it is very easy to let things go and, as a result, have work accumulate as the semester progresses. There is danger in allowing work to pile up as the semester goes on; you may get so far behind that you'll become discouraged and will not want or be able to spend the time required to catch up. Many students drop or withdraw from a course for this exact reason. One excellent way to be sure you will keep up with your courses is to follow a study-time schedule. Developing this schedule is discussed in the next chapter of this part of the text.

Directions: *Read each of these situations and offer possible solutions to each problem.*

1. Because of an error in his class schedule, Sam missed the first class meeting of his criminal justice course. What should he do?

   talk to instructor after class

2. Suppose that you are confused about what is expected of you for a term-paper assignment given by your biology instructor. You decide to talk to your instructor but discover that you have other classes scheduled during each of his office hours. What should you do?

   discuss with him at the break time.

3. Suppose you are taking a course in sociology. The instructor assigns several textbook chapters each week and has recommended that you outline each chapter. She conducts class discussions on brief readings distributed in class that relate to chapter topics. Weekly quizzes and class assignments are given, evaluated, and returned to students. How would you organize these various course materials?

   set different time to study

4. Suppose your business management professor distributes study guides for each unit on which he lectures. There is no text—only his lectures and a book of readings on topics related to the lectures. He gives the class twenty essay questions before each exam and tells you that four will be on the test. How would you organize the materials and prepare for these exams?

LEARNING YOUR WAY AROUND

The expression *learning your way around,* means several things. First, it means learning the location of various buildings, offices, and classrooms on campus. Second, and most important, it means knowing where to go for things you need, what policies affect you, whom to talk to, and how and where to get information you need. Finally, it means being aware of what is going on around you—such as new courses being offered, a new sports team forming, a freshman class picnic on a Sunday afternoon, visiting lecturers on campus, and the schedule for free movies.

There is substantial evidence that students who are active and involved with the college scene around them are more likely to be successful than those who participate only by attending class and returning home. In order to get involved, however, you have to learn your way around. It is important to become familiar with the various offices, services, and student activities on campus. It is equally important to be fully familiar with the rules and policies that may affect you.

Information Sources

The college provides several sources of general information for all students. These are described below.

The College Catalog: The college catalog contains official information about your college, including its rules and policies and course and curriculum information. It explains which courses are required for the degree you seek and the amount and type of credit each course carries. The catalog also explains course numbering systems and indicates what courses must be taken before others (prerequisites). Important deadlines are also listed in the catalog. For example, most catalogs will indicate the last date on which you can withdraw from a course, when you must file for a pass/fail grade, and when to file for graduation. Catalogs usually explain how semester averages, often called grade or quality point averages, are computed and give the minimum averages required at various times during enrollment.

The Student Newspaper: Most colleges subsidize, or financially support, a student newspaper published at least weekly during the academic semester. In addition to feature articles about issues and events on campus, you will find notices of upcoming activities sponsored by various student groups, announcements about changes in college policies, and information on important dates and deadlines. The student paper is usually free. Pick up a copy each time it is issued and look through it.

Brochures and Pamphlets: Pick up and read brochures and pamphlets that you see. They provide a quick way of learning about some of the new and unusual groups or events on campus. Some offices that offer services to students—such as the counseling center, financial aid office, and learning labs—prepare and distribute brochures to make students aware of their services.

Bulletin Boards: On bulletin boards near or outside various department offices, you will find several types of important information. Last-minute information, such as room changes and class cancellations, may be posted. Department information, such as faculty office hours, course changes, and student adviser assignment lists, may also be up.

College Services/Offices

A large portion of every college's budget goes toward providing a variety of support services for students. Some of the most common student service offices are listed below, along with a brief description of what they offer. Try to locate each of these offices on your campus and become familiar with the specific services offered by each.

The Counseling and Testing Center: This office provides useful information and advice on establishing a major, choosing a career, and handling personal problems. If you are undecided about which degree or major to choose, you are not alone. About 60 to 70 percent of college students change their majors at least once. If you make a change, it is most important to make the change that is best for you, and the counseling center can often help you make this decision. Many centers also offer vocational testing that may help identify career areas that are suited to your interests. At community colleges, this office often provides information on and assistance with transferring to four-year colleges.

The Financial Aid Office: Because obtaining tuition assistance awards, loans, and scholarships is sometimes quite complicated, most colleges have a special office whose primary function is to help students receive all possible financial assistance. Smaller colleges sometimes designate one staff member in the counseling center to help with financial aid. In any case, find out who is responsible for financial aid at your college and visit that person's office. Do not be one of the many students who finds out too late, after the deadline for application, that he or she was eligible for some type of aid.

The Library: Most students think of the library only as a place where books are stored, but a library also offers many valuable services. The library may loan records or films; it often houses coin-operated photocopying machines; it may provide listening rooms, typing rooms, and study rooms. Many libraries operate an interlibrary loan system through which you can borrow books from other libraries.

The people who work in a library are perhaps more important than any particular thing that is kept there. While you may think of librarians as people who check out and shelve books, you will find that college librarians are valuable to talk to. They can help you locate information, suggest a focus and direction for approaching a topic, and help you organize your research. Even though librarians always look busy, do not hesitate to ask them questions. There is always at least one librarian, usually located in the reference area, whose primary responsibility is to assist students.

Visit the library, look around, and be ready to use it effectively when you get your first class assignment this semester. Take a tour, and obtain a copy of the library's floor plan if one is available.

Many libraries are now using computers to help users locate information more easily. For example, in some libraries the card catalog drawers have disappeared and have been replaced by computer terminals that you can draw information from about what books the library owns and where those books are located. The terminals are easy to use and produce information faster than a manual search. Many systems, too, can tell you whether a particular book is already checked out, saving you time in searching for a book that is not available. See Chapter 18 for a description of computerized data-base searches.

Now complete the "Do You Know Your Library Checklist" shown in Figure 1-1.

The Placement Office: Although you are not looking for a full-time job right now, it is wise to learn what services the placement office offers. (At small colleges this office may be part of the counseling center.) Placement offices maintain a listing of current full- and part-time job openings. Some placement offices also, upon request, establish a placement file containing a student's background information, transcripts, and references. While at the college a student can use this service to collect and organize job-related information. Later, when applying for a job, the student can request that his or her file be sent to potential employers.

The Student Health Office: Most colleges have some type of health clinic or office to help students who become ill or injured while on campus. Find out what particular services your clinic offers. Does it dispense medicines? Make referrals to area physicians? Offer free tests?

FIGURE 1-1   Do You Know Your Library? Checklist

Do you know . . .	Yes	No
1. the library's hours?	✓	
2. the procedure for checking out books and periodicals?	✓	
3. what is the usual loan period for books?	✓	
4. what fees are assessed for late books?	✓	
5. where the reference section is located?	✓	
6. how the card catalog system works or how to operate the computerized card catalog?	✓	
7. how books are arranged on the shelves?	✓	
8. where to find the reference librarian?	✓	
9. where the photocopy machine is located?		✓
10. how to request a book the library does not own through an interlibrary loan?	✓	
11. how to find out if the library owns a particular issue of a periodical?		✓
12. what types of nonprint materials (videotapes, film, microfilm, recording) the library owns?	✓	
13. the function of the reserve desk?		✓
14. what newspapers and popular magazines the library subscribes to?		✓
15. whether library orientation tours or workshops are available?		✓

The Computer Lab: Many colleges have a lab that provides student access to computers. Usually there is someone available to assist you in their operation. Many students find a computer's word-processing capability extremely helpful in writing papers.

The Reading-Learning Lab: Most colleges now have a center that offers students help with reading, learning, and studying for their college courses. While the services offered by learning labs vary greatly from college to college, check to see if the lab at your college offers tutorial services, self-instructional learning modules, or minicourses at any time during the semester. Some labs offer brushup courses in skills like spelling, punctuation, and usage; basic math computation (percentages, fractions, and so forth); and term-paper writing. Check to see if your college's lab offers anything that could help you become a more successful student.

The Student Center: This building or area houses many of the social and recreational services available to students. Snack bars, theaters, game rooms, lounges, and offices for student groups are often located there. The Student Center is a good place to meet people and to find out what is happening on campus.

The Registrar's (Student Records) Office: This office keeps records on courses you take as well as grades you receive and mails your grades to you at the end of each semester. These records keep track of when you graduate and what degree you receive.

The Bursar's (Student Accounts) Office: All financial records are kept by this office. The people who work there send tuition bills and collect tuition payments.

Department Offices: Each discipline or subject area usually has a department office that is located near the offices of the faculty members who are in that department. The department secretary works there, and the department chairperson's office is usually in the same location.

The Student Affairs Office: The Student Affairs (or Student Activities) Office plans and organizes extracurricular activities. This office can give you information on various athletic, social, and religious functions that are held on campus.

EXERCISE 4

Directions: *If you have learned your way around your campus, you should be able to answer the following questions:*

1. Beyond lending books, what services does your library offer? List as many other library services as you were able to discover. Also list the hours the library is open.

    Mon — Thurs 8:30AM — 9 PM, Fri 8:30 — 1PM

    film, typewriter, computer, Microfish

2. List at least five student activities (clubs, teams) that the college sponsors.

3. How would you request a transcript to be sent to an employer?

    request from Administration desk

4. Does the college allow you to take courses on a pass/fail or satisfactory/ unsatisfactory basis instead of receiving a letter grade? When and how may you elect to take this type of grade?

5. Where is the student health office located?

_____

6. How often is the student newspaper published? Where is it available?

_____

7. What is the last day that you can withdraw from a course this semester?

_____

8. Where would you go to change from one curriculum to another?

_____

9. What is meant by grade point or quality point average and how is it computed?

_____

10. Does the college offer any brushup courses in skills such as spelling, punctuation, or basic math computation?

_____

11. Does your department office have a bulletin board or other ways to communicate information to its students?

_____

12. What courses are required in your major or curriculum next semester?

_____

13. How many and what types of elective courses are you allowed to take?

_____

14. How would you get involved in student government?

_____

15. Where would you refer a friend who needs help with a drug or alcohol problem?

_____

MANAGING STRESS

College is a new and challenging experience, and new and challenging experiences tend to produce stress. Stress is a common problem for college students because college represents a dramatic change in life-style—socially, economically, or academically—and changes in life-style may affect you psychologically, emotionally, and even physically. Many college students feel pressure to perform well and earn good grades. This pressure also contributes to stress. Stress is often created by the inability to manage your time effectively. If you are unable to complete all your assignments or unable to meet important work or family obligations, it is natural to feel worried and upset. Finally, minor annoyances, often caused by living or functioning in a new and unfamiliar environment, produce stress. For example, the roommate or family member who is always playing a stereo when you want to study, or a group of people talking at the next table in the library, becomes upsetting.

Although limited amounts of stress keep us active and alert, too much stress is harmful and produces negative psychological and physical effects. Stress can also interfere with concentration and often affects academic performance. If you are worried about getting good grades, you may feel stressed when taking quizzes and exams and, as a result, may not score as well as you normally would.

Symptoms of Stress

Although individuals react to stress and pressure differently, some common symptoms are:

short-temperedness	listlessness
feeling rushed	headaches
difficulty concentrating	queasiness, indigestion
weight loss	worn-out feeling, fatigue

At other times stress manifests itself in irrational thinking; small problems are seen as overwhelming; minor annoyances are exaggerated into serious confrontations. A disagreement with a friend may become a major conflict or argument, or receiving an order of cold French fries from the snack bar may seem more important than it is.

Do a Stress Audit

Stress often builds gradually as the semester progresses. Consequently, some students do not realize when they are suffering from stress. Periodically, throughout the semester, do a stess audit, or assessment. Take a few minutes to analyze your life-style and how you are handling the new demands of college. Use the questions shown in Figure 1-2 as a guide. Add your own questions that reflect your priorities and commitments. For example, a single parent might add a question such as "I feel as if I'm not spending enough time with my children."

Complete the stress audit now, at the beginning of the semester or term, and record your score. Then around midterm time, complete the audit again. Complete the audit once again during or just before final exam week. If your score increases by more than 1 or 2 points, you'll know you are being affected by stress.

How to Reduce Stress

How you manage your life can reduce or prevent stress. Here are a few suggestions:

FIGURE 1-2　A Stress Audit

Directions: *Respond to each of the following statements by answering yes, no, or sometimes.*	Yes	No	Some-times
1. I seldom get 6 to 8 hours of sleep.	✓		
2. I am having difficulty staying in contact with friends and family.			✓
3. I feel as if I don't have enough time in a week to get everything done.			✓
4. Having at least one healthy meal per day at which I can sit down and relax is unusual.	✓		
5. I seldom find time to do some things for fun each week.		✓	
6. I worry about money regularly.		✓	
7. Smoking or use of alcohol has begun or increased recently.		✓	
8. I have more conflicts and disagreements with friends than I used to.		✓	
9. I am staying involved with social or religious activities.	✓		
10. I am losing or gaining weight.		✓	
11. My usual level of physical activity or exercise has decreased.		✓	
12. I seldom find time to confide in friends.		✓	
13. My course work seems more demanding.		✓	
14. I resent the time I have to spend with routine chores.		✓	
15. I find myself confused or listless more than usual.		✓	
16. I seem to get colds and other minor illnesses (headaches, upset stomachs) more frequently.		✓	
17. I have difficulty concentrating on my assignments.			✓
18. I spend time worrying about grades.		✓	
19. I am more short-tempered or more impatient than I used to be.		✓	
20. I find myself unable to meet deadlines and am losing track of details (appointments, chores, promises to friends, etc.)		✓	

Scoring: Give yourself one point for each "Yes" answer.

Score #1 ___3___ Date _____

Score #2 _____ Date _____

Score #3 _____ Date _____

Manage Your Time Effectively: Time management can significantly reduce stress by allowing you to feel in control and certain that you will have time to accomplish necessary tasks. Refer to Chapter 2 for specific time management strategies.

Eliminate Stressors: Once you've identified a source of stress, eliminate it if possible. If, for instance, a part-time job is stressful, quit it or find another that is less stressful. If a roommate is causing stress, attempt to rearrange your living conditions. If a math course is creating stress, take action: go to the learning lab or math lab for assistance or inquire about tutoring.

Accentuate Your Accomplishments: When you feel pressured, stop and review what you have already accomplished that day and that week. This review will give you confidence that you can handle the work load. A positive attitude goes a long way in overcoming stress.

Get Involved with Campus Activities: Some students become so involved with their course work that they do little else but study or worry about studying. In fact, they feel guilty or stressed when they are not studying. Be sure to allow some time in each day to relax and have fun. Campus activities provide a valuable means of releasing tension and taking your mind off your work.

Avoid Simultaneous Life Changes: College is a major change in lifestyle and is stressful in itself. Therefore, try to avoid additional major changes, such as marriage, initiating a conflict about religion with parents, or starting a new job.

Establish a Daily Routine: To eliminate daily hassles and make daily tasks as simple as possible, establish a daily routine. A routine eliminates the need to make numerous daily small decisions, thereby giving you a sense of "smooth sailing."

Seek Knowledgeable Advice: If stress becomes an insurmountable problem, seek assistance from the student counseling center. The office may offer workshops in stress reduction techniques such as relaxation or biofeedback training.

Get Physical Exercise: Exercise often releases tension, promotes a general feeling of wellness, and improves self-concept. Many students report that as little as 30 minutes of exercise produces immediate relaxation and helps them to place daily events into perspective.

Eat Nutritious Meals: Strength and endurance are affected by diet. When you feel rushed, eating available snacks rather than taking time to buy or prepare lunch or dinner or going to the dining hall may be tempting. Consuming large amounts of snack food may produce fluctuations in your blood sugar level, which can cause headaches or queasiness. During rushed, stressful times, such as exam days, nutritious food can help you keep calm and think more clearly. In general, try to eat fruits, vegetables, and protein; avoid refined sugar, large amounts of caffeine, and high-calorie, low-nutrient snacks.

Get Adequate Amounts of Sleep: Sleep allows the body time to replenish energy and recover from the daily demands placed on it. The amount of sleep one needs is highly individual. Discover how much you need by noticing patterns. For several weeks, analyze how well your day went and consider how much sleep you had the night before. Soon you will recognize patterns: you may notice irritability or "bad" days when you are short on sleep, or you might find you have caught a cold after a hectic weekend with little sleep. Try to respond to body signals rather than let work load or the expectations of others control your schedule.

EXERCISE 5

Directions: *Analyze the following situations and answer the questions that follow.*

A student living in a dorm goes home for holidays and end-of-quarter breaks. Before each holiday or term end, she rushes to finish papers, catch up on reading, and study for exams or finals. She studies late each evening and pays little attention to her health. Each time she arrives home, she gets sick—once she had a severe cold, another time stomach flu, another time an ear infection. Her parents blamed dorm life, thinking she caught illnesses from other students.

1. How can you explain this student's pattern of illness?

   eating disorder

2. Have you observed or experienced similar reactions to stress?

   _____

3. What would you suggest she do to overcome this pattern? Offer specific suggestions.

   more control + regular exercise + eating

SUMMARY

College is a new experience. To be successful you must learn what is expected of you and how to approach new learning and study demands. This chapter presented numerous practical suggestions for achieving success in college. You must set your own operating rules, take responsibility for your own learning, and focus on and evaluate ideas. Active learning is essential; you must become actively involved with reading assignments, lectures, and class activities. Getting the right start in college is important. You should get to know other students, your instructor, and your advisor and get organized for each of your courses. As a new student you should learn your way around campus and become familiar with the services the college offers and the activities it sponsors. Identify information sources and the services your college offers.

Stress can affect academic performance. Symptoms of stress include fatigue, short-temperedness, listlessness, indigestion, and irrational thinking. Stress can be reduced by exercising, eating nutritious meals, getting enough sleep, managing time, eliminating stressors, emphasizing accomplishments, avoiding life changes, maintaining a routine, and, if necessary, seeking advice or counseling.

2

Organizing Your Time

Use this chapter to:

1. *Analyze how you currently spend your time.*
2. *Find out how much time is needed for reading and study.*
3. *Learn how to manage your time more effectively.*

Managing your time is a skill that directly affects your success in college. It also determines whether college becomes a nightmare of pressures, deadlines, and overdue assignments or an enjoyable experience in which you work hard and also have fun and take advantage of the social life it offers. Let's look at how a few students are handling the heavy work load of college courses.

John is at a ball game with Susan. They both have difficult majors and have exams and papers due that week. They are enjoying the game and are not even thinking about their studies.

Sam and Pat are also at the ball game, but they are not having as much fun. Sam has an exam on Monday and Pat has a term paper due soon. Sam feels guilty that he's taking time away from studying, and Pat finds that she keeps thinking about her paper. Because both are worrying about something, neither is much fun to be with.

What is the difference between the two couples? Why are John and Susan having a good time despite the pressures of their studies, while Sam and Pat are not? The answer lies in how each has managed his or her time. John and Susan are keeping up with their work and can afford the "time off" from study to go to the game. Also, they have set aside sufficient time for study and know they will get their work done. Sam and Pat, on the other hand, have not organized their time. They haven't reserved specific times for study and do not plan ahead in getting their assignments done. They often find themselves short on time with work piling up. As a result, they feel guilty about time used for anything but study. Even when they are not studying, they are thinking or worrying about studying.

Throughout this chapter you will learn how to manage your time effectively so you can avoid these problems and get the most out of college both academically and socially.

ESTABLISHING YOUR PRIORITIES

One of the first steps in getting organized and succeeding in college is to set your priorities—to decide what is and is not important to you. For most college students, finding enough time to do everything they *should* do and everything they *want* to do is nearly impossible. They face a series of conflicts over the use of their time and are forced to choose between a variety of activities. Here are a few examples:

Want to: *Should do:*

1.   Watch late movie   *vs.*   get good night's sleep
2.   Go to hockey game   *vs.*   work on term paper
3.   Go out with friends *vs.*   finish psychology reading assignment

These day-to-day choices can be frustrating and use up valuable time as you weigh the alternatives and make decisions. Often, these choices can be narrowed down to wanting to take part in an enjoyable activity while knowing you should be studying, reading, or writing a paper. At other times, it may be a conflict between two things you need to do, one for your studies, another for something else important in your life.

One of the best ways to handle these frequent conflicts is to identify your priorities. Ask yourself, What is most important to me? What activities can I afford to give up? What is least important to me when I am pressured for time? For many students, studying is their first priority. For others with family responsibilities, caring for a child is their first priority with attending college next in importance.

By clearly establishing and following your priorities, you will find that much worry and guilt are eliminated. Instead, you'll feel that you are on target, working steadily toward the goals you have established.

EXERCISE 1 ────────────────

Directions: *Consider your plans for the next several days. List as many "want to" activities as you can with their corresponding "should do" activities.*

Make apt with place study

check on the library

ANALYZING YOUR TIME

Once you've established your priorities, the next step in managing your time is relatively easy. This step—analyzing and planning your time—will enable you to reserve time for both leisure activities and college course work. You can reserve enough time to study for an exam in psychology, time for library research, and time for reading biology assignments. To do this, you must determine how much time is available and then decide how you will use it.

Let's begin by making some rough estimates. First, estimate the number of reading and study hours you need per week. For each course that you are taking, estimate how many hours per week you would need to spend, outside of class time, in order to get the grade you want to earn. Be honest; indicate what grade you can realistically achieve. When estimating time, consider how much time you need to study, how many assignments there are, how fast you normally read, and how difficult the subject is for you. As a general rule of thumb, many instructors expect you to spend two hours of preparation, study, or review for each hour spent in class. This figure, however, is just an estimate; some students will need to spend more time, while others can spend less. Once you are well into each of your courses and begin to see how you are doing, you can modify your estimates on the chart in Figure 2-1. When you are finished, add up the hours and fill in the total.

Now, let's see if you have enough time available each week to earn the grades you indicated on the chart. To find out, analyze your actual time commitments. Fill in Figure 2-2, estimating the time you need for each activity. Remember to indicate how much time each actually takes. Do not indicate an hour for lunch if you usually take only ten or fifteen minutes for a quick sandwich. When you have completed the chart, total the hours per week to discover your actual weekly time commitment.

Now that you know your total committed time per week, it is easy to see how much time you have left to divide between, on the one hand, reading, and study for your courses and leisure activities on the other. Each week has 168 hours. Just copy your committed time from Figure 2-2 and subtract:

$$
\begin{array}{r}
168 \text{ hours in one week} \\
- \underline{} \text{ total committed time} \\
\hline
\underline{} \text{ hours available}
\end{array}
$$

Name of Course	Desired Grade	Hours per Week Needed

Total Hours _____

FIGURE 2-1   Estimated Study Time Per Course

	Hours per Day	Hours per Week
Sleep	7 hrs	49
Breakfast	½ hrs	.35
Lunch	1 hrs	7.0
Dinner	1.5	10.5
Part- or full-time job	50.0	50.0
Time spent in classes	3.15	3.15
Transportation time	2	20
Personal care (dressing, shaving, etc.)	2	2.0
Household/family responsibilities (cooking dinner, driving mother to work, etc.)	14	140

Total committed time per week _____

FIGURE 2-2   Weekly Time Commitment

Are you surprised to see how many hours per week you have left? Look back to Figure 2-1 and see how many hours you estimated you needed to earn a particular grade in each course and write the hours on the first blank. Now answer this question: Do you have enough time available for reading and study to achieve the grades you want?

Estimated hours needed for grades _____ hours
Actual study hours available _____ hours

If your answer to the question was no, one of two things is probably true. Either you were unrealistic in your estimate of committed time, or you really are committed to such a point that it is unrealistic to take as many courses as you are taking and aim toward the grades you indicated. There are several alternatives to consider if your time is overcommitted. Can any activity be dropped or done in less time? Can you reduce the number of hours you work, or can another family member split some time-consuming responsibilities with you? If you are unable to reduce your committed time, consider taking fewer college courses or adjusting your expected grades to more achievable levels.

If your answer to the question was yes, you are ready to begin to develop a schedule that will help you use your available time more effectively. You are probably concerned at this point, however, that the above time analysis did not take into account social and leisure activities. That omission was deliberate up to this point.

While leisure time is essential to everyone's well-being, it should not take precedence over college course work. Most students who develop and follow a time schedule for accomplishing their course work are able to devote reasonable amounts of time to leisure and social activities. They also find time to become involved with campus groups and activities—an important aspect of college life.

BUILDING YOUR TIME SCHEDULE

A study-time schedule is a weekly plan of when and what you will study. It identifies specific times for studying particular subjects as well as times for writing papers, conducting library research, and completing homework assignments for each course.

The major purpose in developing a study-time schedule is to allow you to decide in advance how you will divide your available time between study and leisure activities. A schedule will eliminate the need to make frustrating last-minute choices between "should" and "want to" activities.

The sample study-time schedule in Figure 2-3 was developed by a freshman student. Read it carefully.

Your Own Schedule

Now that you have seen a sample schedule, you can begin to build your own schedule. Fill in the blank schedule shown in Figure 2-4, following steps 1–7:

1. Write *class* in all the time blocks that you spend attending class and labs.
2. If you have a part-time job, write *work* in the appropriate time blocks.
3. Write *trans.* in those portions of the time blocks in which you travel around or to and from campus and to and from work.
4. Block off with an X realistic amounts of time for breakfast, lunch, and dinner.
5. Also block off and write P in blocks of time committed to personal, family, and household responsibilities.
6. Block out reasonable amounts of time, especially on weekends, for having fun and relaxing. For example, mark off the time when your favorite television show is on or for going to see a movie.
7. Include any appointments, such as with the doctor or dentist or for a haircut.

The empty time blocks are those available for study and for leisure activities. Look through the following hints before you attempt to decide which subject you will study at what time.

1. Study difficult subjects first. It is tempting to get easy things and short assignments out of the way beforehand, but do not give in to this approach. When you start studying, your mind is fresh and alert and you are at your peak of concentration. This is the time you are best equipped to handle difficult subjects. Thinking through complicated problems or studying complex ideas requires all the brain power you have, and you have most at the beginning of a study session.
2. Leave the routine and more mechanical tasks for last. Activities like recopying papers or alphabetizing a bibliography for a research paper do not require a high degree of concentration and can be left until you are tired.
3. Schedule study for a particular course close to the time when you attend class; that is, plan to study the evening before the class meets or at a time after the class meeting. If a class meets on Tuesday morning, plan to study Monday evening, or Tuesday afternoon or evening. If you place

	Monday	Tuesday	Wednesday	Thursday	Friday	Saturday	Sunday
7:00							
8:00							
	TRANSPORTATION TIME						
9:00	History class	Psychology class	History class	Psychology class	History class		
10:00	review History notes; read assignment	study	review History notes; read assignment	TRANSPORTATION	review History notes	type Chemistry Lab report	revise English paper
11:00	Math class	Psychology	Math class	study Psychology	Math class	(other typing)	review history assignment
12:00	LUNCH / Math	LUNCH	English Composition	LUNCH	English Composition		
1:00	Math homework	review lab procedures	class	Math homework	class	draft English paper	
2:00	Chemistry class		Chemistry class / LUNCH	read Chemistry	Chemistry class / LUNCH	read Psychology chapter	Math homework
3:00	TRANSPORTATION	Chemistry Lab	TRANSPORTATION		TRANSPORTATION		read and study Chemistry
4:00						review Psychology notes	study Chemistry
5:00	DINNER	TRANSPORTATION / DINNER	DINNER	DINNER	DINNER		
6:00	WORK	write lab report, start reading new Chemistry chapter; type	WORK	read English assignment	WORK		plan next week's study
7:00							
8:00		English Composition		revise returned Composition			
9:00							
10:00							
11:00							

FIGURE 2-3 Example of a Study-Time Schedule

study time and class time close together, it will be easier to relate class lectures and discussions to what you are reading and studying.

4. Build into your schedule a short break before you begin studying each new subject. Your mind needs time to refocus—to switch from one set of facts, problems, and issues to another.

5. Short breaks should also be included when you are working on just one assignment for a long period of time. A 10-minute break after 50–60 minutes of study is reasonable.

6. When reading or studying a particular subject, try to schedule two or three short, separate blocks of time for that course rather than one long, continuous block. As will be explained in the next chapter on principles

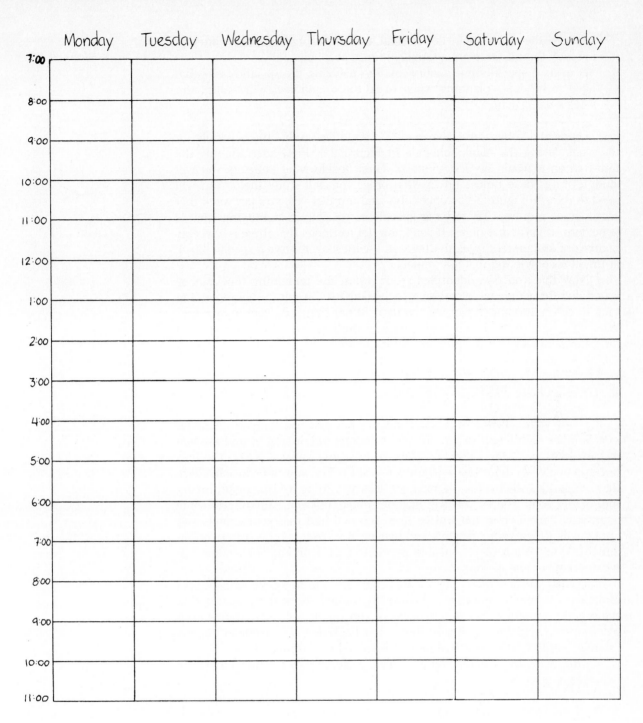

	Monday	Tuesday	Wednesday	Thursday	Friday	Saturday	Sunday
7:00							
8:00							
9:00							
10:00							
11:00							
12:00							
1:00							
2:00							
3:00							
4:00							
5:00							
6:00							
7:00							
8:00							
9:00							
10:00							
11:00							

FIGURE 2-4   Study-Time Schedule

of learning, you are able to learn more by spacing or spreading out your study time than you are by completing it in one sitting.

7. Schedule study sessions at times when you know you are usually alert and feel like studying. Do not schedule a study time early on Saturday morning if you are a person who does not really wake up until noon, and try not to schedule study time late in the evening if you are usually tired by that time.

8. Plan to study at times when your physical surroundings are conducive to

study. If the dinner hour is a rushed and confusing time, don't attempt to study then if there are alternative times available.

9. Set aside a specific time each week for analyzing the specific tasks that need to be done, planning when to do them, and reviewing your prior week's performance.

Using the suggestions above, plan a tentative study-time schedule for the week, using the blank schedule in Figure 2-4. First, identify only the times when it would be best to study. Then decide what subjects you will study during these times and in what order you will study them. You will need to refer to Figure 2-1 to check the total number of hours per week that each course requires. Try to be as specific as possible in identifying what is to be done at particular times. If you know, for example, that there is a weekly homework assignment in math due each Wednesday, reserve a specific block of time for completing that assignment.

Now that you have identified study times, the remaining time can be scheduled for additional leisure and social activities. Analyze this remaining time to determine how it can best be used. What things do you enjoy most? What things do you do just because you have nothing else to do? Plan specific times for activities that are most important to you.

USING YOUR TIME SCHEDULE

Using your schedule will be a challenge because it will mean saying no in a number of different situations. When friends call or stop by and ask you to join them at a time when you planned to study, you will have to refuse, but you could let them know when you will be free and offer to join them then. When a friend or family member asks you to do a favor—like driving him or her somewhere—you will have to refuse, but you can suggest some alternative times when you will be free. You will find that your friends and family will accept your restraints and may even respect you for being conscientious. Don't you respect someone who gets a lot done and is successful in whatever he or she attempts?

Try out the schedule that you have built for one week. Be realistic and make adjustments where they are obviously needed. Mark these changes on the schedule itself. Do not stop to decide if you should follow or change each block on the schedule. Doing so forces you back into the "want to" versus "should" conflict that the schedule was designed to eliminate.

After using the schedule for one week, evaluate it by asking yourself the following questions:

1. Did you over- or underestimate the amount of time you needed for each course? (The time will vary, of course, from week to week, so be sure to allow enough for those heavy times of the semester—midterm and final exam weeks.)
2. Did you notice some conflicts? Can they be resolved?
3. Did you find some scheduled study times particularly inconvenient? Can they be rearranged?
4. Did it help you to get more work done?

Revise your schedule and then try the revised schedule for the next week. Within a week or two you will have worked out a schedule that will carry you through the remainder of the semester. You will be using your time effectively and getting the grades that you have decided you want. Best of all, frustrating day-to-day conflicts over time will be eliminated.

TIME-SAVING TIPS FOR STUDENTS WITH BUSY SCHEDULES

Here are a few suggestions that will help you to make the best use of your time. If you are an older student with family responsibilities who is returning to college, or if you are trying both to work and to attend college, you will find these suggestions particularly valuable.

1. *Use the telephone.* When you need information or must make an appointment, phone rather than visit the office. To find out if a book you've requested at the library has come in, for example, phone the circulation desk.
2. *Set priorities.* There may be days or weeks when you cannot get every assignment done. Many students work until they are exhausted and leave remaining assignments unfinished. A better approach is to decide what is most important to complete immediately and which assignments could, if necessary, be completed later.
3. *Use spare moments.* Think of all the time that you spend waiting. You wait for a class to begin, for a ride, for a friend to call, for a pizza to arrive. Instead of wasting this time, you could use it to review a set of lecture notes, work on review questions at the end of a chapter, or review a chemistry lab setup. Always carry with you something you can work on in spare moments.
4. *Learn to combine activities.* Most people think it is impossible to do two things at once, but busy students soon learn that it is possible to combine some daily chores with routine class assignments. Some students, for example, are able to go to a laundromat and, while there, outline a history chapter or work on routine assignments during breaks. Others review formulas for math or science courses or review vocabulary cards for language courses while walking to classes.
5. *Use lists to keep yourself organized and to save time.* A daily "to do" list is helpful in keeping track of what daily living/household tasks and errands as well as course assignments need to be done. As you think of things to be done, jot them down. Then look over the list each morning and try to find the best way to get everything done. You may find, for instance, that you can stop at the post office on the way to the bookstore, thus saving yourself a trip.
6. *Do not be afraid to admit you are trying to do too much.* If you find your life is becoming too hectic or unmanageable, or if you are facing pressures beyond your ability to handle them, consider dropping a course. Don't be too concerned that this will put you behind schedule for graduation. More than half of all college students take longer than the traditional time expected to earn their degrees. Besides, you may be able to pick up the course later during a summer session or carry a heavier load another semester.

PROCRASTINATION

Have you ever felt that you should work on an assignment, and even wanted to get it out of the way, but could not get started? If so, you may have been a victim of procrastination—putting off tasks that need to be done. Although you know you should review your biology notes this evening, for instance, you procrastinate and do something else instead. Tedious, difficult, or uninteresting tasks are often those that we put off doing. It is often these

Procrastination   **29**

very tasks, however, that are essential to success in college courses. The following suggestions can help you to overcome or control a tendency to procrastinate and put you on track for success.

Give Yourself Five Minutes to Start

If you are having difficulty beginning a task, say to yourself that you will work on it for just five minutes. Often, once you start working, motivation and interest build and you will want to continue working.

Divide the Task into Manageable Parts

Complicated tasks are often difficult to start because they are long and seem unmanageable. Before beginning such tasks, spend a few minutes organizing and planning. Divide each task into parts, and then devise an approach strategy. In other words, list what needs to be done and in what order. In devising an approach strategy for a one-hour biology exam on the topic of cells, one student wrote the following list of subtopics to review:

atoms and molecules   cell organization
organic molecules   cell functioning
cell theory   cell division

She then decided the order in which she would study these topics, the study strategy she would use, and the time she would devote to each.

Clear Your Desk

Move everything from your desk except materials for the task at hand. With nothing else in front of you, you are more likely to start working and less likely to be distracted from your task while working.

Start Regardless of What You Do

If you are having difficulty getting started, do something rather than sit and stare, regardless of how trivial it may seem. If you are having trouble writing a paper from rough draft notes, for example, start by recopying the notes. Suddenly you'll find yourself rearranging and rephrasing them, and you'll be well on your way toward writing a draft.

Recognize When You Need More Information

Sometimes procrastination is a signal that you lack skills or information. You may be avoiding a task because you're not sure how to do it. You may not really understand why you use a certain procedure to solve a type of math problem, for example, so you feel reluctant to do math homework. Or selecting a term-paper topic may be difficult if you aren't certain of its purpose or expected length. Overcome such stumbling blocks by discussing them with classmates or with your professor.

Think Positively

As you begin a task, send yourself positive messages such as "I'll be able to stick with this," or "It will feel great to have this job done." Avoid negatives such as "This is so boring" or "I can't wait to finish."

Recognize Escape Routes

Some students escape work by claiming they haven't enough time to get everything done. Close analysis of their time usage often reveals they are wasting valuable time by following one or more escape routes. One route is to needlessly spend time away from your desk—returning library books, going out to pick up take-out food, dropping off laundry, and so on. Another escape route is to overdo routine tasks: meticulously cleaning your room, pressing clothing, or polishing the car. Doing things by hand also consumes time: copying a friend's notes rather than photocopying them, or balancing your checkbook by hand rather than using a calculator. Analyze your time carefully to detect and avoid any escape routes such as these.

Avoid "The Great Escape"—Television

For some students television poses the greatest threat to keeping to their study-time schedule, and certainly it is often the cause of procrastination. If a TV set is on, it is tempting to watch whatever is showing. To overcome this temptation, turn it on and off at specific times for particular programs you want to see. Don't leave it on between programs you intend to watch; you'll probably continue watching.

EXERCISE 2 ────────────────

Directions: *Read each situation described, and then answer the questions that follow. Discuss your responses with another student or write your answers in the spaces provided.*

1. In analyzing his amount of committed time, George Andrews filled in a chart as follows:

Sleep	56
Breakfast, lunch, dinner (total)	14
Job	35
Time in classes	23
Transportation	10
Personal care	15
Household/family	20
Total	173

   George has to have at least a part-time job in order to pay for school. He is enrolled in science lab technology, so he must spend a lot of class hours in lab. He estimates that he needs 30 hours per week to maintain a high B average this semester. If he schedules this amount of time, he will have virtually no time for leisure and recreation. Look at his chart again. What could he do? What are his choices? Try to find as many alternatives as you can.

_____

_____

2. Susan is a serious student but is having difficulty with her accounting course. She has decided to spend all day Sunday studying accounting. She plans to lock herself in her room and not come out until she has reviewed four chapters. What is wrong with her approach? What study plan would be more effective?

_____

_____

3. Mark realizes that he has three assignments that have to be completed in one evening. The assignments are to revise an English composition, to read and underline ten pages in his anatomy and physiology text, and to recopy a homework assignment for sociology. He decides to get the sociology assignment out of the way first, then do the English composition (because English is one of his favorite subjects), and read the anatomy and physiology text last. Evaluate Mark's plan of study.

_____

_____

4. You are taking a course in music appreciation, and your instructor often asks you to listen to a certain part of a concert on FM radio or to watch a particular program on television. Since you cannot predict when these assignments will be given or at what time you need to complete them, what could you do to include them in your weekly study schedule?

_____

_____

5. Sam Smith is registered for the following courses, which meet at the times indicated:

Business Management 905	T–Th 12–1:30 P.M.
English 101	M–W–F 11 A.M.–12 NOON
Math 201	T–Th 9–10:30 A.M.
Biology 601	Class M–W–F, 2–3 P.M.; lab W, 3–5 P.M.
Psychology 502	M–W–F 9–10 A.M.

The work load for each course is as follows:

English	One 250-word essay per week
Math	A homework assignment for each class, which takes approximately one hour to complete; a quiz each Thursday

Biology	Preparation for weekly lab; one chapter to read per week; a one-hour exam every three weeks
Business Management	Two chapters assigned each week; midterm and final exams; one term paper due at the end of the semester
Psychology	One chapter to read per week; one library reading assignment per week; four major exams throughout the semester

Because Sam has a part-time job, he has the following times available for study:

between his classes
evenings: Tuesday, Wednesday
afternoons: Monday, Thursday, and Friday
weekends: Saturday morning, all day and evening Sunday

What study schedule would you recommend for Sam? Indicate the times he should study each subject and what tasks he should work on.

SUMMARY

The ability to use time effectively greatly increases a student's degree of success in college. This chapter presented specific suggestions for analyzing and organizing your time. You began the chapter by analyzing your current time commitments and determining how much time you have available to meet college course demands. Next you were asked to estimate the amount of time each course requires per week to earn a certain grade and to determine the total amount you need to spend on course work each week. The chapter then offered steps in planning and using a weekly study-time schedule and making necessary adjustments to meet the course load you have assumed. Finally, the chapter presented some time-saving tips for busy students and discussed the problem of procrastination.

3

Principles of Learning and Memory

Use this chapter to:
1. *Find out how forgetting, learning, and memory work.*
2. *Learn principles that will help you learn.*

Now that you are involved with your courses and have become familiar with your campus, it is time to consider how to be successful in your courses.

Think of the courses you are taking this semester and why you are taking them. Most likely, some are required courses, and others you have elected on the basis of interest, convenience, advice, or need. Now think of what you want from each course. At the very minimum, of course, you want to pass. To do so, you must *learn* enough to complete assignments, to pass exams, and to write acceptable papers. You are probably taking certain courses to *learn* a skill, such as math, writing, accounting, or data processing. In others you are *learning* a new academic discipline, such as anthropology, psychology, ecology, or sociology. Regardless of the type of course you are taking, you have one overall goal—to learn.

FORGETTING

Have you ever wondered why you cannot remember what you have just read? Have you noticed students in your classes who seem to remember everything? Do you wonder why you can't? The answer is not that these other students are brighter than you are or that they have studied twice as long as you have. Instead, they have learned *how* to learn and to remember; they have developed techniques for effective learning.

Forgetting, defined as the loss of information stored in memory, is a normal, everyday occurrence. It happens because other information interferes with or prevents you from recalling the desired information. Psychologists have extensively studied the rate at which forgetting takes place. For most people, forgetting occurs very rapidly immediately after learning and then

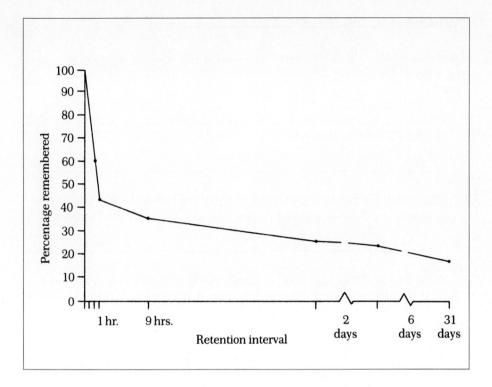

FIGURE 3-1   The Retention Curve

levels off over time. Figure 3-1 demonstrates just how fast forgetting normally occurs and how much information is lost. The figure depicts what is known as the retention curve, and it shows how much you are able to remember over time.

The retention curve has serious implications for you as a learner. Basically, it suggests that unless you are one of the lucky few who remember almost everything they hear or read, you will forget a large portion of the information you learn unless you do something to prevent it. For instance, the graph shows that your recall of learned information drops to below 50 percent within an hour and to about 30 percent within two days.

Fortunately, there are specific techniques to prevent or slow down forgetting. These techniques are what the remainder of this book is all about. Throughout the book you will learn techniques to enable you to identify what to learn (pick out what is important) and to learn it in the most effective way. Each technique is intended to help you remember more and to slow down your rate of forgetting. For instance, in Chapter 13 you will learn a system for reading to learn and remember more. In Chapter 14 you will learn how taking notes during class lectures can help you learn and remember what the lecture is about.

Before we go on to present these specific techniques, however, it is useful that you understand a little about the learning and memory process and why forgetting occurs. Once you know how learning occurs, you will be able to see why and how the various techniques suggested throughout the book are effective. Each reading and study technique is based on the learning and memory process and is designed to help you learn in the most efficient way.

Directions: *Apply the information you have learned about the rate of forgetting to each of the following reading-study situations. Refer to Figure 3-1.*

1. How much information from a textbook chapter can you expect to recall two days after you read it?

    _____

2. How much information presented in a lecture last week can you expect to remember this week if you do not take any notes on the lecture?

    _____

3. What do you think your level of recall would be if you took notes on a particular lecture but did not review your notes for two weeks?

    _____

4. Why would it be necessary to take notes on a film shown in class if you have to write a reaction paper on it that evening?

    _____

HOW PEOPLE LEARN AND REMEMBER

Three stages are involved in the memory process: encoding, storage, and retrieval. First, information enters the brain from a variety of sources. This process is known as *encoding*. In reading and study situations, information is entered primarily through reading or listening. This information lingers briefly in what is known as *sensory storage* and is then either *stored* or discarded. Momentary or brief storage is called *short-term memory*. Next, information in your short-term memory is either forgotten or transferred into more permanent storage. This permanent storage is called *long-term memory*. Anything you want to remember for more than a few seconds must be stored in your long-term memory. To place information in long-term memory it must be learned in some way. Finally, information can be brought back or remembered through a process known as *retrieval*. Figure 3-2 is a visual model of the learning and memory processes. Refer to it frequently as you read the sections that explain each stage.

How Encoding Works

Every waking moment your mind is bombarded with a variety of impressions of what is going on around you. Your five senses—hearing, sight, touch, taste, and smell—provide information about the world around you. Think for a moment of all the signals your brain receives at a given moment. If you are reading, your eyes transmit not only the visual patterns of the words, but also

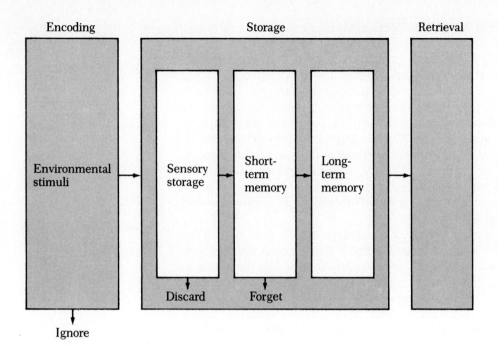

FIGURE 3-2   A Model of Memory

information about the size and color of the print. You may hear a door slamming, a clock ticking, a dog barking. Your sense of smell may detect perfume or cigarette smoke; your sense of touch or feeling may signal that a pen you are using to underline will soon run out of ink or that the room is chilly. When you listen to a classroom lecture, you are constantly receiving numerous stimuli—from the professor, from the lecture hall, from students around you. All these environmental stimuli are transmitted to your brain for a very brief sensory storage and interpretation.

How Sensory Storage Works

Information received from the sense organs is transmitted through the nervous system to the brain, which accepts and interprets it. The information lingers briefly in the nervous system for the brain to interpret it; this lingering is known as sensory storage.

How does your mind handle the barrage of information conveyed by your senses? Thanks to what is known as *selective attention,* your brain automatically sorts out the more important signals from the trivial ones. Trivial signals, such as insignificant noises around you, are ignored or discarded. Through skills of concentration and attention, you can train yourself to ignore other more distracting signals, such as a dog barking or people talking in the background.

Although your sensory storage accepts all information, data is kept there only briefly, usually less than a few seconds. Then the information either fades or decays or is replaced with incoming new stimuli. The function, then, of sensory storage is to retain information long enough for you to selectively attend to it and transmit it to your short-term memory.

How Short-Term Memory Works

Short-term memory holds the information acquired from your sensory storage system. It is used to store information you wish to retain for only a few seconds. A telephone number, for example, is stored in your short-term memory until you dial it. A lecturer's words are retained until you can record them in your notes. Most researchers agree that short-term memory lasts much less than one minute, perhaps 20 seconds or less. Information can be kept or maintained longer if you practice or rehearse the information (repeating a phone number, for example). When you are introduced to someone, then, unless you repeat or rehearse the person's name at the time of introduction, you will not be able to remember it. New incoming information will force it out of your short-term memory.

Your short-term memory is limited in capacity as well as in time span. Research conducted by the psychologist George Miller suggests that we have room in our short-term memories to store from five to nine bits (or pieces or sets) of information at a time—that is, an average of seven. If you try to store more than seven, earlier items are "bumped out." The size of each bit, however, is not limited to a single item. You can group items together to form a longer bit or piece. Known as the Number Seven Theory, this finding is useful in both daily and academic situations.* When you read a textbook chapter or listen to a lecture, for example, your short-term memory is unable to retain each piece of information you receive. It is necessary to rearrange the information into groups or sets—ideas or topics. To retain information beyond the limitations of short-term memory, it must be transferred to long-term memory for more permanent storage.

EXERCISE 2 _____

Directions: *Use your knowledge of the memory process to answer the following questions.*

1. Observe and analyze the area in which you are sitting. What sensory impressions (sights, sounds, touch sensations) have you been ignoring due to selective attention?

   _____

2. Can you remember what you ate for lunch three weeks ago? If not, why not?

   _____

3. Use your knowledge of the Number Seven Theory to explain why dashes are placed in your Social Security number after the third and fifth numbers and after the area code and the first three digits of your phone number.

   _____

* George Miller, "The Magic Number Seven plus or minus two; Some limits on our capacity for processing information," *Psychological Review,* 63 (1956): 81–97.

4. Explain why two people are able to carry on a deep conversation at a crowded, noisy party.

_____

5. Explain why someone who looks up a phone number and then walks into another room to dial it might forget the number.

_____

Learning: The Transfer from Short- to Long-Term Memory

To retain information beyond the brief moment you acquire it, it must be transferred to long-term memory for permanent storage. There are several processes by which to store information in long-term memory: rote learning, rehearsal, and recoding.

Rote Learning: Rote learning involves repetition of information in the form in which it was acquired in sensory storage. Learning the spelling of a word, memorizing the exact definition of a word, or repeating a formula until you can remember it are examples. Material learned through this means is often learned in a fixed order. Rote learning is usually an inefficient means to store large quantities of information.

Elaborative Rehearsal: Used at this stage, rehearsal involves much more than simple repetition or practice. Elaborative rehearsal is a thinking process. It involves connecting new material with already learned material, asking questions, and making associations. It is a process of making the information meaningful and "fitting" it into an established category or relating it to existing memory stores. This form of rehearsal is discussed in more detail later.

Recoding: Recoding is a process of rearranging, rephrasing, changing, or grouping information so that it becomes more meaningful and easier to recall. Expressing ideas in your own words is a form of recoding, or you might record information from a reading assignment by outlining it. Taking notes in lectures is also a form of recoding, as is writing a term paper that summarizes several reference sources.

Rehearsal and recoding are the underlying principles on which many learning strategies presented later in this book are based. Chapter 11, for example, discusses textbook underlining and marking. Underlining is a form of rehearsal. In deciding which information to underline, you review the information and sort the important from the unimportant. When you make marginal notes, you recode the information by classifying, organizing, labeling, or summarizing it.

EXERCISE 3 _____

Directions: *Decide whether each of the following activities primarily involves rote learning, elaborative rehearsal, or recoding.*

1. Learning a formula in economics for computing the rate of inflation.

_____

2. Relating the ideas and feelings expressed in a poem read in your English literature class to your personal experience.

   _____

3. Making a chart that compares three political action groups.

   _____

4. Learning metric equivalents for U.S. units of volume and weight.

   _____

5. Drawing a diagram that shows the processes by which the Constitution can be amended.

   _____

EXERCISE 4 _____

Directions: *Use your knowledge of the memory process to answer the following questions.*

1. Two groups of students read the same textbook chapter. One group underlined key ideas on each page; the second group paraphrased and recorded the important ideas from each page. Explain why the second group received higher scores on a test based on the chapter than did the first group.

   _____

2. On many campuses, weekly recitations or discussions are scheduled for small groups to review material presented in large lecture classes. What learning function do these recitation sections provide?

   _____

3. After lecturing on the causes of domestic violence, a sociology instructor showed her class a videotape of an incident of domestic violence. What learning function(s) did the film provide? How would the tape help students remember the lecture?

   _____

4. A text that contains photographs is often easier to learn from than one without them. What learning function do the pictures perform?

   _____

How Long-Term Memory Works

Long-term memory is your permanent store of information. Unlike short-term memory, long-term memory is nearly unlimited in both span and capacity. It contains hundreds of thousands of facts, details, impressions, and experiences that you have accumulated throughout your life.

Once information is stored in your long-term memory, you recall or pull it out through a process known as retrieval. Academic tasks requiring you to retrieve knowledge include math or science problems, quizzes and exams, and papers. Retrieval is integrally tied to storage. The manner in which information is stored in your memory affects its availability and the ease with which you can retrieve it. For example, suppose you have studied a topic but find that on an exam you are unable to remember much about it. There are several possible explanations: (1) you never completely learned (stored) the information in the first place; (2) you did not study (store) the information in the right way; (3) you are not asking the right questions or using the right means to retrieve it; or (4) you have forgotten it. Later in this chapter you will learn principles that will enable you to store information effectively to retard forgetting.

EXERCISE 5 _____

Directions: *For each of the following activities, decide whether it involves encoding, storage, and/or retrieval.*

1. Taking an essay exam. _____

2. Listening to a lecture. _____

3. Taking notes on a film shown in class. _____

4. Solving a homework problem in mathematics. _____

5. Balancing a ledger in accounting. _____

EXERCISE 6 _____

Directions: *Use your knowledge of how memory works to explain each of the following situations.*

1. A student spends more time than anyone else in her class preparing for the midterm exam, yet she cannot remember important definitions and concepts at the time of the exam. Offer several possibilities that may explain her dilemma.

   _____

2. Try to recall the sixth number of your Social Security number without repeating the first five. What does this show about how you learned (rehearsed) your number?

   _____

3. A computer science instructor begins a class session by handing out a quiz. One student is surprised and says he did not know there would be a quiz. All the other students recall the instructor announcing the quiz

the week before. The student has never been absent or late for class. Why does he not know about the quiz?

_____

4. A business instructor plans to lecture on the process of job-stress analysis. Before class she draws a diagram of this process on the chalkboard. During the lecture she refers to it frequently. Why did the instructor draw the diagram?

_____

5. A student is studying a difficult chapter in biology. Her roommate asks her a question, but she does not answer. The roommate assumes she is angry at her for interrupting her study and storms out of the room. What is the cause of the misunderstanding?

_____

6. Suppose you are reading a section of your history text. You come across an unfamiliar word and so look up its meaning. Once you have looked up the word, you find that you must reread the section. Why?

_____

7. A political science instructor is discussing an essay on world terrorism. He begins the discussion by asking his students to recall recent terrorist acts and how they were resolved. How is the instructor helping his students learn the content of the essay?

_____

8. A sociology instructor asks her students to read and write a summary of a journal article she has placed on reserve in the library. How is she helping her students learn the material?

_____

PRINCIPLES OF LEARNING

Now that you know how the memory process works, it is appropriate to consider ways in which you can learn most effectively. This section presents a summary of principles of learning. Each has specific applications for learning material contained in college texts or presented in class lectures.

Principle 1: Intent to Remember

What were you wearing seventeen months ago at this time? What did you eat for lunch on March 18, 1991? Why can't you answer these questions? The answer, of course, is simple: because you did not store the information; there was no need to remember what you were wearing or eating. One of the most obvious principles related to memory is that you remember only what you intend to remember—that which you identify as worth remembering.

To further illustrate this principle, draw the face side of a one-dollar bill in the space provided below before you read any more.

Now, did you include each of the following: the face of George Washington, the seal of the Department of the Treasury, the Federal Reserve Bank seal, the signature of the treasurer of the United States, the signature of the secretary of the Treasury, the words *Federal Reserve Note*, serial numbers, the series date, the words *UNITED STATES OF AMERICA*, and so on? Did you put all of these things in the right places? Most likely you were not able to reproduce a dollar bill accurately, and just think of how often you have looked at one. You did not remember the details on the bill because, whenever you looked at one, you had no *intention* of remembering it.

Application: Intent to remember has direct applications to both textbook reading and lecture notetaking. As you read or listen, you should select what you intend to remember by sorting out the important ideas from those that are relatively unimportant.

This principle also provides the basis for the techniques of prereading and active reading (presented in Chapters 5 and 6). You will learn that prereading is a method of getting an overview, or advance picture, of what is important and worth remembering in a textbook chapter before you read it completely. Prereading really tells you, in advance of a complete reading, what material you should intend to remember. Suppose you discover through prereading a chapter in an astronomy text that the chapter discusses the location, physical properties, and appearance of eight planets. Then you can establish an intent to remember. As you read, you will plan on identifying and remembering the name, location, properties, and appearance of each planet. The technique of active reading involves forming questions to guide your reading. It requires that, for each dark print (or boldface) heading within a textbook chapter, you form a question; as you read, you then try to find the answer to the question. The answer to your question is what you intend to remember.

Principle 2: Meaningfulness

Material that is meaningful, or makes sense, is easier to learn and remember than meaningless information. It would be easier to learn a list of meaningful words than a list of nonsense words. Try the following experiment to test the accuracy of this statement.

Directions:

1. *Read through list 1 below, spending a maximum of 15 seconds.*
2. *Now, cover list 1 with your hand or a piece of scrap paper, and write down in the space provided on the next page as many items as you can remember.*
3. *Follow steps 1 and 2 for each of the other three lists.*
4. *Check to see how many items you had correct on each of the four lists.*

List 1	List 2	List 3	List 4
KQZ	BLT	WIN	WAS
NLR	TWA	SIT	THE
XOJ	SOS	LIE	CAR
BTK	CBS	SAW	RUN
YSW	NFL	NOT	OFF

List 1	List 2	List 3	List 4
_____	_____	_____	_____
_____	_____	_____	_____
_____	_____	_____	_____
_____	_____	_____	_____

Did you recall more items on list 2 than on list 1? Why? Did you remember more items on list 4 than on list 3? As you must now realize, after list 1, each list became more meaningful than the one before it. The lists progressed from nonsense syllables to meaningful letter groups to words and, finally, to words that, when strung together, produced meanings. This simple experiment demonstrates that you are able to remember information that is meaningful more easily than information that has no meaning.

Let's look at some other examples of the principle of meaningful learning. Consider phone numbers. Some are easy to remember; others are not. Would it be easy to remember the phone number of your local take-out pizza shop if the phone number were 825-3699? Probably not. Would it be easier to remember if you realized that the digits in the phone number correspond to letters on the phone dial that spell *take-out*? Yes. The word *take-out* has a particular meaning to you because you are using the phone number to order a take-out item.

Application: The principle of meaningful learning is critical in all textbook reading situations. It affirms the necessity of understanding (comprehending) what you read. If you do not understand a concept or idea, it is not meaningful and you will not be able to remember it. As you read, to be sure that you are comprehending, try to explain what you have read in your own words. If you cannot, you probably have not understood the material.

Several of the reading and study techniques presented in this text are, in part, based on the principle of meaningfulness. The technique of prereading, in which you become acquainted with the overall organization and content of a selection before you begin to read it, makes the reading process more meaningful. Active reading also makes reading more meaningful: You are

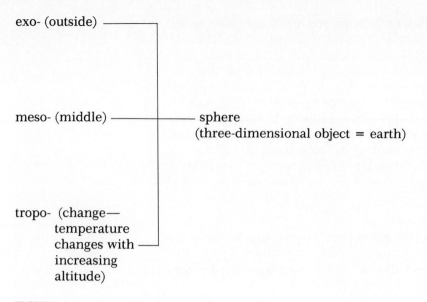

exo- (outside) ─────────┐

meso- (middle) ──────────┼─── sphere
                         │   (three-dimensional object = earth)

tropo- (change—   │
    temperature
    changes with ───────┘
    increasing
    altitude)

FIGURE 3-3   Word Meaning as a Memory Aid

reading to find specific information. The techniques of underlining and marking textbooks and taking lecture notes also give further meaning and organization to the materials to be studied.

Now suppose that, while learning vocabulary for an astronomy course, you discover you have to learn the terms for the lower, middle, and upper layers of the atmosphere. The terms are *troposphere, mesosphere,* and *exosphere.* One way to learn these words would be to memorize each word and its corresponding meaning. A better way would be to recognize that the root *sphere* in each refers to a three-dimensional object—in this case, the earth. The prefix, or beginning part of each word, in some way describes the atmosphere in relation to the earth. *Tropo-* means "change," and it is in this lower layer of the earth's atmosphere that the temperature changes with increasing altitude. The prefix *meso-* means "center or middle," so *mesosphere* is the center layer of the atmosphere. The prefix *exo-* means "outside or external," so it is the exosphere that is the uppermost or outer layer of the atmosphere (see Figure 3-3). It is by learning the meanings of the root *sphere* and the prefixes as well as connecting them with specific astronomical meanings that the terms become more meaningful and are easier to remember.

Principle 3: Categorization and Labeling

Categorization is the restructuring, or reorganizing, of information into meaningful groups for easier recall. Suppose you had to remember to buy the following items at the supermarket and couldn't write them down: apples, milk, toothpaste, eggs, pepperoni, shampoo, celery, deodorant, salami, cheese, pork chops, and onions. What could you do to make recall of the items easier? One thing you could do is classify the items by organizing them in the categories shown in these headings:

Toiletries	*Dairy*	*Meat*	*Fruits/ Vegetables*
toothpaste	milk	pepperoni	apples
deodorant	cheese	salami	onions
shampoo	eggs	pork chops	celery

By classifying the items in these categories, you are, first of all, making the information meaningful—it is organized according to aisles or departments within the store. Second, you have placed a label on each group of items. The labels "Toiletries," "Dairy," and so forth can serve as "memory tags" that will help you to remember to buy the items you classified under each category. Using memory tags may be compared to knowing which cupboard door to open in your kitchen when you are looking for something. If you know which door to open, locating a can of soup is relatively easy. But if you do not know where the canned items are stored, locating the soup could be difficult. In trying to remember your list of supermarket shopping items, if you can remember the category "Dairy," recalling the particular items you want to buy becomes a simpler task.

Application: Try to categorize information as you read it—either in your mind or on paper. In the following passage, you could classify the information into the two categories indicated by the headings in the diagram that follows.

Responsibility for the administration and enforcement of immigration laws rests primarily with the Secretary of State and the Attorney General.

The Secretary of State discharges most of his responsibilities through the Bureau of Security and Consular Affairs authorized by the 1952 act. This bureau embraces the Passport Office and Visa Office. These, in turn, carry on their work with the aid of American diplomatic and consular officers abroad, who, since 1924, have been charged with primary responsibility for selecting immigrants before they embark.

The Attorney General performs most of his function in this field through the Immigration and Naturalization Service, which has a staff in all sections of the country and at important ports of entry. A board of appeals, established by the Attorney General and responsible to him, reviews appeals from orders and actions of agents of the Immigration and Naturalization Service. Hearing officers are not bound, however, to observe the standards of fairness prescribed by the Administrative Procedrues Act.

—Ferguson and McHenry, *The American System of Government,* p. 213

Secretary of State	*Attorney General*
↓	↓
Bureau of Security and Consular Affairs	Immigration and Naturalization Service
↓	↓
Passport and Visa Offices	Staff at ports of entry
↓	↓
American diplomatic and consular officers	Board of Appeals
↓	
Selection of immigrants	

Several reading-study techniques suggested in this book employ the principle of categorization. As you take lecture notes (Chapter 14), for example, you arrange, classify, and categorize information. As you use the recall clue system for studying those lecture notes, you continue to apply the principle of labeling and grouping—categorizing information. As you underline and mark a textbook (Chapter 11), you perform a similar task.

Principle 4: Association

New information is easier to learn and remember if you can connect it with previously learned or familiar information. For instance, it is easy to remember your new license plate if it is 1776 US. You can associate, or connect, the new license plate with an already well-learned date and event, in this case the date the United States became independent. Or you can remember and recognize the shape of Italy on a map if you associate it with a boot.

In an American history course, it would be easier to understand and recall various battles in the Civil War if you had visited the cities in which they occurred and could form associations between the details of the battles and specific geographic points that you recall from your visits.

Application: As you read, always try to make connections between the new material and what you already know. You will see that the recall clue system for studying your notes (Chapter 14) relies heavily upon the principle of association. As you read each recall clue written in the margins of your notes, you attempt to relate, or associate, the clue with the corresponding facts in the notes.

Principle 5: Spaced Study

The length of time and spacing between reading-study lessons directly affects how much you learn. Generally, it is more effective to space or spread out study sessions rather than to study in one or two large blocks of time. In fact, research has shown that when periods of study are divided into units separated by breaks, the total time necessary to memorize information is significantly reduced.

Spaced learning and study has several advantages. First, it is likely that by spacing out your study you are reducing the possibility of becoming fatigued—both physically and mentally. Second, there is some evidence that, even when you stop studying and take a break, a certain amount of rehearsal continues to take place.

Finally, dividing your study time into small blocks is psychologically rewarding. When you finish a block, you will feel that you have made progress and are accomplishing something.

Application: The most direct application of this principle occurs as you organize daily and weekly study schedules, as discussed in Chapters 2 and 4. In addition, the use of the study card system described in Chapter 16 will also help you apply this learning principle to your work.

Principle 6: Consolidation

As you learn new information, your mind organizes that information and makes it fit with existing stored information. This process is called *consolidation*. Think of it as a process in which information settles, gels, or takes shape. Consolidation occurs when you briefly hold information in your memory, as you make notes, outline, or summarize what you read or hear in lecture. Consolidation also seems to occur once you've stopped studying: Your mind continues to mull over—sift, sort, and organize—what you have just learned. Often this consolidation occurs subconsciously while you are doing something else. Consolidation lends strong support to the principle of spaced study. Since consolidation occurs following a study session, if you schedule several short sessions rather than one long one, you are allowing consolidation to occur several times, rather than only once.

Application: You can facilitate consolidation by reviewing material shortly after your initial learning. For example, review your lecture notes shortly after taking them, or review your textbook underlining the day after reading the chapter. The techniques of underlining, summarizing, outlining, and mapping discussed in Chapters 11 and 12 employ the principle of consolidation.

Principle 7: Mnemonic Devices

Mnemonics are memory tricks, or aids, that you can devise to help you remember information. Mnemonics include rhymes, anagrams, words, nonsense words, sentences, or mental pictures that aid in the recall of facts. Do you remember this rhyme: "Thirty days hath September,/April, June, and November./ All the rest have thirty-one/ except February, alone,/ which has twenty-eight days clear/ and twenty-nine in each leap year"? The rhyme is an example of a mnemonic device. It is a quick and easy way of remembering the number of days in each month of the year. You may have learned to recall the colors in the spectrum by remembering the name *Roy G. Biv;* each letter in this name stands for one of the colors that make up the spectrum: *R*ed, *O*range, *Y*ellow, *G*reen, *B*lue, *I*ndigo, *V*iolet.

The Chicago Police Department once developed an anagram to help officers remember what steps to follow when called to the scene of a crime. The officers' responsibility is to make a *preliminary* investigation by following the procedure below. Notice the word that is spelled by the first letters of the steps in the procedure.

P — Proceed to the scene.
R — Render assistance to the injured.
E — Effect the arrest of the perpetrator.
L — Locate and identify witnesses.
I — Interview complainant and witnesses.
M — Maintain the scene and protect evidence.
I — Interrogate suspects.
N — Note all conditions, events, and remarks.
A — Arrange for collection of evidence.
R — Report the incident fully and accurately.
Y — Yield responsibility to detectives.

—Wilson and McLaren, *Police Administration,* p. 353

Application: Mnemonic devices are useful when you are trying to learn information that has no inherent organization of its own. You will find the principle useful in reviewing texts and lecture notes as you prepare for exams.

Principle 8: Visualization

Recent research indicates that the brain's functions are divided between the left and right brain. The left brain handles verbal learning and the logical processing of information, while the right brain controls visual processes and more creative and insightful thought. Reading and writing are primarily left brain processes. However, if you can engage your right brain as well as your left in learning, you will increase the number of channels through which learning can occur, thereby enhancing learning effectiveness.

Visualization involves creating a mental or visual picture to be learned; it engages your right brain in the learning process. You might visualize the events in a short story for a literature class by imagining events, characters, or setting. Or for an American history class, you might visualize the panic on the day of the 1929 stock market crash. Drawing diagrams, charts, or graphs is also a form of visualization. In biology, for example, you might draw a diagram that shows how mitosis occurs. In a social problems class you might construct a chart listing types and impacts of military spending.

Application: As you read, attempt to create mental pictures of events and processes. Chapter 12 discusses how to construct visual and organizational charts and diagrams.

Principle 9: Elaboration

You have learned that information is transferred from short- to long-term memory through rehearsal. In most situations, rehearsal should involve more than mere repetition of material to be learned; instead, it must incorporate *elaboration*—thinking about and reacting to content. You might think of elaboration as expansion, evaluation, or application of ideas. Elaboration can involve asking questions, or thinking about implications, exceptions, similarities, or examples. You may look for relationships or connect the material to other course content. For a business marketing course, a student was studying discount pricing stuctures in which she learned various types of discounts a seller may give. To elaborate on this material the student

> thought of real-life situations in which she had seen or received these discounts;
>
> considered the impact of discounts on profit objectives (a topic previously studied); and
>
> compared the various types of discounts and identified when and by what type of business each might be used.

Through the above processes, the student actively worked with the concept of discount pricing.

Application: Elaboration is a useful means of study and review. It may occur as you read, as well. Outlining and textbook marking require elaboration, since you must discover and describe relationships among ideas. Elaboration is particularly useful in preparing for essay exams. It is also an excellent means of reviewing material in preparation for a class discussion or for generating ideas for writing assignments.

Principle 10: Periodic Review

The retention curve shown in Figure 3-1 demonstrates how quickly and dramatically forgetting occurs. Periodic review is useful to combat forgetting. Periodic review means returning to and quickly reviewing previously learned material on a regular basis. Suppose you have learned the material in the first three chapters of your criminology text during the first two weeks of the course. Unless you review that material, you are likely to forget it and have to relearn it by the time your final exam is given. You might establish a periodic review schedule in which every three weeks or so you quickly review these chapters.

Numerous studies have documented that review immediately following learning increases retention. In fact, review done right after learning is more valuable than an equal amount of time spent reviewing several days later.

Application: Periodic review of previously learned material is difficult and time-consuming unless the material is reduced and organized. Techniques such as underlining, outlining, mapping, and summarizing make periodic review easier to accomplish.

EXERCISE 7 _____

Directions: *Apply your knowledge of the memory process and principles of learning in answering the following questions.*

1. You are studying the principal causes of war in a political science course. Your textbook identifies fourteen such causes. What learning principles would you use to learn this material?

   _____

2. A student is taking a chemistry course. Each week the instructor assigns two textbook chapters. In addition, a weekly lab and lab report are required. In class the instructor performs experiments, solves sample problms, and explains basic principles and laws. Suggest a periodic review plan for the student.

   _____

3. How would you use the principle of association when studying the essential features of effective speaking styles for a speech communication course? The features are accuracy, simplicity, coherence, and appropriateness.

   _____

4. The psychologist Abraham Maslow classified fundamental human needs into five categories, now known as Maslow's hierarchy. How would you use the principle of elaboration in learning this hierarchy? From most to least basic, the five levels are physiological needs, safety needs, belongingness and love needs, esteem needs, and self-actualization (self-fulfillment) needs.

   _____

5. How would you use the principle of visualization in learning the law of demand in an economics class? The law states that the price of a product and the amount purchased are inversely related: If the price rises, the quantity demanded falls; if the price falls, the quantity demanded increases.

_____

6. For the first time, you are required to learn the metric system—the metric equivalents for measures of volume, weight, and temperature. How could you make this learning task as meaningful as possible?

_____

7. Vanessa is taking a business mathematics course. She does well on homework and weekly quizzes that deal with one specific type of problem. However, on one-hour exams in which she faces several different types of problems, she scores poorly. How might she improve her performance on exams?

_____

8. The textbook for your English class is an anthology (collection) of essays, each by a different author. For each class session your instructor assigns and discusses one essay. You have been reading each essay and taking notes on your instructor's discussion. Now a midterm exam has been announced that will consist of only one question. What principle(s) of learning would be useful in preparing for this exam?

_____

9. A nursing student is studying the various life stages (infant, toddler, adolescent, and so on) and the cognitive, physiological, and psychological developments at each stage. What principles of learning would be useful to her?

_____

10. Decide how you could organize (categorize) each of the following sets of information.

a. pollutants and their environmental effects
b. problems faced by two-career families
c. effects of terrorism
d. causes of the Vietnam War

a. _____

b. _____

c. _____

d. _____

SUMMARY

This chapter presented an overview of learning and memory processes and offered practical ways to learn more efficiently. Forgetting occurs very rapidly unless specific steps are taken to retain information.

To prevent forgetting, it is necessary to understand how learning and memory work. Three stages are involved in the memory process: encoding, storage, and retrieval. Encoding is the process through which information enters your brain through your various senses. This information lingers briefly in sensory storage, where it is interpreted. Next, the information is either stored briefly in short-term memory or discarded and forgotten. Then you must either transfer information into the more permanent long-term memory or allow it to be forgotten. Transferring facts from short- to long-term memory involves rote learning, elaborative rehearsal, and recoding. A number of learning principles influence how well information is stored in long-term memory. These include the intent to remember, meaningfulness, categorization, association, spaced study, consolidation, mnemonic devices, visualization, elaboration, and periodic review.

PART TWO

Strategies for Active Learning

To those unfamiliar with the game, basketball might seem to be only a matter of placing a ball in a basket while preventing the opposing team members from doing the same. Similarly, football might appear to be a simple process of scoring field goals and touchdowns. Players must develop skill in running, blocking, tackling, and passing; they must learn plays, rules, and penalties; they must practice and draw on their past experience to anticipate the opposing team's actions.

Studying and learning in college courses may at first appear a simple process of reading textbooks and attending classes. Like football, however, studying and learning are complex activities involving skills, knowledge, strategies, and experience. A student must be actively involved in selecting what to learn from text and lecture, learning various learning strategies, selecting a strategy that suits the material to be learned, applying the strategy effectively, and evaluating the quality of the learning. The primary purpose of this section of the book is to introduce you to numerous strategies that will enable you to become actively involved in the learning process.

Chapter 4 focuses on getting ready to learn. The chapter enables you to analyze how you learn most effectively, describes techniques for improving your concentration, discusses text organization, and demonstrates how to discover what you already know about a topic. Chapter 5 presents the techniques of prereading and predicting. Prereading is a means of familiarizing yourself with the content and organization of a chapter before beginning to read it. Predicting involves anticipating difficulty, content, and organization. Chapter 6 describes strategies for focusing and monitoring your learning. You learn how to develop purposes and guide questions, to select appropriate reading/learning strategies, and to monitor your comprehension and learning effectiveness.

4

Setting the Stage for Learning

Use this chapter to:

1. *Analyze your learning style.*
2. *Establish and maintain concentration.*
3. *Learn about your textbooks.*
4. *Activate your background knowledge and experience.*

A freshman business major failed several required courses. Wisely, the student discussed her situation with her academic adviser. When her adviser asked her to describe how she approaches reading and learning tasks, she summarized her approach. "To read, I sit down with the book and try to concentrate. I underline, too. Then, to study I reread the chapters and study my class notes." What is wrong with this student's approach to reading and learning?

This student is obviously spending time reading and learning, but not getting results. Her problem is her approach: she is viewing reading and learning as separate, distinct, single-step unrelated processes. Actually, reading and learning are multi-stage, interrelated activities that involve planning and preparation, processing information, and application and evaluation. A model of active learning is shown in Figure 4-1. Each stage involves specific activities that make learning occur more easily and increase retention.

Stage 1. Planning and Preparation is a getting ready to learn step. It involves analyzing your learning style, establishing and maintaining concentration, familiarizing yourself with the materials you will use, discovering what you already know about the subject, briefly looking over the specific assignment to become familiar with its content and organization, making predictions, defining your purposes for reading, and selecting an appropriate reading strategy. These strategies will be discussed later in this chapter and in Chapters 5 and 6.

Stage 2. Processing the Information is the taking in of information through reading. Reading, however, involves much more than reading each word and sentence successively. While reading, a successful reader keeps track (monitors) comprehension, selects what is important to learn, and understands how the information is organized. Chapters 6 to 11, and 14 address these skills.

	Analyze Learning Style
Stage 1:	Establish Concentration
	Activate Your Knowledge and
	Experience
Planning and Preparation	Preread
	Predict
	Define Purposes
	Select Reading Strategy

	Read
Stage 2:	Monitor Comprehension
Processing the Information	Select What to Learn
	Organize

	Assess Learning Strategy
Stage 3:	Revise and Modify
	Critically Evaluate
Evaluation and Application	Apply
	Integrate

FIGURE 4-1   A Model of Active Reading and Learning

Stage 3. Evaluation and Application involve the assessment, revision, and modification of strategies and the evaluation, integration, and application of the information. In this stage you critically evaluate the content, consider its use and application, and make connections with other course content. These skills are discussed in Parts Four and Five of the text.

Now that you have studied the model in Figure 4-1, you can see the source of the business student's problem; her approach to reading and study is very limited. As you work through the remainder of this book, you will learn numerous strategies to use before, during, and after reading. These strategies will enable you to handle the demands of college courses and meet expectations set by your professors.

ANALYZING YOUR LEARNING STYLE

Have you noticed some types of tasks are easier to learn than others? Have you also discovered that some study methods work better than others? Have you observed that a study method that works well for a classmate does not work as well for you? These differences can be explained by what is known as learning style. Just as you have a unique personality, so do you have a unique learning style. Each person differs in how they learn and in the methods and strategies they use to learn. Your learning style can, in part, explain why some courses are easier than others, and why you can learn better from one instructor than another. Learning style can also account for why certain assignments are difficult and why you find some learning tasks easy and others more challenging.

To begin to understand learning style, think of everyday tasks and activities that you have learned to do easily and well. Think of others that are always troublesome. For example, is reading maps easy or difficult? Is drawing and sketching easy or difficult? Can you assemble items easily? Are tasks that require physical coordination (such as racquetball) difficult? Can you remember the lyrics to popular songs easily? Now, using the space provided below, begin to make a 2-column list of types of tasks that require learning that are easy and those that are difficult. This activity will require careful thought and should take 10 minutes or more to complete, but it is a very important starting point to understanding your learning style.

One student's sample list is shown in Figure 4-2. You may study this list for items to include in your list, but do not limit yourself to activities listed there. List at least 10 activities in each column.

Easy Tasks

1. _Assembling object_
2. _Drawing_
3. _Math_
4. _Craft_
5. _sports_
6. _Gardelning_
7. _painting_
8. _cooking_
9. _____
10. _____
11. _____
12. _____
13. _____
14. _____
15. _____

Difficult Tasks

1. _Creating writing_
2. _making speed_
3. _Summoary_
4. _____
5. _____
6. _____
7. _____
8. _____
9. _____
10. _____
11. _____
12. _____
13. _____
14. _____
15. _____

Patterns (to be filled in later) _____.

Once you have completed your list review it and look for patterns. Are you good at tasks that require certain abilities and weak with others requiring

FIGURE 4-2   A Sample Task Analysis

Easy	*Difficult*
Remembering names	Assembling objects
Organizing things	Sports
Cooking	Reading maps
Memorizing	Listening to directions
Writing	Remembering faces
Reading novels	Painting
Doing crossword puzzles	Drawing
Caring for house plants	Creative writing
Gardening	Making speeches
Math	Remembering music
	Crafts (ceramics, etc.)
	Typing

different abilities? Here are a few patterns to look for. Are you strong or weak with activities that require you to

_____ read and write
_____ visualize objects
_____ solve problems
_____ listen and remember
_____ use your hands
_____ perform mechanical tasks
_____ follow directions carefully
_____ be creative
_____ organize things
_____ work with others
_____ work with numbers
_____ focus on details

Review your list now and mark items that together suggest a pattern. If you are having difficulty discovering a pattern, ask a classmate to analyze your list. Then, if you are still having trouble, add five or more new items to each column and check with your instructor. In the space marked "Pattern" beneath your lists, write what you have discovered.

Now that you have noticed some pattern to what is easy and difficult to learn, you are ready to focus on your academic learning style to discover what techniques and strategies can help you learn most efficiently. Complete the following Learning Style Questionnaire before continuing.

Learning Style Questionnaire

Directions: Each item presents two alternatives. Select the alternative that best describes you. In cases in which neither choice suits you, select the one that is closer to your preference. Write the letter of your choice in the blank to the right of each item.

Part One

1. I would prefer to
    (a) follow a set of oral directions

   or

    (b) follow a set of written directions
2. I would prefer to
    (a) attend a lecture given by a famous psychologist

   or

    (b) read an article written by the psychologist
3. I am better at
    (a) remembering faces

   or

    (b) remembering names
4. Is it easier to learn new information
    (a) using images (pictures)

   or

    (b) using language
5. I prefer classes in which the instructor
    (a) uses films and videos

   or

    (b) lectures and answers questions
6. To obtain information about current events I would prefer to
    (a) watch TV news

   or

    (b) read the newspaper
7. To learn how to operate a fax machine, I would prefer to
    (a) go to a demonstration

   or

    (b) consult a manual

1. _a_

2. _a_

3. _a_

4. _a_

5. _a_

6. _a_

7. _a_

Part Two

1. I prefer to
    (a) learn facts and details

   or

    (b) construct theories and ideas
2. I would prefer a job involving
    (a) following specific instructions

   or

    (b) reading, writing, and analyzing
3. I prefer to
    (a) solve math problems using a formula

   or

    (b) discover why the formula works
4. I would prefer to write a term paper explaining
    (a) how a process works

   or

    (b) explaining a theory

1. _b_

2. _a_

3. _a_

4. _a_

5. I prefer tasks that require 5. _a_
    (a) careful, detailed following of instructions

or

    (b) reasoning and critical analysis

6. For a criminal justice course I would prefer to 6. _b_
    (a) discover how and when a law can be used

or

    (b) learn how and why it became law

7. To learn more about the operation of a highspeed 7. _b_
computer printer, I would prefer to
    (a) work with several types of printers

or

    (b) understand the principles on which they operate

Part Three

1. To solve a math problem, I would prefer to 1. _a_
    (a) draw or visualize the problem

or

    (b) study a sample problem and use it as a model

2. To remember things best, I 2. _b_
    (a) create a mental picture

or

    (b) write it down

3. Assemblying a bicycle from a diagram would be 3. _b_
    (a) easy

or

    (b) challenging

4. I prefer classes in which I 4. _a_
    (a) handle equipment or work with models

or

    (b) participate in a class discussion

5. To understand and remember how a machine works, I would 5. _a_
    (a) draw a diagram

or

    (b) write notes

6. I enjoy 6. _a_
    (a) drawing or working with my hands

or

    (b) speaking, writing, and listening

7. If you were trying to locate an office on an unfamiliar 7. _b_
university campus, would you prefer a student to
    (a) draw you a map

or

    (b) tell you how to find the office

Part Four

1. For a grade in biology lab, I would prefer to 1. _a_
    (a) work with a lab partner

or

    (b) work alone

2. When faced with a difficult personal problem, I prefer to   2. __a__
    (a) discuss it with others

or

    (b) resolve it myself

3. Many instructors could improve their classes by   3. __a__
    (a) including more discussion and group activities

or

    (b) allowing students to work on their own more frequently

4. When listening to a lecture or speaker, I respond more to   4. __a__
    (a) the person presenting the ideas

or

    (b) the ideas themselves

5. When on a team project, I prefer   5. __a__
    (a) to work with several team members

or

    (b) to divide up tasks and complete those assigned to me

6. I   6. __a__
    (a) frequently try to shop, run errands, and work with friends

or

    (b) seldom try to shop, run errands, and work with friends

7. A job in a busy office is   7. __a__
    (a) more appealing than working alone

or

    (b) less appealing than working alone

Part Five

1. To make decisions I rely on   1. __b__
    (a) my experiences and "gut" feelings

or

    (b) facts and objective data

2. To complete a task, I   2. __a__
    (a) can use whatever is available to get the job done

or

    (b) must have everything I need at hand

3. I prefer to express my ideas and feelings through   3. __b__
    (a) music, song, or poetry

or

    (b) direct, concise language

4. I prefer instructors who   4. __a__
    (a) allow students to select what and how to learn

or

    (b) make their expectations clear and explicit

5. I tend to   5. __a__
    (a) challenge and question what I hear and read

or

    (b) accept what I hear and read

6. I prefer   6. _b_
        (a) essay exams
    or
        (b) objective exams
7. In completing an assignment I prefer to   7. _a_
        (a) figure out my own approach
    or
        (b) be told exactly what to do

To score your questionnaire, record the total number of choice a's you selected and the total number of choice b's for each part of the questionnaire. Record your totals in the scoring grid provided below.

Scoring Grid

Parts	Total # of Choice A	Total # of Choice B
Part One	_____ Auditory	_____ Visual
Part Two	_____ Applied	_____ Conceptual
Part Three	_____ Spatial	_____ Verbal
Part Four	_____ Social	_____ Independent
Part Five	_____ Creative	_____ Pragmatic

Now, circle your higher score for each part of the questionnaire. The word below the score you circled indicates an aspect of your learning style. The next section explains how to interpret your scores and describes these aspects.

Interpreting Your Scores

The questionnaire was divided into five parts; each part identifies one aspect of your learning style. Each of these five aspects is explained below.

Part One: Auditory or Visual Learners This score indicates the sensory mode you prefer when processing information. Auditory learners tend to learn more effectively through listening, while visual learners process information by seeing it in print or other visual modes including film, picture, or diagram. If you have a higher score on auditory than visual, you tend to be an auditory learner. That is, you tend to learn more easily by hearing than by reading. A higher score in visual suggests strengths with visual modes of learning.

Part Two: Applied or Conceptual Learners This score describes the types of learning tasks and learning situations you prefer and find most easy to handle. If you are an applied learner you prefer tasks that involve real objects and situations. Practical, real-life learning situations are ideal for you. If you are a conceptual learner, you prefer to work with language and ideas; practical applications are not necessary for understanding.

Part Three: Spatial or Nonspatial Learners This score reveals your ability to work with spatial relationships. Spatial learners are able to visualize or "mentally see" how things work or how they are positioned in space. Their strengths may include drawing, assembling things, or repairing. Nonspatial learners lack skills in positioning things in space. Instead they tend to rely on verbal or language skills.

Part Four: Social or Independent Learners This score reveals your preferred level of interaction with other people in the learning process. If you are a social learner you prefer to work with others—both peers and instructors—closely and directly. You tend to be people-oriented and enjoy personal interaction. If you are an independent learner, you prefer to work and study alone. You tend to be self directed or self-motivated, and often goal oriented.

Part Five: Creative or Pragmatic Learners This score describes the approach you prefer to take toward learning tasks. Creative learners are imaginative and innovative. They prefer to learn through discovery or experimentation. They are comfortable taking risks and following hunches. Pragmatic learners are practical, logical, and systematic. They seek order and are comfortable following rules.

Using Learning Style to Learn More Effectively

Now that you have recognized some features of your learning style, the next step is to use this information to become a more efficient learner. Awareness of *how you learn* best should influence *how you study*. For example, an auditory-social learner may find it effective to discuss textbook readings with a classmate. A visual-independent learner may find it more effective to write an outline and prepare charts summarizing chapter content. Chapter 6 will discuss selecting reading-study strategies with consideration given to learning style.

Awareness of weaknesses or limitations in your learning style can also improve your learning efficiency. Once you are aware of which tasks or activities may be more difficult, you can take steps to strengthen your approach. For example, a visual learner may find it helpful to improve his or her listening and notetaking skills. An independent learner may discover that exerting leadership when placed within group activities may give him or her a sense of control and make the situation more comfortable. Figure 4-3 describes activities that are useful in compensating for limitations in learning style.

Several Words of Caution

Ideally, through activities in this section and the use of the questionnaire, you have discovered more about yourself as a learner. However, several words of caution are in order.

FIGURE 4-3 Compensating for Learning Style Limitations

If You Are Weak in . . .	*You Can Improve if you . . .*
Auditory learning	□ sharpen your listening skills (see Ch. 14) □ work on notetaking skills (see Ch. 14) □ focus your concentration during class lectures (see Ch. 4) □ take a public speaking course; you'll get a lot of listening practice □ carry cards to write down information presented orally □ summarize oral information (see Ch. 12) □ study with a classmate who is an auditory learner
Visual learning	□ learn when and how to draw diagrams □ learn mapping (see Ch. 12) □ copy and practice redrawing visuals your instructors provide □ practice redrawing visuals included in your textbook □ study the function of graphics (see Ch. 10) □ study with a classmate who is a visual learner □ learn to notice and read visuals and graphics (see Ch. 10)
Applied learning	□ pay attention to applications □ ask and answer the question "How can I use this information?" □ study discussion questions in textbook chapters □ make notes during class discussions that focus on application (see Ch. 15) □ write summaries of steps, directions, processes, procedures □ use visuals □ find practical uses for ideas □ ask how something works rather than why it is the way it is
Conceptual learning	□ ask and answer questions such as "Why is this important? How do we know? Why is it this way? What would happen if . . . ?" □ look for the larger picture—how ideas relate □ try to create models and theories □ group information and ideas and create labels □ look for organizational patterns (see Ch. 9) □ summarize class notes and reading assignments □ use prereading extensively (see Ch. 5) □ make connections between readings □ connect lectures to assigned readings
Spatial learning	□ translate diagrams and drawings into language

	☐ record steps and processes in language
	☐ study and redraw textbook diagrams
	☐ summarize function and key points of diagrams in language (see Ch. 12)
Social learning	☐ get socially involved with classmates
	☐ pay attention to people's feelings
	☐ learn about body language
	☐ join groups or clubs to interact with people with shared interests
	☐ get to know someone in each class
Independent learning	☐ work on time management skills (see Ch. 2)
	☐ set and carry out goals (see Ch. 4)
	☐ set time limits for tasks (see Ch. 4)
Creative learning	☐ use free-writing (brainstorming) (see Ch. 18)
	☐ exercise your creativity by imaging and visualizing
	☐ study with a creative learner
Pragmatic learning	☐ develop organizational skills
	☐ set goals and time limits (see Ch. 4)
	☐ write summaries for processes and procedures (see Ch. 12)
	☐ spend time each week organizing course materials
	☐ study with a pragmatic learner
	☐ use outlining to organize information (see Ch. 12)

---

1. The questionnaire is an informal indicator of your learning style. Other more formal and more accurate measures of learning style are available. These include:

   Kolb's Learning Style Inventory
   Myers-Briggs Type Indicator

   These tests may be available through your college's Counseling, Testing, or Academic Skills Center.

2. There are many more aspects of learning style than those identified through the questionnaire in this chapter. To learn more about other factors, one or more of the tests listed above would be useful.

3. Learning style is *not* a fixed unchanging quality. Just as personalities can change and develop, so can learning style change and develop through exposure, instruction, or practice. For example, as you experience more college lectures, your skill as an auditory learner may be strengthened.

4. It is not necessary to be clearly strong or weak in each aspect. Some students, for example, may be able to learn equally well spatially or verbally. If there was very little difference between your two scores on one or more parts of the questionnaire, then you may have strengths in both areas.

5. When most students discover the features of their learning style, they recognize themselves. A frequent comment is "Yep, that's me." If, for some reason, you feel the description of yourself as a learner is incorrect,

then do not make changes in your learning strategies based on the information. Instead, discuss your style with your instructor or consider taking one of the tests listed above.

ESTABLISHING AND MAINTAINING CONCENTRATION

Do these comments sound familiar?

"I just can't concentrate!"
"I've got so much reading to do; I'll never be able to catch up!"
"I try to study, but nothing happens."
"I waste a lot of time just trying to get started."

A first step in setting the stage for learning is to establish and maintain a level of concentration that permits optimum learning. Concentration is a necessary condition to both learning and study. Regardless of your intelligence or the skills and talents you possess, unless you can keep your mind on the tasks at hand, you will find reading, learning, and studying difficult and frustrating. This section presents two methods of improving your concentration—excluding distractions and focusing your attention.

Excluding Distractions

It is impossible to eliminate all the sources of distraction and interruption, but if you can control several of the factors that interfere with concentration you will improve your ability to concentrate. Effective ways of controlling, if not eliminating, distractions are discussed in this section.

Choose a Place with Minimum Distraction

The place of physical location you choose for reading and study determines, in part, the number of distractions or interruptions you will have. If you try to read or study in a place where there is a lot of activity (doors slamming, people talking, a radio playing, machines running, and so forth), you will probably find that your mind wanders.

Choose a place where there is a minimum of distraction. If your home or dorm is too busy and noisy, study in a quiet place on campus. Try various student lounge areas, or check out study areas in the library. Empty classrooms are also good possibilities.

Establish a Study Area

Try to read and study in the same place rather than wherever it seems convenient at the time. There is a psychological advantage to working in the same place regularly. As with many other activities, you build a mental association, or connection, between an activity and the place where it occurs. If you sit down at a table set for dinner, for example, you expect to eat dinner. If you always sit in the same comfortable chair to watch television, eventually you expect to relax and watch television every time you sit in that chair. This psychological expectation also applies to reading and studying. If you become accustomed to working at a particular desk, you build up an association between the place—your desk—and the activity—reading and studying. Eventually, when you sit down at the desk, you expect to read or study. Your expectation makes the tasks at hand much easier; you do not have to convince yourself to work. Instead, you are almost automatically ready to read or study when you sit down at the desk.

In choosing a regular place to read, be sure you do not select a place you already associate with a different activity. Don't try to read in your TV chair or stretched out across your bed; you have already built associations with your chair and bed as places to relax or sleep.

Eliminate Distracting Clutter

Once you've organized a study area, keep it clear of possible distractions. Don't keep bills to be paid or letters to be answered on the desk where you study. Also do not keep photos, mementos, or interesting magazines that may draw your mind away from study near or on your desk.

Have Necessary Materials Available

When you sit down to read or study, be sure that all the materials you need are readily available. These might include a dictionary, pens, pencils, paper, a calculator, index cards, a calendar, a clock, and so on. Surrounding yourself with these materials will also help to create a psychological readiness for reading or studying. Furthermore, if you have to get up to locate any of these items, you break your concentration and take the chance of being distracted from the task at hand.

Study at Peak Periods of Attention

The time of day or night when you read or study may influence how easy or difficult it is to shut out distractions. Most people have a time limit for how long they can keep their minds on one thing. This is called *attention span*. Attention span changes from subject to subject, from book to book, from lecturer to lecturer, and from one time of day to another. People experience peaks and valleys in attention span at different times of the day. Some people are very alert in the early morning; others find they are most alert at midday or in the early evening. To make concentration easier, try to read and study during the peaks of your attention span. Choose the times of day when you are most alert and when it is easiest to keep your mind on what you are doing. If you are not aware of your own peaks of attention, do a quick analysis of your effectiveness. Over a period of several days, keep track of when you read and studied and how much you accomplished each time. Then look for a pattern.

Control Noise Levels

Some students find it difficult to concentrate in a completely quiet room. Others need some background noise in order to concentrate. Most students find some middle ground, or compromise, between total silence and a loud, noisy background. Research suggests that the volume of background music that interferes with concentration varies with individuals. A noise level that is distracting to one student may not disturb another. To find out how much background noise you can take, try different levels and see which seems best suited for you.

Pay Attention to Your Physical State

How you feel physically greatly influences how well you can concentate. If you are tired or sleepy, concentration will be difficult. If you are hungry, you will find that your thoughts drift toward what you'll have to eat when you're finished. If you feel sluggish, inactive, and in need of exercise, concentration will also be difficult. Try to schedule reading or studying at times when your physical needs are not likely to interfere. Also, if while reading, you find that you are hungry, tired, or sluggish, stop and try to correct the problem. Take a break, have a snack, or get up and walk around. If you are physically or mentally exhausted, however, it is usually best to stop and find a better time to complete the assignment.

EXERCISE 1 _____

Directions: *Decide what might interfere with studying in each of the following situations. Write your answer in the space provided.*

1. You are studying while stretched out on your bed.

    _____

2. You begin studying immediately after you get home from a vigorous basketball team practice.

    _____

3. You are studying while playing a tape you just purchased.

    _____

4. You are studying in an easy chair in front of the television.

    _____

5. You are studying on campus in the snack bar or cafeteria at noon, between your eleven o'clock and one o'clock classes.

    _____

6. You are studying at a table in the library and some friends decide to join you.

    _____

7. You are studying at your friend's house while you wait for her to get ready to go shopping.

    _____

Directions: *As you read an assignment this evening, be alert for distractions. Each time you lose your concentration, try to identify the cause. List below the items that distracted you and, if possible, describe a way to eliminate the distraction.*

1. _____

2. _____

3. _____

4. _____

Focusing Your Attention

Focusing your attention on what you are reading or studying will improve your concentration. By directing your attention to what you are reading or studying, you will find that your mind wanders less often, and that you are able to complete reading and study assignments more efficiently.

Establish Goals and Time Limits

Psychologically, establishing and achieving goals are positive, rewarding experiences. It makes you feel good and proves that you are accomplishing something. Use this psychological principle to help focus on what you are reading or studying. For each reading assignment you have, give yourself a goal to work toward. Instead of just sitting down and beginning, first figure out how much you can accomplish in a specific amount of time. Set a time limit and work toward meeting it. Working under time pressure will help you focus your attention because you will be aware that distractions and daydreaming cost you time and delay you in meeting your goal. Then when you achieve your goal, you will feel positive and know that you have accomplished something worthwhile.

Begin by establishing long-range goals. In Figure 4-4 you can see how one student set up study goals for the week. In Figure 4-5 the student has made his weekly goals more specific and detailed by setting time goals, day by day, for completing each assignment.

In setting goals and time limits, be as realistic and as specific as possible. For example, instead of deciding to study economics for two hours, set three more specific goals: review Chapter 2—½ hour; read and underline Chapter 3—1 hour; review lecture notes—½ hour.

EXERCISE 3 _____

Directions: *Review your class assignments, reading assignments, quizzes, and papers, including exams, for the next week of classes. Write a set of weekly reading/study goals that list what you hope to accomplish in each of your courses.*

Data Processing   *Review Chapters 2 + 3*
Edit and review 3 sets of class notes

English   *Type paper due Wed.*
Do draft of ideas for next paper.

Ecology   *Prepare for Lab on Friday.*
Read and understand Chapter 6
Review Chapter 5.

Psychology   *Start research for 1st project.*
Review for quiz #1 on Friday.

Speech Comm.   *Do draft of ideas for Speech #2*
Write reaction paper to film
shown on Tues.

FIGURE 4-4   Weekly Readings/Study Goals

EXERCISE 4 _____

Directions: *Using the weekly reading/study goals you prepared for Exercise 3, develop a set of daily reading/study goals that specify when you will complete each assignment and how much time you expect to spend on each.*

Reward Yourself

Setting and meeting goals within a time limit is one type of reward that can help you focus your attention. Other types of rewards can be used to help you keep your mind on what you are doing: daily activities you enjoy—such as watching television, eating, making phone calls—can be used as rewards if you arrange them to follow periods of reading and studying. You might, for example, plan to call a friend after you finish working on your math problems. In this situation, calling a friend becomes a reward for finishing your math assignment. Of, if you plan to rewrite your English composition before watching a favorite television program, the program becomes a reward for finishing your revision of the written assignment.

Get Interested in the Subject

Interest is a major factor in keeping your attention focused. Hardly anyone has difficulty concentrating on a magazine article that is highly interesting or keeping his or her mind on a film or television show he or she wants to see. It is when the subject matter is not extremely interesting that the problem of daydreaming occurs. Although you cannot change a dull subject to make it interesting, there are a few things you can do to create or develop your interest in the subject. Try the following suggestions:

1. Read critically. As you read, look for ideas that you can question or disagree with. Look for points of view, opinions, statements that are not supported.
2. Try to predict or anticipate the author's thoughts. See if you can predict what the author is leading up to or what point he or she will make next.

Mon.	Read Data Processing Chap. 2	1 hr.
	Edit Monday's class notes (D.P.)	15 mins.
	Draft ideas for Speech reaction paper	½ hr.
	Read Economics Chap. 6	1½ hr.
Tues.	Type English composition	½ hr.
	Proofread composition	15 mins.
	Review Chaps. 2 & 3 Psychology for quiz	2 hrs.
Wed.	Read Data Processing Chap. 3	1½ hr.
	Edit Wed. class notes in D.P.	10 mins.
Thurs.	Draft ideas - English composition	½ hr.
	Read Lab manual p. 152-160 and list procedures	45 min.
	Review Chapters 4 & 5 for Psychology quiz	2 hrs.
Fri.	Edit Fri's class D.P. notes	10 min.
Sat.	Review Economics Chap. 5	½ hr.
	Write and revise reaction paper for speech	1½ hr.
Sun.	Go to library - start Psychology research	2 hrs.

FIGURE 4-5 Daily Reading/Study Goals

3. Try to connect, or see the relationship between, new material and information you already have learned. Does the new material expand, alter, or contradict ideas you had before?

Use Writing to Focus Your Attention

Physical activities—such as writing and underlining—when combined with the mental activities of reading, reviewing, and memorizing, will help you focus your attention. By underlining, marking, outlining, or taking notes, you keep your mind active and involved. By deciding whether each idea is important enough to underline or write down, you are forced to think about, or pay attention to, each idea. To test the value of writing as you learn, try the following:

EXPERIMENT _____

Directions: *Below are listed two sets of words, which you will try to memorize. Follow each of the three steps right after you read the step. Do not read through all three steps before beginning.*

1. Read the words in set A once. Then reread them. Without looking, write down as many of the words as you can remember on a separate piece of paper.
2. Read the words in set B once. Then copy the words on a piece of paper. Without looking at the words or your copy of them, write down as many words as you can remember.
3. Check to see how many words you have correct on each list.

Set A			*Set B*		
MOM	COP	MOP	CAT	TAR	PAT
FAT	TAP	ARE	SAM	DAD	HOP
RAM	FAR	LAP	MAT	CAR	HAS
	RAM			RAT	

Most likely, you were able to remember more words in set B. Although you spent approximately the same amount of time learning the words in sets A and B, writing the words in B improved your ability to remember. This experiment demonstrates the value of combining writing with reading and remembering.

Vary Your Activities

Ability to focus on a particular subject will improve if you try not to force your concentration on only one type of activity for a long period of time. You might plan your study schedule so that you read sociology for a while, then work on math problems, and finally switch to writing an English paper. This plan would be much more effective than one with all reading activities— reading sociology, then reading chemistry, then reading an essay for English. As you vary the type and nature of your study activities, you are using different mental processes and different skills. The change from one skill or mental process to another will be refreshing and make concentration easier.

Keep a Distractions List

As you are reading or studying, often you will think of something you should remember to do. For example, a dental appointment you've scheduled for the next afternoon may flash through your mind. Although this flash does help you remember, it interferes with your concentration. To overcome these mental reminders flashing through your mind as you study, keep a distractions list. Have a separate sheet of paper nearby. Each time one of these mental reminders occurs, jot it down. You will find that by writing it down on paper, you will temporarily eliminate it from your memory. Use the same paper to record other ideas and problems that distract you. A distractions list might look like this:

Dentist - Tues. 2 p.m.
call Sam
buy Mother's Day Card
return library books

Use the Tally System to Build Your Attention Span

As mentioned earlier, your attention span is the length of time you can keep your mind focused on a particular subject without interference or distraction. An easy way to increase your attention span is to monitor, or keep track of, how many times you are distracted during a specified period of time (half an hour). Make a tally, or count, of distractions. Each time you think about something other than what you are studying, make a mark on the paper. Total your marks at the end of the specified time. Check yourself again, and try to reduce the number of distractions by 10 percent. Do not keep this tally every time you read or study anything, or you will rely on the technique to force your concentration. Instead, use it once every few days until you have sufficiently increased your concentration.

EXERCISE 5 _____

Directions: *Over the next week, try to build your attention span using the tally system suggested above. Record the results below.*

	Reading/Study Assignment	*Time Period*	*Number of Distractions*
1.			
2.			
3.			
4.			

LEARN ABOUT YOUR TEXTS

A first step in preparing to read and learn is to become familiar with the content and organization of each of your texts. Many students mistakenly buy their required texts the first few days of class, stack them on their desk, and wait until an assignment is given to open them. Before that first assignment, however, it is a good idea to discover how each book is organized and determine what useful study aids each contains. Spend 5 to 10 minutes becoming familiar with each of your texts. Check each of the following:

1. *The title and subtitle.* These are more than names or labels. They define the scope and purpose of the text as well as indicate its organization and level of difficulty. For example, an early American history textbook subtitled *Readings and Perspectives* indicates that the text is made up of articles and essays written by different authors which were chosen to provide the reader with various viewpoints on the subject.
2. *The author(s).* In many cases, the name will be unfamiliar, but as you acquire knowledge in new fields of study, you will begin to recognize names of authorities.
3. *The publication or copyright data.* It is always useful to be aware of how up to the date the text is. Especially in rapidly developing fields, a text written several years ago may be seriously outdated.

4. *The table of contents.* The table of contents provides a brief outline of the entire text. It lists all the major topics covered in the text and indicates how the text is organized.
5. *The preface or "To the Student."* This introductory portion of the text describes the text's organization and use. The preface may contain the following important information:
   □ Why the author wrote the text (his or her purpose in writing)
   □ From whom the book was written (audience)
   □ The author's major points of emphasis
   □ The author's particular slant or focus on the subject
   □ How the author organized the book
   □ Important references or authorities consulted when writing
   □ Suggestions on how to use the text
   □ Limitations or weaknesses of the text
6. *Learning aids.* Numerous learning aids are included in most textbook chapters. Before beginning to use any text, be sure to identify what it contains to help you learn more efficiently. The most common learning aids are described in Figure 4-6.
7. *References.* Some texts include a list of references at the end of each chapter or at the end of the book. This reference list is particularly useful when you have completed an assignment or do a term paper that requires you to locate other information sources. The reference list frequently contains some of the most useful or most authoritative books and articles on a given subject.
8. *Answer Key.* Texts and workbooks may contain a complete or selective answer key to assist you in checking your answers to problems and exercises.
9. *Appendix.* The appendix, located at the end of a text, is made up of extra information and materials that the author wanted to include in the text. Frequently, these are things that help students learn more about

FIGURE 4-6   Textbook Learning Features

Learning Aid	Description/Function
Chapter objectives	Focus your attention on key topics
Chapter overview or outline	Reflects content and organization of the chapter
Marginal notations	Offer commentary, pose questions, provide illustrations, examples, identify key vocabulary
Problem sets	Apply chapter content; useful for self-testing and review
Review questions	Test your recall of important concepts and ideas
Discussion questions	Provoke thought, reveal applications, integrate information
New terminology list	Lists new terms introduced in the chapter
Chapter summary	Reviews key points
Suggested readings	Provides additional reference sources

the subject matter, or items that must be referred to regularly. In an American history text, for example, appendixes might include a copy of the Constitution, of the Declaration of Independence, a map of the United States, and a list of the terms of office of American presidents.

10. *Glossary.* A glossary is an alphabetical listing of new vocabulary words that are used in the text. The meaning of each word is also included. Located in the back of the text, the glossary serves as a minidictionary.

11. *Index.* This alphabetical list of topics covered is useful in locating specific information in the text.

EXERCISE 6 ⎯⎯⎯⎯⎯⎯⎯⎯⎯⎯⎯⎯⎯⎯

Directions: *Each of the following three excerpts is taken from the preface of an introductory sociology textbook. Read each excerpt and then describe how each text differs in its approach to the study of sociology.*

1. STARTING SOCIOLOGY

The central issue is this: Sociologists are interested in how social influences and social processes of *any* type shape human behavior. Why, for example, does a dedicated political radical "change his stripes" upon graduation from college? Why does a "woman with everything" throw it all over for a nontraditional life-style? Why do people in American society, in significant numbers, "do drugs" when the evidence is overwhelming that continued usage frequently leads to personal and community disaster?

Finding the answers to such questions is not always easy. One reason for the difficulty is that human behavior is extremely complex and can be examined in many different ways. Consequently, a number of different approaches to its study have developed over the years, each claiming to make a unique contribution to our knowledge.[1]

2. SOCIOLOGY—AN INTRODUCTION

As in the first edition, our purpose in writing this text is to convey both the excitement of sociology and its relevance to students' lives. We feel that the excitement of sociology comes from its subject matter: social life and social organization. Sociology encompasses all aspects of society, including those that involve us in a direct and personal way: family life, community change, religion, and gender inequality, to name just a few. It involves a unique way of looking at the world in which we live, forcing us to question the obvious and understand how society and behavior are patterned and organized. More and more people are discovering that sociology provides them with unique skills and abilities: in research methods, in applying social theory in the working world, and in using their knowledge and understanding of social processes, organization, and change.[2]

3. AMERICA'S PROBLEMS

We wrote this book because we felt that the United States faces both unprecedented challenges and unprecedented opportunities as we move toward the twenty-first century and that meeting those challenges will require the best and most careful analysis of social issues we can muster. We believed that students should be introduced to the complex—

and often difficult—research bearing on the most important debates about social problems today, and that without that kind of exposure, they would be poorly prepared to participate in shaping American society in the future. We still share these beliefs. More than ever, we see the need for a book that can interpret the forces underlying contemporary changes in American society, and do so in a way that is accessible and interesting to students. We have tried to write a textbook for people who don't like textbooks—one that achieves depth without being stuffy and formal, that teaches without being pedantic, that is up-to-date and timely while staying in touch with the best traditions of social science.[3]

EXERCISE 7 _____

Directions: *Evaluate the front and end matter of one of your textbooks. Place a check mark in the appropriate box in the following list if the particular feature is present.*

CHECKLIST   Textbook Features

Preface

- ☐ The purpose of the text is stated.
- ☐ The intended audience is indicated.
- ☐ The preface explains how the book is organized.
- ☐ The author's credentials are included.
- ☐ Distinctive features are described.
- ☐ Major points of emphasis are discussed.
- ☐ Aids to learning are described.

Table of Contents

- ☐ Brief table of contents is included.
- ☐ The chapters are grouped into parts or sections.
- ☐ Thought pattern(s) throughout the text are evident.

Appendix

- ☐ Useful tables and charts are included.
- ☐ Supplementary documents are included.
- ☐ Background or reference material is included.

Glossary

- ☐ The text contains a glossary.
- ☐ Word pronunciation as well as meaning is provided.

Index

- ☐ A subject index is included.
- ☐ A name index is included.

EXERCISE 8 _____

Directions: *Evaluate one of your textbooks to discover what learning/study aids it contains. Use the following chart.*

Chapter preview

☐ What preview format is used?
☐ What is its primary purpose?
☐ How could it be used for review?

Marginal notes

☐ What format is used?
☐ How can these notes be used for study and review?

Review questions

☐ Do the questions provide an outline of chapter content (compare them with chapter headings)?
☐ What type(s) of thinking do they require? Are they primarily factual, or do they require critical thinking?

Discussion questions

☐ What topics are emphasized?
☐ Do these questions suggest applications, practical problems, hypothetical situations?

Key terminology

☐ How many, if any, words are already familiar?
☐ How difficult do you predict the chapter to be?

Chapter summary

☐ Does it list the main topics the chapter will cover?

Suggested readings

☐ What types of sources are listed?
☐ To which topics do they refer?

ACTIVATE YOUR KNOWLEDGE AND EXPERIENCE

Before beginning to read or learn about any topic, it is helpful to discover what you already know about it. Two principles of learning—meaningfulness and association—are relevant here (see Chapter 3). By discovering what you already know about a topic, you will make new learning more meaningful and will have identified familiar material to which you can associate new learning. Thus learning will occur more easily and retrieval will become more efficient. You will find, too, that reading material becomes more interesting once you have connected its topic with your own experience. Comprehension will be easier, too, since you will have already thought about some of the ideas presented in the material.

Suppose you are about to begin reading a chapter in a business textbook on advertising that discusses objectives of advertising, construction and design of ads, and production of ads. Before you begin reading the chapter, you should spend a minute or two recalling what you already know about these topics. Activate your background information and experience with the topic by using one or more of the following technqiues.

1. *Ask questions and try to answer them.* You might ask questions such as "What are the objectives of advertising?" In answering this question you will realize you already know several objectives: to sell a product, to introduce a new product, to announce sales or discounts, and so forth.

2. *Relate the topic to your own experience.* For a topic on the construction and design of ads, think about ads you have heard or read recently. What similarities exist? How do they begin? How do they end? Most likely, this process will lead you to realize that you already know something about how ads are designed.

3. *Free associate.* On a scrap sheet of paper, jot down everything that comes to mind about advertising. List facts and questions, or describe ads that you have recently heard or seen. This process will also activate your recall of information.

At first, you may think you know very little or nothing about a particular topic. However, by using one of the above techniques, you will be surprised to find that there are very few topics about which you know nothing at all. For example, suppose you were about to read a biology chapter on genetics— at first you may think you know nothing about it. Complete Exercise 9, to discover what you do know about genetics.

EXERCISE 9 ———————————

Directions: *For the topics of genetics, write a list of questions, experiences, or associations. (Hint: think of inherited family traits and characteristics, ask questions about eye and hair color.) When you have finished, compare your work with the student sample shown in Figure 4-7.*

What color of eye is dominant?
Is tendency to be overweight inherited?
What do genes do?
How many do we have?
What is genetic engineering?
Are aspects of personality inherited?
Can environment influence genetics?
Why do some woman have facial hair?
Can genes be defective? If so, what happens?
What do chromosomes do?
Is hair loss hereditary?
Can a person have two eyes each of a
different color?

FIGURE 4-7   A Student Sample

EXERCISE 10 _____

Directions: *Activate your knowledge and experience about each of the following topics. Use one of the techniques described above for each topic. Use each technique once.*

Topics

1. Creativity
2. Aggressive behavior
3. Body language

When you have finished, answer the questions below.

1. Did you discover you knew more about the topics than you initially thought?
2. Which technique worked best? Why?
3. Might the technique you choose depend on your subject matter?

EXERCISE 11 _____

Directions: *One topic covered in the sample textbook chapter included in Appendix A (pages 426–428) is sources of stress. Activate your knowledge about this topic using one of the techniques described in this section. Then turn to the sample chapter and assess how many sources of stress you correctly identified.*

EXERCISE 12 _____

Directions: *Select a chapter from one of your textbooks. Use one of the techniques described in this section to discover what you already know about the subject of the chapter.*

SUMMARY

Reading and learning are multi-stage, interrelated processes that involve planning and preparation. This chapter helps you set the stage for learning—to get ready to learn and study actively and efficiently.

Awareness of how you learn is essential to effective learning. The chapter helps you analyze your learning style using the Learning Style Questionnaire and discusses how to compensate for learning style limitations.

Establishing and maintaining concentration is also essential to learning. The chapter offers suggestions for excluding distractions and focusing your attention. Familiarity with each of your texts and the learning aids they contain contributes to effective learning. Learning aids include chapter objective, chapter overview, marginal notations, problem sets, review and discussion questions, new terminology lists, chapter summary, and suggested readings. Finally, familiarity with the subject to be learned enhances learning. The chapter describes three methods for discovering what you already know about a subject—questioning, relating to previous experience, and free association.

5

Prereading and Predicting

Use this chapter to:
1. *Use prereading to get interested in what you are reading and to increase retention.*
2. *Make predictions about content and organization.*

Do you check for traffic before crossing a street? Do you check the depth of a pool before diving in? What do you do to an article or chapter before you read it, before you "jump in"? In this chapter you will become acquainted with the technique of prereading—a useful way of checking any written material before you read it. Just as most people check traffic before crossing a street or water depth before diving, efficient readers check printed materials before reading to become generally familiar with the overall content and organization. The first section of this chapter will demonstrate the technique of prereading.

Once you are familiar with a piece of writing, the next step is to make predictions about the material. You might make predictions, or educated guesses, about how difficult or interesting the material will be, what topics will be discussed, or how the author will approach the subject. You might also anticipate how the material will be organized—how it progresses from one idea to another. The second portion of this chapter will direct you in making accurate and useful predictions.

HOW TO PREREAD

Your overall purposes in prereading are to identify the most important ideas in the material and note their organization. You look only at specific parts and skip over the rest. The portions to look at in prereading a textbook chapter are described in the following paragraphs. Later you will learn how to adapt this procedure to other types of material.

Read the Title and Subtitle

The title provides the overall topic of the article or chapter; the subtitle suggests the specific focus, aspect, or approach toward the overall topic.

Read the Introduction or First Paragraph

The introduction, or first paragraph if there is no introduction, serves as a lead-in to the chapter. It gives you an idea of where the material is starting and where it is heading.

Reading Each Major Heading

The headings function as labels or topic statements for what is contained in the sections that follow them. In other words, a heading announces the major topic of each section.

Read the First Sentence Under Each Heading

The first sentence frequently tells you what the passage is about or states the central thought. You should be aware, however, that in some types of material or in certain styles of writing the first sentence does not function as a central thought. Instead, the opening sentence may function as a transition or lead-in statement, or may be written to catch your interest. If the first sentence seems unimportant, read the last sentence; often this sentence states or restates the central thought.

Note Any Typographical and Graphical Aids

Italics are used to emphasize important terms and definitions by using slanted (italic) type to distinguish them from the rest of the passage. Notice any material that is numbered 1, 2, 3, lettered a, b, c, or presented in list form. Graphs, charts, pictures, and tables are other means of emphasis and are usually meant to point out what is important in the chapter. Be sure to read the captions for pictures and the legends on graphs, charts, or tables. Notice words in italics or dark print—usually a definition follows.

Read the Last Paragraph or Summary

The summary or last paragraph gives a condensed view of the chapter and helps you identify key ideas. Often the summary outlines the key points in the chapter.

Read Quickly Any End-of-Article or End-of-Chapter Material

This might include references, study questions, vocabulary lists, or biographical information about the author. These materials will be useful later as you read and study the article or chapter, and it is important, as part of prereading, to note if such materials are included. If there are study questions, it is useful to read them through quickly since they will indicate what is important in the chapter. If a vocabulary list is included, rapidly skim through it to identify terms you will need to learn as you read.

DEMONSTRATION OF PREREADING

The textbook chapter excerpt seen in Figure 5-1 has been included to demonstrate what it is like to preread. This chapter excerpt is taken from an introductory text, *Psychology*, by Wade and Tavris (HarperCollins, 1990). Features of this text are referred to frequently; the complete chapter is included in Appendix A. To illustrate how prereading is done, these pages have been specially marked. Everything that you should look at or read has been shaded. Preread this exerpt now, reading only the shaded portions of each page.

Now that you have seen what it is like to preread, you are ready to test the technique and observe its benefits. Turn to the sample textbook chapter "Health, Stress, and Coping" in Appendix A (page 419). You have already preread two pages. Preread the entire chapter. You should not spend more than five minutes. When you finish, answer each question in the following exercise.

EXERCISE 1 _____

Directions: *Answer each of the following questions after you have preread the sample textbook chapter in Appendix A. Mark T after statements that are true and F after those that are false. Do not look back in the chapter to locate the answers. When you finish, check your answers in the answer key and write your score in the space indicated.*

1. There is a connection between stress and illness. ___T___

2. Stress has become a topic for study only within the past 20 years. ___F___

3. Learning to live with a source of stress is not discussed in the chapter. ___F___

4. Some psychologists believe that small daily aggravations create stress. ___T___

5. Most people who suffer stress become ill. *not* ___F___

6. Friends can help a person cope with stress. ___T___

7. Four major sources of stress are bereavement, life events, daily hassles, and continuing problems. ___T___

8. Reappraisal and avoidance are means of coping with stress. *loke* ___T___

9. Relaxation has proven ineffective in coping with stress. ___F___

10. Negative emotions and loss of control may affect health. ___T___

Score (number right): _____

Look back at your score on the quiz in Exercise 1. Most likely you got at least half of the questions right, perhaps more. This quiz was a test of the main ideas that were presented in the chapter. You can see, then, that pre-reading does familiarize you with the chapter and enables you to identify and remember many of the main ideas it contains. Actually, each part of the chapter that you read while prereading provided you with specific information about the organization and content of the chapter. The following exercise emphasizes how each step in the prereading process provides you with useful information about the material to be read.

EXERCISE 2 ─────────────────

Directions: *Listed below are various parts of an actual textbook chapter or article to which you would refer in prereading. Read the parts; then answer the question that follows.*

1. *Sample text*
   Title: *Introductory Psychology*
   Subtitle: *Selected Case Studies and Readings*
   Question: What further information does the subtitle provide about the text content?

   _____

   _____

2. *Sample article*
   Title: "Psychologists Have Proof of ESP"
   Source: *Today's Women* magazine
   Question: Answer with yes or no. Would you expect this article to
   a. be technical?
   b. be highly factual with careful references?
   c. contain accounts of individuals with ESP?
   d. contain opinions?
   e. contain references for further study?

3. *Sample text*
   Section heading: Culture and Technology
   Subheadings: Historical Roots and Trends
   Recent Technological Changes
   Predicted Long-Range Effects
   Question: What clues do you have about how the author arranged ideas in this section of the text?

   _____

   _____

4. *Sample text*
   Title: *Business Management*
   Subtitle: *An Organizational Perspective*
   Copyright: 1981

(Text continued on page 88.)

Some sources of stress

What are the stressors that might affect the immune system and thus lead to illness? Some psychologists study the significant events that disrupt our lives and take an emotional toll. Others count nuisances, the small straws that break the camel's back. Still others emphasize continuing pressures.

Life events. Years ago, Thomas Holmes and Richard Rahe (1967) identified 43 events that seemed to be especially stressful. By testing thousands of people, they were able to rank a series of "life-change events" in order of their disruptive impact. Holmes and Rahe then assigned each event a corresponding number of "life-change units" (LCUs). At the top was death of a spouse (100 LCUs), followed by divorce (73), imprisonment (63), and death of a close family member (63). Not all of the events were unpleasant. Marriage (50) was on the list, as were pregnancy (40), buying a house (31), and Christmas (12). Among people who had become ill, the large majority had had 300 LCUs or more in a single year.

Later studies found numerous flaws in the idea that *all* life events are stressful and lead to illness. First, many of the items on the Holmes-Rahe scale are the *result* of psychological problems or illness, not their cause (such as "problems at work" and "major changes in sleeping habits") (Hudgens, 1974). Second, some events become more stressful once a person is already depressed or ill (Dohrenwend, 1979). Third, as we saw in Chapter 14, many expected changes, such as retirement or having the children leave home, are not especially stressful for most people. Happy, positive events are not related (thank goodness) to illness or poor health (Taylor, 1986). Finally, simply counting "life-change units" is not enough: Having 17 things happen to you in one year is not necessarily stressful unless you feel overwhelmed by them (Cohen, Kamarck, & Mermelstein, 1983; Sarason, Johnson, & Siegel, 1978).

Bereavement and tragedy. Some events, of course, are more shocking to the system, psychologically and physically, than others. The events at the top of the Holmes-Rahe list, death of a spouse and divorce, are powerful stressors that are linked to a subsequent decline in health. Widows and widowers are more susceptible to illness and physical ailments, and their mortality rate is higher than expected (Calabrese, Kling, & Gold, 1987). Divorce also often takes a long-term health toll. Divorced adults have higher rates of emotional disturbance, heart disease, pneumonia, and other diseases than comparable adults who are not divorced (Jacobson, 1983; Weiss, 1975).

Bereaved and divorced people may be vulnerable to illness because, feeling unhappy and lonely, they don't sleep well, they stop eating properly, and they consume more drugs and cigarettes. But animal and human studies suggest that separation *itself* creates changes in the cardiovascular system, a lowered white blood cell count, and other abnormal responses of the immune system (Laudenslager & Reite, 1984; Stein, Keller, & Schleifer, 1985). You may recall from Chapters 10 and 13 that attachment appears to be a basic biological need of the

FIGURE 5-1 Prereading

species, and broken attachments affect us at a basic cellular level. But the quality of the attachment is as important as its presence. Unhappily married individuals show the same decline in immune function as unhappy divorced people (Kiecolt-Glaser et al., 1987a).

Sadly, many people suffer shocking experiences that are not on the Holmes-Rahe list—experiences about which they feel so secret, and dirty, that the secret itself adds to the stress. (See "A Closer Look at Psychoneuroimmunology" for a fascinating case study of how this field's findings have yielded a therapeutic suggestion for recovery from trauma.)

Daily hassles. Some psychologists argue that we handle most of the big problems of life relatively well; it's the daily grind that can get us down. "Hassles" are the irritations and frustrations of everyday routines, such as thoughtless roommates, traffic, bad weather, annoying arguments, broken plumbing, lost keys, and sick cats. Some research suggests that hassles are better predictors of psychological and physical symptoms than are life changes (DeLongis et al., 1982). In one study of 75 married couples, the frequency of daily hassles was related to later health problems such as flu, sore throats, headaches, and backaches (DeLongis, Folkman, & Lazarus, 1988).

How do you cope with headaches and hassles? These airplane passengers, frustrated about a canceled flight, show the many possible responses to life's annoyances: amused friendliness, sullen acceptance, efforts to get information, and just plain gloom.

Of course, a major event, such as divorce, often increases the number of hassles a person must contend with (new financial pressures, custody questions, moving) and might make a person more intolerant of small hassles. By and large, though, people's reports of being hassled are independent of life events. In a study of 210 police officers, the most stressful things they reported were not the dramatic dangers you see on television, but daily paperwork, annoyance with ''distorted'' accounts of the police in the press, and the snail-like pace of the judicial system (Grier, 1982).

Notice, though, that when people report that something is a hassle, they are really reporting their feelings about it. The activity itself might be neutral. A young mother who says that making meals every day is a hassle is revealing her attitudes and emotions about this chore. Perhaps because she has so many other things to do every day, preparing dinner feels to her like the last straw. Her husband might look forward to cooking as an enjoyable way to reduce tension. So the measure of ''hassles,'' like that of ''stressful events,'' may be confounded with existing symptoms of emotional distress (Dohrenwend & Shrout, 1985).

Continuing problems. Many stress researchers believe that people have a good ability to withstand acute (short-term) stress, even a massive blow. The real problem, they say, occurs when stress becomes interminable: working in a pressure-cooker occupation; living with a tyrannical parent; living with discrimination because of your color, religion, gender, or age; feeling trapped in a situation you can't escape.

Under conditions of chronic stress, many people do not show physical adaptation to the stressor. In a study of 34 people who were taking care of a relative with advanced Alzheimer's disease—a relentless source of stress if there ever was one—the caregivers had significantly lower percentages of T lymphocytes and helper T lymphocytes than the control group and showed other abnormalities of the immune system. Their immune systems were apparently not adapting to the chronic stress (Kiecolt-Glaser et al., 1987b).

Prolonged or repeated stress (from occupations such as air traffic controller or from circumstances such as unemployment) is associated with heart disease, hypertension, arthritis, and immune-related deficiencies (Taylor, 1986). Black men in America who live in stressful neighborhoods (characterized by poverty, high divorce and unemployment rates, crime, and drug use) are particularly vulnerable to hypertension and related diseases (Gentry, 1985; Harburg et al., 1973). Female clerical workers who feel they have no support from their bosses, who are stuck in low-paying jobs without hope of promotion, and who have financial problems at home are the women most at risk of heart disease (Haynes & Feinleib, 1980).

FIGURE 5-1   *(Continued)*

What is "stressful" about stress?

In general, health psychologists today believe that life changes *are* related to your state of health, although the relationship is weak (Cohen & Edwards, 1989). Something else is going on between the event and your response to it. One of those things, as by now you can guess, is your perception of how stressful an event, a "hassle," or an accumulation of events is. In turn, feeling overwhelmed by stress depends on whether or not you feel you can *control* it. What seems to be most debilitating about chronically stressful situations is the feeling of powerlessness, of having no control over what happens. People can tolerate years of difficulty if they feel they can *control* events or at least *predict* them (Laudenslager & Reite, 1984). These are not necessarily the same thing. You may not be able to control the stressful experience of an exam, but you can usually predict and prepare for it. When people know that they will be going through a hard time or living in a stressful environment, they can take steps to reduce stress. We will return to this important topic of control later.

QUICK ■ QUIZ

We hope these questions are not sources of stress for you.

1. Steve is unexpectedly called on in class to discuss a question. He doesn't have the faintest idea of the answer, and he feels his heart start to pound and his palms to sweat. He is in the _____ phase of the GAS.
2. Which of the Holmes-Rahe "life-change events" has the strongest relationship to immune problems and illness? **(a)** marriage, **(b)** bereavement, **(c)** taking an exam, **(d)** moving, **(e)** hassles
3. Maria works in a fast-food shop. Which aspect of the job is likely to be *most* stressful for her? **(a)** the speed of the work, **(b)** the predictable routine, **(c)** feeling unable to make any changes in her job, **(d)** the daily demands from customers

Answers:
1. alarm 2. b 3. c

Question: What does this information tell you about the usefulness and limitations of the material contained in this text?

_____

_____

5. *Sample text*

Title: *Biology*

Chapter title: "The Human Animal: An Introduction"

Chapter summary:

We are vertebrates. As such, we have a bony, jointed supporting endoskeleton that includes a skull and a vertebral column exclosing the central nervous system. Our bodies contain a coelom that is divided by a muscle, the diaphragm, into two major compartments, the abdominal cavity and the thoracic cavity.

Our bodies are organized into tissues and organs. Tissues are groups of cells that are structurally, functionally, and developmentally similar. Various types of tissues are grouped in different ways to form organs, and organs are grouped to form organ systems. The four principle tissue types of which our bodies are made are epithelial tissue, connective tissue, muscle, and nerve. Epithelium serves as a covering or lining for the body and its cavities. Glands are composed of specialized epithelial cells. Their secretions include mucus, perspiration, milk, saliva, hormones, and digestive enzymes. Connective tissues are characterized by their capacity to secrete substances, such as collagen and other fibers, that make up the intercellular matrix. They serve to support, strengthen, and protect the other tissues of the body. Muscle cells are specialized for contraction. Muscle is categorized as striated muscle or smooth muscle. In striated muscle, which includes cardiac and skeletal muscle, the stripped pattern is due to regular assemblies of specialized proteins, actin and myosin. Smooth muscle, or involuntary muscle, is under the control of the autonomic nervous system, whereas striated muscle (with the exception of cardiac muscle) is under somatic control. Nerve cells, or neurons, are specialized for the conduction of an electrical impulse. Neurons consist of dendrites, a cell body, and an axon. Neurons are surrounded and supported by neuroglia or Schwann cells.

A multicellular animal processes nutrients to yield energy and structural materials. It regulates its internal environment, a process known as homeostasis. It coordiates the activities of its many tissues and organ systems in response to changes in both the internal and external environments. These integration and control systems characteristically function through negative feedback loops. Finally, as dictated by its genes, the organism reproduces itself.

–Curtis, *Biology,* p. 670

Question: The chapter will emphasize
a. the human as a vertebrate
b. the organization and functioning of the human body
c. the four principal tissue types
d. integration and control systems

6. *Sample text*

Title: *Organizational Behavior and Performance*

Chapter title: "Leadership"

Chapter introduction:

Leadership is one of the most important elements affecting organizational performance. For the manager, leadership is activity through which the goals and objectives of the organization are accomplished. Leadership has been the focus of attention of behavioral scientists because leaders have a significant effect on the behavior, attitudes, and preformances of employees.

Leadership has been studied for a number of years, resulting in numerous theories and models. Like motivation, no universally accepted theoretical framework of leadership has been developed. This chapter will examine the development of leadership theory from early studies to current situational approaches. We will first examine the concept of influence as one foundation of leadership, and then discuss the three main theoretical approaches to leadership—trait, behavioral, and situational theories. Finally, we will present some contemporary issues in leadership and combine the presented material in an integrative model that stresses the importance of a manager's developing the ability to *diagnose* a situation and alter his or her style of leadership in the most effective manner.

–Szilagyi and Wallace, *Organizational Behavior and Performance*, p. 317

Questions: a. Describe the chapter's organization.

_____

b. The chapter will focus primarily on
   1. historical approaches in leadership
   2. current problems in leadership
   3. diagnosing a leadership style
   4. theories of leadership

7. *Sample text*

Title: *Our Changing Economy*

Subtitle: *An Introduction to Economics*

Chapter title: "Why Are There Economic Systems?"

Graphic aids: The chapter includes the following graphic aids:
   a. a graph showing the relationship between production of various types of goods and price
   b. a "Beetle Bailey" cartoon that illustrates that choice is associated with cost
   c. a picture of various objects that have been used as money in various cultures throughout the world

Question: What clues do the graph, cartoon, and picture give you about the chapter content?

_____

_____

8. *Sample text*

Title:	*The World Today*
Subtitle:	*Its Patterns and Cultures*
Chapter title:	"The Orient"
Section headings:	This chapter is divided into four major sections:

    a. The Heritage of the Past in the Orient
    b. How the People of the Orient Make a Living
    c. New Directions for India, Pakistan, and Southeast Asia
    d. The People's Republic of China, Democracy, and the Uncommitted Orient

Question: By noting the section titles within this chapter, what do you expect about the organization and content of the chapter?

_____

_____

PREREADING SPECIFIC TYPES OF MATERIAL

Textbook Chapters

This technique of prereading is highly effective when used in reading textbook chapters. When approaching a lengthy textbook chapter, first preread it entirely, noting only major groups of ideas. Then divide the chapter into smaller segments or sections and preread, then read, each section.

Articles and Essays

When prereading magazine articles, essays, or excerpts included within a book, in addition to the items listed earlier under the section "How to Preread," be sure to pay particular attention to:

1. *The title.* It often suggests the topic and author's focus, although sometimes it is intended to catch your interest.
2. *The author.* Check to see who wrote the material. If you are able to recognize the author's name, then you can form a set of expectations about the content of the article.
3. *The source.* When prereading material reprinted from another source, use the footnote or acknowledgment at the beginning or end to determine where the material was originally published. How much you accept of what is said depends on the type of publication the article appeared in. For example, you would expect an article on aggression published in *Newsweek* to be more factual than an article on the same topic published in a supermarket tabloid.

Reference Material

When you are collecting information for a class assignment or research paper, prereading is a valuable technique to use to identify sources that contain the information you need. When you have identified a book that appears to contain information on the topic you are researching, take a few moments to preread before checking it out of the library or using valuable time reading it unnecessarily. By prereading you may find that the source does not contain information you need, that it is too general or too detailed for your purpose, or that it only contains information you have already collected from another source.

To preread reference material, first check the index and table of contents. Then, if your topic is listed, quickly preread the appropriate sections or chapters to determine if they contain information that suits your purpose.

Newspapers

Information in newspaper articles is structured differently from most other types of writing. In contrast to most material in which the first few sentences are introductory, the opening sentences in news stories frequently carry the *most* important information. As the article progresses, the facts presented become more and more detailed, and you find more background information. To preread a news article, then, read the headline, the first few lines, and section headings; then glance through the rest of the article, picking up details such as names, dates, and places.

Textbooks

Always become familiar with the scope and organization of a textbook before beginning to read a specific assignment. Refer to Chapter 4 "Learn About Your Texts" for specific suggestions.

Research Reports/Journal Articles

Titles of research reports and journal articles usually reveal the subject matter and may suggest conclusions as well.

Formats of articles depend on the journal in which they are printed, as well as the academic discipline they represent. Many begin with an abstract, which summarizes the author's purpose, methodology, and findings. If an abstract is included, this is sufficient to preread. If there is no abstract, then preview as you would a textbook chapter, reading the introduction, headings, and summary or conclusion.

Material Without Headings

Earlier in this chapter you learned that when prereading you should read boldface (dark print) headings. However, much material is written without these convenient labels of section content. In articles and chapters without headings, prereading becomes more time consuming because you must read the first sentence of each paragraph. As you will see later in the text, by reading the first sentence of each paragraph, you are often reading the main idea of the paragraph. Articles or chapters without headings may still have introductory and concluding portions, graphic material, and questions at the end. You can also get ideas from the organization of the material. Is it a list of ideas on the topic? Is it a series of events? If you can see this, you will know what to expect in the rest of the article or chapter.

Research studies suggest that prereading does increase comprehension and improve recall. Several studies show that prereading is a useful technique for reading textbook chapters. In a classic study done by McClusky,* college students were divided into two groups. One group was taught how to use headings and summaries for prereading; the other group received no instruction. Both groups were given a selection to read and comprehension questions to answer. Results of the study indicated that the group who used headings and summaries read 24 percent faster and just as accurately as the students who did not preread.

Prereading is effective for several reasons. First, prereading helps you get interested in and involved with what you will read. It activates your thinking. Through prereading, you become familiar with the material or gain advance information about it. You become acquainted with the general subject of the material, you discover who wrote it, and you learn when and where it was published. You also become aware of the main subtopics and how they are organized. Because you know what to expect, then, reading the material completely will be easier.

Second, prereading helps bring to mind what you already know about the subject, thereby making the material more meaningful and interesting.

Third, prereading provides you with a mental outline of the material you are going to read. As you read the headings of a chapter, you are actually forming a mental outline of the chapter. You begin to anticipate the sequence of ideas; you see the relationships of topics to one another; you recognize what approach and direction the author has taken in writing about his or her subject. With this outline in mind, the actual reading is a much simpler task. Reading the chapter becomes a matter of filling in the parts of the outline with the proper details.

Fourth, prereading is useful because it enables you to apply several principles of learning. Through prereading, you identify what is important, thus establishing an intent to remember. Prereading also facilitates meaningfulness by allowing you to become familiar with the basic content and organization of the material. Because prereading also provides an additional repetition of the major points, it functions as a type of rehearsal that enhances recall.

Prereading is used best with expository, factual material that is fairly well organized. Knowing this, you can see that prereading is not a good strategy to use when reading materials such as novels, poems, narrative articles, essays, or short stories. However, you will find it fairly easy to adapt the prereading technique to various types of writing you read.

EXERCISE 3 ———————————————

Directions: *Select a chapter from one of your textbooks. To be practical, choose a chapter that you will be assigned to read in the near future. After prereading it, answer the following questions.*

1. What is the major topic of the chapter?

———————————————————————————

* H. Y. McClusky, "An Experiment on the Influence of Preliminary Skimming on Reading," *Journal of Educational Psychology,* 25 (1934): 521–29.

2. How does the author subdivide or break down this topic?

_____

3. What approach does the author take toward the subject? (Does he or she cite research, give examples, describe problems, list causes?)

_____

4. Can you construct a very general mental outline of the chapter?

_____

MAKING PREDICTIONS

Do you predict what a film will be about and whether it's worthwhile based on a coming attractions preview? Do you anticipate what a party will be like before attending? This type of prediction or anticipation is typical and occurs automatically. Do you predict what a chapter will discuss before you read it?

Research studies of how good and poor readers read demonstrate that efficient readers frequently predict and anticipate both before and while reading both content and organization of the material. For example, from the title of a textbook chapter, you can predict the subject and, often, how the author will approach it. A business management textbook chapter titled "Schools of Management Thought: Art or Science?" indicates the subject—schools of management—but also suggest that the author will classify the various schools as artistic (creative) or scientific. Similarly, author, source, headings, graphics, photographs, chapter previews, and summaries, all of which you may check during prereading, provide additional information for anticipating content.

Making accurate predictions involves drawing on your background knowledge and experience. It is a process of making connections between what you already know about the subject and the clues you picked up from prereading. Now, use your knowledge and experience to predict the topic and/or approach of each of the following essays:

"The Threat of Radon Gas"
"The Motion Picture? Art or Industry?"
"Art as Social Commentary"

Did you predict that the first essay will discuss possible health risks of radon gas, that the second will debate whether motion pictures are an art form or a business product, and that the third essay will describe how art provides a vehicle for reacting to or commenting on our society?

Efficient readers frequently make predictions about organization as well as context. That is, they anticipate the order or manner in which ideas or information will be presented. For instance from a chapter section titled "The History of World Population Growth" you can predict that the chapter will be organized chronologically, moving ahead in time as the chapter progresses. A chapter titled "Behavioral vs. Situational Approaches to Leadership" suggests that the chapter will compare and contrast the two approaches to leadership.

As efficient readers read, they also confirm, reject, or revise their initial predictions. For example, a student read the heading "Types of Managers" and anticipated the section to describe different management styles. Then he began reading:

TYPES OF MANAGERS

Now that you have an idea of what the management process is, consider the roles of managers themselves. It is possible to classify managers by the nature of the position they hold. This section will review some of the major categories of managers. The next section will identify how these differences affect a manager's job.

Thus, he revised his prediction—realizing that managers would not be classified by style—but by the position they hold.

Making predictions and anticipating content and organization are worthwhile and important for several reasons. First, it focuses your attention on the material. Second, the process of confirming, rejecting, or revising predictions is an active one—it forces concentration and facilitates comprehension. Third, once you know what to expect in a piece of reading, you will find that it is easier to read.

EXERCISE 4 _____

Directions: *For the textbook chapter described below, predict which of the following topics might appear in the chapter, and place a checkmark next to each.*

Textbook Title: *Psychology: An Introduction*
  Chapter: Human Development Before Birth
  Headings: The Mechanics of Heredity
        Prenatal Development: Influences Before Birth

Topics _____ 1. cognitive abilities of newborns

_____ 2. sex determination

_____ 3. auditory stimulation of infants

_____ 4. intellectual deficits

_____ 5. fetal alcohol syndrome

_____ 6. dominant and recessive genes

_____ 7. observing perceptual development

_____ 8. chromosome abnormalities

_____ 9. siblings as behavioral role models

_____ 10. upper limb development

EXERCISE 5 _____

Directions: *Below are listed a textbook title, chapter title, and chapter headings. For each of the statements listed, place a checkmark in front of the statements you predict might appear in the chapter. If possible, also indicate the section in which it is most likely to appear. (Indicate by marking 1, 2, 3, 4, or 5 to correspond to the headings in successive order.)*

Textbook Title: *America's Problems: Social Issues and Public Policy*
Chapter Title: The Family
Headings: Some Trends in Family Disruption
The Consequences of Family Disruption
Inequality in the Family: Division of Labor in the Home
Work, Family, and Social Supports
The Family as a Crucible of Violence

Statements:

_____ 1. Divorce creates social and personal stress for both children and parents.

_____ 2. Sex-role stereotypes dictate how much males contribute to housekeeping chores.

_____ 3. Street crime takes an enormous toll on citizens, and only rarely results in prosecution by the courts.

_____ 4. Child and spouse abuse is aggravated by poverty and gender inequality.

_____ 5. The continued concentration of minorities in low-paying jobs is a reflection of inequality.

_____ 6. Lack of day care for single-parent families creates insurmountable problems.

_____ 7. Changing health care policies have reduced public responsibilities for family health care maintenance.

EXERCISE 6 _____

Directions: *The sample textbook chapter in Appendix A is titled "Health, Stress, and Coping." Make a list of topics you predict it will cover. Next, read the chapter headings and chapter summary. Then review your list of predictions and place a check next to those the chapter will address.*

EXERCISE 7 _____

Directions: *Select a chapter from one of your textbooks. Preread the chapter and then write a list of predictions about the chapter's content or organization.*

SUMMARY

Prereading is a technique that allows the reader to become familiar with the material to be read before beginning to read it completely. The technique involves checking specific parts of an article or textbook chapter that provide the reader with a mental outline of the content of the material. Prereading makes the actual reading of the material easier and helps the reader understand and remember what he or she reads. In prereading, the reader should note items such as the following: title and subtitle; the author and source; publication or copyright date; introduction or first paragraph; each major heading and the first sentence under it; typographical aids (italics, maps, pictures, charts, graphs); summary of last paragraph; and end-of-chapter or end-of-article materials.

Predicting, or anticipating, content and organization is an extension of prereading. It is a process of making connections between what you already know about the subject and the clues you picked up during prereading. Efficient readers not only make predictions, they continually revise and modify them as they read.

6

Focusing and Monitoring Your Learning

Use this chapter to:

1. *Establish purposes for reading.*
2. *Select appropriate reading strategies.*
3. *Monitor your comprehension.*
4. *Assess the effectiveness of your learning.*

To those unfamiliar with the game, basketball might seem to be only a matter of placing a ball in a basket while preventing the opposing team members from doing the same. Similarly, football might appear to be a simple process of scoring field goals and touchdowns. Players of these games know, however, that each is a complex process involving skill, knowledge, and experience. Players devise a game plan or strategy as they play, evaluate, and revise the game plan to suit the conditions at hand. Football players must develop skill too, in running, blocking, tackling, and passing; they must learn plays, rules, and penalties.

Reading, too, may at first appear to be a simple physical process—moving one's eyes across lines of print. Like football, however, reading is a complex activity involving skill, knowledge, and experience. A skillful reader defines a game plan that includes purposes and strategies for reading. A reader must also apply skills in recognizing words, understanding main ideas and details, and following organizational development.

The purpose of this chapter is to help you develop a "game plan" for reading. You will learn to set purposes for reading, select appropriate strategies, monitor your comprehension, and assess and revise the effectiveness of the strategies you selected.

DEFINE YOUR PURPOSES FOR READING

Have you ever read a complete page or more and then not remembered a thing you read? Have you wandered aimlessly through paragraph after paragraph, section after section, unable to remember key ideas you have just read, even when you were really trying to concentrate? If these problems sound familiar, you probably began reading without a specific purpose in mind. That is, you were not looking for anything in particular as you read. Perhaps the single most important thing to do to understand and remember more of what you read is to identify your purposes—to decide what facts and ideas you are looking for, and then read to find them.

By now, you are probably beginning to see the relationship of prereading and predicting, discussed in the last chapter, to identifying purposes for reading. Prereading and predicting help you to identify the topics that are included in the assignment. The next step is to develop guide questions that will focus your attention and lead you through the material.

Developing Guide Questions

Most textbook chapters use boldface headings to organize chapter content. The simplest way to establish a purpose for reading is to change each heading into one or more questions that will guide your reading. As you read, you then look for the answers. For a section with the heading "The Hidden Welfare System," you could ask the questions, What is the hidden welfare system? and How does it work? As you read that section, you would actively search for answers. Or for a section of a business textbook titled "Taxonomy of Organizational Research Strategies," you could pose such questions as, What is a taxonomy? or What research strategies are discussed and how are they used?

The excerpt printed below is taken from a psychology textbook chapter on sensation and perception. Before reading it, formulate several guide questions and list them here. Read to find the answers. After you have read the article, fill in the answers below.

Question 1: _____

_____

Answer: _____

_____

Question 2: _____

_____

Answer: _____

_____

CLASSIFYING THE SENSES

Most people learn quite early about the five basic senses: vision, audition, taste, smell, and touch. Few learn that this five-way classification dates to the Greek philosopher Aristotle, and just as few know that in fact there are many more than five senses and that Aristotle's classification is largely arbitrary. For example, touch (or the skin senses as they are more properly called) tells much more than how things "feel"; it also registers temperature, vibration, pain, and many other properties. Similarly, such perceptual experience of the world results from the senses working in close coordination. Locating an object often depends on eyes, ears, and touch working simultaneously. You will, for example, find it harder to tell where a sound originates with your eyes closed than with them open. Last, people sense the position of their limbs (the kinesthetic sense) and state of balance with respect to gravity (vestibular sense) without drawing on the five classical senses.

–Roediger et al., *Psychology*, p. 35

Most likely, you developed questions such as, What are the senses? and How are they classified? Then, as you read the section, you found out that, in addition to the five basic senses, there are also kinesthetic and vestibular senses. You also discovered that the five-way classification of sensory perception, dating back to Aristotle, is not completely accurate as well as somewhat arbitrary. Did the guide questions help you focus your attention and make the passage easier to read?

Some students find it helpful to jot down their guide questions in the margins of their texts, next to the appropriate headings. These questions are then available for later study. Reviewing and answering your questions is an excellent method of review.

Formulating the Right Questions

Guide questions that begin with *What, Why,* and *How* are especially effective. *Who, When,* and *Where* questions are less useful because they can often be answered through superficial reading or may lead to simple, factual, or one-word answers. *What, Why,* and *How* questions, however, require detailed answers that demand more thought, and, as a result, they force you to read in more depth in order to construct acceptable answers.

A section in a history text titled "The Fall of the Roman Empire," for example, could be turned into a question such as, When did the Roman Empire fall? For this question, the answer is merely a date. This question, then, would not guide your reading effectively. On the other hand, questions such as, How did the Roman Empire fall? What brought about the fall of the Roman Empire? or What factors contributed to the fall of the Roman Empire? would require you to recall important events and identify causes or reasons.

Here are a few examples of effective guide questions:

Heading	*Effective Guide Questions*
Management of Stress in Organizations	What types of stress occur? How is it controlled?
Theories of Leadership	What are the theories of leadership? How are they applied or used?
Styles of Leader Behavior	What are the styles of leader behavior? How do they differ? How effective are they?

EXERCISE 1 ⎯⎯⎯⎯⎯⎯⎯⎯⎯

Directions: *Assume that each of the following is a boldface heading within a textbook chapter and that related textual material follows. In the space provided, write questions that would guide your reading.*

1. Operating System Aids to Efficient Merging of Computer Files

    _____

    _____

2. Natural Immunity and Blood Types

    _____

    _____

3. Production of Electromagnetic Waves

    _____

    _____

4. Physical Changes in Adolescence

    _____

    _____

5. Sociological Factors Related to Delinquency

    _____

    _____

6. The Circular Flow of Spending, Production, and Income

    _____

    _____

7. Influence of "Experts" on Child-rearing Practices

    _____

    _____

8. Appraisal of Job Performance and Effectiveness

    _____

    _____

9. Inheritance of Physical Characteristics

    _____

    _____

_____

_____

Written Materials Without Headings

In articles and essays without headings, the title often provides a general overall purpose, and the first sentence of each paragraph can often be used to form a guide question about each paragraph. In the following paragraph, the first sentence could be turned into a question that would guide your reading.

Despite its recent increase in popularity, hypnotism has serious limitations that restrict its widespread use. First of all, not everyone is susceptible to hypnotism. Second, a person who does not cooperate with the hypnotist is unlikely to fall into a hypnotic trance. Finally, there are limits to the commands a subject will obey when hypnotized. In many cases, subjects will not do anything which violates their moral code.

From the first sentence you could form the question: What are the limitations of hypnotism? In reading the remainder of the paragraph, you would find three limitations: (1) Some people cannot be hypnotized; (2) the subject must cooperate or hypnosis will not occur; and (3) subjects will not follow commands to do what they believe is wrong.

EXERCISE 2 _____

Directions: *Assume that each of the following sentences is the first sentence of a paragraph within an article that does not contain boldface headings. Beside each sentence, write a guide question.*

First Sentence	*Question*
1. Historically, there have been three major branches of philosophical analysis.	_____ _____ _____
2. Scientists who are studying earthquakes attribute their cause to intense pressures and stresses that build up inside the earth.	_____ _____ _____
3. The way in which managers and employees view and treat conflict has changed measurably over the last fifty years.	_____ _____ _____

4. In the Marxist view, the government serves as an agent of social control.

    _____

    _____

    _____

5. Perhaps it will be easier to understand the nature and function of empathetic listening if we contrast it to deliberative listening.

    _____

    _____

    _____

6. The different types of drill presses for performing drilling and allied operations vary in design and specific function.

    _____

    _____

    _____

7. To read data from a disk, the operating system has to know the sector and the track that contain the data.

    _____

    _____

    _____

8. In addition to the price of a good or service, there are dozens, perhaps hundreds, of other factors and circumstances affecting a person's decision to buy or not to buy.

    _____

    _____

    _____

9. Although sometimes used interchangeably, poor nutritional states can be categorized as malnutrition, undernutrition, or overnutrition.

    _____

    _____

    _____

10. Among the most important changes of the twentieth century is the rise of large governments.

    _____

    _____

Are Guide Questions Effective?

A number of research studies have been conducted to test whether establishing purposes by forming guide questions improves understanding and recall of information. These studies confirm the effectiveness of guide questions and indicate that students who read with a purpose have a higher percentage of recall of factual information than students who read without a specific purpose.

In one experiment conducted by Frase and Schwartz,* for example, 64

* L. T. Frase and B. J. Schwartz, "Effect of Question Production and Answering on Prose Recall," *Journal of Educational Psychology,* 67 (1975): 628–635.

college students were divided into two groups. Both groups were given a passage to read and study. One group (Group A) was directed to construct and write out questions based on the text; the other group (Group B) was simply directed to study the material. The results were as follows:

Group	Percentage of Recall
Group A	72%
Group B	53%

The group that established a purpose for reading by forming questions recalled 19 percent more than the group that read without establishing a purpose.

Developing guide questions fulfills an essential principle of learning: the intent to remember. It focuses your attention on what is important—on what you are supposed to read and remember. Guide questions also force you to read actively—to sort out, process, and evaluate ideas to determine if they answer your guide question.

EXERCISE 3 _____

Directions: *Turn to the sample textbook chapter included in Appendix B (pages 457–471). Beginning with the heading "Homeotherms," form questions that would be useful in guiding your reading. Work through the next five pages, listing the questions you formed in the space provided below. Then read these pages and answer your questions on a separate sheet of paper.*

_____

_____

_____

_____

_____

EXERCISE 4 _____

Directions: *Choose a three-to-four-page selection from one of your textbooks. Select pages that have already been assigned or that you anticipate will be assigned. For each heading, form and record guide questions that establish a purpose for reading. Then read the selection and answer your questions.*

SELECT APPROPRIATE READING/LEARNING STRATEGIES

Many students approach all their assignments in the same way, only to find out later that a different approach would have produced better results and saved valuable time. Here is an example:

Jason was preparing for a midterm examination in human anatomy and physiology. As soon as the date of the exam was announced he began to prepare detailed outlines of each chapter. The night before the exam, while studying with a classmate, he discovered that a system of testing himself by drawing and labeling diagrams and making tables and function charts would have been a more active and effective means of learning.

This student approached his assignment mechanically and routinely. Instead, he should have analyzed the learning task and considered how to accomplish it most effectively.

In selecting the right reading/learning strategy, you should consider four factors or variables: learner characteristics, text characteristics, performance activities, and instructors advice and expectations. These factors are diagrammed in Figure 6-1.

Learner Characteristics

Learner characteristics refer to the traits, features, and knowledge you bring to the situation. In Chapter 4 you assessed your learning style and discovered or confirmed a great deal about how you learn most effectively. Now is the time when that information is most useful. The learning strategy you select for a particular assignment should, if possible, be one that capitalizes on your strengths as a learner. Figure 6-2 shows types of reading/learning strategies that correspond to various learning styles.

In addition to learning style, your background knowledge and experience

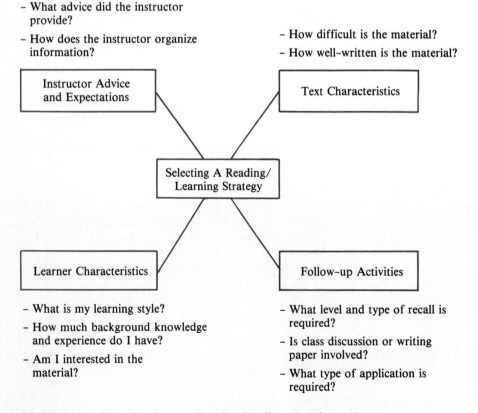

FIGURE 6-1   Selecting Appropriate Reading/Learning Strategies

should also be considered. When reading about a subject in which you have little background, you can expect the material to be difficult and require more time; more careful reading is necessary than for a subject with which you are familiar. Additional strategies to aid comprehension and recall may also be needed—outlining or paraphrasing, for example. It is very possible that members of the same class taking the same course from the same instructor may need to use very different reading/learning strategies. Let's consider a biology class, for example. One student is a biology major who has strong interest and plenty of background knowledge of the field. She is accustomed to reading scientific and technical material and has already discovered approaches that work for her. Another student, a communications major, taking biology as his one required science course, however, has a much more difficult task. Unaccustomed to reading scientific material, he must develop new strategies and revise old ones to make them "work" in biology. Similarly, a student who has always been "poor" in math must approach a math course differently than one who has always found math easy to understand. Even when working within a field with which you are generally familiar, you may, at times, encounter topics of which you have little awareness. When you find yourself working with material in which you have relatively little background knowledge or experience, use the following suggestions:

1. Increase your "usual" study time.
2. Plan more frequent, as well as longer reading study sessions. Unfamiliar material is best learned through frequent, regular learning.
3. Engage more sensory modes than you normally use.
4. Include more writing activities (see Chapter 13), even if you are an auditory learner.
5. Increase your effort to learn specialized and technical vocabulary. (See Chapter 19.)
6. Use all available or optional study aids. Depending on the course, review books, exercise workbooks, study guides, taped lectures, or tutoring may be available.
7. Talk with your instructor. When you anticipate that a course will be difficult, it usually is. Plan ahead; talk with the instructor and seek his or her advice on how to approach the course.
8. Talk with other students, but not only those earning top grades in the course. Try to discover a variety of reading/learning strategies.

Interest is a third learner characteristic. In general, lack of intent poses many of the same problems and limitations as lack of knowledge or experience. The suggestions listed above, then, are useful and appropriate. In addition, try to generate interest. Do not just say "this is boring"; instead, try to find some portion of the material that does interest you. For instance, suppose you are a math major taking a required sociology course. Make it your "special interest" to assess how statistical data is collected and analyzed and how research is conducted. A business student taking a required literature course might look for themes that are relevant today in business, such as competition, determination of values, leadership, role models, influence and control, or decision making.

Text Characteristics

The nature of the material you will read and learn is a key factor in deciding how to approach it. Later, in Chapter 21, you will read more about what text factors influence difficulty.

FIGURE 6-2   Learning Styles and Reading/Learning Strategies

If Your Learning Style Is . . .	*Then the Reading/Learning Strategies to Use Are . . .*
Auditory	☐ tape lectures ☐ tape review notes ☐ discuss/study with friends (Ch. 16) ☐ talk aloud when studying ☐ tape self-test questions and answers (Ch. 13)
Visual	☐ draw diagrams, charts, maps (see Chs. 10, 12) ☐ use mapping (see Ch. 12) ☐ use visualization (Ch. 3) ☐ use films, videos when available ☐ use computer-assisted instruction if available
Applied	☐ think of practical situations to which learning applies ☐ associate ideas with their application ☐ take courses with lab or practicum ☐ use case studies, examples, and applications to cue your learning
Conceptual	☐ organize materials that lack order (Ch. 12) ☐ use outlining (Ch. 12) ☐ focus on organizational patterns (see Ch. 9)
Spatial	☐ use mapping (Ch. 12) ☐ use outlining (Ch. 12) ☐ draw diagrams, make charts and sketches (Chs. 10, 12) ☐ use visualization (Ch. 3)
Nonspatial	☐ translate diagrams and drawings into language ☐ record steps, processes, procedures in words ☐ write summaries (Ch. 12) ☐ write your interpretation next to textbook drawings, maps, graphics
Social	☐ form study groups ☐ find a study partner ☐ interact with instructor ☐ work with a tutor ☐ take courses with class-discussion format (Ch. 15)
Independent	☐ use computer-assisted instruction, if available ☐ consider independent study courses

	□ enroll in courses using traditional lecture-exam format
	□ purchase review books, study guides, if available
	□ use self-testing (Ch. 13)
Creative	□ ask questions about chapter content and answer them
	□ use annotation to record impressions and reactions (Ch. 11)
	□ take courses that involve exploration, experimentation, or discussion
Pragmatic	□ write summaries and outlines (Ch. 12)
	□ write lists of steps, processes, procedures
	□ paraphrase difficult material (Ch. 13)
	□ use SQ3R (Ch. 13)
	□ focus on problem-solving, logical sequence
	□ use a structured study environment

Figure 6-3 lists important factors to consider. Once you've identified difficulty factors, the next step is to select a strategy to compensate for these factors. For example, when reading material that is poorly organized, outlining is a useful strategy to help you determine the relationship of ideas. Or for material in which summaries are lacking, writing summaries is appropriate.

Performance Activities

A third important factor to consider when selecting a reading/learning strategy is how you will use or apply the information. Often, you'll be taking some type of quiz, test, or exam. As you will see in Chapter 17, the type of exam you will take, essay or objective, for example, influences how you should

Complicated subject matter

Conceptually difficult subject matter

Complex charts or diagrams

Lengthy material

Poor organization

Few learning aids (study questions, sample problems)

Lack of headings

Frequent use of technical vocabulary

Lack of summaries

FIGURE 6-3   Factors That Signal Difficulty

prepare for it. If the exam is open-book or an oral exam, still different strategies are needed. Other times, instead of an exam you may be preparing to write a research paper, participate in a class discussion, or get ready for a lab; each of these situations also demands unique learning strategies.

There is one very important rule to follow in selecting a learning strategy: choose the strategy that most directly parallels the activity for which you are preparing. Think of how a long-distance runner prepares for a race or how a rock group warms up for a concert, or how a football team readies itself for a game. Each prepares by practicing the skills or activities they must perform. In the same way, you should prepare for exams by doing the actual activity required. For example, to prepare for an essay exam, you should write, or to prepare for a math exam you should practice solving problems. Figure 6-4 lists common performance tasks and describes suitable learning strategies.

Instructor Advice and Expectations

Any advice your instructor offers about how to study is of utmost importance. If your professor recommends a particular method of study or review, by all means use it. He or she is an expert in his or her field and, as a teacher, is skilled and experienced in helping you learn that subject matter. Many instructors do not offer explicit advice on how to study; instead you will have to pick up on clues and indirect advice. For example, if you notice that an instructor uses charts to organize information during lectures, you can infer that charting may be a useful study method as well.

The approach your instructor takes toward a particular topic also provides

FIGURE 6-4   Selecting Reading/Learning Strategies

Task	*Reading/Learning Strategy*	*Chapter Reference*
Essay exams	Predict sample questions and draft responses	17
Problem-solving exams	Create sample problems	17
Objective exams	Review underlining, organize information using index cards; study sheets	11, 16
Open-book exams		17
Oral presentations	Make notes; rehearse presentations	15
Labs	Familiarize yourself with purpose and procedures; highlight; jot down questions	15, 18
Research papers	Locate and organize information using index cards	18
Class discussions	Read for key points, issues, and themes; make notes and list of questions	15
Reaction or critique papers	Make notes as you read; underline; annotate; record reactions, feelings	18

clues about how to study. If your instructor is most interested in factual recall of information, you would handle the material differently than if he or she expects you to interpret, react, or criticize ideas. As you will see later in the chapter, class exams are also useful clues in assessing and revising learning strategies. The type of questions your instructor asks should provide clues about how to study. If, for instance, your instructor includes a fair number of questions that force you to apply information to practical or hypothetical situations, then you will need to build a step into your study approach in which you consider possible applications of the material. Here are a few additional hints:

1. Pay attention when an instructor gives an assignment. Does he or she indicate why it is being given, what to focus on, or parts to pay attention to?
2. Notice what parts of the assignment and what types of information the instructor emphasized during class lectures or discussions. Does he or she focus on facts, problems, procedures, concepts, historical significance, or trends and patterns? The instructor's focus usually provides clues about what is important.
3. Study your course syllabus or course outline. Pay special attention to the course objectives, if they are included. Objectives list what the course is to accomplish and translate to what type of learning is expected. Study the course outline, noticing how topics connect and relate.
4. Consider how your instructor will evaluate you. Will he or she require papers, exams, quizzes? You will learn more about taking exams in Chapter 17, and the type of activity for which you are preparing will determine, in part, your reading/study approach. If, for example, you will take only essay exams in a particular course, you know the emphasis is on ideas— trends or concepts and not specific dates, names, and places.

If you are experiencing difficulty in a course, talk with your instructor during office hours. Describe the strategies you are using and ask for his or her reaction. Take along samples of your work, notes, outlines, or study sheets.

EXERCISE 5 _____

Directions: *On a separate sheet, analyze each of the following assignments. Decide what is expected in each assignment. Then suggest an approach that might be effective.*

1. Writing an analysis of a poem by John Donne for your English composition and introduction to literature class.
2. Reading a chapter in a criminology textbook in preparation for a class discussion and, eventually, an essay exam.

EXERCISE 6 _____

Directions: *List all the assignments you have been given for this week in each of your courses. Then answer the following questions.*

1. How do the assignments differ?
2. How do your learner characteristics vary?
3. What guidance or clues, if any, has your instructor provided?
4. For what performance activities are you preparing?
5. How will you vary your approach to each assignment?

MONITOR YOUR COMPREHENSION

For many daily activities you maintain an awareness or "check" on how well you are performing them. In sports such as racquetball, tennis, or bowling, you know if you are playing a poor game; you actually keep score and deliberately try to correct errors and improve your performance. When preparing a favorite food, you often taste it as you work to be sure it will turn out as you want. When washing your car, you check to be sure that you have not missed any spots.

A similar type of checking should occur as you read. You should be aware of, or monitor, your performance. You need to "keep score" of how effectively and efficiently you are comprehending. However, since reading is a mental process, it is more difficult to monitor than bowling or cooking. There is very little clear, observable evidence to suggest whether you are on the right track when reading. Comprehension is also difficult to keep track of because it is not always either good or poor. You may understand certain ideas you read and be confused by others. At times, comprehension may be incomplete, you may miss certain key ideas and not know you missed them.

Recognizing Comprehension Signals

Think for a moment about what occurs when you read material you can understand easily and then compare this to what happens when you read complicated material that is difficult for you to understand. When you read certain material, does it seem that everything "clicks"—that is, do ideas seem to fit together and make sense? Is that "click" noticeably absent at other times?

Read each of the following paragraphs. As you read, be alert to your level of understanding of each.

PARAGRAPH 1

The two most common drugs that are legal and do not require a prescription are caffeine and nicotine. Caffeine is the active ingredient in coffee, tea, and many cola drinks. It stimulates the central nervous system and heart and therefore is often used to stay awake. Heavy use—say, seven to ten cups of coffee per day—has toxic effects, that is, acts like a mild poison. Prolonged heavy use appears to be addicting. Nicotine is the active ingredient in tobacco. One of the most addicting of all drugs and one of the most dangerous, at least when obtained by smoking, it has been implicated in lung cancer, emphysema, and heart disease.

–Geiwitz, *Psychology: Looking at Ourselves*, p. 276

PARAGRAPH 2

In the HOSC experiment, two variables were of sufficient importance to include as stratification (classification) variables prior to the random assignment of class sections to treatments. These two stratification variables were science subject (biology, chemistry, or physics) and teacher's understanding of science (high or low). Inclusion of these two variables in the HOSC design allowed the experimenter to make generalizations about the HOSC treatment in terms of science subject matter and the teacher's understanding of science. Even if the HOSC experiments had selected a completely random sample of American high school science teacher–class sections, generalizations regarding the effectiveness of the HOSC treatment would only be possible in terms of the factors included in the experimental design. . . .

–Lohnes and Cooley, *Introduction to Statistical Procedures*, p. 11.

Did you feel comfortable and confident as you read paragraph 1? Did ideas seem to lead from one to another and make sense? How did you feel while reading paragraph 2? Most likely you sensed its difficulty and felt confused. Unfamiliar words were used and you could not follow the flow of ideas, so that the whole passage didn't make sense.

As you read paragraph 2, did you know that you were not understanding it? Did you feel confused or uncertain? Table 6-1 lists and compares common signals that may assist you in monitoring your comprehension. Not all signals appear at the same time, and not all signals work for everyone. As you study the list, identify those positive signals you sensed as you read paragraph 1 on common drugs. Then identify the negative signals that you sensed when reading about the HOSC experiment.

TABLE 6-1   Comprehension Signals

Positive Signals	*Negative Signals*
Everything seems to fit and make sense; ideas flow logically from one to another.	Some pieces do not seem to belong; the material seems disjointed.
You understand what is important.	Nothing or everything seems important.
You are able to see where the author is leading.	You feel as if you are struggling to stay with the author and are unable to predict what will follow.
You are able to make connections among ideas.	You are unable to detect relationships; the organization is not apparent.
You read at a regular, comfortable pace.	You often slow down or reread.
You understand why the material was assigned.	You do not know why the material was assigned and cannot explain why it is important.
You can express the main ideas in your own words.	You must reread and use the author's language to explain an idea.
You recognize most words or can figure them out from context.	Many words are unfamiliar.
You feel comfortable and have some knowledge about the topic.	The topic is unfamiliar, yet the author assumes you understand it.

EXERCISE 7 _____

Directions: *Read the section "Principles of Heat Balance" in the sample textbook chapter reprinted in Appendix B (pages 459–462). Monitor your comprehension as you read. After reading the section, answer the following questions.*

1. How would you rate your overall comprehension? What positive signals did you sense? Did you feel any negative signals?
2. Test the accuracy of your rating in question 1 by answering the following questions based on the material you read.
   a. Name and explain three means of heat transfer.
   b. Explain the difference between a poikilotherm and a homeotherm. Give an example of each.
   c. Identify the two primary sources of heat gain on which living organisms depend.
   d. How does an organism's size affect heat transfer?
3. Check your answers in the Answer Key. In what sections was your comprehension strongest?
4. Did you feel at any time that you had lost or were about to lose comprehension? If so, go back to that section now. What made that section difficult to read?

EXERCISE 8 _____

Directions: *Select a three-to-four page section of a chapter in one of your textbooks. Read the section and then answer questions 1, 3, 4, in the above exercise.*

Monitoring Techniques

At times signals of poor comprehension do not come through clearly or strongly enough. In fact, some students think they have understood what they read until they are questioned in class or take an exam. Only then do they discover that their comprehension was incomplete. Other students find that they comprehend material on a surface, factual level, but do not recognize more complicated relationships and implied meanings, or do not see implications and applications. Use the following monitoring techniques to determine if you really understand what you read.

1. *Establish checkpoints.* Race car drivers make pit stops during races for quick mechanical checks and repairs; athletes are subject to frequent physical tests and examinations. These activities provide an opportunity to evaluate or assess performance and to correct any problems or malfunctions. Similarly when reading it is necessary to stop and evaluate.

As you preread a textbook assignment, identify reasonable or logical checkpoints: points at which to stop, check, and if necessary, correct your performance before continuing. Pencil a checkmark in the margin to designate these points. These checkpoints should be logical breaking points where one topic ends and another begins, or where a topic is broken down into several subtopics. As you reach each of these checkpoints, stop and assess your work using the techniques described below.

2. *Use your guide questions.* Earlier in this chapter, you learned how

to form guide questions using boldface headings. These same questions can be used to monitor your comprehension while reading. When you finish a boldface-headed section, stop and take a moment to recall your guide question and answer it mentally or on paper. Your ability to answer your questions will indicate your level of comprehension.

3. *Ask connection questions.* To be certain that your comprehension is complete and that you are not recalling only superficial factual information, ask connection questions. Connection questions are those that require you to think about content. They force you to draw together ideas and to discover relationships between the material at hand and other material in the same chapter, in other chapters, or in class lectures. Here are a few examples.

> What does this topic have to do with topics discussed earlier in the chapter?
> How does this reading assignment fit with the topics of this week's class lectures?
> What does this chapter have to do with the chapter assigned last week?
> What principle do these problems illustrate?

Connection questions enable you to determine whether your learning is meaningful—whether you are simply taking in information or whether you are using the information and fitting it into the scheme of the course. The best time to ask connection questions is before beginning and after you have finished a chapter of each major section.

4. *Use internal dialogue.* Internal dialogue, mentally talking to yourself, is another excellent means of monitoring your reading and learning. It involves rephrasing to yourself the message the author is communicating or the ideas you are studying. If you are unable to express ideas in your own words, your understanding is very likely incomplete. Here are a few examples of its use.

a. While reading a section in a math textbook, you mentally outline the steps to follow in solving a sample problem.
b. You are reading an essay that argues convincingly that the threat of nuclear war is real. As you finish reading each stage of the argument, you rephrase it in your own words.
c. As you finish each boldface section in a psychology chapter, you summarize the key points.

EXERCISE 9 _____

Directions: *Refer to the subsection "Alarms and Adaptation" (pages 423–425) in the sample textbook chapter reprinted in Appendix A. Write a list of guide and connection questions you could pose for this section.*

Guide Questions

_____

_____

_____

_____

_____

_____

_____

_____

EXERCISE 10 _____

Directions: *Choose a section from one of your own textbooks. Read it and monitor your comprehension using both guide and connection questions. List your questions on a separate sheet of paper.*

EXERCISE 11 _____

Directions: *Select another section from one of your textbooks and experiment with the technique of internal dialogue to monitor your comprehension. In the space provided below, describe the technique you used and evaluate its effectiveness.*

_____

_____

_____

_____

Strengthening Your Comprehension

You have learned how to recognize clues that signal strong or weak understanding of reading material and how to monitor your comprehension. This section will offer some suggestions to follow when you realize you need to strengthen your comprehension.

1. *Analyze the time and place in which you are reading.* If you've been reading or studying for several hours, mental fatigue may be the source of the problem. If you are reading in a place with numerous distractions or interruptions, lack of concentration may contribute to comprehension loss. (See Chapter 4 for suggestions on how to monitor and improve your concentration.)
2. *Rephrase each paragraph in your own words.* You might need to approach extremely complicated material sentence by sentence, expressing each in your own words.
3. *Read aloud sentences or sections that are particularly difficult.* The auditory feedback that oral reading provides often aid comprehension.

4. *Do not hesitate to reread difficult or complicated sections.* In fact, at times several readings are appropriate and necessary.
5. *Slow down your reading rate.* On occasion simply reading more slowly and carefully will provide you with the needed boost in comprehension.
6. *Write guide questions next to headings.* Refer to your questions frequently and jot down or underline answers.
7. *Write a brief outline of major points.* This will help you see the overall organization and progression of ideas. (See Chapter 13 for specific outlining techniques.)
8. *Underline key ideas.* After you've read a section, go back and think about and underline what is important. Underlining forces you to sort out what is important, and this sorting process builds comprehension and recall. (Refer to Chapter 11 for suggestions on how to underline effectively.)
9. *Write notes in the margins.* Explain or rephrase difficult or complicated ideas or sections.
10. *Determine if you lack background knowledge.* Comprehension is difficult, or at times impossible, if you lack essential information that the writer assumes you have. Suppose you are reading a section of a political science text in which the author describes implications of the balance of power in the Third World. If you do not understnad the concept of balance of power, your comprehension will break down. When you lack background information, take immediate steps to correct the problem:

Consult other sections of your text, using the glossary and index.
Obtain a more basic text that reviews fundamental principles and concepts.
Consult reference materials (encyclopedias, subject or biographical dictionaries).
Ask your instructor to recommend additional sources, guidebooks, or review texts.

EXERCISE 12 _____

Directions: *The following two passages have been chosen for their difficulty. Monitor your comprehension as you read each, paying attention to both positive and negative signals. After you have read each passage, list the signals you received (refer to Table 6-1) and indicate what you could do to strengthen your comprehension.*

PARAGRAPH 1

Throughout the last quarter-century, the debate regarding international economic development has been conducted principally between the traditionalists (whose analyses focus on modernization strategies) and the radicals (who prefer to concentrate on the intrinsic characteristics of the international system that perpetuate dependency). More recently, however, a number of scholars have suggested new approaches to the problem. One, for example, has noted that neither of the two dominant theories can explain the late development of some countries because economic advancement is not necessarily tied to exclusively economic factors. This observation leads to the conclusion that disparate paths to development must consider such local sociological factors as traditions, motives, attitudes, and religious influences upon traditionalism and modernism.

–Jones, *The Logic of International Relations*, pp. 212–213

Positive signals: _____

Negative signals: _____

Strengthen comprehension by: _____

_____

PARAGRAPH 2

Any form of law has as its incentives a variety of normative, utilitarian and coercive sanctions. An individual may drive his automobile lawfully because he fears the consequences of wrongdoing (fear of coercive sanction), or as a matter of personal safety (utilitarian sanction) or a contribution to orderly social coexistance (normative sanction). Likewise among states, compliance with rules of law is rather consistent, and is grounded in normative and utilitarian motives. Governments do generally regard reciprocal behavior as mutually beneficial, and are often sensitive to international pressures. They wish to avoid reprisals and embarrassing declarations and resolutions brought on by improper behavior, except when perceived needs exceed the risk of external criticism.

–Jones, *The Logic of International Relations*, p. 495.

Positive signals: _____

Negative signals: _____

Strengthen comprehension by: _____

_____

EXERCISE 13 _____

Directions: *Select three brief sections from your most difficult textbook. Choose three of the suggestions for strengthening your comprehension and list them below. Try out each suggestion on one textbook section. Evaluate and describe the effectiveness of each.*

	Suggestion	*Evaluation*
1.	_____	_____
2.	_____	_____
3.	_____	_____

MONITOR YOUR LEARNING

When you purchase a new product or brand, such as frozen yogurt or new takeout pizza, you don't know if you like it until you try it. The same is true of learning strategies. You won't know if they work until you try them. Some amount of experimentation and trial-and-error testing is necessarily involved. You can expect some strategies to work better than others, a few not to work at all, and occasionally find one that works perfectly the first time. Usually you have to modify and adopt the first strategy you select. It may take at least two or three study sessions to perfect a strategy. But once you've found the right strategy, it should work for the course for the entire semester.

Monitoring, evaluating, and revising your learning strategies is essential. This activity should occur at three times: while you study, after you study, and when you get the results of the exam you were preparing for.

The following list of questions will help you:

During Study

Am I concentrating?
Is this learning strategy working?
Am I accomplishing what I intended?
Am I spending too much or too little time?

After Study

Did I learn what I intended?
Was the strategy effective in terms of time?
What problems did I encounter?
What additional review is necessary?
What could I have done differently?

Return of Exam

Is my grade higher or lower than I expected? Why?
What items did I miss or where did I lose points?
Is there a pattern to the types of questions I missed? If so, how can I
    change my study strategy to include this?
Is there a strategy that would have been more effective?

EXERCISE 14 _____

Directions: *Select an assignment you must complete for one of your courses. Choose a strategy, apply it, and then aswer the "During Study" and "After Study" questions listed above.*

EXERCISE 15 _____

Directions: *Evaluate the following situation and answer the questions that follow.*

For an anatomy and physiology course, the class is assigned one chapter each week. The instructor gives an exam after every four chapters. One student read and underlined each chapter, but failed the first exam. She was angry and disappointed when papers were returned and crumpled and discarded her exam paper as she left the classroom. Later, the student told a friend she knew she would have to study harder and longer for the next exam.

1. What obvious mistake did the student make?
2. Should the student study harder for the next exam or differently?
3. Offer specific suggestions for how the student might revise her study strategies.
4. The student seems to think that spending more time would improve her grade. Do you agree with this assumption? Why?

Suppose you have discovered that you are a visual and applied learner and you are reading a chapter in your business textbook on motivation. You are reading about Maslow's need-hierarchy theory that states that people in organizations are motivated to perform by a desire to satisfy a set of internal needs. To capitalize on your strengths as a visual learner, you might draw a diagram of the needs, arranging them in order of importance. As an applied learner, you would think of an example of each need and include it in your diagram. For instance, as an example of the social need, you might think of friendship with co-workers.

SUMMARY

This chapter emphasizes active reading strategies prior to, during, and after reading. Before reading, it is helpful to establish a purpose for reading by developing guide questions. Then, once you are familiar with the assignment and have defined your purposes, the next step is to select appropriate reading and learning strategies. To do so you must consider four factors: (1) your learning characteristics, (2) the characteristics of the material, (3) your instructor's expectations, and (4) the type of follow-up activities required.

As you read an assignment, keep track of your comprehension by picking up both positive and negative comprehension signals. Four comprehension monitoring techniques are (1) establishing checkpoints, (2) using guide questions, (3) asking connection questions, and (4) using internal dialogue. As you study and review, you should monitor the effectiveness of your learning by asking questions during study, after study, and after an exam is returned.

PART THREE

Understanding Content

Can you remember how you were taught to read? Do you remember going to reading class or having reading groups in elementary school? Can you remember using readers (series of books with stories) and then answering questions on what you read? Did you use workbooks with drills and exercises that taught you about vowel sounds and syllables? You probably can remember some or all of these things because reading was a regular part of each day's instruction in elementary school.

Now, do you remember going to reading class in junior or senior high school? Probably not. Most secondary schools throughout the country do not offer reading classes as a regular part of each year's curriculum. In effect, then, reading instruction stopped for you at the end of grade six. This general practice of discontinuing reading instruction at the end of elementary school has serious implications and has directly affected how well you can read now, as you enter college.

When you finished sixth grade, you probably were reading at least at sixth-grade level. You achieved this level through the direct instruction and practice you received in grades one through six. Then, after you entered seventh grade, reading was no longer taught. Instead, it was left up to you to raise your reading skills to the seventh-grade level by the end of seventh grade, to the eighth-grade level by the end of eighth grade, and so forth. The assumption that you could improve your reading skills on your own continued throughout the remainder of your secondary education.

What occurs as a result of this lack of direct instruction is that some students are able to increase their own reading ability while others are not. Most students are able to make some improvement; that is, not many students still read at a sixth-grade level when in the twelfth grade. But on the other hand, a large percentage of students do not read at a twelfth-grade level at the end of twelfth grade.

continued

continued

More and more college students are not beginning college immediately after completing high school. Instead, they are returning to education after working, raising a family, or serving in the military. Many of these students have not read or studied textbook material for several years. As a result, their reading and study skills are "rusty" from lack of use.

The purpose of Part Three is to help you make up, or compensate, for the lack of reading instruction during secondary school or a time lapse in your educational experience. This part will present some of the most important higher-level reading skills that should have been taught to all students as they began to read more complex and difficult assigned material. The chapters are primarily concerned with how to understand content and how to remember more, most efficiently. Chapters 7 and 8 focus on the sentence and the paragraph. Chapter 9 describes the structure of textbook chapters, discusses types of supporting information, and presents organizational patterns commonly used in academic writing. Chapter 10 offers strategies for understanding graphics and for reading technical writing.

7

Understanding Sentences

Use this chapter to:

1. *Learn how to grasp quickly the meaning of a sentence.*
2. *Discover how to use punctuation as an aid to comprehension.*
3. *Learn how to approach complicated sentences.*

Along with words and phrases, sentences are basic units of meaning to consider when we try to improve reading rate and comprehension. Clear, accurate understanding of sentences is essential to all other comprehension skills and to the effective reading and study of textbook chapters.

A sentence is commonly defined as a group of words that express a complete thought or idea. A sentence must be about one thing—the *subject*—and some action that happens in relation to the subject—the *verb*. In some situations, instead of expressing action the verb links or connects two parts of the sentence. Together, the subject and verb form the *core parts* of the sentence and carry its essential meaning. Sentences can contain many other parts, however, and they can vary widely in pattern and complexity. To read a sentence effectively, it is necessary to develop the ability to recognize the structure of a sentence as well as to identify the core parts that convey the essential meaning of the sentence. Knowledge of sentence structure is also very important to improving your own writing skills. As you learn how to comprehend sentences more effectively, you will also be learning how to write them clearly and correctly.

Before beginning to develop skill in recognizing core parts of a sentence, you must understand the difference between complete and incomplete thoughts. A complete thought is one that supplies enough information to give you the full meaning that is being expressed by the writer. Incomplete thoughts give you only partial information. After reading an incomplete thought, you are left with a question about (1) what happened, or (2) to whom or what something happened. The following examples show the difference between groups of words that are complete sentences and those that are not complete sentences because they do not fully express the writers' meanings.

Example 1A: Slipped off the side of the road into the ditch during a winter storm.

In this sentence, you know what happened (something or someone slipped into the ditch), but you do not know what or who slipped. You do not now whether it was a truck, bus, car, or careless driver that went into the ditch.

Example 1B: The tractor-trailer slipped off the side of the road into the ditch during a winter storm.

Sentence 1B is complete. Now you know that what slipped off the road and went into the ditch was a tractor-trailer.

Example 2A: This chapter, an excellent summary of the current economic problems in Russia.

In this sentence, there is a subject, "chapter," and some information is given about the subject—"an excellent summary of current economic problems in Russia." The sentence is not complete because there is no action; nothing is happening in relation to the chapter. You do not know what is being said about the chapter—whether it is boring, or whether it is difficult to read.

Example 2B: This chapter, an excellent summary of the current economic problems in Russia, presents some very useful graphs.

Example 2B is a complete sentence because you now know what the chapter does—it presents useful graphs.

You can see that unless a group of words contains a subject and a verb, it does not express a complete thought.

EXERCISE 1 _____

Directions: *Read each of the following groups of words. Mark an S in the blank if the words form a sentence. Mark an N if they do not form a sentence.*

   S   1. Finance companies raise funds by selling commercial paper and by issuing stocks and bonds.[1]

   N   2. A second feature of the preoperational stage of child growth and development.

   N   3. Becoming less dependent on sensory-motor responses and more capable of processing language.

   S   4. A computer gets data from input devices and sends data to output devices.[2]

   N   5. The energy that is used in business and industry in the form of electricity.

   N   6. Added to the problem of racial unrest caused by court-ordered busing.

   S   7. In the rigid atmosphere created in many public schools by so many rules and regulations, creativity is often stifled.[3]

   N   8. Islands and peninsulas that are inhabited by fewer than one hundred people.

   S   9. Archimedes' principle states that an immersed body is buoyed up by a force that is equal to the weight of the fluid it displaces.

   S   10. Often a misplaced comma or other punctuation mark can change a sentence's meaning.

IDENTIFYING CORE PARTS

As you can see from the preceding examples and exercise, the two core parts of the sentence—the subject and the verb, or the subject and the action—must be present for a group of words to convey a complete thought. For a group of words to be considered a sentence in written English, three conditions must be met. The group of words must (1) contain a subject, (2) contain a verb, and (3) express a complete thought. To read and understand a sentence, you should be able to quickly identify these core parts. Read this sentence: The battleship sank. The sentence consists only of the core parts: the subject—*battleship*—and the verb or action—*sank*. Now read this sentence: After the battle, the ship sank. The core parts are still easy to identify—*ship* and *sank*. However, in addition to conveying the basic message that the ship sank, the sentence contains an additional piece of information—*when* it sank.

In each of the following examples, the core parts are underlined.

The <u>children lined up</u> according to height.

The <u>books fell</u> off the desk.

Most psychological <u>principles can be applied</u> by everyone.

The average <u>American consumes</u> six gallons of beer each year.

After her own illness, the <u>physician was</u> more sympathetic to her patient's concerns and fears.

In reading these examples, you probably noticed the words and phrases that were not core parts of the sentences and contained additional information that in some way described or further explained the chief thoughts in the sentences. In the last sentence, for example, the important thought is that the physician was sympathetic. The other parts of the sentence tell *when* she was more sympathetic (after her own illness), suggest *why* she was more sympathetic (due to her experience with illness), and tells to *whom* she was more sympathetic (to her own patients).

Objects

In some sentences, the verb has an object or thing it refers to that completes the meaning of the sentence. You might think of the object as the person, place, or thing upon whom or to which the action is performed. The object is often called the receiver of the action. Not all sentences have an object, however. Here are a few sentences in which the object is underlined.

The psychology instructor discussed a <u>theory of motivation</u>.
  —A theory of motivation is *what* the instructor discussed.

Accountants use <u>computerized programs</u> to complete routine computations.
  —Computerized programs are *what* accountants use.

Researchers have investigated <u>the differences in communication styles</u>.
  —Differences in communication styles are *what* researchers have investigated.

Sentence Modifiers

Once you have identified the core parts of a sentence, the next step is to determine how the meaning of those core parts is changed or modified by the remainder of the sentence. These remaining parts, called *modifiers,* provide you with further information about one of the core parts. Notice how each of the underlined modifiers expands, alters, or limits the meaning of the following sentences.

After showing the film, the instructor gave a quiz.
—The modifier tells *when* the quiz was given.

Dr. Ling, my philosophy instructor, assigns one chapter per week.
—The modifier indicates *who* Dr. Ling is.

Everyone except engineering majors is required to take a philosophy course.
—The modifier limits by giving an exception.

Multiple Core Parts

Some sentences may have more than one subject or more than one verb. Read this sentence. The bookstore and library were closed. There are two subjects—*bookstore* and *library.* Next, consider the following sentence: The professor gave an assignment and canceled class. The instructor performed two actions—*gave* and *canceled.* Here are a few more examples of sentences that contain multiple core parts.

Diet and exercise both contribute to weight loss.

Quick weight loss schemes deceive consumers and discourage them from trying legitimate plans.

Local businesses and private citizens organized the scholarship fund and solicited donations throughout the community.

You should have noticed that sentence 1 contains two subjects, sentence 2 has two predicates, and sentence 3 contains both two subjects and two predicates.

To read a sentence accurately, you must notice and understand the relationship between the modifiers and the core parts. In some cases, modifiers provide relatively unimportant additional information to which you should pay little attention. At other times, modifiers qualify, limit, or restrict the meaning of the core parts and significantly alter their meaning, as in the following sentence:

Those congressmen hoping for a pay increase voted against the budget cut.

Here the underlined portion is essential; you would not fully understand the sentence unless you know that not all congressmen, but only those hoping for a pay increase, voted against the cut.

Directions: *Read each of the following sentences, underline the subject and verb, and circle the object if present.*

1. My sister took her car to the garage for repairs.
2. The library was closed for the entire week due to a flu epidemic.
3. The textbook contains exercises intended to increase reading speed.
4. Most governments in today's world claim to be democratic.
5. Storage, processing, and retrieval are essential data processing functions.
6. Reports such as the check-and-earnings statement are essential to operating a business.
7. Some companies issue written warranties to induce consumers to purchase their products.
8. Life insurance needs are determined by subtracting the financial resources that will be available at death from the financial losses likely to result from the death.[4]
9. An audit, a procedure designed to increase the quality of health care, is required of all Joint Commission—accredited hospitals.[5]
10. Numerous authors have researched delinquency and offered subcultural theories.

RECOGNIZING COMBINED IDEAS

Many sentences that you read in textbooks and reference material express more than one idea. Often, a writer combines closely related ideas into one sentence to make the connection between them clearer and easier to understand.

There are two basic sentence patterns commonly used to combine ideas—coordinate and subordinate. Each type provides the reader with clues about the relationship and relative importance of the ideas.

Coordinate Sentences

Coordinate sentences express ideas that are equally important. They coordinate, or tie together, two or more ideas. This is done for three reasons: (1) to emphasize their relationship, (2) to indicate their equal importance, and/or (3) to make the material more concise and easier to read. In the following example notice how two related ideas are combined.

1. Marlene was in obvious danger.
2. Joe quickly pulled Marlene from the street.

Combined sentence:
Marlene was in obvious danger, and Joe quickly pulled her from the street.

In this case the combined sentence establishes that the two equally important events are parts of a single incident.

As you read coordinate sentences, be sure to locate two sets of core parts. If you do not read carefully or if you are reading too fast, you might miss the second idea. Often you can recognize a sentence that combines two or more ideas by its structure and punctuation. Although a later section of this chapter discusses punctuation in more detail, basically, coordinate ideas are combined by using either a semicolon or a comma along with one of the following words: *and, but, or, either-or, neither-nor.* Here are a few examples:

The students wanted the instructor to cancel the class, <u>but</u> the instructor decided to reschedule it.

The union members wanted to strike<u>;</u> the company did nothing to discourage them.

Some students decided to take the final exam, <u>and</u> others chose to rely on their semester average.

Subordinate Sentences

Subordinate sentences contain one key, important idea and one or more less important, or subordinate, ideas that explain the key idea. These less important ideas have their own core parts, but they depend on the base sentence to complete their meaning. For example, in the following sentence you do not fully understand the meaning of the underlined portion until you read the entire sentence.

<u>Because Diane forgot to make a payment</u>, she had to pay a late charge on her loan.

In this sentence, the more important idea is that Diane had to pay a late charge. The reason for the late charge is presented as background information that amplifies and further explains the basic message.

As you read subordinate sentences, be sure to notice the relationship between the two ideas. The idea of lesser importance may describe or explain a condition, cause, reason, purpose, time, or place. Here are a few additional examples of sentences that relate ideas. In each the base sentence is underlined and the function of the less important idea is indicated in parentheses above it.

(*description*)
<u>My grandfather</u>, who is eighty years old, <u>collects stamps</u>.

(*time*)
<u>American foreign policy changed</u> when we entered the Vietnam War.

(*condition*)
Unless my class is dismissed early, <u>I'll be late for my dental appointment</u>.

(*reason*)
Since I failed my last history exam, <u>I decided to drop the course</u>.

EXERCISE 3

Directions: *Read each of the following and decide whether it is a coordinate or a subordinate sentence. Mark C in the space to the right if the sentence is coordinate. Mark S if it is subordinate, and underline the more important, key idea.*

1. The personnel office eagerly accepted my application for a job, and I expect to receive an offer next week. _____
2. Since it is difficult to stop smoking, the individual who wants to quit may find group therapy effective. _____
3. Birth control is interference with the natural rhythms of reproduction; some individuals object to it on this basis. _____
4. Computers have become part of our daily lives, but their role in today's college classrooms has not yet been fully explored. _____
5. Marriage consists of shared experiences and ambitions, and both are influenced by the values of each partner. _____
6. As far as we can tell from historical evidence, humankind has inhabited this earth for several million years. _____
7. Because sugar is Cuba's main export, the Cuban economy depends upon the worldwide demand for and price of sugar. _____
8. The personnel manager who accepted my application is well known for interviewing all likely candidates. _____
9. Even though a feather and a brick will fall equally fast in a vacuum, they fall quite differently in the presence of air. _____
10. We never learn anything in a vacuum; we are always having other experiences before and after we learn new material. _____

EXERCISE 4

Directions: *Choose a page from one of your textbooks. Read each sentence and underline all coordinate sentences. Place brackets [ ] around all subordinate sentences.*

EXERCISE 5

Directions: *Turn to the sample textbook chapter included in Appendix B of this text. Beginning with the section headed "Principles of Heat Balance" on page 459, read each sentence and underline the core parts of each. Continue reading and underlining until you finish the page. For coordinate sentences, underline both sets of core parts. For subordinate sentences, underline the core parts in the more important, key idea.*

Directions: *Select one page from a chapter in a textbook you are currently reading. After you have read each sentence, underline its core parts. For coordinate sentences, underline both sets of core parts. For subordinate sentences, underline the core parts in the more important, key idea.*

PAYING ATTENTION TO PUNCTUATION

Read the following paragraph.

some of the earliest philosophical speculations were concerned with what the material world is made of is each substance such as rock or wood infinitely divisible so that its subdivisions always yield the same properties as the whole substance or is there some level of structure below which the subdivisions will show new properties and forms the greek philosopher Democritus 460–370 b.c. suggested that the material objects of our experience are actually made up of fundamental units.

–Berman and Evans, *Exploring the Cosmos,* p. 4.

Reading this paragraph was awkward and difficult because all punctuation was deleted. None of the words were separated from each other; you had no clues as to what words belonged together. Paying attention to punctuation can make reading easier. It helps comprehension in several ways:

1. It separates different pieces of the sentence from one another.
2. It suggests thought or idea groupings.
3. It provides clues to the relative importance of ideas within the sentence.

Each type of punctuation mark has specific functions. Those punctuation marks most useful to sentence comprehension are described below.

The Comma

The comma has a number of different uses, but in each case it separates some type of information from other parts of the sentence. The different uses of the comma are explained below.

The Introductory Use: The comma can be used to separate introductory, beginning, or opening parts of a sentence from the main part of the sentence. These parts may connect what will be said in one sentence with what has already been said in a previous sentence, provide some background information, set the scene or time frame, or offer some qualifying information or considerations. These introductory comments are less important, and tend to explain or modify the sentence's main thought. The following examples show how commas can be used to separate introductory phrases from the main sentence.

Not surprisingly, it is not only the size of America's corporations that is at issue.

Use in Subordinate and Coordinate Sentences: Commas are used along with a conjunction (*and, or but, nor, for*), to separate complete thoughts in coordinate sentences. In subordinate sentences, the comma may be used to separate the key idea from the less important idea that explains it.

<u>When atoms interact with one another</u>, new particles are formed.

The Parenthetical Use: The comma can be used to separate additional information from the main part of the sentence. Writers occasionally interrupt the core sentence to add some extra (parenthetical) information that is important but not crucial to the sentence meaning. They use a comma before and after this parenthetical information. This use of a comma helps you tell important from less important information and should aid you in identifying the sentence's core parts.

Each of the sentences in the following examples illustrates the parenthetical use of the comma.

Dolphins, <u>as a matter of fact</u>, are very friendly creatures that frequently come to the rescue of people.

Drugs and alcohol, <u>experts warn</u>, are an unsafe and dangerous combination.

The Coal Mine Safetry Act, <u>one of the first federal efforts to enforce safety standards</u>, reduced worker productivity.

The Serial Use: Whenever several items are presented in a list, or series, in a sentence, they are separated by commas. In all cases, the items in a series are equal and consistent in how they are connected or related to the core parts of the sentence. Read each of the following sentences, which are examples of the serial use of the comma. Notice how the underlined items in the series have a parallel or equal relationship to one another.

Each state maintained its <u>sovereignty</u>, <u>freedom</u>, and <u>independence</u>.

Social adjustment requries that an <u>individual maintain himself independently</u>, <u>be gainfully employed</u>, <u>and conform to the social standards set by the community</u>.

EXERCISE 7 ————————————————

Directions: *In each sentence that follows, cross out the part or parts that you identify as of lesser importance in the sentence based on the use and placement of commas.*

1. ~~In the nineteenth century,~~ industrialization made a strong impact on society.
2. ~~That is,~~ no member of the Congress should serve more than three years in any six.
3. How is it, ~~then,~~ that we perceive depth as a third dimension?
4. ~~Perhaps even more important,~~ when humans think, they know they are thinking.

5. Graphite, on the other hand, is made of carbon layers stacked one on top of the other, like sheets of paper.

The Semicolon

The primary use of the semicolon is to separate two very closely related ideas that have been combined into a coordinate sentence. Sentences 1 and 2 in the following examples can be combined using a semicolon to form sentence 3.

1. They bought the house at a very low price.
2. The former owner had to sell immediately and move to another city.
3. They bought the house at a very low price; the former owner had to sell immediately and move to another city.

When you are reading a sentence that contains a semicolon, be alert for two separate ideas and two sets of core parts. When a semicolon is used, you know that the two ideas have equal weight or importance. Each of the following sentences contains two ideas separated by a semicolon. The core parts of each sentence are underlined.

The <u>fishermen caught</u> fifteen trout; <u>they cooked</u> them over an open fire.

All <u>objects radiate</u> some form of electromagnetic radiation; the <u>amount depends</u> on their temperature and physical state.

Occasionally, a semicolon is used to separate sentence parts that, if divided by commas, would be confusing or difficult to read. To illustrate this use of the semicolon, the following example has been written in two versions.

1. Speakers at the conference included Dr. Frank, a biologist, Dr. Flock, a philosopher, and Professor Smich, a geneticist.
2. Speakers at the conference included Dr. Frank, a biologist; Dr. Flock, a philosopher; and Professor Smich, a geneticist.

As you read the first version of the sentence, you are not sure whether the speakers include Dr. Frank and a biologist or whether it was Dr. Frank who was being described as a biologist. The use of the semicolon in the second version makes it clear that Dr. Frank is the biologist.

The Colon

The colon is most often used to introduce a list, statement, or quotation. The colon tells you, the reader, that some type of additional information, which further explains the main idea of a sentence, is to follow. The colon also serves as a marker indicating that the sentence's core parts precede the colon.

The causes of the war can be divided into three categories: social, economic, and political. (Here the colon indicates that a list of categories will follow.)

Chomsky described two levels of language: One underlying or deep structure involved with meaning, and a surface level used in ordinary conversation. (The colon in this example signals that an explanation of the two levels of language is to follow.)

The Dash

The dash is most commonly used in a sentence to separate unessential or parenthetical elements from the core sentence, when using a comma would be confusing. This usage also assists the reader in separating core parts from supporting information.

At least three sports—basketball, football, and tennis—are continually gaining television fans.

EXERCISE 8 ─────────────────────

Directions: *Using punctuation as a guide, underline the core parts of each sentence.*

1. Steel, for instance, is mostly iron, with various other metals added, such as chromium, nickel, vanadium, manganese, or zirconium.
2. Among the physical traits that, added together, separate humans from all other animals, there are three of overwhelming significance: a skeleton built for walking upright; eyes capable of sharp, three-dimensional vision in color; and hands that provide both a powerful grip and nimble manipulations.[6]
3. Unfortunately, though, despite recent medical advances, the cause of mental retardation cannot be determined in most cases.
4. For a hundred years, changes in the environment, caused by humans using fossil fuels, clearing large forest areas, and excavating the land, have rapidly accelerated.
5. Throughout history, man has been puzzled and exasperated by the strange duality of his nature—half animal, half angel—and much religious and philosophical teaching has been an attempt to understand and integrate these two sides of human nature.[7]
6. Poverty and mild retardation go hand in hand, yet the vast majority of individuals from poverty neighborhoods are not mentally retarded.[8]
7. Like horses, human beings have a variety of gaits; they amble, stride, jog, and sprint.[9]
8. Evolutionary biologists have made this much clear to us: each species is a product of its genes and its environment.[10]
9. Anthropologists have accumulated a vast store of evidence to support their theory: tools and artifacts, such as those unearthed in Choukoutien, and the bones of animals who were contemporaries.[11]
10. Infant apes and monkeys, as they grow up, must learn a code of behavior, much as a human child has to do; all the members of a group are linked by an elaborate system of communication that uses both sounds and gestures and shows considerable sophistication.[12]

DECIPHERING COMPLICATED SENTENCES

Many sentences are short, direct, and straightforward and, as such, are easy to comprehend. Others, however, are complicated by the addition of numerous facts and the expression of complex relationships. In the following example, a simple sentence is compared with a complicated one. Facts that explain and clarify the core meaning were added, resulting in a complicated second sentence.

Simple sentence: Abnormal behavior is the product of biochemical processes in the brain.

Complicated science: Many professionals in the field of psychology, especially those with medical backgrounds, believe that most, if not all, abnormal behavior is the product of biochemical processes in the brain of the affected individual.

The sentence is complicated by the addition of three pieces of information: (1) who believes abnormal behavior is biochemically caused—"many professionals in the field of psychology, especially with medical backgrounds"; (2) the qualifying statement "most, if not all"; and (3) whose brain—"of the affected individual."

The key to understanding a complicated sentence is to unravel it, identifying its core parts and analyzing how each additional piece (fact) modifies the meaning of the core. The following steps are useful.

Step 1: Locate the Core Parts. Establish what the sentence is about and what action is occurring. Be alert for compound subjects or verbs. Many complicated sentences may express more than one idea and have more than one set of core parts.

Step 2: Study the Modifiers. Identify how each remaining piece of the sentence alters its meaning. Does it describe the subject? Does it tell when, why, how, or where the action occurred?

Step 3: Paraphrase. Express the sentence's basic meaning in your own words without referring to the sentence. If necessary, split it into two or more basic sentences. This step provides the best test of whether you actually understood the sentence.

Step 4: Check Vocabulary. If step 3 fails, then difficult or technical vocabulary may be interfering with your comprehension. Check your text's glossary or consult the dictionary.

Here is an example of this four-step procedure:

Because of Washington's loss of world military superiority, the changing role of the Third World, the deterioration of American control over Western allies, and political changes in the United States affecting the conduct of foreign relations, the United States has, since the demise of détente, taken a militaristic stance.[13]

Step 1: Locate the Core Parts.

(subject)   (verb)   (object)
The United States   has taken   a militaristic stance.

Step 2: Study the Modifiers. The first part of the sentence gives four reasons why the United States has taken a militaristic stance. The phrase "since the demise of détente" indicates when this action occurred.

Step 3: Paraphrase. The sentence might be paraphrased as follows:

The United States has taken a militaristic stance since the demise of détente.

This statement expresses the key idea. Details include that this has occurred because of (1) U.S. loss of world power, (2) the changing role of Third World countries, (3) the breakdown of control over allies, and (4) political changes in the United States.

Step 4: Check the Vocabulary. If necessary, check the meaning of words such as "détente," "demise," and "militaristic."

EXERCISE 9 _____

Directions: *Read each of the following sentences, using the procedure suggested above. Paraphrase each sentence in the space provided.*

1. Multiple personality is a reaction, usually caused by stress, in which the patient manifests two or more systems of personality, each of which has distinct, well-developed emotional and thought processes and represents a unique personality.

   caused by stress

   _____

   _____

2. In trying to identify the causes of problem drinking, some researchers have stressed the role of genetic factors, while others have viewed it as an inability to adjust to the stress of life or as a social phenomenon.

   Problem drinking is caused by genetic factors and the effects of stress

3. Some individuals do not go through the normal process of grieving, perhaps because of their personality makeup or as a consequence of the particular situation: the individual may, for instance, be stoical about his or her feelings or may have to manage the affairs of the family.[14]

   Some individuals do not grieve because of personality factors or in particular situation

4. Policies that encourage industries to pack up and move from one state to another, or out of the country, in search of lower labor costs, lighter taxes, and fewer regulations, are policies that, whatever their intention, ultimately promote racial inequality through their disproportionate impact on minority workers.[15]

   Racial inequality is promoted by industries moving from state to state

5. Beyond the volume and quality of arms transferred to troubled regions by the Soviet Union and the United States, the Soviet bloc has demonstrated a superior willingness to arrange deliveries [of arms] on schedules that could not be met by the West, thus enabling it to influence events in regional hotspots at critical junctions, while Western arms have generally been much slower to arrive.[16]

The soviet Union is more willing and able to deliver arms faster than the United stated

EXERCISE 10 _____

Directions: *Select several pages from one of your more difficult textbooks. Quickly look through these pages and locate ten long or complicated sentences. Then paraphrase each.*

Troublesome Types of Sentences

Sentences may be complicated because they are packed with information that modifies and explains the key idea. However, sentences can also be troublesome if they follow unusual or unfamiliar sentence patterns. As you learned earlier in the chapter, many sentences follow the subject-verb-object pattern. When this pattern is not followed or is modified, sentences become more difficult to read. Three types of difficult sentence patterns are described below.

Reversed Order of Events: Most sentences present ideas in chronological order—the order in which they occur, as in the following sentence:

After class, I went to the bookstore.

However, when the order of events presented in the sentence is presented differently from the way they actually occurred, the reader must make a mental switch or transformation, reversing the order of events in his or her mind, as in the following:

I went to the bookstore after class.

The above switch is easy to make. However, when the ideas become more complex and less familiar, the switch is more difficult, and sometimes easy to miss:

The industrial workers become proletarians where before they were serfs.[17]

Here, you must transform the sentence by thinking, "the workers were serfs, then they became proletarians."

When reading reverse-order sentences, stop and establish the correct order of events before continuing to read.

EXERCISE 11 _____

Directions: *For each of the following sentences, list the events in correct chronological order.*

1. American intervention in the Vietnam War followed earlier French involvement.

    _____

2. Although it has subsequently been revised and extended, the Omnibus Crime Control and Safe Streets Act, when passed in 1968, was intended to establish a massive campaign against lawlessness.

    _____

3. In computing federal income tax owed, in order to consult a tax table, you must compute your adjusted gross income and taxable income.

    _____

4. In computing net cost, before you subtract cash discount, you must subtract trade discounts from the list price.

    _____

5. Prior to a presidential review of the proposed federal budget, the Office of Management and Budget holds hearings and reviews its assessment of the economy.

    _____

Distance Between Subject and Verb: In most sentences the verb (action) closely follows the subject, as in the sentence:

Effective <u>managers share</u> a number of common characteristics.

However, some writers place additional information between the subject and verb, as in the following:

<u>Chief executive officers</u> who are successful at acquiring considerable power and using it to control others <u>tend to share</u> a number of common characteristics.

When the subject and verb are split, the reader is forced to carry mentally an incomplete idea while he or she reads additional information about the subject before reaching the action of the sentence. For this type of sentence, make an effort to hold in mind the subject until you reach the verb. Reread if necessary.

EXERCISE 12 _____

Directions: *For each of the following sentences underline the subject and verb.*

1. Industry, the second and more modern form of production, displaced feudalism.

    _____

2. Israel, surrounded by boundaries easily crossed by hostile tanks and infantry and further limited by its tiny size, is severely hindered in national defense by its geography.

    _____

3. Crimes committed in the course of one's occupation by those who operate inside business, government, or other establishments, in violation of their sense of loyalty to the employer or client, are among the most difficult to identify.

    _____

4. A distinguished panel of educators and lawyers, which recently concluded that the only just system of punishment is one based on retribution, proposed a maximum penalty for all crimes but murder of five years' imprisonment.[18]

    _____

5. Currency and things that can be changed into currency very easily, such as bank accounts, stocks, bonds, Treasury bills, and the like, are termed liquid assets.[19]

    _____

Inverted Sentence Order: As you learned earlier in the chapter, the most common, normal order of a sentence is subject-verb-object, as in the following:

Ted studied his chemistry textbook.

Occasionally, however, a writer will reverse this normal order, creating sentences such as

The chemistry textbook was studied by Ted.

The order is object-verb-subject. Sentences of this type use a verb form called the passive voice (and are often intended to focus the reader's attention on the object rather than the action). Reading such sentences requires a mental switch or transformation to place the sentence in normal order.

Here is a more challenging example:

The twentieth century has seen a radical alteration in the world position of the United States.[20]

In this sentence, you must make a mental switch. The sentence might be paraphrased as follows:

The United States has experienced a severe change in its world position during the twentieth century.

EXERCISE 13 ───────────────

Directions: *Paraphrase each of the following sentences, transforming the sentence to normal sentence order.*

1. Some of the most influential research linking mental illness to the state of the economy has been done by the sociologist M. Harvey Brenner.[21]

   ───

2. A major reason for the fairly impressive gains in income by black women, as compared to Hispanic women, was found to be the much greater rate of employment.

   ───

3. It has been argued that women's growing role in the work force has moved them toward economic equality with men, even if they have not yet attained that goal.

   ───

4. It is suggested, for example, that the "love bonds" between parent and child are important to regulating the aggressive drive and that destructive behavior is prevented by the formation of stable human relationships in early childhood.[22]

   ───

5. It is widely agreed that there has been a profound shift in the way Americans earn their livings in the twentieth century, especially during the last quarter.

   ───

SUMMARY

The sentence, one of the basic units of meaning, is defined as a group of words that expresses a complete thought or idea. All complete sentences must have two essential components; these are called core parts. First, a sentence must have a subject; it must be about a person, thing, or idea. Second, a sentence must express some type of action; something must happen to or be done by the subject. To understand a sentence, the reader must be able to recognize these core parts. Many sentences combine two or more sets of core parts for the purpose of showing relationships between them.

Punctuation is an aid to the reader in comprehending sentence meaning and identifying the core parts of the sentence. Each type of punctuation mark gives the reader specific information about the relative importance of ideas and the location of core parts within the sentence.

Deciphering complicated sentences is a four-step process: Locate the core parts, study the modifiers, paraphrase, and check vocabulary. Types of complicated sentences include reversed order of events, split subject and verb, and inverted sentence order.

8

Understanding Paragraphs

Use this chapter to:

1. *Find out what to look for as you read a paragraph.*
2. *Increase your recall of paragraph content.*

The *paragraph* can be defined as a group of related sentences about a single topic. Just as sentences have specific components—core parts—paragraphs also contain particular elements that are necessary for complete meaning to be conveyed.

THREE ESSENTIAL ELEMENTS OF A PARAGRAPH

The *topic,* the one thing the paragraph is about, is the unifying factor, and every sentence and idea contained in the paragraph relate to the topic. The *main idea,* what the author wants to communicate about the topic, is the central or most important thought in the paragraph. Every other sentence and idea in the paragraph is related to the main idea. The sentence that expresses this idea is called the *topic sentence. Details* are the proof, support, explanation, reasons, or examples that explain the paragraph's main idea.

Each of the following examples contains a group of sentences, but only one is a paragraph. Only that one has the three essential elements. Identify the paragraph.

Cats frequently become aggressive when provoked. Some plants require more light than others due to coloration of their foliage. Some buildings, due to poor construction, waste a tremendous amount of energy.

Some plants require more light than others due to coloration of their foliage. Some plants will live a long time without watering. Plants are being used as decorator items in stores and office buildings.

Some plants require more light than others due to coloration of their foliage. Plants with shades of white, yellow, or pink in their leaves need more light than plants with completely green foliage. For example, a Swedish ivy plant with completely green leaves requires less light per day than a variegated Swedish ivy that contains shades of white, yellow, and green in its leaves.

In the first example, the sentences were unrelated; each sentence was about a different thing, and there was no connection among them.

In the second example, each sentence was about plants—the common topic; however, the sentences together did not prove, explain, or support any particular idea about plants.

In the third example, each sentence was about plants, and all sentences were about one main idea—that some plants need more light than others due the coloration of their leaves. Thus, the third example is a paragraph; it has a topic—plants; a main idea—that plants require varying degrees of light due to coloration; and supporting details—the example of the Swedish ivy. The first sentence functions as a topic sentence.

In order to understand a paragraph, a reader must be able to identify the topic, main idea, and details easily. In the following paragraph, each of these parts is identified.

Topic sentence { As societies become industrialized, the distribution of workers among various economic activities tends to change in a predictable way. In the early stages, the population is engaged in agriculture and the collection of raw materials for food and shelter. But as technology develops, agricultural workers are drawn into manufacturing and construction.

Topic: distribution of workers

Details

This chapter will focus on identifying these essential elements of the paragraph and enable you to read paragraphs more easily. Although emphasis is on reading paragraphs, you will find this information useful in your own writing as well. Just as a reader must identify these elements, so must a writer structure his or her paragraph using these elements.

HOW TO IDENTIFY THE TOPIC

The topic of a paragraph is the subject of the whole paragraph. It is the one thing that the whole paragraph is about. Usually, the topic of a paragraph can be expressed in two or three words. To find the topic of a paragraph, ask yourself this question: What is the one thing the author is discussing throughout the paragraph? Read the following example.

Magazines are a channel of communication halfway between newspapers and books. Unlike newspapers or books, however, many of the most influential magazines are difficult or impossible to purchase at newsstands. With their color printing and slick paper (in most cases), magazines have become a showplace for exciting graphics. Until the 1940s most consumer (general) magazines offered a diverse menu of both fiction and nonfiction articles and miscellany such as poetry and short humor selections. With television providing a heavy quotient of entertainment for the American home, many magazines discovered a strong demand for nonfiction articles, their almost exclusive content today.

–Agee, Ault, and Emery, *Introduction to Mass Communication,*
p. 153.

In the example, the author is discussing one topic—magazines—throughout the paragraph. Notice how many times the word *magazines* is repeated in the paragraph. Frequently, the repeated use of a word can serve as a clue to the topic of a paragraph.

EXERCISE 1

Directions: *Read each of the following paragraphs and then select the topic of the paragraph from the choices given.*

1. The organization of both branches of Congress is based on political party lines. The *majority party* in each house is the one with the greatest number of members. Being the majority party is quite important because that party chooses the major officers of the branch of Congress, controls debate on the floor, selects all committee chairmen, and has a majority on all committees. For almost thirty years, the Democratic party was the majority party in both the House and the Senate; the Republicans were the minority party. In the 1980 elections the GOP ("Grand Old Party") won control of the Senate for the first time in twenty-eight years. Thus the Republicans became the majority party in the Senate, although the Democrats remained the majority party in the house.

   –Wasserman, *The Basics of American Politics*, pp. 94–95

   a. political parties
   b. majority parties in Congress
   c. the Republican majority
   d. branches of Congress

2. The absence of instincts in people leads to a *variety* of behavior that is not observed in other animals. Whereas a cornered rat *always* exhibits the same automatic and predictable aggressive reaction, a "cornered" human being may not necessarily act the same way. Imagine a young boy, say 6 or 7 years old, walking in the woods one day who happens upon a bear cub. He does not know yet that it is dangerous to be near the young of wild animals. When the boy sees how playful the cub is, he begins to run and play with it. Shortly, the mother bear returns and finds this fellow cavorting with her cub. The adult bear, *instinctively* perceiving a threat to her young, *automatically* reacts. She growls and makes other noises indicating her intent to attack and chases the boy through the woods into a small box canyon. The boy, like the proverbial rat, finds himself "cornered" and must turn to face his adversary. What will he do?

   –Levin and Spates, *Starting Sociology*, pp. 44–45

   a. a boy facing a bear
   b. instinctive behavior
   c. variety in human behavior
   d. variety in animal behavior

3. Technological advancements in microcircuitry have enabled engineers to develop computers that can perform diagnostic and control functions in a host of conventional devices. For example, as you push the buttons of a microwave oven or photocopying machine, or even as you drive your car, it is likely that your actions are monitored and trans-

lated into action by an internal computer. The same can be said for dishwashers, refrigerators, sewing machines, lawn mowers, power hand tools, heating and cooling equipment, intrusion alarms, telephones, television, stereo systems, word processors, military vehicles and weapons, and industrial robots. The computers in such applications are "special-purpose" computers, designed to perform a specific function in that particular device.

–Miller and Heeren, *Mathematical Ideas,* p. 629

a. diagnostic and control capabilities
b. monitoring functions
c. special-purpose computers
d. microcircuitry and control functions

4. The simple word "to" has caused a great deal of confusion in many areas of science. For example, consider the phrase, "Birds migrate southward to escape winter." The statement seems harmless enough, but if interpreted literally, it implies that the birds have a goal in mind, or that they are moving under the directions of some conscious force that compels them to escape winter. Philosophers have termed such assumptions *teleology.* (*Teleos* is Greek for *end* or *goal.*) It is commonly used in reference to ideas that go beyond what is actually verifiable and generally implies some inner drive to complete a goal or some directing force operating above the laws of nature.

–Wallace, *Biology: The World of Life,* pp. 31–32

a. forces operating above the laws of nature
b. confusion in language
c. literally interpreted statements
d. teleological assumptions

5. Pain sensations are generally classified by their sites of origin. Cutaneous pain originates from skin pain receptors and generally shows both fast and slow properties. In contrast, visceral pain comes from visceral organs and other deep tissues. This pain is generally of the slow, "aching" variety, which is difficult to localize. Frequently, visceral pain may be referred to other parts of the body supplied by the same spinal nerve (the dermatomal rule), known as *referred pain.* Also, visceral pain of the abdomen may cause overlying abdominal muscles to contract. This increased rigidity of the abdominal wall is called "guarding."

–Davis, Holtz, and Davis, *Conceptual Human Physiology,* pp. 195–196

a. classifying pain by site of origin
b. visceral organ pain
c. guarding in the abdominal wall
d. referred pain

6. Effective listening means listening with a third ear. By this I mean trying to listen for the meanings behind the words and not just to the words alone. The way words are spoken—loud, soft, fast, slow, strong, hesitating—is very important. There are messages buried in all the cues that surround words. If a mother says, "Come *in* now" in a soft, gentle voice, it may mean the kids have a few more minutes. If she says, "Come in NOW" there is no question about the meaning of the command. To listen effectively we have to pay attention to facial ex-

pressions and eye contact, gestures and body movement, posture and dress, as well as to the quality of the other person's voice, vocabulary, rhythm, rate, tone, and volume. These nonverbal cues are a vital part of any message. Listening with our third ear helps us to understand the whole message.

–Weaver, *Understanding Interpersonal Communications*, p. 117

a. meaning cues in listening
b. facial cues
c. the ways words are spoken
d. listening techniques

7. Corporations may obtain short-term funds through the use of promissory notes, trade credit, etc. Long-term debt of the corporation is usually in the form of bonds issued by the corporation. *Bonds* are, in a sense, long-term promissory notes of the corporation. Bonds have a face value, which is usually in $1,000 denominations, and a maturity date, at which time the principal must be repaid. In addition, each certificate has a stated interest rate. The issuing corporation is obligated to pay the bondholder an amount of money equal to the interest percentage of the face value of the bond. For example, a bond with a face value of $1,000 and a 6 percent interest rate would require a payment of $60 a year until the bond matured.

–Pickle and Abrahamson, *Introduction to Business,* p. 45

a. promissory notes
b. types of corporate debt
c. how bonds work
d. interest rates on bonds

8. To become part of the *official* data on crime, activities must be known to legal officials and must be appropriately labeled by them. Activities become known to the police, and hence become eligible for official labeling as crimes, in two ways. The most common way is for a member of the public to notify the police of a "crime" or "possible crime." The less common way is for the police to directly witness an activity that they then label crime. Police rely heavily on citizens bringing suspected crimes to their attention. This means that most actions that eventually become official crimes do so only because they have been evaluated as "crimes" or "possible crimes" by the public, who then bring them to the attention of the police. Here we see the importance of unofficial (public) evaluations and behavior in the production of *official* crime data.

–Barlow, *Introduction to Criminology,* p. 99

a. evaluating possible crimes
b. criminal activity
c. collection of official crime data
d. direct witnessing of criminal behavior

9. The Bill of Rights is an inexhaustible source of potential conflicts over rights. Clearly, the Constitution meant to guarantee the right to a fair trial as well as a free press. But a trial may not be fair if press coverage inflames public opinion so much that an impartial jury cannot be found. In one famous criminal trial an Ohio physician, Sam Sheppard, was accused of the murder of his wife. The extent of press coverage

rivaled that of a military campaign, and little of it sympathized with Dr. Sheppard. Found guilty and sent to the state penitentiary, Sheppard appealed his conviction to the Supreme Court. He argued that press coverage had interfered with his ability to get a fair trial. The Supreme Court agreed, claiming that the press had created a virtual "Roman circus," and reversed Sheppard's conviction.

–Lineberry, *Government in America*, p. 142

a. the purpose of the Bill of Rights
b. conflicts between fair trials and the free press
c. rights of the free press
d. the Sheppard trial

10. A mixture of copper and tin in a molten state will cool to form a harder, stronger, and more durable solid than either copper itself or tin itself. This solid is bronze, historically the first of the materials we call *alloys*. Brass, a mixture of copper and zinc, is another alloy. Steels are alloys of iron with carbon, often with the addition of other elements for special purposes, like chromium for rustlessness and silicon for high permeability. Gallium arsenide is a newer alloy that is a semiconductor used in electronics for such solid-state devices as the light-emitting diodes in calculator readouts. All alloys are made by basically the same process, by mixing two or more molten metals in varying proportions and letting the mixture cool and solidify.

–Hewitt, *Conceptual Physics*, p. 169

a. manufacture of bronze alloys
b. uses of alloys
c. the process of cooling and solidifying metal alloys
d. production of alloys

EXERCISE 2 _____

Directions: *For each of the following paragraphs, read the paragraph and write the topic in the space provided. Be sure to limit the topic to two or three words.*

1. Energy conservation in the short run and long run will require creative solutions in all areas of business. A few innovative solutions have already surfaced which indicate that business understands the importance of saving energy. The makers of Maxwell House coffee developed a method to save natural gas. The first step in making instant coffee is to brew the coffee just as people do at home, except in 1000-gallon containers. The heat to brew the coffee had come from burning natural gas, and the process left Maxwell House with tons of coffee grounds. The company then had to use trucks (that burned gasoline) to cart the coffee grounds away. Maxwell House realized it could save most of the cost of the natural gas (and the gasoline cost) by burning the grounds to get the heat to brew subsequent batches of coffee. Natural gas is now used only to start the coffee grounds burning.

–Kinnear and Bernhardt, *Principles of Marketing*, pp. 79–81

Topic: _____

2. What happens when your feelings about yourself are weak or negative? Since you tend to act consistently with the feelings you have about yourself, this can be a damaging or destructive situation. For example, what if you perceive yourself as a failure in school? This attitude may be a result of something as insignificant as misunderstanding directions for an assignment, or it may have developed over a long period of time: having to compete with a very successful brother or sister, having a string of unsympathetic teachers, or not gaining enough positive reinforcement at home for schoolwork. Whatever the cause, it is likely that once you start thinking of yourself as a failure, you will begin to act the part. Because of poor study habits, inadequate reading, and lack of participation in class, a poor grade may result, reinforcing your feeling. Such negative feelings feed upon themselves and become a vicious cycle, a cycle that will begin to encompass all your thoughts, actions, and relationships.

   —Weaver, *Understanding Interpersonal Communications,* p. 52

   Topic: _____

3. A human being can handle only so much information at one time. This has to do not only with the capability of the human brain to decipher material but also with the various ways that emotions get bound to certain experiences. Often the root causes for conflict are closely tied to our emotional response pattern. In such cases, as sure as conflicts are bound to come up, so are the emotions that go along with them. If we are having an emotionally involving experience, it is difficult to take on and fully comprehend a new "load" of information at the same time. Our senses are preoccupied. If someone else tries to share some vital news with us while our feelings are thus tied up, interpersonal conflicts may result. We may experience this when we try to listen to a classroom lecture just after we've heard some upsetting news. The intensity of the emotional experience overshadows any material the teacher could offer. We simply don't have room for any more information.

   —Weaver, *Understanding Interpersonal Communications,* p. 265

   Topic: _____

4. One prominent theory in biological circles is that humans are by nature, or instinctively, aggressive. This argument has been helped along by influential studies of animal behavior. Konrad Lorenz's book, *On Aggression,* may be taken as a case in point. According to Lorenz, nature has armed animals with an instinct for aggression for three reasons: (1) to ensure that stronger animals succeed in mating the most desirable females of their kind, thus helping to perpetuate "good" qualities in future generations; (2) to ensure that each individual has sufficient physical space for securing food, raising young, and so on (defense of physical space is called *territoriality*); and (3) to maintain hierarchies of dominance, and through them a stable, well-policed society.

   —Barlow, *Introduction to Criminology,* p. 147

   Topic: _____

5. We can identify almost any object or event as a *pattern* or bundle of features. To define a dog, for example, we begin with a set of features: four legs, a hairy coat, a tail. Of course, this list so far describes a cat as well as a dog. So we add further features like round pupils (cats have vertical slits) and smooth tongues (cats' tongues are sandpapery). More features might distinguish a particular dog: a spot around the left eye, for example. Such features as antlers and flippers must be absent. Finally, we should allow some leeway for features that might be *missing* in a particular dog, such as a tail that has been bobbed. When we think about it this way, we see that the category "dog" is itself a complex, abstract concept. Most theories of human pattern recognition hold that our visual system uses features of these sorts in recognizing objects.

   –Roediger et al., *Psychology,* p. 129

   Topic: _____

6. Particularly after 1972, when Richard Nixon packed away so much extra money from his campaign that his staff was doling it out to Watergate burglars as "hush money," there has been grave concern about money in politics. One key aspect of this concern is the worry over the cost of elections. In 1984, our nation footed a bill of more than $1 billion for elections. (However, this included all elections—national, state, and local—and presidential expenditures are incurred only once every four years.) Horror stories about expensive campaigns have become a staple of American journalism.

   –Lineberry, *Government in America,* p. 251

   Topic: _____

7. Although they can process and move information rapidly (sometimes at the speed of light), computers are passive electronic machines awaiting human commands. If a computer fails to understand the particular command, it will not work. If it receives an incorrect command, it will work incorrectly. Likewise, integrated software, word processors, electronic mail systems, dictaphones, and all other computerized devices used to speed the flow of information in the automated office cannot convert poor writing to good. Anyone with programming experience knows that instructions to a computer demand the same precise phrasing, logical organization, and exact punctuation required of any good letter, memo, or report. Otherwise, the message will not be understood by the recipient—machine or human.

   –Dumont and Lannon, *Business Communications,* p. 8

   Topic: _____

8. Unlike courtship, dating serves a number of important functions prior to and in addition to mate selection. For adolescents, as well as for increasing numbers of dating adults, dating is a form of recreation that allows people to enjoy not only a leisure activity but each other's company as well. For adolescents it is also a means of socialization in which young people learn the social and interpersonal skills that will allow them to interact meaningfully with one another throughout their lives. They also learn about sexuality and intimacy . . . , and through

their dates establish status in their peer groups. . . . Girls tend to bring a person-centered orientation to dating, while boys bring a body-centered orientation, and within the dating context, both learn to integrate intimacy and sexuality . . .

–Fuhrmann, *Adolescence, Adolescents,* p. 114

Topic: _____

9. Automated radio has made large gains, as station managers try to reduce expenses by eliminating some of their on-the-air personnel. These stations broadcast packaged taped programs obtained from syndicates, hour after hour, or material delivered by satellite from a central program source. The closely timed tapes contain music and commercials, along with the necessary voice introductions and bridges. They have spaces into which a staff engineer can slip local recorded commercials. By eliminating disc jockeys in this manner, a station keeps its costs down but loses the personal touch and becomes a broadcasting automation. For example, one leading syndicator, Satellite Music Network, provides more than 625 stations with their choice of seven different 24-hour music formats that include news and live disc jockeys playing records.

–Agee, Ault, and Emery, *Introduction to Mass Communications,* p. 225

Topic: _____

10. Interestingly, it can take hours to digest a meal that required only minutes to eat. Obviously, we can eat food faster than we can digest it, so some degree of storage is needed within the digestive tract. The stomach is specialized to meet this need. The human stomach is a pouchlike enlargement of the gut tube that stores food as it is eaten and gradually releases it into the intestine for complete processing. . . . Because of its storage function, the tunica mucosa and tunica submucosa of the stomach are specialized for distention as food enters the stomach. These two layers of the stomach show longitudinal folds, or rugae, that can flatten as the stomach is stretched. The tunica muscularis of the stomach is also specialized for distention. The smooth muscle of this layer can be stretched without increasing its contraction strength, or tone. This allows the stomach to hold large quantities of food without increasing the pressure of its contents.

–Davis, Holtz, and Davis, *Conceptual Human Physiology,* p. 462

Topic: _____

HOW TO FIND THE MAIN IDEA

The main idea of a paragraph tells you what the author wants you to know about the topic. The main idea is usually directly stated by the writer in one or more sentences within the paragraph. The sentence that states this main idea is called the *topic sentence.* The topic sentence tells what the rest of the paragraph is about. In some paragraphs, the main idea is not directly stated in any one sentence. Instead, it is left to the reader to infer, or reason out.

To find the main idea of a paragraph, first decide what the topic of the paragraph is. Then ask yourself these questions: What is the main idea—what is the author trying to say about the topic? Which sentence states the main idea? Read the following paragraph.

The Federal Trade Commission has become increasingly interested in false and misleading packaging. Complaints have been filed against many food packagers because they make boxes unnecessarily large to give a false impression of quantity. Cosmetics manufacturers have been accused of using false bottoms in packaging to make a small amount of their product appear to be much more.

In the preceding paragraph, the topic is false packaging. The main idea is that the Federal Trade Commission is becoming increasingly concerned about false or misleading packaging. The author states the main idea in the first sentence, so it is the topic sentence.

WHERE TO FIND THE TOPIC SENTENCE

Although the topic sentence of a paragraph can be located anywhere in the paragraph, there are several positions where it is most likely to be found. Each type of paragraph has been diagrammed to help you visualize how it is structured.

First Sentence

The most common placement of the topic sentence is first in the paragraph. In this type of paragraph, the author states the main idea at the beginning of the paragraph and then elaborates on it. For example:

<u>The good listener, in order to achieve the purpose of acquiring information, is careful to follow specific steps to achieve accurate understanding.</u> First, whenever possible the good listener prepares in advance for the speech or lecture he or she is going to attend. He or she studies the topic to be discussed and finds out about the speaker and his or her beliefs. Second, on arriving at the place where the speech is to be given, he or she chooses a seat where seeing, hearing, and remaining alert are easy. Finally, when the speech is over, an effective listener reviews what was said and reacts to and evaluates the ideas expressed.

Usually, in this type of paragraph, the author is employing a deductive thought pattern in which a statement is made at the beginning and then supported through the paragraph.

Last Sentence

The second most common position of the topic sentence is last in the paragraph. In this type of paragraph, the author leads or builds up to the main idea and then states it in a sentence at the very end. For example:

Whenever possible, the good listener prepares in advance for the speech or lecture he or she plans to attend. He or she studies the topic to be discussed and finds out about the speaker and his or her beliefs. On arriving at the place where the speech is to be given, he or she chooses a seat where seeing, hearing, and remaining alert are easy. And, when the speech is over, he or she reviews what was said and reacts to and evaluates the ideas expressed. <u>Thus, an effective listener, in order to achieve the purpose of acquiring information, takes specific steps to achieve accurate understanding.</u>

The thought pattern frequently used in this type of paragraph is inductive. That is, the author provides supporting evidence for the main idea first, and then states it.

Middle of the Paragraph

Another common placement of the topic sentence is in the middle of the paragraph. In this case, the author builds up to the main idea, states it in the middle of the paragraph, and then goes on with further elaboration and detail. For example:

Whenever possible, the good listener prepares in advance for the speech or lecture he or she plans to attend. He or she studies the topic to be discussed and finds out about the speaker and his or her beliefs. <u>An effective listener, as you are beginning to see, takes specific steps to achieve accurate understanding of the lecture.</u> Furthermore, on arriving at the place where the speech is to be given, he or she chooses a seat where it is easy to see, hear, and remain alert. Finally, when the speech is over, the effective listener reviews what was said and reacts to and evaluates the ideas expressed.

First and Last Sentences

Sometimes an author uses two sentences to state the main idea or state the main idea twice in one paragraph. Usually, in this type of paragraph, the writer states the main idea at the beginning of the paragraph, then explains or supports the idea, and finally restates the main idea at the very end. For example:

<u>The good listener, in order to achieve the purpose of acquiring information, is careful to follow specific steps to achieve accurate understanding.</u> First, whenever possible the good listener prepares in advance for the speech or lecture he or she is going to attend. He or she studies the topic to be discussed and finds out about the speaker and his or her beliefs. Second, on arriving at the place where the speech is to be given, he or she chooses a seat where seeing, hearing, and remaining alert are easy. Finally, when the speech is over, he or she reviews what was said and reacts to and evaluates the ideas expressed. <u>Effective listening is an active process in which a listener deliberately takes certain actions to ensure that accurate communication has occurred.</u>

Directions: *Read each of the following paragraphs and underline the topic sentence.*

1. At least four types of sensation are usually lumped together as the sense of touch: pressure, pain, warmth, and cold. The skin contains various receptors that act together in ways that are still a bit mysterious, and it is not uniformly sensitively to all of these properties across its entire surface. When a small square of skin is touched with tiny needles that have been heated or chilled, some areas in the square sense only heat, some only cold, and some neither. Likewise, the skin is not uniformly sensitive to touch. If two pointed objects are pressed against the skin simultaneously, they often will be felt as one. The distance by which they must be separated to be experienced as two objects rather than one (a measurement called the *two-point threshold*) varies over the body as well; it is much greater on the back than on the fingertips, for instance.

    –Roediger et al., *Psychology*, p. 110

2. Much of what we know about how consumers behave is based on theories and research from the field of psychology, the study of individual behavior. In analyzing consumers' purchase decision processes, such psychological factors as motivation, perception, learning, personality, and attitudes are important to understand, since they can help explain the *why* behind consumer behavior. It is virtually impossible to directly determine the influence of these factors; thus, it must be inferred. It is impossible to observe directly what is going on in a buyer's mind. Often the consumers themselves do not know why they behave as they do. Other times they do know, but may not be willing to tell the researcher the true reasons for their behavior. So, marketers must study the psychological factors that are relevant to their products or services.

    –Kinnear and Bernhardt, *Principles of Marketing*, p. 149

3. The first all-electronic computer, ENIAC (Electronic Numerical Integrator and Calculator), was developed at the University of Pennsylvania in 1947 for a cost of $487,000. The device stood two stories high, covered fifteen thousand square feet, weighed some thirty tons, and contained 18,000 vacuum tubes (which failed at a rate of about one every seven minutes). Since that time, a revolution in miniaturization, mass production, and economic competition has brought about computers smaller than typewriters, twenty times faster than ENIAC, more powerful and much more reliable, and readily available to the average citizen. The cost of a million calculations is now measured in cents, rather than in tens of thousands of dollars. It is said that if the same rate of advancement had been possible in the automobile industry over the past thirty years, a Rolls-Royce would now cost less than $3 and would go more than two million miles on a gallon of gasoline.

    –Miller and Heeren, *Mathematical Ideas*, p. 628

4. An understanding of the eye's ability to form images of both near and distant objects requires a basic knowledge of certain principles of optics. Light travels through air at an incredibly fast rate, approximately

300,000 kilometers/second. Light also travels through other transparent media, such as water and glass, but more slowly. When light rays pass from one medium into another of a different density, the rays are bent unless they strike the surface of the second medium at a perfectly perpendicular angle. The extent of this bending, or refraction, of light varies with the angle between the light rays and the surface of the medium. . . .

–Davis, Holtz, and Davis, *Conceptual Human Physiology,* pp. 201–202

5. Business, labor, and farmers all fret over the impacts of government regulations. Even a minor change in government regulatory policy can cost industries large amounts or bring windfall profits. Tax policies also affect the livelihoods of farmers, firms, and workers. How the tax code is written determines whether people and producers pay a lot or a little of their incomes to the government. Because government often provides subsidies (to farmers, small businesses, railroads, minority businesses, and others), every economic group wants to gets its share of direct aid and of government contracts. And in this day of the global economic connection, business, labor, and farmers alike worry about import quotas, tariffs (fees placed on imports), and the soundness of the dollar. In short, white-collar business executives, blue-collar workers, and khaki-collar farmers seek to influence government because regulations, taxes, subsidies, and international economic policy all affect their economic livelihoods. Let us take a quick tour of some of the major organized interests in the economic policy arena.

–Lineberry, *Government in America,* p. 313

6. All sounds are waves produced by the vibrations of material objects. In pianos and violins, the sound is produced by the vibrating strings; in a clarinet, by a vibrating reed. The human voice results from the vibration of the vocal cords. In each of these cases a vibrating source sends a disturbance through the surrounding medium, usually air, in the form of longitudinal waves. The *loudness* of sound depends on the amplitude of these waves, that is, on how much air is set into motion. The *pitch* of sound is directly related to the frequency of the sound waves, which is identical to the frequency of the vibrating source. The pitches produced by lower frequencies are heard as low bass tones, and higher pitches are produced by higher frequencies. (We will treat pitch and loudness further in the next chapter.) The human ear can normally hear sounds made by vibrating bodies of frequencies in the range between 16 and 20,000 hertz. Sound waves with frequencies below 16 hertz are called *infrasonic,* and those with frequencies above 20,000 hertz are called *ultrasonic.* We cannot hear infrasonic and ultrasonic sound waves.

–Hewitt, *Conceptual Physics,* p. 294

7. Union membership has traditionally come from the ranks of the blue-collar employees in manufacturing. However, the number of blue-collar employees has declined so that they account for only about 30 percent of the total labor force in the United States, and this trend is expected to continue. White-collar employees comprise almost 54 percent of the labor force, service employees about 14 percent, and agricultural employees just over 2 percent. Future union growth will depend upon the success of unions in organizing employees in occupations other than blue-collar, such as government employees,

office-clerical employees, and educators. Even professional athletes are unionized.

–Pickle and Abrahamson, *Introduction to Business,* p. 189

8. Critics of advertising argue that most ads are tasteless and wasteful assaults on consumers' senses. Since products and services in monopolistically competitive markets are, by definition, close substitutes, product characteristics are difficult to differentiate with *actual* differences. Rather, critics point out that advertising creates only imagined differences. A large number of competitive firms have the incentive to advertise in this manner, creating a confusing array of messages to consumers. In this view, advertising allocates demand among competitors without increasing the total demand for the product. To increase the total demand for the product, such as fast-food hamburgers, cat food, or breakfast cereal, advertising must reduce either consumers' savings or their expenditures on other goods. If advertising is unsuccessful at this task, the critics allege, it is unproductive because it merely allocates demand among competing firms producing goods that are fundamentally alike.

–Ekelund and Tollison, *Economics,* p. 233

9. When robbery is studied as work it does not look very different from many legitimate business pursuits. The popular myth depicting robbery as a senseless, violent act of plunder perpetrated by equally senseless and violent individuals can be upheld on some occasions. But a robbery is more accurately pictured as having characteristics that lie on a number of continua, of which three of the more important are *planning, organizing,* and *skill at victim management.* Those who make robbery a regular pursuit are likely to be found in robberies at the high end of these continua; those who are opportunists, or who indulge in robbery in a repetitive but sporadic and unsystematic manner, will be involved in robberies at the low end. Thus robberies committed by professionals tend to exhibit high levels of planning, organization, and victim-management skills; those committed by opportunists out for a fast buck tend to exhibit little in the way of planning and organization, and it may be in robberies committed by such individuals that we find confusion, fear, and disorder when it comes to handling their own and the victim's stresses and tensions.

–Barlow, *Introduction to Criminology,* p. 196

10. In the photosynthesis of green plants, as the energy of sunlight falls on the green pigment in the leaves, carbon dioxide and water are used to make food, and water and oxygen are released. The release of oxygen by those first photosynthesizers was a critical step in the direction of life's development. In a sense, the production of oxygen falls into the "good news–bad news" category. It's good news for us, of course, since we need oxygen, but as oxygen began to replace hydrogen as the most prevalent gas in the atmosphere, it sounded the death knell for many of the early heterotrophs. This is because oxygen is a disruptive gas, as we know from seeing the process of rusting. . . . So, in the early days of life on the planet, many life forms were destroyed by the deadly and accumulating gas.

–Wallace, *Biology: The World of Life,* p. 48

RECOGNIZING DETAILS

The details in a paragraph are those facts and ideas that prove, explain, support, or give examples of the main idea of the paragraph. Once the topic and main idea have been identified, recognizing the supporting details is a relatively simple matter. The more difficult job involved is the selection of the few key, or most important, details that clearly support the main idea.

All details in a paragraph relate to and in some way expand the paragraph's main idea, but not all these details are completely essential to the author's central thought. Some details are just meant to describe; others are meant to provide added, but not essential, information; still others are intended merely to repeat or restate the main idea.

On the other hand, the key supporting details within a paragraph are those statements that carry the primary supporting evidence needed to back up the main idea. To find the key supporting details in a paragraph, ask yourself, What are the main facts the author uses to back up or prove what he or she said about the topic?

In the following paragraph, the topic sentence is underlined twice; the key supporting details are underlined once. Notice how the underlined details differ, in the type and importance of the information they provide, from the remaining details in the paragraph.

> Some analysts attribute this downturn in [employee satisfaction] to "blue-collar blues" or "white-collar woes" attendant on <u>jobs that have become boring, routine, and mundane.</u> Others suggest that the problem has less to do with the jobs than with <u>changes in the employees themselves.</u> Many managers, for example, have become less confident and loyal to their firms in the face of acquisitions, mergers, and cutbacks that have changed their companies and resulted in a loss of 500,000 managerial jobs since 1979. Many employees who devoted all their energies to their employer may now believe that their energies were misplaced. Young employees are more cynical than were their parents and have expectations about buying power and life-style that have been disappointed. Many of these employees place family life and other nonwork interests above their jobs and refuse promotions and transfers. Finally, highly trained <u>professional employees may identify more with their professions than with their employers. The satisfaction of a professional employee often depends on the degree to which his or her professional skills are recognized and used by the employer.</u>
>
> –Szilagyi and Wallace, *Organizational Behavior and Performance,*
> p. 75

All the underlined details give the primary reasons why employees are dissatisfied with their jobs. The details in the remainder of the paragraph offer examples or explain these reasons further.

EXERCISE 4 ───────────

Directions: *Each of the following statements could function as the topic sentence of a paragraph. After each statement are sentences containing de-*

tails that may relate to the main idea statement. Read each sentence and make a checkmark beside those with details that can be considered primary support for the main idea statement.

1. *Topic sentence:*

    Licorice is used in tobacco products because it has specific characteristics that cannot be found in any other single ingredient.

    Details:

    _____ a. McAdams & Co. is the largest importer and processor of licorice root.

    _____ b. Licorice blends with tobacco and provides added mildness.

    _____ c. Licorice provides a unique flavor and sweetens many types of tobacco.

    _____ d. The extract of licorice is present in relatively small amounts in most types of pipe tobacco.

    _____ e. Licorice helps tobacco retain the correct amount of moisture during storage.

2. *Topic sentence:*

    Many dramatic physical changes occur during adolescence between the ages of 13 and 15.

    Details:

    _____ a. Voice changes in boys begin to occur at age 13 or 14.

    _____ b. Facial proportions may change during adolescence.

    _____ c. The forehead tends to become wider, and the mouth widens.

    _____ d. Many teenagers do not know how to react to these changes.

    _____ e. Primary sex characteristics begin to develop for both boys and girls.

3. *Topic sentence:*

    The development of speech in infants follows a definite sequence or pattern of development.

    Details:

    _____ a. By the time an infant is six months old, he or she can make twelve different speech sounds.

    _____ b. Before the age of three months, most infants are unable to produce any recognizable syllables.

    _____ c. During the first year, the number of vowel sounds a child can produce is greater than the number of consonant sounds he or she can make.

    _____ d. During the second year, the number of consonant sounds a child can produce increases.

    _____ e. Parents often reward the first recognizable word a child produces by smiling or speaking to the child.

4. *Topic sentence:*

    The two main motives for attending a play are the desire for recreation and the need for relaxation.

    Details:

    _____ a. By becoming involved with the actors and their problems members of the audience temporarily suspend their personal cares and concerns.

    _____ b. In America today, the success of a play is judged by its ability to attract a large audience.

    _____ c. Almost everyone who attends a play expects to be entertained.

    _____ d. Plays allow the audience to release tension, which facilitates relaxation.

_____ e. There is a smaller audience that looks to theater for intellectual stimulation.

5. *Topic sentence:*

In some parts of the world, famine is a constant human condition and exists due to a variety of causes.

Details:

_____ a. In parts of Africa, people are dying of hunger by the tens of thousands.

_____ b. Famine is partly caused by increased population.

_____ c. Advances in medicine have increased life expectancies, keeping more people active for longer periods of time.

_____ d. Agricultural technology has not made substantial advances in increasing the food supply.

_____ e. Due to the growth of cities, populations have become more dense, and agricultural support for these population centers is not available.

6. *Topic sentence:*

The amount of alcohol a person consumes has been found to depend on a number of socioeconomic factors such as age, sex, ethnic background, and occupation.

Details:

_____ a. Some religions prohibit consumption altogether, and most encourage moderation.

_____ b. The lowest proportion of drinkers is found among people with an educational level of below sixth grade.

_____ c. People in a lower socioeconomic level drink more than people in a higher socioeconomic levels.

_____ d. In some cultures drinking is common at meals, but these same cultures disapprove of drunkenness.

_____ e. Farm owners have the highest proportion of nondrinkers, while professionals and businessmen have the highest proportion of drinkers.

7. *Topic sentence:*

An individual deals with anxiety in a variety of ways and produces a wide range of responses.

Details:

_____ a. Anxiety may manifest iteself by such physical symptoms as increased heart activity or labored breathing.

_____ b. Fear, unlike anxiety, is a response to real or threatened danger.

_____ c. Psychologically, anxiety often produces a feeling of powerlessness, or lack of direct control over the immediate environment.

_____ d. Temporary blindness, deafness, or the loss of the sensation of touch are examples of extreme physical responses to anxiety.

_____ e. Some people cannot cope with anxiety and are unable to control the neurotic behavior associated with anxiety.

8. *Topic sentence:*

An individual's status or importance within a group affects his or her behavior in that particular group.

Details:

_____ a. High-status individuals frequently arrive late at social functions.

_____ b. Once a person achieves high status, he or she attempts to maintain it.

_____ c. High-status individuals demand more privileges.

_____ d. Low-status individuals are less resistant to change within the group structure than persons of high status.

_____ e. There are always fewer high-status members than low-status members in any particular group.

9. *Topic sentence:*

An oligopoly is a market structure in which only a few companies sell a certain product.

Details:

_____ a. The automobile industry is a good example of an oligopoly, although it gives the appearance of being highly competitive.

_____ b. The breakfast cereal, soap, and cigarette industries, although basic to our economy, operate as oligopolies.

_____ c. Monopolies refer to market structures in which only one industry produces a particular product.

_____ d. Monopolies are able to exert more control and fixation of price than oligopolies.

_____ e. In the oil industry, because there are only a few producers, each producer has a fairly large share of the sales.

10. *Topic sentence:*

Advertising can be used to expand consumer choice as well as to limit it.

Details:

_____ a. Food stores that typically advertise their "specials" each Wednesday in the local paper are encouraging consumer choice.

_____ b. Department store advertising often makes the consumer aware of new products and styles, as well as of current prices of products.

_____ c. Misleading or excessive advertising is usually rejected by the consuming public.

_____ d. Exaggerated claims made by some advertisers serve to limit the consumer's actual knowledge and free choice of products.

_____ e. Advertising that provides little or no factual information, but attempts to make the brand name well known, actually restricts consumers' free choice.

EXERCISE 5 _____

Directions: *Read each paragraph and identify the topic and location of the main idea. Write each in the space provided. Then underline the key supporting details.*

1. Compared with vision and audition, taste is relatively poorly developed in humans. People often attribute the pleasure of eating good food to the sense of taste, but more often it is the smell that induces enjoyment. You have noticed, of course, that food resembles cardboard in flavor when a head cold congests your nasal passages. The tongue, which registers taste, is actually sensitive to a mere handful of properties, notably salty, sweet, sour, and bitter. These properties are detected by the 10,000 or so *taste buds* that line the tongue; taste buds live only a few days and then are replaced by new ones. Different taste buds are sensitive to different sensory properties, and they are not distributed uniformly on the tongue. . . . For example, the tip of the tongue is more responsive to sweetness, the base of the tongue to bit-

terness. However, most individual taste buds actually respond to more than one taste, so a substance's taste probably arises from the pattern of neural activity across many taste buds. . . . Of course, the tongue also senses the texture and temperatures of foods, which may add considerably to the enjoyment of eating.

–Roediger et al., *Psychology,* p. 109

Topic: _____

Main idea: _____

2. In the economic sense, *utility* refers to the power that goods or services have to satisfy a human want. There are four types of utility: form, possession, place, and time. Form utility is produced when raw materials are extracted from nature and their structure or shape is changed so that they satisfy a human want. For example, wheat is ground into flour by the miller, and then the flour is converted into bread by a bakery. Form utility is a production utility. The other three types of utilities are included in the marketing process. If goods or services are to satisfy individuals, they must be in their possession (possession utility). For this to happen, goods and services must be moved from the place where they have limited usefulness to the location where they have maximum usefulness in fulfilling consumer wants (place utility). Furthermore, if goods (or services) are to be of value to the final consumers, they must be available when they are demanded (time utility). For example, an appliance dealer stocks more air-conditioning units during the spring and summer months, when demand is greatest.

–Pickle and Abrahamson, *Introduction to Business,* pp. 201–202

Topic: _____

Main idea: _____

3. Perhaps we can best describe a theory by showing how one can be developed. Suppose someone comes up with an idea—one that explains certain observed phenomena in nature. At first, it is regarded as just that, an idea. But after it has been carefully described and its premises precisely defined, it may then become a *hypothesis*—an idea that can be tested. In a sense, the hypothesis is the first part of an "if . . . then" statement. The "then" predicts the result of the hypothesis, so one can know by testing if the hypothesis is sound. A hypothesis can also stand as a provisional statement for which more data are needed. If rigorous, carefully controlled testing supports the hypothesis, more confidence will be placed in it, until it finally gains the status of a theory. The theory itself, however, may remain unproven and unprovable. A hypothesis, then, is a possible explanation to be tested, whereas a *theory* is a more-or-less verified explanation that accounts for observed phenomena in nature.

–Wallace, *Biology: The World of Life,* p. 28

Topic: _____

Main idea: _____

4. Freewriting is nothing more than putting down on paper all your thoughts exactly as they occur to you when you start thinking about writing a paper. And, as you know from having listened closely to your own thoughts, while your mind is working it jumps from idea to idea with little apparent order. Nor do the ideas come out as complete sentences. Nevertheless, there is value to committing this jumble of thoughts to paper despite their apparent randomness. Many writers, including professionals, use freewriting not only because they find it helps them to discover ideas about the topic that they did not know they had, or to make connections that had not previously occurred to them, but also because it helps clear out any minor annoyances that may be blocking their creativity. It is also useful because it provides a starting point on a project that seems, at first glance, too complex to organize coherently. In freewriting you begin with whatever is on the top of your mind and let your thoughts go where they choose. At this point, you forget about organizing, forget about correcting, forget about revising, since in this initial stage these concerns will only interrupt the free flow of your ideas.

–Anselmo et al., *Thinking and Writing in College,* p. 13

Topic: _____

Main idea: _____

5. The importance of formal organizations in modern complex societies can hardly be overestimated. Every day, we deal with some sort of formal organization in connection with work, food, travel, health care, police protection, or some other necessity of life. Organizations enable people who are often total strangers to work together toward common goals. They create levels of authority and channels of command that clarify who gives orders, who obeys them, and who does which tasks. They are also a source of continuity and permanence in a society's efforts to meet specific goals. Individual members may come and go, but the organization continues to function. Thus formal organizations make it possible for highly complex industrialized societies to meet their most fundamental needs and pursue their collective aspirations.

–Eshleman and Cashion, *Sociology,* pp. 121–122

Topic: _____

Main idea: _____

6. Matter exists in four states: *solid, liquid, gaseous,* and *plasma.* In all states the atoms are perpetually moving. In solid state the atoms and molecules vibrate about fixed positions. If the rate of molecular vibration is increased sufficiently, molecules will shake apart and wander throughout the material, vibrating in nonfixed positions. The shape of the material is no longer fixed but takes the shape of its container. This is the liquid state. If more energy is put into the material and the molecules vibrate at even greater rates, they may break away from one another and assume the gaseous state. H_2O is a common example of this changing of states. When solid, it is ice. If we heat the ice, the increased molecular motion jiggles the molecules out of their fixed positions, and we have water. If we heat the water, we can reach a stage

where continued molecular vibration results in a separation between water molecules, and we have steam. Continued heating causes the molecules to separate into atoms; if we heat the steam to temperatures exceeding 2000°C, the atoms themselves will be shaken apart, making a gas of free electrons and bare nuclei called plasma.

—Hewitt, *Conceptual Physics,* p. 160

Topic: _____

Main idea: _____

7. There are two kinds of government expenditures: direct purchases of goods and services and transfer payments. *Direct purchases* of newly produced goods and services include such items as missiles, highway construction, police and fire stations, consulting services, and the like. In other words, the government purchases real goods and services. *Transfer payments* are the transfers of income from some citizens (via taxation) to other citizens; these are sometimes called *income security transfers* or payments. Examples of transfer payments are Social Security contributions and payments, Aid to Families with Dependent Children, food stamp programs, and other welfare payments. These transfers do not represent direct purchase by the government of new goods and services, but they influence purchases of goods and services in the private sector. They are a growing part of government's role in the mixed economy.

—Ekelund and Tollison, *Economics,* p. 58

Topic: _____

Main idea: _____

8. Ordinary comparison shows similarities between two things *of the same class* (two computer keyboards, two technicians, two methods of cleaning dioxin-contaminated sites). Analogy, on the other hand, shows some essential similarity between two things of *different classes* (report writing and computer programming, computer memory and post office boxes.) Analogies are good for emphasizing a point (e.g., Rain in our state is now as acidic as vinegar). Analogies are especially useful in translating something abstract, complex, or unfamiliar to laypersons—as long as the easier subject is broadly familiar to readers. For instance, an analogy between trite language and TV dinners (to make the point that both are effortless but unimpressive) would be lost on anyone who has never tasted a TV dinner. Analogy, therefore, calls for particularly careful analysis of audience.

—Dumont and Lannon, *Business Communications,* p. 83

Topic: _____

Main idea: _____

9. One hallmark of the postindustrial society is a revolution in communications. Information is processed and transmitted almost instantaneously, with a resultant explosion in both the amount of knowledge

available and the speed with which it is communicated. Information doubles every five and one-half years. . . . Simultaneously, cultural change is more rapid today than ever before, and these two situations have made young people frequently better informed than their elders. . . . In times of slower cultural change, the older generation held the wisdom of the society, which they passed down to the younger generation as they saw fit. This is not so in a time of rapid change; young people are often exposed to more, sooner, than are their parents, and we are witnessing in postindustrial society the phenomenon of youth influencing societal standards. Mead . . . points to attitudes toward racism, sexuality, drug use, and popular music and art as areas in which this phenomenon is most obvious. And any parent who has tried to help an elementary school child with "computer literacy" homework is acutely aware that the child is gaining knowledge of which the parent never dreamed. In the last decades of the twentieth century, it may not be unlikely for a twenty-year-old to seem woefully old-fashioned to a fifteen-year-old!

–Fuhrmann, *Adolescence, Adolescents,* pp. 34–35

Topic: _____

Main idea: _____

10. Content theories of individual motivation focus on the question of what it is that energizes, arouses, or starts behavior. The answers to this question have been provided by various motivational theorists in their discussions of the needs or motives that drive people and the incentives that cause them to behave in a particular manner. A need or motive is considered an internal quality of the individual. Hunger (the need for food) and a steady job (the need for security) are seen as motives that arouse people and may cause them to choose a specific behavioral act or pattern of acts. Incentives, on the other hand, are external factors associated with the goal or end result the person hopes to achieve through his or her actions. The income earned from a steady day of work (motivation by a need for security) is valued by the person. It is this value or attractiveness that is the incentive.

–Szilagyi and Wallace, *Organizational Behavior and Performance,* p. 94

Topic: _____

Main idea: _____

UNSTATED MAIN IDEAS

Occasionally, a writer does not directly state the main idea of a given paragraph in a topic sentence. Instead, he or she leaves it up to the reader to infer, or reason out, what the main idea of the paragrpah is. This type of paragraph contains only details or specifics that relate to a given topic and substantiate an unstated main idea. To read this type of paragraph, start as you would for paragraphs with stated main ideas. Ask yourself the question for finding the topic: What is the one thing the author is discussing throughout the paragraph? They try to think of a sentence about the topic that all the details included in the paragraph would support.

Read the paragraph in the following example. First, identify the topic. Then study the details and think of a general statement that all the details in the paragraph would support or prove.

Suppose a group of plumbers in a community decide to set standard prices for repair services and agree to quote the same price for the same job. Is this ethical? Suppose a group of automobile dealers agree to abide strictly by the used car blue book prices on trade-ins. It this ethical? Two meat supply houses serving a large university submit identical bids each month for the meat contract. Is this ethical?

This paragraph describes three specific instances in which there was agreement to fix prices. Clearly, the main idea of the author is whether price collusion is ethical, but that main idea is not directly stated in a sentence anywhere within the passage.

EXERCISE 6 ——————————————

Directions: *In each of these paragraphs, the main idea is not directly stated. Read the paragraph, identify the topic, and write it in the space provided. Then write a sentence that expresses the main idea of the passage.*

1. The first Congress consisted of 26 senators and 65 represntatives. With each new state added to the union, the Senate has grown by two, so that it now has 100 members. As the nation's population grew, the size of the House of Representatives grew also. In 1922 the Congress passed a law setting the maximum size of the House at 435 members, where it remains today. . . . In the first House each member represented around 50,000 citizens. The average representative now serves some 550,000 constituents.

    –Wasserman, *The Basics of American Politics*, p. 87

    Topic: ———————————————————————————

    Main idea: ——————————————————————————

    ——————————————————————————————

2. *Job analysis* involves the systematic collection of all information about a job to determine its requirements. This information should be obtained from a number of sources, such as the person performing the task, the immediate supervisor, observation by work-study specialists, and labor union representatives, in unionized companies. From the job analysis, a job description is prepared. The *job description* identifies the authority of the task, its location in the company, and the activities and major responsibilities of the job. Whereas the job description describes the task, the *job specification* focuses on people. It outlines the personal qualifications essential for completing the task, such as education, experience, mental and visual abilities; the supervisory responsibility for the position; the physical requirements of the task; accountability; the complexity of duties; working conditions; and work relations expected with others. This information is critical for human

resource managers as they assist line managers in completing the staffing process.

–Pickle and Abrahamson, *Introduction to Business*, p. 152

Topic: _____

Main idea: _____

_____

3. In probability, each repetition of an experiment is called a *trial*. The possible results of each trial are *outcomes*. An example of a probability experiment is the tossing of a coin. Each trial of the experiment (each toss) has two possible outcomes, heads and tails, abbreviated h and t, respectively. If the two outcomes, h and t, are equally likely to occur, then the coin is not "loaded" to favor one side over the other. Such a coin is called *fair*. For a coin that is not loaded, this "equally likely" assumption is made for each trial.

–Miller and Heeren, *Mathematical Ideas*, p. 483

Topic: _____

Main idea: _____

_____

4. In 1914, for example, more than 70 percent of Russia's people still worked in agriculture. They had to compete against the efficient foreign farmers, who drove prices down. The tsarist minister of finance, who oversaw a program of grain export to attract foreign loans, stated that "we may go hungry, but we will export." Export Russia did, but the famine of 1891 devastated the peasants in the European provinces of the country. Other farming classes also endured difficult times during the century, especially the Irish peasants, who in the 1840s suffered under the weight of the potato famine. The peasants of southern and eastern Europe had to struggle to maintain a tenuous existence.

–Wallbank et al., *Civilization Past and Present*, p. 556

Topic: _____

Main idea: _____

_____

5. Constructing a speech in a fashion that reveals the major conflicts between persons or groups is one way of gaining and holding attention. Another way of generating a sense of conflict is to use a narrative aproach in retelling the story of a recent controversy. This is especially true if the audience senses they are getting inside information—incidents and events not generally known. In generating a sense of conflict, be certain that your representation of events is as accurate as possible. If you are detailing the sides of a controversy to audience members who belong to one or the other side, you can expect them to

be critical of your depiction of their respective positions. Also be wary of using a "straw man" approach—setting up a sham conflict and then resolving it. The effectiveness of your message depends on the audience's perception of the sincerity and accuracy of your description.

–Ehninger et al., *Principles and Types of Speech Communications*, p. 46

Topic: _____

Main idea: _____

_____

6. As we noted earlier, when carbohydrates are taken into the body in excess of the body's energy requirements, they are stored temporarily as glycogen or, more permanently, as fats. Conversely, when the energy requirements of the body are not met by its immediate intake of food, glycogen and, subsequently, fat are broken down to fill these requirements. Whether or not the body uses up its own storage molecules has nothing to do with the molecular form in which the energy comes into the body. It is simply a matter of whether these molecules, as they are broken down, release sufficient numbers of calories.

–Curtis, *Biology*, p. 61.

Topic: _____

Main idea: _____

_____

7. A sudden explosion at 200 decibels can cause massive damage in a fraction of a second; however, routine exposure to sounds less than 100 decibels can also cause significant hearing loss. Hearing loss from loud sounds is called *stimulation deafness*. Most people report such hearing loss for up to several hours after listening to a rock concert in an enclosed area. Not surprisingly, then, more permanent hearing loss is an occupational hazard for rock musicians, because they are exposed to such intense sound levels so frequently. It also occurs in many other occupations where people are exposed to loud noises for extended periods.

–Zimbardo, *Psychology and Life*, p. 169

Topic: _____

Main idea: _____

_____

8. No one has ever "seen" motivation, just as no one has ever "seen" learning. All we see are changes in behavior. To explain these observed changes, we make *inferences* about underlying psychological and physiological variables—"educated hunches" that are formalized in the concept of motivation. Among the words most commonly associated with motivation are *goals*, *needs*, *wants*, *intentions*, and *purposes*;

all of which relate to factors that cause us to act. Two motivational terms that are frequently used by researchers in this area are *drive* and *motive*. Psychologists usually use the label *drive* to mean motivation for action that is assumed to be primarily biologically instigated, as in hunger. They often use *motive* to refer to psychologically and socially instigated motivation, which is generally assumed to be, at least in part, learned. A motive can be either conscious or nonconscious (in the ways we distinguished between them in chapter 7).

–Zimbardo, *Psychology and Life*, p. 376

Topic: _____

Main idea: _____

_____

9. For most of earth's history, the land was bare. A billion years ago, seaweeds clung to the shores at low tide and perhaps some gray-green lichens patched a few inland rocks. But, had anyone been there to observe it, the earth's surface would generally have appeared as barren and forbidding as the bleak Martian landscape. According to the fossil record, plants first began to invade the land a mere half billion years ago. Not until then did the earth's surface truly come to life. As a film of green spread from the edges of the waters, other forms of life—the heterotrophs—were able to follow. The shapes of these new forms and the ways in which they lived were determined by the plant life that preceded them. Plants supplied not only their food—their chemical energy—but also their nesting, hiding, stalking, and breeding places.

–Curtis, *Biology*, p. 573

Topic: _____

Main idea: _____

_____

10. A contract is not enforceable by law if it provides for actions that are not acceptable by law. Any contract that calls for criminal or civil wrongs is not a valid contract. For example, a contract in which one person agrees to beat up another person in exchange for money is not a valid and enforceable contract because it calls for a criminal act. In addition, a contract between two businesses that provides for price fixing is not a valid enforceable contract because it requires action that is a civil wrong under law.

–Pickle and Abrahamson, *Introduction to Business*, p. 417

Topic: _____

Main idea: _____

_____

EXERCISE 7 ——————————————

Directions: *Turn to the sample textbook chapter included in Appendix B of this text. In the section "Homeotherms" on pages 464–467, read each paragraph and identify the topic and main idea. Then place brackets around the topic and underline the sentence that expresses the main idea.*

EXERCISE 8 ——————————————

Directions: *Select a three-page section from a textbook that you have been assigned to read. After reading each paragraph, place brackets around the topic and then underline the sentence stating the main idea. If any of the paragraphs have an unstated main idea, write a sentence in the margin that summarizes the main idea. Continue reading and marking until you have completed the three pages.*

SUMMARY

A paragraph is a group of related sentences about a single topic. A paragraph has three essential elements:

1. Topic: the one thing the entire paragraph is about
2. Main idea: a direct statement or an implied idea about the topic
3. Details: the proof, reasons, or examples that explain or support the paragraph's main idea

A paragraph, then, provides explanation, support, or proof for a main idea (expressed or unexpressed) about a particular topic. A topic sentence expressing the main idea of the paragraph may be located anywhere within the paragraph, but the most common positions for this sentence are first, last, in the middle, or both first and last.

While most paragraphs contain a topic sentence that directly states the main idea of the paragraph, occasionally an author will write a paragraph in which the main idea is not stated in any single sentence. Instead, it is left up to you, the reader, to infer, or reason out, the main idea. To find the main idea when it is unstated, ask yourself the following question: What is the one thing (topic) this paragraph is about, and what is the author saying about this thing (main idea)?

9

Following Thought Patterns in Textbooks

Use this chapter to:
1. *Understand the structure of ideas in textbooks.*
2. *Learn to recognize patterns of thought in textbooks.*

In college you will read a variety of materials; however, *most* of what you read will be textbooks, which are unique, highly organized information sources. If you become familiar with their organization and structure and learn to follow the writers' thought patterns, you will find that you can read them more easily. The skills you learn in reading textbooks can be applied to other types of reading, including articles and essays.

Reading a chapter can be compared to watching a football game. You watch the overall progression of the game from start to finish, but you also watch individual plays and notice how each is executed. Furthermore, you observe how several plays work together as part of a game strategy or pattern. Similarly, when reading a chapter, you are concerned with the progression of ideas. But you are also concerned with each separate idea and how it is developed and explained. Finally, you are concerned with how the ideas and details work together to form a pattern.

This chapter focuses on three important features of textbook chapters: (1) their overall structure or progression of ideas, (2) types of details used to explain each idea, and (3) organizational patterns (how ideas fit together).

RECOGNIZING THE STRUCTURE OF IDEAS

A texbook is divided into parts, each successively smaller and more limited in scope than the other one before it. As a general rule, the whole text is divided into chapters; each chapter may be divided into sections; each section is subdivided by headings into subsections; and each subsection is divided into paragraphs. Each of these parts has a similar structure. Just as each paragraph has a main idea and supporting information, each subsection, section, or chapter has its own key idea and supporting information.

Locate the Controlling Idea and Supporting Information

The controlling idea in a textbook section is the broad, general idea the writer is discussing throughout the section. It is the central, most important thought that is explained, discussed, or supported throughout the section. It is similar to the main idea of the paragraph, but is a more general, more comprehensive idea that takes numerous paragraphs to explain.

The controlling idea, then, is developed or explained throughout the section. Subheadings are often used to divide a section into smaller units. Each subsection, or group of paragraphs, explains one idea or major concept, the central thought. Each paragraph within a subsection provides one main idea that supports or explains the central thought. As you read each paragraph, you should understand its function and connection to the other paragraphs in the section. The end of each section is an ideal checkpoint for monitoring your comprehension. Although the number of subheadings and paragraphs will vary, the structure of textbook sections is usually consistent (see Figure 9-1).

Read the section in Figure 9-2, "Sources of Stress," from a chapter in the book *Psychology* by Roediger et al. titled "Emotion and Stress." (*Note:* ellipses [. . .] indicate text omitted from the original.)

Notice that paragraph 1 of the section introduces the subject: stress. The paragraph then defines stress, states that it has a variety of causes, and gives some examples of stressful situations. The last sentence of the first paragraph states the controlling idea of the section: The most common sources of stress will be discussed. The subheadings divide the remaining text, and each identifies one source of stress. Each group of paragraphs under a sub-

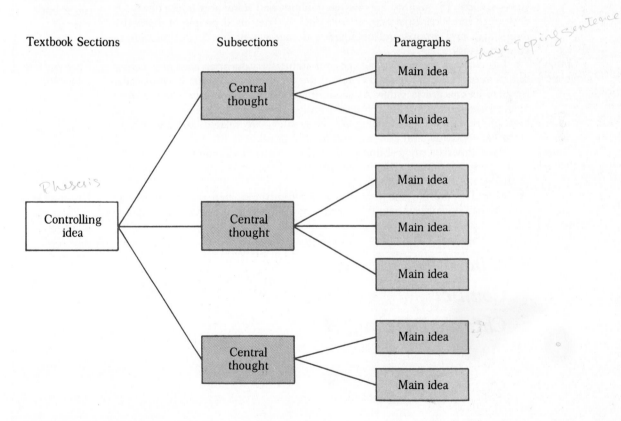

FIGURE 9-1   Organization of a Textbook Section

SOURCES OF STRESS

Introduction
of subject

1 When emotions are prolonged or excessive, the associated physiological changes can become detrimental to health. *Stress* is a general term that refers to physiological and psychological reactions to certain events in the environment. Generally, stress is created by a perceived threat to an individual's physical or psychological well-being, and the feeling that he or she is unable to deal with it. Prolonged or excessive emotion is only one source of stress. The list of things that bring on stress varies widely from individual to individual. Some events, such as the death of a loved one, cause stress for almost everyone; otherwise, the context of the event and the individual's appraisal of the event determine whether or not stress occurs. Retirement, for instance, threatens self-esteem and induces great stress in some people; it presents a welcome opportunity to do different things for others. Keeping the importance of the individual's perceptions in mind, we shall consider the most common sources of stress.

Examples

Definition

Controlling
idea of
section

Life Changes

Central
thought of
section

2 One general source of stress is life change. Any change in life that requires adaptation may cause some stress whether or not the change is beneficial. The greater the degree of change and necessary adaptation required, the greater the stress will be. To quantify life change, Holmes and Rahe and their colleagues developed the *Social Readjustment Scale (SRRS)*. They used people of many different ages and groups and obtained wide agreement on the seriousness of various events. . . .

Description of
scale that
measures
change

Topic
sentence

3 Life changes take place at all ages but, naturally, how often each kind occurs differs at each age. Illness and death in the family, for example, become more frequent as one grows older. At some time most people will experience most of the stress-producing life changes. Studies using this scale have found that high life-change scores—totaling 300 or greater—are related to frequency of ailments, accidents, and athletic injuries.

Frequency of
changes

Topic
sentence

4 Some theorists suggest that modern society produces more stress than did earlier periods of human life, in part because of the large number and rapidity of changes people now endure. . . .

Comparison
with previous
times

Topic
sentence

5 Irwin G. Sarason and his colleagues recently modified the Holmes-Rahe scale by having subjects rate the severity of the perceived positive or negative impact of each relevant event. . . .

Description of
revision of
scale to
measure
changes

Minor Annoyances
....
Conflict
....
Chronic Discomfort
....

FIGURE 9-2   Excerpt from Emotion and Stress

heading explains one source of stress (its central thought). Each paragraph beneath a subheading contributes one key piece of information (its main idea) that explains or supports the central thought. Then, within each paragraph, the main idea is supported with facts and details.

In the first subsection on life changes, the first sentence in paragraph 2 states the central thought of that section. Within that paragraph, life changes are discussed and a measurement scale is described. Each subsequent paragraph discusses one aspect of life change. Paragraph 3 is about how often changes occur; paragraph 4 compares the frequency of life changes in modern society with previous times; and paragraph 5 describes a measurement scale that rates life changes as positive or negative.

This example shows that the subheadings divided the section into four parts, or subsections. The section began with a general discussion of the subject and was divided into four smaller topics. This progression of ideas from large to small, general to particular, is typical of most textbooks. When you are familiar with and can follow this progression, your textbooks will seem more logical and systematic and easier to read.

EXERCISE 1 ————————————

Directions: *Turn to the beginning of Chapter 6 on page 97 of this text and complete the following instructions.*

1. The controlling idea of the chapter is expressed in the first three introductory paragraphs. Underline it.
2. The dark-print headings divide the chapter into four parts, each of which is further divided by subheadings. How many main points are included under each?

EXERCISE 2 ————————————

Directions: *Read the subsection "Living with the Problem" beginning on page 436 of the psychology sample textbook chapter reprinted in Appendix A. Complete the following instructions.*

1. The controlling idea is presented in the first paragraph. Underline that idea.
2. The remaining paragraphs develop and explain this idea. For each paragraph, underline the main idea. Review your underlining. Notice how each paragraph provides further information about the delivery of health care.

EXERCISE 3 ————————————

Directions: *Choose a three- to four-page section from one of your textbooks that you have already read, then answer the following questions.*

1. What is the overall topic or subject discussed in this section?

_____

2. What is the controlling idea?

_____

_____

3. Is the section divided by subheadings? If so, underline the central thought in each subsection.

TYPES OF SUPPORTING INFORMATION

Authors use various types of supporting information to explain a controlling idea of a textbook section. Recognizing these types of supporting information is the key to understanding *how* the author develops and connects his or her ideas.

Examples

Usually a writer gives an example to make an idea practical and understandable. An example shows how a principle, concept, problem, or process works or can be applied in a real situation. In the following paragraph, notice how the writer explains how situations influence purchase behavior by giving the example of a tire blow out.

> The situations consumers find themselves in can also have direct influence on their purchase behavior. Consider, for example, the consumer behavior of a person who has a tire blow out one block away from a service station. The amount of information sought and the number of alternatives considered would vary substantially depending upon the status of the spare tire. Without a good spare, the consumer might purchase a new tire from the nearby gas station, particularly if it were the only seller of tires in the area. If, on the other hand, the spare was in good shape, the consumer might take considerable time in buying another tire, looking at which store had tires on sale and perhaps calling or visiting several stores to identify and evaluate the alternative.
>
> –Kinnear and Bernhardt, *Principles of Marketing*, p. 148

As you read examples, be sure to look for the connection between the example and the concept it illustrates. Remember, examples are important only for the ideas they illustrate.

Description

An author uses description to help you visualize the appearance, organization, or composition of an object, a place, or a process. Descriptions are usually detailed and are intended to help you create a mental picture of what is being described. Read the following description of the stylistic features of various artists' work.

To turn now to our central topic, style in art, we can all instantly tell the difference between a picture by Van Gogh and one by Norman Rockwell or Walt Disney, even though the subject matter of all three pictures is the same, for instance, a seated woman. How can we tell? By the style, that is, by line, color, medium, and so forth—all of the things we talked about earlier in this chapter. Walt Disney's figures tend to be built up out of circles (think of Mickey Mouse), and the color shows no modeling or traces of brush strokes; Norman Rockwell's methods of depicting figures are different, and Van Gogh's are different in yet other ways. Similarly, a Chinese landscape, painted with ink on silk or on paper, simply cannot look like a Van Gogh landscape done with oil paint on canvas, partly because the materials prohibit such identity and partly because the Chinese painter's vision of landscape (usually lofty mountains) is not Van Gogh's vision. In short, we recognize certain *distinguishing characteristics* that mark an artist, or a period, or a culture, and these constitute the style.

–Barnet, *A Short Guide to Writing About Art,* p. 40

You should be able to visualize, for example, what Walt Disney's figures look like or features of a Chinese landscape. Each detail contributes a bit of information which, when added to other bits, reveals its composition.

Facts and Statistics

Another way to support an idea is to include facts or statistics that provide information about the main or controlling idea. Read the following passage, and notice how facts and statistics are used to support the idea that age is a limiting factor in the war against poverty.

Another limitation of the success of the War on Poverty involves age rather than residence or region. Most of the people who officially moved out of poverty, especially in the 1970s, were older. And even their relative gains began to be reversed in the early 1980s.

Between 1970 and 1978, the number of poor people over 65 dropped by almost a million and a half. Most of this decline resulted from improved Social Security benefits. But this didn't mean that the low-income aged achieved genuine comfort and security. Many still lived uncomfortably close to the poverty line, and the poverty rate for the elderly remains higher than that of most other groups. (And the Social Security system itself, of course, has become ever more precarious in the face of economic stagnation and political criticism.)

–Currie and Skolnick, *America's Problems,* p. 115

When reading factual support or explanations, remember these questions: *What? When? Where? How?* and *Why?* They will lead you to the important facts and statistics contained in the passage.

Citation of Research Evidence

In many fields of study, authors support their ideas by citing research that has been done on the topic. Authors report the results of surveys, experiments, and research studies to substantiate theories or principles or to lend support to a particular viewpoint. The following excerpt from a social problems textbook reports the results of research conducted to describe the extent of family violence.

> One of the most extensive recent studies of family violence, conducted by the sociologists Murray Straus, Richard Gelles, and Suzanne Steinmetz, concluded that "violence between family members is probably as common as love." . . . On the basis of a sample survey of more than 2,000 families, the researchers estimated that in the course of a year, about one-sixth of married people have engaged in at least one act of violence against their spouse, ranging from pushing, shoving, or "throwing something" to "beating up spouse" and "using a knife or gun." And that over the course of their marriages, more than one-fourth of the spouses would be involved in an act of violence. The researchers argued that those figures probably *underestimated* the amount of serious violence between husbands and wives, partly because many failed to report or admit family violence and partly because the study didn't include divorced couples, who might be expected to have experienced even higher levels of violence while married. The informal estimate was that *50 to 60 percent of couples* had engaged in violence at some point over the course of their marriages.
>
> –Currie and Skolnick, *America's Problems*, pp. 266–267

When reading research reports, keep the following questions in mind. They will help you see the relationship between the research results and the author's controlling idea.

1. Why was the research done?
2. What did it show?
3. Why did the author include it?

EXERCISE 4 _____

Directions: *Read the following passages and identify the type of supporting information or detail that is used in each.*

1. Colors in your photographs will vary depending on the time of day that you made them. Photographing very early or late in the day can produce strikingly beautiful pictures simply because the light is not its usually "white" color.

    In the earliest hours of the day, before sunrise, the world is essentially black and white. The light has a cool, shadowless quality. Colors are muted. They grow in intensity slowly, gradually differentiating themselves. But right up to the moment of sunrise, they remain pearly and flat.

    As soon as the sun rises, the light warms up. Because of the great amount of atmosphere that the low-lying sun must penetrate, the light that gets through is much warmer in color than it will be later in the day—that is, more on the red or orange side because the colder blue hues are filtered out by the air. Shadows, by contrast, may look blue because they lack gold sunlight and also because they reflect blue from the sky.

The higher the sun climbs in the sky, the greater the contrast between colors. At noon, particularly in the summer, this contrast is at its peak. Film for use in daylight is balanced for midday sunlight, so colors appear accurately rendered. Each color stands out in its own true hue. Shadows at noon are more likely to be neutral black.

–Upton, *Photography,* p. 232

Type of detail: _____

2. In the early 1960s, for example, Thorsten Sellin and Marvin Wolfgang (1964) asked samples of judges, police, and university students to rate the seriousness of 141 offenses. They found much agreement. A later survey of adults in Baltimore (Rossi et al., 1974) again found much consensus on a similar list of illegal acts. But, this study did find a prominent difference among white and black respondents: blacks rated violence among family and friends lower in seriousness than did whites. Thus, although there may be general agreement on crime seriousness, subgroups of the population may not share the general attitude toward particular crimes.

The most recent, and by far the most extensive, study confirms these earlier findings (Wolfgang et al., 1985). A total of 204 crimes were rated by a national sample of sixty thousand respondents (though no one person rated more than 25 offenses). . . . Overall, there was broad consensus. Violent crimes were rated more serious than were property offenses, and drug dealing was taken seriously, as was virtually any offense that had the potential for harming or killing more than one person. The study showed also that people evaluate crimes according to their consequences for the victims, and not surprisingly, respondents who had been victims of crime tended to assign higher seriousness scores than did others. Whites tended generally to assign higher scores than did minority groups.

–Barlow, *Introduction to Criminology,* p. 9

Type of detail: _____

3. The Earth's crust and the uppermost part of the mantle are known as the *lithosphere.* This is a fairly rigid zone that extends about 100 km below the Earth's surface. The crust extends some 60 km or so under continents, but only about 10 km below the ocean floor. The continental crust has a lower density than the oceanic crust. It is primarily a light granitic rock rich in the silicates of aluminum, iron, and magnesium. In a simplified view, the continental crust can be thought of as layered: On top of a layer of igneous rock (molten rock that has hardened, such as granite) lies a thin layer of sedimentary rocks (rocks formed by sediment and fragments that water deposited, such as limestone and sandstone); there is also a soil layer deposited during past ages in the parts of continents that have had no recent volcanic activity or mountain building.

Sandwiched between the lithosphere and the lower mantle is the partially molten material known as the *asthenosphere*, about 150 km thick. It consists primarily of iron and magnesium silicates that readily deform and flow under pressure.

–Berman and Evans, *Exploring the Cosmos*, p. 145

Type of detail: _____

4. Human beings, like all other animals, learn quickly to react to stimuli in their environments; we learn to sort out stimuli (experiences) into various categories of things or events in order to predict consequences. But, unlike most other animals, humans can go beyond sorting, even beyond understanding consequences—they can seek *coherence* in their environments. (1) We can *generalize* and *anticipate*. A baby who burns its hand on a hot stove, a match, and a metal sheet sitting in the sun quickly learns that "hot objects produce pain"; the baby can re-member past instances of pain and anticipate future pain when it no-tices even previously unexperienced "hot objects" in its surroundings. (2) We search for *coherent structures* in our environments. Young children soon learn to seek relationships between and among items in their environment. They learn early that one set of furniture comprises a bedroom; another set, a kitchen; and another set, a playroom; they soon learn that living and dead objects are treated differently. By early elementary school, children can determine what is "foreground" or "figure" in a picture, and what is "background" or supporting detail. An important part of environmental control is understanding relation-ships between and among the environmental elements. (3) Structures become so important to us psychologically that we learn to *fill in or complete* missing elements. If someone says to you, "One, two, three, four," you almost automatically continue, "five, six, seven, eight." Car-toonists can draw a few features of a famous person, and most readers will be able to identify the person in question. This is because we all have what Gestalt psychologists term the "drive to complete," the need to complete missing elements and thus make sense out of some stim-ulus.

–Ehninger, *Principles and Types of Speech Communication*, pp. 151–152

Type of detail: _____

5. As we'll see, infant death rates in this country are crucially affected by race. But it is important to realize that America's problem of infant mortality goes beyond race as well—even the *white* rate of infant death in the United States is higher than the rates in much of Western Europe and Japan.

   Our high rates of infant mortality are a major reason why . . . Americans' life expectancy, especially for men, is somewhat lower than that of people in many other industrial societies. Life expectancy at birth is a tricky statistic; it represents an average of the chances of dying at any point in the life cycle. Thus, the fact that an American male at birth, at the end of the 1970s, could expect to live almost four years less than a Japanese and three years less than a Swede largely reflects the much higher chance that the American male might die during his first year. But these differences also persist through childhood and adolescence into young adulthood. In the mid-1970s, an American girl aged 1 to 4 had nearly twice the chance of dying as a Swedish girl those ages; a young American woman aged 15 to 24 had almost twice the chance of death faced by a young British woman. . . .

–Currie and Skolnick, *America's Problems*, pp. 266–267

Type of detail: _____

6. Sociologist Rosabeth Moss Kanter spent seven months studying a typical suburban nursery school located in the Midwest. According to Kanter, the teachers in this school believed that children who followed orders and exerted self-control were mentally healthy children. As a result, the teachers constantly urged the children to adapt to the planned classroom routine, and they set up a round of activities each day conducive to promoting, in Kanter's terms, the *organization child*—the child who is most comfortable when those in authority provide supervision, guidance, and roles to be fulfilled. In requiring children to adapt to such experiences, Kanter concludes, the schools both reflect and support the trends toward bureaucratization of life in American society.

   Similar conclusions have also been reached by Harry L. Gracey, a sociologist who studied classrooms in an eastern elementary school. One part of Gracey's research focused on kindergarten, which he came to call *academic boot camp*. Kindergarten works to teach the student role to children not previously conditioned to organized schooling. The content of the student role is "the repertoire of behavior and attitudes regarded by educators as appropriate to children in school." Such behaviors include willingness to conform to teacher demands and to perform the "work" at hand without resistance. Educators believe that children who have successfully learned the student role in kindergarten will function smoothly in the later grades.

–Neubeck, *Social Problems*, pp. 93–94

Type of detail: _____

7. There are really only two ways to gather information from human subjects about what they are currently doing, thinking, or feeling. One way is to watch what they do, the technique of observation; the other is to ask them, the technique of surveys. The many approaches included in each type of technique have several advantages and disadvantages. Firms frequently use both techniques to minimize disadvantages.

   There is a great variety of observational studies. A researcher stands near the entrance to a theater and observes the approximate age and sex of patrons entering the theater during certain times of the day and days of the week. Researchers comb through the garbage cans of Arizona residents (with permission) to identify what is being thrown away and, by inference from the packages, what is being bought. Toy manufacturers watch from behind one-way mirrors to see how children react to and play with prototypes of toys they are thinking of introducing. Observers in public places—airports, doctors' offices— watch to see how subjects read newspapers and magazines (front to back, right-hand or left-hand page). Researchers call on households and take a "pantry audit" to learn the quantity and brands of certain items on the kitchen or bathroom shelves.

–Russ and Kirkpatrick, *Marketing,* p. 92

Type of detail: _____

8. How many languages are spoken in the world today? Estimates range from three thousand to five thousand, but no one is really certain. . . . As many as three thousand different languages used by South American Indians alone have been named in the literature, but this high number is deceptive. Problems in identifying separate languages are many. In the South American studies, in many cases a single language has been identified by more than one name. Furthermore, many of the language studies that are available are of poor quality, making it difficult to tell whether the language described by one linguist is the same as that described by another. Some languages named are now extinct; other categories overlap or are inappropriate. Once such categories are eliminated, there appear to be only three hundred to four hundred Indian languages currently spoken in South America. Yet as Sorenson (1973: 312) has concluded, "the linguistic map of South America remains impressionistic at best," and similar problems exist elsewhere.

–Howard, *Contemporary Cultural Anthropology,* p. 80

Type of detail: _____

9. Otherwise known as the Landrum-Griffin Act, the Labor-Management Reporting and Disclosure Act of 1959 is aimed primarily at establishing guidelines for eliminating improper activities by either labor or management. One provision of the Act provides protection for the rights of union members. All union members may nominate candidates for union leadership, vote in union elections, attend union meetings, and vote on union matters. The Act also provides for filing reports that describe the organization, financial dealings, and business practices of the union and its officers and certain employees. Guidelines were established for handling union funds. The filing of the anticommunist affidavit required under the Taft-Hartley Act was repealed.

While the closed shop was declared illegal under the Taft-Hartley Act, the Landrum-Griffin Act exempted the construction industry by substituting a seven-day probationary period instead of the usual thirty-day period. As a practical matter, employers prefer to hire union members rather than nonunion members who would have to be replaced in seven days.

–Pickle and Abrahamson, *Introduction to Business,* p. 185

Type of detail: _____

10. The concept of *mafia* was also important in the Italian heritage. It refers not to the organization but, rather, to "a state of mind, a sense of pride, a philosophy of life, and a style of behavior which Sicilians recognize immediately." To describe someone as a *mafioso* does not necessarily mean that he is a member of the Mafia: it may simply mean that he is a man who is respected and held in awe. He is a man who seeks protection not through the law but by his own devices; he is a man who commands fear; he is a man who has dignity and bearing; he is a

man who gets things done; he is a man to whom people come when in need; he is a man with "friends."

—Barlow, *Introduction to Criminology*, p. 297

Type of detail: _____

RECOGNIZING ORGANIZATIONAL PATTERNS

You have seen that textbook sections are structured around a controlling idea and supporting information and details. The next step in reading these materials effectively is to become familiar with how information is organized.

Recognition of organizational patterns is a useful learning device. It is based on the principle of meaningfulness (see Chapter 3), which states that meaningful things are easier to learn and remember than those that are not. When you fit details into a pattern, you connect them so that each one helps you recall the rest. By identifying how the key details in a paragraph or passage form a pattern, you are making them more meaningful to you and, as a result, making them easier to remember.

Patterns are forms of schemata, or sets of familiar information. Once you recognize that a paragraph or passage follows a particular pattern, its organization becomes familiar and predictable.

Six organizational patterns are commonly used in textbook writing; definition, time sequence, comparison-contrast, cause-effect, problem-solution, and enumeration. A summary chart of these patterns is shown in Figure 9.3 at the end of the chapter.

To help you visualize each pattern, a diagram will be presented for each. Later, in Chapter 12, you will see that these diagrams, also called maps, are useful means of organizing and retaining information.

These patterns may also appear together in various combinations, producing a mixed pattern. For each of these patterns, particular words and phrases are used to connect details and lead from one idea to another. These words are called *directional words* because they indicate the direction or pattern of thought. A chart (Figure 9.4) summarizing types of directional words appears at the end of this chapter.

Definition

One of the most obvious patterns is definition, which you will find in textbooks of most academic subjects. Each academic discipline has its own language or specialized terminology (see Chapter 19). One of the primary tasks of authors of introductory course textbooks, then, is to introduce their readers to this new language. Therefore, you will find many textbook sections in which new terms are defined.

Suppose you were asked to define the word *comedian* for someone unfamiliar with the term. First, you would probably say that a comedian is a person who entertains. Then you might distinguish a comedian from other types of entertainers by saying that a comedian is an entertainer who tells jokes and makes others laugh. Finally, you might mention as examples the names of several well-known comedians who have appeared on television. Although you may have presented it informally, your definition would have followed the standard, classic pattern. The first part of your definition tells what general class or group the term belongs to (entertainers). The second part tells what distinguishes the term from other items in the same class or category. The third part includes further explanation, characteristics, examples, or applications.

This pattern can be visualized as follows:

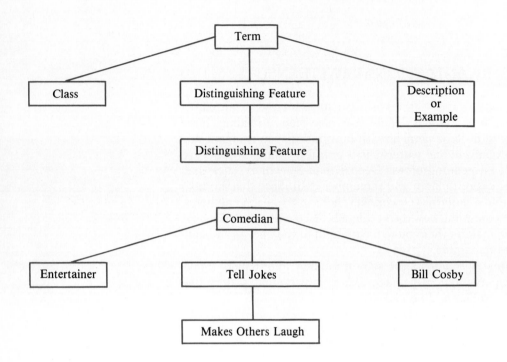

Read the following definition of *prejudice* taken from a sociology textbook.

> *Prejudice* is a rigid, emotional attitude often based on inadequate data, characterized by stereotyped thinking and involving a tendency to respond negatively toward certain identifiable groups or members of these groups. Prejudice does not involve any overt action or behavior, although it may serve as a stimulus to behavior. As it is an attitude, it is a hidden or covert characteristic, which people may or may not reveal to others.
>
> Prejudice is emotional, it involves feelings. These feelings are negative and are often revealed in the words used to describe a group. After the Japanese attacked Pearl Harbor, strong prejudice against them existed in this country. The Japanese were described as cunning, crafty, wily, slippery, shifty, treacherous, evasive, and underhanded, all obviously undesirable traits. Such negative connotations are also attached to the word *black*. For example, blacken, blackguard, Black Hand, blackleg, black magic, blackmail, and Black Mass. Of course, the word *white* can be used emotionally and negatively, as in white flag, white elephant, white feature, white-livered, and white plague.
>
> –Wright and Weiss, *Social Problems,* p. 165

This definition has three parts: (1) The general class is stated first; (2) the distinguishing characteristics are then described; and (3) further explanation and examples are given. The first sentence states the general class—

emotional attitude. The same sentence also gives distinguishing characteristics. The remainder of the passage further explains and gives examples of prejudice. When reading definitions, be sure to look for each of these parts. Passages that define often use directional words and phrases such as:

refers to	can be defined as
means	consists of
is	

EXERCISE 5

Directions: *Define each of the following terms by identifying the class to which it belongs and describing its distinguishing characteristics.*

1. adolescence

2. automatic teller

3. cable television

4. computer

5. advertising

Time Sequence

One of the clearest ways to describe events, processes, procedures, and development of theories is to present them in the order in which they occurred. The event that happened first appears first in the passage; whatever occurred last is described last in the passage.

The time sequence pattern can be visualized as follows:

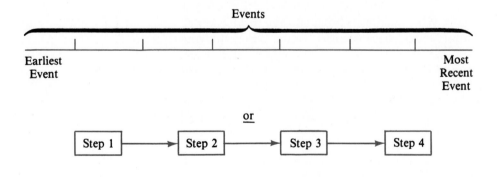

The first drawing is often called a time line; the second a process diagram.

Notice in the following example how the writer proceeds through time, describing the process of preparing a computer program.

In the process of preparing a computer program to solve a particular problem the programmer performs a number of tasks. One thing that must be done is to code the program. As we have seen, this involves writing the instructions in the program. Before coding can begin, however, the programmer must first understand the problem to be solved and then plan the solution procedure.

Understanding the problem involves determining the requirements of the problem and deciding how they can be met. The programmer must know what the program is required to do: what output must be produced and what computations must be performed. The programmer must also determine what resources (including input) are available to meet these requirements.

Once the problem is understood, the programmer can begin to design a program to solve it. The sequence of steps that is necessary to solve the problem must be carefully planned. This program-designing activity does *not* involve coding the program. Before coding can start, the programmer must think through the solution procedure completely because the sequence of steps must be carefully planned. The programmer sometimes writes down the solution procedure in rough notes using English or draws a diagram that represents the solution graphically.

After the solution to the problem has been planned, the program can be coded. The programmer uses his or her knowledge of the computer language, an understanding of the problem to be solved, and the program design determined previously. With this background, the programmer writes the program to solve the problem.

–Nickerson, *Fundamentals of Structured COBOL*, p. 24

This excerpt could be visualized as follows:

Steps in Preparing a Computer Program

Material using this pattern is relatively easy to read because you know what order the writer will follow. When reading sequential, organized material, pay attention to the order of and connection between events. When studying this material, remember that the order is often as important as the events themselves. To test your memory and to prepare information for study, list ideas in their correct order, or draw a process diagram or time line.

The time sequence pattern uses directional words to connect the events described or to lead you from one step to another. The most frequently used words are:

first	before	following
second	after	last
later	then	during
next	finally	when
as soon as	meanwhile	until

Directions: *For each of the following topic sentences, make a list of directional words you expect to be used in the paragraph.*

1. Advertising has appeared in magazines since the late 1700s.
2. Large numbers of European immigrants first began to arrive in the United States in the 1920s.
3. The first step in grasping a novel's theme is reading it closely for literal content, including plot and character development.
4. After leaving Spain, strong winds blew Columbus and his ships into the middle of the Atlantic.
5. The life-cycle of a product is the stages a product goes through from when it is created to when it is no longer produced.

Comparison-Contrast

Many fields of study involve the comparison of one set of ideas, theories, concepts, or events with another. These comparisons usually examine similarities and differences. In anthropology, one kinship category might be compared with another; in literature, one poet might be compared with another; in biology, one theory of evolution might be compared with another. You will find that the comparison-contrast pattern is common in the textbooks used in these fields.

The comparison-contrast pattern can be visualized in several ways. For material that considers both similarities and differences, the following map is effective.

Topics A and B

Similarities	*Differences*
_____	_____
_____	_____
_____	_____

For example:

Professor Miller and Professor Wright

Similarities	*Differences*
both require class attendance	Miller assigns term paper
both give essay exams	Wright demands class participation
both have sense of humor	age

For material that focuses primarily on differences, you might use the following:

	Topic A	Topic B
Feature #1	_____	_____
Feature #2	_____	_____
Feature #3	_____	_____

For example:

Feature	Professor Smith	Professor Jones
teaching style	lecture	discussion
class atmosphere	formal	casual
type of exam	multiple choice	essay

A comparison-contrast pattern can be organized three ways. A writer who is comparing two famous artists, X and Y, could use any of the following procedures:

1. Discuss the characteristics of artist X and artist Y and summarize their similarities and differences.
2. Consider their similarities first, then discuss their differences.
3. Consider both X and Y together for each of several characteristics. For instance, discuss the use of color by X and Y, then discuss the use of space by X and Y, then consider the use of proportion by X and Y.

Read the following paragraph, and try to determine which of the preceding patterns is used.

> In their original work both Darwin and that other great innovator who followed him, Gregor Mendel, used deductive reasoning to great effect. Both these giants of biology had been trained in theology. As a result, they were well acquainted with an intellectual tradition based on deduction. And since induction is difficult to apply in a field where so little can be directly observed, perhaps theology provided some of the essential intellectual tools both men needed to develop a viewpoint so different from prevailing theological thinking.
>
> Darwin and Mendel are linked in another fundamental way. Darwin could not explain how successful traits are passed on to successive generations, exposing this theory of natural selection to growing criticism. When Mendel was rediscovered, geneticists were paying a lot of attention to mutations. They still felt that natural selection of variants had a minor part in evolution. The major factor, they believed, was sudden change introduced by mutation. Not until the 1930s did biologists realize, at last, that Darwin's theory of natural selection and Mendel's laws of genetics were fully compatible. Together the two form the basis of population genetics, a major science of today.
>
> –Laetsch, *Plants: Basic Concepts in Botany*, p. 393

This excerpt can be visualized as follows:

> **Darwin and Mendel**
>
> *Similarities*
>
>   both trained in theology
>
>   both giants of biology
>
>   both developed different viewpoint
>
>   held compatible theories

The passage compares the characteristics of the work of Darwin and Mendel. The first paragraph presents their use of deductive reasoning. The second paragraph describes the compatibility of their theories.

In comparison-contrast passages, the way ideas are organized provides clues to what is important. In a passage that is organized by characteristics, the emphasis is placed on the characteristics. A passage that groups similarities and then differences emphasizes the similarities and differences themselves rather than the characteristics.

Directional words indicate whether the passage focuses on similarities, differences, or both:

Similarities	*Differences*
also	unlike
similarly	on the other hand
like	instead
likewise	despite
too	nevertheless
as well as	however
both	in spite of

EXERCISE 7

Directions: *For each of the following topic sentences, predict the content of the paragraph. Will it focus on similarities, differences, or discuss both? Also, if you predict the passage will discuss* both *similarities and differences, predict the organization of the paragraph that will follow. (Refer to the three types of organization given above.)*

1. Two types of leaders can usually be identified in organizations: informal and formal.

    Content: _____ *Organization:* _____

2. The human brain is divided into two halves, each of which is responsible for separate functions.

    Content: _____ *Organization:* _____

3. Humans and primates, such as gorillas and New World monkeys, share many characteristics, but are clearly set apart by others.

    Content: _____ *Organization:* _____

4. Interpersonal communication is far more complex than intrapersonal communication.

    Content: _____ *Organization:* _____

5. Sociology and psychology both focus on human behavior.

    Content: _____ *Organization:* _____

Cause-Effect

Understanding any academic discipline requires learning *how* and *why* things happen. In psychology it is not sufficient to know that people are often aggressive; you also need to know why and how people exhibit aggression. In physics it is not enough to know the laws of motion; you also must understand why they work and how they apply to everyday experiences.

The cause-effect pattern arranges ideas according to why and how they occur. This pattern is based on the relationship between or among events. Some passages discuss one cause and one effect—the omission of a command, for example, causing a computer program to fail.

This relationship can be visualized as follows:

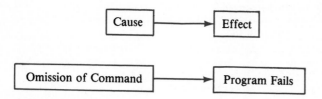

Most passages, however, describe multiple causes or effects. Some may describe the numerous effects of a single cause, such as unemployment producing an increase in crime, family disagreements, and diminishing self-esteem.

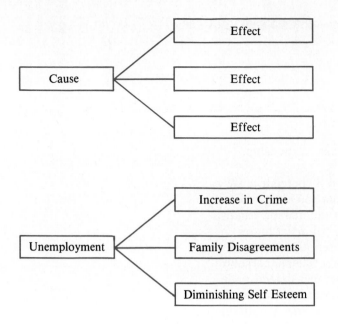

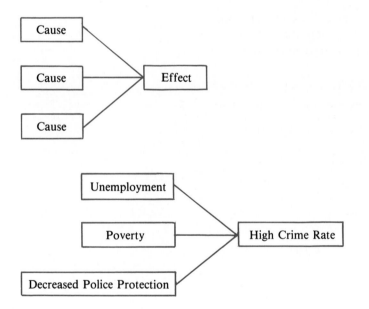

Others may describe the numerous causes of a single effect, such as increased unemployment and poverty along with decreased police protection causing a higher crime rate.

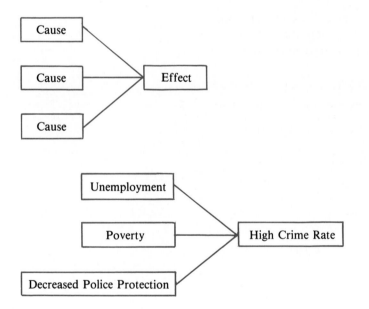

Still others may present multiple causes and effects, such as unemployment and poverty producing an increase in crime and in family disputes.

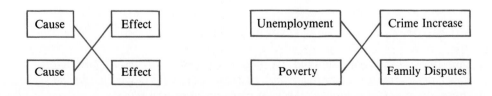

Read the following passage, taken from a business marketing text, and determine which of the following patterns is used:

1. single cause–single effect
2. multiple causes–single effect
3. single cause–multiple effects
4. multiple causes–multiple effects

Then draw a diagram in the margin, describing this relationship.

> Many new products do not succeed—from 30 percent to 90 percent, in fact, depending on which estimate you choose. The reason may be inaccurate information about the market, bad estimates of how the market or the competition will react to the product, or just unfortunate timing. More often, the causes of failure are related to the four components of a seller's marketing mix. The product itself, for example, is sometimes defective, despite previous research and testing. The assortment of colors, or flavors, or package sizes might be wrong. Sometimes the product is not different enough for buyers to perceive any point of competitive superiority. Or perhaps it is too different and too complicated in operation to attract buyers. Its quality, performance, or some other characteristic may disappoint buyers who expected more.
>
> The initial price may be too high or too low. Production and marketing costs may have been underestimated. Competitors may cut their prices, either in the test marketing step to distort the seller's findings, or in the commercialization step, or in both.
>
> –Russ and Kirkpatrick, *Marketing,* p. 241

The passage offers numerous reasons why new products fail. Numerous causes, then, produce a single effect.

When you read and study ideas organized in a cause-effect pattern, focus on the connection between or among events. To make relationships clearer, determine which of the four cause-effect patterns is used. Directional words can help you determine the cause-effect relationship.

Causes	*Effects*
because	consequently
because of	as a result
since	one result is
one cause is	therefore
one reason is	thus

EXERCISE 8 _____

Directions: *From the following list of section headings from an American Government textbook, predict which sections will be developed using the cause-effect pattern. Place a check in front of those you select.*

_____ 1. How Public Policies Affect Income

_____ 2. Explaining the Decline of Isolationism in America

_____ 3. Tasks of Political Parties

_____ 4. The Affirmative Action Issue

_____ 5. Political Parties: How Party Loyalty Shifts

_____ 6. Why Bureaucracies Exist

_____ 7. The Organization of National Political Parties

_____ 8. How Lobbyists Shape Policy

_____ 9. Types of Special Interest Groups

_____ 10. The Nature of the Judicial System

Enumeration

The primary function of textbooks is to present information. If there is a relationship or connection between or among ideas, this connection is usually emphasized and used to organize information. Many types of information, however, have no inherent order or connection. Lists of facts, characteristics, parts, or categories can appear in any order; thus writers use a pattern called enumeration. In this pattern, the information is often loosely connected with a topic sentence or controlling idea: "There are several categories of . . ." or "There are three types of . . ." and so forth. This listing pattern, sometimes called classification, divides a topic into subgroups or groups items according to a common charactertistic.

Read the following paragraph, observing how the pattern proceeds from one type of neuron to another.

> Neurons come in many different shapes and sizes. Scientists usually classify them into three types: sensory neurons, motor neurons, and interneurons. . . . _Sensory neurons_ receive and convey information about the environment. Their dendrites pick up signals directly from specialized _receptor cells_ that respond to light, pressure, and other external stimuli. The retinas of each eye, for example, are made up of thousands of receptor cells. Sensory neurons pass information about the environment on to other neurons, and this process enables us to see, hear, touch, smell, and taste. . . . Whereas information is conveyed to the brain via sensory neurons, _motor neurons_ carry signals from the brain and spinal cord to the muscles, organs, and glands of the body. The third and by far most common type of neuron in the human brain is the _interneuron,_ which connects one neuron with another.

–Roediger et al., _Psychology,_ p. 39

One key to reading and studying this pattern is to be aware of how many items are enumerated so you can check your recall of them. It is also helpful to note whether the information is listed in order of importance, frequency, size, or any other characteristic. This will help you organize the information for easier recall.

one	first
anther	second
also	finally
too	for example
for instance	in other words

Directional words are very useful in locating items in a list. As a writer moves from one item in a list to another, he or she may use directional words to mark or identify each point.

EXERCISE 9 _____

Directions: *For each of the following topic sentences, supply three pieces of information that might be contained in the paragraph.*

1. There are magazines designed for almost every possible special interest and every conceivable type of person.
2. Humans have more than just five senses; within the broad category of touch there are many different kinds of sensation that can be felt.
3. The category of mammals contains many widely different kinds of animals.
4. Scientists find life hard to define, except by describing its characteristics.
5. Because the purpose of a résumé is to sell the qualities of the person writing it, it should include several important kinds of information.

Problem-Solution

Many academic disciplines are concerned with defining problems, conducting research, and examining possible solutions. Consequently, problem-solution is a common pattern used in textbooks. For example, an ecology text may describe various solutions to control environmental pollution. A mathematics text formally presents solutions to various problems.

The problem-solution pattern is closely tied to the cause-effect pattern, since solutions are causally related to problems. The overall pattern often hinges on if . . . then relationships. For example:

Solution

If chemical solution waste dumping is outlawed, *then* there will be less polution in the local rivers.

Problem

More than one step or action may be necessary to produce a solution, and at times several conditions may exist simultaneously that cause the problem. Other times, an author may analyze a problem, identify causes, but not offer a direct solution. For example, a social problem text may analyze conditions that create abuse of the welfare system, but not propose a comprehensive solution.

Read the following excerpt, identify the problem, and sketch how it might be most effectively mapped. In this excerpt the problem discussed is women's persistent poverty. It could be mapped as follows:

> Many women find themselves placed in an inescapable poverty syndrome. Numerous factors contribute to this persistence of poverty. First, many women without higher education or skilled training are relegated to low paying jobs, usually within the service or agricultural fields. Factors within our economy and social system prevent these women from advancing beyond their entry level, low paying jobs. Their low paying jobs do not provide fringe benefits such as overtime pay, vacations, leaves, or unemployment or medical insurance. Lacking these benefits, many women are unable to seek further education or retraining. Sexual division of labor within the home requires many women to spend long hours in childcare and household upkeep, again preventing them from seeking advancement through education.

Causes	Problem
1. job segregation	women's persistent poverty
2. women's economy	
3. sexual division of labor in family	

The following map is effective in visualizing and recalling ideas presented in problem-solution patterns. Do not expect to always be able to fill in both causes and solutions.

Causes	Problem	Solution(s)
_____	_____	_____
_____	_____	_____
_____	_____	_____

Directional words for the problem-solution pattern may include some of the words that suggest a cause-effect pattern as well as the following:

the problem is . . .	causes
Why does . . .	What happens when
if . . . then . . .	suppose

EXERCISE 10 _____

Directions: *For each of the following topic sentences, identify the problem and predict whether the paragraph will focus on causes, solutions, or both.*

1. There is growing controversy today about the need to cut trees in national forests for commercial lumber production; numerous alternative proposals are currently under discussion.
2. The overcrowding in federal and state prisons has led some social scientists to consider other methods of crime deterrence.
3. Steps can be taken to restore or identify fossils archaeologists discover that are damaged.
4. When writing the Constitution, its framers recognized that the fundamental rights of the people had to be protected by the government.
5. Perhaps the most difficult part of a job interview is being asked an unexpected question for which you do not have a ready answer.

Mixed Patterns

In many texts, sections and passages combine one or more patterns. In defining a concept or idea, a writer might explain a term by comparing it with something similar or familiar. In describing an event or process, a writer might include reasons for or causes of an event, or explain why the steps in a process must be followed in the prescribed order.

Read the following paragraph and determine what two patterns are used.

Psychologists have long puzzled over how the perceptual systems generally achieve constancy. Why don't people appear to shrink as they walk away? The constancies can be understood by first examining the distinction between proximal and distal stimuli. *Proximal* (nearby) *stimuli* are the physical energy patterns that strike the sensory receptors. The retinal image is a proximal stimulus, as is the sound pattern that strikes our eardrums. *Distal* (distant) *stimuli* are the objects at a distance that give rise to the proximal stimuli. The existence of the perceptual constancies demonstrates that perceptual experience is tied more closely to distal stimuli than to proximal stimuli. Thus, if you pick up this book and move it closer to you and then farther away, you will perceive the book's size and shape to remain the same; the distal stimulus, the book itself, does remain the same in size and shape, although the proximal stimulus, the retinal image of the book, fluctuates over a large range.

–Roediger et al., *Psychology,* p. 141

Two terms—*proximal* and *distal stimuli*—are defined, but for purposes of explanation, the terms are also compared. You can see, therefore, that the paragraph combines a definition pattern with a comprehension-contrast pattern. Because the primary purpose of the paragraph is to define the terms, the predominant pattern is definition.

When reading mixed patterns, do not be overly concerned with identifying or labeling each pattern. Instead, look for the predominant pattern that carries the overall organization.

Figures 9-3 and 9-4 present a review of the various organizational patterns and of directional words commonly used with each pattern. Although this chapter has focused on the use of these patttrns in textbook writing, you will find such patterns in other academic situations as well. For example, your professor may organize his or her lecture using one or more of these patterns and use directional words to enable you to follow the line of thought. On exams, especially essay exams, you will find questions that require you to organize information using one or more of the organizational patterns. (Refer to Chapter 17 for more information on essay exam questions.)

Organizational patterns and directional words are also useful in organizing your own ideas and presenting them effectively in written form. As you write papers and complete written assignments, these patterns will provide a basis for relating and connecting your ideas and presenting them in a clear and understandable form. The directional words are useful as transitions, leading your reader from one idea to another.

EXERCISE 11 _____

Directions: *Assume that each of the following sentences or groups of sentences is the beginning of a textbook section. Based on the information contained in each, predict what organizational pattern is used throughout the passage. Look for directional words to help you identify the pattern.*

1. In large businesses, clerical jobs are usually very specialized in order to accomplish the work to be done in the most efficient manner. As a result, clerical work is very often routine and highly repetitive. _____

2. There are clear limitations to population growth and the use of natural resources. First, the food supply could be exhausted due to water, mineral, and soil depletion. _____

3. Unlike the statues of humans, the statues of animals found in Stone Age sites are quite lifelike. _____

4. When a patient enters a mental hospital, he is carefully tested and observed for twenty-four hours. Then a preliminary decision is made concerning medication and treatment. _____

5. One shortcoming of the clinical approach in treating mental illness is that definitions of normal behavior are subjective. Another shortcoming of the approach is that it assumes that when a patient has recovered he will be able to return to his previous environment. _____

6. Most of the world's news is transmitted by western news agencies. Third World nations regard this dominance as oppressive and feel action must be taken to develop their communication networks. _____

FIGURE 9-3 Organizational Pattern Summary

Pattern	Characteristics
Definition	Explains the meaning of a term or phrase Consists of class, distinguishing characteristics, and explanation
Time sequence	Describes events, processes, procedures
Comparison-contrast	Discusses similarities and/or differences among ideas, theories, concepts, objects, or persons
Cause-effect	Describes how one (or more) things cause or are related to another
Problem-solution	Focuses on if . . . then relationships; identifies problems, discusses causes and solutions
Enumeration	Organizes lists of information: characteristics, features, parts, or categories

FIGURE 9-4 A Summary of Directional Words

Thought Pattern		Directional Words
Definition		refers to, means, can be defined as, consists of
Time sequence		first, second, later, before, next, as soon as, after, then, finally, meanwhile, following, last, during, when, until
Comparison-contrast	*Similarities:*	also, similarly, like, likewise, too, as well as, both
	Differences:	unlike, on the other hand, instead, despite, nevertheless, however, in spite of
Cause-effect	*Causes:*	because, because of, since, one cause is, one reason is
	Effects:	consequently, as a result, one result is, therefore, thus
Problem-solution		why does . . . , if . . . then, causes, suppose, what happens when . . .
Enumeration		one, another, also, too, for instance, first, second, finally, for example, in other words

EXERCISE 12 _____

Directions: *Read each of the following passages and identify the predominant organizational pattern used in each.*

1. FAMILY STUDIES

Another method used to measure a genetic influence on behavior is to study families. Family members have similar genes. You share half your genes with your mother and half with your father. On average you also share half your genes with your brothers and sisters. However, most families also live together. So if families share a common trait it could be related to their common genes, to their common environment, or both.

One way to get around this problem is to study adopted children. Heston (1970) found subjects born to schizophrenic mothers who were permanently separated from them before they were one month old and were reared in foster or adoptive homes. Another group of children who also had been separated from their biological mothers before reaching one month of age and were reared in foster homes were used as controls. Their mothers had no record of psychiatric problems. As adults, the children of schizophrenic mothers showed significantly greater incidence of schizophrenia than the control subjects. These data, consistent with those from the twin studies, evidence a possible genetic factor in schizophrenia.

In another type of family study investigators measure a trait within a family over generations. The pattern of appearance of a trait in family members over generations can suggest specific hypotheses as to how genes are related to a trait. Not all genes are directly reflected in observable traits (phenotype is not the same as genotype). An example of this is a characteristic of genes termed *recessiveness*. Recessive genes will not be expressed in the phenotype unless both members of a pair of genes are the same. Blue eyes are produced by recessive genes. If one parent contributes genes for brown eyes and the other contributes genes for blue eyes, the child's eyes will be brown; the blue eye gene is recessive, the brown eye gene is dominant. Two brown-eyed parents could have a blue-eyed child if they both carried the recessive eye genes, and these recessive genes were contributed to the child by both parents.

–Roediger et al., *Psychology*, p. 78

Organizational pattern: _____

2. COSMOLOGICAL SPECULATIONS AFTER GREEK COSMOLOGY

Whether the universe "have his boundes or bee in deed infinite and without boundes" was the profound question English astronomer Thomas Digges (1546?–1595) asked himself. It appeared in Digges's 1576 book *Perfit Description of the Celestial Orbes*. A few decades later Galileo too wrote of an infinite and unbounded universe in his *Dialogues*, which was probably prompted by the fact he had seen with his telescope that the Milky Way consists of myriads of stars.

What is the Milky Way? Swedish philosopher Emanuel Swedenborg (1688–1772) speculated in 1734 that the stars formed one vast collection, of which the solar system was but one constituent. Thomas Wright (1711–1786) of England theorized in his 1750 work, *An Original Theory of the Universe*, that the Milky Way seems to be a bright band of stars because the sun lies inside a flattened slab of stars. He also suggested that there were other Milky Ways in the universe. Immanuel Kant (1724–1804), the noted philosopher, went beyond Wright's idea, suggesting in 1755 that the small oval nebulous objects seen with telescopes were other systems of stars or "island universes"; the phrase captured popular fancy a century and a half later. . . .

Besides these speculations observational evidence was also accumulating that could be used to reveal the structure of the Milky Way. In 1785 Herschel gave the first quantitative proof that the Milky Way was a stellar structure shaped like a flat disk, a grindstone. Since Herschel and others did not suspect that starlight might be dimmed by obscuring material between the stars, he deduced that the sun was near the center of the system.

–Berman and Evans, *Exploring the Cosmos*, pp. 333, 336

Organizational pattern: _____ Time sequence + Define

3. **MINORITIES AND THE JOB MARKET**

Work, or the lack of work, crucially determines the way all of us live, so it isn't surprising that the distinctive pattern of significant gains for some groups in the minority population coupled with stagnation and even decline for others is intimately connected to the fortunes of minorities in the job market.

Untangling these issues is difficult because several different factors in the job market may contribute, simultaneously or in various combinations, to the inequality of minority and white income. One source of that inequality may be differences in the amount of work— or, put another way, the risks of not working—between the groups. Another may be differences in the earnings they receive when they do work. Both of these, in turn, are partly reflections of the kinds of jobs different groups typically hold, for this affects both the wages or salaries they receive when they work and the chances they face of being unemployed or intermittently employed. And all of these factors differ in their impact not only among the various minority groups but also among men and women within those groups.

–Currie and Skolnick, *America's Problems*, p. 161

Organizational pattern: _____ Cause + effect

4. **BIOGRAPHY OF KARL MARX**

Born in the ancient German Rhineland city of Trier, the son of middle-class Jewish parents who had converted to Protestantism, Karl Marx studied law. Significantly, for the development of his theories, he joined a circle of intellectuals who considered themselves to be young Hegelians. Despite his father's wishes, he switched to the study of philosophy, in which he received his Ph.D. at Jena in 1841. At that point his academic career came to an end, as he failed to receive a university teaching position.

Marx returned to the Rhineland where he began writing for a local liberal newspaper. He was struck by the inequities he saw around him, and as he read more deeply in the works of classical economists and French socialists, he became more aware of the economic factors in history. He moved to Paris, where he met Friedrich Engels (1820–1895), whose father owned a factory near Manchester, England, and struck up a close, lifelong friendship with him. Marx' views and activities moved the Prussian authorities to request the French government to expel him, and he went on to Belgium. His studies, personal observations of the working classes, and discussions with Engels on the condition of the factory workers in Britain sharpened his distaste for capitalism.

—Wallbank et al., *Civilization Past and Present*, Vol. 2, p. 605

Organizational pattern: ___Time Sequence___

5. **PAIN**

Perception of pain is not well understood. We could not live without the capacity to experience pain because if we did not notice painful stimuli, we might well depart before the stimuli did. Some people feel no pain, that is, they lack sensitivity to it; while this might seem advantageous, they are in constant danger of serious yet undetected injury (Melzack, 1973). Pain does not always occur from damage to bodily tissues; amputees experience "phantom limb" pain in arms or legs long since severed. Psychiatric patients sometimes report severe pain for which no organic cause can be found (Veilleux & Melzack, 1976).

One explanation of pain is in terms of the *gate-control theory* of Melzack and Wall (1965). According to that theory, sensations of pain result from activation of certain nerve fibers that lead to specific centers of the brain responsible for pain perception. When these fibers are activated, say by an injury, the neural "gate" to the brain is opened for pain sensations. The theory also postulates another set of neural fibers that, when activated, reduce the effects of the pain fibers and "close the gate" on the pain sensations. The theory proposes that neural activity arising from other stimuli (e.g., those producing general excitement) may close the gate to pain signals. The important idea is that signals from the brain can be sent to other parts of the body to modify the incoming pain signals.

Gate-control theory may help explain some common phenomena of pain. For example, it has been reported that patients feel less pain when dentists working on them play music; the music may help close the gate for pain. Similarly, Melzack (1970) reports that amputees feel less phantom limb pain when the stump is massaged. The massaging may activate fibers that close the gate to pain.

—Roediger et al., *Psychology*, p. 111

Organizational pattern: ___definition   cause + effect___

6. **INFORMAL AND FORMAL EDUCATION**

In nonindustrial societies most educational instruction is given by example; learning results from observation and imitation of relatives, peers, and neighbors. Children see how adults perform tasks and how they behave. At first, children's imitation is in the form of play—making toy bows and arrows and shooting at insects or making mud pies. Play slowly disappears as children begin to take a more substantial role in community work. From an early age children accompany their parents on their daily round of activities, watching and then assisting until eventually they are able to preform required adult tasks on their own. Some education in small-scale societies is more formalized. This is especially true of more esoteric subjects such as magic, curing, and playing a musical instrument. Sometimes formal education is also of a more universal nature, as when all Mardudjara male children are isolated for weeks and given instruction about religious and legal traditions in preparation for initiation.

In large-scale societies formal education tends to be more pervasive. Individuals are instructed formally in a wider range of topics and they spend more time in specialized institutional settings, or schools. This is is not necessarily because there is more to learn; rather, it reflects a shift of emphasis in the way people are taught and who is responsible for their instruction. In most large-scale societies some governmental authority or large institution such as the church assumes a primary role in education, resulting in a loss of instructional autonomy at the family and community level. In such situations education functions not simply to provide instruction, but also to promote homogeneity and a sense of identification with the state that supersedes more local and personal loyalties. The aim is to promote a common national culture.

–Howard, *Contemporary Cultural Anthropology*, pp. 250–251

Organizational pattern: _____ Compa _____

7. **CAPITAL**

Capital is [a] produced means of production. Capital consists of goods we have produced but that we keep aside and use to produce other goods and services. *Capital goods* are thus distinguished from *consumer goods*, which we can use directly. Tools and machines, transportation and communication networks, buildings and irrigation facilities are capital goods. Farmers save a portion of their grain crop to use for seed in the next planting season. Their seed grain is a capital good which allows them to produce more in the future.

Education (including all types of training in useful skills) may be thought of as *human capital*. To build capital requires that we give up something today for something in the future. Like the farmers who give up grain, students give up jobs—and parents give up trips abroad—all for the opportunity to develop a stock of capital. Human capital is an important basis for the growing prosperity of U.S. workers.

The word "capital" is sometimes also used to mean a stock of money, as in *financial capital*, but this is not what we mean when we speak of capital as a factor of production. Financial capital is provided to business firms for construction of real capital goods. This is the way individuals help to save in the current period for the sake of greater production in the future.

–Chisholm and McCarty, *Principles of Economics*, p. 22

Organizational pattern: _____ defin _____

8. **INTERPERSONAL VERSUS MASS COMMUNICATION**

Both interpersonal and mass communication are important in marketing. Personal selling requires interpersonal communication, while advertising, sales promotion, and publicity use mass communication techniques. . . .

A mass communication, such as an advertisement in a magazine, can more accurately deliver the same message to a larger audience than can an interpersonal communication, such as a salesperson's presentation to a customer. The latter changes with each attempt to communicate. The cost of reaching an individual through the mass media is substantially lower as well. However, mass communication is one-way; it has less likelihood of gaining the potential audience's selective attention, and it suffers from slow, and many times, inaccurate feedback.

Interpersonal communication has the benefits of being fast, and allowing two-way feedback. A buyer can respond instantly to a salesperson's presentation, and the salesperson can ask for clarification of the response. This greater flexibility in feedback allows the communicator to counter objections from the buyer and thus attain a greater change in attitude and behavior than is possible with mass communication. Interpersonal communication is much more efficient than mass communication. Unfortunately, interpersonal communication used for a large audience is slow and very expensive. One must thus compare the efficiency of using a particular type of communication with the cost involved. This comparison of communication efficiency with cost leads to what has been referred to as the *communication-promotion paradox*.

–Kinnear and Bernhardt, *Principles of Marketing*, pp. 438–439

Organizational pattern: ___ compare _____

9. **SOCIETY**

Culture is not created in a vacuum, nor by isolated individuals. It is the product of humans interacting in groups. From their parents and from others around them, humans learn how to act and how to think in ways that are shared by or comprehensible to people in their group. Humans are by nature social animals. From birth to death, humans are biologically conditioned to live not as separate individuals, but as members of groups. Since the beginning of human evolution, our survival has been a cooperative enterprise. Even hermits do not escape the rest of humanity, for everything they think, know, or believe has been conditioned by others. Culture is a group effort and is *socially shared*.

We sometimes speak of those who share the same cultural perceptions and modes of behavior as members of a society. A *society* is a collection of people who are linked to one another, either directly or indirectly, through social interaction. It is through their common experiences that members of a society evolve shared cultural attributes. Culture and society are complementary concepts; they are two sides of the same coin. Without culture, societies as we know them could not exist, for there would be no common basis for interpreting one another's behavior. Similarly, without a society there would be no culture, for there would be no interaction by which people could share their knowledge, values, and beliefs. The sharing of culture comes about through interaction, and predictable interaction is made possible through values and attitudes that people hold in common.

–Howard, *Contemporary Cultural Anthropology*, pp. 5–6

Organizational pattern: ___ defi _____

10. THE PHYSICS OF LIGHT

The two properties of light most important for the study of the psychology of vision are intensity and wavelength. The *intensity* of light affects the psychological experiences of *brightness* and *lightness* perception. In general, the more intense a light source, the brighter a light will appear. When light illuminates an object, part of it is absorbed and part reflected; the perceived lightness of an object depends on the proportion of light that is reflected. There is more to the perception of brightness and lightness, however, than intensity. A blacktop road will appear black whether it is seen in the evening, when there is relatively little light falling on it, or in broad daylight. In fact, a blacktop road in the noonday sun reflects more light to the eye than does a white shirt worn indoors in the evening. (You can verify that with any light meter, such as one built in many cameras.) Yet the road looks black and the shirt looks white. This is one of many bits of evidence that the eye is much more complicated than a camera.

The second important property of light is *wavelength,* which affects the light's perceived color, or *hue.* Wavelength is the distance between adjacent wave crests, and it is measured in *nanometers,* or billionths of a meter. As the wavelength of light increases through the visible spectrum, which ranges roughly from 400 to 750 nanometers, humans perceive the color of the light as changing from violet through blue, green, yellow, and orange to red at the longest wavelengths. . . . Color perception, however, involves factors other than the registration of wavelength. For example, many colors such as brown, pink and even white are not in the spectrum. (Have you ever seen brown in a rainbow?) Such colors embody several different wavelengths, and the visual system in effect mixes the wavelengths to produce perception of a nearly infinite variety of colors.

–Roediger et al., *Psychology,* pp. 86–87

Organizational pattern: _____ Enumeration _____

EXERCISE 13 _____

Directions: *Refer to the biology sample textbook chapter reprinted in Appendix B. Using headings and first sentences of sections, predict and record the organizational patterns that are used in the chapter.*

EXERCISE 14 _____

Directions: *Refer to the first section of the psychology sample textbook chapter reprinted in Appendix A. Using subheadings and first sentences of paragraphs, predict and record the organizational patterns that are used in the section.*

SUMMARY

Textbooks are unique, highly organized sources of information. Becoming familiar with their organization and structure and learning to follow the writer's thought patterns are important textbook reading skills. A textbook is divided into parts: chapters, sections, subsections, and paragraphs. Although each is successively smaller in size and more limited in scope, each follows a similar organization and is built around a single idea with details that support and explain it. Textbook writers explain ideas by providing various types of supporting information: examples, description, facts and statistics, and citation of research evidence. These supporting details are often organized into one or more organizational patterns: definition, time sequence, comparison-contrast, cause-effect, problem-solution, and enumeration.

10

Reading Graphics and Technical Writing

Use this chapter to:
1. *Read graphics more effectively.*
2. *Develop strategies for reading technical writing.*

Highly detailed specific information is often an integral part of course content. For instance, a sociology course may involve crime-rate statisics, a chemistry course is concerned with characteristics of atomic particles, an art history course focuses on historical periods.

These kinds of highly specialized information are presented through two unique vehicles: (1) graphics and (2) technical writing. Graphics refers to all forms of visual representations of information, including maps, charts, tables, diagrams. Textbooks in many academic disciplines employ graphics to organize and present information. Technical writing is the compact, precise, and detailed presentation of factual information intended for practical use or application. Applications may include, for example, solving a problem in chemistry, writing a computer program, or operating a fax machine. College courses in the sciences, applied technologies, business, and specialized careers all demand technical reading skills. The purpose of this chapter is to present strategies for reading graphics and for approaching technical writing.

READING GRAPHICS

Graphics are pictorial representations of information—or information pictures. They condense information and allow the reader to study and evaluate it quickly and efficiently. The following activity demonstrates the functions of graphics.

Read the paragraph below and answer the questions that follow.

An experiment was done to study the effect of smell on taste. Subjects were given a drop of a substance on their tongues and asked to identify it. Each of twelve substances was administered twice—once the subject was allowed to smell, the second time smelling was prevented. The results in terms of percentage of correct identification are: apricots with smell 58%, without smell 4%; chocolate with smell 90%, without smell 4%; cherry with smell 79%, without smell 4%; dill pickle juice with smell 45%, without smell 4%; garlic with smell 56%, without smell 4%; grape juice with smell 58%, without smell 10%; lemon with smell 84%, without smell 40%; onion with smell 47%, without smell 18%; root beer with smell 56%, without smell 4%; water with smell 84%, without smell 70%; wine with smell 58%, without smell 17%.

1. For what substances is there the greatest taste recognition difference between smell and no smell?
2. What substance is more recognizable using both taste and smell?
3. What substance is most recognizable using taste and no smell?
4. For what substance is there least difference in recognition between smell and no smell?

The above paragraph is repetitious and tedious to read; answering the questions required rereading and culling through the data. Now, suppose you had been given the graph shown in Figure 10-1 instead of the above paragraph. Check the correctness of your answers using the graph. Clearly, the

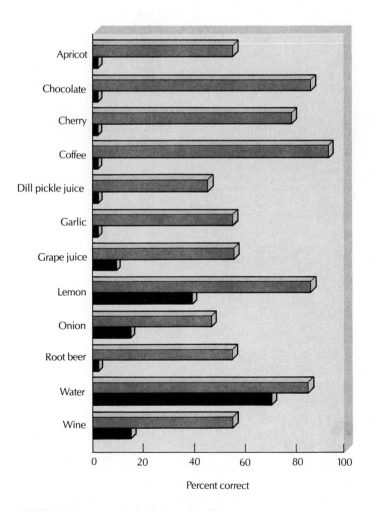

Taste test
The gray bars show the percentages of people who could identify a substance dropped on their tongues when they were able to smell it. The black bars show the percentages who could identify a substance when they were prevented from smelling it. (From Mozell et al., 1969.)

FIGURE 10-1   A Sample Bar Graph[1]

graph makes the results of the experiment much clearer and easy to understand.

Graphics, then, not only condense information, they also reveal trends and allow the reader to assess patterns, notice variations, and interpret information.

Some students are tempted to skip over graphs, tables, and diagrams. Stopping to study graphics requires time and seems to interrupt the flow of reading. Others think, incorrectly, that since the accompanying text explains the graphic, the graphic is unimportant. Actually, graphics are usually *more* important than the paragraphs that surround them. They are included to call your attention to, emphasize, and further explain the subject at hand.

Here is a general strategy for reading graphics. More specific suggestions for each type of graphic will follow.

1. *Read the title or caption.* The title will identify the subject and may suggest what relationship is being described.
2. *Determine how the graphic is organized.* Read the column headings or labels on the horizontal and vertical axis.
3. *Identify the variables.* Decide what is being compared to what or what relationship is being described.
4. *Anticipate the purpose.* Based on what you have seen, predict what the graphic is intended to show. Is its purpose to show change over time, describe a process, compare costs, or present statistics?
5. *Determine scale, values, or units of measurement.*
6. *Study the data to identify trends or patterns.* Note changes, unusual statistics, unexplained variations.
7. *Draw connections with the chapter content.* Take a moment to discover why the graphic was included and what concepts or key point it illustrates or explains.
8. *Make a brief summary note.* In the margin jot a brief note summarizing the trend or pattern the graphic emphasizes. Writing will crystallize the idea in your mind and your note will be useful for reviewing.

TYPES OF GRAPHICS

There are various types of graphics; each accomplishes specific purposes for the writer and each describes a particular relationship.

Tables

A table is an organized display of factual information, usually numbers or statistics. Its purpose is to present large amounts of information in a condensed and systematically arranged form. The arrangement allows comparisons between or among data. Take a few minutes to study the table in Figure 10-2, then use the tips shown below.

1. *Determine how the data is classified or divided.* The table shown in Figure 10-2 classifies the national origins of U.S. immigrants from 1821 to 1927 by decade. Europe is subdivided by region.
2. *Make comparisons and look for trends or patterns.* This step involves surveying the rows and columns, noting how each compares with the

Year	Total Immigrants	Total Europe	Europe			Western Hemisphere	Asia	Other
			North and West	East and Central	South and Other			
		No. (%)	No. (%)	No. (%)	No. (%)	No. (%)	No. (%)	No. (%)
1821–1830	144	99 (69.2)	96 (67.1)	——	3 (2.1)	12 (8.4)	——	32 (22.4)
1831–1840	599	496 (82.8)	490 (81.8)	——	1 (1.0)	33 (5.5)	——	70 (11.7)
1841–1850	1,713	1,599 (93.3)	1,592 (92.9)	2 (0.1)	5 (0.3)	62 (3.6)	——	53 (3.1)
1851–1860	2,598	2,453 (94.4)	2,432 (93.6)	3 (0.1)	21 (0.8)	75 (2.9)	42 (1.6)	29 (1.1)
1861–1870	2,315	2,065 (89.2)	2,032 (87.8)	12 (0.5)	21 (0.9)	167 (7.2)	65 (2.8)	19 (0.8)
1871–1880	2,812	2,272 (80.8)	2,070 (73.6)	127 (4.5)	76 (2.7)	405 (14.4)	124 (4.4)	11 (0.4)
1881–1890	5,247	4,738 (90.3)	3,778 (72.0)	624 (11.9)	331 (6.3)	425 (8.1)	68 (1.3)	16 (0.3)
1891–1900	3,688	3,559 (96.5)	1,641 (44.5)	1,210 (32.8)	704 (19.1)	41 (1.1)	70 (1.9)	18 (0.5)
1901–1910	8,795	8,136 (92.5)	1,909 (21.7)	3,914 (44.5)	2,313 (26.3)	361 (4.1)	246 (2.8)	53 (0.6)
1911–1920	5,736	4,376 (76.3)	998 (17.4)	1,916 (33.4)	1,463 (25.5)	1,141 (19.9)	195 (3.4)	23 (0.4)
1921–1930	4,107	2,477 (60.3)	1,302 (31.7)	591 (14.4)	587 (14.3)	1,516 (36.9)	99 (2.4)	16 (0.4)
1931–1940	528	348 (65.9)	205 (38.8)	58 (11.0)	85 (16.1)	160 (30.3)	15 (2.8)	5 (0.9)
1941–1950	1,035	622 (60.1)	492 (47.5)	48 (4.6)	82 (7.9)	355 (34.3)	32 (3.1)	26 (2.5)
1951–1960	2,516	1,328 (52.8)	445 (17.7)	611 (24.3)	272 (10.8)	996 (39.6)	151 (6.0)	40 (1.6)
1961–1970	3,322	1,239 (37.3)	394 (11.9)	419 (12.6)	426 (12.8)	1,579 (47.6)	445 (13.4)	58 (1.9)
1971–1980	4,384	801 (18.3)	188 (4.3)	246 (5.6)	368 (8.4)	1,929 (44.0)	1,634 (37.3)	19 (0.4)
1981–1987	4,068	446 (11.0)	156 (3.9)	199 (4.9)	91 (2.2)	1,580 (38.9)	1,902 (46.7)	140 (3.4)

Note: Numbers are given in thousands.

FIGURE 10-2   A Sample Table[2]

others. Look for similarities, differences, and sudden changes of variations. Underline or highlight unusual or outstanding data. At first, the data may seem overwhelming, as in Figure 10-2. A table such as this requires you to spend a few minutes just scanning columns and getting used to the data. For example, for the table in Figure 10-2, there is a notable, sudden decline in immigration between 1931 and 1940. Immigration was particularly high between 1901 and 1910. It is also notable that there is an increase in percentage of Asian immigration in the last three decades and a corresponding reduction in European immigration.

3. *Draw conclusions*. Decide what the data means and what it suggests about the subject at hand. Look for clues, or sometimes direct statements, in the paragraphs that correspond to the table about the purpose of the graph. You can conclude from Figure 10-2 that there is a trend toward immigration by Asians and a decrease in immigration by Europeans.

EXERCISE 1 ————————————————

Directions: *Study the table in Figure 10-3 and answer the questions that follow.*

1. What can you conclude about the influence of labor unions in the work force?
2. What trends are evident about women in the work force?
3. What trends are evident about married women in the work force?

Year	Total Number of Workers	Males as % of Total Workers	Females as % of Total Workers	Married Women as % of Female Workers	% of Labor Force Unemployed	% of Workers in Labor Unions
1870	12,506,000	85	15	NA	NA	NA
1880	17,392,000	85	15	NA	NA	NA
1890	23,318,000	83	17	13.9	4 (1894 = 18%)	NA
1900	29,073,000	82	18	15.4	5	3
1910	38,167,000	79	21	24.7	6	6
1920	41,614,000	79	21	23.0	5 (1921 = 12%)	12
1930	48,830,000	78	22	28.9	9 (1933 = 25%)	7
1940	53,011,000	76	24	36.4	15 (1944 = 1%)	27
1950	59,643,000	72	28	52.1	5	25
1960	69,877,000	68	32	59.9	5.4	26
1970	82,049,000	63	37	63.4	4.8	25
1980	108,544,000	58	42	59.7	7.0	23
1986	117,835,000	55	45	58.5	7.0	18

Note: NA = not available.

FIGURE 10-3   A Sample Table[3]

Graphs

There are two primary types of graphs: bar and linear. Each plots a set of points on a set of axes.

Bar Graphs: A bar graph is often used to make comparisons between quantities or amounts. It is particularly useful in showing changes that occur with passing time. Bar graphs usually are constructed to emphasize differences. The graph shown in Figure 10-4 displays the percentage of women in selected occupations. It facilitates comparison between occupations and it is easy to see at a glance which occupations have high and low percentages of women.

Multiple Bar Graphs: A multiple bar graph displays at least two or three comparisons simultaneously. Figure 10-5 compares male and female participation in the labor force by age group.

Stacked Bar Graphs: A stacked bar graph is an arrangement of data in which, instead of arranging bars side by side they are placed one on top of another. This variation is often used to emphasize whole/part relationships; that is, to show what part of an entire group or class a particular item holds. Stacked bar graphs also allows numerous comparisons. The graph in Figure 10-6 allows you to see the portion of sales and the portion of operating profit that is attributable to each of the types of products or lines of businesses. This graph, surprisingly, makes at least 35 comparisons. It compares:

1.   Sales vs. operating profit for each year (5 comparisons)
2.   Sales of building products vs. energy products each year (5 comparisons)
3.   Profits of building products vs. energy products each year (5 comparisons)

PERCENTAGE OF WOMEN IN SELECTED OCCUPATIONS

An example of a bar chart.
SOURCE: U.S. Bureau of Labor Statistics

Occupation	Percentage
Accountants	38.6%
Bank & Financial Officers	37.1%
College & University Teachers	35.4%
Computer Specialists	28.5%
Lawyers & Judges	15.4%
Managers	28.0%
Pharmacists	23.8%
Sales Workers	45.4%

FIGURE 10-4   A Sample Bar Graph[4]

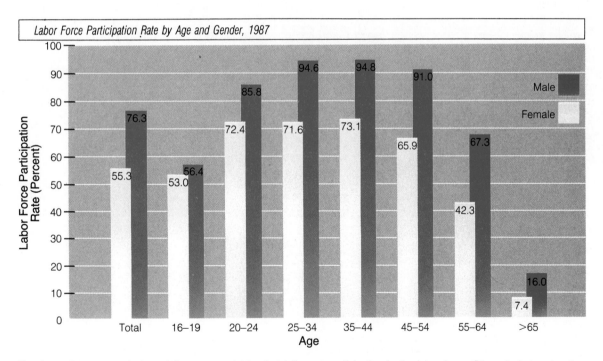

Labor Force Participation Rate by Age and Gender, 1987

Gender and age are only two of the many variables that influence participation in the labor force. Others include education spouse's income or other family income, race, and number and age of children in the family.

Source: *Statistical Abstract of the United States,* 1987, p. 377; *Economic Report of the President,* 1987.

FIGURE 10-5   A Multiple Bar Graph[5]

LINES OF BUSINESS
(in millions)

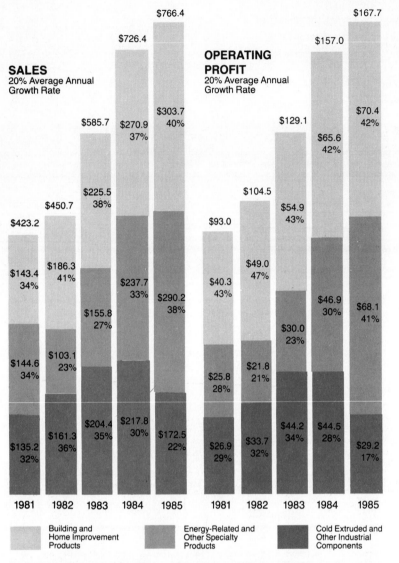

SALES
20% Average Annual
Growth Rate

OPERATING PROFIT
20% Average Annual
Growth Rate

| | Building and Home Improvement Products | Energy-Related and Other Specialty Products | Cold Extruded and Other Industrial Components |

The Oil-Field and Related Products, Personal Communications, and a portion of the Other industry segments, as presented in the Segment Information Note to the financial statements, are included in the Energy-Related and Other Specialty Products line of business. The Transportation-Related and the remaining portion of Other industry segments are included in the Cold Extruded and Other Industrial Components line of business.

FIGURE 10-6   A Sample Stacked Bar Graph[6]

4. Sales of energy products vs. industrial each year (5 comparisons)
5. Profits of energy products vs. industrial each year (5 comparisons)
6. Sales of building products vs. industrial each year (5 comparisons)
7. Profits of building products vs. industrial each year (5 comparisons)

Linear Graphs: A linear, or line, graph plots and connects points along a vertical and horizontal axis. A linear graph allows more data points than a bar graph. Consequently it is used to present more detailed and/or larger quantities of information. A linear graph may compare two variables; if so, then it consists of a single line. More often, however, linear graphs are used to compare relationships among several sets of variables and multiple lines are included. The graph shown in Figure 10-7 compares suicide death rates across eight age categories for black and white males and females.

Linear graphs are usually used to display continuous data—data that is connected in time or events occurring in sequence. The data in Figure 10-7 are continuous as they move from teenage years to age 85.

Single linear graphs can display one of three general relationships: positive, negative, or independent. Each of these is shown in Figure 10-8.

> *Positive relationships.* When both variables increase or decrease simultaneously, the relationship is positive and is shown by an upwardly sloping line. Graph A shows the relation between years of education and income. As one's years in school increase, so does one's income.
> *Inverse (or negative) relationships.* Inverse relationships occur when, as one variable increases, the other decreases, as shown in Graph B. Here, as one's educational level increased, the number of chil-

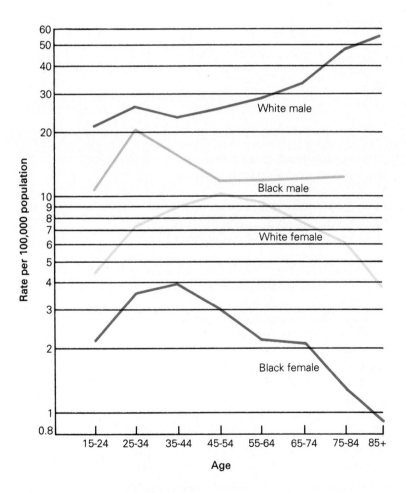

FIGURE 10-7   A Linear Graph[7]

Suicide death rates in the United States (1982) by age, race, and sex. (From Weed, 1985)

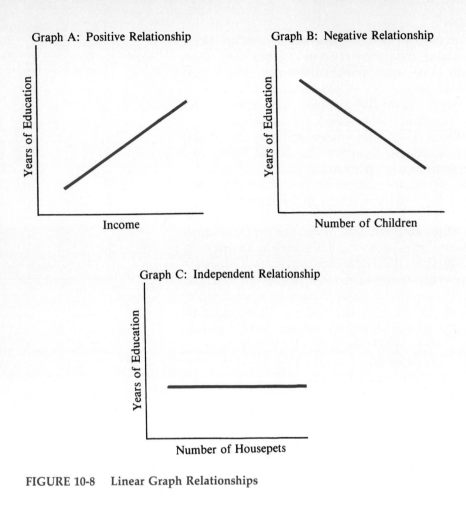

FIGURE 10-8   Linear Graph Relationships

dren one has decreased. The inverse relationship is shown by a
line or curve that slopes downward and to the right of point of
origin.

Independent relationship. When the variables have no effect on or relationship to one another, the graph appears as in Graph C. This
graph demonstrates that the education had no effect on the number
of housepets.

The linear graph in Figure 10-7 shows a positive relationship between age
and suicide death rate for white and black females until they reach ages 45–
54 and 34–44, respectively. After that age a negative relationship is evident.
For black males at first there is a positive relationship, then a negative relationship, and finally an independent relationship. From these three relationships, you probably realized that linear graphs may suggest a cause and effect
relationship between the variables. A word of caution is in order here. Do not
assume that since two variables change, one is the cause of the other. Once
you have determined the trend and the nature of the relationship a linear
graph describes, be sure to jot these down in the margin next to the graph.
These notes will be a valuable timesaver as you review the chapter.

EXERCISE 2 _____

Directions: *Study the graphs shown in Figures 10-9 through 10-11 and answer the corresponding questions.*

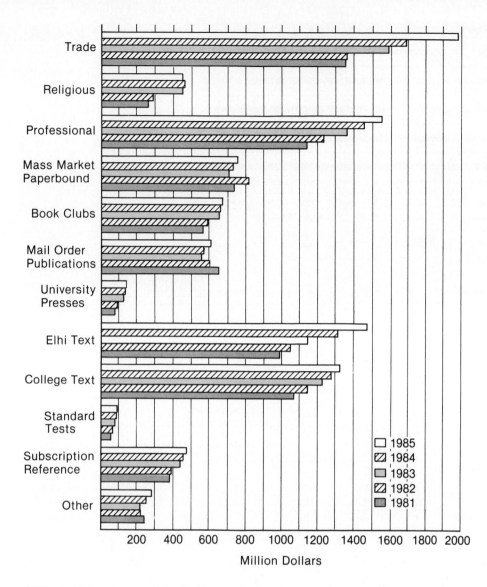

FIGURE 10-9   A Sample Multi-Bar Graph[8]

Figure 10-9: A Multiple Bar Graph

1. What is the purpose of the graph in Figure 10-9?
2. What type of book sold the most in 1985?
3. What type of books sold less in 1985 than in the previous year?
4. What type of print media has the largest market share? Which have the smallest?
5. What conclusions can you draw about the overall sales of books?

Figure 10-10: A Stacked Bar Graph

1. What industry has the largest percentage of plans in the 3–5 year range?
2. For all industries considered together, what percentage of plans tend to be 3–5 year plans?
3. What industry has the smallest percentage of plans in the 6–10 year range?

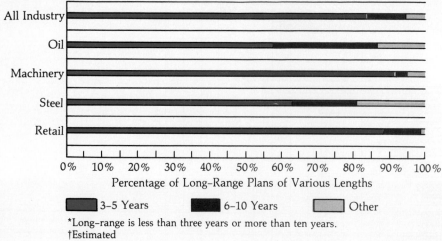

How Long is a Long-Range Plan?

All Industry

Oil

Machinery

Steel

Retail

0% 10% 20% 30% 40% 50% 60% 70% 80% 90% 100%

Percentage of Long-Range Plans of Various Lengths

■ 3–5 Years   ■ 6–10 Years   □ Other

*Long–range is less than three years or more than ten years.
†Estimated

Source: L. W. Rue (December 1973). The how and who of long–range planning. *Business Horizons,* 29.

FIGURE 10-10   A Stacked Bar Graph[9]

Figure 10-11: A Linear Graph

1. What variables does Figure 10-11 compare?
2. At what stages are women more satisfied than men?
3. Is there a positive, negative, or independent relationship between marital satisfaction and child rearing?
4. At what stage(s) is men's satisfaction increasing while women's satisfaction is decreasing?
5. What overall trend does this graph display?

Charts

Four types of charts are commonly used in college textbooks: pie charts, organizational charts, flowcharts, and pictograms. Each is intended to display a relationship, either quantitative or cause-effect.

Pie Charts: Pie charts, sometimes called circle graphs, are used to show whole/part relationships or to show how given parts of a unit have been divided or classified. They enable the reader to compare the parts to each other as well as to compare each part to the whole.

Organizational Charts: An organizational chart divides an organization, such as a corporation, a hospital, or a university, into its administrative parts, staff positions, or lines of authority. Figure 10-12 displays the organization of the marketing division of Coca-Cola. It indicates there are four major subdivisions and depicts divisions of responsibility for each.

Flowcharts: A flowchart is a specialized type of chart that shows how a process or procedure works. Lines or arrows are used to indicate the direction (route or routes) through the procedure. Various shapes (boxes, circles, rectangles) enclose what is done at each stage or step. You could draw, for example, a flowchart to describe how to apply for and obtain a student loan

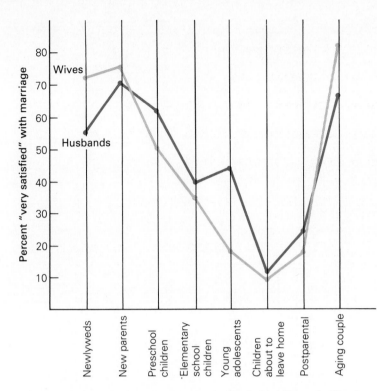

Marital satisfaction at various stages in family life. (After Rollins & Feldman, 1970)

FIGURE 10-11　　A Linear Graph[10]

or how to locate a malfunction in your car's electrical system. The flowchart shown in Figure 10-13, taken from a business management textbook, describes how groups function. The chart reveals a five-step process and describes the components of each step.

To read flowcharts effectively, use the following suggestions:

1. Decide what process the flowchart shows.
2. Next, follow the chart, using the arrows and reading each step. Start at the top or far left of the chart.
3. When you've finished, summarize the process in your own words. Try to draw the chart from memory without referring to the text. Compare your drawing with the chart and note discrepancies.

Pictograms: A combination of a chart and a graph, a pictogram uses symbols or drawings (such as books, cars, or buildings), instead of numbers, to represent specified quantities or amounts. This type of chart tends to be visually appealing, makes statistics seem realistic, and may carry an emotional impact. For example, a chart that uses stick-figure drawings of pregnant women to indicate the number of abortions performed each year per state may have a more significant impact than statistics presented in numeric form. A sample pictogram is shown in Figure 10-14. This pictogram uses symbols to represent various energy sources, an oil drum to represent oil, for example. (DOE is an abbreviation for Department of Energy.) The size of the symbol suggests its relative importance. The pictogram compares actual energy use in 1982 with the DOE forecast against the public's forecast.

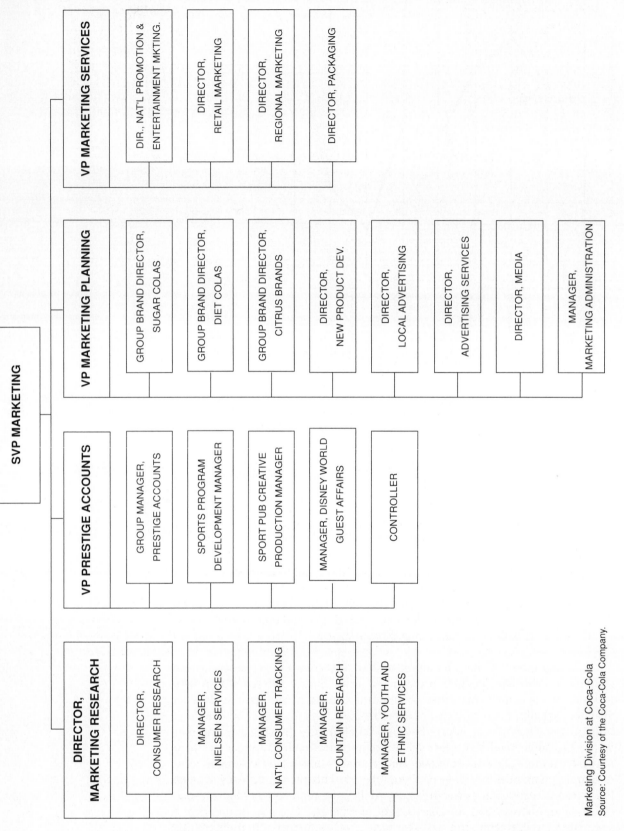

SVP MARKETING

DIRECTOR, MARKETING RESEARCH
- DIRECTOR, CONSUMER RESEARCH
- MANAGER, NIELSEN SERVICES
- MANAGER, NAT'L CONSUMER TRACKING
- MANAGER, FOUNTAIN RESEARCH
- MANAGER, YOUTH AND ETHNIC SERVICES

VP PRESTIGE ACCOUNTS
- GROUP MANAGER, PRESTIGE ACCOUNTS
- SPORTS PROGRAM DEVELOPMENT MANAGER
- SPORT PUB CREATIVE PRODUCTION MANAGER
- MANAGER, DISNEY WORLD GUEST AFFAIRS
- CONTROLLER

VP MARKETING PLANNING
- GROUP BRAND DIRECTOR, SUGAR COLAS
- GROUP BRAND DIRECTOR, DIET COLAS
- GROUP BRAND DIRECTOR, CITRUS BRANDS
- DIRECTOR, NEW PRODUCT DEV.
- DIRECTOR, LOCAL ADVERTISING
- DIRECTOR, ADVERTISING SERVICES
- DIRECTOR, MEDIA
- MANAGER, MARKETING ADMINISTRATION

VP MARKETING SERVICES
- DIR., NAT'L PROMOTION & ENTERTAINMENT MKTING.
- DIRECTOR, RETAIL MARKETING
- DIRECTOR, REGIONAL MARKETING
- DIRECTOR, PACKAGING

Marketing Division at Coca-Cola
Source: Courtesy of the Coca-Cola Company.

FIGURE 10-12   A Sample Organizational Chart[11]

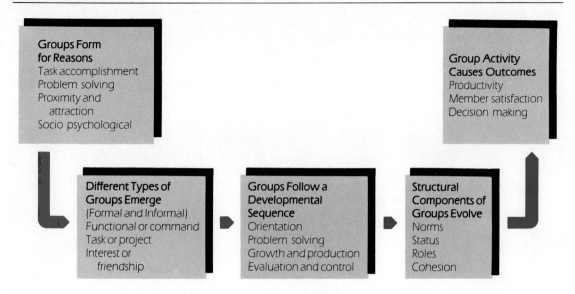

FIGURE 10-13   A Sample Flowchart[12]

EXERCISE 3 _____

Directions: *Study the charts shown in Figures 10-15 and 10-16 and answer the corresponding questions.*

Figure 10-15: A Pie Chart

1. What soft drink brand has the highest percentage of market shares?
2. In what order are the "pieces of the pie" arranged?
3. Is this chart more effective than a bar graph displaying the same data? Why or why not?

Figure 10-16: A Flowchart

1. What process does this flowchart describe?
2. List the steps in the order in which they occur.
3. At what stage in developing a sales promotional event would a manager decide which employees should perform specific tasks for that event?
4. At what stage would a manager of a large discount store decide to revise an advertising plan after a promotional event failed to achieve an expected sales increase?

Diagrams

Diagrams often are included in technical and scientific as well as business and social science texts to explain processes. Diagrams are intended to help you visualize relationships between parts and understand sequences. Figure 10-17 taken from a biology textbook, depicts a plant stem and illustrates the process by which a plant's history is revealed by stem growth.

Reading diagrams differs from reading other types of graphics in that diagrams often correspond to fairly large segments of text, requiring you to

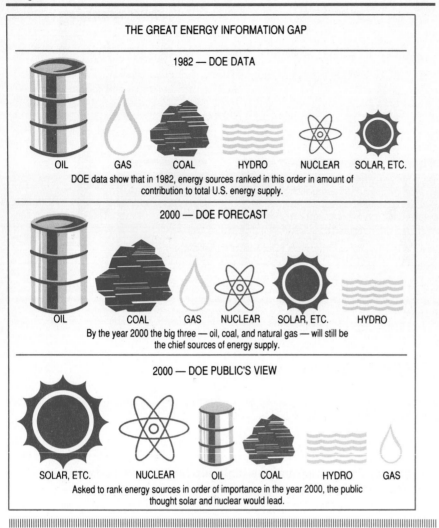

THE GREAT ENERGY INFORMATION GAP

1982 — DOE DATA

OIL   GAS   COAL   HYDRO   NUCLEAR   SOLAR, ETC.

DOE data show that in 1982, energy sources ranked in this order in amount of
contribution to total U.S. energy supply.

2000 — DOE FORECAST

OIL   COAL   GAS   NUCLEAR   SOLAR, ETC.   HYDRO

By the year 2000 the big three — oil, coal, and natural gas — will still be
the chief sources of energy supply.

2000 — DOE PUBLIC'S VIEW

SOLAR, ETC.   NUCLEAR   OIL   COAL   HYDRO   GAS

Asked to rank energy sources in order of importance in the year 2000, the public
thought solar and nuclear would lead.

FIGURE 10-14   A Sample Pictogram[13]

Top Five Soft Drink Brands
(Percent of Market Share)

Diet Pepsi
4.3
Other Brands 45.0
Dr. Pepper
4.9
diet Coke 9.3
Pepsi Cola
17.6
Coca-Cola classic
18.9%

FIGURE 10-15   A Sample Pie Chart[14]

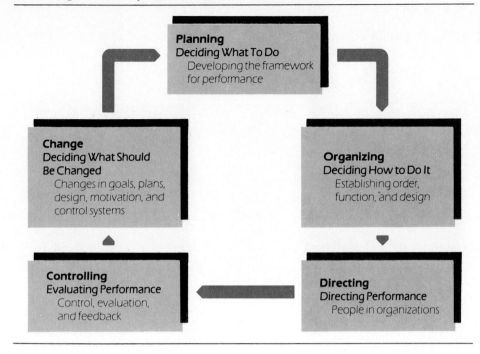

FIGURE 10-16   A Sample Flowchart[15]

switch back and forth frequently between the text and the diagram to determine what part of the process each paragraph refers to.

Because diagrams of processes and their corresponding text are often difficult, complicated, or highly technical, plan on reading these sections more than once. Use the first reading to grasp the overall process. In subsequent readings, focus on the details of the process, examining each step and understanding its progression.

One of the best ways to study a diagram is to redraw it without referring to the original, including as much detail as possible. Or, test your understanding and recall of the process explained in a diagram by explaining it, step by step in writing, using your own words.

EXERCISE 4 _____

Directions: *Study the diagram shown in Figure 10-18 and answer the questions below.*

Figure 10-18: A Diagram

1. What is the purpose of the diagram?
2. What amendment process is most commonly used?
3. Name two processes that have never been used?

Photographs

Although sometimes considered an art form instead of a graphic, photographs are used in place of words to fulfill purposes similar to other

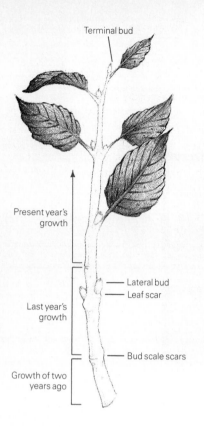

Terminal bud

Present year's growth

Last year's growth

Lateral bud
Leaf scar

Bud scale scars

Growth of two years ago

The growth area of a stem. One can read a bit of the plant's history by noting the distance between bud scale scars, the distance being greater for good years when the stem has been able to grow rapidly.

FIGURE 10-17   A Sample Diagram[16]

graphics—to replace verbal descriptions to present information. Photographs also are used to spark your interest, and, often, to draw out an emotional response or feeling. The caption on a photograph often provides a clue to its intended meaning. As you study a photograph ask: What is my first overall impression? What details did I notice first? These questions will lead you to discover the purpose of the photograph.

Maps

Maps describe relationships and provide information about location and direction. They are commonly found in geography and history texts, and also appear in ecology, biology, and anthropology texts. While most of us think of maps as describing distances and locations, maps also are used to describe placement of geographical and ecological features such as areas of pollution, areas of population density, or political data (voting districts).

When reading maps, use the following steps:

1. Read the caption. This identifies the subject of the map.
2. Use the legend or key to identify the symbols or codes used.
3. Note distance scales.

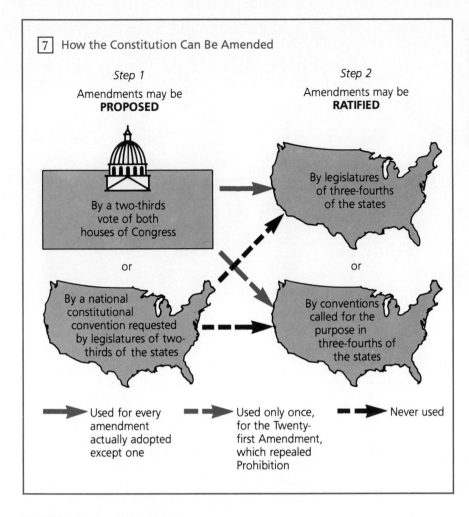

The Constitution set up two alternative routes for proposing amendments and two for ratifying them. Only one of the four possible combinations has really been used, but there are persistent calls for a constitutional convention to propose some new amendment or another. (Amendments to permit school prayers, to make abortion unconstitutional, and to require a balanced national budget are recent examples.)

7 How the Constitution Can Be Amended

Step 1
Amendments may be
PROPOSED

Step 2
Amendments may be
RATIFIED

By a two-thirds
vote of both
houses of Congress

or

By a national
constitutional
convention requested
by legislatures of two-
thirds of the states

By legislatures
of three-fourths
of the states

or

By conventions
called for the
purpose in
three-fourths of
the states

→ Used for every amendment actually adopted except one

⇢ Used only once, for the Twenty-first Amendment, which repealed Prohibition

⇢ Never used

FIGURE 10-18   A Diagram[17]

4. Study the map, looking for trends or key points. Often the text that accompanies the map states the key points the map illustrates.
5. Try to visualize, or create a mental picture of, the map.
6. As a learning and study aid, write, in your own words, a statement of what the map shows.

Now, refer to the map shown in Figure 10-19, taken from a business textbook.

This map shows geographic sources of various types of products. The map enables the reader, at a glance, to identify states heavily involved with production and those relatively uninvolved. Regions within particular states heavily involved are also clearly identifiable.

EXERCISE 5 _____

Directions: *Study the photographs shown in Figure 10-20 and answer the questions that follow.*

1. What are the photographs intended to emphasize?
2. What does this set of photographs show that a paragraph could not?
3. List several cultural differences that these photographs reveal.

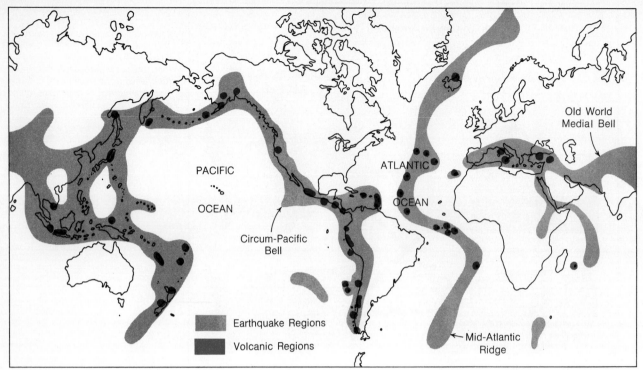

Earthquake-volcanic hazard zones.

Schematic map of main areas of earthquakes and volcanic activity during the most recent geological period (i.e., that most relevant to human beings). Note the concentration into three main zones. The most important is the circum-Pacific zone or girdle which accounts for about 80 percent of all earthquake activity. The Old World medial belt running from the Mediterranean to Indonesia accounts for most of the remaining activity with the mid-Atlantic ridge forming a third and less active region.

FIGURE 10-19   A Sample Map[18]

EXERCISE 6 ————————————————

Directions: *Indicate what type of graphic(s) would be most useful in presenting each of the following sets of information.*

1. Damage done to ancient carved figures by sulfur dioxide in the air.
2. A comparison of the types of products the United States imports with those it exports.
3. Changes in worker productivity each year from 1970 to 1990 in Japan, France, Germany, and the United States.
4. The probabilities of being murdered for various racial and ethnic groups in the United States.
5. Foreign revenue, total revenue, foreign operating profit, foreign assets, and total assets for the ten largest American multinational corporations.
6. Living arrangement (one parent, two parents, neither parent) for white, black, Spanish origin children under 18 years old in 1960, 1970, 1980, and 1990.
7. The basic components of a robot's manipulator arm.
8. A description of how the AIDS virus affects the immune system.
9. Sites of earliest Neanderthal discoveries in Western Europe.
10. Number of receipts of, and profits for, three types of businesses: proprietorships, corporations, and partnerships.

Marriage ceremonies in different cultures vary even more than family structure. Note the different styles of dress and the different degrees of solemnity in the above photographs. The one on top depicts a marriage in the United States, the one on the bottom a marriage in Southeast Asia.

FIGURE 10-20   A Sample Photograph[19]

READING TECHNICAL WRITING

Technical writing is commonly thought of as something science or engineering students read. Actually, technical writing is by no means restricted to traditional technical or scientific fields. Technical writing is what most of us are called on to read in our daily lives as well as in many academic courses. Here are a few examples of situations, both everyday and academic, that require technical reading.

Everyday Situations

1. Reading directions to set up your programmable telephone.
2. Assembling a bicycle from printed instructions.
3. Consulting a repair manual to troubleshoot problems in your car's engine.

Academic Situations

1. Reading end-of-the-year financial reports to assess a corporation's financial health for a business class project.
2. Consulting the *Journal of Abnormal Psychology* to complete a psychology term paper on characteristics of the manic depressive personality.
3. Referring to a technical manual to find out how to save a file on a new word-processing program.

Technical writing, then, is an important part of everyday activities and of many academic disciplines. Technical reading skills are essential in both the everyday and academic world. This portion of the chapter will discuss and describe technical writing and offer suggestions for reading it effectively.

How Technical Writing Is Different

You already know that technical writing is different, but do you know how it differs from other types of writing? Take a moment now to activate what you already know about technical writing.

EXERCISE 7 _____

Directions: *List below as many ways as you know that technical writing differs from nontechnical writing.*

_____   _____

_____   _____

_____   _____

_____

Now, expand your knowledge by comparing several sample pieces of writing, one of which is a technical one. All excerpts below concern the same topic: birds. After you have read all three, complete Exercise 8.

Sample 1: An Essay

"You would know the heron if you saw it," the stranger continued eagerly. "A queer tall white bird with soft feathers and long thin legs. And it would have a nest perhaps in the top of a high tree, made of sticks, something like a hawk's nest."

Sylvia's heart gave a wild beat; she knew that strange white bird, and had once stolen softly near where it stood in some bright green swamp grass, away over at the other side of the woods. There was an open place where the sunshine always seemed strangely yellow and hot, where tall, nodding rushes grew, and her grandmother had warned her that she might sink in the soft black mud underneath and never be heard of more. Not far beyond were the salt marshes just this side the sea itself, which Sylvia wondered and dreamed much about, but never had seen, whose great voice could sometimes be heard above the noise of the woods on stormy nights.[20]

Sample 2: A Poem

> At once a voice arose among
> The bleak twigs overhead
> In a full-hearted evensong
> Of joy unlimited;
> An aged thrush, frail, gaunt, and small
> In blast—beruffled plume,
> Had chosen thus to fling his soul
> Upon the growing gloom.[21]

Sample 3:

FINCH, any of a large group of small, primarily arboreal, seed-eating birds, most frequently found in the temperate areas of the Americas, Eurasia, and Africa, but sometimes in deserts and arctic areas.

Finches make up the family Fringillidae of the order Passeriformes; a heterogeneous group, they have been divided into several subfamilies Cardnelinae and Fringillinae, which include the goldfinches, grosbeaks, crossbills, rosy finches, siskins, redpolls, chaffinches, and bramblings.

Finches are small, compact birds, usually 3 to 10 inches (10–27 cm.) long. They vary in color from brown to gray to combinations of yellow, purple, red, green, blue, black, and white. The sexes are often colored alike, but in some species the males are more brightly colored than the females. The voices of the finches vary from soft rudimentary notes to loud musical songs.

A finch's bill is adapted for cracking or extracting seeds and is generally large at the base and conical in shape. The bills range in size from the slender, needlelike bill of the goldfinch to the massive seed-cracking bills of the grosbeaks. Studies of the small hawfinch have shown that its bill is equipped with massive muscles that give it a crushing power of from 60 to 159 pounds (27–72 kg.), so that it can crack the seeds of cherries and olives. The crossbill also has a specialized bill that permits the bird to open pine cones and extract the seeds.[22]

Sample 1, an excerpt from an essay titled "A White Heron," presents an everyday description of the heron—a sense of oddness and awkwardness is revealed through the description.

Sample 2 is an excerpt from a poem titled "The Darkling Thrush," by Thomas Hardy. Here the bird and its song are presented in contrast to a gloomy depressing scene. The thrush is . . .

Sample 3, an excerpt from an encyclopedia entry on finches, presents factual information about the bird's appearance and habitat.

EXERCISE 8 _____

Directions: *By comparing and contrasting the three excerpts shown above, list additional features of technical writing that you have discovered. Then compare your list with the information given in Figure 10-21.*

Tips for Reading Technical Material

Use the following suggestions to read technical material.

Adjust Your Reading Rate: Because technical writing is factual and contains numerous illustrations, diagrams, and sample problems, adjust your reading rate accordingly. Plan on spending twice as long reading a technical textbook as you spend on reading other nontechnical texts.

Plan on Rereading: Do not expect to understand everything the first time you read the assignment. It is helpful to read an assignment once rather quickly to get an overview of the processes and procedures it presents. Then reread it to learn the exact steps or details.

Preread Carefully: Because technical material often deals with unfamiliar subject matter for which you have little background knowledge, prereading is particularly important.

Alternate Between Reading Text and Studying Graphics: Drawings and illustrations are referred to frequently in surrounding text. Consequently, it is often necessary to alternate between text and graphics. Page arrangement is often confusing and the diagram to which a paragraph refers may not be on the same page. Other times, a diagram may appear before it is referred to in the text. Use the following strategy:

1. Notice the types of illustrations and drawings as you preread the material.
2. As soon as a graphic is mentioned in the text, locate and study it. Identify its purpose and determine its organization. Titles, captions, and labels are important.
3. If a graphic appears before its text reference, notice its title, and keep reading until it is introduced.
4. Plan to stop reading frequently to refer to graphics. For instance, reading about the function of specific parts of a piece of equipment, each time a specific part is mentioned, refer to the diagram and locate the part. Then read the description of its function.

Use Visualization: Visualization is a process of creating mental pictures or images. As you read, try to visualize the process or procedure being described. Make your image as specific and detailed as possible. Visualization will make reading these descriptions easier, as well as improve your ability to recall details. Here are a few examples of how students use visualization.

FIGURE 10-21 Characteristics of Technical Writing

Characteristic	Description
Purpose	To supply the reader with needed information. To perform a task, understand a situation, solve a problem, make a decision.
Fact density	Facts are abundant and usually are presented as compactly as possible.
Exact word choice	Meaning must be clear and without possibility of confusion or misinterpretation.
Technical/Specialized vocabulary	Because meaning must be exact, technical or specialized vocabulary is often introduced. These words have specific meanings within the field or discipline and often serve as shortcuts to lengthy descriptions or details that would be necessary if using nonspecialized language.
Abbreviations and notation systems	An extensive system of abbreviation and notations (signs and symbols) is used. These are also shortcuts to writing out complete words or meanings and are often used in diagrams, formulas, and drawings.
Graphics	Most technical writing contains numerous drawings, charts, tables, diagrams, or graphs. They are included to clarify, enabling you to visualize, and emphasize key information.
Examples and sample problems	Technical textbooks often contain numerous examples and sample problems. These are included to illustrate how information is used and instructions are applied.
Specific formats	Technical writing often follows specific formats. A lab report follows a specific organization. A psychologist case report has specific categories. Research reports in the sciences typically have a statement of problem, a description of experimental design, and so forth.

A nursing student reading about methods of arranging intravenous tubing for administering two solutions simultaneously visualized the arrangement of clamps, tubing, and bottles.

A communications student studying types of nonverbal communication visualized himself using each form.

Now read the following description of paramecia and try to visualize as you read.

If you should find yourself with a microscope and unable to resist examining the water of a scummy pond, you would likely find great numbers of tiny protozoans. Some of these would be covered with tiny, hairlike cilia. Protists that bear cilia at some stage in the life cycles comprise the phylum **ciliophora.** The most familiar of these are the **Paramecia.** Paramecia (singular, Paramecium) are recognizable by their slipper shape, which is maintained by their outer thickened membrane, the **pellicle.** The **pellicle,** while holding its form, is flexible enough to enable the paramecium to bend around objects as it furiously swims through the water propelled by the wavelike actions of the **cilia** covering its body. Behind its rounded anterior (or front) end lies a deep **oral groove** into which food is swept by other cilia. The food is then forced through a mouthlike pore **(cytostome)** at the end of the groove and into a bulbous opening, which will break away and move into the cytoplasm as a food **food vacuole.**[23]

✳ Tips for Studying Technical Material

Use the following suggestions to learn technical material.

Study Daily: Because technical material is unfamiliar, frequent contact with the material is necessary for retention.

Reserve Large Blocks of Time: Large blocks of time are often necessary to complete projects, lab write-ups, or problem sets. Also, technical material requires a particular mind set, which, once you've established it, is worth continuing.

Learn Technical Vocabulary: Understanding the technical vocabulary in your discipline is essential. For technical and applied fields, it is especially important to learn to pronounce technical terms and use them in your speech and writing. To establish yourself as a professional in the field and to communicate effectively with other professionals, it is vital to speak and use the language. Use the suggestions in Chapter 19 for learning specialized terminology.

Study by Drawing Diagrams and Pictures: While your textbook may include numerous drawings and illustrations, there is not sufficient space to have drawings for every process. An effective learning strategy is to draw diagrams and pictures whenever possible. These should be fast sketches; be concerned with describing parts or processes and do not worry about artwork or scale drawings. For example, a student studying air conditioning and refrigeration repair drew a quick sketch of a unit he was to repair in his lab before he began to disassemble it, and referred to sketches he had drawn in his notebook as he diagnosed the problem.

Focus on Concepts and Principles: Because technical subjects are so detailed, many students get lost with details and lose sight of the concepts and principles to which the details relate. Keep a sheet in the front of your notebook for easy reference on which you record information you need to refer to frequently. Include constants, conversations, formulas, metric equivalents, and commonly used abbreviations.

Integrate Lab, Lecture, and Classroom Activities: Many technical courses have a required lab. Because the lab is scheduled separately from the lecture and has its own unique format, you may fail to see the lab as an integral part of the course. The lab is intended to help you understand and apply principles and techniques used in your course and provides you with an opportunity to ask pertinent questions. Use the following tips for handling lab work:

☐ Be prepared before going to lab. Read the manual or assignment once to understand its overall purpose and a second time to understand the specific procedures. Make notes or underline key information.
☐ Ask questions before you make a mistake. Since procedures can be time consuming to repeat, ask questions first.
☐ Be sure you understand the purpose of each step before you perform it.
☐ Analyze your results and do the follow-up report as soon as possible. The best time to study your results is while the experiment and procedures are still fresh in your mind. If you finish the lab work early, stay and discuss results and interpretations with other students or your lab instructor.
☐ Follow the required format closely when writing your report.

Make Use of the Glossary and Index: Due to the large number of technical terms, formulas, and notations you will encounter, often it is necessary to refer back to definitions and explanations. Place a paper clip at the beginning of the glossary and a second at the index so you can find them easily.

Underline Selectively: Everything looks and often is important in texts, and it is easy to fall into the habit of over-underlining. Avoid this pitfall by reading a paragraph or section before underlining. Then go back and mark only key terms and concepts. Do not try to underline all useful facts. Refer to Chapter 11 for suggestions on how to underline effectively.

Use Outlining: Many students find outlining to be an effective study and review technique. Some texts may include chapter outlines; even though your text may have one, make your own. It is the process of making the outline that is important. Outlining forces you to decide what information is important and how it is related, and then to express the ideas in your own words. Refer to Chapter 12 for specific suggestions on taking outline notes.

Learn Processes and Procedures: Procedures, directions, installations, repairs, instructions, and diagnostic checking procedures all follow the process pattern. To read materials written in this pattern, you must not only learn the steps, but learn them in the correct order. To study process material, use the following tips:

1.   Prepare study sheets that summarize each process. For example, a psychology student learning the steps in motor development of infants wrote the summary sheet shown in Figure 10-22.

Month(s)	Activity
1½	raise head—45 degrees
3	roll—front to back
4	sit w/support
6	sit alone
7–12	crawl and creep
7	pull to stand
9	sidestepping
11	stand alone
12	walk

FIGURE 10-22   A Sample Summary Sheet

2. Test your recall by writing out the steps from memory. Recheck periodically by mentally reviewing each step.
3. For difficult or lengthy procedures, write each step on a separate index card. Shuffle the pack and practice putting them in the correct order.
4. Be certain you understand the logic behind the process. Figure out why each step is done in the specified order.

EXERCISE 9 ——————————————

Directions: *Using the sample textbook chapter in Appendix A, read the section on p. 449 titled "And Coping with Friends." Then write a summary sheet summarizing the steps in the reaction.*

SUMMARY

Compact, detailed, and highly specific information, an integral part of many courses, is presented in two common forms—graphics and technical writing.

Graphics condense information and allow the reader to assess patterns, identify trends, observe variations, and interpret information. The chapter presents a step-by-step procedure for reading graphics and discusses types of graphics: tables, bar graphs, including multiple bar graphs and stacked bar graphs, linear graphs, pie charts, organizational charts, flowcharts, pictograms, diagrams, photographs, and maps.

Technical writing is unique and distinct from other types of writing. Characteristics of technical writing are described in the chapter and suggestions given for reading technical writing. Suggestions for studying technical writing are also included.

PART FOUR

Learning from Texts

Do you think of your textbooks as just something to read? If so, you may not be using them to full advantage. A textbook is much more than a book of chapters, parts of which are assigned by instructors at various times during the semester. Textbooks are actually learning tools or devices. A text is often one of your primary sources of information for a course, and it is a valuable teaching-learning tool when used effectively.

Textbooks are written for the purpose of presenting information about a subject that students need to know. Textbook authors, most of whom are college teachers, attempt to present the information in such a way that it can be learned easily by students. They use a variety of methods and include a variety of learning aids, all of them to help students learn the content of their texts. As a student, you want to be aware of these methods and learning aids and know how to use them to make reading and studying easier.

Since the textbook is most often your primary source of information in a college course, you will need to become familiar with techniques for effectively studying and learning textbook material. You will want to know how to learn as you read, and you will want to master the technique of marking a textbook as you read. Once you have identified and marked important information, you will want to organize it to make learning easier.

The textbook chapters reprinted in the appendixes of this book have been included for purposes of demonstration and practice. They are, however, only samples. While they have many similarities to other textbook chapters, do not expect to find every textbook chapter organized or presented exactly like these. The sample chapters have been included so that you can try out the techniques and suggestions given in this unit. You will notice, also, that the sample chapters are used many times throughout the unit to show how particular techniques are applied or to illustrate particular aspects of effective textbook reading.

continued

continued

Chapter 11 presents techniques for underlining and marking textbooks. Methods of organizing information, including outlining, summarizing, and mapping, are described in Chapter 12. Chapter 13 offers two study and review strategies: learning through writing and the SQ3R reading/learning system.

11

Textbook Underlining and Marking

> **Use this chapter to:**
> 1. *Learn to underline textbooks effectively.*
> 2. *Develop a system of textbook marking.*

As you have already discovered, most college courses have lengthy and time-consuming reading assignments. Just completing reading assignments is a big job. Have you begun to wonder how you will ever go back over all those textbook chapters when it is time for an exam?

THE PROBLEM OF TEXTBOOK REVIEW

Let's suppose that it takes you at least four hours to read carefully a forty-page chapter for one of your courses. Assume that your text has ten chapters of approximately forty pages each. It would take a total of forty hours, then, to read completely through the text once. Suppose that your instructor is giving a final exam that will cover the entire text. If the only thing you did to prepare for the final was to reread the whole text, it would take close to another forty hours to study for the exam; but one additional reading is no guarantee that you will pass the exam.

There is a technique you could have used to review and study the chapters of your text adequately at exam time. You could have underlined and marked important ideas and facts as you were first reading the chapters. Then, when you were ready to review, you would have had to read and study only what you marked. If you had marked or underlined 15 to 20 percent of the chapter material, you would have cut down your rereading time by 80 to 85 percent, or thirty-two hours! Of course, to prepare effectively for the exam, it would have been necessary to review in other ways besides rereading, but you would have had time left in which to use these other ways.

HOW TO UNDERLINE TEXTBOOKS

To learn how to underline textbooks effectively, start with the following guidelines:

1. Read first; then underline. As you are reading to develop skill in underlining, it is better, at first, to read a paragraph or section first, and then go back and underline what is important to remember and review. Later, when you've had more practice underlining, you may be able to underline while you read.
2. Read the boldface headings. Headings are labels, or overall topics, for what is contained in that section. Use the headings to form questions that you expect to be answered in the section.
3. After you have read the section, go back and underline the parts that answer your questions. These will be parts of sentences that express the main ideas, or most important thoughts, in the section. In reading and underlining the following section, you could form questions like those suggested and then underline as shown:

Questions to ask: What is the propositional form?
What is the narrative form?

PROPOSITIONAL VS. NARRATIVE FORM

Finally, speaking styles can differ greatly in another important way: Some styles are highly *propositional*—that is, they are dominated by an argumentative method of composition; while other styles are highly *narrative*—that is, they are dominated by storytelling. When using a propositional form of speaking, the speaker offers a series of claims or assertions and supports each one with evidence the audience should consider important. When using a narrative form, the speaker offers a story which contains a message or "moral" the audience should consider compelling.

–Ehninger, *Principles and Types of Speech Communication,* p. 230

4. As you identify and underline main ideas, look for important facts that explain or support the main idea and underline them too.
5. When underlining main ideas and details, do not underline complete sentences. Underline only enough so that you can see what is important and so that your underlining makes sense when you reread. Notice how only key words and phrases are underlined in the following:

DEFINING FROM ORIGINAL SOURCES

Sometimes you can reinforce a series of feelings or attitudes you wish an audience to have about a concept by telling them where the word came from: "*Sincere* comes from two Latin words: *sine,* meaning 'without,' and *ceres,* meaning 'wax.' In early Rome, a superior statue was one in which the artisan did not have to cover his mistake by putting wax into flaws. That statue was said to be *sine ceres*—'without wax.' Today, the term *a sincere person* carries some of that same meaning. . . ." This is called an *etymological definition* when you trace a word's meaning back into its original language. It's termed a *genetic definition* when you explain where the idea rather than the word comes from. You could, for instance, explain the American concept of freedom of speech by looking at important discussions of that idea in eighteenth-century England, and then showing how the American doctrine took its shape from our ancestors' British experiences. <u>Defining from original sources</u>, either of the word or of the idea, <u>gives</u> an <u>audience</u> a <u>sense of continuity</u> and at times <u>explains certain nuances of meaning</u> we cannot explain any other way.

–Ehninger, *Principles and Types of Speech Communication*, p. 232

ASPECTS OF EFFECTIVE UNDERLINING

For your underlining to be effective and useful to you as you study and review, it must follow four specific guidelines: (1) the right amount of information must be underlined; (2) the underlining must be regular and consistent; (3) it must be accurate; and (4) it must clearly reflect the content of the passage. Suggestions for and examples of each of these guidelines are given in the following paragraphs.

Underline the Right Amount

Students frequently make the mistake of underlining either too much or too little. If you underline too much, the passages you have marked will take you too long to reread when studying. If you underline too little, you won't be able to get any meaning from your underlining as you review it. To get an idea of each mistake, study the passages below.

Too Much Underlining. <u>The Shah attempted rapid modernization of his country</u> [Iran]. <u>He sent thousands of young Iranians abroad for an education, subsidized new industries</u>, and introduced some <u>land reforms</u>. He <u>purchased</u> huge quantities of <u>arms</u>. Some $14 billion worth was bought from the United States alone. This crash <u>program of modernization</u>, however, <u>was his undoing</u>. It caused many <u>areas of friction and discontent</u>. <u>Inflation rose</u> rapidly to <u>50 percent</u> annually. Bad planning placed too much emphasis on industrry and the cities, <u>neglecting agriculture and the villages</u>. Thousands of peasants flocked to the cities, especially Teheran, where <u>areas of slums and blight sprang up</u>. But worst of all, the <u>rapid modernization threatened the integrity of the Iranian cultural fabric</u>.

–Wallbank et al., *Civilization Past and Present*, p. 953

Too Little Underlining. The <u>Shah attempted rapid modernization</u> of his country [Iran]. He sent thousands of young Iranians abroad for an education, subsidized new industries, and introduced some land reforms. He purchased huge quantities of arms. Some $14 billion worth was bought from the United States alone. This crash <u>program of modernization</u>, however, <u>was his undoing</u>. It caused many areas of friction and discontent. <u>Inflation</u> rose rapidly to <u>50 percent</u> annually. Bad planning placed too much emphasis on industry and the cities, neglecting agriuclture and the villages. Thousands of peasants flocked to the cities, especially Teheran, where areas of slums and blight sprang up. But worst of all, the rapid <u>modernization threatened</u> the integrity of the <u>Iranian cultural fabric</u>.

Effective Underlining.   The <u>Shah</u> attempted <u>rapid moderniza-tion</u> of his countgry [<u>Iran</u>]. He sent thousands of young Iranians abroad for an education, subsidized new industries, and intro-duced some land reforms. He purchased huge quantities of arms. Some $14 billion worth was bought from the United States alone. This <u>crash program of modernization</u>, however, <u>was his undoing</u>. It caused many areas of friction and discontent. <u>Inflation rose rapidly</u> to <u>50 percent</u> annually. Bad planning placed too much emphasis on industry and the cities, neglecting agriculture and the villages. Thousands of <u>peasants flocked</u> to the <u>cities</u>, espe-cially Teheran, where areas of <u>slums and blight sprang up</u>. But worst of all, the rapid modernization <u>threatened</u> the integrity of the <u>Iranian cultural fabric</u>.

Almost all of the first passage is underlined. To underline nearly all the passage is as ineffective as not underlining at all because it does not sort out or distinguish important from unimportant information. In the second pas-sage, only the main point of the paragraph is underlined, but very sketchily— not enough detail is included. The underlining in the third passage is effective; it identifies the main idea of the paragraph and includes sufficient detail to make the main idea clear and understandable.

As a rule of thumb, try to underline no more than one-quarter to one-third of each page. This figure will vary, of course, depending on the type of material you are reading. Here is another example of effective underlining. Notice that approximately one-third of each paragraph is underlined.

"HIGH-TECH" CRIME: THE CRIMINAL AND THE COMPUTER

<u>Technological change advances criminal opportunities</u> as well as noncriminal ones. Nowhere is this more in evidence than in the realm of electronics. We live in an era of high technology, one in which electronic brains and silicon chips rule much of the behavior of people and machines. The more computers we have and the more things we can get them to do, the more opportuni-ties there are for computer crime. Estimates of the <u>annual losses</u> from <u>computer-related crimes</u> go as high as <u>$5 billion</u>, and in all likelihood the figure will go much higher (Kolata, 1982).

The <u>range of computer crimes</u> is <u>vast</u> and <u>growing</u>. . . . <u>Em-bezzlement</u>, industrial <u>espionage</u>, <u>theft of services</u> (for example, using a computer that belongs to someone else for one's private business), <u>invasion of privacy</u>, <u>copyright</u> violations, <u>destruction of information</u> or programs, <u>falsification of data</u>, and a host of fraud-ulent transactions are just a few of the computer-related abuses that have come to light.

The <u>potential for computer crime</u> is <u>staggering</u>, and that fact is now recognized in legislative and enforcement circles. But most of the <u>preventive work</u> so far initiated is <u>privately organized</u> and <u>paid for</u>. Hundreds of companies have sprung up in recent years peddling advice and technology to counteract the new breed of high-tech criminal.

—Barlow, *Introduction to Criminology*, p. 252

Develop a Regular and Consistent System of Underlining

As you develop your textbook underlining skills, you should focus on this second guideline: Develop a system for deciding what type of information you will underline and how you will mark it. First, decide what type of information you want to mark. Before marking anything, decide whether you will mark only main ideas or whether you will mark main ideas and details. You should also decide whether you will underline or mark definitions of new terminology and, if so, how will you distinguish them from other information marked in the paragraph. Second, it is important to use whatever system and type of underlining you decide on consistently so that you will know what your underlining means when you review it. If you sometimes mark details and main ideas and other times underline only main ideas, you will find that, at review time, you are unsure of what passages are marked in what way, and you will be forced to reread a great deal of material.

You may decide to develop a system for separating main ideas from details, major points from supporting information. When you review underlining done this way, you will immediately know what is the most important point of the paragraph or section, and you will not get bogged down in the details—unless you need to. One such system uses double underlining for main points and single underlining for details. Another system might be to use asterisks to distinguish the main points. A third choice might be to use two colors of ink to distinguish main ideas and details.

Each of the following paragraphs has been underlined using one of the suggested systems. You will notice that the paragraphs vary in the type of information marked in each.

VERSION 1

MODELING VIOLENCE

✳ Many scholars believe that aggression is learned, just like any other behavior. One prominent theory is that we learn it by imitation or modeling the behavior of people we "look up to." Albert Bandura (1973) showed that the behavior of aggressive models is readily imitated by experimental subjects, whether observed in the flesh or via film. In one well-known experiment, Bandura played a film of a woman sitting on, beating, kicking, and hacking an inflatable doll. After witnessing the film, nursery school children, when placed in a room with a similar doll, duplicated the women's behavior and also engaged in other aggressive acts.

–Barlow, *Criminology,* p. 140

VERSION 2

MODELING VIOLENCE

Many scholars believe that aggression is learned, just like any other behavior. One prominent theory is that we learn it by imitation or modeling the behavior of people we "look up to." Albert Bandura (1973) showed that the behavior of aggressive models is readily imitated by experimental subjects, whether observed in the flesh or via film. In one well-known experiment, Bandura played a film of a woman sitting on, beating, kicking, and hacking an inflatable <u>doll</u>. After witnessing the film, nursery <u>school children</u>, when placed in a room with a similar doll, <u>duplicated the woman's behavior</u> and also engaged in other aggressive acts.

VERSION 3

MODELING VIOLENCE

Many scholars believe that <u>aggression is learned</u>, just like any other behavior. One <u>prominent theory</u> is that we <u>learn it by imitation or modeling</u> the <u>behavior</u> of <u>people</u> we "<u>look up to.</u>" Albert Bandura (1973) showed that the behavior of aggressive models is readily imitated by experimental subjects, whether observed in the flesh or via film. In one <u>well-known experiment</u>, Bandura played a film of a <u>woman</u> sitting on, <u>beating, kicking,</u> and hacking an inflatable <u>doll</u>. After witnessing the film, nursery school <u>children</u>, when placed in a room with a similar doll, <u>duplicated the woman's behavior</u> and also engaged in other aggressive acts.

EXERCISE 1 _____

Directions: *Read the following passage. Then evaluate the effectiveness of the underlining, making suggestions for improvement.*

SCARCITY OF HUMAN FOSSILS

Humans are a maddeningly <u>poor source of fossils.</u> In 1956, the paleontologist <u>G. H. R. von Koenigswald</u> calculated that if all the then-<u>known fragments of human beings</u> older than the Neandertal people were gathered together they could be comfortably <u>displayed on a medium-sized table.</u> Although many more fossils of early hominids have been found since then, discoveries are still rare.

Why are human fossils so scarce? <u>Why can one go to good fossil sites almost anywhere in the world and find millions of shell remains</u> or thousands of bones of extinct reptiles and mammals, while peoples earlier than Neandertal are known from only a handful of sites at which investigators, working through tons of deposits, pile up other finds by the bushel basket before recovering a single human tooth?

There are many reasons. First, the <u>commonness of marine fossils</u> is a direct reflection of the <u>abundance of these creatures</u> when they were alive. It also reflects the tremendous span of time during which they abounded. Many of them swarmed through the waters of the earth for hundreds of millions of years. When they died, they sank and were covered by sediments. <u>Their way of life</u>—their life in the water—<u>preserved them</u>, as did their extremely durable shells, the only parts of them that now remain. <u>Humans,</u> by contrast, have never been as numerous as oysters and clams. They <u>existed in small numbers,</u> reproduced slowly and in small numbers, and lived a relatively long time. They were more intelligent than, for example, dinosaurs and were perhaps less apt to get mired in bogs, marshes, or quicksands. Most improtant, their way of life was different. They were <u>not sea creatures</u> or riverside browsers but <u>lively, wide-ranging food-gatherers and hunters.</u> They often lived and died in the open, where their bones could be gnawed by scavengers and bleached and decomposed in the sun and rain. In hot climates, particularly in tropical forests and woodlands, the soil is likely to be markedly acid. Bones dissolve in such soils, and early humans who lived and died in such an environment would have had a very poor chance of leaving remains that would last until today. Finally, <u>human ancestors</u> have been on <u>earth only a few million years.</u> There simply has not been as much time for them to scatter their bones about as there has been for some of the more ancient species of animals.

–Campbell, *Humankind Emerging,* pp. 22–23

EXERCISE 2 _____

Directions: *Read each paragraph or passage and then underline the* main idea *and* important details *in each. You may want to try various systems of underlining as you work through this exercise.*

1. **GENERAL BUYING POWER INDEXES**

   It is possible to estimate the market potential in specific regions for many products by using indexes of relative buying power. The index may be either a *single-* or *multiple-factor* index. For example, a single-factor index might use summary Internal Revenue Service income data, by state, as a measure of market potential. If total American market potential for a product is estimated to be $100 million, and all potential buyers have incomes over $50,000, and California has 20 percent of all people with incomes above $50,000, then the estimated potential in California would be $20 million ($100 million $\times$ .2).

   In industrial markets, a widely accepted single-factor index is the *Sales & Marketing Management Survey of Industrial Purchasing Power.* This annual index uses data on the value of shipments of industrial goods. The index is organized according to categories of the Standard Industrial Classification industry groups and uses geographic area as its measure of potential. For example, it would report the value of paper products shipped into the New England area.

   It is usually more accurate to use *multiple factors* to construct an index. One very well-known consumer market index is the *Sales & Marketing Management Survey of Buying Power.* It is constructed by weighting population by two, effective buying income by five, and total retail sales by three. Data in this index are provided at the state, county, and city level. For example, if Texas is rated as having 10 percent of buying power, then 10 percent of the total American market potential would be allocated to Texas.

   –Kinnear and Bernhardt, *Principles of Marketing,* p. 223

2. **TYPES OF INTERVIEW QUESTIONS**

   Because the communicative basis of interviews is made up of questions and answers, a skilled interviewer must be practiced in phrasing and organizing useful questions. Six types of questions are often asked. *Primary questions* introduce some topic or area of inquiry, while *follow-up questions* probe more deeply or ask for elaboration or clarification. Thus, if you are interviewing a local newspaper editor for a feature article, you might begin with "What background did you have before becoming editor?" and follow up with "Would you elaborate on your experience as a copy editor—what did you do in that position?" You also will develop *direct questions* ("How long have you been the editor?") and *indirect questions* ("What is your goal for the paper five years from now?"). Direct questions allow you to gather information quickly, while indirect probes let you see interviewees "thinking on their feet," structuring materials and responses and exploring their own minds. Interviewers also employ both *open* and *closed* questions. A closed question specifies the direction of the response—"Do your editorials serve to create public concern about local issues?" An open question allows the interviewee to control the categories of response—"How do you perceive your role in the community?" Closed questions require little effort from the interviewee and are easy to "code" or record; open questions allow interviewers to observe the interviewee's habits, to let them feel in control of the interaction. Of course, these various types of questions overlap: You can use a direct or indirect question as your primary question; a closed question can be direct ("Do you function most as editor, reporter, or lay-out specialist?") or indirect ("Of the various jobs you perform—editor, reporter, lay-out specialist—which do you enjoy the most?"). Overall, primary, direct, and closed questions tend to produce a lot of "hard" information quickly; follow-up, indirect, and open questions produce more thought and interpretation—grounds for understanding and analyzing interviewees and their motivations, capacities, and expectations. As you plan interviews, learn to blend questions of all six types—to build an *interview schedule*.

An interview schedule is your effort to organize specific questions so as to elicit systematically the materials and opinions you are seeking. Like any other organizational pattern, an interview schedule should have a rationale, one which *(1)* permits you to acquire systematic information or opinion, and (2) seems reasonable to the interviewee, avoiding confusing detours and repetitions. Interview schedules normally are built in one of two forms: the *traditional schedule* and the *branching schedule*.

–Ehninger, *Principles and Types of Speech Communication*, pp. 142–143

3. **ANALYZING THE PROBLEM OF UNEMPLOYMENT**

The Employment Act of 1946 set forth the goal of maintaining maximum employment. The law made it the clear responsibility of the federal government to establish policies for achieving this goal.

An effective policy for full employment depends first on correct analysis of the sources of unemployment. Identifying these sources will enable policymakers to design effective programs to correct each type. Economists have classified unemployment into three categories, depending on the cause: frictional, cyclical, and structural.

Frictional Unemployment.   Economists define normal full employment as the condition that exists when approximately 97 to 98 percent of the civilian labor force is employed. The remaining 2 or 3 percent are unemployed because of *frictional unemployment*—unemployment caused by difficulties in the movement of workers from job to job or among workers entering the labor force for the first time.

Frictional unemployment is necessary and even desirable in a dynamic economy. It is a reflection of the healthy growth or decline of different sectors of the economy. Markets and production techniques are constantly changing to reflect changes in consumer demand. Workers must move out of declining industries and into expanding industries. If there were no frictional unemployment, expanding industries would have to bid up the wages of employed workers, aggravating tendencies toward inflation.

In recent years, frictional unemployment has come to constitute a larger portion of total employment. This is primarily because of the growing numbers of married women and teenagers in the job market, with typically higher rates of entry and re-entry into the labor force than adult male workers.

Frictional unemployment is, by definition, temporary. Its effects may be relieved by better job information and aids to worker mobility. For example, workers can be provided job counseling, or they can be paid grants to finance a move to a new location where jobs are more plentiful.

Cyclical Unemployment. The term "mass unemployment" brings to mind the more awesome evil of *cyclical unemployment*—unemployment associated with cycles of economic activity. The Great Depression provides the best example of this type of unemployment. During the Great Depression, the unemployment rate reached as high as 25 percent of the labor force.

Typically, economic activity grows in spurts. Periods of great optimism and growth are followed by slower growth or decline. Once homes are equipped with video recorders, microwave ovens, and personal computers, demand for consumer goods diminishes. Retailers cut back on inventories and cancel orders to wholesalers. The whole economic system seems to pause before the next round of innovations brings on a new outpouring of gadgets, and the cycle begins again.

Cyclical swings in employment are most severe in industries producing durable goods. The purchase of an auto, refrigerator, or sewing machine can be postponed if family heads are worried about their jobs. Cyclical swings are less severe in the production of nondurable goods and services. Purchases of food, clothing, and health services, for instance, cannot generally be postponed.

When consumer demand declines, blue-collar production workers are more likely to suffer unemployment than professional or supervisory workers. One reason is the specialized functions of the latter workers, which the firm cannot afford to lose to other firms. Another is the fact that many professional workers are covered by contracts that protect their jobs.

Federal economic policy to stimulate consumer demand was developed following the Depression as a means of controlling cyclical unemployment. Expansionary fiscal and monetary policies make cyclical unemployment less a threat to our economic system today than in former years.

Structural Unemployment. More threatening to our prosperity and social health is the growing problem of structural unemployment. *Structural unemployment* is caused by an imbalance between the structure of the labor force, on the one hand, and the requirements of modern industry, on the other. When available labor skills fail to correspond to the needs of industry, there is unemployment. Substantial unemployment may persist even though there are job vacancies. Structural unemployment is worsened by the entry of untrained workers (such as teenagers) into the labor force.

The greatest needs in business today are for skilled workers and for workers in the growing service sector. For example, there are extreme shortages of workers in machine trades, engineering, nursing, transport, and finance. Federal and state programs to train workers in new skills, better job information and counseling, and private on-the-job training can help relieve structural unemployment.

–McCarty, *Dollars and Sense: An Introduction to Economics,* pp. 213–214

Underline Accurately

A third guideline for marking textbooks is to be sure that the information you underline accurately conveys the thought of the paragraph or passage. In a rush, students often overlook the second half of the main idea expressed in a paragraph, miss a crucial qualifying statement, or mistake an example of contrasting idea for the main idea. Read the paragraph in the following example and evaluate the accuracy of the underlining.

It has long been established that the American legal court system is an open and fair system. Those suspected to be guilty of a criminal offense are given a jury trial in which a group of impartially selected citizens are asked to determine, based upon evidence presented, the guilt or innocence of the person on trial. In actuality, however, this system of jury trial is fair to everyone except the jurors involved. Citizens are expected and, in many instances, required to sit on a jury. They have little or no choice as to the time, place, or any other circumstances surrounding their participation. Additionally, they are expected to leave their job and accept jury duty pay for each day spent in court in place of their regular on-the-job salary. The jury must remain on duty until the case is decided.

In the preceding paragraph, the underlining indicates the main idea of the paragraph: The legal system that operates in American courts is open and fair. The paragraph starts out by saying that the legal system has long been established as fair but then goes on to say (in the third sentence) that the system is actually unfair to one particular group—the jury. In this case, the student who did the underlining missed the real main statement of the paragraph by mistaking the introductory contrasting statement with the main idea.

Make Your Underlining Understandable for Review

As you underline, keep the fourth guideline in mind: Be certain that your underlining clearly reflects the content of the passage so that you will be able to reread and review it easily. Try to underline enough information in each passage so that the passage reads smoothly when you review it.

Read these two versions of underlining of the same passage. Which underlining is easier to reread?

VERSION 1

Capital may be thought of as manufactured resources. Capital includes the tools and equipment that strengthen, extend, or replace human hands in the production of goods and services: hammers, sewing machines, turbines, bookkeeping machines, and components of finished goods. Capital resources permit "roundabout" production: through capital, goods are produced indirectly by a kind of tool, rather than directly by physical labor. To construct a capital resource requires that we postpone production of consumer goods today so that we may produce more in the future. (Economists do not think of money as capital, since money by itself cannot produce anything at all. However, money is a convenient means of exchanging resources used in production.)

VERSION 2

   Capital may be thought of as manufactured resources. Capital includes the tools and equipment that strengthen, extend, or replace human hands in the production of goods and services: hammers, sewing machines, turbines, bookkeeping machines, and components of finished goods. Capital resources permit "roundabout" production: through capital, goods are produced indirectly by a kind of tool, rather than directly by physical labor. To construct a capital resource requires that we postpone production of consumer goods today so that we may produce more in the future. (Economists do not think of money as capital, since money by itself cannot produce anything at all. However, money is a convenient means of exchanging resources used in production.)

   –McCarty, *Dollars and Sense,* pp. 213–214

   A good way to check to see if your underlining is understandable for review is to reread only your underlining. If parts are unclear right after you read it, you can be sure it will be more confusing when you reread it a week or a month later. Be sure to fix ineffectual underlining in one paragraph before you continue to the next paragraph. You may find it useful, at first, to use a pencil for underlining. Then, when the underlining in a passage needs revising, you can accomplish this easily by erasing.

TESTING YOUR UNDERLINING

   As you are learning underlining techniques, it is important to check to be certain that your underlining is effective and will be useful for review purposes. To test the effectiveness of your underlining, take any passage that you have underlined in Exercise 2 and reread only the underlining. Then ask yourself the following questions:

1. Have I underlined the right amount or do I have too much or too little information underlined?
2. Have I used a regular and consistent system for underlining?
3. Does my underlining accurately reflect the meaning of the passage?
4. As I reread my underlining, is it easy to follow the train of thought or does the passage seem like a list of unconnected words?

Directions: *Turn to the section of psychology sample chapter in Appendix A of this text titled "The Social Side of Health and Well-Being" (pages 447– 451). Now read this section and underline the main ideas and important details. When you have finished, test your underlining. Use the four preceding questions for testing your underlining. Make any changes that will make your underlining more consistent, accurate, or understandable.*

EXERCISE 4 _____

Directions: *Choose a three- to four-page passage from one of your text-books. Read the selection and underline main ideas, the important details, and key terms that are introduced. When you have finished, test your underlining using the four questions above, and make any changes that will improve your underlining.*

MARKING A TEXTBOOK

As you were underlining paragraphs and passages in the earlier part of this chapter, you may have realized that underlining alone is not sufficient, in many cases, to separate main ideas from details and both of these from new terminology. You may have seen that underlining does not easily show the relative importance of ideas or indicate the relationship of facts and ideas. Therefore, it is often necessary to mark, as well as underline, selections that you are reading. Suggestions for marking are shown in Table 11-1.

Two versions of the same paragraph, excerpted from *Conceptual Human Physiology* by Davis, Holtz, and Davis, follow. The first version contains only underlining, while in the second both underlining and marking are used. Which version more easily conveys the meaning of the passage?

VERSION 1

EPILEPSY

Epilepsy is a disorder that affects the excitable cells, or neurons, of the nervous system; neurons of the brain, usually those of the cerebral cortex, become hyperactive, or hyperexcitable. This neuronal hyperactivity leads to the development of *seizures (convulsions)* that tend to recur on a chronic basis. Seizures include brief episodes of uncontrollable motor, sensory, or psychic disturbances that interrupt the individual's normal activities.

Epilepsy may be idiopathic (essential), in which no brain pathology can be identified, or it may be symptomatic, or secondary, to a previous brain disease or injury. Conditions that may produce epilepsy are head injuries, including birth injuries; brain tumors; inflammatory conditions of the brain; hypoglycemia, or low blood sugar; toxic conditions, such as uric acid buildup or alcohol withdrawal; or lack of oxygen to the brain cells. The development of epilepsy seems to depend on a combination of genetic and environmental factors, in which persons with a genetic predisposition

TABLE 11-1   Textbook Marking

Type of Marking	Example
Circling unknown words	*def* . . . redressing the apparent (asymmetry) of their relationship . . .
Marking definitions	*def* To say that the balance of power favors one party over another is to introduce a disequilibrium.
Marking examples	*ex* . . . concessions may include negative sanctions, trade agreements . . .
Numbering lists of ideas, causes, reasons, or events	. . . components of power include ①self-image, ②population, ③natural resources, and ④geography
Placing asterisks next to important passages	* Power comes from three primary sources . . .
Putting question marks next to confusing passages	? → . . . war prevention occurs through institutionalization of mediation . . .
Making notes to yourself	*check def in soc text* . . . power is the ability of an actor on the international stage to . . .
Marking possible test items	T There are several key features in the relationship . . .
Drawing arrows to show relationships	. . . natural resources . . . control of industrial manufacture capacity
Writing comments, noting disagreements and similarities	*Can terrorism be prevented through similar balance?* . . . war prevention through balance of power is . . .
Marking summary statements	*sum* . . . the greater the degree of conflict, the more intricate will be . . .

have greater chances of developing epilepsy when environmental conditions favor it.

VERSION 2

EPILEPSY

def   (Epilepsy) is a <u>disorder</u> that affects the excitable cells, or neurons, of the <u>nervous system</u>; neurons of the brain, usually
those of the cerebral cortex, become <u>hyperactive</u>, or hyperex-
Symptoms   citable. This neuronal hyperactivity leads to the development
of *seizures* (convulsions) that tend to recur on a <u>chronic basis</u>.

Seizures include brief episodes of uncontrollable motor, sensory, or psychic disturbances that interrupt the individual's normal activities. ①

2 types

Epilepsy may be idiopathic (essential), in which no brain pathology can be identified, or it may be symptomatic, or secondary, to a previous brain disease or injury. Conditions that

Causes

may produce epilepsy are head injuries, including birth injuries; brain tumors; inflammatory conditions of the brain; hypoglycemia, or low blood sugar; toxic conditions, such as uric acid buildup or alcohol withdrawal; or lack of oxygen to the brain cells. The development of epilepsy seems to depend on a combination of genetic and environmental factors, in which persons with a genetic predisposition have greater chances of developing epilepsy when environmental conditions favor it.

As you can see, in Version 2 the two types of epilepsy are easy to identify. Numbering the types makes them immediately noticeable and distinguishes them from the remainder of the passage.

Summary Words

Writing summary words or phrases in the margin is one of the most valuable types of textbook marking. It involves pulling together ideas and summarizing them in your own words. This summarizing process forces you to think and evaluate as you read and makes remembering easier. Writing summary phrases is also a good test of your understanding. If you cannot state the main idea of a section in your own words, you probably do not understand it clearly. This realization can serve as an early warning signal that you may not be able to handle a test question on that section.

To illustrate effective marking of summary phrases, the following sample passage has been included. First, read through the passage. Then look at the marginal summary clues.

DATA

Computers process data. A computer gets data from input devices and sends data to output devices. It stores data in internal storage and in auxiliary storage. It performs computations and makes logical decisions using data. The instructions in a program tell the computer how to process the data.

Data must be arranged or organized in a way that makes it easier to process. In this subsection we explain the main concepts of data organization. We also discuss data input and output.

DATA ORGANIZATION

Data is composed of symbols or *characters*. There are three basic types of characters: *numeric characters* or *digits* (0, 1, . . . , 9), *alphabetic characters* or *letters* (A, B, . . . , Z), and *special characters* (comma, decimal point, equal sign, and so forth). A *blank* or *space* is considered a special character; it is often very important in computer data processing.

3 types of characters

Although a single character can represent data, more often groups of characters convey information. A related group of characters, representing some unit of information, is called a *field*. For example, a person's name is a field; it is a group of characters that conveys specific information. A social security number is also a field. Similarly, a person's address, pay rate, age, and marital status are fields. A field usually contains several characters but can consist of a single character (such as a code field for marital status).

field

If a field contains only numeric characters, it is called a *numeric field* and we say that it contains *numeric data*. For example, a person's pay rate is a numeric field. A field that can contain any type of characters is called an *alphanumeric field;* that is, it contains *alphanumeric data*. For example, a street address (such as 123 MAIN ST.) consists of digits (123), letters (MAIN ST), and special characters (blank spaces and a period). Hence it is alphanumeric data and forms an alphanumeric field. Sometimes we refer to a field that contains all numbers as alphanumeric. For example, a social security number, which consists of nine digits, is a numeric field; but it may also be called an alphanumeric field. *Alphanumeric* means that the field can contain *any type of characters; numeric* means that the field can contain *only numeric characters.*

numeric data

alphanumeric data

Fields are grouped together to provide information about a single entity such as a person or event. Such a related group of fields is called a *record*. For example, all of the fields containing information about a single employee (such as employee name, social security number, address, pay rate, and so on) form an employee information record.

record

Finally, all of the records that are used together for one purpose are called a *file*. For example, all of the employee information records for a business make up the employee information file. The file consists of as many records as there are employees in the business.

file

To summarize, data is composed of numeric, alphabetic, and special characters. A group of related characters is called a field. A field can be numeric or alphanumeric. A record is a group of related fields and a file is a group of related records.

–Nickerson, *Fundamentals of Structured COBOL*, pp. 8–9

Summary notes are most effectively used in passages that contain long and complicated ideas. In these cases it is simpler to write a summary phrase in the margin than to underline a long or complicated statement of the main idea and supporting details.

To write a summary clue, try to think of a word or phrase that accurately states in brief form a particular idea presented in the passage. Summary words should "trigger" your memory of the content of the passage.

EXERCISE 5 _____

Directions: *Read the following textbook selection. Then mark as well as underline important information contained in the passage.*

BASIS OF SOCIAL ORGANIZATION

Although monkeys and apes differ from each other in important ways, they share many characteristics. Of these, certainly the most interesting is that they are all social species (except perhaps the orangutan) and their societies are highly organized. We first need to ask ourselves several questions. What are the advantages of social life? Why are so many mammal and bird species social and why have the Hominoidea developed this characteristic to such lengths? Four kinds of advantage are usually proposed by zoologists:

1. Several pairs of eyes are better than one in the detection of predators and in their avoidance. Defense by a group is also far more effective. Three or four male baboons constitute an impressive display and can frighten any predator, even a lion. A single baboon is a dead baboon.
2. Food finding and food exploitation and handling, as well as defense (of a carcass, for example) are more efficient at times when food is in fairly ample supply. We shall see that in some monkeys social groups subdivide when food is sparse and widely scattered.
3. Reproductive advantages accrue from social groups because regular access to the opposite sex is ensured.
4. Social groups permit extensive socialization with peers and elders and the opportunity for learning from them. Among animals such as the higher primates, this is a factor of the greatest importance.

These factors are probably the most important in bringing about the selection of social life in animals such as primates. Although considerable variation may occur within a species, especially under different environmental conditions, only a few Old World primate species (including the gibbons and siamang, a large gibbon) normally live in groups consisting only of an adult male, female, and young. The remaining seventy-odd species of Old World primates all live in social groups that number as high as five hundred individuals but most commonly number between ten and fifty.

But how are these societies organized? Far from being a structureless collection of rushing, squalling animals, primate societies are remarkably stable and usually serene and quiet. Order is maintained in primate societies through a complex interrelationship of several factors. One factor is the animals' prolonged period of dependence: infant apes and monkeys, like human infants, are far from self-sufficient, and maintain a close relationship with their mothers longer than most other animals.

–Campbell, *Humankind Emerging*, pp. 131–132

IS UNDERLINING AN EFFECTIVE MEANS OF PREPARATION FOR STUDY?

In a classic study conducted by Willmore,* a group of college students were each taught four study techniques: underlining, outlining, SQ3R (discussed in Chapter 13), and reading. The students then applied each of the four techniques to four different chapters in a college text. Tests were given

* D. J. Willmore, "A Comparison of Four Methods of Studying a College Textbook." Ph.D. diss., University of Minnesota, 1966.

on each chapter. Students scored significantly higher on the test when they used underlining as a study technique than when using any of the other three methods.

WHY UNDERLINING AND MARKING WORK

Underlining and marking are effective ways to prepare for study for several very important reasons. First, the process of underlining forces you to sift through what you have read to identify important information. This sifting or sorting helps you keep your mind on what you are doing. Second, underlining and marking keep you physically active while you are reading. The physical activity helps to direct or focus your concentration on what you are reading. Third, when you are underlining you are forced to weigh and evaluate what you read. In other words, you must think about and react to what you are reading in order to decide whether to underline it. Fourth, underlining helps you to see the organization of facts and ideas as well as their connections and relationships to one another because you are forced to look for these things in order to mark and underline effectively. Finally, underlining demonstrates to you whether you have understood a passage you have just read. If you have difficulty underlining, or your underlining is not helpful or meaningful after you have finished reading, you will know that you did not understand the passage.

EXERCISE 6 ————————————————

Directions: *Turn to the section of the psychology sample textbook chapter, pp. 447–451, that you underlined to complete Exercise 3. Review the section and add marking and summary words that would make the section easier to study and review.*

EXERCISE 7 ————————————————

Directions: *Select a three- to four-page selection from one of your textbooks. Underline and mark main ideas, important details, and key terms. Include summary words, if possible.*

SUMMARY

Reading textbook chapters is a long and time-consuming process. As you read, you encounter a considerable amount of information that you know you will need to study and review for your next exam or quiz. To be able to locate this information quickly when you study, it is necessary to underline and mark important information as you read. Without a system of underlining and marking, it would be necessary to reread an entire chapter in order to review it effectively. This chapter offers step-by-step instructions for underlining and marking textbooks.

After offering some general suggestions to follow in underlining, four specific guidelines for effective underlining are given: (1) underline the right amount, (2) develop a regular and consistent system of underlining, (3) underline accurately, and (4) make your underlining understandable for review. A system for marking as well as underlining is discussed. Marking involves the use of marginal notes, summary words, and symbols that can make a passage easier to review.

12

Methods of Organizing Information

Use this chapter to:

1. *Learn how to organization information for easier learning.*

2. *Learn how to condense information and pull ideas together.*

3. *Learn how to develop visual study aids.*

Do you feel overwhelmed by the volume of facts, dates, events, ideas, definitions, formulas, principles, and theories you must learn in each course? Do you wonder if you will be able to learn all of them?

The key to learning large amounts of information is to organize and condense it. Basically, this involves looking for patterns, differences, similarities, or shared characteristics and then grouping, rearranging, and reducing the information into manageable pieces. To do this, you will have to think about the information and look for the relationships and connections. This in itself is a form of review and rehearsal that will facilitate learning. Three methods of organizing information—outlining, summarizing, and using visual and organizational charts and diagrams—will be discussed in this chapter. As you learn these methods, you will see that they are based on many of the learning principles outlined in Chapter 3, especially meaningfulness and categorization. You will also see that the methods are unique; each uses a different format and varies in the way information is treated. The method you select for a particular course will depend on the type of material, the type of learning required, and the characteristics of your learning style.

The first step in using any of these methods is to sort the information and to identify what is to be learned. If you have underlined and marked your reading assignments and have taken notes on important ideas in class lectures, you have completed this first step.

ORGANIZING BY OUTLINING

Outlining is an effective way of organizing the relationship among ideas. From past experiences, many students think of an outline as an exact, detailed, organized listing of all information in a passage; they consider outlining as routine copying of information from page to page and, therefore, avoid doing it.

Actually, an outline should *not* be a recopying of ideas. Think of it, instead, as a means of pulling together important information and recording it to show how ideas interconnect. It is a form of note-taking that provides a visual picture of the structure of ideas within a textbook chapter.

Outlining has many advantages, one being that you learn while you write it. Outlining forces you to think about the material you read and to sort out the important ideas from those that are less important. Because it requires you to express ideas in your own words and to group them together, you are able to test whether you have understood what you read. Finally, thinking about, sorting, and expressing ideas in your own words is a form of repetition, or rehearsal, and helps you to remember the material.

How to Develop an Outline

To be effective, an outline must show (1) the relative importance of ideas, and (2) the relationship between ideas. The easiest way to achieve this is to use the following format:

I. Major topic
   A. First major idea
      1. First important detail
      2. Second important detail
   B. Second major idea
      1. First important detail
         a. Minor detail or example
      2. Second important detail
II. Second major topic
   A. First major idea

Notice that the more important ideas are closer to the left margin, while less important details are indented toward the middle of the page. A quick glance at an outline indicates what is most important, and how ideas support or explain one another.

Here are a few suggestions for developing an effective outline:

1. Don't get caught up in the numbering and lettering system. Instead, concentrate on showing the relative importance of ideas. How you number or letter an idea is not as important as showing what other ideas it supports or explains. Don't be concerned if some items don't fit exactly into outline format.
2. Be brief; use words and phrases, never complete sentences. Abbreviate words and phrases where possible.
3. Use your own words rather than "lifting" most of the material from the text. It is acceptable to use the author's key words and specialized terminology.
4. Be sure that all information underneath a heading supports or explains it.
5. All headings that are aligned vertically should be of equal importance.

Now study the sample outline in Figure 12-1, which is based on the sample textbook section "The Social Side of Health and Well-Being." To refer to this section, turn to page 447 in Appendix A.

I. Social Side of Health and Well-Being
   A. Alameda and Tecumsah studies
      1. types of social ties
         a. marriage
         b. friends and relatives
         c. church
         d. other groups
      2. people with fewer networks died sooner
   B. when friends help you cope
      1. types of support
         a. emotional support – concern and affection
         b. cognitive guidance – evaluate problems and plan
         c. tangible support – resources and services
      2. effects of friends on health
         a. average stress – support had no effect
         b. above ave. stress – support reduced stress
         c. below ave. stress – support harmful
   C. coping with friends
      1. stressful aspects of friendship
         a. contagion effect – depression may rub off on you when you help a friend
         b. network stress – friend's problems become yours
         c. burdens of care – too many friends = stress and exhaustion
      2. factors determining whether support helps
         a. amount – too much can be bad
         b. timing
         c. source – support better coming from one who understands the problem
         d. density – too many friends in a tight group can make it difficult to change

FIGURE 12-1   A Sample Outline

How Much Information to Include

Before you begin to outline, decide how much information to include. An outline can be very brief and cover only major topics, or at the other extreme, it can be very detailed, providing an extensive review of information.

How much detail you include in an outline should be determined by your purpose for making it. For example, if you are outlining a collateral reading assignment for which your instructor asked that you be familiar with the author's viewpoint and general approach to a problem, then little detail is needed. On the other hand, if you are outlining a section of an anatomy and physiology text for an upcoming objective exam, a much more detailed outline is needed. To determine the right amount of detail, ask yourself, What do I need to know? What type of test situation, if any, am I preparing for?

When to Use Outlining

Outlining is useful in a variety of situations.

1. When using reference books or reading books you do not own, outlining is an effective way of taking notes.
2. When reading material that seems difficult or confusing, outlining forces you to sort ideas, see connections, and express them in your own words.
3. When you are asked to write an evaluation or critical interpretation of an article or essay, it is helpful to outline briefly the factual content. The outline will reflect development and progression of thought and help you analyze the writer's ideas.
4. In courses where order or process is important, an outline is particularly useful. In a data processing course, for example, in which various sets of programming commands must be performed in a specified sequence, an outline would be a good way to organize the information.
5. In the natural sciences, in which classifications are important, outlines help you record and sort information. In botany, for example, one important focus is the classification and description of various plant groups. An outline would enable you to list subgroups within each category and to keep track of similar characteristics.

EXERCISE 1 _____

Directions: *Write a brief outline of the textbook excerpt entitled "Society" on page 197, passage 9.*

EXERCISE 2 _____

Directions: *Write a brief outline of Chapter 13, "Study and Review Strategies," beginning with page 262 of this text. Assume you are preparing for an essay exam on the chapter.*

EXERCISE 3 _____

Directions: *Write a brief outline of this chapter. Assume you are preparing for a multiple-choice exam on the chapter.*

Directions: *Choose a section from one of your textbooks, and write a brief outline reflecting the organization and content of that section.*

SUMMARIZING

A summary is a brief statement or list of ideas that identifies the major concepts in a textbook section. Its main purpose is to record the most important ideas in an abbreviated and condensed form. A summary is briefer and less detailed than an outline. It goes one step beyond an outline by pulling together the writer's thoughts and making general statements about them. In writing a summary or making summary notes, you may indicate how the writer makes his or her point or note the types of supporting information the writer provides.

Writing a summary forces you to go beyond separate facts and ideas and consider what they signify as a whole. Summarizing encourages you to consider questions such as, What is the writer's main point? and How does the writer prove or explain his or her ideas? It is also a valuable study technique that will clarify the material.

How to Summarize

While most students think of a summary as a correctly written paragraph, when written for your own study and review purposes it may be in either paragraph or note format. If you choose a note format, however, be sure that you record ideas and not just facts. Here are a few suggestions for writing useful summaries:

1. Start by identifying the author's main point; write a statement that expresses it.
2. Next, identify the most important information the writer includes to support or explain his or her main point. Include these main supporting ideas in your summary.
3. Include any definitions of key terms or important new principles, theories, or procedures that are introduced.
4. The amount of detail you include, if any, will depend on your purpose for writing the summary and on the type and amount of recall that you need.
5. Although examples are usually not included in a summary, include several representative examples if you feel the material is complex and cannot be understood easily without them.
6. Depending on the type of material you are summarizing, it may be appropriate to indicate the author's attitude and approach toward the subject and to suggest his or her purpose for writing.
7. Try to keep your summary objective and factual. Think of it as a brief report that should reflect the writer's ideas, not your evaluation of them.
8. Let your purpose guide and determine the amount and type of information you include in your summary.

Now read the summary in Figure 12-2, based on the section "The Social Side of Health and Well-Being," beginning on page 447 of the sample textbook chapter reprinted in Appendix A. After you have studied the sample summary, compare it with the outline of the same material shown in Figure 12-1.

> Social ties are important for health. Studies show that people with fewer ties die earlier than those with more ties. Friends provide emotional, cognitive and tangible support. Support from friends had no effect on people with average stress levels. High stress levels are reduced by support and low stress levels are increased by support from friends. In different cultures different numbers of friends are necessary for well-being. Friendships can also add stress through the contagion effect, network stress, and burdens of care. The helpfulness of support from friends is determined by the amount, timing, source and density of support.

FIGURE 12-2   A Sample Summary

When to Use Summaries

Summaries are particularly useful in learning situations in which factual, detailed recall is not needed.

Preparing for Essay Exams: Summarizing ideas to be learned for possible exam topics is an excellent way to study for an exam. Because essay exam questions often require you to summarize information you have learned on a particular topic, writing summaries is a way to practice taking the exam, simulating real conditions.

Reading Literature: When reading literature, you are most often required to interpret and react to the ideas presented. To do so, you must be familiar with the basic plot (in fiction) or literal presentation of ideas (in nonfiction). Seldom, however, are you required to learn and recall specific actions, events, or facts. Writing a plot summary (describing who did what, when, and where) for fiction and a content summary for nonfiction are useful means of review.

Collateral Reading Assignments: In many undergraduate courses, instructors give additional reading assignments in sources other than your own text. These assignments may be given to supplement information in the text, to present a different or opposing viewpoint, to illustrate a concept, or to show practical applications. Usually, in-depth recall of particular facts and information is not expected. Your instructor probably wants you to understand the main points and their relation to topics covered in the text or in class; therefore, a fairly detailed summary would be a useful study aid for collateral readings.

Laboratory Experiments/Demonstrations: A summary is a useful means of recording the results of a laboratory experiment or class demonstration in a natural science course. While laboratory reports usually specify a format that includes careful reporting of procedures and listing of observations, a summary is often included. Reviewing summaries is an efficient way of recalling the purpose, procedure, and outcome of lab and classroom experiments conducted throughout the semester.

EXERCISE 5 _____

Directions: *Write a brief summary of the textbook excerpt subtitled "Capital," page 196 of this text (item 7).*

EXERCISE 6 _____

Directions: *Write a summary of the section "Adaptations to Extreme Temperatures," beginning on page 468 of the sample textbook chapter reprinted in Appendix B.*

EXERCISE 7 _____

Directions: *Refer to the section from one of your textbooks that you used to complete Exercise 4 on page 251. Write a summary of the information presented in this section.*

CONCEPT MAPPING: A VISUAL MEANS OF ORGANIZING IDEAS

Concept mapping is a visual method of organizing information. It involves drawing diagrams to show how ideas or concepts in an article or chapter are related. Mapping provides a picture or visual representation of how ideas are developed and connected. Maps group and consolidate information and make it easier to learn. The extent to which you make use of mapping will depend on your learning style. Some students, especially those with a visual learning style, prefer mapping to outlining. Other students find mapping to be freer and less tightly structured than outlining. The degree to which you use mapping will also depend on the types of courses you are taking. Some types of information are more easily learned by using mapping than are others.

Maps can take numerous forms. You can draw them in any way that shows the relationships of ideas. Figure 12-3 shows two sample maps. Each was drawn to show the organization of the section on comprehension monitoring in Chapter 6 in this book. Refer to page 254, then study each map.

For an additional example of a concept map, refer to page 425 in Appendix A. Here a concept map is used to present a model of stress.

How to Draw Concept Maps

Think of a map as a picture or diagram that shows how ideas are connected. Use the following steps in drawing a map.

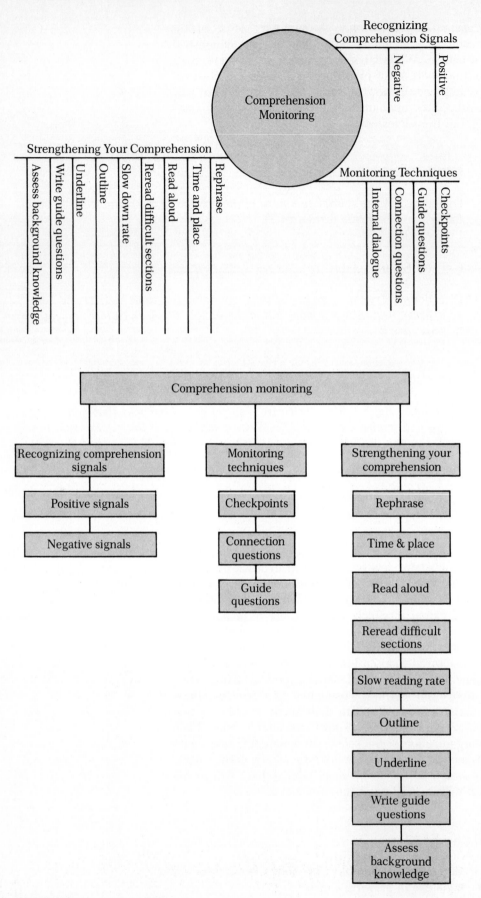

FIGURE 12-3　Sample Maps

1. Identify the overall topic or subject and write it in the center or at the top of the page.
2. Identify the major supporting information that relates to the topic. State each fact or idea on a line connected to the central topic.
3. As you discover details that further explain an idea already mapped, draw a new line branching from the idea it explains.

How you arrange your map will depend on the subject matter and how it is organized. Like an outline, it can be either quite detailed or very brief, depending on your purpose.

EXERCISE 8 _____

Directions: *Draw a concept map showing the organization of any section of Chapter 1 in this text.*

EXERCISE 9 _____

Directions: *Draw a concept map showing how the section "Sources of Stress" reprinted in the psychology sample textbook chapter (page 426) is organized.*

EXERCISE 10 _____

Directions: *Select a section from one of your textbooks. Draw a concept map that reflects its organization.*

Types of Concept Maps

Concept maps may take numerous forms. This section presents five types of maps useful for organizing specific types of information: time lines, process diagrams, part/function diagrams, organizational charts, and comparison-contrast charts.

Time Lines

In a course in which chronology of events is the central focus, a time line is a useful way to organize information. To visualize a sequence of events, draw a single horizontal line and mark it off in yearly intervals, just as a ruler is marked off in inches, then write events next to the appropriate year. The time line in Figure 12-4, for example, was developed for an American history course in which the Vietnam War was being studied. It shows the sequence of events and helps you to visualize them.

EXERCISE 11 _____

Directions: *The following passage reviews the ancient history of maps. Read the selection and then draw a time line that helps you visualize these*

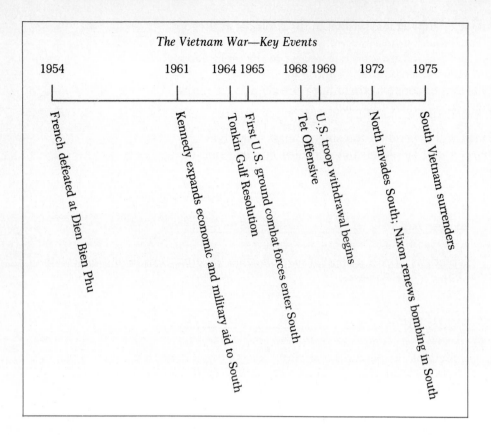

FIGURE 12-4   A Time Line

historical events. (Remember that B.C. refers to time before Christ and numbers increase as time moves back in history.)

In Babylonia, in approximately 2300 B.C., the oldest known map was drawn on a clay tablet. The map showed a man's property located in a valley surrounded by tall mountains. Later, around 1300 B.C., the Egyptians drew maps that detailed the location of Ethiopian gold mines and that showed a route from the Nile Valley. The ancient Greeks were early mapmakers as well, although no maps remain for us to examine. It is estimated that in 300 B.C. they drew maps showing the earth to be round. The Romans drew the first road maps, a few of which have been preserved for study today. Claudius Ptolemy, an Egyptian scholar who lived around 150 A.D., drew one of the most famous ancient maps. He drew maps of the world as it was known at that time, including 26 regional maps of Europe, Africa, and Asia.

Process Diagrams

In the natural sciences as well as other courses such as economics and data processing, processes are an important part of course content. A diagram that describes visually the steps, variables, or parts of a process will aid learning. A biology student, for example, might use Figure 12-5, which describes the food chain and shows how energy is transferred through food consumption from lowest to highest organisms. Notice that this student in-

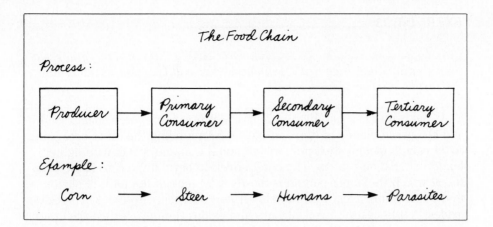

FIGURE 12-5   A Process Diagram

cluded an example, as well as the steps in the process, to make the diagram clearer.

Another example of a process diagram is found on page 469 of the biology sample textbook chapter in Appendix B. It explains how heat is exchanged between a mammal and its environment.

EXERCISE 12 _____

Directions: *The following paragraph describes the process through which malaria is spread by mosquitoes. Read the paragraph and then draw a process diagram that shows how this process occurs.*

Malaria, a serious tropical disease, is caused by parasites, or one-celled animals, called protozoa. These parasites live in the red blood cells of humans as well as in the female anopheles mosquitoes. These mosquitoes serve as hosts to the parasites and carry and spread malaria. When an anopheles mosquito bites a person who already has malaria, it ingests the red blood cells that contain the malaria parasites. In the host mosquito's body, these parasites multiply rapidly and move to its salivary glands and mouth. When the host mosquito bites another person, the malaria parasites are injected into the victim and enter his or her blood stream. The parasites again multiply and burst the victim's blood cells, causing anemia.

Part/Function Diagrams

In courses that deal with the use and description of physical objects, labeled drawings are an important learning tool. In a human anatomy and physiology course, for example, the easiest way to study the parts and functions of the inner, middle, and outer ear is to use a drawing of the ear. Study it and sketch a drawing of the ear; then test your recall of ear parts and their function.

An example of a part/function diagram appears on page 465 of the biology sample textbook chapter in Appendix B. It shows how the human skin is involved in temperature regulation.

Directions: *The following paragraph describes the earth's structure. Read the paragraph and then draw a diagram that will help you visualize how the earth's interior is structured.*

At the center is a hot, highly compressed *inner core,* presumably solid and composed mainly of iron and nickel. Surrounding the inner core is an *outer core,* a molten shell primarily of liquid iron and nickel with lighter liquid material on the top. The outer envelope beyond the core is the *mantle,* of which the upper portion is mostly solid rock in the form of olivine, an iron-magnesium silicate, and the lower portion chiefly iron and magnesium oxides. A thin coat of metal silicates and oxides (granite), called the *crust,* forms the outermost skin.

–Berman and Evans, *Exploring the Cosmos,* p. 145

Organizational Charts

When reviewing material that is composed of relationships and structures, organizational charts are useful study aids. In a business management course, suppose you are studying the organization of a small temporary clerical employment agency. If you drew and studied the organizational chart shown in Figure 12-6, the structure would become apparent and easy to remember.

EXERCISE 14 _____

Directions: *The following paragraph describes one business organizational structure that is studied in business management courses. Read the paragraph and then draw a diagram that will help you visualize this type of organization.*

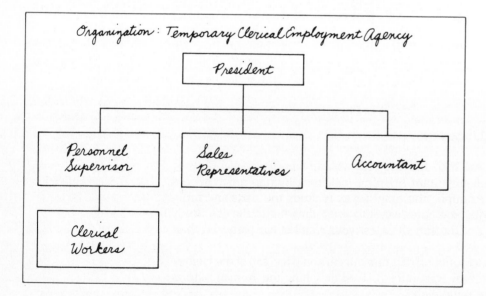

FIGURE 12-6   An Organizational Chart

It is common for some large businesses to be organized by *place*, with a department for each major geographic area in which the business is active. Businesses that market products for which customer preference differs from one part of the country to another often use this management structure. Departmentalization allows each region to focus on its own special needs and problems. Often the president of such a company appoints several regional vice-presidents, one for each part of the country. Then each regional office is divided into sales districts, each supervised by a district director.

Comparison-Contrast Charts

A final type of visual aid that is useful for organizing factual information is the comparison-contrast chart. Based on the categorization principle of learning, this method of visual organization divides and groups information according to similarities or common characteristics. Suppose in a marketing and advertising course you are studying three types of market survey techniques: mail, telephone, and personal interview surveys. You are concerned with factors such as cost, level of response, time, and accuracy. In your text this information is discussed in paragraph form. To learn and compare this information in an efficient manner, you could draw a chart such as the one shown in Figure 12-7.

EXERCISE 15 _____

Directions: *The following passage describes the major physical differences between humans and apes. Read the selection and then arrange the information into a chart that would make the information easy to learn.*

Numerous physical characteristics distinguish humans from apes. While apes' bodies are covered with hair, the human body has relatively little hair. While apes often use both their hands and feet to walk, humans walk erect. Apes' arms are longer than their legs, while just the reverse is true for humans. Apes have large teeth, necessary for devouring coarse, uncooked food, and long canine teeth for self-defense and fighting. By comparison, human teeth are small and short. The ape's brain is not as well developed as that of the human being. Humans are capable of speech, thinking, and higher-level reasoning skills. These skills enable humans to establish culture, thereby placing the quality and level of human life far above that of apes.

Humans are also set apart from apes by features of the head and face. The human facial profile is vertical, while the ape's profile is *prognathous,* with jaw jutting outward. Humans have a chin; apes have a strong lower jaw, but no chin. Human nostrils are smaller and less flaring than those of the ape. Apes also have thinner, more flexible lips than human beings.

Man's upright walk also distinguishes him from apes. The human spine has a double curve to support his weight, while an ape's spine has a single curve. The human foot is arched both vertically and horizontally, but, unlike the apes, is unable to grasp objects. The human torso is shorter than that of apes. It is important to note that many of these physical traits, while quite distinct, differ in degree rather than in kind.

Market Survey Techniques

Type	Cost	Response	Accuracy
Mail	usually the cheapest	higher than phone or personal interview	problems with misunderstanding directions
Phone	depends on availability of WATS line	same as personal interview	problems with unlisted phones and homes w/out phones
Personal interview	most expensive	same as phone	problems with honesty when asking personal or embarrassing questions

FIGURE 12-7   A Comparison-Contrast Chart

EXERCISE 16 _____

Directions: *Refer to the sections "Poikilotherms" and "Homeotherms" in the biology sample textbook chapter, pages 462–467. Draw a comparison-contrast chart that analyzes traits of these two types of animals.*

EXERCISE 17 _____

Directions: *Draw a process diagram that shows how temperature regulation occurs in mammals. Refer to the section of the biology sample texbook chapter titled "The Mammalian Thermostat," pages 465–466.*

EXERCISE 18 _____

Directions: *Draw a concept map that describes the principles of heat balance. Refer to the section in the biology sample textbook chapter titled "Principles of Heat Balance," pages 459–462.*

EXERCISE 19 _____

Directions: *Draw a part/function diagram or process map that describes the heat conserving mechanisms in the legs of an Arctic animal. Refer to pages 468–470 in the biology sample textbook chapter in Appendix B.*

SUMMARY

This chapter explained how to organize and condense information so that it is easy to learn and remember. Three methods of organizing information were presented: outlining, summarizing, and mapping.

Outlining is a form of organizing information that provides a visual picture of the ideas. An outline indicates the relative importance of ideas and shows the relationship between these ideas. Summarizing is the process of recording the most important ideas of a passage in a condensed, abbreviated form. Mapping presents a visual representation of the information while showing relationships. The five types discussed are time lines, process diagrams, part/function diagrams, organizational charts, and comparison-contrast charts.

13

Study and Review Strategies

Use this chapter to:

1. *Use writing to learn.*
2. *Develop systems of study.*
3. *Adapt your study systems.*

Even though you have read a textbook chapter and underlined or outlined it, you cannot be certain that you have learned the material or will be able to apply it on exams. Study and review must follow reading and organizing. Study and review involve the transfer of information from short- to long-term memory. As you learned in Chapter 3, there are three means of doing this: rote learning, elaborative rehearsal, and recoding. In this chapter, we will focus on methods of study and review, particularly those involving elaborative rehearsal and recoding.

LEARNING THROUGH WRITING

Writing is a form of recoding, or processing information by rearranging, rephrasing, or regrouping it so it becomes more meaningful and easier to recall. Outlining, summarizing, and mapping, each described in the previous chapter, are forms of writing and recoding and do contribute to learning. This section will discuss three other ways to use writing to learn: paraphrasing, self-testing, and keeping a learning journal.

Paraphrasing

A paraphrase is a restatement of a passage's ideas in your own words. The author's meaning is retained but your wording, *not* the author's, is used. We use paraphrasing frequently in everyday speech. For example, when you relay a message from one person to another you convey the meaning but do not use the person's exact wording. A paraphrase can be used to make a passage's meaning clearer and often more concise. Paraphrasing is also an effective learning and review strategy in several situations.

First, paraphrasing is useful for material for which exact, detailed comprehension is required. For example, you might paraphrase the steps in solv-

What does the separation of the two halves of the heart have to do with efficiency? The two halves are essentially two hearts, one serving the lungs, the other serving the body. When CO_2-laden blood enters the right atrium from the large veins (the *superior vena cava* from above and the *inferior vena cava* from below), it is pumped from the atrium to the right ventricle. Contraction of the right ventricle sends the blood through the *pulmonary arteries* to the lungs. Here the blood picks up oxygen and releases carbon dioxide before returning to the left atrium via the *pulmonary veins*. The left atrium pumps the blood into the left ventricle, which then contracts to send the blood into the large aorta, which immediately branches before looping downward, carrying the blood on the first leg of its long journey through the body, bearing its gift of oxygen.

Wallace, 434

Blood-filled CO_2 enters the right atrium of the heart from the superior vena cava and the inferior vena cava. It is pumped to the right ventricle where a contraction moves it through the pulmonary arteries into the lungs where it exchanges CO_2 for O_2 and then returns through the pulmonary veins to the left atrium. From the left atrium it is pumped to the left ventricle, then to the large aorta and from there it carries O_2 to the rest of the body.

FIGURE 13-1   A Sample Paraphrase

ing a math problem, the process by which a blood transfusion is administered, or the levels of jurisdiction of the Supreme Court. Figure 13-1 shows a paraphrase written by a biology student studying the functioning of the human heart.

Paraphrasing is also a useful way to be certain you understand difficult or complicated material. If you can express the author's ideas in your own words, you can be certain you understand it, and if you find yourself at a loss for words—except for those of the author—you will know your understanding is incomplete. Figure 13-2 shows two students' paraphrases of an excerpt of a difficult essay. Paraphrase #1 shows that the student had difficulty—the student wrote in generalities and was unable to connect ideas. In contrast, paraphrase #2 carries the meaning of the passage and demonstrates the student's level of understanding.

Paraphrasing is a useful strategy when working with material that is stylistically complex, poorly written, or overly formal, awkward, or biased. Many technical manuals, for example, are poorly written and require the reader to struggle to obtain meaning. An essay written in the 1700s may use language patterns different from those you are accustomed to. In such situations, it is helpful to cut through the language barrier and express the content as simply as possible in your own words. Figure 13-3 shows how a student simplified a complicated discussion about the disappearance of oral poetry from Germany.

Use the following suggestions to paraphrase effectively.

1. Read slowly and carefully.
2. Read the material through entirely before writing anything.

PASSAGE: CARL ROGERS AND SELF-THEORY

Carl Rogers (b. 1902), a clinical psychologist, developed his theory of personality from observations he made while practicing psychotherapy. At the heart of Rogers's (1970b) theory is the self-concept. In his clinical experience, Rogers came to realize that his clients (a term he prefers to "patients") usually expressed their problems in terms of a sense of themselves as an "I" or "me." Such statements led Rogers to conclude that the self—the body of perceptions we think of as "I" or "me"—is a vital part of human experience. Rogers defines *self* or *self-concept* as an organized pattern of perceived characteristics along with the values attached to those attributes. People can have positive self-concepts, in which they feel good about themselves, or negative self-concepts, in which they may actually dislike themselves. How people view themselves, according to the humanistic approach, is the single most important aspect of personality functioning. The self-concept need not reflect "objective reality"; an individual may be at the top of her profession and appear happy and successful yet view herself as a failure. In fact, the self-concept comes in two parts: the *actual-self* and the *ideal-self*. The ideal-self is similar to Freud's concept of the ego-ideal. A positive self-concept arises when close agreement exists between the actual and the ideal selves. A large discrepancy between the two results in an unhappy, dissatisfied individual.

Roediger, p. 51.

PARAPHRASE #1: DEMONSTRATES LACK OF UNDERSTANDING

Carl Rogers was a clinical psychologist who practiced psychotherapy. He noticed that people talk about their problems using "I" and "me" a lot. This is self-concept and is an important part of the human experience. People can be positive or negative but this is not always the same as it objectively is in reality. There are two parts—the actual-self and the ideal-self, which is like Freud's ego-ideal.

PARAPHRASE #2: DEMONSTRATES UNDERSTANDING

Carl Rogers' theory of personality contains the idea of self-concept—the way in which a person views himself and judges himself—as an important part of human experience. A person's self-concept is not always the same as who they are in reality. Self-concepts can be negative or positive and have two parts—actual and ideal.

FIGURE 13-2 A Comparison of Paraphrases

The heroic oral poetry of the ancient Germanic peoples, which survived in Iceland and was there committed to writing, disappeared gradually from among the continental Germans in the course of the Middle Ages, and for a long time no adequate substitute took its place. Heathen gods and heathen manners were honored in those poems, and the Church could not approve of either, much less foster their preservation in writing. Thus the numerous German dialects came to be represented during their "old" period, roughly from 500 A.D. to 1000 A.D., almost exclusively by utilitarian and devotional works, and no secular literature worthy of the name was created.

–Parzival

PARAPHRASE

Germanic heroic oral poetry, although written down in Ireland, slowly disappeared from Germany in the Middle Ages because it celebrated heathen religion which would not be tolerated by the Church. German dialects were thus not written until they became old (500 A.D. to 1000 A.D.) and then only in religious and practical contexts.

FIGURE 13-3   Paraphrasing to Simplify

3. As you read, pay attention to exact meanings and relationships among ideas.
4. Paraphrase sentence by sentence.
5. Read each sentence and express the key idea in your own words. Reread the original sentence; then look away and write your own sentence. Then reread the original and add anything you missed.
6. Don't try to paraphrase word by word. Instead work with ideas.
7. For words or phrases you are unsure of or that are not words you feel comfortable using, check a dictionary to locate a more familiar meaning.
8. You may combine several original sentences into a more concise paraphrase.
9. Follow the author's arrangement (order) of ideas unless you have a specific reason for changing them.
10. When finished, reread your paraphrase and compare it with the original for completeness and accuracy.

EXERCISE 1 _____

Directions: *Write a paraphrase for each of the following excerpts.*

1. As Morris Cohen once said, one of the most fascinating problems about human behavior is why men violate the laws in which they believe. This is the problem that confronts us when we attempt to explain why delinquency occurs despite a greater or lesser commitment to the

usages of conformity. A basic clue is offered by the fact that social rules or norms calling for valued behavior seldom if ever take the form of categorical imperatives. Rather, values or norms appear as *qualified* guides for action, limited in their applicability in terms of time, place, persons, and social circumstances. The moral injunction against killing, for example, does not apply to the enemy during combat in time of war, although a captured enemy comes once again under the prohibition. Similarly, the taking and distributing of scarce goods in a time of acute social need is felt by many to be right, although under other circumstances private property is held inviolable. The normative system of a society, then, is marked by what Williams had termed *flexibility;* it does not consist of a body of rules held to be binding under all conditions.[1]

–Kelly, *Deviant Behavior,* p. 104

2. The *stomach* is a muscular sac that churns the food as it secretes mucus, hydrochloric acid, and enzymes that begin the digestion of proteins. The food is meanwhile sealed in the stomach by two sphincters, or rings of muscles, one at either end of the stomach. After the mixing is completed, the lower sphincter opens and the stomach begins to contract repeatedly, squeezing the food into the small intestine. A fatty meal, by the way, slows this process and makes us feel "full" longer. This is also why we're hungry again so soon after a low-fat Chinese dinner.

The *small intestine* is a long convoluted tube in which digestion is completed and through which most nutrient products enter the bloodstream. Its inner surface is covered with tiny, fingerlike projections called *villi,* which increase the surface area of the intestinal lining. Furthermore, the surface area of each villus is increased by about 3000 tiny projections called *microvilli.* Within each villus is a minute lymph vessel surrounded by a network of blood capillaries. While the digested products of certain fats move directly into the lymph vessel, the products of protein and starch digestion move into the blood capillaries.

–Wallace, *Biology: The World of Life,* p. 443

3. *Section 7.* (1). All bills for raising revenue shall originate in the House of Representatives; but the Senate may propose or concur with amendments as on other bills.

(2). Every bill which shall have passed the House of Representatives and the Senate, shall, before it become a law, be presented to the President of the United States; if he approve he shall sign it, but if not he shall return it, with his objections to that House in which it shall have originated, who shall enter the objections at large on their journal, and proceed to reconsider it. If after such reconsideration two thirds of that House shall agree to pass the bill, it shall be sent, together with the objections, to the other House, by which it shall likewise be reconsidered, and if approved by two thirds of that House, it shall become a law. But in all such cases the votes of both Houses shall be determined by yeas and nays, and the names of the persons voting for and against the bill shall be entered on the journal of each House respectively. If any bill shall not be returned by the President within ten days (Sundays excepted) after it shall have been presented to him, the same shall be a law, in like manner as if he had signed it, unless the Congress by their adjournment prevent its return, in which case it shall not be a law.

–U.S. Constitution

EXERCISE 2 _____

Directions: *Write a paraphrase of the section titled "Cold-blooded and Warm-blooded," p. 462 in the sample textbook chapter included in Appendix B.*

EXERCISE 3 _____

Directions: *Write a paraphrase of a two- to three-paragraph excerpt from one of your textbooks—choose a passage that is difficult or stylistically complex.*

Self-Testing

Have you ever taken an exam for which you studied hard and felt prepared only to find out you earned just an average grade? Although you spent time reviewing, you did not review in the right ways; you probably focused on recalling factual information. Many college professors demand much more of their students than factual recall of textbook and lecture content. They expect their students to react, evaluate, and apply ideas. They require their students to be able to compare and synthesize sources and integrate ideas.

Consequently, a study approach that includes only factual recall is inadequate. Strategies such as rereading, underlining, writing an outline, and drawing maps are useful and important because they do enable you to learn literal content. However, you must use additional and different strategies to focus on interpretation, application, and evaluation.

Interpretation, application, and evaluation are thinking techniques. They involve skills such as problem-solving, comparing and contrasting, synthesizing, and analyzing. Writing can facilitate and clarify your thinking. Writing is a way of "seeing your ideas." Once you've seen some, others will follow. Writing, then, is a way of generating ideas, discovering relationships, and revealing applications.

Self-testing is a study strategy that uses writing to discover and relate ideas. It involves writing possible exam questions and drafting answers to them. This activity combines the use of factual recall with interpretation and evaluation. Self-testing is an active strategy that gets you involved with the material and forces you to think about, organize, and express ideas in your own words. Self-testing is also a sensible and effective way to prepare for an exam. How would you prepare for a typing or keyboarding exam?—by keyboarding. How would you prepare to run a marathon?—by running. Similarly, you should prepare for an exam by testing yourself.

Constructing potential test questions is fun and challenging and can be done with a classmate or in groups. It is usually best to write answers yourself, however, to get maximum benefit from the technique. After writing, it is very worthwhile to compare and discuss your answers with classmates. If you prefer to work alone, be sure to verify your answers using your text and/or lecture notes.

The kinds of questions that you ask should depend on the type of material you are learning as well as on the types or level of analysis your instructor expects. Figure 13-4 lists sample questions for various types of material you may be required to study.

FIGURE 13-4   Questions to Provoke Thought

Type of Material	Questions
Report of research studies and experiments	What was the purpose of the study?
	What are the important facts and conclusions?
	What are its implications? How can these results be used?
Case studies	What is it intended to illustrate?
	What problems or limitations does it demonstrate?
	To what other situations might this case apply?
Models	How was the model derived?
	What are its applications?
	What are its limitations?
	Do other models of the same process exist?
Current events	What is the significance of the event?
	What impact will this have in the future?
	Is there "historical precedence"?
Supplementary readings	Why did your instructor assign the reading?
	How do they relate to course content?
	What key points or concepts does the reading contain?
	Does the reading present a particular viewpoint?
Sample problems	What processes or concepts does the problem illustrate?
	What is its unique feature?
	How is it similar to and different from other problems?
Historical data (historical reviews)	Why was the data presented?
	What trends or patterns are evident?
	How does it relate to key concepts in the chapter or article?
Arguments	Is the argument convincing?
	How is the conclusion supported?
	What persuasive devices does the author use?

Type of Material	Questions
	Do logical flaws exist?
	Is the author's appeal emotional?
Poetry	What kinds of feelings does the poem evoke?
	What message or statement is the poet making?
	How does the poet use language to create feelings?
Essays	What is the author's purpose?
	What thought patterns are evident?
	How does the author support his key point (thesis)?
Short stories	What does the title mean?
	Beyond the plot, what does the story really mean? (What is the theme?)
	What kinds of comments does it make about life?
	How does the plot, setting, and tone contribute to its overall meaning?

To construct and answer possible test questions, use the following hints:

1. Do not waste time writing multiple-choice or true-false questions. They are time consuming to write and you know the answer before you start.
2. Matching tests are useful, but are limited to information requiring only factual recall.
3. Open-ended questions that require sentence answers are best because they tend to require more levels of thought.
4. Consult Table 17-1 for ideas on how to word your questions.
5. Since you are interested in long-term retention of information, it is best to write the questions one day and answer them a day or two later.
6. As you answer your questions, respond in complete sentences. Writing complete sentences usually involves more careful and deliberate thought and, therefore, your learning will be more complete.
7. Take time to review and critique your answers. This process will also contribute to learning.
8. Rewrite any answers that you found to be poorly done or incomplete. This repetition will facilitate learning.
9. Save your answers and review them once again on the evening before the exam.

Many students who use self-testing as a review strategy are pleasantly surprised when they take their first exam: they discover that some (or many!) of their questions actually appeared on the exam. This discovery boosts their confidence during the exam and saves them time, as well. As you will see later in this chapter, self-testing is an important part of the SQ3R system—a systematic approach to learning and study.

EXERCISE 4 _____

Directions: *Write a list of questions that might be asked on an exam on one of the chapters in this book that you have already read. Answer them and verify their correctness by consulting the chapter.*

EXERCISE 5 _____

Directions: *Write a list of questions for an upcoming exam in one of your courses. Answer each. Save your questions and after you have taken the exam, mark those that appeared on the exam. (Do not expect the actual questions to use the same wording or format as those you constructed.)*

Keeping a Learning Journal

As you have seen throughout this book, there is a wide range of study and review alternatives. Do not expect to know right away what strategies will work for you or what modifications to make. Instead, you will need to experiment with different variations until you are satisfied with the results. Some students find it effective to keep a learning journal—an informal written record of the techniques they have tried, how well they worked, and problems they encountered. Writing the journal helps you to sort and evaluate techniques. The journal also serves as a record and is useful to reread as you revise or consider new approaches. Keep a separate journal—perhaps a spiral or steno notebook or section for each of your most challenging courses. A sample learning journal entry is shown in Figure 13-5. It was written as the student applied several of the techniques in this chapter to her biology textbook.

Your journal may include a wide range of observations, comments, and reactions. Consider including:

- General reactions to course content.
- Unique features of assignments.
- What you like and don't like about the course.
- Problems encountered with a particular assignment.
- Techniques that worked (and *why*).
- Techniques that didn't work (*why* techniques didn't work).
- New ideas for approaching the material.
- Changes you made in using various techniques.
- Enter analysis and reactions to exams when taking and again when returned.

Be sure to date your entries and reference them to particular chapters or assignments. Some students find it helpful to record the amount of time spent on each assignment, as well.

Once you've made several entries for a particular course, reread your entries and look for patterns. Try to discover what you are doing right, what needs changing, and what changes you'll make. Then write an entry summarizing your findings.

EXERCISE 6 _____

Directions: *For each of the courses you are taking this semester, create a learning journal. Experiment with self-testing as a means of review of a*

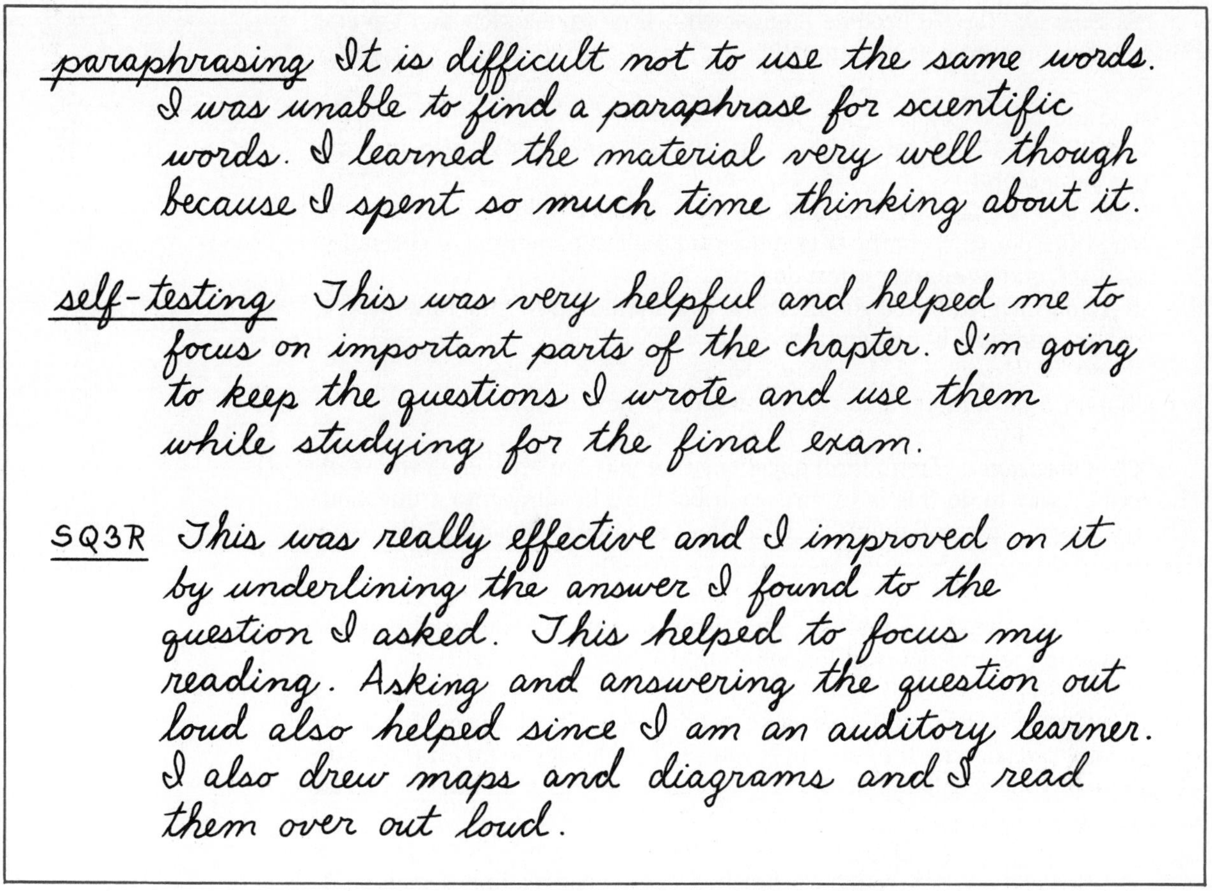

<u>paraphrasing</u> It is difficult not to use the same words. I was unable to find a paraphrase for scientific words. I learned the material very well though because I spent so much time thinking about it.

<u>self-testing</u> This was very helpful and helped me to focus on important parts of the chapter. I'm going to keep the questions I wrote and use them while studying for the final exam.

<u>SQ3R</u> This was really effective and I improved on it by underlining the answer I found to the question I asked. This helped to focus my reading. Asking and answering the question out loud also helped since I am an auditory learner. I also drew maps and diagrams and I read them over out loud.

FIGURE 13-5   Sample Learning Journal

particular chapter in each. Then write a journal entry describing how you used self-testing, how you modified the technique to suit the course, and how effective you felt it to be.

A CLASSIC SYSTEM: SQ3R

In 1941, a psychologist named Francis P. Robinson developed a study-reading system called SQ3R. It is a system that incorporates study and review with reading. The SQ3R system, based on principles of learning theory, was carefully researched and tested. Continuing experimentation has confirmed its effectiveness. Since that time SQ3R has been taught to thousands of college students and has become widely recognized as the classic study-reading system.

As a step toward developing your own personalized system, look at SQ3R as a model. Once you see how and why SQ3R works, you can modify or adapt it to suit your own academic needs.

Steps in the SQ3R System

The SQ3R system involves five basic steps that integrate reading and study techniques. As you read the following steps, some of them will seem similar to the skills you have already learned.

S—Survey: Try to become familiar with the organization and general content of the material you are to read.

1. Read the title.
2. Read the lead-in or introduction. (If it is extremely long, read just the first paragraph.)
3. Read each boldface heading and the first sentence following each.
4. Read titles of maps, charts, or graphs; read the last paragraph or summary.
5. Read the end-of-chapter questions.
6. After you have surveyed the material, you should know generally what it is about and how it is organized.

See Chapter 5 for a more detailed explanation of how to survey.

Q—Questions: Try to form questions that you can answer as you read. The easiest way to do this is to turn each boldface heading into a question. (The section of Chapter 6 titled "Formulating Purposes for Reading" discusses this step in depth.)

R—Read: Read the material section by section. As you read, look for the answer to the question you formed from the heading of that section.

R—Recite: After you finish each section, stop. Check to see if you can answer your question for the section. If you can't, look back to find the answer. Then check your recall again. Be sure to complete this step after you read each section.

R—Review: When you have finished the whole reading assignment, go back to each heading; recall your question and try to answer it. If you can't recall the answer, be sure to look back and find the answer. Then test yourself again.

The SQ3R method ties together much of what you have already learned about active reading. The first two steps activate your background knowledge and establish questions to guide your reading. The last two steps provide a means of monitoring your comprehension and recall.

Why SQ3R Works

Results of research studies overwhelmingly suggest that students who are taught to use a study-reading system understand and remember what they read much better than students who have not been taught to use such a system.

In one research study designed to test the effectiveness of the SQ3R system,* the reading rate and comprehension level of a group of college students were measured before and after learning and using the SQ3R system. After students learned the SQ3R method, the average reading rate increased by 22 percent; the comprehension level increased by 10 percent.

If you consider for a moment how people learn, it becomes clear why study-reading systems are effective. One major way to learn is through repetition. Consider the way you learned the multiplication tables. Through repeated practice and drills, you learned $2 \times 2 = 4$, $5 \times 6 = 30$, $8 \times 9 = 72$,

---

* F. P. Robinson, *Effective Study* (New York: Harper & Row, 1941), p. 30.

and so forth. The key was repetition. Study-reading systems provide some of the repetition necessary to ensure learning. Compared with the usual once-through approach to reading textbook assignments that provide one chance to learn, SQ3R provides numerous repetitions and increases the amount learned.

SQ3R has many psychological advantages over ordinary reading. First, surveying (prereading) gives you a mental organization or structure—you know what to expect. Second, you always feel that you are looking for something specific rather than wandering aimlessly through a printed page. Third, when you find the information you're looking for, it is rewarding; you feel you have accomplished something. And if you can remember the information in the immediate and long-term recall checks, it is even more rewarding.

EXERCISE 7 _____

Directions: *Turn to the sample textbook chapter included in Appendix A of this text. Read the section of the Chapter titled "The Individual Side of Health and Well-Being," beginning on page 440, using the SQ3R method. The following SQ3R worksheet will help you get started. Fill in the required information as you go through each step.*

SQ3R WORKSHEET

   S—*Survey:*   Read the title of the chapter, the introduction, each boldface heading, and the summary, and look at any pictures or graphs included.

1.   What is the chapter about?

_____

2.   What major topics are included?

_____

   Q—*Question 1:*   Turn the first heading into a question.

_____

   R—*Read:*   Read the material following the first heading, looking for the answer to your question.

   R—*Recite:*   Reread the heading and recall the question you asked. Briefly answer this question in your own words without looking at the section. Check to see if you are correct.

_____

_____

   Q—*Question 2:*   Turn the second heading into a question.

_____

R—Read: Read the material following the second heading, looking for the answer to your question.

R—Recite: Briefly answer the question.

_____

_____

Q—Question 3: Turn the third heading into a question.

_____

R—Read: Read the material following the third heading, looking for the answer to your question.

R—Recite: Briefly answer the question.

_____

_____

_____

Continue using the question, read, and recite steps until you have finished each part of the chapter. Then complete the review step.

R—Review: Look over the total chapter by rereading the headings. Try to answer the question you made from each heading.

Answer to Question 1:

_____

_____

Answer to Question 2:

_____

_____

Answer to Question 3:

_____

_____

Check to see that your answers are correct.

UPDATING AND REVISING THE SQ3R SYSTEM

Now that you are familiar with the basic SQ3R system, it is time to modify it to suit your specific needs. As mentioned previously, the SQ3R

FIGURE 13-6   Expanding SQ3R

SQ3R Steps	Additional Strategies
Survey	Preread (Ch. 5)
	Activate your background and experience (Ch. 4)
	Predict (Ch. 5)
Question	Pose guide questions (Ch. 6)
Read	Monitor your comprehension (Ch. 6)
	Underline and mark (Ch. 11)
	Anticipate thought patterns (Ch. 9)
Recite	Outline (Ch. 12)
	Summarize (Ch. 12)
	Map (Ch. 12)
Review	Paraphrase (Ch. 13)
	Self-test (Ch. 13)
	Discovery writing (Ch. 13)
	Review underlining, outlines, maps (Ch. 11, 12)

method was developed in the 1940s, more than fifty years ago. Over the past fifty years, considerable research has been done and much has been discovered about the learning process. Consequently, it is now possible to expand on the original SQ3R method by adding more recent techniques and strategies. Figure 13-6 lists the steps in the SQ3R method and indicates how you can expand each step to make it work better for you. Most of the techniques listed have been described in previous chapters, as indicated in the table.

As shown in Figure 13-6, the Survey step is really a "get ready to read" step, along with the Question step. The Read step becomes much more than simply the "see-words" step. It involves interacting with the text, thinking, anticipating, and reacting. The Recite step can involve much more than answering the questions posed in the Question step. As you identify important information, grasp relationships, and understand key concepts, you might revise your underlining, add to your marking, write notes or questions, self-test, summarize, outline, or draw maps. The final step, Review, can be expanded to include paraphrasing, self-testing, and the review of underlining, annotation outlines, and maps.

In Chapter 4 you completed a learning style questionnaire to discover characteristics of your learning style. These characteristics are important to consider in deciding how to modify SQ3R to work best for you. For instance, if you are a visual learner, you might sketch a map showing the organization of the chapter as part of the Survey step. Then, as part of the Recite step, include additional mapping. An auditory learner, during the Survey step, might predict and tape record what he or she expects the chapter to cover and replay it before and after reading. During the Question step, the questions could also be taped, then played back and answered as part of the Recite step.

Directions: *Review the results of the Learning Style Questionnaire on p. 62. Then write a list of the modifications you might make in the SQ3R method for one of your courses.*

ADAPTING YOUR SYSTEM FOR VARIOUS ACADEMIC DISCIPLINES

Various academic disciplines require different kinds of learning. In an English composition and literature class, for example, you learn skills of critical interpretation, while in a chemistry course you learn facts, principles, and processes. A history course focuses on events, their causes, their significance, and long-term trends.

Because different courses require different types of learning, they also require different types of reading and study; therefore, you should develop a specialized study-reading approach for each subject. The following subjects are some of the most common academic disciplines studied by beginning college students, for which changes in a study-reading system are most important. For each, possible modifications in a study-reading system are suggested.

Mathematics

Sample problems are an important part of most math courses; therefore, you would add a "Study the Problems" step, in which you would try to see how the problems illustrate the theory or process explained in the chapter. This step might also include working through or reviewing additional practice problems.

Literature

When reading novels, essays, short stories, or poetry in a composition and literature class, you are usually asked to interpret, react, and write about what you read. For reading literature, then, you might drop the recite step, use the review step for the literal content (who did what, when, and where?), and add two new steps: "Interpret" and "React." In the interpret step, you would analyze the characters, their actions, and the writer's style and point of view to determine the writer's theme or message. In the react step, you might ask questions such as, What meaning does this have for me? How effectively did the writer communicate his or her message? Do I agree with this writer's view of life? You should make notes about your reactions, which could be a source of ideas if a paper is assigned.

Sciences

When reading and studying biology, chemistry, physics, or another science, prereading is particularly important because most of the material is new. You might quickly read each end-of-chapter problem to discover what principles and formulas are emphasized in that chapter. The sciences emphasize facts, principles, formulas, and processes; therefore, build a "Write" or "Record" step in which you underline, outline, or write study sheets.

Social Sciences

Introductory courses in the social sciences (psychology, sociology, anthropology, economics, politial science) often focus on a particular discipline's basic problems or topics. These courses introduce specialized vocabulary and the basic principles and theories on which the discipline operates.

For social science courses, then, build a "Vocabulary Review" step into your study-reading system. A "Write" or "Underline" step is also needed to provide an efficient method for review and study.

Other Academic Disciplines

This brief chapter does not permit discussion of modifications for every academic discipline. Most likely, you are taking one or more courses not previously mentioned. To adapt your study-reading system to these courses, ask yourself the following questions:

1. What type of learning is required? What is the main focus of the course? Often the preface or the first chapter of your text will answer these questions. The instructor's course outline or objectives may be helpful.
2. What must I do to learn this type of material?

Learn to "read" the instructor of each course. Find out what each expects, what topics and types of information each feels are important, and how your grades are determined. Talk with other students in the course or with students who have already taken the course to get ideas for useful ways of studying.

EXERCISE 9 _____

Directions: *The sample textbook chapters reprinted in the appendixes represent two very different academic disciplines—psychology and biology. How would you modify the SQ3R system to study-read each chapter? Consider chapter features as well as content.*

Psychology

_____

_____

_____

Biology

_____

_____

_____

EXERCISE 10 _____

Directions: *List each of the courses for which you are currently registered. Then briefly indicate what changes in your study-reading system you intend to make for each course.*

_____

_____

_____

_____

_____

_____

SUMMARY

For complete learning to occur, study and review necessarily follow the reading and organizing of information. Writing is one effective means of study and review. This chapter presents three strategies: paraphrasing, self-testing, and journal writing. Paraphrasing is the restatement of a passage's ideas in your own words. Self-testing emphasizes interpretation and application and involves writing possible exam questions and drafting answers to them. A learning journal is a log in which you keep a written record of your reactions, comments, and assessment of learning strategies for individual courses.

The SQ3R method is a classic, five-step method of study and review. The steps are Survey, Question, Read, Recite, and Review. The SQ3R method should be adapted to suit unique characteristics of various academic disciplines. The system can also be expanded to include additional and/or more recent techniques and strategies.

PART FIVE

Classroom Performance Skills

The average college student spends between fifteen and eighteen hours in class each week. Attending class, then, represents a significant portion of a student's weekly schedule. Since such a large amount of time is spent in class each week, it is important to use this time effectively. While attending class, you can actually be doing things to help you learn, make studying easier, and earn better grades. Among the most important classroom skills are notetaking, test-taking, and participating in class discussions.

Taking notes on class lectures is extremely valuable. Class lecture notes are an important source of information and are excellent study aids. Chapter 14 ("Lecture Notetaking Techniques") will show you how to take good notes and suggest how you can use them effectively in study.

Participation in classroom discussions is expected by many college instructors. While you may be reluctant at first to become involved, you will find taking part in discussions an excellent way of keeping yourself interested, learning while in class, and showing the instructor that you are interested and involved. Chapter 15 ("Participating in Class Activities and Projects") will present information on how to prepare for discussions, how to get involved, and how to study for or learn from discussion classes.

Besides the time spent in class each week, students are expected to spend time outside class. One important out-of-class activity is preparation for exams. And, of course, how thoroughly you prepare and study largely determines how well you perform on quizzes and exams. Chapter 16 ("Preparing for Exams") will discuss how to study for exams. Chapter 17 ("Taking Exams") will discuss how to do well on an exam while you are taking it.

Another activity that requires considerable time and effort outside class is writing papers. Some instructors require brief essays, reports, or reaction papers, while others require a research paper. Chapter 18 ("Preparing Written Assignments and Research Papers") offers suggestions for writing all types of papers, and outlines a step-by-step procedure for researching and writing research papers.

14

Lecture Notetaking Techniques

> **Use this chapter to:**
>
> 1. *Find out what information to write down and what to skip during a lecture.*
> 2. *Learn how to take notes so that they are easy to study later.*

WHY NOTETAKING IS IMPORTANT

As you sit in class in which the instructor lectures, it is easy to just sit back and listen, especially if the instructor and the subject are interesting or exciting. At the time information is presented, it may seem that you will always be able to remember it. Unfortunately, memory fades quickly, and a lecture that is vivid in your memory today will be only vaguely familiar several weeks later. Because instructors expect you to remember and apply facts and ideas presented in each lecture throughout the semester, it is necessary to take notes as lectures are given. A set of good lecture notes is a valuable study aid that will help you get good grades in a course.

SHARPENING YOUR LISTENING SKILLS

The first step in taking good lecture notes is to sharpen your listening skills. The average adult spends 31 percent of his or her waking hours listening. By comparison, 7 percent is spent on writing, 11 percent on reading, and 21 percent on speaking. Listening, then, is an essential communication skill. During college lectures listening is especially important; it is your primary means of acquiring information.

Have you ever found yourself not listening to a professor who was lecturing? Her voice was loud and clear, so you certainly could hear her, but you weren't paying attention—you "tuned her out." This situation illustrates the distinction between hearing and listening. Hearing is a passive, biological process in which sound waves are received by the ear. Listening, however, is an intellectual activity involving the processing and interpretation of incoming information. Listening must be intentional, purposeful, and deliberate. You must plan to listen, have a reason for listening, and carefully focus your attention. Use the following suggestions to sharpen your listening skills.

1. *Approach listening as a process similar to reading.* When you read, you not only recognize words, you understand, connect, and evaluate ideas. Similarly, listening is not simply a process of hearing words. It is a comprehension process in which you grasp ideas, assess their importance, and connect them to other ideas. All of the reading comprehension skills you developed in Part Three of this text are useful for listening as well. Focus on identifying main ideas, evaluating the importance and connection of details in relation to the main idea. Be alert for transitions—speakers tend to use them more frequently than writers. Also try to identify patterns of thought to improve both comprehension and recall.

2. *Focus on content, not delivery.* It is easy to become so annoyed, upset, charmed, or engaged with the lecturer as an individual that you fail to comprehend the message he or she is conveying. Force yourself to focus on the content of the lecture and disregard the personal style and characteristics of the lecturer.

3. *Focus on ideas, not facts.* If you concentrate on recording and remembering separate, unconnected facts, you are doomed to failure. Remember, your short-term memory is extremely limited in span and capacity, so while you are focusing on certain facts, it is inevitable that you will ignore some and forget others. Instead, listen for ideas, trends, and patterns.

4. *Listen carefully to the speaker's opening comments.* As your mind refocuses from prior tasks and problems, it is easy to miss the speaker's opening remarks. However, these are among the most important. Here the speaker may establish connections with prior lectures, identify his or her purpose, or describe the lecture's content or organization.

5. *Attempt to understand the lecturer's purpose.* If not stated explicitly, try to reason it out. Is the purpose to present facts, raise and discuss questions, demonstrate a trend or pattern, or present a technique or procedure?

6. *Fill the gap between rate of speech and rate of thinking.* Has your mind ever wandered back and forth during a lecture? Although you may be interested in what the speaker is saying, do you seem to "have time" to think about other things while listening? This is natural, since the rate of speech is much slower than the speed of thought. The average rate of speech is around 125 words per minute, whereas the rate at which you can process ideas is over 500 words per minute. To listen most effectively, use this gap to think about lecture content. Anticipate what is to follow, think of situations in which the information might be applied, pose questions, or make the information "fit" your prior knowledge and experience.

7. *Approach listening as a challenging mental task.* We all know concentration and attention are necessary for reading, yet many of us treat listening as something that should occur without effort. Perhaps due to the constant barrage of spoken words we are bombarded with through radio, television, and conversation, we assume that listening occurs automatically. Lectures, however, are a concentrated form of oral communication that require you to put higher-level attention and thinking skills into gear.

PREPARING FOR A LECTURE CLASS

Before you attend a lecture class, you should become familiar with the main topic of the lecture and be aware of important subtopics and related subjects.

Understanding the lecture and taking notes will be easier if you have some idea of what the lecture is about. If your instructor assigns a textbook chapter that is related to the lecture, try to read the assignment before attending. If you are unable to read the entire chapter before class, at least preread the chapter to become familiar with the topics it covers. If no reading assignment is given in advance, check your course outline to determine the topic of the lecture. Then preread the sections of your text that pertain to the topic.

Once you arrive at a lecture class, get organized before it begins. Take your coat off and have your notebook, pen, and textbook chapter, if needed, ready to use. While waiting for class to begin, try to recall the content of the previous lecture: Think of three or four key points that were presented. Check your notes, if necessary. This process will activate your thought processes, focus your attention on course content, and make it easier for you to begin taking notes right away.

HOW TO TAKE LECTURE NOTES

A good set of lecture notes must accomplish three things. First, and most important, your notes must serve as a record or summary of the lecture's main points. Second, they must include enough details and examples so that you can recall the information several weeks later. Third, your notes must in some way show the relative importance of ideas presented and reflect the organization of the lecture.

Record Main Ideas

The main ideas of a lecture are the points the instructor emphasizes and elaborates. They are the major ideas that the details, explanations, examples, and general discussion support. Instructors frequently give many clues to what is important in a lecture. Here are a few ways speakers show what is important.

Change in Voice: Some lecturers change the tone or pitch of their voices in order to emphasize major points. A speaker's voice may get louder or softer or higher or lower as he or she presents important ideas.

Change in Rate of Speech: Speakers may slow down as they discuss important concepts. Sometimes a speaker goes so slowly that he or she seems to be dictating information. If a speaker giving a definition pauses slightly after each word or phrase, it is a way of telling you that the definition is important and you should write it down.

Listing and Numbering Points: A lecturer may directly state that there are "three important causes" or "four significant effects" or "five possible situations" as he or she begins discussing a particular topic. These expressions are clues to the material's importance. Frequently, a speaker further identifies or emphasizes the separate, particular facts or ideas that make up the "three causes" or "four effects" with words such as *first, second,* and *finally,* or *one effect, a second effect, another effect,* and *a final effect.*

Writing on the Chalkboard: Some lecturers write key words or outlines of major ideas on the chalkboard as they speak. While not all important ideas are recorded on the chalkboard, you can be sure that if an instructor does take the time to write a word or phrase on the chalkboard, it is important.

Use of Audiovisuals: Some instructors emphasize important ideas, clarify relationships, or diagram processes or procedures by using audiovisual aids. Commonly used are overhead projectors that project on a screen previously prepared material or information the instructor draws or writes. Also, an instructor may use movies, filmstrips, videotapes, or photographs to emphasize or describe important ideas and concepts.

Direct Announcement: Occasionally, an instructor will announce straightforwardly that a concept or idea is especially important. He or she may begin by saying, "Particularly important to remember as you study is . . . ," or "One important fact that you must keep in mind is. . . ." The instructor may even hint that such information would make a good exam question. Be sure to mark hints like these in your notes. Emphasize these items with an asterisk or write *exam?* in the margin.

Nonverbal Clues: Many speakers give as many nonverbal as verbal clues to what is important. Often lecturers provide clues to what they feel is important through their movements and actions as well as their words. Some lecturers walk toward their audience as they make a major point. Others may use hand gestures, pound the table, or pace back and forth as they present key ideas. While each speaker is different, most speakers use some nonverbal means of emphasizing important points.

EXERCISE 1 ───────────

Directions: *Select one of your instructors and analyze his or her lecture style. Attend one lecture, and, as you take notes, try to be particularly aware of how he or she lets you know what is important. After the lecture, try to analyze your instructor, using the following questions:*

1. Did the instructor change his or her voice? When? How?

   _____

2. Did his or her rate of speech vary? When?

   _____

3. Did the instructor list or number important points?

   _____

4. Did the instructor use the chalkboard?

   _____

5. Did he or she directly state what was important?

   _____

6. What nonverbal clues did the instructor give?

   _____

Record Details and Examples

A difficult part of taking notes is deciding how much detail to include with the main ideas. Obviously you cannot write down everything, since lecturers speak at the rate of about 125 words per minute. Even if you could take shorthand, it would be nearly impossible to record everything the lecturer says. As a result, you have to be selective and record only particularly important details. As a rule of thumb, record a brief phrase that summarizes each major supporting detail. Try to write down a phrase for each detail that directly explains or clarifies a major point.

If an instructor gives you several examples of a particular law, situation, or problem, be sure to write down in summary form at least one example. Record more than one if you have time. While at the time of the lecture it may seem that you completely understand what is being discussed, you will find that a few weeks later you really do need the example to help you recall the lecture.

Record the Organization of the Lecture

As you write down the main ideas and important details of a lecture, try to organize or arrange your notes so that you can easily see how the lecture is organized. By recording the organization of the lecture, you will be able to determine the relative importance of ideas, and you will know what to pay most attention to as you study and review for an exam.

A simple way to show a lecture's organization is to use indentation. Retain a regular margin on your paper. Start your notes on the most important of the topics at the left margin. For less important main ideas, indent your notes slightly. For major details, indent slightly more. Indent even more for examples and other details. The rule of thumb to follow is this: The less important the idea, the more it should be indented. Your notes might be organized like this:

```
Major topic
   Main idea
      detail
      detail
         example
   Main idea
      detail
      detail
      detail
Major topic
   Main idea
      detail
         example
```

Notice that the sample looks like an outline but is missing the Roman numerals (I, II, III), capital letters (A, B, C), and Arabic numerals (1, 2, 3) that are usually contained in an outline. Also notice, however, that this system of note-taking does accomplish the same major goal as an outline—it separates important information from less important information. This indentation system, like an outline, shows at a glance how important a particular fact or idea is. If the organization of a lecture is obvious, you may wish to use a number or letter system in addition to indenting.

Lectures are often organized using organizational patterns—definition, time sequence, comparison-contrast, cause-effect, problem-solution, or enumeration. An entire lecture may be organized using one pattern; a history lecture, for example, may use the time-sequence pattern throughout. More often, however, several patterns will be evident at various points in a lecture. A psychology professor, for instance, may discuss definitions of motivation and compare and contrast different motivational theories. Refer to Chapter 9 for a review of organizational patterns and the directional words that signal them.

The notes in Figures 14-1 and 14-2 show that effective lecture notes should record main ideas, important details, and examples, and that they should reflect the lecture's organization. Both sets of notes were taken on the same lecture. One set of notes is thorough and effective; the other is lengthy and does not focus on key ideas. Read and evaluate each set of notes.

Make Notetaking Easier

If you record main ideas, details, and examples, using the indentation system to show the lecture's organization, you will take adequate notes. However, there are some tips you can follow to make notetaking easier, to make your notes more complete, and to make study and review easier.

I. Social Stratification
 Def's
  Soc. Strat. - hierarchy of ranks that exist in society
  Status - criteria to find position in soc.
   - depends partly on roles
  2 types
   1. ascribed status - handed down, inherited
    ex.: titles, race, wealth, ethnic background
   2. achieved status - things you control
    ex.: education, jobs

II. Social Mobility
 Def. - how indiv. moves in hierarchy
  - amt. of movement depends on society

 2 Types
  1. caste - ex.: India - no mobility - you inherit class + status
  2. open - large amt. of achieved status - great mobility - ex.: U.S.A.

Soc. 106
9/16

FIGURE 14-1 Notes Showing Lecture Organization

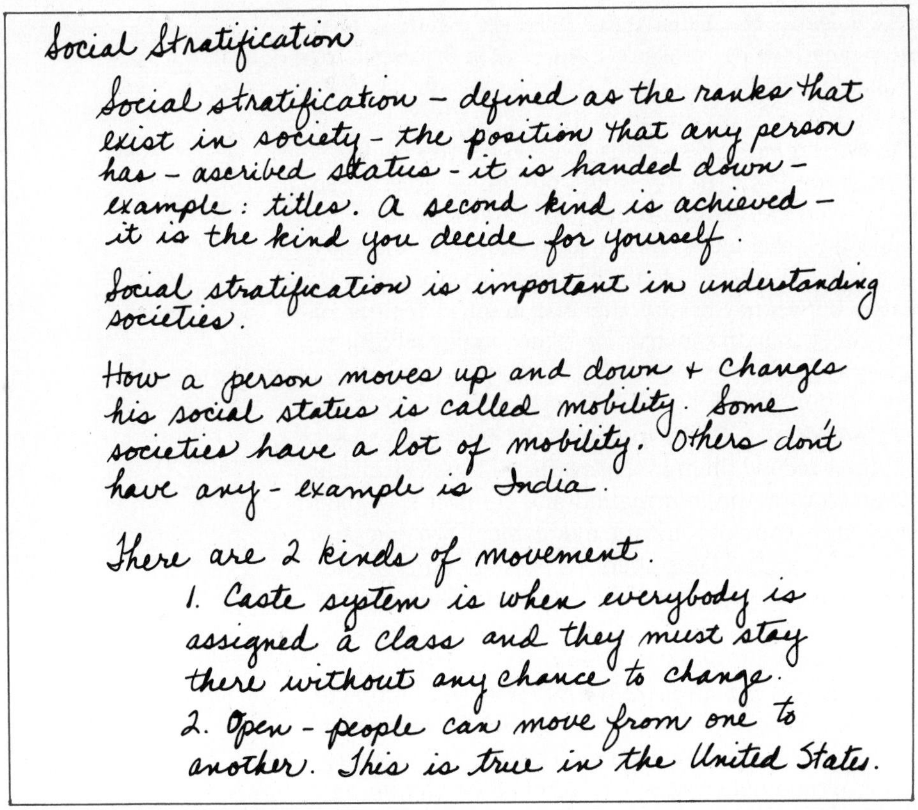

> Social Stratification
>
> Social stratification – defined as the ranks that exist in society – the position that any person has – ascribed status – it is handed down – example: titles. A second kind is achieved – it is the kind you decide for yourself.
>
> Social stratification is important in understanding societies.
>
> How a person moves up and down + changes his social status is called mobility. Some societies have a lot of mobility. Others don't have any – example is India.
>
> There are 2 kinds of movement.
> 1. Caste system is when everybody is assigned a class and they must stay there without any chance to change.
> 2. Open – people can move from one to another. This is true in the United States.

FIGURE 14-2   Less Effective, Unfocused Lecture Notes

Use Ink: Pencil tends to smear and is harder to read.

Use a Standard-sized Notebook and Paper: Paper smaller than 8½″ × 11″ doesn't allow you to write as much on a page, and it is more difficult to see the overall organization of a lecture if you have to flip through a lot of pages.

Keep a Separate Notebook or Section for Each Course: You need to have notes for each course together so that you can review them easily.

Date Your Notes: For easy reference later, be sure to date your notes. Your instructor might announce that an exam will cover everything presented after, for example, October 5. If your notes are not dated, you will not know where to begin to study.

Leave Blank Spaces: To make your notes more readable and make it easier to see the organization of ideas, leave plenty of blank space. If you know you missed a detail or definition, leave additional blank space. You can fill it in later by checking with a friend or referring to your text.

Mark Assignments: Occasionally an instructor will announce an assignment or test date in the middle of a lecture. Of course you will jot it down, but be sure to mark "Assignment" or "Test Date" in the margin so that you can find it easily and transfer it to your assignment notebook.

Mark Ideas That Are Unclear: If an instructor presents a fact or idea that is unclear, put a question mark in the margin. Later, ask your instructor or another student about this idea.

Sit in the Front of the Classroom: Especially in large lecture halls, it is to your advantage to sit near the front. In the front you will be able to see and hear the instructor easily—you can maintain eye contact and observe his or her facial expressions and nonverbal clues. If you sit in the back, you may become bored, and it is easy to be distracted by all the people in front of you. Because of the people seated between you and the instructor, a feeling of distance is created. You may feel that the instructor is not really talking to you.

Don't Plan to Recopy Your Notes: Some students take each day's notes in a hasty, careless way and then recopy them in the evening. These students feel that recopying helps them review the information and think it is a good way to study. Actually, recopying often becomes a mechanical process that takes a lot of time but very little thought. Time spent recopying can be better spent reviewing the notes in a manner that will be suggested later in this chapter.

Avoid Tape-recording Lectures: As a maximum effort to get complete and accurate notes, some students resort to tape-recording each lecture. After the lecture, they play back the tape and take notes on it, starting and stopping the tape as needed. This is a tremendously time-consuming technique and very inefficient in terms of the time spent relative to the amount of learning that occurs. In using the tape system, a student has to spend at least an additional hour in playback for every hour spent in class just to complete his or her notes.

Use Abbreviations: To save time, try to use abbreviations instead of writing out long or frequently used words. If you are taking a course in psychology, you would not want to write out *p-s-y-c-h-o-l-o-g-y* each time the word is used. It would be much faster to use the abbreviation *psy*. Try to develop abbreviations that are appropriate for the subject areas you are studying. The abbreviations shown in Figure 14-3, devised by a student in business

Common words	Abbreviation	Specialized words	Abbreviation
and	+	organization	org.
with	w/	management	man.
compare		data bank	D.B.
comparison	comp.	structure	str.
importance	imp't	evaluation	eval.
advantage	adv	management	
introduction	intro.	by objective	MBO
continued	cont'd.	management	
		information	MIS
		system	
		organizational	
		development	OD
		communication	
		simulations	comm/sim.

FIGURE 14-3   Abbreviations for Use in Notetaking

management, give you an idea of the possibilities. Notice that both common and specialized words are abbreviated.

As you develop your own set of abbreviations, be sure to begin gradually. It is easy to overuse abbreviations and end up with a set of notes that are almost meaningless.

EXERCISE 2 _____

Directions: *Select one set of lecture notes from a class you recently attended. Reread your notes and look for words or phrases you could have abbreviated. Write some of these words in the space provided.*

Word	*Abbreviation*
_____	_____
_____	_____
_____	_____
_____	_____
_____	_____
_____	_____
_____	_____
_____	_____
_____	_____

Overcoming Common Notetaking Problems

Instructors present lectures differently, use various lecture styles, and organize their subjects in different ways. It is therefore common to experience difficulty taking notes in one or more courses. Table 14-1 identifies common problems associated with lecture notetaking and offers possible solutions.

HOW TO EDIT YOUR NOTES

After you have taken a set of lecture notes, do not assume that they are accurate and complete. Most students find that they missed some information and were unable to record as many details or examples as they would have liked. Even very experienced notetakers are faced with these problems. Fortunately, the solution is simple. Do not plan on taking a final and complete set of notes during the lecture. Instead, record just enough during the lecture to help you remember a main idea, detail, or example. Leave plenty of blank space; then, if possible, sit down immediately after the lecture and review your notes. Fill in the missing information. Expand, or make more complete,

TABLE 14-1 Common Notetaking Problems

Problem	Solution
"My mind wanders and I get bored."	Sit in the front of the room. Be certain to preview assignments. Pose questions you expect to be answered in the lecture.
"The instructor talks too fast."	Develop a shorthand system; use abbreviations. Leave blanks and fill them in later.
"The lecturer rambles."	Preview correlating text assignments to determine organizing principles. Reorganize your notes after the lecture.
"Some ideas don't seem to fit anywhere."	Record them in the margin or in parentheses within your notes for reassessment later during editing.
"Everything seems important." _or_ "Nothing seems important."	You have not identified key concepts and may lack necessary background knowledge (see Chapter 6)—you do not understand the topic. Preview related text assignments.
"I can't spell all the new technical terms."	Record them phonetically, the way they sound; fill in correct spellings during editing.
"The instructor uses terms without defining them."	Record terms as used; leave space to record definitions later; consult text glossary or dictionary.
"The instructor reads directly from text."	Mark passages in text; write instructor's comments in the margin. Record page references in your notes.

any details or examples that are not fully explained. This process is called _editing_. It is essentially a process of correcting, revising, and adding to your notes to make them more complete and accurate. Editing notes for a one-hour lecture should take no more than five or ten minutes.

If you are unable to edit your notes immediately after a lecture, it is critical that you edit them that evening. The longer the time lapse between notetaking and editing, the less effective editing becomes. Also, the greater the time lapse, the more facts and examples you will be unable to recall and fill in.

The sample set of lecture notes in Figure 14-4 has been edited. The notes taken during the lecture are in black; the additions and changes made during editing are in color. Read the notes, noticing the types of information added during editing.

HOW TO STUDY YOUR NOTES

Taking and editing lecture notes is only part of what must be done to learn from your instructor's lectures. You also have to learn and review the

Anxiety + Defense Mechanisms   Page 602
                                                    10/12

I. Anxiety
        def gen fear or worry [generalized]
    Levels
        1. moderate - productive
            athletes - higher level of phys. functioning
            test-taking - certain amt helps - keeps you alert
        2. Extreme - uncomfortable   ex: nauseous,
                    extremely nervous, hands shaking.
                - can be reduced by defense mechanism

II. Defense Mech
        def - uncon[scious] devices to protect self and /or keep self
                under control
            ex: student who is hostile toward teacher
                explains it to himself by saying that "the
                                                teacher hates me"
    Types of Def. Mechanism
        1. Repression - to drive out of consciousness
            ex: student - math instructor   student forgets
                to keep app't with math instructor because
                he's afraid he will be told he is failing the
                course.
        2. Regression - reaction to anxiety by going back to less
            mature behavior
            ex: college student applying for job but
                doesn't get it - pouts + says the
                interviewer cheated + hired son of
                his best friend.

FIGURE 14-4   Edited Lecture Notes

notes in order to do well on an exam. To study lecture notes, try to apply the same principles that you use in learning material in your textbooks. (1) Do not try to learn your notes by reading them over and over. Rereading is not an efficient review technique because it takes too much time relative to the amount you learn. (2) As in reading textbook assignments, identify what is important. You must sort out what you will learn and study from all the rest of the information that you have written in your notes. (3) Have a way of checking yourself—of deciding if you have learned the necessary information. In studying textbooks, you use the "Recite" step of the SQ3R method to check your recall of what you have read; you can use fact cards or summary sheets to test your recall further. For studying lecture notes, there is a system that uses similar techniques of study: the *recall clue system.*

The Recall Clue System

The recall clue system helps make the review and study of lecture notes easier and more effective. You will notice that it is very similar to the summary word technique suggested in Chapter 11. To use the recall clue system, follow these steps:

1. Leave a two-inch margin at the left side of each page of notes.
2. The margin stays blank while you are taking notes.
3. After you have edited your notes, fill in the left margin with words and phrases that briefly summarize the notes.

The recall clues should be words that will trigger your memory and help you recall the complete information in your notes. These clues function as memory tags. They help you pull out, or retrieve, from your memory any information that is labeled with these tags. Figure 14-5 shows a sample of notes in which the recall clue system has been used. When you are trying to remember information on an exam, the recall clue from your notes will work automatically to help you remember necessary information.

A variation on the recall clue system that students have found effective is to write questions rather than summary words and phrases in the margin (see Figure 14-6). The questions trigger your memory and enable you to recall the information that answers your question. The use of questions enables you to test yourself, thereby allowing you to simulate an exam situation.

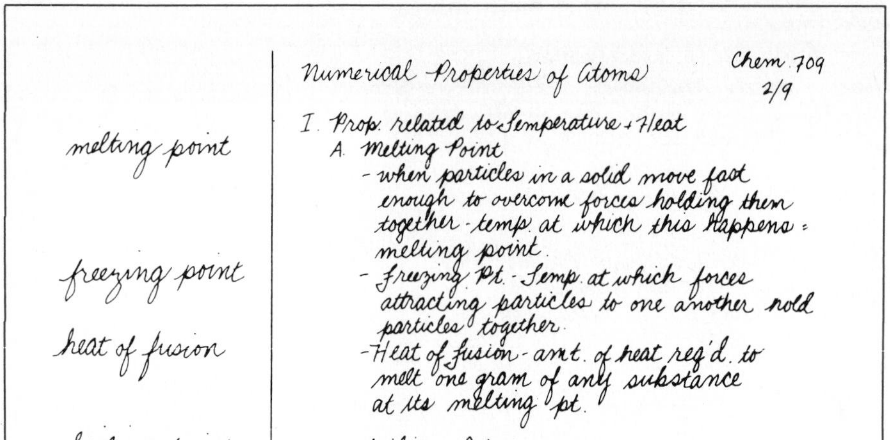

Numerical Properties of Atoms — Chem. 709, 2/9

I. Prop. related to Temperature + Heat

melting point	A. Melting Point - when particles in a solid move fast enough to overcome forces holding them together - temp. at which this happens = melting point.
freezing point	- Freezing Pt. - Temp. at which forces attracting particles to one another hold particles together.
heat of fusion	- Heat of fusion - am't. of heat req'd. to melt one gram of any substance at its melting pt.
boiling point	B. Boiling Point. - Point at which molecules of a liquid begin to escape as gas.
heat of vap.	- Heat of vaporization - am't of heat req'd. to change one gram of liquid to a gas at its boiling pt.
condensation pt.	- Condensation Pt. - point at which gas, cooling, changes back to liquid.
spec. heat	C. Specific Heat ex. beach - sand hot, water cold - why? Sand + H_2O have different spec. heat def. am't of heat needed to raise temp. of a spec. mass of substance by a certain am't.
formula for S.h.	formula - S.h. = $\frac{\text{heat in cals.}}{\text{mass in grams} \times \text{temp diff. in °C}}$ S.h. = $\frac{cal}{g \times °C}$

FIGURE 14-5 Lecture Notes with Recall Clues Added

Role of Advertising

Advertising
- Widely used in our economy.
- Promotes competition; encourages open system.
- definition - presentation of a product/service to broad segment of the population.

what is Advertising?

Characteristics

what are its Characteristics?

1. non-personal - uses media rather than person-to-person contact.
2. paid for by seller
3. intended to influence the consumer.

Objectives

what is the Ultimate Objective?

Ultimate objective - to sell product or service

what are the Immediate Objectives?

Immediate objectives

1. to inform - make consumer aware
   ex. new product available

2. to persuade - stress value, advantages of product.
   ex. results of market research

3. to reinforce - happens after 1 and 2.
   - consumers need to be reminded about prod./service - even if they use it.
   - often done through slogans and jingles.

FIGURE 14-6   Lecture Notes with Recall Questions Added

	Yes	No
1. Notes are titled and dated.		
2. A separate line is used for each key idea.		
3. Less important ideas are indented.		
4. Abbreviations and symbols are used.		
5. The organization of the lecture is apparent.		
6. Words and phrases (not entire sentences) are recorded.		
7. Examples and illustrations are included.		
8. Sufficient explanation and detail are included.		
9. Adequate space is left for editing.		
10. Marginal space is available for recall clues.		

FIGURE 14-7   Notetaking Checklist

Using the Recall Clue System

To study your notes using the recall clue system, cover up the notes with a sheet of paper, exposing only the recall clues in the left margin. Then read the first recall clue and try to remember the information in the portion of the notes beside it. Then slide the paper down and check that portion to see if you remembered all the important facts. If you remembered only part of the information, cover up that portion of your notes and again check your recall. Continue checking until you are satisfied that you can remember all the important facts. Then move on to the next recall clue on the page, following the same testing-checking procedure.

To get into the habit of using the recall clue system, mark off with a ruler a two-inch column on the next several blank pages in each of your notebooks. Then when you open your notebook at the beginning of the class, you will be reminded to use the system.

This chapter has offered numerous techniques and suggestions for taking effective lecture notes. Use the checklist shown in Figure 14-7 to refresh your memory on them and evaluate your own notetaking.

EXERCISE 3 _____

Directions: *Read the sample set of notes in Figure 14-8. Fill in the recall clues or formulate questions that would help you study and learn the notes.*

EXERCISE 4 _____

Directions: *For each course that you are taking this semester, use the recall clue system for at least one week. Use the recall clues to review your notes several times. At the end of the week, evaluate how well the system works for you.*

1. What advantages does it have?

I Psychoanalytic theory - created by Sigmund Freud

  A. free association - major diagnostic techniques in psychoanalysis; patient reports whatever comes to mind / holds nothing back.

  B. repression - psych. process of driving ideas out of consciousness

  C. suppression - conscious of an idea, but won't tell anyone about it.

  D. trauma - particularly disturbing event; most psych. disturbances traceable to a trauma.

  E. interp. of dreams - dreams - fantasies which person believes to be true / have profound influence on personality devlpmt.

  F. Id - power system of personality providing energy.
    1. pleasure principle - all unpleasent events should be avoided.
      a. primary process - normal logic does not operate.
        ex. bizarre dreams, hallucinations

  G. Ego - strategist of personality / concerned w/ what a person CAN do.
    1. reality principle - distinction between real + unreal rather than dist. between pleasure + pain. Satisfies _id_ in a realistic manner.
      a. secondary process - rational, logical, critical.

  H. Superego - "good versus bad", rewards and punishments.
    1. conscience - critical, punitive aspect of superego.

FIGURE 14-8 **Sample Lecture Notes**

2. Did it help you remember facts and ideas?

_____

3. Are there any disadvantages?

_____

SUMMARY

Because many college instructors expect you to remember and apply facts and ideas in their class lectures, it is necessary to take good lecture notes, edit them properly, and develop a system for studying them effectively.

Effective lecture notes should accomplish three things. First, good notes should summarize the main points of the lecture. Well-taken lecture notes are a valuable aid to study. Second, lecture notes should include enough details and examples so that you can completely understand and recall the information several weeks later. Third, the notes should show the relative importance of ideas and reflect the organization of the lecture. The chapter provided specific suggestions on how to accomplish each of these goals and offered numerous tips on how to accomplish each of these goals and offered numerous tips on making notetaking easier.

After taking a set of lecture notes, it is necessary to correct, revise, fill in missing or additional information, and expand your notes to make them more complete. This process of editing your notes results in clearer, more accurate notes from which to study.

Effective study of lecture notes follows many of the same principles and procedures that are used for studying textbook chapters. The recall clue system is a way of making study and review easier and more effective. A two-inch margin at the left of each page of notes is left blank during notetaking. Later, as you reread your notes, you then write in the margin words and phrases that briefly summarize the notes. These phrases, or recall clues, trigger your memory and help you recall information in the notes.

15

Participating in Class Activities and Projects

Use this chapter to:

1. *Learn to ask and answer questions in class.*
2. *Prepare for class discussions.*
3. *Work effectively on group projects.*
4. *Prepare and make oral presentations.*

While the lecture is still the most common method of teaching in college classes, many instructors have recently begun to incorporate more discussion and group activities into their course organization. Considerable research on teaching effectiveness indicates that students learn from each other as well as from the instructor. Consequently, some of your classes will likely involve group projects or assignments, small group or panel discussions, or oral presentations. Also, once you begin to take specialized courses in your major, you will be enrolled in smaller classes or seminars in which group participation is essential.

ASKING AND ANSWERING QUESTIONS

Asking and answering questions in class is an important aspect of many college courses; even in lecture courses, instructors may invite questions at the end of class. For some large lecture courses, you might be required to register for a weekly recitation class. Its purpose is to provide a forum for students to ask and answer questions, as well as to discuss lecture content. Furthermore, in some courses a portion of your grade is determined by your class participation.

Many students are hesitant to ask or answer questions; often because they are concerned about how their classmates and instructor will respond. They fear that their question may seem "dumb" or that their answer may be incorrect. This fear is one that must be conquered early in your college career. Asking questions is often essential to complete and thorough understanding, and you will find that once you've asked a question, other students will be glad you asked because they had the same question in mind. Answering questions posed by your instructor gives you an opportunity to evaluate how well you have learned or understood course content as well as to demonstrate your knowledge. Use the following suggestions to build the habit of asking and answering questions:

1. To get started, as you read an assignment jot down several questions that might clarify or explain it better. Bring your list to class. Refer to your list as you speak, if necessary.
2. When you ask a question, state it clearly and concisely. Don't ramble or make excuses for asking.
3. Remember, most instructors invite and respond favorably to questions; if your question is a serious one, it will be received positively. Don't pose questions for the sake of asking a question. Class time is limited and valuable.
4. In answering questions, formulate your responses mentally before you volunteer them.
5. Think of answering questions as a means of identifying yourself to the instructor as a serious, committed student, as well as a means of learning.

PARTICIPATING IN CLASS DISCUSSIONS

In courses designed to encourage students to think, react to, and evaluate ideas and issues, class discussions are a common form of instruction. Class discussion courses differ from lecture classes in three ways. First, the amount of advance preparations differs greatly. Second, your responsibility and involvement are of a different level and type. Finally, the manner in which you study, review, and are evaluated for group activities is different from techniques used in lecture classes. You may find, for example, that you are graded, in part, on the quality and effectiveness of your participation, rather than solely by tests and exams.

Preparing for Class Discussions

Preparing for a class discussion demands more time and effort than does getting ready for a lecture class. In a lecture class, most of your work comes *after* the class, editing your notes and using the recall clue system to review them. The opposite is true for discussion courses. Most of your work is done *before* you go to class. You must spend considerable time reading, evaluating, and making notes. The following suggestions will help you get ready for a discussion class.

Read the Assignment: Usually a class discussion is about a particular topic (issue problem). Frequently, instructors give textbook or library reading assignments that are intended to give you some background information. The reading assignments are also meant to start you thinking about a topic, show you different points of a view about an issue, or indicate some aspects of a problem. Read carefully the material assigned. Do not just skim through it as you might for a lecture class. Instead, read the assignment with the purpose of learning all the material. Use a variation of the SQ3R method to help you learn, and mark and underline important ideas as you read.

Review: Make Notes for Discussion: After you have read the assign-ment, review it with the purpose of identifying and jotting down the following:

1. Ideas, concepts, or points of view you do not understand. Keep a list of these; you can use the list as a guide to form questions during class.
2. Ideas and points with which you disagree or strongly agree. By jotting these down you will have some ideas to start with if your instructor asks you to react to the topic.
3. Good and poor examples. Note examples that are particularly good or particularly poor. These will help you to react to the topic.
4. Strong arguments and weak arguments. As you read, try to follow the line of reasoning, and evaluate any arguments presented. Make notes on your evaluations; the notes will remind you of points you may want to make during the discussion.

Getting Involved in Class Discussions

Discussion classes require greater, more active involvement and partic-ipation than do lecture classes. In lecture classes, your main concern is to listen carefully and to record notes accurately and completely. In discussion classes, your responsibility is much greater. Not only do you have to take notes, but you also have to participate in the discussion. The problem many students experience in getting involved in discussions is that they do not know what to say or when to say it. Here are a few instances when it might be appropriate to speak. Say something when:

1. You can ask a serious, thoughtful question.
2. Someone asks a question that you can answer.
3. You have a comment or suggestion to make on what has already been said.
4. You can supply additional information that will clarify the topic under discussion.
5. You can correct an error or clarify a misunderstanding.

To get further involved in the discussion, try the following suggestions:

1. Even if you are reluctant to speak before a group, try to say something early in the discussion; the longer you wait, the more difficult it becomes. Also, the longer you wait, the greater the chance someone else will say what you were planning to say.
2. Make your comments brief and to the point. It is probably a mistake to say too much rather than too little. If your instructor feels you should say more, he or she will probably ask you to explain or elaborate further.
3. Try to avoid getting involved in direct exchanges or disagreements with other class members. Always speak to the group, not individuals, and be sure that your comments relate to and involve the entire class.
4. When you feel it is appropriate to introduce a new idea, clue your listeners that you are changing topics or introducing a new idea. You might say something like "Another related question . . . ," or "Another point to consider is . . ."
5. When you think of comments or ideas that you want to make as the discussion is going on, jot them down. Then when you get a chance to

speak, you will have your notes to refer to. Notes help you organize and present your ideas in a clear and organized fashion.

6. Try to keep an open mind throughout the discussion. Leave personal dislikes, attitudes toward other members of the group, and your own biases and prejudices aside.

7. Organize your remarks. First, connect what you plan to say with what has already been said. Then state your ideas as clearly as possible. Next, develop or explain your idea.

8. Watch the group as you speak. When making a point or offering a comment, watch both your instructor and others in the class. Their responses will show whether they understand you or need further information, whether they agree or disagree, whether they are interested or uninterested. You can then decide, based on their responses, whether you made your point effectively or whether you need to explain or defend your argument more carefully.

Notetaking During Class Discussions

While most of your energy in a class discussion is consumed by following and participating in the discussion, it is important to take summary notes while the discussion is going on. Your notes should not be as detailed as they would be for a lecture class; record only the key topics discussed and the important concepts and ideas brought into the discussion.

Editing the notes you take in discussion classes is essential. Because you have so little time and mental energy to devote to notetaking during the discussion, it is very important to fill in and complete your notes later.

Reviewing and Studying for Discussion Classes

Just as preparing for and participating in discussion classes differ from preparing for and participating in lecture classes, so does the review-study process for discussion classes require slightly different techniques from those used for lecture classes. Fortunately, since more work is done prior to attending a discussion class, less is required after it. To review and study for a discussion class, be sure to:

1. Review your notes; use the recall clue system to check your recall of important information.

2. Review any reading assignment given prior to the class discussion. You may want to reread the assignment. Given the new ideas and perspectives introduced in class, you will probably find new ways of approaching and viewing the information presented in the assignment. As you review, be sure to mark and underline any information that you now realize is particularly important or has direct bearing on the discussion.

3. Anticipate possible test or exam questions based on your notes, the reading assignment, and your recall of the discussion. Most likely, your instructor will give you either essay or short-answer questions on exams. Objective questions (true/false, multiple-choice, or matching) would be rather difficult to construct if there is little or no clear base of factual information. Essay or short-answer questions lend themselves more readily to the concerns, purposes, and goals your instructor most likely has for a discussion course. (For specific techniques of preparing for and taking essay

and short-answer exams refer to the next chapter.) Pay particular attention to topics for which your instructor allowed the most discussion time and those with which your instructor seemed to get most involved.

EXERCISE 1 ——————————————————

Directions: Review the section "Some Sources of Stress," beginning on page 426 in the sample textbook chapter reprinted in Appendix A. Assume that you have been assigned this section of the chapter as preparation for a discussion class. What notes would you make and what questions would you be ready to ask as you prepared for the discussion? Record your notes and questions on a separate sheet.

WORKING EFFECTIVELY ON GROUP PROJECTS

Many assignments and class activities involve working with a small group of classmates. For example, a sociology instructor might divide the class into groups and ask each group to brainstorm solutions to economic or social problems of the elderly. Your political science professor might create a panel to discuss the private and collective consequences of voting. Group presentations may be required in a business course, or groups in your American history class might be asked to research a topic.

Group projects are intended to enable students to learn from one another by viewing each other's thinking processes and by evaluating each other's ideas and approaches. Group activities also develop valuable skills in interpersonal communication that are essential in career and work-related situations. Some students are reluctant to work in groups because they feel that they are not in control of the situation; they dislike having their grade depend on the performance of others as well as themselves. Use the following suggestions to make your group function effectively:

1. Select alert, energetic classmates if you are permitted to choose with whom you work.
2. Be an active, responsible participant. Accept your share of the work and expect others to do the same. Approach the activity with a serious attitude, rather than joking or complaining about the assignment. This will establish a serious tone and cut down on wasted time.
3. Because organization and direction are essential for productivity, every group needs a leader. Unless some other competent group member immediately assumes leadership, take a leadership role. While leadership may require more work, you will be in control. (Remember, too, that leadership roles are valuable experiences for your career.) As the group's leader, you will need to direct the group in analyzing the assignment, organizing a plan of action, distributing work assignments, planning, and if the project is long-term, establishing deadlines.
4. Take advantage of individual strengths and weaknesses. For instance, a person who seems indifferent or is easily distracted should not be assigned the task of recording the group's findings. The most organized, outgoing member might be assigned the task of making an oral report to the class.
5. Be assertive. If a group member fails to do his or her share of the work,

clearly express your concern. Be direct and nonthreatening; don't hint about deadlines or angrily accuse the person of ruining your grade.

EXERCISE 2 ————————————————

Directions: *Suppose you are part of a five-member group that is preparing for a panel discussion on gun control for a sociology class. One group member is very vocal and opinionated. You fear she is likely to dominate the discussion. Another group member is painfully shy and has volunteered to do double research if he doesn't have to speak much during the discussion. A third member appears uninterested and tends to sit back and watch as the group works and plans. How should the group respond to each of these individuals? List several possible solutions to each problem.*

PREPARING AND MAKING ORAL PRESENTATIONS

Oral presentations may be group or individual. Groups may be asked to report their findings, summarize their research, or describe a process of procedure. Individual presentations are often summaries of research papers, reviews or critiques, or interpretations of literary or artistic works. Use the following suggestions to make effective oral presentations:

1. Understand the purpose of the assignment. Analyze it carefully before beginning to work. Is the presentation intended to be informative? Are you to summarize, evaluate, or criticize?
2. Collect and organize your information. Refer to Chapter 18 for specific techniques.
3. Prepare outline notes. Use index cards (either 3″ × 5″ or 5″ × 8″) to record only key words and phrases.
4. Consider the use of visual aids. Depending on the type of assignment as well as your topic, diagrams, photographs, or demonstrations may be appropriate and effective in maintaining audience interest.
5. Anticipate questions your audience may ask. Review and revise your notes to include answers.
6. Practice delivery. This will build your confidence and help overcome nervousness. First, practice your presentation aloud several times by yourself. Time yourself to be sure you are within any limits. Then practice in front of friends and ask for criticism. Finally, tape-record your presentation. Play it back, looking for ways to improve it.
7. Deliver your presentation as effectively as possible. Engage your audience's interest by maintaining eye contact; look directly at other students as you speak, and make a deliberate effort to speak slowly; when you are nervous, your speech tends to speed up. Be enthusiastic and energetic.

If you need additional information or help with making oral presentations, consult your college's learning lab or obtain a guidebook on public speaking from your campus library.

As a variation on oral presentations, some instructors might ask each student (or group) to lead one class discussion, or they might organize panel discussions. As in oral presentations, organization is the essential ingredient for these activities. Plan ahead, outlining topics to be discussed, questions to be asked, or issues to confront.

EXERCISE 3 _____

Directions: *You are to make a three-minute oral presentation on learning and study methods you have found effective in a particular course you are taking this semester. Prepare a set of outline notes for your presentation, and practice delivery of your presentation. Then, answer the following questions.*

1. How did you organize your presentation?

   _____

2. Did preparation of your presentation force you to analyze how you learn in the course you chose?

   _____

3. How did you improve your presentation through practice?

   _____

SUMMARY

Although some instructors prefer the lecture method as a means of conducting their classes, others use class activities, discussions, group projects, or oral presentations to direct students' learning. Asking and answering questions is an essential part of some college courses. Asking questions enables you to clarify course content: answering them allows you to evaluate the level and quality of your learning.

Class discussions allow students to learn from each other by assessing and evaluating each other's ideas. A substantial amount of advance preparation is required before you attend discussion classes. Preparation often includes carefully reading any assignments and taking notes for discussion. Your notes might include specific comments, ideas, and questions you could contribute to the discussion. During the class, you are expected to get involved, to participate in the discussion. As the discussion is going on, it is important to take summary notes that can be expanded during a later editing process.

As you review and study after the class discussion, first review your notes and check your recall of the information by using the recall clue system suggested for taking lecture notes. Then review and mark any reading assignment you completed prior to the discussion. Finally, try to anticipate test or exam questions that could be based on your notes, the reading assignment, and your recall of the discussion.

Group projects require you to work closely with other students to complete an assignment. Organization and active participation by each group member are essential to group productivity. Oral presentations, either group or individual, require careful preparation, practice, and effective delivery.

16

Preparing for Exams

Use this chapter to:
1. *Get organized for study and review.*
2. *Find out how to learn the material to be covered in an exam.*

Tests, quizzes, and examinations are important parts of most college courses because they help to determine grades. Tests are also important as learning experiences. Daily or weekly quizzes force you to keep up with reading assignments and attend class regularly. Also, it is through preparing for and taking exams that a student consolidates, or ties together, concepts and facts learned in a course. Finally, it is through the review and study involved in preparing for an exam that information is learned or stored in your memory.

Studying is the most important thing you can do to increase your chance of passing an exam. When exam papers are returned, you may hear comments like "I spent at least ten hours studying. I went over everything, and I still failed the exam!" Students frequently complain that they spend large amounts of time studying and do not get the grades they think they deserve. Usually the problem is that although they did study, they did not study the best way.

A second mistake students make is to begin studying only when the date of an exam is announced. These students may read textbook assignments as they are given, but they hurry through them, planning to study them carefully later. Some students do the same with their lecture notes—they take them but do not edit or review them until an exam is announced. These delay tactics result in last-minute study, or cramming. Research indicates that cramming is *not* an effective learning method and confirms that continuous review, the alternative to cramming, is superior.

The most important steps in preparing for exams are (1) organizing your study and review, (2) identifying what to learn, (3) connecting and synthesizing ideas, and (4) learning and memorizing the material.

ORGANIZING YOUR STUDY AND REVIEW

The timing of your review sessions is crucial to achieving good test results. Organize your review sessions, using the suggestions discussed in the following sections.

Organize Your Time

1. Schedule several review sessions at least one week in advance of an exam. Set aside specific times for daily review, and incorporate them into your weekly schedule. If you are having difficulty with a particular subject, set up extra study times.
2. Spend time organizing your review. Make a list of all chapters, notes, and handouts that need to be reviewed. Divide the material, planning what you will review during each session.
3. Reserve time the night before the exam for final, complete review. Do not study new material during the session. Instead, review the most difficult material, checking your recall of important facts or information for possible essay questions.

When studying for an exam or test, find out whether it will be objective, essay, or a combination of both. If your instructor does not specify the type of exam when he or she announces the date, ask during or after class. Most instructors are willing to tell students what type of exam will be given—sometimes they simply forget to mention it when announcing the exam. If an instructor chooses not to tell you, do not be concerned; at least you have shown that you are interested and are thinking ahead.

Be sure you know what material the exam will cover. Usually your instructor will either announce the exam topics or give the time span that the exam will cover. Also, find out what your instructor expects of you and how he or she will evaluate your exam. Some instructors expect you to recall text and lecture material; others expect you to agree with their views on a particular subject; still others encourage you to recall, discuss, analyze, or disagree with the ideas and information they have presented. You can usually tell what to expect by the way quizzes have been graded or classes have been conducted.

Attend the Class Before the Exam

Be sure to attend the class prior to the exam. Cutting class to spend the time studying, although tempting, is a mistake. During this class the instructor may give a brief review of the material to be covered or offer last-minute review suggestions. Have you ever heard an instructor say "Be sure to look over . . ." prior to an exam? Listen carefully to how the instructor answers students' questions; these answers will provide clues about what the exam will emphasize.

Consider Studying with Others

Consider whether it would help you to study with another person or with a small group of students from your class. Be sure to weigh the following advantages and disadvantages of group study, then decide whether group study suits your learning style.

Group study can be advantageous for the following reasons.

1. Group study forces you to become actively involved with the course content. Talking about, reacting to, and discussing the material aids learning. If you have trouble concentrating or "staying with it" when studying alone, group study may be useful.

2. One of the best ways to learn something is to explain it to someone else. By using your own words and thinking of the best way to explain an idea, you are analyzing it and testing your own understanding. The repetition of explaining something you already understand also strengthens your learning.

Group study can, however, have disadvantages.

1. Unless everyone is serious, group study sessions can turn into social events in which very little study occurs.
2. Studying with the wrong people can produce negative attitudes that will work against you. For example, the "None of us understands this and we can't all fail" attitude is common.
3. By studying with someone who has not read the material carefully or attended classes regularly, you will waste time reviewing basic definitions and facts that you already know, instead of focusing on more difficult topics.

EXERCISE 1 ⎯⎯⎯⎯⎯⎯⎯⎯⎯⎯⎯⎯⎯

Directions: *Plan a review schedule for an upcoming exam. Include material you will study and when you will study it.*

IDENTIFYING WHAT TO STUDY

In preparing for an exam, review every source of information—textbook chapters and lecture notes—as well as sources sometimes overlooked, such as old exams and quizzes, the instructor's handouts, course outlines, and outside assignments. Talking with other students about the exam can also be helpful.

Textbook Chapters

All chapters assigned during the period covered by the exam or relating to the topics covered in the exam must be reviewed. Review of textbook chapters should be fairly easy if you have kept up with weekly assignments, used your own variation of a study-reading system, and marked and underlined each assignment.

Lecture Notes

In addition to textbook chapters, all relevant notes must be reviewed. This too is easy if you have used the notetaking and editing system presented in Chapter 14.

Previous Exams and Quizzes

Be sure to keep all old tests and quizzes, which are valuable sources of review for longer, more comprehensive exams. While most instructors do not repeat the same test questions, old quizzes list important facts, terms, and ideas. The comprehensive exam will probably test your recall of the same information through different types of questions. Pay particular attention to items that you got wrong; try to see a pattern of error. Are you missing certain types of questions? If so, spend extra time on these questions.

Instructor's Handouts

Instructors frequently distribute duplicated sheets of information, such as summary outlines, lists of terms, sample problems, maps and charts, or explanations of difficult concepts. Any material that an instructor prepares for distribution is bound to be important. As you review these sheets throughout the course, date them and label the lecture topic to which they correspond. Keep them together in a folder or in the front of your notebook so that you can refer to them easily.

Outside Assignments

Out-of-class assignments might include problems to solve, library research, written reactions or evaluations, or lectures or movies to attend. If an instructor gives an assignment outside of class, the topic is important. Because of the limited number of assignments that can be given in a course, instructors choose only those that are most valuable. You should, therefore, keep your notes on assignments together for easy review.

Talk with Other Students

Talking with classmates can help you identify the right material to learn. By talking with others, you may discover a topic that you have overlooked or recognize a new focus or direction.

CONNECTING AND SYNTHESIZING INFORMATION

Once you have identified what material must be learned, the next step is to make learning easier by drawing together, or synthesizing, the information. In your close study of chapters and lecture notes, do not get lost in details and lose sight of major themes or processes. When concentrating on details, you can miss significant points and fail to see relationships. Exams often measure your awareness of concepts and trends as well as your recall of facts, dates, and definitions. The following suggestions will help you learn to synthesize information.

Get a Perspective on the Course

To avoid overconcentration on detail and to obtain perspective on the course material, step back and view the course from a distance. Imagine that all your notes, textbook chapters, outlines, and study sheets are arranged on a table and that you are looking down on them from a peephole in the ceiling. Then ask yourself, What does all that mean? When put together, what does it all show? Why is it important?

Look for Relationships

Study and review consist of more than just learning facts. Try to see how facts relate and interconnect. In learning the periodic table of chemical elements, for example, you should do more than just learn names and symbols. You should understand how elements are grouped, what similar properties they share, and how the groups are arranged.

Look for Patterns and the Progression of Thought

Try to see how or why the material was covered in the order it was presented. How does one class lecture relate to the next? To what larger topic or theme are they connected? For class lectures, check the course outline or syllabus that was distributed at the beginning of the course. Since it lists major topics and suggests the order in which they will be covered, your syllabus will be useful in discovering patterns.

Similarly, for textbook chapters, try to focus on the progression of ideas. Study the table of contents to see the connection between chapters you have read. Often chapters are grouped into sections based on similar content.

Watch for the progression or development of thought. Ask yourself, What is the information presented in this chapter leading up to? What does it have to do with the chapter that follows? Suppose in psychology you had covered a chapter on personality traits; next you were assigned a chapter on abnormal and deviant behavior. You would ask yourself, What do the two chapters have to do with each other? In this case, the first chapter on personality establishes the standard or norm by which abnormal and deviant behavior is determined.

Interpret and Evaluate

Do not let facts and details camouflage important questions. Remember to ask yourself, What does this mean? How is this information useful? How can this be applied to various situations? Once you have identified the literal content, stop, react, and evaluate its use, value, and application.

Prepare Study Sheets

The study sheet system is a way of organizing and summarizing complex information by preparing a mini-outline. It is most useful for reviewing material that is interrelated, or connected, and needs to be learned as a whole rather than as separate facts. Types of information that should be reviewed on a study sheet include:

1. Theories and principles
2. Complex events with multiple causes and effects
3. Controversial issues—pros and cons
4. Summaries of philosophical issues
5. Trends in ideas, or data
6. Groups of related facts

Look at the sample study sheet in Figure 16-1, which was made by a student preparing for an exam on the sample textbook chapter included in Appendix A. You will notice that the study sheet organizes information on

	Problem Focused Approach	Emotion Focused Approach
Purpose	solving the problem causing stress	changing or managing the emotions the problems caused
Example	learning about a disability and how to live with it	expressing grief and anger to get it out of your system
How it is Accomplished	1. defining the problem 2. learn about problem and how to fix it 3. take steps to fix the problem	1. reappraisal 2. comparisons 3. avoidance 4. humor

FIGURE 16-1   Sample Study Sheet

two approaches to coping with stress and presents them in a form that permits easy comparison.

To prepare a study sheet, first select the information to be learned. Then outline the information, using as few words as possible. Group together important points, facts, and ideas that relate to each topic.

EXERCISE 2 ⸻⸻⸻⸻⸻⸻

Directions: *Prepare a study sheet for the selection "Some Sources of Stress," beginning on page 426 of the psychology sample chapter reprinted in Appendix A.*

EXERCISE 3 ⸻⸻⸻⸻⸻⸻

Directions: *Prepare a study sheet for a topic you are studying in one of your courses. Include all the information you need to learn in order to prepare for an exam.*

LEARNING AND MEMORIZING

The methods and procedures you use to learn and to remember depend on the type of exam for which you are preparing. You would study and learn information differently for a multiple-choice test than you would for an essay exam.

Exams can be divided into two basic types: objective and essay. Objective tests are short-answer tests in which you choose one or more answers from several that are given, or supply a word or phrase to complete a statement. Multiple-choice, true/false, matching, and fill-in-the-blank questions are types of objective tests. In each of these, the questions are constructed so that the answers you choose are either right or wrong; scoring is completely objective, or free from judgment.

Essay tests require you to write answers to questions in your own words. You have to recall information, organize it, and present it in an acceptable written form. This is different from recognizing the correct answer among given choices, or from recalling a word or phrase. Because essay exams differ from objective tests, you must use different methods in preparing and reviewing for each.

Review for Objective Tests

Objective tests usually require you to recognize the right answer. On a multiple-choice test, for example, you have to pick the correct answer from the choices given. In true/false tests, you have to recognize which two items go together. One goal in reviewing for objective tests, then, is to become so familiar with the course material that you can recognize and select the right answers.

Use Underlining and Marking

Your underlining of reading assignments can be used in several ways for review. First, reread your underlining in each chapter. Second, read the chapter's boldface headings and form a question for each, as you did in the "Question" step in the SQ3R system. Try to answer your question; then check your underlining to see if you were correct. Finally, review special marks you may have included. If, for example, you marked new or important definitions with a particular symbol, go through the chapter once and note these terms, checking your recall of their meanings.

Use the Recall Clues in Your Lecture Notes

Go back through each set of lecture notes and check your recall by using the marginal recall clue system. Test yourself by asking questions and trying to recall answers. Mark in red ink the things you have trouble remembering. Then use a different color of ink the second time you go through your notes, marking information you can't recall.

Use Study Aids

Use all study sheets, outlines, summaries, and organizational charts and diagrams that you have prepared to review and learn course content. To learn the information on a study sheet or outline, first read through it several times. Then take the first topic, write it on a sheet of paper, and see if you can fill in the information under the topic on your study sheet or outline. If you can't recall all the information, test yourself until you have learned it. Continue in this way with each topic.

Use the Index Card System

The index card system is an effective way of reviewing for objective tests. Using $3'' \times 5''$ index cards (or just small sheets of paper), write part of the information on the front, the remainder on the back. To review the dates of important events, write the date on the front, the event on the back; to review vocabulary, put each term on the front of one card, with its definition on the back. See the sample index cards shown in Figure 16-2, which were made by a student preparing for an objective exam on the biology chapter reprinted in Appendix B.

To study these cards, look at the front of each and try to remember what is written on the back. Then turn the card over to see if you are correct. As you go through your pack of cards, sort them into two stacks—those you know and those you do not remember. Then go back through the stack that you don't know, study each, and retest yourself, again sorting the cards into two stacks. Continue this procedure until you are satisfied that you have learned all the information. Go through your cards in this manner two or three times a day for three or four days before the exam. On the day of your exam, do a final, once-through review so that the information is fresh in your mind.

The index card system has several advantages. First, it is time-efficient; by sorting the cards, you spend time learning what you do not know and do not waste time reviewing what you have already learned. Second, by having each item of information on a separate card rather than in a list on a single sheet of paper, you avoid the danger of learning the items in a certain order. If you study a list of items, you run the risk of being able to remember them only in the order in which they are written on the list. When a single item appears out of order on an exam, you may not remember it. By sorting and occasionally shuffling your index cards, you avoid learning information in a fixed order. A third advantage of the index card system is that these cards are easy to carry in a pocket or purse. It is therefore easier for you to space your review of the material. If carried with you, the cards can be studied in spare moments—even when you don't have textbooks or notebooks with you. Moments usually wasted waiting in supermarket lines, doctor's offices, gas stations, or traffic jams can be used for study.

The index card system is more appropriate for learning brief facts than for reviewing concepts, ideas, and principles or for understanding sequences of events, theories, and cause-effect relationships. For this reason it works best when studying for objective tests that include short-answer questions such as "fill in the blanks." This type of question requires you to recall brief facts rather than simply to recognize them.

EXERCISE 4 ————————————————

Directions: *Prepare a set of index cards (at least twenty) for a chapter or section of a chapter that you are studying in one of your courses. Then learn the information on the cards, using the sorting technique described previously.*

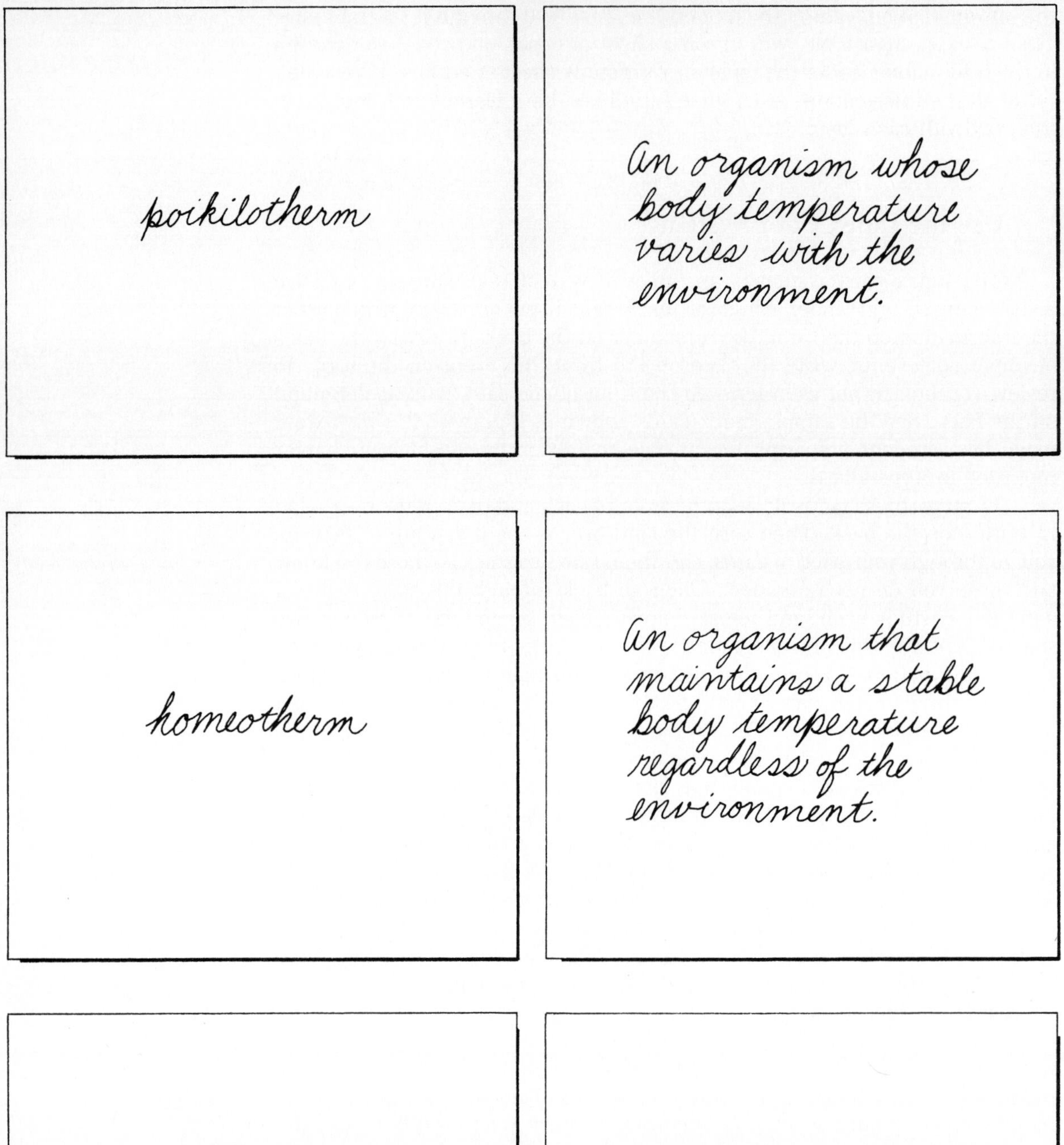

poikilotherm

An organism whose body temperature varies with the environment.

homeotherm

An organism that maintains a stable body temperature regardless of the environment.

primary sources of heat gain

1. Radiant energy
2. Cellular metabolism

FIGURE 16-2   **Sample Study Cards**

Test Yourself

Check to be sure you have learned all the necessary facts and ideas. By testing yourself before the instructor tests you, you are preparing in a realistic way for the exam. If you were entering a marathon race, you would prepare for the race by running—not by playing golf. The same is true of test-taking; preparation requires practice tests that you give yourself—not simply rereading chapters or staring at pages of notes.

Review for Essay Exams

Essay exams demand complete recall. Starting with a blank sheet of paper, you are required to retrieve from your memory all the information that answers the question. Then you must organize that information and express your ideas about it in acceptable written form.

To review for an essay exam, first identify topics that may be included in the exam. Then learn and organize enough information so that you can write about each topic.

Predict Essay Questions: In choosing topics to study, you attempt to predict what questions will be included on the exam. There are several sources from which you can choose topics. First, you can use boldface textbook headings to identify important topics or subtopics. End-of-chapter discussion questions and recall clues written in the margins of your lecture notes may also suggest topics. Remember to check the course outline distributed by your instructor at the beginning of the course. This outline frequently contains a list of major topics covered in the course.

Study the Topics Selected: Once you have made your choices, identify what aspects of the topics you should review. Perhaps the best source of information is your instructor, who probably has been consciously or unconsciously giving clues all semester about what the most important topics are. Train yourself to watch and listen for these clues. Specifically, look for your instructor's approach, focus, and emphasis with respect to the subject matter. Does your history instructor emphasize causes and dates of events? Is he or she more concerned with historical importance and lasting effects of events? Is your ecology instructor concerned with specific changes that a pollutant produces or its more general environmental effects?

After you have identified the aspects of each topic, prepare a study sheet on each. Include all the information you would want to remember if you were going to write an essay on each topic. As you prepare these study sheets, organize the information so that you could write a clear, concise essay on every topic. You might organize the causes of a particular historical event in order of importance or in chronological order. By organizing the information, you will be able to remember it more easily when you take the exam. After your study sheets are prepared, study each one, trying to recall the major subtopics you included. Also, test yourself to see if you can recall the specific facts under each topic.

Use a Key-Word Outline: To improve your memory, and to ensure that you will write an organized essay answer, try the key-word system, which helps you remember information by summarizing each idea with a single word or phrase. You can memorize each key word or phrase in a particular order. Together, these words and phrases form a mini-outline of the ideas or

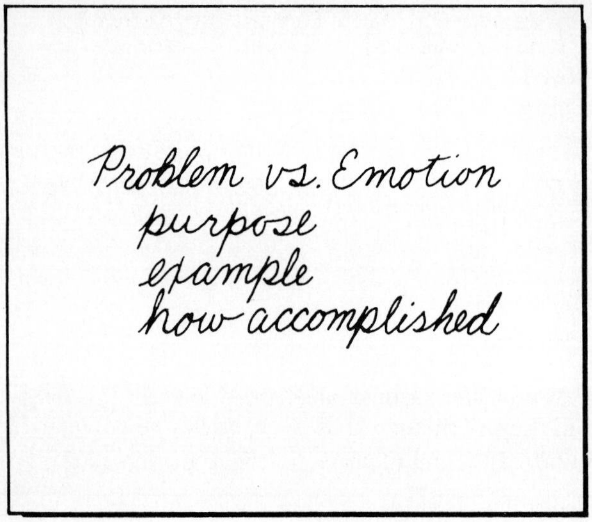

Problem vs. Emotion
purpose
example
how accomplished

FIGURE 16-3   Sample Key-Word Outline

topics you want to include in your essay. You might test the effectiveness of your key-word outline and your ability to recall it by formulating your own exam questions and then writing complete or outline-form answers to the questions. When you are taking the exam, write the key-word mini-outline for each question on a scrap of paper or on the back of the exam paper before you start to write your answer. The outline will be an easy-to-follow guide to all the major points to include in your essay.

Refer again to the sample study sheet in Figure 16-1. The study sheet was made by a student preparing for an essay exam that was to be based in part on the psychology textbook chapter reprinted in Appendix A. Among the topics this student chose to review was stress. She predicted that her instructor might include a question on the approaches to coping with stress. From her study sheet, the student made the key-word list shown in Figure 16-3, which briefly outlines various aspects of the two major approaches to stress. By learning this list, the student will be well prepared to discuss the advantages and disadvantages of the two approaches.

EXERCISE 5 _____

Directions: *Predict several questions that an instructor might ask on an essay exam covering the psychology textbook chapter included in Appendix A (pages 421–454). Write them in the space provided.*

_____

_____

_____

_____

EXERCISE 6 _____

Directions: *Assume you are preparing for an essay exam in one of your courses. Predict several questions that might be asked for one textbook chapter and write them in the space provided.*

_____

_____

_____

EXERCISE 7 _____

Directions: *Choose one of the essay exam questions that you wrote in Exercise 5. Prepare a study sheet that summarizes the information on the topic. Then reduce that information on your study sheet to a key-word outline.*

SUMMARY

Tests, exams, and quizzes are an important part of most college courses because they determine grades and serve as learning experiences. Preparing for an exam involves four steps. The first, organizing for study and review, requires planning and scheduling your time so that all the material is reviewed carefully and thoroughly. In the second step, identifying what to study, suggestions are given for reviewing all sources of information to determine what material is to be learned. Once the material is identified, the next step is to organize and connect the facts and ideas into a meaningful body of information. Learning and memorizing, the final step, require learning the material in a manner that is most appropriate for the type of exam to be taken. For objective exams, study sheets and the index card system should be used. For essay exams, study sheets and key-word outlines are suggested.

17

Taking Exams

Use this chapter to:

1. *Learn how to approach exams in an organized, systematic manner.*
2. *Become test-wise by learning test-taking tips for each type of exam.*

Thorough, careful study and review are the two most important things you can do to ensure that you will get a good exam grade. Test-taking skills and techniques, however, if used to full advantage, can influence your grade by as much as 10 or 15 points. The manner in which you approach the exam, how you read and answer objective tests, and how carefully you read, organize, and write your answer to an essay exam can influence your grade. This chapter will discuss each of these aspects of becoming test-wise and will also discuss a problem that interferes with many students' ability to do well on exams: test anxiety.

GENERAL SUGGESTIONS FOR TAKING EXAMS

The following suggestions will help you approach any exam in an organized, systematic way.

Bring Necessary Materials

When going to any exam, be sure to take along any materials you might be asked or allowed to use. Be sure you have an extra pen, and take a pencil in case you must make a drawing or diagram. Take paper—you may need it for computing figures or writing essay answers. Take along anything you have been allowed to use throughout the semester, such as a pocket calculator, conversion chart, or dictionary. If you are not sure whether you may use them, ask the instructor.

Get There on Time

It is important to arrive at the exam room on time, or a few minutes early, to get a seat and get organized before the instructor arrives. If you are late, you may miss instructions and feel rushed as you begin the exam.

If you arrive too early (fifteen minutes ahead), you risk anxiety induced by panic-stricken students questioning each other, trading last-minute memory tricks, and worrying about how difficult the exam will be.

Sit in the Front of the Room

If you have a choice, the most practical place to sit in an exam room is at the front. There you often receive the test first and get a head start. There, also, you are sure to hear directions and corrections and can easily read any changes written on the chalkboard. Finally, it is easier to concentrate and avoid distractions at the front of the room. At the back, you are exposed to distractions such as a student dropping papers or cheating, or the person in front who is already two pages ahead of you.

Preread the Exam

Before you start to answer any of the questions, quickly page through the exam, noting the directions, the length, the type of questions, and the general topics covered. Prereading provides an overview and perspective of the whole exam. Prereading also helps eliminate the panic you may feel if you go right to the first few questions and find that you are unsure of the answers.

Plan Your Time

After prereading the exam, you will know the numbers and types of questions included. You should then estimate how much time you will spend on each part of the exam. The number of points each section is worth (the point distribution) should be your guide. If, for example, one part of an exam has twenty multiple-choice questions worth one point each and another part has two essays worth forty points each, you should spend much more time answering the essay questions than working through the multiple-choice items. If the point distribution is not indicated on the test booklet, you may want to ask the instructor what it is.

As you plan your time, be sure to allow a minute or two to preread the exam. Also allow three to four minutes at the end of the exam to review what you have done, answering questions you skipped and making any necessary corrections or changes.

To keep track of time, wear a watch. Many classrooms do not have wall clocks, or you may be sitting in a position where the clock is difficult to see.

If you were taking an exam with the following question and point distribution, how would you divide your time? Assume the total exam time is sixty minutes.

Type of Question	Number of Questions	Total Points
Multiple choice	25 questions	25 points
True/false	20 questions	20 points
Essay	2 questions	55 points

You should probably divide your time as indicated:

Prereading	1–2 minutes
Multiple choice	15 minutes
True/false	10 minutes
Essay	30 minutes
Review	3–4 minutes

Because the essays are worth twice as many points as either of the other two parts of the exam, it is necessary to spend twice as much time on the essay portion.

Read the Questions Carefully

Most instructors word their questions so that what is expected is clear. A common mistake students make is to read more into the question than is asked for. To avoid this error, read the question several times, paying attention to how it is worded. If you are uncertain of what is asked for, try to relate the question to the course content. Don't anticipate hidden meanings or trick questions.

EXERCISE 1 _____

Directions: *For each of the exams described below, estimate how you would divide your time.*

1. Time limit: 75 minutes

Type of Question	Number of Questions	Total Points
Multiple choice	20 questions	40 points
Matching	10 questions	10 points
Essay	2 questions	50 points

How would you divide your time?

Prereading	_____ minutes
Multiple choice	_____ minutes
Matching	_____ minutes
Essay	_____ minutes
Review	_____ minutes

2. Time limit: 40 minutes

Type of Question	Number of Questions	Total Points
True/false	15 questions	30 points
Fill-in-the-blank	10 questions	30 points
Short answer	10 questions	40 points

How would you divide your time?

Prereading	_____ minutes
True/false	_____ minutes
Fill-in-the-blank	_____ minutes
Short answer	_____ minutes
Review	_____ minutes

HINTS FOR TAKING OBJECTIVE EXAMS

When taking objective exams—usually multiple choice, true/false, or matching—remember the following hints, which may give you a few more points.

Read the Directions

Before answering any questions, read the directions. Often an instructor may want the correct answer marked in a particular way (underlined rather than circled). The directions may contain crucial information that you must know in order to answer the questions correctly. If you were to ignore directions such as the following and assume the test questions were of the usual type, you could lose a considerable number of points.

True/False Directions

Read each statement. If the statement is true, mark a T in the blank to the left of the item. If the statement is false, add and/or subtract words that will make the statement correct.

Multiple-Choice Directions

Circle all the choices that correctly complete the statement.

Without reading the true/false directions, you would not know that you should correct incorrect statements. Without reading the multiple-choice directions, you would not know that you are to choose more than one answer.

Leave Nothing Blank

Before turning in your exam, be sure you have answered every question. If you have no idea about the correct answer to a question, guess—you might be right. On a true/false test, your chances of being correct are 50 percent; on a four-choice multiple-choice question, your odds are 25 percent.

Students frequently turn in tests with some items unanswered because they leave difficult questions blank, planning to return to them later. Then, in the rush to finish everything, they forget to go back to them. The best way to avoid this problem is to choose what look like the best answers and mark the question numbers with an X or a checkmark; then, if you have time at the end of the exam, you can give them more thought. If you run out of time, at least you will have attempted to answer them.

Look for Clues

If you encounter a difficult question, choose what seems to be the best answer, mark the question so that you can return to it, and keep the item in mind as you go through the rest of the exam. Sometimes you will see some piece of information later in the exam that reminds you of a fact or idea. At other times you may notice information that, if true, contradicts an answer you had already chosen.

Don't Change Answers Without Good Reason

When reviewing your exam answers, don't make a change unless you have a specific reason for doing so. If a later test item made you remember information for a previous item, by all means make a change. If, however, you are just having second thoughts about an answer, leave it alone. Your first guess is usually the best one.

Hints for Taking True/False Tests

When taking true/false tests, watch for words that qualify or change the meaning of a statement; often, just one word makes it true or false. Consider the following oversimplified example:

All dogs are white.

Some dogs are white.

The first statement is obviously false, whereas the second is true. In each statement, only one word determined whether the statement was true or false. While the words and statements are much more complicated on college true/false exams, you will find that one word often determines whether a statement is true or false. Read the following examples:

All paragraphs must have a stated main idea.

Spelling, punctuation, and handwriting *always* affect the grade given to an essay answer.

When taking notes on a lecture, try to write down *everything* the speaker says.

In each of these examples, the italicized words modify—or limit—the truth of each statement. When reading a true/false statement, look carefully for any limiting words, such as *all, some, none, never, always, usually, frequently, most of the time*. To overlook these words may cost you several points on an exam.

Read Two-Part Statements Carefully: Occasionally you may find a statement with two or more parts. In answering these items, remember that both or all parts of the statement must be true in order for it to be correctly marked true. If part of the statement is true and another part is false, then mark the statement false, such as in the following example:

The World Health Organization (WHO) has been successful in its campaign to eliminate smallpox and malaria.

While it is true that WHO has been successful in eliminating smallpox, malaria is still a world health problem and has not been eliminated. Because only part of this statement is true, it should be marked false.

Look for Negative and Double-Negative Statements: Test items that use negative words or word parts can be confusing. Words such as *no, none, never, not, cannot* and beginnings of words such as *in-, dis-, un-, it-,* or *ir-* are easy to miss and always alter the meaning of the statement. For items containing negative statements, make it a habit to underline or circle them as you read.

Statements that contain two negatives such as the following are even more confusing.

It is not unreasonable to expect that Vietnam veterans continue to be angry about their exposure to Agent Orange.

In reading these statements, remember that two negatives balance or cancel out each other. "Not unreasonable," then, can be interpreted to mean "reasonable."

Make Your Best Guess: When all else fails and you are unable to reason out the answer to an item, use these three last-resort rules of thumb:

1. Absolute statements tend to be false. Because there are very few things that are always true and for which there are no exceptions, your best guess is to mark statements that contain words such as *always, all, never,* or *none* as false.
2. Mark any item that contains unfamiliar terminology or facts as false. If you've studied the material thoroughly, trust that you would recognize as true anything that was a part of the course content.
3. When all else fails, it is better to guess true than false. It is more difficult for instructors to write false statements than true statements. As a result, many exams have more true items than false.

EXERCISE 2 _____

Directions: *The following true/false test is based on content presented in the sample chapter in Appendix B of this text. Read each item. Then find and underline the single word that, if changed or deleted, could change the truth or falsity of the statement. In the space provided at the right, indicate whether the statement is true or false by marking T for true and F for false.*

1. Less energy is consumed by a hibernating animal than by an active one.   T

2. All mammals have a layer of subcutaneous fat that functions as a thermostat control.   T

3. Constancy of body temperature is characteristic only of humans.   F

4. An increase in metabolic rate also lowers fuel consumptions.   T

5. Skin receptors for hot and cold are the most important
    source of information about temperature change.   _I_

6. The elevation of body temperature known as a fever is due
    not to a malfunction of the hypothalamic thermostat but to
    its resetting.   ____

7. All terrestrial reptiles are poikilotherms.   _F_

8. All poikilotherms vary their temperature with the environ-
    ment and lose body heat primarily through convection.   _F_

9. A camel would be better adapted to its environment if it had
    all-over fat distribution rather than localized fat deposits in
    its hump.   _F_

10. Most small desert animals are nocturnal.   _F_

Hints for Taking Matching Tests

Matching tests require you to select items in one list that can be paired
with items in a second list. Use the following tips to answer matching tests.

1. Glance through both lists before answering any items to get an overview
    of the subjects and topics the test covers. Next, try to discover a pattern.
    Are you asked to match dates with events, terms with meanings, people
    with accomplishments?
2. Answer the items you are sure of first, lightly crossing off items as they
    are used.
3. Don't choose the first answer you see that seems correct; items later in
    the list may be better choices.
4. If the first column consists of short words or phrases and the second is
    lengthy definitions or descriptions, save time by reverse matching; that
    is, look for the word or phrase in column 1 that fits each item in column 2.

Hints for Taking Short-Answer Tests

Short-answer tests require you to write a brief answer, usually in list or
sentence form, such as asked by the following example.

    List three events that increased U.S. involvement in the Vietnam
    War.

In answering short-answer questions, be sure to:

1. Use point distribution as a clue to how many pieces of information to
    include. For a nine-point item asking you to describe the characteristics
    of a totalitarian government, give three ideas.
2. Plan what you will say before starting to write.
3. Use the amount of space provided, especially if it varies for different items,
    as a clue to how much should be written.

Hints for Taking Fill-in-the-Blank Tests

Items that ask you to fill in a missing word or phrase within a sentence require recall of information rather than recognition of the correct answer. It is important, therefore, to look for clues that will trigger your recall.

1. Look for key words in the sentence and use them to decide what subject matter and topic are covered in the item.
2. Decide what type of information is required. Is it a date, name, place, new term?
3. Use the grammatical structure of the sentence to determine the type of word called for. Is it a noun, verb, or qualifier?

Hints for Taking Multiple-Choice Tests

Multiple-choice exams are among the most frequently used types of exams and are often the most difficult to answer. The following suggestions should improve your success in taking multiple-choice tests.

1. Read all choices first, considering each. Do not stop with the second or third choice, even if you are sure that you have found the correct answer. Remember, on most multiple-choice tests your job is to pick the *best* answer, and the last choice may be better than the preceding answers.
2. Some multiple-choice tests include combinations of previously listed choices, as in the following test item.

> Among the causes of slow reading is (are)
> a. lack of comprehension
> b. reading word-by-word rather than in phrases
> c. poorly developed vocabulary
> d. making too few fixations per line
> e. a and b
> f. a, b, and c
> g. a, b, c, and d

   The addition of choices that are combinations of previous choices tends to be confusing. Treat each choice, when combined with the stem, as a true or false statement. As you consider each choice, mark it true or false. If you find more than one true statement, select the choice that contains the letters of all the true statements you identified.
3. Use logic and common sense. Even if you are unfamiliar with the subject matter, it is sometimes possible to reason out the correct answer. The following item is taken from a history exam on Japanese-American relations after World War II.

> Prejudice and discrimination are
> a. harmful to our society because they waste our economic, political, and social resources
> b. helpful because they ensure us against attack from within
> c. harmful because they create negative images of the United States in foreign countries
> d. helpful because they keep the majority pure and united against minorities

Through logic and common sense, it is possible to eliminate choices b and d. Prejudice and discrimination are seldom, if ever, regarded as positive, desirable, or "helpful," since they are inconsistent with democratic ideals. Having narrowed your answer to two choices, a or c, you can see that choice a offers a stronger, more substantial reason why prejudice and discrimnation are harmful. What other countries think of the United States is not as serious as the waste of economic, political, and social resources.

4. Study items that are very similar. When two choices seem very close and you cannot decide between them, stop and examine each. First, try to express each in your own words. Then analyze how they differ. Often this process will lead you to recognize the correct answer.

5. Look for qualifying words. As in true/false tests, the presence of qualifying words is important. Because many statements, ideas, principles, and rules have exceptions, you should be careful in selecting items that contain such words as *best, always, all, no, entirely,* and *completely,* all of which suggest that something is always true, without exception. Also be careful of statements containing such words as *none, never,* and *worst,* which suggest things that are never true without exception. Items containing words that provide for some level of exception, or qualification, are more likely to be correct; a few examples are *often, usually, less, seldom, few, more,* and *most.*

   In the following example, notice the use of italicized qualifying words:

> In most societies
>   a. values are *highly* consistent
>   b. people *often* believe and act on values that are contradictory
>   c. *all* legitimate organizations support the values of the majority
>   d. values of equality *never* exist alongside prejudice and discrimination

In this question, items c and d contain the words *all* and *never,* suggesting that those statements are true without exception. Thus if you did not know the answer to this question based on content, you could eliminate items c and d on the basis of the level of qualifiers.

6. Some multiple-choice questions require application of knowledge or information. You may be asked to analyze a hypothetical situation or to use what you have learned to solve a problem. Here is an example taken from a psychology text.

> Carrie is comfortable in her new home in New Orleans. When she gets dressed up and leaves her home and goes to the supermarket to buy the week's groceries, she gets nervous and upset and thinks that something is going to happen to her. She feels the same way when walking her four-year-old son Jason in the park or playground.
>
> Carrie is suffering from
>   a. shyness
>   b. a phobia

    c. a personality disorder
    d. hypertension

In answering questions of this type, start by crossing out unnecessary information that can distract you. In the preceding example, distracting information includes the woman's name, her son's name, where she lives, why she goes to the store, and so forth.

7. If a question concerns steps in a process or order of events or any other information that is likely to confuse you, ignore the choices and use the margin or scrap paper to jot down the information as you can recall it. Then select the choice that matches what you wrote.

8. Avoid selecting answers that are unfamiliar or that you do not understand. A choice that looks complicated or uses difficult words is not necessarily correct. If you have studied carefully, a choice that is unfamiliar to you is probably incorrect.

9. As a last resort, when you do not know the answer and are unable to eliminate any of the choices as wrong, guess by picking the one that seems most complete and contains the most information. This is a good choice because instructors are always careful to make the best answer completely correct and recognizable. In doing so, the choice often becomes long or detailed.

10. Make educated guesses. In most instances you can eliminate one or more of the choices as obviously wrong. Even if you can eliminate only one choice, you have reduced the odds on a four-choice item from one in four to one in three. If you can eliminate two choices, you have reduced your odds to one in two, or 50 percent. Don't hesitate to play the odds and make a guess—you may gain points.

HINTS FOR TAKING STANDARDIZED TESTS

At various times in college you may be required to take a standardized test, which is a commercially prepared, timed test used nationally or statewide to measure skills and abilities. Your score compares your performance to large numbers of other students throughout the country or state. The SAT and ACT are examples of standardized tests; many graduate schools require a standardized test as part of their admission process. Here are a few suggestions for taking this type of test.

1. Most standardized tests are timed, so the pace at which you work is a critical factor. You need to work at a fairly rapid rate, but not so fast as to make careless errors.

2. Don't plan on finishing the test. Many of the tests are designed so that no one finishes.

3. Don't expect to get everything right. Unlike classroom tests or exams, you are not expected to get most of the answers correct.

4. Find out if there is a penalty for guessing. If there is none, then use the last twenty or thirty seconds to randomly fill in an answer for each item that you have not had time to do. For every four items that you guess, the odds are that you will get one item correct.

5. Get organized before the timing begins. Line up your answer sheet and test booklet so you can move between them rapidly without losing your place.

HINTS FOR TAKING ESSAY EXAMS

Essay questions are usually graded on two factors: what you say and how you say it. It is not enough, then, simply to include the correct information. The information must be presented in a logical, organized way that demonstrates your understanding of the subject you are writing about. There can be as much as one whole letter grade difference between a well-written and poorly written essay, although both contain the same basic information. This section offers suggestions for getting as many points as possible on essay exams.

Read the Question

For essay exams, reading the question carefully is the key to writing a correct, complete, and organized answer.

Read the Directions First: The directions may tell you how many essays to answer and how to structure your answer, or specify a minimum or maximum length for your answer.

Study the Question for Clues: The question usually includes three valuable pieces of information. First, the question tells you the topic you are to write about. Second, it contains a limiting word that restricts and directs your answer. Finally, the question contains a key word or phrase that tells you how to organize and present answers. Read the essay question in this example:

(key word)   *(limiting word)*   *(topic)*   *(limiting word)*
Compare the causes of the Vietnam War with the causes of the

(topic)
Korean War.

In this example you have two topics—the Vietnam War and the Korean War. The question also contains a limiting word that restricts your discussion to these topics and tells you what to include in your answer. In this sample question, the limiting word is *causes*. It tells you to limit your answer to a discussion of events that started, or caused, each war. Do not include information about events of the war or its effects. The key word in the sample question is *compare*. It means you should consider the similarities, and possibly the differences, in the causes of the two wars. When directed to compare, you already have some clues as to how your answer should be written. One possibility is to discuss the causes of one war and then the causes of the other and finally to make an overall statement about their similarities. Another choice is to discuss one type of cause for each of the wars, and then go on to discuss another type of cause for each. For instance, you could discuss the economic causes of each, then the political causes of each.

There are several common key words and phrases used in essay questions. They are listed in Table 17-1.

Watch for Questions with Several Parts

A common mistake that students often make is to fail to answer all parts of an essay question. Most likely, they get involved with answering the first

TABLE 17-1   Key Words Used in Essay Questions

Key Words	Example	Information to Include
Discuss	Discuss Laetrile as a treatment for cancer.	Consider important characteristics and main points.
Enumerate	Enumerate the reasons for U.S. withdrawal from Vietnam.	List or discuss one by one.
Illustrate	State Boyle's law and illustrate its use.	Explain, using examples that demonstrate or clarify a point or idea.
Compare	Compare the causes of air pollution with those of water pollution.	Show how items are similar as well as different; include details or examples.
Contrast	Contrast the health care systems in the United States with those in England.	Show how the items are different; include details or examples.
Define	Define thermal pollution and include several examples.	Give an accurate meaning of the term with enough detail to show that you really understand it.
Explain	Explain why black Americans are primarily city dwellers.	Give facts and details that make the idea or concept clear and understandable.
Trace	Trace the history of legalized prostitution in Nevada.	Describe the development or progress of a particular trend, event, or process in chronological order.
Evaluate	Evaluate the strategies our society has used to treat mental illness.	React to the topic in a logical way. Discuss the merits, strengths, weaknesses, advantages, or limitations of the topic.
Summarize	Summarize the arguments for and against offering sex education courses in public schools.	Cover the major points in brief form; use a sentence and paragraph form.
Describe	Describe the experimentation that tests whether plants are sensitive to music.	Tell how something looks or happened, including how, who, where, why.
Justify	Justify former President Carter's attempt to rescue the hostages in Iran.	Give reasons that support an action, event, or policy.
Criticize	Criticize the current environmental controls to combat air pollution.	Make judgments about quality or worth; include both positive and negative aspects.
Prove	Prove that ice is a better cooling agent than water when both are at the same temperature.	Demonstrate or establish that a concept or theory is correct, logical, or valid.

part and forget about the remaining parts. Questions with several parts come in two forms. The most obvious form is as follows.

For the U.S. invasion of Granada, discuss the
a. causes
b. immediate effects
c. long-range political implications

A less obvious form that does not stand out as a several-part question includes the following.

Discuss *how* the Equal Rights Amendment was developed and *why* its passage has aroused controversy.

When you find a question of this type, underline or circle the limiting words to serve as a reminder.

Make Notes as You Read

As you read a question the first time, you may begin to formulate an answer. When this occurs, jot down a few key words that will bring these thoughts back when you are ready to organize your answer.

EXERCISE 3 _____

Directions: *Read each of the following essay questions. For each question, underline the topic, circle the limiting word, and place a box around the key word.*

1. Discuss the long-term effects of the trend toward a smaller, more self-contained family structure.
2. Trace the development of monopolies in the late nineteenth and early twentieth centuries in America.
3. Explain one effect of the Industrial Revolution on each of three of the following:
   a. transportation
   b. capitalism
   c. socialism
   d. population growth
   e. scientific research
4. Discuss the reason why, although tropical plants have very large leaves and most desert plants have very small leaves, cactus grows equally well in both habitats.
5. Describe the events leading up to the War of 1812.
6. Compare and contrast the purpose and procedures in textbook marking and lecture notetaking.
7. Briefly describe a complete approach to reading and studying a textbook chapter that will enable you to handle a test on that material successfully.
8. List four factors that influence memory or recall ability, and explain how each can be used to make study more efficient.
9. Summarize the techniques a speaker or lecturer may use to emphasize the important concepts and ideas in a lecture.

10. Explain the value and purpose of the prereading technique, and list the steps involved in prereading a textbook chapter.

Organize Your Answer

As mentioned before, a well-written, organized essay often gets a higher grade than a carelessly constructed one. Read each of these examples and notice how they differ. Each essay was written in response to this instruction on a psychology final exam: Describe the stages involved in the memory process.

EXAMPLE 1

Memory is important to everybody's life. Memory has special ways to help you get a better recollection of things and ideas. Psychologists believe that memory has three stages: encoding, storage, and retrieval.

In the encoding stage, you are putting facts and ideas into a code, usually words, and filing them away in your memory. Encoding involves preparing information for storage in memory.

The second stage of memory is storage. It is the stage that most people call memory. It involves keeping information so that it is accessible for use later in time. How well information is stored can be affected by old information already stored and newer information that is added later.

The third step in memory is retrieval, which means the ability to get back information that is in storage. There are two types of retrieval—recognition and recall. In recognition, you have to be able to identify the correct information from several choices. In recall, you have to pull information directly from your memory without using the recognition type of retrieval.

EXAMPLE 2

Memory is very complicated in how it works. It involves remembering things that are stored in your mind and being able to pull them out when you want to remember them. When you pull information out of your memory it is called retrieval. How well you can remember something is affected by how you keep the information in your mind and how you put it in. When keeping, or storing, information you have to realize that this information will be affected by old information already in your memory. Putting information in your memory is called encoding, and it means that you store facts and ideas in word form in your memory. Information stored in your memory can also be influenced by information that you add to your memory later.

There are two ways you can retrieve information. You can either recognize it or recall it. When you recognize information you are able to spot the correct information among other information. When you recall information you have to pull information out of your head. Recall is what you have to do when you write an essay exam.

While these two essays contain practically the same information, the first will probably receive a higher grade. In this essay, it is easy to see that the writer knows that there are three stages in the memory process and knows how to explain each. The writer opens the essay by stating that there are three stages and then devotes one paragraph to each of the three stages.

In the second essay it is not easy to find out what the stages of memory are. The paragraphs are not organzied according to stages in the memory process. The writer does not write about one stage at a time in a logical order. Retrieval is mentioned first; then storage and retrieval are discussed further. At the end, the writer returns to the topic of retrieval and gives further information.

Here are a few suggestions to help you organize your answer.

1. Think before you start to write. Decide what information is called for and what you will include.
2. Make a brief word or phrase outline of the ideas you want to include in your answer.
3. Study your word outline and rearrange its order. You may want to put major topics and important ideas first and less important points toward the end; or you may decide to organize your answer chronologically, discussing events early in time near the beginning and mentioning more recent events near the end. The topic you are discussing will largely determine the order of presentation.
4. If the point value of the essay is given, use that information as a clue to how many separate points or ideas may be expected. For an essay worth 25 points, for example, discussion of five major ideas may be expected.

Use Correct Paragraph Form

Be sure to write your answers in complete, correct sentences and to include only one major point in each paragraph. Each paragraph should have a main idea, usually expressed in one sentence. The remainder of the paragraph should explain, prove, or support the main idea you state. Also, use correct spelling and punctuation.

Begin Your Answer with a Topic Sentence

Your first sentence should state what the entire essay is about and suggest how you intend to approach it. If a question asks you to discuss the practical applications of Newton's three laws of motion, you might begin by writing, "There are many practical applications of Newton's laws of motion." Then you should proceed to name the three laws and their practical applications, devoting one paragraph to each law. If you have time, your final paragraph may be a summary or review of the major points you covered in the essay.

Make Your Main Points Easy to Find

Because many essay exam readers have a large number of papers to read in a short period of time, they tend to skim (look for key ideas) rather than read everything; therefore, state each main point at the beginning of a new paragraph. For lengthy answers or multipart questions, you might use headings or the same numbering used in the question. Use space (two lines) to divide your answers into different parts.

Include Sufficient Explanation

A frequent criticism instructors make of student essay answers is the failure to explain or to support ideas fully. By following the rule of thumb of only one major idea per paragraph, you avoid this danger and force yourself to explain major points. If you think of answering an essay question as a process of convincing your instructor that you have learned the material, then you are likely to include enough explanation. Another rule of thumb is also useful: Too much information is better than too little.

Avoid Opinions and Judgments

Unless the question specifically asks you to do so, do not include your personal reaction to the topic. When you are asked to state your reactions and opinions, include reasons to support them.

Make Your Answer Readable

Because there is a certain amount of judgment and personal reaction involved as an instructor reads your answer, it is to your advantage to make your paper as easy to read as possible. It is annoying to an instructor to try to read poor handwriting and carelessly written answers.

1. Use ink—it is easier to read and does not smear.
2. Use clean, unwrinkled 8½″ × 11″ paper. Reading a handful of small sheets is difficult and confusing.
3. Number your pages and put your name on each sheet.
4. Do not scratch out sentences you want to omit. Draw a single line through each and write *omit* in the margin.
5. If the paper is thin or ink runs, write on only one side.
6. Leave plenty of space between questions. Leave 1″–2″ margin at each side. The instructor will need space to write comments.

Proofread Your Answer

After you have written an essay, read it twice. Before reading your essay the first time, read the question again. Then check to see that you have included all necessary facts and information and that you have adequately explained each fact. Add anything you feel improves your answer. Then read the essay a second time, checking and correcting all the mechanical aspects of your writing. Check for hard-to-read words and errors in spelling and punctuation. Again, make all necessary corrections.

If You Run Out of Time

Despite careful planning of exam time, you may run out of time before you finish writing one of the essays. If this happens, try to jot down the major ideas that you would discuss fully if you had time. Often, your instructor will give you partial credit for this type of response, especially if you mentioned that you ran out of time.

If You Don't Know the Answer

Despite careful preparation, you may forget an answer. If this should happen, do not leave a blank page; write something. Attempt to answer the question—you may hit upon some partially correct information. The main reason for writing something is to give the instructor a chance to give you a few points for trying. If you leave a blank page, your instructor has no choice but to give you zero points. Usually when you lose full credit on one essay, you automatically eliminate your chance to get a high passing grade.

EXERCISE 4 _____

Directions: *Organize and write a response to one of the following essay questions.*

1. Five organizational patterns are commonly used in textbook writing: comparison-contrast, definition, time sequence, cause-effect, and enumeration. Discuss the usefulness of these patterns in predicting and answering essay exam questions.
2. Describe three strategies that have improved your reading skills. Explain why each is effective.
3. Describe your approach to time management. Include specific techniques and organizational strategies that you have found effective.

CONTROLLING TEST ANXIETY

Do you get nervous and anxious just before an exam begins? If so, your response is normal; most students feel some level of anxiety before an exam. In fact, research indicates that some anxiety is beneficial and improves your performance by sharpening your attention and keeping you alert.

Research also shows that very high levels of anxiety can interfere with test performance. Some students become highly nervous and emotional and lose their concentration. Their minds seem to go blank and they are unable to recall material they have learned. They also report physical symptoms: Their hearts pound, it is difficult to swallow, or they break out in a cold sweat.

Test anxiety is a complicated psychological response to a threatening situation, and it may be related to other problems and past experiences. The following suggestions are intended to help you ease text anxiety. If these suggestions do not help, the next step is to discuss the problem with a counselor.

Be Sure Test Anxiety Is Not an Excuse

Many students say they have test anxiety when actually they have not studied and reviewed carefully or thoroughly. The first question, then, that you must answer honestly is this: Are you in fact *unprepared* for the exam and, therefore, should have every reason to be anxious?

Get Used to Test Situations

Psychologists who have studied anxiety use processes called "systematic desensitization" and "simulation" to reduce test anxiety. Bascially, these are ways of becoming less sensitive or disturbed by tests by putting yourself in testlike conditions. Although these are complicated processes often used by trained therapists, here are a few ways you can use these processes to reduce test anxiety.

1. Become familiar with the building and room in which the test is given. Visit the room when it is empty and take a seat. Visualize yourself taking a test there.
2. Develop practice or review tests. Treat them as real tests and do them in situations as similar as possible to real test conditions.
3. Practice working with time limits. Set an alarm clock and work only until it rings.
4. Take as many tests as possible, even though you dislike them. Always take advantage of practice tests and make-up exams. Buy a review book for the course you are taking, or a workbook that accompanies your text. Treat each section as an exam and have someone else correct your work.

Control Negative Thinking

Major factors that contribute to test anxiety are self-doubt and negative thinking. Just before and during an exam, test-anxious students often think, "I won't do well," "I'm going to fail," "What will my friends think of me when I get a failing grade?" This type of thinking predisposes you to failure; you are telling yourself that you expect to fail. By thinking in this way you prevent or block your chances for success.

One solution to this problem is to send yourself positive rather than negative messages. Say to yourself, "I have studied hard and I deserve to pass," "I know that I know the material," or "I know I can do it!" Remember, being well prepared is one of the best ways to reduce test anxiety.

Compose Yourself Before the Test Begins

Don't take an exam on an empty stomach; you will feel queasy. Have something light or bland to eat. Some students find that a brisk walk outside before going to an exam helps to reduce tension.

Before you begin the test take thirty seconds or so to calm yourself, to slow down, and to focus your attention. Take several deep breaths, close your eyes, and visualize yourself calmly working through the test. Remind yourself that you have prepared carefully and have every reason to do well.

Answer Easy Questions First

To give yourself an initial boost of confidence, begin with a section of the test that seems easy. This will help you to work calmly and you will prove to yourself that you can handle the test.

SUMMARY

This chapter offered suggestions on how to improve exam grades by approaching tests in a systematic, organized manner. This involves taking the necessary materials, arriving on time, deliberately choosing a seat in a non-distracting section of the room, prereading the exam, and planning the time you will devote to various sections of the exam. Techniques for taking objective and essay exams were discussed. In taking any type of objective exam, read the directions carefully, leave nothing blank, and look for clues that will help you recall the information. Specific suggestions were given for taking true/false, matching, short-answer, fill-in-the-bank, and multiple-choice exams. When taking an essay exam, it is important to read the question carefully to determine exactly what type of response your instructor wants. Essay answers should be carefully organized and written in an easy-to-read form. The problem of test anxiety was defined, and several methods for overcoming it were presented.

18

Preparing Written Assignments and Research Papers

Use this chapter to:

1. *Learn how to prepare common types of written assignments.*
2. *Develop a step-by-step procedure for writing research papers.*

Do you have difficulty getting started on writing assignments? When you start writing do you feel as though you have nothing to say? Have you ever worked hard on a paper and still not received a grade that was worth all the time and effort you put in? If you answered yes to any of these questions, your response is typical of many college students. Many students find writing to be a difficult, often frustrating, task. In fact, many professional writers experience the same difficulty generating ideas and getting started. One purpose of this chapter is to offer some practical suggestions for getting started on and successfully completing the most common types of college writing assignments. Another is to provide specific step-by-step procedures for organizing and writing a research paper.

WHY WRITTEN ASSIGNMENTS ARE GIVEN

If you are going to put in all the effort that is required to complete a writing assignment, it often helps to understand why instructors assign them. You know that instructors use papers as a means of evaluating your learning and awarding grades. More important, however, writing assignments are a means of helping you learn. Putting your ideas on paper forces you to think them through, draw them together, and examine how they relate to one another. If you can put important concepts and ideas from the course into your own words, you will retain them longer and begin to put them to use more readily. Often, once you have recorded your ideas, you will find that you need additional information or that you need to read what others have written about the topic. Instructors thus may assign a paper for the purpose of encouraging you to learn more about a particular topic.

How to Take Advantage of Written Assignments

Most students, if given their choice, would rather take an exam than write a paper. Actually, written assignments have several advantages over exams. In fact, you might think of a paper as a golden opportunity to demonstrate what you know. An exam is usually a one-time-only, you-know-it-or-you-don't pressured situation. A written assignment allows you unlimited time, unlimited references, and the opportunity to ask for help from friends or from your instructor. When a paper is assigned, then, think of it as an opportunity to work in an open-ended, nonpressured way. Relax, take your time, and prove what you know.

TYPES OF WRITTEN ASSIGNMENTS

There are several types of writing that an instructor may assign to you. The most common types are listed here along with a brief description of what is usually expected in each.

Essay Exams

Although essay exams are not papers, they do constitute a major portion of assigned writing in some courses. The most important thing to remember in writing essay exams is to answer each question *clearly* and *specifically*. Take time to figure out what the instructor is asking for, then write your essay in direct response to the question (see Chapters 16 and 17 for more information on studying for and taking essay exams).

Essays or Compositions

Many instructors give assignments that require you to present or discuss your own ideas on a particular topic. Often this type of assignment is simply called a paper. A philosophy instructor might ask you, for instance, to write a paper explaining your views on abortion. Usually the instructor specifies the topic or the general subject area to write about. An exception may occur in English composition classes, when you are allowed to select a topic but the instructor specifies *how* you are to write or organize your paper. Often, too, the instructor suggests a particular length, either in number of words or pages.

When a paper of this type is given, listen carefully as the instructor announces and discusses the assignment. At that time, the instructor will often indicate what is expected. Jot down the instructor's exact wording of the assignment so that you can refer to it before you begin writing. Also jot down any examples he or she may give. You might find them useful as a starting point for generating ideas.

If the assignment is unclear or you feel you do not understand what is expected, do not hesitate to check with others in the class or to ask the instructor after class. It is your responsibility to let your instructor know if you do not understand what you are to do. If you decide to speak with your instructor, try to ask specific questions rather than simply saying you do not understand the assignment. By asking specific questions, you are more likely to get information that will help you to complete the assignment.

If you are required to write about a topic that you know little or nothing about, it is worthwhile to spend an hour or so in the library reading about the topic. Once you have learned a little about the topic, you will feel more confident writing about it.

Factual Reports

Another type of writing assignment commonly used in college courses is the report. When you write a report you are expected to present factual information on a particular topic. In a chemistry course, a summary or description of a laboratory experiment might be considered a report. In a psychology class, you might be asked to observe the behavior of a particular group of people and report your observations. In sociology, you might be asked to do a survey and report your findings. Most often your instructor will suggest, or perhaps require, that you follow a particular format. The length will often be dictated by the nature of the assignment. Here are a few specific guidelines for writing reports:

1. Be thorough. Include all important details.
2. Be concise. Express your ideas clearly and in the briefest possible way.
3. Be accurate. Because you are reporting facts or observations, be certain that the information you include is correct.
4. Avoid flowery language, creative or humorous touches.
5. If you do not have sufficient information, be sure to check reference books to acquire what you need. Do not hesitate to use the library if your text does not contain the information you need.
6. If no format is suggested by your instructor, devise a logical format with headings or subheadings before you begin writing.
7. Do not include reactions, opinions, or interpretations of your topic unless your instructor has indicated that you should do so.

Reaction Papers

Unlike a report, a reaction paper should present your opinion on or reaction to a particular topic. You may be asked to react to something you've read, such as a poem or short story, or to describe your feelings about a film, lecture, play, recording, or demonstration. The length of a reaction paper may vary, but it is usually a one- or two-page paper. To write reaction papers effectively, use the following suggestions:

1. Think before you write. Decide what your reactions really are: You may need to review or reread the material (if you are reacting to something you have read) or any notes that you may have.
2. Be sure to state and briefly describe what your reaction paper is about.
3. Organize or group your reactions in some way. Don't just write reactions as they occur to you.
4. As a means of getting started and of collecting ideas, discuss the topic with a friend.

Research Papers

The research paper is the longest and most time-consuming type of writing assignment. Because of the amount of work it requires, the research paper is usually weighted heavily in determining your final course grade. A research paper or "term paper" involves locating information and ideas about a particular topic and organizing them in written form. The first step is to research the topic in the library, locating and reading appropriate books, periodicals, and reference sources. As you read, you should record, in note form, information you may want to include in your paper. Then, once you've collected sufficient information, organize your information and write the paper. (Specific suggestions for writing and researching this type of paper will be presented later in the chapter.)

GENERAL SUGGESTIONS FOR WRITING PAPERS

When they begin working on a paper, many students just pick up a pen and start writing the paper. This is usually not the best way to begin. In writing, as in reading, there are certain things you can do before you begin writing a paper as well as after you have written it that can help ensure that you have produced an acceptable, well-constructed work. The steps, or stages, that most good writers go through in writing a paper are prewriting, organizing, writing, revising, and proofreading.

Prewriting

You might think of prewriting as a process similar to prereading. When prereading (see Chapter 5) you are in a sense getting ready to read, focusing your attention on the material and anticipating the content and organization. When you write, you also need to get ready by making decisions about the purposes, overall organization, and content of what you will write. Here are a few suggestions for how to get off to a good start:

Get Organized: As is true for reading and study, when and where you write is important. Choose a time of day when you can concentrate and a place free of distractions. Have plenty of paper, pens, pencils, and a dictionary available. Begin by reviewing what your assignment is. Reread either your instructor's statement of the assignment, if presented in writing, or your notes on the assignment if it was given orally. As you review, look for clues about what specifically is expected.

Once you are familiar with the nature and scope of the assignment, try to establish a time schedule for its completion. Never try to complete a paper in one evening. You need time to let the paper rest; this allows you to come back to it later to reconsider what you've written in a different perspective and with a critical eye.

Choose a Manageable Topic: In many cases, except for research papers, the topic is defined by your instructor or by the nature of the assignment. In the event that you do have a choice, use the following guidelines:

1. Choose a topic that interests you. You will find that it is much easier to maintain a high level of concentration and motivation if the topic is genuinely interesting. Also, ideas will flow more easily if you are involved with your topic.
2. Choose a topic you know something about. If you do not know much about a topic, it is very difficult—in some cases almost impossible—to

write about it. So, unless you are prepared to learn about a topic before writing about it, avoid topics that you know little about.

3. Choose a topic that can be handled effectively in the length of paper you are writing. For example, you could not do a good job of discussing the general topic "Religions of the World" in a three-page paper. There are many religions in the world, and each has its own set of beliefs, rituals, and codes for living. It would be impossible to discuss each in the length of paper assigned. A much better, more manageable topic would be something like "Changing Trends in Catholicism in the Twentieth Century." This topic is more specific than "Religions of the World" and is a manageable part of that broader topic. Techniques for narrowing a subject to a workable topic will be discussed later in this chapter.

Develop Ideas About the Topic: Once you have chosen a topic, the next step is to generate or develop ideas about your topic. If you have trouble, as many students do, in finding something to say, you might try a technique called free writing. Figure 18-1 shows a portion of free writing on the topic of the changing American family. It works like this: Take a piece of paper and just start writing anything that comes into your mind about the topic. Do not be concerned about whether you are writing in complete sentences or whether the ideas make sense or connect to one another. You might think of free writing as a type of "brainstorming," or thinking of a variety of ideas on a topic. Keep writing continuously for a set period of time, four to five minutes or so. If you cannot think of an idea about the topic, write whatever else comes to mind.

When you've finished, reread what you have written. You will be surprised at the number of different ideas that you have thought of. Then, underline or rewrite those ideas that seem worth including in your paper. An alternative technique to generate ideas is to take five minutes or so and write down all the questions you can think of on your topic. For instance, you might write the following questions about the topic of the role of computers in our daily lives:

How do computers affect our lives?
Have computers changed our way of life?
Who allows computers to influence us?
Do computers invade our right to privacy?
Are computers economically important?
Is computer skill a marketable job skill?
Can computers replace men and women in the work force?

When you're finished, reread the questions, and as you did in free writing, try to identify those that, when answered, would be worth including in your paper.

EXERCISE 1 ————————————————

Directions: *Choose one of the topics listed below. Free-write about that topic for five minutes*

Topics

1. Television watching
2. Sports in America
3. Protecting the environment

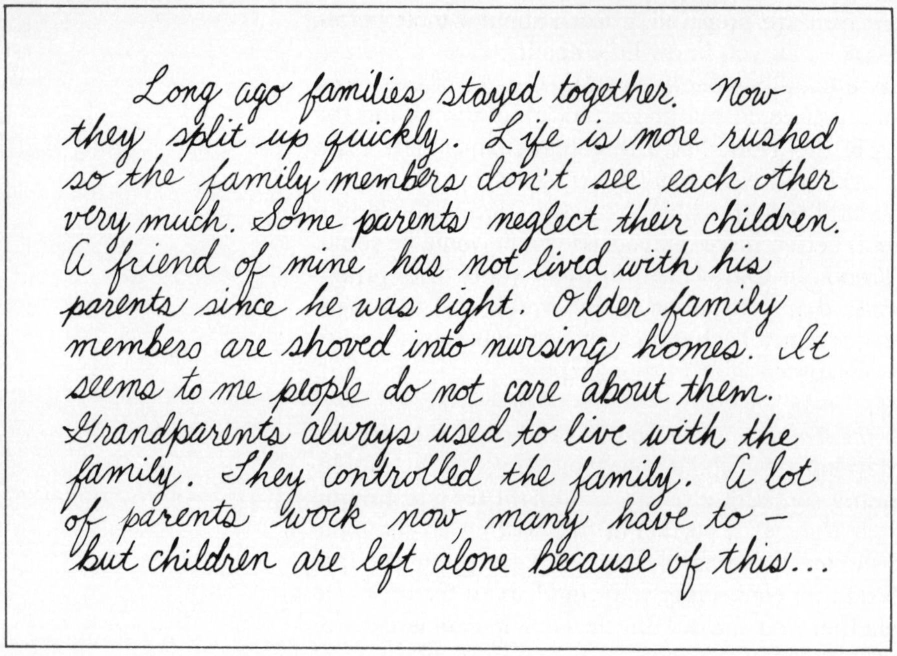

> *Long ago families stayed together. Now they split up quickly. Life is more rushed so the family members don't see each other very much. Some parents neglect their children. A friend of mine has not lived with his parents since he was eight. Older family members are shoved into nursing homes. It seems to me people do not care about them. Grandparents always used to live with the family. They controlled the family. A lot of parents work now, many have to — but children are left alone because of this...*

FIGURE 18-1   An Example of Free Writing

EXERCISE 2

Directions: *Choose one of the topics given below. Write as many questions as you can think of about the topic. Limit your time to five minutes.*

Topics

1. Unemployment and how it affects our lives
2. The value of college education
3. Soap operas

Organizing and Outlining

Once you have identifed some ideas to include in your paper, the next step is to organize them. This involves arranging the ideas in an order that will result in an understandable and well-written paper. The most effective way of organizing your ideas is to make an outline. An outline will help you see the relationship of ideas to one another. To accomplish this, use the following steps:

1. Quickly list the ideas in the order in which you wrote them.
2. Read through the list, looking for ideas that are similar or those that should follow one another.
3. Rewrite your outline, trying to group ideas together so that they are listed in a logical order (an order that would be a sensible approach to discussing your topic).

Writing a Draft

After you have organized your ideas, you are ready to begin writing the first draft of your paper. Here are a few suggestions:

1. Always plan on revising and recopying your paper. Your first draft should never be your final copy.
2. As you begin, be concerned only with getting your ideas down on paper. Do not be concerned with exact word choice or with correct punctuation. You can check and correct those details later.
3. Use your outline as a guide. Discuss the ideas in the order in which they appear in the outline.
4. Be sure to explain each idea completely. A common fault instructors find with student papers is that they do not include enough detail. Try to include, where appropriate, examples, reasons, descriptions, or other supporting information.
5. Do not hesitate to make changes as you think of them.

Revising

Revision is the step that can make a good paper a better one or an unacceptable paper acceptable. Revision involves rereading, rewriting, and making changes to improve both the content and organization of your paper. Here are a few suggestions to follow:

1. Do not revise as soon as you have finished writing. Instead, try to allow a lapse of time between writing and revision. This lapse gives you the distance and objectivity that you do not have immediately on completing your draft.
2. If you have trouble finding anything wrong with your paper, ask a friend to read and criticize it. Also, ask him or her to summarize what your paper said. This will allow you to see if you have expressed your ideas clearly and accurately.
3. To evaluate your own paper, try asking yourself the following questions:
   a. Are the ideas clearly expressed?
   b. Do the ideas tie together to form a unified piece of writing?
   c. Is each major idea supported with facts and details.?

Proofreading

Once you have prepared the final copy of your paper, be sure to read it to detect errors in spelling, punctuation, grammar, and usage. At this point, try to ignore the idea flow and simply check each sentence to be sure that it does not contain errors. To locate spelling errors, try reading the paper backward, word by word. To locate sentence structure errors, read the paper backward sentence by sentence. If your paper is typewritten, also check for typographical errors such as omitted words or sentences and transposed letters.

Although you may not think it is fair, your paper's physical appearance and grammatical correctness will actually influence its grade. It pays to make sure your work is error free. After all, it would be unfortunate to spend a great deal of time and effort on a research paper only to have it downgraded because you did not take a few minutes to proofread and make final corrections.

WRITING RESEARCH PAPERS

In assigning a research paper, your instructor is asking you to learn about a topic and then to organize and summarize what you have learned.

You are expected to learn on your own, using whatever resources and references are available. Completing a research paper involves much more than just writing. It involves topic selection, locating appropriate sources of information, reading, taking notes, and organizing the information. In fact, writing is actually the final step in the process of acquiring and organizing information on a particular topic.

The purpose of this portion of the chapter is to offer general guidelines for completing a successful research paper. After providing some general tips for getting started, the section will present a step-by-step procedure for collecting information and writing the paper.

Tips for Getting Started

The first college research paper you do is always the most difficult. The reason for this is that you are learning *how* to do the paper while doing it. Once you have mastered the techniques for writing research papers, later ones will be much easier and less time consuming. Here are a few tips to help you get started:

1. Find out how important the research paper is by finding out how heavily the paper counts in your final grade. This information will help you to determine how much time and effort you should put into the paper.
2. Get an early start. Even if the paper is not due until the end of the semester, start working on the paper as soon as possible. Starting early may enable you to produce a good rather than barely acceptable paper. Also, if you have not done a research paper before, you will need time to become familiar with the process.

    There are several other advantages to starting early. You will find books and references readily available in the library, while if you wait until everyone is working on papers, popular sources will be in use or checked out by other students. Also, starting early gives you time to acquire information you may need from other libraries through interlibrary loan services. Finally, an early start allows you time to think, to organize, and even to make mistakes and be able to correct them.
3. Ask your instructor for advice. If you experience difficulty, ask your instructor for help with a particular problem. Through their experience with the subject matter, instructors are often able to suggest alternate approaches to the topic, recommend a particular reference, or suggest a different organization. However, do not go to see your instructor until you have wrestled with the problem and find yourself at a standstill. When you do see your instructor, take your notes, outlines, and rough drafts.

STEPS IN WRITING A RESEARCH PAPER

In paging through the remainder of this chapter, you might think that writing a research paper is a very complicated process. You will see that eleven steps are shown and that they appear to be fairly detailed. If you follow each step, however, you will discover that you are carefully led through a fairly routine process of focusing your paper, collecting information, and writing the paper. The steps are:

1. Narrow your topic.
2. Determine the purpose of the paper.

3. Locate appropriate sources of information.
4. Refine the topic through further reading.
5. Write a tentative thesis statement.
6. Collect information.
7. Form an outline.
8. Write a first draft.
9. Revise the draft.
10. Prepare the final copy.
11. Prepare the bibliography.

Step 1: Narrow Your Topic

Choosing and narrowing your topic is critical to producing a good paper. If you begin with an unmanageable topic, regardless of how hard you work, you will be unable to produce an acceptable paper. Also, your task is much easier if you choose a manageable topic—one for which information is readily accessible and understandable. Some instructors might require that you select a topic within a specific subject area; others may accept any topic that pertains to the course. In either case choice is involved.

The most important consideration in selecting a topic is to choose one that is neither too broad nor too narrow. If you choose a topic that is too broad, it will be impossible for you to cover all its aspects adequately. On the other hand, if it is too specific, you may have difficulty finding enough to write about. For most students, the tendency is to select a topic that is too general.

Suppose you are taking a course in ecology and the environment and you have been assigned a fifteen-page research paper. Your instructor will allow you to choose any topic related to the course of study. You have always been interested in environmental pollution and decide to do your research paper on this subject. Because there are many causes of pollution, many types of pollution, and many effects of pollution, both immediate and long-term, you realize that the general topic of environmental pollution is much too broad. To narrow or limit this topic, you might choose one type of pollution—such as water pollution—and then decide to research its causes or effects. Or you might decide to limit your topic to a study of the different types of chemicals that pollute the air.

It is often necessary to narrow your topic two or three times. The process of narrowing a topic might be diagrammed as shown in Figure 18-2.

Once you have a subject area or a broad topic in mind, try to think of ways your topic could be subdivided. Often you will first have to acquire some general background about the subject. For ideas to start with, check the card catalog in the library under your subject and read the subject headings that immediately follow it to see how the subject is divided. Also, check an encyclopedia to see how the subject is divided, then skim quickly through to learn a little about the topic. Depending on your subject, you may also wish to consult other texts in the subject area to get a brief overview of the field. Make a list of possible topics. As an alternate approach, make a list of questions that might be asked about the subject. Each of your questions suggests a possible division of your subject. You may find it necessary to further limit these divisions as you gather information.

EXERCISE 3 _____

Directions: *Assume that one of your instructors has assigned a research paper on one of the following subjects. Choose a subject and narrow it to a topic that is manageable in a ten- to twenty-page paper. If necessary, check the card catalog, an encyclopedia entry, or various texts in the field. Use an outline like the one shown below.*

Subjects

1. Clothing styles and fashion
2. Test-tube babies
3. Sports
4. Death
5. Pornography

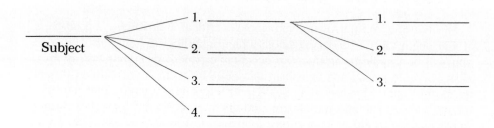

Step 2: Determine the Purpose of the Paper

Once you have narrowed your topic, the next step is to determine the purpose of your paper. You should decide whether you want to prove something about your topic, inform others about it, or explain or analyze it. In some cases, your purpose may have already been defined by your instructor when he or she assigned the research paper. Most of the time, however, you will need to decide how you will approach your topic. To determine your approach, ask yourself, What do I want to accomplish by writing this paper? Whatever approach you select will directly affect how you proceed from this point. The type of sources you consult, the amount of reading you do, and the thesis that you state and develop are each shaped by your purpose.

Step 3: Locate Appropriate Sources of Information

Your campus library, its librarians, and its reference materials are the keys to locating appropriate sources of information on your topic. If you have not used the library on your campus, take a half hour or so to visit the library

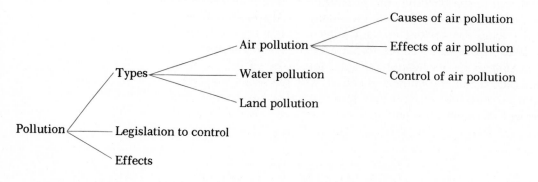

FIGURE 18-2   Narrowing a Topic

just to become acquainted with its organization and the services it offers. Do not try to begin researching your topic until you know what is available in the library and how to use it. Be sure to find out:

1. how the card catalog is organized
2. how the books are arranged on the shelves
3. where the reference section is located
4. whether a reference librarian is available
5. whether there is a photocopy machine
6. where periodicals (journals and magazines) are located
7. the procedure for checking out books and periodicals
8. whether your library participates in an interlibrary loan system
9. if a floor plan of the library is available

If you feel lost in the library or find that you are unfamiliar with many of the reference materials, check to see what assistance the library has to offer. Some libraries offer one- to two-hour workshops on library usage and research skills; others have pamphlets, brochures, or videotapes that provide basic information on using the campus library. If none of these services is available, ask the reference librarian for assistance. After all, a reference librarian's primary responsibility is to assist students in using the library.

Rules of Thumb for Locating Sources: When you are generally familiar with the library, you are ready to begin locating sources of information. There are several rules of thumb to follow:

1. Proceed from general to specific. Locate general sources of information first; then, once you have an overview of the topic, locate more detailed references on particular aspects of the topic.
2. Locate as many sources as possible. Your research paper is expected to cover your topic thoroughly. In collecting information, therefore, you must be sure that you do not overlook important aspects of the topic. By locating and checking as many references as possible, you can be certain that you have covered the topic completely. Once you have read several sources, it is possible to skim additional sources, checking to see what new information is provided.
3. Record all sources used. Many students waste valuable time by failing to keep a complete record of all references used. An important part of any research paper is the bibliography, or list of all the references you use to write the paper (see Step 11, page 351). To prepare this bibliography in the easiest way possible, just write down each source as you use it. If you forget to do this, you will have to spend additional time later, checking back and trying to locate each source you used.

    The easiest way to record bibliographical information is to use a separate 3″ × 5″ index card for each source. Later you will see that the cards enable you to alphabetize your references easily. To avoid wasting time recopying or rewriting information, record it in the exact form in which it should appear in the bibliography.
4. Ask for assistance. If you have difficulty locating information or if you are not certain that you have exhausted all possible sources, ask the reference librarian for assistance. Most librarians are ready and willing to guide serious students in their research.

Using the Card Catalog: The key to every library is the card catalog. It is an easy-to-use record of all the books and periodicals that the library owns.

Two, three, or more separate cards are filed for each book in the library. Each book may be listed by author, by title, and by subject(s) covered. The card briefly describes what the book includes and contains a call number that you can use to locate the book on the shelf. The card catalog, then, is one of the first places to start in researching a topic.

Using Reference Materials: In addition to its holdings of books and periodicals, libraries have a reference section that contains general references, sources that cannot be checked out. Among the most common reference materials are encyclopedias, dictionaries, periodical indexes, almanacs, biographical dictionaries, atlases, and statistical handbooks. Also, many libraries contain a reserve section in which instructors "reserve," or place on restricted use, important, useful sources that many students wish to use. The reference librarian is available to assist you in using these sources.

Conducting Data Base Searches: Most libraries offer computerized data-base searches. Once you supply the computer with specific topics that pertain to your subject, the computer is connected by telephone lines to a data bank and provides you with a list of sources relating to your topic. Data-base searches are often used when more traditional searches within the library fail to yield sufficient sources. If you are considering using a data-base search, discuss your research problem with a librarian. He or she may suggest alternatives or, if a search is appropriate, assist you with the process. The process involves:

1. Listing topics, synonyms, and related terminology that describe your subject.
2. Listing related topics that you do *not* wish to research.
3. Limiting the scope of the search. For example, you may limit it to certain years, certain types of publications, certain languages.

You should be aware that some libraries require you to pay a fee for this service. Costs may be substantial, depending on the percentage of cost your college chooses to absorb.

Step 4: Refine the Topic Through Further Reading

To become familiar with the range and scope of your topic and to acquire background information, it is useful to read or skim several general sources of information. Your purpose at this point is to learn enough about your topic to be able to refine the direction, or focus, of your paper. Again a good starting point is the encyclopedia. The entry will provide you with an overview of your topic and may suggest directions on the general subject of which your topic is part, or books written on the subject.

Since your purpose is to get an overview of the topic, do not try to read everything. You might read parts of the material and skip others. Do not try to take notes on your reading yet. Instead, just jot down on index cards references that would be useful for later, more thorough reading. Also, jot down any ideas that might come to mind about how to approach, to further limit, or to organize your topic. Continue sampling general sources until you find that most of what you are reading is no longer new and that you have already read it in another source.

Step 5: Write a Tentative Thesis Statement

A thesis statement is a one-sentence statement of what your paper is about. It states the idea you will develop throughout the paper. You might think of a thesis statement as similar to the topic sentence of a paragraph or the central thought of a passage. Each states, in a general way, what the paragraph or passage is about. Similarly, the thesis statement indicates to your reader what your paper will be about.

Here are a few examples of thesis statements that could be written for the topic of effects of air pollution:

> Air pollution has had a dramatic effect on the lives of twentieth-century Americans.

> Air pollution has been the primary cause of numerous health-related problems for Americans.

> Public concern over the long-range effects of air pollution has forced industrial reform.

Notice that each specifically states what the writer intends to show about air pollution and its effects.

Since you have so far done only preliminary reading and research, your thesis statement is only tentative. You should plan on changing, revising, or narrowing this statement as you proceed through the remaining steps. Right now your thesis statement should express the idea you *think* your paper will explain or discuss. In a sense, the thesis statement further narrows your topic by limiting your paper to a specific focus or approach.

EXERCISE 4 ————————————————

Directions: *Assume that each of the following is the topic of a research paper. For each, write a thesis statement that suggests a direction of development or focus for the topic.*

1. *Topic:* Cigarette Smoking and Health

   Thesis statement: ————————————————

   ——————————————————————

2. *Topic:* The Progress of the Women's Movement

   Thesis statement: ————————————————

   ——————————————————————

3. *Topic:* The Draft for Women

   Thesis statement: ————————————————

   ——————————————————————

4. *Topic:* Choosing a Career

   Thesis statement: _____

   _____

5. *Topic:* Gay Rights

   Thesis statement: _____

   _____

Step 6: Collect Information: Reading and Notetaking

Now that you have written a tentative thesis statement, the next step is to collect and record the information that supports your thesis.

Reading Reference Material: In reading reference material, you clearly define your purpose for reading; you are looking for facts and ideas that will help you prove, explain, or support your thesis statement. However, reading reference sources is very different from reading textbooks. In textbooks you are reading for retention and recall of most of the information presented. When reading reference material, on the other hand, not all information is useful or important. Also, you are not trying to remember everything you read; instead, when you find a useful piece of information, you can write it down for later reference.

Prereading is a valuable skill in identifying sources that may contain information on your topic. Once you have located a book in the card catalog and then found it on the library shelves, take a few minutes to preview it to determine if it contains useful information before you check it out. You can save yourself valuable time and avoid carrying home armloads of books by prereading to select only appropriate, usable sources.

Because high retention is not required when reading reference material you can afford to skim, scan, or skip large portions of material (see Chapter 22 for skimming and scanning techniques). In fact, trying to read everything, regardless of whether you use it in your paper, would be an extremely inefficient use of time.

Taking Notes: The manner and form in which you take notes largely determines whether writing your paper will be a relatively simple or extremely difficult, time-consuming task. The next two steps, developing an outline and writing the paper, require that the information you collect be in a form that can be rearranged or placed in a specific order.

One effective way to take notes is to use index cards; 5″ × 8″ and 4″ × 6″ sizes are best. Some students prefer to use separate full sheets of paper. Use a separate card or sheet of paper for each different subtopic, or different aspect of your topic. Record the author's last name and the pages you used in the upper right corner. In the upper left corner, write the subtopic that the notes are concerned with. Be sure to write on only one side of the cards. A sample note card or sheet might look like the one shown in Figure 18-3.

Here are a few suggestions for taking good research notes:

1. Record the information in your own words, instead of copying the author's words. By recording the author's wording, you run the risk of using the

> Violence - how it's learned   Barlow p. 125-6
>
> violence learned through imitation + modelling.
>   -experiments by Bandura show that children
> pick up behavior patterns of adults they know or respect.
>   ex. Child views film of woman beating/kicking a doll/
>   then child is given similar doll.
>   Child performs similar violent behavior
>   as woman.
>   -patterns may be learned from watching adults
>   on T.V.
> patterns are retained through life + generalized to
> other situations
> reward + punishment play imp't role in this type of learning.

FIGURE 18-3   A Sample Note Card

author's wording in your paper, perhaps without realizing that you have done so. Whenever you use an author's words instead of your own, you are required to give the author credit by indicating the author and source from which the material was taken. The same rule applies when you use someone's idea, theory, or argument that is not common knowledge. Failure to give credit is known as plagiarism and means that you have borrowed someone else's words and ideas without acknowledging them. Plagiarism is a serious error, and many institutions penalize students who either knowingly or unknowingly plagiarize.

2. Try to summarize and condense information. You will find that it is impossible to record all the information you find, so whenever possible try to state the facts and ideas as concisely and as briefly as possible.

3. Record information only once. As you continue reading, eventually you will find the same information appearing and reappearing in various sources. If you have already made a note once, do not spend time writing it again. Occasionally you may need to check back through your notes to see what you've already recorded. You might, however, want to note the fact that there is common agreement in a number of sources about the information.

4. Record useful quotations. If you find a statement that strongly supports your thesis, you may want to quote it in your paper. Copy it down exactly and place it in quotation marks in your notes, along with its source.

Step 7: Form an Outline

Once you are satisfied that you have collected sufficient information, take a few moments to reread and organize your note cards. Try to group them together by subtopic. You may find some subtopics that overlap and others that can be grouped together under a more general subtopic. Remember to change the subtopic written in the upper left corner of the card for any cards that you reclassify.

Next, sort your cards in separate piles according to subtopic. Then, with each pack of cards or sheets laid out in front of you, try to arrange them in some logical order or sequence. You might arrange your subtopics chronologically, in order of importance, or by cause-effect. Often your purpose for writing, your thesis statement, or the content of the paper will dictate the order or arrangement. You can use the organizational patterns you learned to identify in reading paragraphs as a means of organizing your paper. Arrange your information in a manner that supports your thesis statement. Once you have done this, you have a tentative outline. To record this arrangement, list the subtopics in order. When you can see how the ideas relate to one another, reread your outline and revise it. Check each subtopic to be sure that it directly supports your thesis statement.

Step 8: Write a First Draft

Using your outline as a guide and your note cards to provide the specific facts and information, start writing the first draft of your paper. Your paper should have a brief introduction of one or two paragraphs, a body, and a conclusion or summary. In the introduction you should lead up to and state the thesis of the paper. Before starting it, you might lead up to it by supplying necessary background information or by providing a context.

The body, which comprises most of the paper, should explain and discuss the thesis statement. Each idea should be directly related to and support the thesis statement. Finally, in the conclusion or summary you should draw together the ideas you presented and bring the paper to a close. That is, in the last several paragraphs, try to review the major points you presented and connect them, once again, to the thesis statement.

Step 9: Revise the Draft

Once you have written a first draft, the next step is to reread, evaluate, and revise it. As with any other type of paper, revision is a critical step and can make a difference in the grade you earn.

When revising your paper, ask yourself the following questions:

1. Does each paragraph directly support the thesis statement?
2. Are the ideas expressed clearly and concisely?
3. Are the major points connected to one another as well as to the thesis statement?
4. Is there sufficient explanation and support for the thesis statement?

After you have reread your paper and made changes, ask someone else to read your paper. Then ask the person to identify the thesis statement and to summarize the supporting information. If he or she is unable to do so or does so incorrectly, then you may not have communicated your message effectively.

Some students find it necessary to go through more than one revision, especially if their first drafts are weak or poorly organized. Also, you may sometimes find that you need more information, in which case you must go back to the research stage to check new sources. Do not be discouraged by these additional steps; remember, the first few times you write a research paper, you are learning *how* to do the assignment. Therefore some extra time and effort may be required initially.

Step 10: Prepare the Final Copy

Once you are satisfied that you have made sufficient revision to produce a good research paper, you are ready to prepare the final copy for submission. It is generally agreed that a typewritten copy is strongly desirable. Some instructors require typewritten copy; most prefer it to handwritten papers. If you have poor, illegible handwriting, your instructor may become annoyed while reading the paper and may unconsciously react to your paper negatively or critically. A typewritten copy, on the other hand, presents a neat appearance and suggests that you care enough about your work to present it in the best possible form.

An important part of preparing a final copy, regardless of whether it is handwritten or typed, is proofreading. Once you have prepared the final copy, be sure to take the time to read it through and correct spelling, punctuation, and grammar. If you are weak in one or more of these areas and cannot easily recognize your own errors, ask a friend to proofread your paper and point out or mark the errors.

Step 11: Prepare the Bibliography

The final steps to completing a research paper are to prepare a list, or bibliography, of all the sources that you used to write the paper, and to prepare any endnotes necessary. Endnotes list in consecutive order the sources from which you have taken quotations or which contained unique or specialized information particular to a certain source. Endnotes are called footnotes if placed at the bottom of each page rather than in a consecutive list at the end of the paper. You will need to consult a handbook to determine the specialized format endnotes require.

As mentioned earlier, if you kept careful records as you collected your information, preparing a bibliography is a relatively simple task. In the bibliography you simply list alphabetically all the sources you consulted. Also, you must use a consistent form for listing the information. Depending on your instructor, as well as the subject area with which you are working, different formats may be expected. Although each format requires basically the same information, arrangement of information as well as punctuation may vary. Some instructors may specify a particular format, while others may accept any standard, consistent format. If your instructor prefers a particular format, by all means use it.

It is well worth the initial cost to purchase a handbook or style guide that explains a particular format. Among the most commonly used handbooks that explain how to do a bibliography as well as how to handle many of the other stylistic features of research papers are

The MLA Handbook for Writers of Research Papers, 3rd ed. (New York: Modern Language Association, 1988).
Turabian, Kate L. *A Manual for Writers*, 5th ed. (Chicago: University of Chicago Press, 1987).

SUMMARY

Written assignments and research papers are an important part of many college courses. There are several types of writing that instructors assign: essay exams, essays or compositions, factual reports, reaction papers, and research papers. Writing a good paper involves much more than picking up a pen and starting to write. The steps involved in writing any type of paper are prewriting, organizing, writing, revising, and proofreading. Writing a research paper is a process of acquiring and organizing information on a particular topic. It involves selecting an appropriate topic, locating useful sources of information, reading, taking notes, and organizing information. This chapter presented some tips for getting started and then outlined a step-by-step approach for completing a research paper. The steps are as follows:

1. Narrow your topic.
2. Determine the purpose of the paper.
3. Locate appropriate sources of information.
4. Refine the topic through further reading.
5. Write a tentative thesis statement.
6. Collect information.
7. Form an outline.
8. Write a first draft.
9. Revise the draft.
10. Prepare the final copy.
11. Prepare the bibliography.

PART SIX

Vocabulary Development

Vocabulary development is crucial to the development of effective and efficient reading. *Vocabulary* means the ability to recognize individual words and to associate meaning with the particular combination of letters that form a word.

Words are symbols; they are groups of letters that stand for, or represent, either a physical object or an idea. The word *table* can call to our minds a physical reality—an object with a flat, plane surface, usually supported by four perpendicular legs, and used for holding objects or for eating dinner. The word *love*, on the other hand, does not represent a physical object; it symbolizes the feeling of one person toward another. The combination of the letters *t-a-b-l-e* or *l-o-v-e* has no real meaning in itself; it is only when the combination of letters is associated with a particular object or idea that it becomes meaningful. Take, for example, *hoglag;* you can read it, you can pronounce it, but it has no meaning for you (it is a nonsense word). You have not built up any associations between this combination of letters and a physical object or idea. The major task involved in building vocabulary, then, is to increase the number of associations you can make between words (combinations of letters) and the physical objects or ideas they stand for.

The number of word-meaning associations you have acquired defines your vocabulary level. Adult vocabulary levels vary greatly—some adults are functionally illiterate, whereas others have attained an amazing mastery of words. The average adult knows the meanings of thousands of words. Since you, as a college student, are above the educational level of most adults, you should strive to develop your vocabulary beyond an average adult level.

There are a number of methods you can use to develop your vocabulary. Those presented in this part of the text are limited to those that are the most practical and immediately beneficial.

Chapter 19 is concerned with expanding both general and

continued

continued

specialized (discipline-related) vocabulary. Suggestions are given for developing a sense of word awareness, and useful reference sources are discussed. A vocabulary card system for learning and remembering new words is also presented.

Chapter 20 presents a practical method of figuring out the meaning of an unknown word in a sentence, paragraph, or passage. By using the words around an unknown word, or its *context,* it is often possible to determine the meaning of the word. The chapter will focus on specific techniques for effectively using clues in the context to derive word meanings. It also discusses analyzing word parts—prefixes, roots, and suffixes—as a means of unlocking word meaning and of building vocabulary. Tables of common prefixes, roots, and suffixes are included.

19

Expanding Your Vocabulary

Use this chapter to:

1. *Learn how to expand your vocabulary.*
2. *Learn the best way to pick up new terminology introduced in a course.*

A strong vocabulary can be a valuable asset, both in college and later in your career. Considerable research evidence suggests that students who are the most successful in school are those with the largest vocabularies. Other research ties job advancement to vocabulary level. In one study, successful business executives were found to have the highest vocabulary of any occupational group.

Your vocabulary is also an important personal characteristic upon which people form first but lasting impressions of you. Your vocabulary reveals a lot about you and is particularly important in job interviews, oral class presentations, discussion group classes, and papers and exams that you write.

How would you rate your vocabulary? Many students answer either "good" or "terrible," but vocabulary knowledge is not an either/or, two-choice situation. Try the following quiz, which will help you realize that vocabulary ability is much more than "Either I know the word or I don't." Do not be concerned with how you score on the quiz; its purpose is to make a point, not to measure your vocabulary level.

VOCABULARY QUIZ

1. Read through the following list of words. If you can define the word, mark *D* in the space provided. If you've heard or seen the word before and have a general idea of what it means, mark *G* in the space. If the word is completely unfamiliar, mark *U*.

acrid	_____	interlude	_____
peripheral	_____	peregrine	_____
liquidate	_____	juror	_____
jaded	_____	litigation	_____
interior	_____	kumquat	_____
interject	_____		

2. How many different meanings can you think of for the word *run*?

_____

3. What does the word *cones* mean when used in a human anatomy and physiology course?

_____

4. Could a fugue be played at a concert?

_____

5. Does a cake baking in an oven have a fetid odor?

_____

6. You have probably heard the French expression *faux pas*. Can you define it?

_____

7. Use the word *credit* in a sentence in which it does not refer to college course work or a credit card.

_____

8. All of the following words mean "unable to do something." How do they differ in meaning? When would you use each?

    incapable   powerless   incompetent

_____

_____

Now check your answers in the Answer Key.

From this quiz, you should see that expanding your vocabulary involves much more than just looking up words you don't know. It involves learning new meanings and uses for words you already know. It involves taking vaguely familiar words that have an unclear or fuzzy meaning and sharpening their focus so you can put them to use. It involves learning specialized or technical meanings of everyday words for particular academic disciplines. Finally, it involves learning new words, both general and technical, that you have never heard or seen before.

GENERAL APPROACHES TO VOCABULARY EXPANSION

Expanding your vocabulary requires motivation, positive attitudes, and skills, the first of which is most important. To improve your vocabulary, you must be willing to work at it, spending both time and effort to notice and learn new words and meanings. Keep in mind that intent to remember is one of the principles of learning (see Chapter 3). Unless you intend to remember new words you hear or read, you will probably forget them. Your attitude toward reading will also influence the extent to which your vocabulary develops. If you enjoy reading and you read a broad range of subjects, you will frequently encounter new words. On the other hand, if you read only when required to do so, your exposure to words will be limited. Finally, your skills in using reference sources, in handling specialized terminology, and in organizing a system for learning new words will influence your vocabulary development.

The remainder of this chapter will focus on the skills you need to build your vocabulary. Before you continue, however, read the following suggestions for expanding your vocabulary.

Read Widely: One of the best ways to improve your vocabulary is by reading widely and diversely, sampling many different subjects and styles of writing. Through reading you encounter new words and new uses for familiar words. You also see words used in contexts that you had not previously considered.

College is one of the best places to begin reading widely. As you take elective and required courses, you are exposed to new ideas, as well as the words that express them clearly and succinctly. While you are a student, use the range of required and elective reading to expand your vocabulary.

Look for Five-Dollar Words to Replace One-Dollar Words: Some words in your vocabulary are general and vague. While they convey meaning, they are not precise, exact, or expressive. Try to replace these one-dollar words with five-dollar words that convey your meaning more directly. The word *good* is an example of a word that has a general, unclear meaning in the following sentence:

The movie was so good, it was worth the high admission price.

Try substituting the following words in the preceding sentence: exciting, moving, thrilling, scary, heart-tugging. Notice how each of these gives more information than the word *good*. These are the types of words you should strive to use in your speech and writing.

Build a Sense of Word Awareness: Get in the habit of noticing new or unusual words when reading and listening. Learn to pay attention to words and notice those that seem useful. One of the first steps in expanding your vocabulary is to develop a sense of word awareness. At the college level, many new words you learn do not represent new concepts or ideas. Instead, they are more accurate or more descriptive replacements for simpler words and expressions that you already know and use. Once you begin to notice words, you will find that many of them automatically become part of your vocabulary.

Your instructors are a good resource for new words. Both in formal classroom lectures and in more casual discussions and conversations, many instructors use words that students understand but seldom use. You will hear new words and technical terms that are particular to a specific academic discipline.

Other good sources are textbooks, collateral reading assignments, and reference materials. If you are like most students, you understand many more words than you use in your own speech and writing. As you read, you will encounter many words you are vaguely familiar with but which you cannot define. When you begin to notice these words, you will find that many of them become part of your vocabulary.

Consider Working with a Vocabulary Improvement Program: If you feel motivated to make improvements in a concentrated program of study, consider setting aside a block of time each week to work with a vocabulary improvement program. A variety of paperbacks on the market are designed to help you improve your vocabulary. The average bookstore should have several to choose from. Also, microcomputer programs, some in game formats, are available to strengthen general vocabulary. Check with your college's learning lab or library to see what is available.

USING REFERENCE SOURCES

Once you have developed a sense of word awarness and have begun to identify useful words to add to your vocabulary, the next step is to become familiar with the references you can use to expand your vocabulary.

Dictionaries: Which One to Buy

A common question students ask is, Which dictionary should I buy? There are several types of dictionaries, each with its own purpose and use. A pocket or paperback dictionary is an inexpensive, shortened version of a standard desk dictionary. It is small enough to carry with you to your classes and costs around five dollars.

A desk dictionary is a more complete, thorough dictionary. Although a pocket dictionary is convenient, it is also limited. A pocket edition lists about 55,000 words, whereas a standard desk edition lists up to 150,000 words. Also, the desk edition provides much more complete information about each word. Desk dictionaries are usually hardbound and cost over twenty dollars.

Several standard dictionaries are available in both desk and paperback editions. These include the *Random House Dictionary of the English Language, Webster's Collegiate Dictionary,* and the *American Heritage Dictionary of the English Language.*

Another type is the unabridged dictionary, which can be found in the reference section of any library. The unabridged edition provides the most complete information on each word in the English language.

Deciding whether to purchase a desk or pocket dictionary will depend on your needs as well as what you can afford. It would be ideal to have both. A pocket dictionary is sufficient for checking spelling and for looking up common meanings of unfamiliar words. To expand your vocabulary by learning additional meanings of words or to do any serious word study, you need a desk dictionary.

Use of the Dictionary

Most students are familiar with the common uses of a dictionary: (1) to look up the meaning of words you don't know, and (2) to check the spelling of words. A dictionary can be useful in many other ways because it contains much more than just word meanings. For most entries you will find a pronunciation key, word origin, part(s) of speech, variant spellings, and synonyms. At the beginning or end of many desk dictionaries you will find information on language history and manuscript form, lists of symbols, and tables of weights and measures.

A dictionary is the basic tool for expanding your vocabulary. Get in the habit of consulting your dictionary whenever you see or hear a somewhat familiar word that you don't use and can't define precisely. Locate the word, read each meaning, and find the one that fits the way the word was used when you read or heard it. Use the vocabulary card system suggested later in this chapter to record and learn these words.

EXERCISE 1 ——————————————

Directions: *Use a desk dictionary to answer the following questions.*

1. What does the abbreviation *obs.* means?

2. What does the symbol *c.* stand for?

3. How many meanings are listed for the word *fall*?

4. How is the word *phylloxera* pronounced? (Record its phonetic spelling.)

5. What is the plural spelling of *addendum*?

6. Can the word *protest* be used other than as a verb? If so, how?

7. The word *prime* can mean first or original. List some of its other meanings.

8. What does the French expression *savoir faire* mean?

9. List three synonyms for the word *fault*.

10. List several words that are formed using the word *dream*.

Thesauruses

A thesaurus, or dictionary of synonyms, is a valuable reference for locating a precise, accurate, or descriptive word to fit a particular situation. Suppose you are searching for a more precise term for the expression *looked over*, as used in the following sentence:

My instructor looked over my essay exam.

The thesaurus lists the synonyms seen in Figure 19-1. Right away you can identify a number of words that are more specific than the phrase *looked over*. The next step, then, is to choose a word from the entry that most closely suggests the meaning you want to convey. The easiest way to do this is to "test out" or substitute various choices in your sentence to see which one is most appropriate; check the dictionary if you are not sure of a word's exact meaning.

Many students misuse the thesaurus by choosing words that do not fit the context. *Be sure to use words only when you are familiar with all their shades of meaning.* Remember, a misused word is often a more serious error than a wordy or imprecise expression.

The most widely used thesaurus was originally compiled by the English scholar Peter Roget and is known today as *Roget's Thesaurus;* it is readily available in an inexpensive paperback edition.

EXERCISE 2 ━━━━━━━━━━━━━━━━━━

Directions: *Replace the underlined word or phrase in each sentence with a more descriptive word or phrase. Use a thesaurus to locate your replacement.*

1. When Sara learned that her sister had committed a crime, she was <u>sad</u>.
2. Compared to earlier chapters, the last two chapters in my chemistry text are <u>hard</u>.
3. The instructor spent the entire class <u>talking about</u> the causes of inflation and deflation.
4. The main character in the film was a <u>thin</u>, talkative British soldier.
5. We went to see the film that won the Academy Award for the best picture; it was <u>great</u>!

Subject Area Dictionaries

Many academic disciplines have specialized dictionaries that list important terminology used in that field. They have specialized meanings and suggest how and when to use a word. For the field of music there is *The New Grove Dictionary of Music and Musicians,* which lists and defines the specialized vocabulary of music. Other subject area dictionaries include *Taber's Cyclopedic Medical Dictionary, A Dictionary of Anthropology,* and *A Dictionary of Economics.*

Be sure to check if there is a subject area dictionary for your courses and area of specialization. Most of these dictionaries are available only in hardbound copies and are likely to be expensive. Many students, however, find them to be worth the initial investment. You will find that most libraries have copies of specialized dictionaries in their reference section.

VERBS **12. see, behold, observe, view, witness, perceive, discern, spy,** espy, descry, **sight,** have in sight, make out, spot [coll.], twig [coll.], discover, notice, distinguish, recognize, ken [dial.], **catch sight of,** get a load of [slang, U.S.], take in, look on or upon, cast the eyes on or upon, **set or lay eyes on, clap eyes on** [coll.]; pipe, lamp, nail, peg [all slang]; **glimpse,** get or catch a glimpse of; see at a glance, see with half an eye; see with one's own eyes.

13. look, peer, direct the eyes, turn or bend the eyes, lift up the eyes; **peek, peep,** pry, take a peep or peek; play at peekaboo or bopeep; get an eyeful [coll., U.S.].

14. look at, take a look at, take a gander at [slang, U.S.], have a looksee [slang, U.S.], look on or upon, gaze at or upon; **watch, observe,** pipe [slang], **view, regard;** keep in sight or view, hold in view; look after, follow; spy upon.

15. scrutinize, survey, eye, ogle, contemplate, look over, give the eye [slang], give the once-over or double-O [slang, U.S.]; examine, **inspect** 484.31; size up

[coll.], take one's measure [slang].

16. gaze, gloat, fix ~, fasten or **rivet** the eyes upon, keep the eyes upon; eye, ogle; **stare,** look [coll.], goggle, **gape, gawk** [coll.], gaup or gawp [dial.], gaze open-mouthed; crane, crane the neck; rubber, **rubberneck,** gander [all slang, U.S.]; look straight in the eye, look full in the face, hold one's eye or gaze, stare down; strain the eyes.

17. glare, glower, look daggers.

18. glance, glimpse, glint, cast a glance, glance at or upon, take a glance at, take a slant or squint at [slang].

19. look askance or **askant,** give a sidelong look, cut one's eye [slang], glime [dial.]; squint, look asquint; cock the eye; **look down one's nose** [coll.].

20. leer, leer the eye, look leeringly, give a leering look.

21. look away, avert the eyes; look another way, break one's eyes away, stop looking, turn away from, turn the back upon; drop one's eyes or gaze, cast one's eyes down; avoid one's gaze, cut eyes [coll.].

FIGURE 19-1   A Sample Thesaurus Entry

EXERCISE 3 ————————————————

Directions: *List below each course you are taking this term. Using your campus library, find out if a subject area dictionary is available for each discipline. If so, list their titles below.*

Course   *Subject Area Dictionary*

_____   _____

_____   _____

_____   _____

_____   _____

LEARNING SPECIALIZED TERMINOLOGY

Each subject area can be said to have a language of its own—its own set of specialized words that makes it possible to describe and discuss accurately topics, principles and concepts, problems, and occurrences related to the subject area.

One of the first tasks facing both college instructors and textbook authors is the necessity of introducing and teaching the specialized language of an academic field. This task is especially important in introductory, first-semester courses in which a student studies or encounters the subject area for the first time. In an introduction to psychology course, for instance, you often start by learning the meaning of *psychology* itself—what the study is devoted to, what it encompasses, how it approaches situations, events, and problems. From that point you move on to learn related terms: *behavior, observations, hypothesis, experiment, variables, subjects,* and so forth.

Often the first few class lectures in a course are introductory. They are devoted to acquainting students with the nature and scope of the subject area and to introducing students to the specialized language.

The first few chapters within a textbook are introductory too. They are written to familiarize students with the subject of study and acquaint them with its specialized language. In one economics textbook, thirty-four new terms were introduced in the first two chapters (forty pages). In the first two chapters (twenty-eight pages) of a chemistry book, fifty-six specialized words were introduced. A sample of the words introduced in each text is given below. From these lists you can see that some of the words are words of common, everyday usage that take on a specialized meaning; others are technical terms used only in the subject area.

New Terms: *Economics Text*	*New Terms:* *Chemistry Text*
capital	matter
ownership	element
opportunity cost	halogen
distribution	isotope
productive contribution	allotropic form
durable goods	nonmetal
economic system	group (family)
barter	burning
commodity money	toxicity

EXERCISE 4 ─────────────────

Directions: *Turn to the biology sample textbook chapter in Appendix B, pages 457–471. Identify as many new terms as you can and record them in the space provided below.*

Total Specialzied Words: _____

Examples of Specialized Vocabulary:

_____

_____

_____

_____

EXERCISE 5 ─────────────────

Directions: *Select any two textbooks you are currently using. In each, turn to the first chapter and check to see how many specialized items are introduced. List the total number of terms. Then list several examples.*

Textbook 1: _____   *Textbook 2:* _____
                    (title)   *(title)*

Total specialized words: _____   *Total specialized words:* _____

   Examples of Specialized Words: *Examples of Specialized Words:*

1. _____   1. _____

2. _____   2. _____

3. _____   3. _____

4. _____   4. _____

5. _____   5. _____

Recognition of specialized terminology is only the first step in learning the language of a course. More important is the development of a systematic way of identifying, marking, recording, and learning the specialized terms. Since new terminology is introduced in both class lectures and course textbooks, it is necessary to develop a procedure for handling the specialized terms in each.

Specialized Terminology in Class Lectures

As a part of your notetaking system, develop a consistent way of separating new terms and definitions from other facts and ideas. You might circle or draw a box around each new term; or as you edit your notes (make revisions, changes, or additions to your notes after taking them), underline each new term in red; or mark "def." in the margin each time a definition is included. The mark or symbol you use is a matter of preference; the important thing is to find some way to identify definitions for further study. In addition, as part of your editing process, check each definition to be sure that it is complete and readable. Also, if you were not able to record any explanation or examples of new terms, add them as you edit. If the definitions you recorded are unclear, check with a friend or with your instructor. The last step in handling new terminology presented in class lectures is to organize the terms into a system for efficient study. One such system will be suggested later in this chapter.

Specialized Terminology in Textbooks

Textbook authors use various means to emphasize new terminology as they introduce it. In some texts, new vocabulary is printed in italics, boldface type, or colored print. Other texts indicate new terms in the margin of each page. Still the most common means of emphasis, however, is a "new terms" or "vocabulary list" at the beginning or end of each chapter.

While you are reading and underlining important facts and ideas, you should also mark new terminology. Be sure to mark and to separate definitions from other chapter content. (The mark or symbol you use is your choice.)

Occasionally in textbooks you may meet a new term that is not defined or for which the definition is unclear. In this case, check the glossary at the back of the book for the meaning of the word. Make a note of the meaning in the margin of the page.

The glossary, a comprehensive list of terms introduced throughout the text, is an aid that can help you learn new terminology. At the end of the course, when you have covered all or most of the chapters, the glossary can be used to review terminology. Use the glossary to test yourself; read an entry, cover up the meaning and try to remember it, then check to see if you were correct. As you progress through a course, however, the glossary is not an adequate study aid. A more organized, systematic approach to learning unfamiliar new terms is needed.

THE VOCABULARY CARD SYSTEM

Once you have identified and marked new terminology, both in your lecture notes and in your textbook, the next step is to organize the words for study and review. One of the most efficient and practical ways to accomplish this is the vocabulary card system. Use a $3'' \times 5''$ index card for each new term. Record the word on the front and the meaning on the back. If the word is particularly difficult, you might also include a guide to its pronunciation. Underneath the correct spelling of the word, indicate in syllables how the word sounds. For the word *eutrophication* (a term used in chemistry meaning "overnourishment"), you could indicate its pronunciation as "you-tro-fi-kay'-shun. On the back of the card, along with the meaning, you might want to include an example to help you remember the term more easily. A sample vocabulary card, front and back, is shown in Figure 19-2.

Use these cards for study, for review, and for testing yourself. Go through your pack of cards once, looking at the front and trying to recall the meaning on the back. Then reverse the procedure; look at the meanings and see if you can recall the terms. As you go through the pack in this way, sort the cards into two piles: words you know and words you don't know. The next time you review the cards, use only cards in the "don't know" pile for review. This sorting procedure will help you avoid wasting time reviewing words you have already learned. Continue to review the cards until you are satisfied that you

Front of Card

conglomerate
con-glom'-er-it

Back of Card

def.: an organization comprising two or more companies that produce unrelated products.
ex.: Nichols Company owns a shoe factory, vineyards in France, soft drink factories, and Sara Jane pastry company.

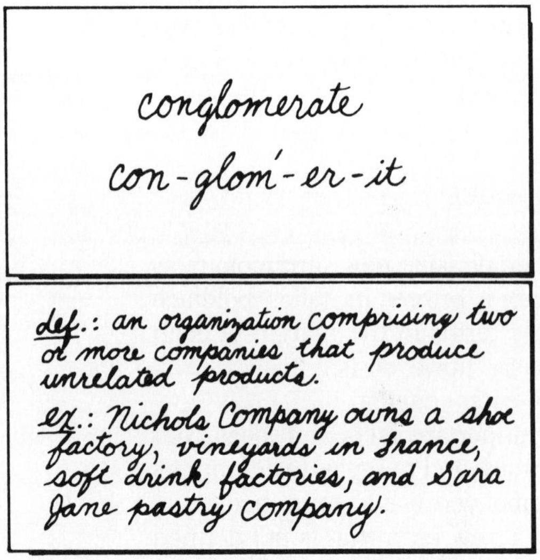

FIGURE 19-2   A Sample Vocabulary Card

have learned each new term. To prevent forgetting, it will be necessary to review the entire pack of cards periodically.

EXERCISE 6 ——————————————

Directions: *Select two or three sets of notes on a particular topic from any course you are taking. Prepare a set of vocabulary cards for the new terms introduced. Review and study the cards.*

EXERCISE 7 ——————————————

Directions: *Select one chapter from any of the textbooks you are currently using. Prepare a vocabulary card for each new term introduced in the chapter. Review and study the cards.*

SUMMARY

Vocabulary is an important personal asset that can directly contribute to your success in college and later in your career. Expanding your vocabulary is a relatively simple process and does not require large investments of time or money. All that is needed is a sense of word awareness, familiarity with information sources, and a system for learning new words.

Developing a sense of word awareness means paying attention to and noticing words. Good sources of new words, both general and specialized, include your instructors and textbooks, as well as collateral readings and reference sources. References that are useful in expanding your vocabulary include the dictionary, the thesaurus, and subject-area dictionaries. Specialized terminology, those words used within an academic discipline, are especially important to learn. While taking notes and reading textbooks, pay special attention to these words. Once general and specialized vocabulary have been identified, the vocabulary card system provides an easy and efficient way to learn each.

20

Effective Use of Context and Word Parts

Use this chapter to:

1. *Learn techniques to figure out the meaning of a word from the words around it.*

2. *Learn the types of clues that can suggest the meaning of a particular word in a sentence, paragraph, or passage.*

3. *Learn how to figure out word meanings using prefixes, roots, and suffixes.*

What should you do when you are reading a passage and you come to a word you don't know? If your instructor asked this question, you might reply, "I'd look the word up in the dictionary." And as you said this, you would know that in fact you don't often take the time to check the dictionary and were only giving an answer you thought your instructor wanted to hear and would agree with.

Actually, looking up a word in a dictionary is not the first thing to do when you meet a word you don't know. In fact, a dictionary is your last resort, something to turn to when all else fails. Instead, it is best to try to figure out the meaning of the word from the words around it in a sentence, paragraph, or passage that you are reading. Very often, among these surrrounding words are various types of clues that make it possible to reason out the meaning of the unknown word. The words around an unknown word that contain clues to its meaning are referred to as the *context*. The clues themselves are called *context clues*. There are four basic types of context clues that you can use in determining word meanings in textbook material: *definition, example/illustration, contrast,* and *logic of the passage*.

If a word's context does not provide clues to its meaning, you might try breaking it into parts. Analyzing a word's parts, known as its *prefix, root,* and *suffix,* also provides clues to its meaning.

USING CONTEXT CLUES

Definition Context Clues

The most obvious type of context clue is a direct statement of the meaning of a new term by an author. Usually this occurs in textbook writing when the author is aware that the word is new to the reader and takes the time to give an accurate definition of the term. In the first chapter of a chemistry book, the term *chemical reaction* is defined:

> A <u>chemical reaction</u> is an interaction involving different atoms, in which chemical bonds are formed, or broken, or both.[1]

Some writers signal you directly that they are presenting a definition with expressions such as "Mass is . . ." or "Anthropology can be defined as . . . ." Other writers, however, are less direct and obvious when they include a definition. Parentheses may be used to give a definition, partial definition, or synonym of a word, as in the following sentence:

> Scientists measure temperature with two scales: the <u>Celsius</u> (or centrigrade) scale (C), and the <u>Kelvin</u> (or thermodynamic) scale (K).[2]

Or an author may employ the parenthetical use of commas or dashes to include a brief definition or synonym within the sentence:

> To begin with, he (Mendel) needed <u>true-breeding plants,</u> plants that showed little variation from generation to generation.[3]
>
> *or*
>
> The importance of <u>bipedalism</u>—two-leggedness—cannot be over-estimated.[4]

Finally, an author may simply insert a synonym directly within the sentence:

> Another central issue, that of the right of a state to withdraw or <u>secede</u> from the Union, was simply avoided.[5]

EXERCISE 1 _____

Directions: *In each sentence, locate the part of the sentence that gives a definition or synonym of the underlined word. Underline this portion of the sentence.*

1. A <u>democracy</u> is a form of government in which the people effectively participate.[6]
2. The amount of heat that it takes to melt one gram of any substance at its melting point is called the <u>heat of fusion</u>.[7]
3. <u>Linoleic acid</u> is an essentially fatty acid necessary for growth and skin integrity in infants.[8]
4. When a gas is cooled, it <u>condenses</u> (changes to a liquid) at its condensation point.[9]

5. But neither a monkey nor an ape has thumbs long enough or flexible enough to be completely <u>opposable</u>, able to reach comfortably to the tips of all the other fingers, as is required for our delicate yet strong precision grip.[10]

Example/Illustration Context Clues

Authors frequently explain their ideas and concepts by giving specific, concrete examples or illustrations. Many times, when an example is given that illustrates, or explains, a new term, you can figure out the meaning of the term from the example. Suppose, for instance, that you frequently confuse the terms *fiction* and *nonfiction* and you are given the following assignment by your instructor: *Select any nonfiction book and write a critical review; you can choose from a wide range of books such as an autobiography, sports, "how-to" manuals, commentaries on historical periods, or current consumer-awareness paperbacks.* From the examples given, you can easily see that *nonfiction* refers to books that are factual, or true.

Writers sometimes give you an advance warning or signal that they are going to present an example or illustration. Phrases that signal an example or illustration to follow include *for example, for instance, to illustrate, such as, included are,* and so on. Read the following examples:

Some everyday, common <u>solutions</u> include gasoline, antifreeze, soda water, seawater, vodka, and ammonia.

Specifically, management of a New York bank developed a strategic plan to increase its customers by making them see banks as offering a large variety of services rather than just a few <u>specialized services</u> (cashing checks, putting money into savings accounts, and making loans).[11]

EXERCISE 2 _____

Directions: *Read each sentence and write a definition or synonym for each underlined word. Use the illustration/example context clue to help you determine word meanings.*

1. Since then a near <u>symbiotic</u> relationship has developed between the player and the fan in the stands watching him—that phrase "I just die when the Chiefs (or the Rams, or the Mets, or whatever)" . . . the fan's forefinger raised to denote that his team (and he) are Number One, the "we did it, we did it," and the self-satisfied smiles on the faces of the people coming down the stadium ramps after their teams have won.[12]

    or the Rams, or the Mets or whatever

2. The play contained a variety of <u>morbid</u> events: the death of a young child, the suicide of her mother, and the murder of an older sister.

    a murder

3. Psychological disturbances are sometimes traceable to a particular <u>trauma</u> in childhood. For example, the death of a parent may produce long-range psychological effects.

   produce long-range psychological effect

4. To <u>substantiate</u> his theory, Watson offered experimental evidence, case study reports, testimony of patients, and a log of observational notes.

   prove

5. There are many <u>phobias</u> that can seriously influence human behavior; the two most common are claustrophobia (fear of confined spaces) and acrophobia (fear of heights).

   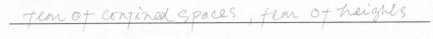

   fear of confined spaces, fear of heights

6. <u>Homogeneous</u> groups, such as classes of all boys, or social organizations of high-IQ people, or country clubs of wealthy families, have particular roles and functions.

   same identity.

Contrast Context Clues

It is sometimes possible to figure out the meaning of an unknown word from a word or phrase in the context that has an opposite meaning. To use a simple example, in the sentence "Sam was thin, but George was obese," a contrasting or opposite description is set up between George and Sam. The word *but* signals that an opposite or contrasting idea is to follow. By knowing the meaning of *thin* and knowing that George is the opposite of thin, you figure out that *obese* means "not thin," or *fat*.

Most often when an opposite or contrasting meaning is given, there is a signal word or phrase in the sentence which indicates a change in the direction of the thought. Most commonly used are these signal words or phrases: *on the other hand, however, while, but, nevertheless, on the contrary.* Note the following example.

> The Federalists, from their <u>pessimistic</u> viewpoint, believed the Constitution could protect them by its procedures, while the more positive Anti-Federalists thought of the Constitution as the natural rights due to all people.

In the preceding example, if you did not know the meaning of the word *pessimistic*, you could figure it out because a word appears later in the sentence that gives you a clue. The sentence is about the beliefs of two groups, the Federalists and the Anti-Federalists. The prefix *anti-* tells you that they hold opposite or differing views. If the Federalists are described as "pessimistic" and their views are opposite those of the Anti-Federalists, who are described as "more positive," you realize that *pessimistic* means the opposite of positive, or *negative*.

Here is another example:

Most members of Western society marry only one person at a time, but in other cultures polygamy is common and acceptable.

In this sentence, by the contrast established between Western society and other cultures, you can infer that *polygamy* refers to the practice of marriage to more than one person at a time.

EXERCISE 3 _____

Directions: *Read each sentence and write a definition or synonym for each underlined word. Use the contrast context clue to help you determine the meaning of the word.*

1. The philosopher was vehement in his objections to the new grading system, while the more practical historian, on the other hand, expressed his views calmly and quietly.

   _____

2. The mayor was very dogmatic about government policy, while the assistant mayor was more lenient and flexible in his interpretations.

   _____

3. Instead of evaluating each possible solution when it was first proposed, the committee decided it would defer judgment until all possible solutions had been proposed.

   _____

4. The tenacious islanders responded reluctantly to the government compromise on land settlement, whereas the immigrants agreed immediately to the government offer.

   _____

5. Cultures vary in the types of behavior that are considered socially acceptable. In one culture, a man may be ostricized for having more than one wife, while in other cultures, a man with many wives is an admired and respected part of the group.

   _____

Context Clues in the Logic of a Passage

One of the most common ways in which context provides clues about the meaning of an unknown word is through logic or general reasoning about the content of a sentence, or about the relationship of ideas within a sentence. Suppose that before you read the following sentence you did not know the meaning of the word *empirical*.

Some of the questions now before us are empirical issues that require evidence directly bearing on the question.[13]

From the way *empirical* is used in the sentence, you know that an empirical issue is one that requires direct evidence, and from that information you can infer or reason that *empirical* has something to do with proof or supporting facts.

Now suppose that you did not know the meaning of the term *cul-de-sac* before reading the following sentence:

> A group of animals hunting together can sometimes maneuver the hunted animal into a <u>cul-de-sac</u>: out onto a peak of high land, into a swamp or river, or into a gully from which it cannot escape.[14]

From the mention of the places into which a hunted animal can be maneuvered—a gully, a peak, or a swamp—you realize that the hunters have cornered the animal and that *cul-de-sac* means a blind alley or a situation from which there is no escape.

EXERCISE 4

Directions: *Read each of the following sentences and write a synonym or definition for each underlined word or term. Look for logic of the passage context clues to help you figure out the meaning of each.*

1. The lecturer stumbled frequently and misquoted his sources; however, he <u>redeemed</u> himself by injecting humor and sarcasm into the lecture.

   _____

2. The two philosophical theories were <u>incompatible</u>: one acknowledged the existence of free will; the other denied it.

   _____

3. When the judge pronounced the sentence, the convicted criminal shouted <u>execrations</u> at the jury.

   _____

4. The police officer was <u>exonerated</u> by a police review panel of any possible misconduct or involvement in a case of police bribery.

   _____

5. The editor would not allow the paper to go to press until certain passages were <u>expunged</u> from an article naming individuals involved in a political scandal.

   _____

EXERCISE 5

Directions: *Each of the following sentences contains an underlined word or phrase whose meaning can be determined from the context. Underline the part of the sentence that contains the clue to the meaning of the underlined words. Then, in the blank below, identify what type of context clue you used.*

1. Separation of powers is the principle that the powers of government should be separated and put in the care of different parts of the government.[15]

   _____

2. Samples of moon rock have been analyzed by uranium dating and found to be about 4.6 billion years old, or about the same age as the earth.[16]

   _____

3. Like horses, human beings have a variety of gaits; they amble, stride, jog, and sprint.[17]

   _____

4. In the past, malapportionment (large differences in the populations of congressional districts) was common in many areas of the country.[18]

   _____

5. Tremendous variability characterizes the treatment of the mentally retarded during the medieval era, ranging from treatment as innocents to being tolerated as fools to persecution as witches.[19]

   _____

EXERCISE 6 ⸻

Directions: *Read each of the following paragraphs. For each underlined word, use context to determine its meaning. Write a synonym or brief definition in the space provided.*

1. Popular writings on mental disorders are being continually supplemented by dramatic presentations in the theaters, in the movies, and on television. In addition, the daily press regularly carries accounts of the behavior of seemingly demented persons and often seeks to lend legitimacy to its accounts by citing commentary by mental health professionals, who more often than not have never examined the offender. Such "armchair" diagnoses are probably useless, or worse, in the majority of cases. We seem to have an insatiable curiosity about bizarre behavior, and most of us avidly seek and devour the newspaper, radio, and TV accounts available on the subject. Though we surely learn some things from these accounts, we also may be narrowing our perspective: such accounts are written for the popular media; they are typically simplified and can appear to give answers when, in fact, they barely succeed in posing the correct questions.

   –Coleman, *Abnormal Psychology and Modern Life*, p. 10.

a. supplemented _____

b. legitimacy _____

c. citing _____

d. insatiable _____

e. avidly _____

2. **EVOLUTIONISM**

A central topic in many areas of psychology is the contributions of *nature*, or hereditary influences, and *nurture*, or environmental influences to behavioral development. This issue has its origins in the evolutionary theory developed by Charles Darwin. His theory maintains three principles: (a) all species evolved over millions of years; (b) differences between species are because of hereditary differences; and (c) differences within a species are related to differences among its members in terms of their individual differences in fitness. Those most fit to adapt to environmental changes and challenges passed on their genes and reproduced more of their kind. These ideas were based on Darwin's careful observations of species throughout the world during his five-year journey on the ship *Beagle* and were presented in *Origin of Species* (1859) and *Descent of Man* (1871).

Evolutionary theory challenged the doctrine of *creationism*, which asserted that all species were created by an act of God, with humans being a special case of direct divine creation. Just as Copernicus' theory of the universe moved the earth out of the center of the solar system, Darwin's theory pushed man and woman out of the center arena of existence by giving them a common ancestry with animals. Darwin's doctrine further shook notions of homo sapien supremacy by dragging human origin down from the heavens into the muck of evolutionary slime.

–Zimbardo, *Psychology and Life,* p. 13.

a. nature _____

b. nurture _____

c. maintains _____

d. evolved _____

e. adapt _____

f. creationism _____

g. divine _____

h. arena _____

3. Scarcity is not the same as poverty. Even the rich have to reckon with scarcity. The wealthy individual who can afford to give millions of dollars to a favorite charity or to endow a university with a building that

will bear his or her name must still choose among benefactions. For most of us the problem of choice is far more urgent. We schedule our limited time so that each activity yields the greatest possible reward—hours for economics and chemistry and minutes for errands. We allocate our limited funds so that our expenditures yield the greatest possible usefulness—gym shoes and bus fare this week, but the laundry will have to wait.

–Chisholm, *Principles of Economics*, p. 20.

a. endow _____

b. benefactions _____

c. allocate _____

d. expenditures _____

4. That Darwin was the founder of the modern theory of evolution is well known. In order to understand the meaning of his theory, however, it is useful to look briefly at the intellectual climate in which it was formulated. Aristotle (384–322 B.C.), the first great biologist, believed that all living things could be arranged in a hierarchy. This hierarchy became known as the Scala Naturae, or ladder of nature, in which the simplest creatures had a humble position on the bottommost rung, mankind occupied the top, and all other organisms had their proper places between. Until the end of the last century, many biologists believed in such a natural hierarchy. But whereas to Aristotle living organisms had always existed, the later biologists (at least those of the Occidental world) believed, in harmony with the teachings of the Old Testament, that all living things were the products of a divine creation. They believed, moreover, that most were created for the service or pleasure of mankind. Indeed, it was pointed out, even the lengths of day and night were planned to coincide with the human need for sleep.

–Curtis, *Biology*, p. 1.

a. formulated _____

b. *Scala Naturae* _____

c. hierarchy _____

d. harmony _____

e. divine _____

f. coincide _____

ANALYZING WORD PARTS

Mark and Elaine were taking a course in biology. While walking to class one day, Mark complained to Elaine, "I'll never be able to learn all this vocabulary!" Does this sound familiar? They agreed that they needed some system, since learning each new word separately would be nearly impossible. Have you felt the same way in some of your courses?

The purpose of this section is to present a system of vocabulary learning. This system works for specific courses in which a great deal of new terminology is presented as well as for building your overall, general vocabulary. The approach is based on analyzing word parts. Many words in the English language are made up of word parts called *prefixes, roots,* and *suffixes.* Think of these as beginnings, middles, and endings of words. These word parts have specific meanings and when added together can help you figure out the meaning of the word as a whole. Let's begin with a few words from biology:

poikilotherm   homeotherm   endotherm   ectotherm

Each of these terms appeared in the biology sample textbook chapter in Appendix B on temperature regulation in various life forms. You could learn the definition of each term separately, but learning would be easier and more meaningful if you could see the relationship between the terms.

Each of the four words has as its root *-therm,* which means heat. The meaning of the prefix, or beginning, of each word is given below:

poikilo- = changeable
homeo- = same or constant
endo-   = within
ecto-   = outside

Knowing these meanings can help you determine the meaning of each word:

poikilotherm = organism with variable body temperature (i.e.,
                cold-blooded)
homeotherm = organism with stable body temperature (i.e.,
                warm-blooded)
ectotherm   = organism that regulates its temperature by taking
                in heat from the environment or giving off heat
                to the environment
endotherm   = organism that regulates its temperature internally

When you first start using this method you may not feel as if you're making progress; in this case you had to learn four prefixes and one root to figure out four words. However, what may not be obvious as yet is that these prefixes will help unlock the meaning of numerous other words, not only in the field of biology but also in related fields and in general vocabulary usage. Here are a few examples of words using each of the above word parts:

therm-	*poikilo-*	*homeo- (homo-)*	*ecto-*	*endo-*
thermal	poikilocyte	homeostasis	ectoparasite	endocytosis
thermodynamics	poikilocytosis	homogeneous	ectoderm	endoderm

The remainder of this section will focus on commonly used prefixes, roots, and suffixes that are used in a variety of academic disciplines. In various combinations, these will unlock the meanings of thousands of words. For example, more than ten thousand words begin with the prefix *non-.*

Once you have mastered the prefixes, roots, and suffixes given in this chapter, you should begin to identify word parts that are commonly used in each of your courses. For example, a partial list made by one student for his

Psychology

neuro-	nerves, nervous system	path-	feeling, suffering
phob-	fear	homo-	same
auto-	self	hetero-	different

FIGURE 20-1   A Sample List of Prefixes

psychology course is shown in Figure 20-1. Keep these lists in your course notebooks or use index cards, as described later in this chapter.

Before learning specific prefixes, roots, and suffixes, it is useful to be aware of the following:

1. In most cases, a word is built upon at least one root.
2. Words can have more than one prefix, root, or suffix.
   a. Words can be made up of two or more roots (*geo / logy*).
   b. Some words have two prefixes (*in / sub* / ordination).
   c. Some words have two suffixes (beauti / *ful / ly*).
3. Words do not always have a prefix and a suffix.
   a. Some words have neither a prefix nor a suffix (read).
   b. Others have a suffix but no prefix (read / *ing*).
   c. Others have a prefix but no suffix (*pre* / read).
4. Roots may change in spelling as they are combined with suffixes. Some common variations are noted on page 379.
5. Sometimes you may identify a group of letters as a prefix or root but find that it does not carry the meaning of the prefix or root. For example, in the word *internal*, the letters *inter* should not be confused with the prefix *inter*-, meaning "between." Similarly, the letters *mis* in the word *missile* are part of the root and are not the prefix *mis*-, which means "wrong" or "bad."

Prefixes

Prefixes, appearing at the beginning of many English words, alter or modify the meaning of the root to which they are connected. Table 20-1 lists common prefixes grouped according to meaning.

EXERCISE 7 _____

Directions: *Use the prefixes listed in Table 20-1 to help determine the meaning of each of the underlined words in the following sentences. Write a brief definition or synonym for each. If you are unfamiliar with the root, you may need to check a dictionary.*

1. The instances of <u>abnormal</u> behavior reported in the mass media are likely to be extreme.

_____

_____

TABLE 20-1   Common Prefixes

Prefix	Meaning	Sample Word
Prefixes indicating direction, location, or placement		
circum-	around	circumference
com-, col-, con-	with, together	compile
de-	away, from	depart
ex-/extra-	from, out of, former	ex-wife
hyper-	over, excessive	hyperactive
inter-	between	interpersonal
intro-/intra-	within, into, in	introduction
mid-	middle	midterm
post-	after	post-test
pre-	before	premarital
re-	back, again	review
retro-	backward	retrospect
sub-	under, below	submarine
super-	above, extra	supercharge
tele-	far	telescope
trans-	across, over	transcontinental
Prefixes referring to amount or number		
bi-	two	bimonthly
equi-	equal	equidistant
micro-	small	microscope
mono-	one	monocle
multi-	many	multipurpose
poly-	many	polygon
semi-	half	semicircle
tri-	three	triangle
uni-	one	unicycle
Prefixes meaning "not" (negative)		
a-, an-, ab-	not	asymmetrical
anti-	against	antiwar
contra-	against, opposite	contradict
dis-	apart, away, not	disagree
mis-	wrong, bad	misunderstand
non-	not	nonfiction
pseudo-	false	pseudoscientific
un-	not	unpopular

2. The two theories of language development are not fundamentally incompatible, as originally thought.

   _____

3. When threatened, the ego resorts to irrational protective measures, which are called defense mechanisms.

   _____

4. Freud viewed the interplay among the id, ego, and superego as of critical importance in determining behavioral patterns.

   _____

5. The long-term effects of continuous drug use are irreversible.

   _____

EXERCISE 8 _____

Directions: *Write a synonym or brief definition for each of the following underlined words. Check a dictionary if the root is unfamiliar.*

1. a substandard performance _____

2. to transcend everyday differences _____

3. telecommunications equipment _____

4. a hypercritical person _____

5. a retroactive policy _____

6. superconductive metal _____

7. extracurricular activities _____

8. postoperative nursing care _____

9. a blood transfusion _____

10. antisocial behavior _____

11. to misappropriate funds _____

12. a microscopic organism _____

13. a monotonous speech _____

14. a pseudointellectual essay _____

15. a polysyllabic word _____

Roots

Roots carry the basic or core meaning of a word. Hundreds of root words are used to build words in the English language. Thirty of the most common and most useful are listed in Table 20-2. Knowing the meanings of these roots will assist you in unlocking the meanings of many words. For example, if you know that the root *dic-* or *dict-* means "tell" "say," then you would have a clue to the meanings of such words as *predict* (to tell what will happen in the future), *contradiction* (a statement that is contrary or opposite), and *diction* (wording or manner of speaking).

TABLE 20-2   Common Roots

Root	Meaning	Sample Word
aster, astro	star	astronaut
aud, audit	hear	audible
bio	life	biology
cap	take, seize	captive
chron(o)	time	chronology
corp	body	corpse
cred	believe	incredible
dict, dic	tell, say	predict
duc, duct	lead	introduce
fact, fac	make, do	factory
geo	earth	geophysics
graph	write	telegraph
log, logo, logy	study, thought	psychology
mit, miss	send	dismiss
mort, mor	die, death	immortal
path	feeling, disease	sympathy
phono	sound, voice	telephone
photo	light	photosensitive
port	carry	transport
scop	seeing	microscope
scrib, script	write	inscription
sen, sent	feel	insensitive
spec, spic, spect	look, see	retrospect
tend, tent, tens	stretch, strain	tension
terr, terre	land, earth	territory
theo	god	theology
ven, vent	come	convention
vert, vers	turn	invert
vis, vid	see	invisible
voc	call	vocation

Directions: *Write a synonym or brief definition for each of the underlined words. Consult Tables 20-1 and 20-2 as necessary.*

1. a <u>monotheistic</u> religion _____

2. a <u>subterranean</u> tunnel _____

3. a <u>chronicle</u> of events _____

4. a <u>conversion</u> chart _____

5. <u>exportation</u> policies _____

6. leading an <u>introspective</u> life _____

7. to <u>speculate</u> on the results _____

8. <u>sensuous</u> music _____

9. a <u>versatile</u> performance _____

10. an <u>incredible</u> explanation _____

11. infant <u>mortality</u> rates _____

12. <u>tensile</u> strength of a cable _____

13. a <u>vociferous</u> crowd _____

14. a logical <u>deduction</u> _____

15. a <u>corporate</u> earnings report _____

Suffixes

Suffixes are word endings that often change the part of speech of a word. For example, adding the suffix *-y* to a word changes it from a noun to an adjective and shifts the meaning—for example, *cloud, cloudy.* Often several different words can be formed from a single root word with the addition of different suffixes. Here are a few examples:

Root: *Class*
classify
classification
classic

Common suffixes grouped according to meaning are listed in Table 20-3.

Directions: *Write a synonym or brief definition of each of the underlined words. Consult a dictionary if necessary.*

TABLE 20-3 Common Suffixes

Suffix	Sample Word
Suffixes that refer to a state, condition, or quality	
-able	touchable
-ance	assistance
-ation	confrontation
-ence	reference
-ic	aerobic
-ible	tangible
-ion	discussion
-ity	superiority
-ive	permissive
-ment	amazement
-ness	kindness
-ous	jealous
-ty	loyalty
-y	creamy
Suffixes that mean "one who"	
-ee	employee
-eer	engineer
-er	teacher
-ist	activist
-or	editor
Suffixes that mean "pertaining to" or "referring to"	
-al	autumnal
-ship	friendship
-hood	brotherhood
-ward	homeward

1. <u>terrorist</u> activities _____

2. a <u>graphic</u> description _____

3. a <u>materialistic</u> philosophy _____

4. <u>immunity</u> to disease _____

5. <u>impassable</u> road conditions _____

6. a speech <u>impediment</u> _____

7. <u>intangible</u> property _____

8. <u>instinctive</u> behavior _____

9. interrogation techniques _____

10. the communist sector _____

11. obvious frustration _____

12. global conflicts _____

13. in deference to _____

14. piteous physical ailments _____

15. Supreme Court nominee _____

EXERCISE 11 _____

Directions: *The following list of terms were taken from the psychology sample textbook chapter Appendix A. Write a brief definition of each. Consult the sample chapter or a dictionary, if necessary.*

1. psychosocial model of health _____

2. psychosomatic medicine _____

3. dysfunctional behavior _____

4. nonadaptive behavior _____

5. posttraumatic stress disorder _____

6. retrospective studies _____

7. prospective studies _____

8. cognitive restructuring _____

9. reappraising stressors _____

10. biofeedback techniques _____

SUMMARY

One of the easiest and most practical ways of determining the meaning of an unknown word is to study carefully how the word is used in the sentence, paragraph, or passage in which it is found. The context—the words around an unknown word—frequently contains various types of clues that help you figure out the meaning of the unknown word. There are four basic types of context clues that are useful in determining the meaning of words in factual material. These types of clues are described in the following list:

Definition: A brief definition or synonym of an unknown word may be included in the sentence in which the word is used.

Example/illustration: Writers may explain their words and ideas by giving specific, concrete examples of them. When an example is given to illustrate or explain a new term or concept, it is sometimes possible to figure out the meaning of an unknown word from the example.

Contrast: The meaning of an unknown word can sometimes be determined from a word or phrase in the context that has the opposite meaning.

Logic of the passage: The meaning of an unknown word can sometimes be determined through reasoning or applying logic to the content of the sentence or paragraph.

Learning word parts—prefixes, roots, and suffixes—is a system of vocabulary learning. This approach enables you to figure out the meaning of an unknown word by analyzing the meanings of its parts. Tables of common prefixes, roots, and suffixes were presented in the chapter.

PART SEVEN

Reading Efficiency Techniques

Most adults, including college students, are inefficient readers: They do not make the best possible use of their reading time, and they do not apply skills that would enable them to read faster. They read all types of material at the same rate, and they are always careful to read everything. Many adults have the capacity to read twice as fast as they usually read.

The purpose of this part of the book is to discuss situations in which you could read faster and to present techniques that will enable you to do so. Chapter 21 discusses the factors that affect how fast you read and then suggests reading rates for four different categories of reading. You are given an opportunity to measure your own reading rate for each category. Finally, the chapter offers suggestions on how to read faster.

Chapter 22 considers situations in which it is not necessary to read everything and offers specific techniques for selective reading. The chapter suggests a procedure for *skimming*—getting an overview, or general picture, of an article—and a procedure for *scanning*—rapidly looking through material to locate a particular piece of information.

21

Improving Your Rate and Flexibility

Use this chapter to:

1. *Find out how fast you read and how your rate compares to that of other college students.*
2. *Learn how to adjust your rate to suit your purpose and the material you are reading.*
3. *Find out how to increase your overall reading rate.*

Reading rate, the speed at which you read, is measured in words per minute (wpm). Do you read 100 wpm, 200 wpm, 300 wpm, 400 wpm? At what rate should you be reading? Are you a fast or a slow reader? You should be able to read at 100, 200, 300, and 400 wpm; you should be both a fast *and* a slow reader. These answers may seem strange or even contradictory, but they are nevertheless true. Your reading rate should change in different situations and with different types of reading material. There are a number of variables that determine what your reading rate should be on any particular printed page. The purpose of this chapter is to present these variables that affect reading rate and to show you how to adjust, or vary, your reading rate to deal with them. In this chapter you will also measure your reading rate and learn how to increase it.

FACTORS THAT INFLUENCE READING RATE

There are literally hundreds of factors that influence how fast you read. These variables also affect your comprehension of what you read. Factors that influence both reading rate and comprehension can be divided into three general categories: text characteristics, reader characteristics, and reader's purpose. *Text characteristics* are the features of the printed material that influence how easy or difficult it is to read. The skills and traits of a person that determine or affect rate and comprehension are called *reader characteristics. Reader's purpose* refers to the reason the material is read and the level of comprehension needed.

Text Characteristics

The way writers write, the words they use, how they put words together, and how clearly they can express ideas all contribute to how easy it is to read a passage and how fast it can be read.

EXPERIMENT _____

Try the following experiment. First, read each of the following passages:

PASSAGE 1

War is usually thought of as a political conflict. However, there are many causes of this political conflict. It may arise from economic problems. Or it may stem from conflicts between racial or ethnic groups. Cultural differences between countries may also contribute to political conflict. Individual personalities of leaders are also involved in wars. To study war, then, we must study many different fields such as economics, history, and psychology.

PASSAGE 2

In studying the fourteen theories of the origins of war which follow, the reader will discover that while war is typically regarded as a political phenomenon, it springs not only from political events, but from economic motives, from ethnic and racial conflict, from cultural and anthropological differences, from individual personalities and sometimes from psychopathology. A comprehensive study of the causes of war necessarily carries one into the literatures of politics, economics, history, philosophy, psychiatry, social psychology, anthropology, psychology and other pertinent fields of study. In keeping with the central concept of this book, then, this chapter seeks not to present a single comprehensive theory of the causes of war, but a comparative and comprehensive review of the several principal theories.

–Jones, *The Logic of International Relations*, p. 397

Which passage seemed easier? The passages are approximately the same length, but they differ greatly in many other features—primarily characteristics that contribute to difficulty. Passage 1 is written at a fourth-grade level, while Passage 2 is at a college level.

Look again at each passage; what features of the writing make Passage 1 easier or Passage 2 more difficult? Try to list below as many differences as you can:

Passage 1   *Passage 2*

_____   _____

_____   _____

_____   _____

_____   _____

There are a great many differences between those two passages. Some of the obvious differences are:

1. Passage 1 uses brief, relatively simple sentences. The words are short; the vocabulary is easy. The passage contains clear examples, and the terms are clearly defined.
2. In Passage 2, the sentences are longer and more complex. The words are longer and more difficult. The passage is more detailed and complicated, and words with specialized, technical meanings are used.

Linguists, people who study language, could list many other differences between the two passages. Very technical or subtle features of language, called linguistic variables, have been found to affect how easily a passage may be understood. Linguistic variables include the total number of syllables, the number of times a word is repeated, and the arrangement of words within a sentence. However, some variables have a greater effect than others and are more useful to note; these are sentence length, vocabulary difficulty, and the sophistication of the concepts being discussed.

Sentence Length: A passage with very long sentences can make reading more difficult and will force you to read more slowly. Try reading the following sentence; notice how the length of the sentence seems to hold you back and slow you down.

> Caught in global recession and inflation, forced by Washington to revalue their currency in a direction injurious to their prosperity and once again conscious of their vulnerability to foreign economic decisions, the Japanese also saw domestic capital flow out to lucrative investment opportunities elsewhere.
>
> –Jones, *The Logic of International Relations*, p. 99

Vocabulary: A passage with difficult or unfamiliar vocabulary can have the same effect—understanding becomes difficult or impossible, and your rate of reading is extremely slow. Try the following:

> The liberal-cynical criminologist is skeptical about the perfectability of crime control efforts, and locates criminogenic forces in the basic structure and institutions of society, but he still retains a belief in the continued viability of American society in its present form.
>
> –Barlow, *Introduction to Criminology*, p. 26

Ideas and Concepts: In addition to these mechanical features of language, ideas and concepts also affect difficulty. Even when written in fairly simple language, an article may discuss complicated ideas or follow a sophisticated line of reasoning. In the following sample, you will notice that, although the language used is clear and direct, a difficult concept is discussed.

> The whole universe may have an overall curvature. If it is negatively curved, it is open-ended and extends without limit; if it is positively curved; it closes in on itself. The surface of the earth, for example, forms a closed curvature; so that if you travel along a geodesic, you come back to your starting point. Similarly, if the

universe were positively curved, it would be closed; so that if you could look infinitely into space through an ideal telescope, you would see the back of your own head! (This is assuming that you waited a long enough time or that light traveled infinitely fast.)

–Hewitt, *Conceptual Physics*, p. 587.

While you can do nothing to change the characteristics of writing that affect difficulty, you can change how you approach the writing. You can deliberately slow down if you encounter a passage with long, complicated sentences or an article that presents difficult concepts or complicated arguments. Or you can deliberately speed up when you find a passage with simple, unsophisticated vocabulary. In other words, you can *adjust* your rate to the characteristics of the reading material.

Reader's Characteristics

A second set of factors that influences how fast you are able to read and how well you comprehend is related to you, the reader. Here is only a partial list of the many things about you that affect your reading speed.

Your Vocabulary Level: If your general reading vocabulary level is high, you will not encounter many words that you do not know, and your speed will be unaffected. On the other hand, if your reading vocabulary is weak and you meet several unknown words in every paragraph, you will find that you lose speed as you pause to look for context clues to their meaning.

Your Comprehension Ability: Your level of skill in understanding sentences and paragraphs will affect your rate. If you have trouble locating the core parts of a sentence or cannot identify the topic, main idea, and details of a paragraph, then your rate will suffer as you spend time looking for and understanding these elements.

Your Physical State: How you feel physically affects both rate and comprehension. If you are extremely tired, or just recovering from the flu, you will not be able to perform at your peak level. Concentration may become a problem, or you may not be able to force yourself to stay awake. If you are hungry, or if the room is extremely hot or cold, your reading performance may also be affected.

Your State of Mind: Just as your physical state can affect your reading rate, so can your mental or emotional state. If you are depressed or worried, you may not be able to concentrate easily; if you are excited or anxious about something, your mental state may not be conducive to effective reading.

Your Interest in the Material: Your interest in what you are reading influences how fast and with what degree of comprehension you read. If you are reading about a topic that interests you, you are likely to read faster and with more understanding than if you are reading about a subject in which you have little or no interest.

Your Background Knowledge: The amount of knowledge you have of a topic partially determines how well you will be able to read about it. Suppose you are assigned to read a passage taken from the middle of an introductory botany textbook. If you have completed a course in botany, the passage will probably be understandable and easy enough to read. On the other hand, if you have never studied botany, the passage may be extremely difficult and confusing; it will be necessary to read very slowly, and you might have to stop to look up any unfamiliar terms and concepts.

Reader's Purpose

Your purpose for reading is an important factor related to both rate and comprehension. If you are reading a magazine article for enjoyment, your purpose is different from when you are reading a textbook chapter to prepare for an exam. If you are paging through the newspaper, your purpose differs from your purpose when you are reading a poem for your English literature class.

Your reading rate is determined partly by your purpose for reading. There are four basic types of reading, ranging from an extremely slow analysis to an extremely rapid overview of the material. Each type is related to a specific kind of material, has a definite purpose, and is done at a certain speed. These are summarized in Table 21-1.

DEVELOPING YOUR READING FLEXIBILITY

As you can see from Table 21-1, no one should have just one reading rate. Instead, your reading rate should vary according to *what* you are reading

TABLE 21-1   Types of Reading

Method of Reading	Range of Speed	Purpose in Reading	Types of Material
Analytical	Under 100 wpm	Detailed comprehension: analysis, evaluation, critique	Poetry, argumentative writing
Study-reading	150–250 wpm	High comprehension and high recall	Textbooks, library research
Casual reading	250–400 wpm	Moderate comprehension of main ideas, enertainment, enjoyment, general	Novels, newspapers, magazines
Accelerated reading	Above 600 wpm	Overivew of material, rapid location of a specific fact	Reference material, magazines, novels, nonfiction

and *why* you are reading it. Adjusting your rate in response to the material and to your purpose for reading is called *reading flexibility.*

Learning to adjust your rate according to style, content, and purpose will require a conscious effort at first. If you are now in the habit of reading everything at the same pace, as most college students are, then you will need to force yourself to make an assessment of the particular reading material before deciding how fast you can read it. When you use the technique of prereading, you are only a small step away from adjusting your rate. By prereading, you familiarize yourself with the overall content and organization of the material. You may also include, as part of your prereading, a step in which you pay particular attention to the overall difficulty of the material. While prereading, you will sample enough of the actual writing to be able to assess the level of complexity of both the language and the content.

Deciding how much to speed up or slow down for a particular article is a matter of judgment. You will find through experience that you will be able to judge how much you can afford to alter your speed. It is not important to know precisely how much to increase your speed. Rather, the important thing is to develop the skill of *flexibility.* Here is a step-by-step procedure you can follow that will help you build the habit of varying your reading rate.

1. Choose a time and place for reading that will help rather than hinder your concentration. Choose a time when you are alert and your state of mind is conducive to study.
2. Preread the material. As you preread, assess the difficulty of both the writing style and the content. Are there a lot of difficult words? Are the sentences long and complicated? How factual is the material? How much background information do you have on the subject?
3. Define your overall purpose for reading. Your purpose will determine the level of comprehension and the degree of retention that you require. Are you reading for enjoyment, looking up facts, or reading a text chapter to prepare for an exam?
4. Decide what rate would be appropriate for reading this particular material.
5. After you've finished the first page of the reading material, stop and evaluate. Are you understanding and remembering what you are reading? Can you summarize the ideas in your own words?

MEASURING YOUR READING FLEXIBILITY

You now realize that the type of material you read and how you approach it determine, in part, your reading rate. Most students want to know whether they are fast or slow readers, or above or below average. Also, you can measure your reading flexibility if various types of materials are used and the purpose for reading each is defined.

Before beginning to measure your rate for each type of reading listed on the chart in Table 21-2, you will need to know how to figure out your words per minute, which is the unit of measurement used in computing reading rate.

How to Compute Words per Minute (wpm)

1. After you have chosen a passage in a book or article, count the total number of words in any three lines. Divide the total by three and round

TABLE 21-2 Reading Rate

Method of Reading	Average Speed	Your Speed (wpm)
Analytical	Below 100 wpm	_____
Study-reading	150–250 wpm	_____
Casual reading	250–400 wpm	_____
Accelerated	Above 600 wpm	_____

it off to the nearest whole number. This will give the average number of words per line.

2. Count the number of lines in the article or book by counting the number of lines of one page and multiplying that number by the total number of pages. Multiply the number of words per line by the total number of lines. This will give you a fairly accurate estimate of the total number of words.

3. Time yourself as you read, using a watch with a second hand. Record both minutes and seconds of your starting time (for example, 4:20 18). Start reading when the second hand of the clock reaches twelve. Record your finishing time. Subtract your starting from your finishing time.

4. Divide your total reading time into the total number of words. To do this, round off the number of seconds to the nearest quarter of a minute and then divide. For example, if your total reading time was 3 minutes and 12 seconds, round it off to 3.25 minutes and then divide. Your answer will be your words-per-minute score.

The following example illustrates computation of words per minute.

Total number of words on 3 lines: 23
Divide by 3 and round off: $23 \div 3 = 7\frac{2}{3} = 8$
Number of lines in article: 120
Multiply number of words per line by number of lines:
$8 \times 120 = 960$ (total words)
    Subtract finishing time   1:13 22
      from starting time   <u>1:05   </u>
                         8 minutes 22 seconds
Round off to nearest ¼ minute: 8½ minutes
Divide time into total number of words:
    $960 \div 8.5 = 112$ + a fraction (your reading rate)

Measuring Your Analytical Reading Rate

1. Select a poem or a passage from a complicated essay in an English textbook, or choose an extremely detailed description of a process from another of your texts, or pick a discussion of a controversial issue that you plan to analyze carefully.

2. Estimate the number of words, read the material, time yourself, and compute your words-per-minute score. Record your wpm in the chart in Table 21-2.

3. Check your comprehension; could you now write a paper analyzing and reacting to what you read?

Measuring Your Study-Reading Rate

Choose a passage from one of your textbooks that you have not read but expect will be assigned. Assume that you will have to pass an exam on the material later in the course. Then follow steps 2 and 3 given above.

Measuring Your Casual Reading Rate

Choose a passage of several pages from a novel you are reading or select several pages from a magazine article that interests you. Timing yourself, read it only for enjoyment or general information. Then compute your wpm, and fill in the chart in Table 21-2.

Measuring Your Accelerated Reading Rate

Choose a magazine article on a subject that interests you. It should be at least one page in length. Assume that you are in a hurry and do not have time to read the entire article but that you want to know what major ideas the article contains. Quickly read through the article, reading certain portions and skipping others. Try to read less than half of the material. Time yourself as you read, compute your wpm score, and record it in Table 21-2.

Interpreting Your Results

If your reading rate was nearly the same for each type of reading, then you do not vary your speed according to purpose and type of material. Review the suggestions on page 392 for developing your reading flexibility, then deliberately speed up or slow down as you read various types of material.

If each of your rates was below average, this suggests that you are a slow reader. When students learn that their rate is low, their first impulse is to work on improving their reading speed. Usually, however, this approach is ineffective. A slow reading rate is more often a symptom than a cause. A slow rate is to reading as chills and fever are to a cold. The chills and fever are not the cause of the cold; rather they are symptoms that let you know you have a cold. Similarly, a slow reading rate suggests that something else is wrong. Usually, the problem is comprehension—you are having difficulty understanding what you read. If your reading rate is slow, do not simply try to read faster. Instead, work on the cause—comprehension skills. Focus on developing the comprehension skills presented in Part Three of this text.

SUGGESTIONS FOR READING FASTER

To read faster, you must improve your capacity to process information rapidly. Instead of thinking about your eyes and how they move, concentrate on getting information quickly from the printed page. Reading faster involves understanding ideas and how they interrelate.

By working through this book, you have learned numerous skills and techniques that have improved your comprehension. Many techniques that improve comprehension also improve rate. Reading faster is often a combination of pushing yourself to higher reading speeds on different types of materials and learning and applying several new techniques. The following suggestions will help you to read faster.

Avoid Roadblocks to Reading Efficiency

There is a group of poor reading habits that are carryovers from when you first learned to read. These are (1) moving your head as you read, (2) moving your lips as you read, and (3) using your finger or pen to keep your place on the line. Each of these habits can slow you down and contribute to poor comprehension.

Moving Your Head: When children learn to read, they have difficulty moving only their eyes straight across a line of print. Because of this lack of eye control, many children move their heads from left to right as they proceed across the line. While this habit may be necessary for children, it is not for adults with adequate visual control. Some adults, however, have never eliminated the habit. Moving the head rather than just the eyes prevents adult readers from reading at even a normal reading rate and also creates strain and muscular fatigue. Ask someone to check to see if you move your head while reading; this person should check when you are not consciously thinking about this problem.

If you have this habit, it is probably a very old one that will require effort to overcome. One of the easiest ways to break it is to sit with your elbow up on your desk with your hand cupping your chin. If you start to move your head, you will feel your hand and forearm move, and this will remind you to correct the habit.

Moving Your Lips: Lip movement while reading silently is also a carryover from beginning reading experiences. Most students are taught to read orally first. Later on, when making the change from mostly oral to mostly silent reading in second or third grade, many children move their lips. Eventually, when the changeover is completed, lip movement should be eliminated. For some students, however, this habit hangs on. For an adult, lip movement limits rate improvement. The average adult rate of speech (pronouncing words out loud) is 125 words per minute, while the average adult rate for silent reading is 250 to 300 words per minute. You can see that moving your lips can really slow your silent reading down—by as much as half. However, there is one situation in which lip movement may be appropriate. When you are reading something that is extremely difficult or complicated, you may find that moving your lips or even whispering aloud as you read helps you to understand the material.

Young children are sometimes broken of the habit of lip movement by having them hold a pencil horizontally between their lips as they read. When their lips move, the pencil wiggles or drops. This technique is not appropriate for adults, but you may wish to try a more sophisticated version. Sit in a position so that part of your hand or your fingers touch your lips. If you move your lips while reading, you will feel the movement on your hand or fingers.

Keeping Your Place on the Line: Another bad habit left over from childhood reading is keeping your place on a line of print by moving your finger or a pen, pencil, or index card across the line as you read. Children are sometimes allowed to do this because they lack the eye control to keep their eyes from jumping from line to line or to move their eyes straight across one line smoothly. For adults, however, this habit results in a very slow word-by-word reading.

The solution to this problem is simple—tightly grasp the book with both hands. This will prevent you from following across the line with your finger or another object. Be careful you don't cheat and slide your thumb down the margin as a guide to where you are on the page. If you have tried unsuccessfully to control this habit, an eye exam is advisable. Inability to keep one's place on the line is one symptom of a need for corrective lenses.

Preread to Familiarize Yourself with the Material

In Chapter 5 you learned that prereading is a means of improving your comprehension by becoming familiar with the organization and content of material before you begin to read it. In addition to improving your comprehension, prereading increases your reading speed. Because prereading enables you to anticipate the flow of ideas, you will find yourself able to read the material more rapidly.

Try to Eliminate Regressions

As your eyes move across a line, they normally proceed from left to right. Occasionally, instead of moving to the next word, your eyes move backward, or regress, to a word in the same line or in a line already read. Regressions (backward movements) scramble word order, thus creating confusion that slows your pace. Although even very good readers make regressions, your rate and comprehension will improve if you can reduce the number of regressions. The following suggestions will help you eliminate or reduce regressions.

1. Be conscious of the tendency to regress, and force yourself to continue reading. Do not allow yourself to regress until you have finished a sentence. Then, if the meaning is still unclear, reread the entire sentence.
2. If you frequently regress to a word or phrase on a previous line, you might try sliding a 5″ × 8″ index card down the page as you read. Use the card to cover the lines you have finished reading. This technique will help break the habit of regression because when you look back, the line will be covered.
3. Although it is not a good habit to form, try guiding your eye movement by using a pen or your finger to force yourself continually forward. Move your finger across each line at a speed with which your eyes can keep pace. The forward motion of your finger or pen will guide your eye and force it along in a left-to-right pattern.

Read in Meaning Clusters

Most college students read word by word, looking at each word and then moving to the next one. A more efficient way to read is to combine words that naturally go together. Try not to think of a sentence as a string of single words. Instead, think of it as several word clusters, or phrases. Look at the following sentence:

The math instructor told her class about the quiz.

"The" does not convey any meaning by itself. While "math" does have meaning, it is intended to describe the next word, "instructor." Rather than reading the first three words separately, try to think of them together as a meaningful phrase—"the math instructor." The remainder of the sentence could then be read as two additional phrases: "told her class" and "about the quiz."

The following brief paragraph has been divided into meaningful word groups separated by slashes. Read the paragraph; as you read, try to see and think of each cluster as a unit of thought rather than as two or three separate words.

> In order / to protect themselves / against loss / drivers purchase /
> liability insurance. / There are / two types of / liability insurance. /
> Bodily injury liability / provides payment / if you / are injured / in
> an accident. / Property damage liability / covers you / when your
> car / damages the property / of others.

Notice that words that make sense together are grouped together. Words are grouped with the words they explain or modify.

To see if you can group words into meaningful clusters, divide the following paragraph with slashes. The first line has been done for you.

> The United States / has changed / in the past one hundred years /
> from an agricultural economy / to an industrial economy / and
> has become / the world's first / service economy. What does the
> term *service* mean? There is no widely accepted definition in
> marketing. In fact, there is no clear distinction between those
> firms that are part of a marketing channel for products and those
> firms that market services. Restaurants are often classified as
> food distributors because they compete with supermarkets, but
> restaurants also provide services to customers.

> –Kinnear and Bernhardt, *Principles of Marketing,* p. 654

Once you begin reading in word clusters, you will find that meaning falls into place more easily, thus enabling you to read somewhat faster.

Learn to Pace Yourself

An established method of improving your reading rate is *pacing,* which requires maintaining a preestablished rate. Pacing means pushing yourself to read faster than your normal speed while maintaining your level of comprehension. There are numerous ways to pace yourself in order to increase your speed; among the most common methods are:

1. *Use an index card.* Slide a 3″ × 5″ card down the page as you read, moving it so that it covers up lines as they are read. This technique will force you along and keep you moving rapidly. Move the card down the page at a fixed pace, and try to keep up while reading. How fast you move the card will depend on the size of print and the length of the line, and will then vary for each new piece of material you read. At first you will need to experiment to find an appropriate pace. Try to move at a pace that is slightly uncomfortable and that you are not sure you can maintain.
2. *Use your hand or index finger, or a pen or pencil.* Use your hand or index

finger, pen or pencil in the same manner as the index card. Using your hand does not completely obstruct your view of the page and allows you to pick up clues from the layout of the page (to see that a paragraph is ending, that a graphic example is to follow, and so on).

3. *Use a timer or clock.* Start by measuring what portion of a page you can read in a minute. Then set a goal for yourself: Determine how many pages you will attempt to read in a given period of time. Set your goal slightly above what you measured as your current rate. For example, suppose in a particular book you can read half a page in a minute. You might set as your goal to read five pages in nine minutes (forcing yourself to read a little more than a half page per minute). The next day, try to read five pages in eight or eight and a half minutes. Use an alarm clock or timer to let you know when you have used up your time.

EXERCISE 1 _____

Directions: *Select a magazine or newspaper article that you are interested in or a section of a paperback you are reading. Using one of the pacing techniques described in this section, try to increase your current reading speed by approximately 50 wpm. Record your results in the space provided.*

Article title: _____

Estimated number of words: _____

Finishing time: _____

Starting time: _____

Reading time: _____

Words per minute: _____

Estimated level of comprehension: _____

Use Rereading to Build Speed

Although rereading is not an effective way to learn, it is an effective method of building your reading speed. Rereading at a slightly faster pace prepares you for reading new material faster. Rereading gets you moving at a faster rate and serves as a practice or "trial run" for reading new material faster.

To reread for speed increase, use the following steps:

1. Select an article or passage and read it as you normally would for careful or leisure reading.
2. Time yourself and compute your speed in words per minute after you finish reading.
3. Take a break (five minutes or so). Then reread the same selection. Push yourself to read faster than you read the first time.
4. Time yourself and compute your speed once again. You should be able to reread the selection at a faster rate than you read it initially.

5. Read a new selection, pushing yourself to read almost as fast as you *reread* the first selection.

EXERCISE 2 _____

Directions: *Choose two magazine or newspaper articles that you are interested in reading. Follow the preceding steps for rereading to build speed. Record your results below.*

ARTICLE 1

Title: _____

Estimated number of words: _____

First reading
    Time: _____

    Words per minute: _____

Second reading
    Time: _____

    Words per minute: _____

ARTICLE 2

Title: _____

Estimated number of words: _____

First reading
    Time: _____

    Words per minute: _____

SUMMARY

Reading rate is influenced by three factors: text characteristics, reader's characteristics, and reader's purpose. Text factors refer to the features of language that determine the difficulty of what you read. These include sentence length, vocabulary, and complexity of ideas.

Reader's factors refer to those characteristics, skills, and habits that affect reading rate which you, the reader, have developed. Among the most important variables are your vocabulary level, level of comprehension, physical and mental state, interest in the material, and familiarity with the subject.

While both writer's and reader's factors directly influence your rate, a third major factor also determines how fast you read—your purpose for reading. Depending on the amount and type of information you must retain, your reading rate should fluctuate widely. The ability to adjust your reading rate as determined by the type of material and your purpose for reading is called *reading flexibility*.

This chapter focused on the development of reading flexibility. It established four categories of reading and provided four different reading situations for measuring your rate and flexibility. Finally, general suggestions for reading faster were offered.

22

Skimming and Scanning

Use this chapter to:

1. *Learn to adjust your rate to what you are reading and your purpose for reading it.*

2. *Learn techniques for skimming and scanning.*

Can you think of any situation in which it would not be necessary to read every word on a printed page? Consider the telephone directory. Have you ever read all the words on any page of it? The answer is obvious; each time you look up a phone number, you read selectively, picking out only the information you need and skipping everything else. Think of other types of printed material that you read the same way. List them below:

_____   _____

_____   _____

_____   _____

_____   _____

_____   _____

Your responses might have included bus schedules, television program listings, theater schedules, want ads, and dictionaries.

There are many types of printed material that do not require thorough, beginning-to-end, careful reading. This chapter discusses situations in which you can afford to skip material as well as types of material for which it is not necessary to read everything. The chapter also presents a systematic approach to help you decide what to read and what to skip.

WHEN DON'T YOU HAVE TO READ EVERYTHING?

Before you begin to read selectively, you must accept the notion that there is nothing sacred about the printed word. Many students erroneously think that anything that appears in print must be true, valuable, and worth reading. Actually, the importance and value of printed information are affected by whether you need to learn it or whether you can use it in a practical way. Depending on the kind of material and your purpose for reading it, many times you may need to read only some parts and skip over others. You might read selectively when:

1. *A high level of comprehension is not needed.* If you are not trying to remember a major portion of the facts and details, then you might concentrate on reading only main ideas. This method of reading only main ideas is called *skimming*. Specific techniques for skimming are presented later in the chapter.
2. *You are searching for specific information.* If you are looking up the date of a historical event in your history text, you would skip over everything in the chapter except the exact passage that contains the information. This technique of skipping everything except the specific information for which you are looking is called *scanning*. Practice in scanning technqiues is included later in the chapter.
3. *You are familiar with what you are reading.* In a college chemistry course, for example, you might find that the first few chapters of your text are very basic if you have already studied high school chemistry. You could afford to skip basic definitions and explanations and examples of principles that you already know. Do not, however, decide to skip an entire chapter or even large sections within it; there just may be some new information included. You may find that more exact and detailed definitions are given or that a new approach is taken toward a particular topic.
4. *The material does not match your purpose in reading.* Suppose, in making an assignment in your physics text, your instructor told you to concentrate only on theories, laws, and principles presented in the chapter. As you begin reading the chapter, you find that the first topic discussed is Newton's law of motion, but the chapter also contains a biographical sketch of Newton giving detailed information about his life. Since your purpose in reading the chapter is to focus on theories, laws, and principles, it would be appropriate to skip over much of the biographical information.

TYPES OF MATERIAL TO SKIP

Just as there are situations when it is appropriate to skip over information, there are also various types and styles of writing in which it is possible to skip information. Some writers include many examples of a particular concept or principle. If, after reading two or three examples, you are sure that you understand the idea being explained, just quickly glance at the remaining examples. Unless they present a new aspect or different point of view, skip over them.

Other writers provide detailed background information before leading into a discussion of the intended topic. If a chapter starts out by summarizing information that was covered in a chapter you just read last week, it would not be necessary to read this information again carefully unless you feel you need to review.

EXERCISE 1 _____

Directions: *Each of the following items suggests a reading situation and describes the material to be read. After reading each item, decide whether the reader should (a) read the material completely; (b) read parts, and skip other parts; or (c) skip most of the material.*

1. Your history instructor has assigned each student to read a historical novel for the purpose of getting a realistic picture of what life was like and how people lived during a certain period. As you are reading, you come to a detailed two-page description of the type of gowns southern women wore to a particular party. How should you read these two pages? _____

2. You are doing research for a sociology term paper on the world population explosion. You are looking for information and statistics on recent population trends. You have located several books from the 1940s on the topic of population growth in the United States. How would you read these books? _____

3. Your nursing instructor has just returned a test on a chapter describing the nursing process. She indicates that the class's overall performance on this test was poor and suggests that the chapter be reviewed. You received a grade of 79 on the test. How should this chapter be reread? _____

4. Your biology professor has assigned a number of brief outside readings along with the chapters in your regular textbook. He has put them on reserve in the college library for the use of all his classes. This is the only place they can be used. He did not say whether you would be tested on them. How would you read them? _____

5. You have just attended English class, where your instructor discussed Milton's *Paradise Lost*. During his discussion he made numerous references to Dante's *Inferno*. You have never read this second work but think it's important to know something about it. How would you read it? _____

SKIMMING TECHNIQUES

As you know, the term *skimming* refers to the process of reading only main ideas within a passage and simply glancing at the remainder of the material. Skimming is used to get an overall picture of the material, to become generally familiar with the topics and ideas presented, or to get the gist of a particular work. Usually skimming is an end in itself; that is, skimming is all that you intend to do with the article. You do not intend to read it more completely later. You are willing to settle for an overview of the article, giving up a major portion of the details.

At this point, you may be thinking that skimming seems similar to the technique of prereading. If so, you are correct. Prereading is actually a form of skimming. To be more precise, there are three forms of skimming: *preread skimming, skim-reading,* and *review skimming.* Preread skimming assumes that you plan to read the entire article or chapter and that you are prereading as a means of getting ready to read. Skim-reading refers to situations in which skimming is the only coverage you plan to give the material. Review skimming assumes you have already read the material and are going back over it as a means of study and review.

Prereading has already been discussed in Part Two, Chapter 5. Methods of review after reading are part of the reading-study systems, such as SQ3R, discussed in Part Four, Chapter 12. Therefore, this chapter will focus on skim-reading techniques.

DEMONSTRATION OF SKIMMING

The sample passage in Figure 22-1 has been included to demonstrate what skimming is like. The parts of the passage that should be read while skimming appear in color print.

The passage is taken from a sociology text on courtship and marriage. It appears at the end of a chapter that discusses masculine and feminine roles and conflicts. The article is included not as part of the chapter, but as an additional reading selected to give a perspective on or interpretation of the topic discussed in the chapter itself. Since the article is not factual and not part of the text itself, skimming it for main ideas is appropriate.

How to Skim-Read

Your purpose in skimming is to get an overall impression of the content of a reading selection. The technique of skimming involves selecting and reading those parts of the selection that contain the most important ideas and merely glancing at the rest of the material. Below is a step-by-step procedure to follow in skimming for main ideas.

1. Read the title. If the piece is an article, check the author, publication date, and source.
2. Read the introduction. If it is very long, read only the first paragraph completely. Read the first sentence of every other paragraph. Usually the first sentence will be a statement of the main idea of that paragraph.
3. Read any headings and subheadings. The headings, when taken together, form an outline of the main topics that are covered in the material.
4. Notice any pictures, charts, or graphs; these are usually included to emphasize important ideas, concepts, or trends.
5. If you do not get enough information from the headings or if you are working with material that does not have headings, read the first sentence of each paragraph.
6. Glance at the remainder of the paragraph.
   a. Notice any italicized or boldface words or phrases. These are key terms used throughout the selection.
   b. Look for any lists of ideas within the text of the material. The author may use numerals, such as (1), (2), (3), in the list or may include signal words such as *first, second, one major cause, another cause.*
   c. Look for unusual or striking features of the paragraph. You may notice a series of dates, many capitalized words, or several large-figure numbers.
7. Read the summary or last paragraph.

EXERCISE 2 _____

Directions: *Skim each of the following selections. Then summarize each article in the space provided.*

Selection 1: "To Lie or Not to Lie? The Doctor's Dilemma"

_____

_____

_____

Selection 2: "Aging and Death"

_____

_____

_____

Selection 3: "Getting Those *!@#%" Machines to Work

_____

_____

_____

1. TO LIE OR NOT TO LIE? THE DOCTOR'S DILEMMA

–Sissela Bok

Should doctors ever lie to benefit their patients—to speed recovery or to conceal the approach of death? In medicine as in law, government, and other lines of work, the requirements of honesty often seem dwarfed by greater needs: the need to shelter from brutal news or to uphold a promise of secrecy; to expose corruption or to promote the public interest.

What should doctors say, for example, to a 46-year-old man coming for a routine physical checkup just before going on vacation with his family who, though he feels in perfect health, is found to have a form of cancer that will cause him to die within six months? Is it best to tell him the truth? If he asks, should the doctors deny that he is ill, or minimize the gravity of the prognosis? Should they at least conceal the truth until after the family vacation?

Doctors confront such choices often and urgently. At times, they see important reasons to lie for the patient's own sake; in their eyes, such lies differ sharply from self-serving ones.

Studies show that most doctors sincerely believe that the seriously ill do not want to know the truth about their condition, and that informing them risks destroying their hope, so that they may recover more slowly, or deteriorate faster, perhaps even commit suicide. As one physician wrote: "Ours is a profession which traditionally has been guided by a precept that transcends the virtue of uttering the truth for truth's sake, and that is 'as far as possible do no harm.' "

Armed with such a precept, a number of doctors may slip into deceptive practices that they assume will "do no harm" and may well help their patients. They may prescribe innumerable placebos, sound more

Taking Psychology with You

When a Friend Is Suicidal

Suicide is a scary subject, surrounded by mystery and myth. It can be frightening to those who find themselves fantasizing about it, and it is devastating to the family, friends, and acquaintances of those who go through with it. In the United States, most people who commit suicide are over the age of 45, but suicide rates are rapidly increasing among young people. Suicide is the second highest cause of death (after car accidents) among college students.

People who attempt suicide have different motives. Some believe they have no reason to live; some feel like failures in a world where (they think) everyone else is happy and successful; some want revenge against those who (they think) have made them suffer. But they all share the belief that life is unendurable and that suicide is the only solution. This belief may be rational, in the case of people who are terminally ill and in pain, or it may be the distorted thinking of someone suffering from depression.

Friends and family members can help prevent a suicide by knowing the difference between fact and fiction, and by recognizing the danger signs.

1. *There is no "suicidal type."* Most adolescents who try to commit suicide are isolated and lonely. Many are children of divorced or alcoholic parents. Some have problems in school and feel like failures. But others who are vulnerable to suicide attempts are college students who are perfectionistic, self-critical, and highly intelligent. The former may feel like ending their lives because they can foresee no future. The latter may feel suicidal because they do not like the futures they foresee.

2. *Take all suicide threats seriously.* Many people fail to take action when a friend talks about committing suicide. Some believe the friend's intentions but assume there is nothing they can do. "He'll just do it at another place, another time," they think. In fact, most suicides occur during an acute crisis. Once the person gets through the crisis, the desire to commit suicide fades. One researcher tracked down 515 people who had attempted suicide by jumping off the Golden Gate Bridge many years earlier. After those attempts, fewer than 5 percent had actually committed suicide in the subsequent decades (Seiden, 1978).

Others believe that if a friend is *talking* about suicide, he or she won't really *do* it. This belief is also false. Few people commit suicide without signaling their intentions. Most are ambivalent: "I want to kill myself, but I don't want to be dead—at least not forever." Most suicidal people don't want death, but relief from the terrible pain of feeling that nobody cares, that life is not worth living. Getting these thoughts and fears out in the open is an important first step.

3. *Know the danger signs.* A depressed person may be at risk of trying to commit suicide if he or she:

- Has tried to commit suicide before.
- Has become withdrawn, apathetic, and socially isolated.
- Reveals specific plans for carrying out the suicide.
- Expresses no concern about the usual deterrents to suicide, such as hurting the family, breaking religious rules, or the fact that suicide is an irreversible action.
- Suddenly seems to be coming out of a severe depression. The risk of suicide increases when the person begins to recover. No one knows why this is so. Perhaps deeply depressed people lack the energy to carry out a suicide. Perhaps making the decision to end their suffering causes them to feel better.

4. *Take constructive action.* If you believe your friend is in danger of suicide, trust your judgment. Do not be afraid to ask, "Are you thinking of suicide?" This question does not "put the idea" in anyone's mind. If your friend is contemplating the action, he or she will probably be relieved to talk about it, and you will know that it is time to find help (Beck, Kovacs, and Weissman, 1979). Let your friend talk—without criticism, argument, or disapproval. Don't try to talk your friend out of it by debating whether suicide is right or wrong, and don't put on phony cheerfulness ("Everything will be all right"). If your friend's words or actions scare you, say so. By listening nonjudgmentally, you are showing that you care. By allowing your friend to unburden his or her grief, you help the person get through the immediate crisis.

Most of all, don't leave your friend alone. If necessary, get the person to a counselor, health professional, or emergency room of a hospital; or call a local suicide hot line. Don't worry about "doing the wrong thing." In an emergency, the worst thing you can do is nothing at all.

FIGURE 22-1   An Example of Skimming

encouraging than the facts warrant, and distort grave news, especially to the incurably ill and the dying.

But the illusory nature of the benefits such deception is meant to bestow is now coming to be documented. Studies show that, contrary to the belief of many physicians, an overwhelming majority of patients do want to be told the truth, even about grave illness, and feel betrayed when they learn they have been misled. We are also learning that truthful information, humanely conveyed, helps patients cope with illness: helps them tolerate pain better, need less medication, and even recover faster after surgery.

Not only do lies not provide the "help" hoped for by advocates of benevolent deception; they invade the autonomy of patients and render them unable to make informed choices concerning their own health, including the choice of whether to *be* a patient in the first place. We are becoming increasingly aware of all that can befall patients in the course of their illness when information is denied or distorted.

Dying patients especially—who are easiest to mislead and most often kept in the dark—can then not make decisions about the end of life: about whether or not to enter a hospital, or to have surgery; about where and with whom to spend their remaining time; about how to bring their affairs to a close and take leave.

Lies also do harm to those who tell them: harm to their integrity and, in the long run, to their credibility. Lies hurt their colleagues as well. The suspicion of deceit undercuts the work of the many doctors who are scrupulously honest with their patients; it contributes to the spiral of litigation and of "defensive medicine," and thus it injures, in turn, the entire medical profession.

Sharp conflicts are now arising. Patients are learning to press for answers. Patients' bills of rights require that they be informed about their condition and about alternatives for treatment. Many doctors go to great lengths to provide such information. Yet even in hospitals with the most eloquent bill of rights, believers in benevolent deception continue their age-old practices. Colleagues may disapprove but refrain from remonstrating. Nurses may bitterly resent having to take part, day after day, in deceiving patients, but feel powerless to take a stand.

There is urgent need to debate this issue openly. Not only in medicine, but in other professions as well, practitioners may find themselves repeatedly in straits where serious consequences seem avoidable only through deception. Yet the public has every reason to be wary of professional deception, for such practices are peculiarly likely to become ingrained, to spread, and to erode trust. Neither in medicine, nor in law, government, or the social sciences can there be comfort in the old saw, "What you don't know can't hurt you."

2. **AGING AND DEATH**

–James Geiwitz

Grow old along with me!
The best is yet to be,
The last of life, for which
*   the first was made,*

–Robert Browning

Aging and death are two subjects that are generally avoided in conversation. When they come up, an uneasy atmosphere develops. Growing old generally elicits bad jokes at best, and death is discussed in euphemisms—"passed away," "kicked the bucket," "the late————."

Why do Americans have such strong negative reactions to growing old and to dying? Perhaps the fear of death is understandable, since what happens next is totally unknown, and uncertainty is always a little frightening. But why do millions of Americans dye their hair, have "face-lifts" and other cosmetic surgery, and otherwise spend so much time, energy, and money on the effort to keep looking young?

AGING: PSYCHOLOGICAL ASPECTS

Some of the reasons the American culture is so youth-oriented have to do with its rapidly changing, super-industrial status. In some cultures, particularly in the past, the wisdom of the "elders" was highly valued. They had experience: They knew what was likely to happen and what to do in a variety of situations. In our culture, the elders know about things that no longer exist. Often they are bewildered about events. Old people are no longer respected for their wisdom; they are "out of date."

Ironically, it is the super-industrial cultures that have the most old people. Advances in medical science have doubled the percentage of United States citizens over the age of 65 in this century alone. At the same time, our society has pressed to make earlier retirements possible and, in some industries, required.

Retirement means an abrupt change in habits. For some people, it is an unhappy switch from an active, productive life into what feels like uselessness. The daily routine of a job disappears, leaving the retired person plenty of spare time—but for what? Some people are unable to seek out new friends and activities. These men and women, disabled by the physical ailments of old age or restricted by the loss of income that comes with retirement, may be forced to leave their homes and move in with their children or go to a nursing home. No longer able to direct their own lives, they become dependent on other people. They may feel that all their choices have been taken away: What they eat, whom they see, where they go may all be decided for them. Sources of stimulation often become fewer. A person may spend day after day within the same room or rooms, with only brief periods of human contact. Even in a family situation the elderly person may be ignored much of the time. However, there are increasing numbers of social help agencies that can work to alleviate these problems, and a loving family can sometimes find new activities or jobs that will give the aging relative a sense of being a valuable part of the household.

It is important to realize that the changes we face at retirement *can* be dealt with, just like changes at any other time of life. For many people, retirement is an opportunity, a chance to do things they never had time to do before. As you might expect, people who adjusted well to life before retirement are the best adjusted after retirement. But in both youth and age, adjustment is an active process. The people who are happiest in retirement are those who seek out new activities, like gardening and volunteer social work, to replace the ones no longer available to them. They also seek out social companions who share their interests, instead of sitting in sullen isolation, lamenting the deaths of friends and how no one visits them anymore. They may even join the Gray Panthers, a radical political organization for old people that lobbies for the rights and benefits of the elderly: improved bus service, tax reforms, new health laws.

AGING: BIOLOGICAL ASPECTS

Biologically, aging may be defined as a decline in the ability of the body to avoid or fight off the effects of accidents, disease, and other types of stress. Thus, most people die of a disease, not "natural causes." There is good evidence that each of us has an alloted time in life that can be shortened by disease or accident, but not lengthened. Medical science has increased the *average* lifespan in many countries by saving the lives of infants and young people, but it has had little effect among the very old. For example, if all cancer (a prime killer of the elderly) were eliminated, the average lifespan would increase by only 1.5 years.

It is very difficult to distinguish between "pure" aging and the effects of various chronic diseases that often come with age. These diseases include arthritis—inflammation of the joints, causing pain and decreased dexterity and mobility—and arteriosclerosis—hardening and thickening of the arteries. Arthritis makes it hard for the victim to move around and to do certain things. Arteriosclerosis causes increased blood pressure, which may cause headaches and generally poor circulation. Poor circulation, in turn, makes adjustment to cooler temperatures more difficult; and poor blood circulation to the brain may result in some problems in processing information.

A classic study of *healthy* men between the ages of 65 and 91 compared their physical and mental abilities to those of another group of men, average age 21. The older men proved as fit as the younger men on a number of variables. Measures of blood flow to the brain and oxygen consumption during exercise did not differ between groups. The older subjects were superior in non-timed tests of intelligence, such as vocabulary, and poorer in tests requiring speed or involving reaction time. The reaction-time tests showed the most marked results. By and large, however, there were very few differences between the healthy old men and healthy young men. This indicates the validity of a definition of aging as increasing susceptibility to diseases, diseases which may cause many of the symptoms we often incorrectly attribute to aging itself.

Of course, many physical changes are directly related to aging. Hair may become gray (or disappear altogether); the skin wrinkles; the senses become less acute and the bones more brittle, making accidents more likely and more serious. There is some evidence that pain becomes less painful, so not all changes are for the worse. And contrary to popular myth, people up to and even over 80 years old are capable of enjoying sexual intercourse—and many do.

DEATH AND DYING

Death and dying are sad, depressing subjects to most of us. No matter how prepared we are, or however strongly we may believe in a life after death, the loss of a close friend or relative is painful. The bereaved—those who have lost a loved one to death—are often faced with serious problems of adjustment, including coping with loneliness, sorrow, and the simple tasks of day-to-day living. There is a funeral, a will to be read and executed, expressions of sympathy to be accepted and responded to. These institutionalized aspects of the mourning period may help, as Freud once suggested, to spread the grief over several days. But soon they are over, and then comes the crying, the depression, the difficulty in sleeping, concentrating, and remembering, the lack of appetite for food and for life—the most common symptoms in a study of over 100 people who had lost a husband or wife.

During the period of bereavement, which often lasts a year or two, grief at least slightly affects the person's ability to function. For someone who has lost a spouse, the probability of a fatal illness, accident, or suicide is slightly higher during this period; these symptoms may be related to others, such as heavy drinking.

But what is death like for the person who is dying? From interviews with over 200 dying patients, one psychiatrist identified five attitudes experienced by these patients, often but not always in sequence (Kübler-Ross, 1970). *Denial* is usually the first stage. The patient says, in effect, "No! Not me!" Patients even choose to ignore obvious symptoms instead of openly confronting their own fears. This stage is followed by *anger:* The patient demands, "Why me? Why now?"

In the third stage, called *bargaining,* the patient seeks for a pardon or at least a postponement. Often he or she tries to make a bargain, secretly or openly, with God or "fate" or even Satan. One woman's bargain was "If I can only be allowed to live to see my son marry. . . ." She managed to get the hospital staff to teach her self-hypnosis to control the pain so that she could attend her son's wedding.

The fourth stage is *depression,* which develops as the patient realizes the loss of everything and everybody he or she loves is close at hand. This "preparatory" sorrow is probably necessary for the final stage, *acceptance.* In this fifth and last stage, the patient usually weans himself away from the world, desiring less and less contact with an increasingly small number of close friends. Acceptance was perhaps best expressed by Stewart Alsop, the noted journalist, just before he died: "A dying man needs to die as a sleepy man needs to sleep, and there comes a time when it is wrong, as well as useless, to resist."

One of the most important points brought out in Kübler-Ross's studies is the dying person's need to talk about his or her fears and feelings about death. In fact, Kübler-Ross believes that if we were more open in thinking and talking about our deaths throughout our lives, we would live fuller lives and die with much less trauma and struggle. Death is, after all, one of the inescapable facts of human experience, and should be allowed to take a less fearsome and more accepted position in our daily lives.

3. **GETTING THOSE *!@#% MACHINES TO WORK**

—Wade & Tauris, pp. 186–187

Your new VCR, the salesperson assures you, is state-of-the-art. It will enable you to preprogram the recording of umpteen shows over a period of umpteen days; you can record one show while watching another . . . it practically makes your coffee for you in the morning. "I'll take it!" you say. Three weeks later you're still trying to figure out how to set the current time of day, never mind recording programs.

Why are modern "conveniences" so often inconvenient to use? Why is it so hard to open a milk carton, adjust water temperature in a one-faucet shower, or put someone on hold in a modern office telephone system? **Human factors psychology**—also called ergonomics—has some of the answers. Psychologists in this fast-growing field design human-machine systems that optimize human abilities while minimizing error (Smither, 1988). Their goal is to come up with equipment, tasks, and work settings that take into account the sensory, perceptual, and motor abilities and limitations of human beings. Knowing that people react more quickly to green signals than to red or blue, or that reaction time with the hand is 20 percent faster than with the foot, can be critical in the design of an airplane control panel. Knowing that fluorescent lighting minimizes shadows and diffuses light can reduce the stress of office workers.

But what about those milk cartons, faucets, and telephones? One psychologist who studies human perception estimates that an adult must readily discriminate among 30,000 different everyday objects (Biederman, 1987). In *The Psychology of Everyday Things* (1988), cognitive psychologist Donald Norman shows that many of these objects are engineered with little thought for how the human mind works. It can be a major challenge to figure out how to use a new washing machine, camera, or sewing machine, or set a digital watch. And it's not the *people* that are stupid. A well-known engineer, the founder of a major data-processing equipment company, once confessed at an annual meeting that he couldn't figure out how to heat a cup of coffee in the company's microwave oven.

A good product, Norman observes, conveys information regarding its use by means of its visible structure instead of forcing the user to rely on memory. One useful design concept, borrowed from the study of perception, is called *affordance* (Gibson, 1979). Affordance refers to the way perceived and actual properties of a thing determine how it can be used. A flat horizontal bar on a door *affords* no action except pushing, so it's a good idea to have such a bar on a door that is supposed to be pushed. A door that is supposed to be pulled should have a different kind of hardware, such as a small, narrow, vertical bar. (Can you think of other possibilities?) When affordances are taken advantage of, says Norman, you know what to do with an object just by looking; you don't need pictures, labels, or instructions.

Good design also requires *visibility*: Crucial distinctions must be visually obvious. What good is a telephone that has a dozen fancy features if you need to read the manual every time you perform an operation, or if the lettering on the phone is so small you can't read it? (One of us has such a phone. Switches used for the programming of numbers are on the side, labeled by tiny raised black letters, and the phone itself is black. You can't decipher the labels unless you lift the phone up, turn it on its side, and hold it 2 inches away from your face.)

And then there's the matter of *mapping*, the relationship between controls and their results. Most stoves have two burners in front and two in back. The controls, however, are often arranged in a row. It's hard to know which control goes with which burner unless there are labels. The solution: Arrange the controls in a rectangular configuration that matches that of the burners, or arrange the burners in a semicircle to achieve a left-to-right arrangement like that of the controls.

If you are clever, you can overcome problems of poor design by making your own modifications, using perceptual principles in this chapter.

For example, if you want knobs or switches to be easily distinguishable, you can apply the Gestalt principles on page 184: The objects should have different colors, textures, or shapes and be spatially separated. (Control-room operators in one nuclear power plant solved the problem of similar nobs on two adjacent switches by placing distinctively shaped beer-keg handles over them, one labeled Heineken's, the other Michelob.) At the very least, we can learn to recognize good and bad design and adjust our buying habits accordingly. "Give mental prizes to those who practice good design: send flowers," advises Norman. "Jeer those who don't: send weeds."

SCANNING TECHNIQUES

Scanning is a method of selective reading that is used when you are searching for a particular fact or the answer to a question. Scanning can best be described as a looking rather than a reading process. As you look for the information you need, you ignore everything else. When you finish scanning a page, the only thing you should know is whether it contained the information you were looking for. You should *not* be able to recall topics, main ideas, or details presented on the page. You already use the technique of scanning daily: you regularly scan telephone books, television listings, and indexes. The purpose of this section is to help you develop a rapid, efficient, approach for scanning.

Use the following step-by-step procedure to become more skilled in rapidly locating specific information:

1. State in your mind the specific information you are looking for. Phrase it in question form if possible.
2. Try to anticipate how the answer will appear and what clues you might use to help you locate the answer. If you are scanning to find the distance between two cities, you might expect either digits or numbers written out as words. Also, a unit of measurement, probably miles or kilometers, will appear after the number.
3. Determine the organization of material: it is your most important clue to where to begin looking for information. Especially when you are looking up information contained in charts and tables, the organization of the information is crucial to rapid scanning.
4. Use headings and any other aids that will help you identify which sections might contain the information you are looking for.
5. Selectively read and skip through likely sections of the passage, keeping in mind the specific question you formed and your expectations of how the answer might appear. Move your eyes down the page in a systematic way. While there are various eye movement patterns, such as the "arrow pattern" (straight down the middle of the page) or the "Z pattern" (zig-zagging down the page), it is best to use a pattern that seems comfortable and easy for you.
6. When you reach the fact you are looking for, you will find that the word or phrase will stand out, and you will notice it immediately.
7. When you have found the needed information, carefully read the sentences in which it appears in order to confirm that you have located the correct information.

Directions: *Scan each paragraph or passage to locate the answer to the question stated at the beginning of each.*

1. *Question:* In what unit is energy measured?

   Passage:

   Work is done in lifting the heavy ram of a pile driver, and, as a consequence, the ram acquires the property of being able to do work on a body beneath when it falls. When work is done in winding a spring mechanism, the spring acquires the ability to do work on an assemblage of gears to run a clock, ring a bell, or sound an alarm. And when a battery is charged, it may in turn do the work of a wound spring. In each case, something has been acquired. When work is done on an object, something is given to the object, which, in many cases, enables it to work. This "something" may be a physical separation of attracting bodies; it may be a compression of atoms in the material of a body; or it may be a rearrangement of electric charges in the molecules of a body. This something that enables a body to do work is called *energy.* Like work, energy is measured in joules. It appears in many forms, which we will discuss in subsequent chapters. We shall give attention here to the two forms of mechanical energy: potential energy and kinetic energy.

   –Hewitt, *Conceptual Physics,* p. 82

2. *Question:* What was Hitler's promise?

   Passage:

   In September the United States requested, and Hitler and Mussolini agreed to, a big-power crisis conference at Munich. Included were the two Fascist leaders and the premiers of Britain and France (but not of the Soviet Union), who met to discuss the Czech crisis and how war might be averted. At Munich the democratic leaders took Hitler at his word that he would make no further demands if given the Sudetenland, and the Allies abandoned Czechoslovakia to its fate. Prime Minister Chamberlain returned to London with the wishful declaration that he had achieved "peace in our time," on the grounds of Hitler's promise that this was "the last territorial claim which I have to make in Europe." These are now remembered as some of the most tragic statements in diplomatic history.

   –Jones, *The Logic of International Relations,* p. 54

3. *Question:* In what phase of advertising is the largest number of workers employed?

   Passage:

   More than 400,000 persons are employed in all phases of advertising in this country. This estimate by industry spokespersons includes those who create or sell advertising for an advertiser, medium, or service, but not the thousands behind the scenes such as printers, sign painters, and clerical workers. Manufacturing and service concerns employ the largest number of advertising workers. Next in order are the mass media, including radio, television, magazines, outdoor, direct mail, and transportation advertising departments. Following them are retail establishments, advertising agencies, wholesalers, and miscellaneous specialty companies.

–Agee, Ault, and Emery, *Introduction to Mass Communications*, p. 365

4. *Question:* Why was an Irish militia supposedly formed?

Passage:

Revolution in American also brought drastic changes to Ireland. Before 1775, that unhappy island, under English rule, had endured centuries of religious persecution, economic exploitation, and political domination. During the war, however, Henry Gratton (1746–1820) and Henry Flood (1732–91), two leaders of the Irish Protestant gentry, exploited English weakness to obtain concessions. An Irish militia was formed, supposedly to protect the coasts against American or French attacks. With thousands of armed Irishmen behind them, the two leaders resorted successfully to American methods. In February 1782, a convention in Dublin, representing 80,000 militiamen, demanded legislative independence, which the English Parliament subsequently granted. An Irish legislature could now make its own laws, subject to veto only by the English king. Ireland thus acquired a status denied the American colonies in 1774.

–Wallbank et al., *Civilization Past and Present*, Vol. 2, p. 533

5. *Question:* How does the cost of in-home retailing compare with suburban rates?

Passage:

In-home retailing involves the presenting of goods to customers in a face-to-face meeting at the customer's home or by contacting the customer by telephone. This solicitation can be done without advance selection of consumers or follow-ups based upon prior contact at stores, or by phone or mail. The well-known Tupperware party fits in this category. Here a person has a social gathering where everyone knows a sales presentation will be made. Besides Tupperware, the largest companies operating in this type of retailing are Avon (cosmetics), Electrolux (vacuum cleaners), Amway (household products), World Book (encyclopedia and books), Shaklee (food supplements), Home Interiors and Gifts (decorative items), L. H. Stuart (jewelry and crafts), Stanley Home Products (household products), and Kirby (vacuum cleaners). Despite the great cost savings of having no store and no inventory, labor costs make this form of retailing expensive. Expenses are estimated to average about 50 percent of sales, compared to about 26 percent for all retailing.

–Kinnear and Bernhardt, *Principles of Marketing*, p. 388

6. *Question:* What agreement was violated when West Germany was incorporated into NATO?

Passage:

Far from accepting the role of antagonist in world politics and in the strategic arms race, the Kremlin seeks to defend its island of socialism from capitalist encirclement. Bolstering their traditional fears of exposed borders, the Soviets have experienced overt attempts by Japan and the West to bring down their power. Japanese and American landings in Siberia at the close of the First World War, shortly after the Bolshevik Revolution of 1917, were historic signals of the need to maintain rigorous defense against the capitalist industrialized states. More recently, American efforts after the Second World War to influence Soviet policy in Eastern Europe through atomic monopoly have accentuated the need for vigilance. NATO in particular, and the string of anti-Soviet alliances in general, added further to the need. Incorporation of West Germany into NATO in apparent violation of the Potsdam Agreement of 1945 was the ultimate sign of American intentions of maintaining anti-Soviet tension throughout Europe; the Kremlin responded by forming the Warsaw Pact. Soviet arms policy, far from being the cause of the balance of terror, is a response to the capitalist (specifically American) political and strategic threats.

–Jones, *The Logic of International Relations,* p. 387

7. *Question:* What race of inmates are victimized in prisons?

Passage:

In Bowker's view, racial and ethnic group victimization is the most significant and widespread. It used to be that the minority black inmates were the object of victimization, but now it appears that in many prisons it is the whites, especially the middle-class whites, who are victimized by black inmates. Leo Carroll's (1974) research at a New England state prison confirms the direction of interracial aggression, as does a more recent study of Stateville, the Illinois penitentiary at Joliet. In Stateville, James Jacobs (1977) found four highly cohesive gangs whose reputation and power dominated interracial contacts and radiated throughout the prison. The Black P. Stone Nation, the Devil's Disciples, and the Vicelords are blank gangs; the Latin Kings is made up of Hispanic inmates. Their exploitation of other prisoners is extensive.

–Barlow, *Introduction to Criminology,* p. 465

8. *Question:* What is a spiff?

Passage:

Manufacturers often sponsor *contests* with prizes like free merchandise, trips, and plaques to dealers who reach certain specified sales levels. Additionally, they may get free *merchandise allowances* or even *money bonuses* for reaching sales performance goals. Once in a while, there is a sweepstakes, where "lucky" dealers can win substantial prizes. For example, Fisher-Price Toys had great success with a sweepstakes that gave cooperating dealers a chance to win a trip to Puerto Rico. These types of programs may also be directed at in-store sales personnel for their individual sales performances. A direct payment by a manufacturer to a channel member salesperson is called a *spiff.* This is very common at the consumer level for consumer durables and cosmetics, and at the wholesale level for beer and records. Another version of a spiff is when retailers pay their salespeople to push certain items. Clearly, this practice makes it possible for consumers to be deceived by a salesperson attempting to earn *push money*. As a result, these types of payments are controversial.

–Kinnear and Bernhardt, *Principles of Marketing*, p. 495

9. *Question:* What were the objectives of the New Deal?

Passage:

In the 1932 elections, Franklin D. Roosevelt, only the third Democrat to be elected to the presidency since 1860, overwhelmed Hoover by assembling a coalition of labor, intellectuals, minorities, and farmers. The country had reached a crisis point by the time he was to be inaugurated in 1933, and quick action had to be taken in the face of bank closings. Under his leadership, the New Deal, a sweeping, pragmatic, often hit-or-miss program, was developed to cope with the emergency. The New Deal's three objectives were relief, recovery, and reform. Millions of dollars flowed from the federal treasury to feed the hungry, create jobs for the unemployed through public works, and provide for the sick and elderly through such reforms as the Social Security Act. In addition, Roosevelt's administration substantially reformed the banking and stock systems, greatly increased the rights of labor unions, invested in massive public power and conservation projects, and supported families who either needed homes or were in danger of losing the homes they inhabited.

–Wallbank et al., *Civilization Past and Present*, Vol. 2, p. 781

10. *Question:* Why does the tide come in rapidly at the Bay of Fundy?

Passage:

Ocean tides are complicated because of the presence of interfering land masses and friction with the ocean bottom. Because of these complications, the tides break up into smaller "basins of circulation," where a tidal bulge travels around the basin like a circulating wave that travels around a small basin of water when it is tilted properly. There is always a high tide someplace in the basin, although at a particular locality it may be hours away from an overhead moon. In midocean the variation in the water level—the range of the tide—is usually a meter or two. This range varies in different parts of the world; it is greatest in some Alaskan fjords and is most notable in the basin of the Bay of Fundy, between New Brunswick and Nova Scotia in southeast Canada, where tidal differences sometimes exceed 15 meters. This is largely due to the ocean floor, which funnels shoreward in a V-shape. The tide often comes in faster than a person can run. Don't dig clams near the water's edge at low tide in the Bay of Fundy!

–Hewitt, *Conceptual Physics*, p. 134

SUMMARY

Many adults feel that it is important to read every word on a printed page. This mistaken notion is often responsible for a slow, inflexible rate of reading. Actually, there are many types of material that do not require a thorough, beginning-to-end, careful reading. There are also many situations in which reading everything is not necessary—situations in which selective reading (reading some parts and skipping others) is more appropriate. It is effective to read selectively in situations in which you need only main ideas, you are looking for a specific fact or answer to a question, you are highly familiar with the content of the material, or the material contains information that does not relate to your purpose for reading. Finally, there are certain types of material and styles of writing in which it is possible to skip information.

In situations where it is appropriate to read selectively, the techniques of skimming and scanning are useful. Skimming is a process of reading only main ideas and simply glancing at the remainder of the material. There are three basic types of skimming: preread skimming, skim-reading, and review skimming. The type of skimming used depends on the reader's purpose. Scanning is a method of selective reading that is used when searching for a particular fact or answer to a question.

Sample Textbook Chapter

Health, Stress, and Coping
(from Wade/Tavris, *Psychology*)

CHAPTER 15

Health,
Stress,
and
Coping

Rule No. 1 is, don't sweat the small stuff.
Rule No. 2 is, it's all small stuff.
And if you can't fight and you can't flee, flow.

ROBERT ELIOT, M.D.

Stressful events can hit at any time. How would you react to a "bolt from the blue"?

■ Bill and his father have been battling for years. Bill feels that he can never do anything right, that his father is always ready to criticize him for the slightest flaw. Now that he has left home, Bill has more perspective on their relationship, but one thing hasn't changed. Every time his father comes to visit, Bill breaks out in a mysterious rash.

■ Tanya has never told anyone about a shattering experience she had as a child. She is afraid to reveal her secret, sure that no one will understand or sympathize. But the memory haunts her in daydreams and nightmares.

■ Josh is walking home from school one night when three young men grab him, threaten to kill him, and steal his watch and wallet. Josh is relieved to be alive, but he finds that he can't get over this experience. Months later, he still feels humiliated and angry, and dreams of revenge.

■ Lucy, who is already late for class, gets stuck in a traffic jam caused by a three-car accident. As she walks in the door, her instructor reprimands her for being late. Rushing to get her notes together for an overdue research paper, Lucy spills coffee all over herself and the documents. By noon Lucy has a splitting headache and feels exhausted.

All of these people are certainly under "stress," but, as you see, this word covers a multitude of experiences. It includes occasional but recurring conflicts (Bill and his father), a traumatic experience or a sudden event that shatters your sense of safety (Tanya, Josh), and a collection of small irritations that can wear you down (Lucy). Is there a link between these "stresses" and health or illness?

In this chapter, we will explore the psychology of health and illness, stress and coping, in the context of daily life. We will look at some findings from the new field of **health psychology**, which studies all psychological aspects of health and illness, such as the psychological influences on how people stay healthy, why they become ill, and how they respond when they do get ill (Taylor, 1986). A related field, called **behavioral medicine**, is an interdisciplinary approach to health and illness. Researchers in behavioral medicine come from many different backgrounds, such as medicine, nutrition, and physiology, as well as psychology.

Scientific psychology and medicine have typically used a *pathogenic* approach, focusing on the causes of a problem or an illness (from *patho-*, "disease" or "suffering," and *-genic*, "producing"). But health psychologists also want to know what generates health, by taking the *salutogenic* approach (from *salut*, "health"). According to Aaron Antonovsky (1979, 1984), the pathogenic approach divides the world into the healthy and the sick, although many healthy people have occasions of "dis-ease" and many sick people are able to get along in life. It seeks a single cause to a problem, such as "Type A causes heart attacks," and it has led us to assume that all stress is bad. In emphasizing the people who are at "high risk" of becoming ill, it ignores the majority who, though at risk, stay well.

The pathogenic approach, says Antonovsky, asks, "How can we eradicate this or that stressor?" The salutogenic approach asks instead, "How can we learn to

health psychology *A field within psychology that studies psychological aspects of health and illness.*
behavioral medicine *An interdisciplinary field that studies behaviors related to the maintenance of health, the onset of illness, and the prevention of disease.*

558

live, and live well, with stressors, and possibly even turn [them] to our advantage?'' To find out, health psychologists also study the exceptions—the people who theoretically should become sick but don't, the people who transcend difficult problems instead of giving in to them.

Modern research in health psychology, as we will see in this chapter, is very promising. But some of its findings, unfortunately, have been misused to foster two common misconceptions: Illness is ''all in the mind'' and curing illness just requires the right attitude, or ''mind over matter.'' In the conclusion, we will consider the contributions of health psychology and its limitations.

The Nature of Stress

Throughout history, ''stress'' has been one of those things that everyone has experienced but few can define (Elliott & Eisdorfer, 1982). Why has it been so difficult to agree on something all of us have felt?

Alarms and adaptation

In his 1956 book, *The Stress of Life,* Canadian physician Hans Selye (1907–1982) popularized the idea of stress and advanced its study. Selye noted that many environmental factors—heat, cold, pain, toxins, viruses, and so on—throw the body out of equilibrium, forcing it to respond. These factors, called *stressors*, include anything that requires the body to mobilize its resources. The body responds to a stressor with an orchestrated set of physical and chemical changes, which, as we saw in Chapter 9, prepare an individual to fight or flee. To Selye, ''stress'' consisted of this package of reactions, which he called the **General Adaptation Syndrome** (with the memorable acronym GAS). Usually, the body will meet the challenge of the environment and *adapt* to the stress.

The general adaptation syndrome has three phases:

1. In the *alarm phase*, the organism mobilizes to meet the threat. This is a basic package of biological responses that allows a person to fight or flee no matter what the stressor is: trying to cross a crowded intersection or trying to escape a cross rattlesnake.

2. In the *phase of resistance*, the organism attempts to resist or cope with a threat that continues and cannot be avoided. During this phase, the body's physiological responses are above normal—a response to the original stressor—but this very mechanism makes the body more susceptible to *other* stressors. For example, when your body has mobilized to fight off the flu, you may find you are more easily annoyed by minor frustrations. In most cases, the body will eventually *adapt* to the stressor and return to normal.

3. If the stressor persists, it may overwhelm the body's resources. Depleted of energy, the body enters the *phase of exhaustion*, becoming vulnerable to fatigue, physical problems, and eventually illness. The very reactions that allow the body to resist short-term stressors—boosting energy, tensing muscles in preparation for action, shutting out signs of pain, closing off digestion, raising blood pressure—are unhealthy as long-range responses. Tense muscles can cause headache and neck pain. Increased blood pressure can become chronic hypertension. Closing off digestion for too long can lead to digestive disorders.

General Adaptation Syndrome (GAS) *According to Hans Selye, the bodily reactions to environmental stressors.*

Who has more "stress"—and whose stress counts? *Many media stories emphasize the "stress" faced by white-collar workers and managers of companies. They are less concerned with the stress faced by assembly line workers and laborers. Why do you think this might be so? Which group* is *under more stress—powerful people in highly competitive and complicated jobs, or powerless people in boring and predictable jobs?*

Stress is a bane of modern civilization because our physiological alarm mechanism now chimes too often. Today, when the typical stressor is a mammoth traffic jam and not a mammoth mammal, the fight-or-flight response often gets revved up with nowhere to go. When your teacher announces that you will have an unexpected exam, you don't really need to respond as if you were fighting for your life, but your body will still sweat to dispose of excess body heat. When you see your sweetheart flirting with someone else, you don't really need to breathe hard to get oxygen to your muscles, as you would if you were fleeing to safety.

Not all stress is bad, however. Some stress, which Selye called **eustress**, is positive and feels good, even if it also requires the body to produce short-term energy: competing in an athletic event, falling in love, working hard on a project you enjoy. Selye did not believe that all stress could be avoided or that people should aim for a stress-free life, which is an impossible goal. "Just as any inanimate machine gradually wears out," he said, "so does the human machine sooner or later become the victim of constant wear and tear." The goal is to minimize the wear and tear, not get rid of it.

Selye recognized that psychological stressors (such as emotional conflict or grief) can be as important as physical stressors (such as heat, toxic chemicals, or noise). He also observed that some factors *mediate* between the stressor and the stress. A warm climate or a nutritious diet, for example, can soften the impact of an environmental stressor such as pollution. Conversely, a harsh climate or a poor diet can make such stressors worse. But by and large, Selye concentrated on the biological responses that result from a person's attempt to adapt to environmental demands. He defined a stressor as any event that produces the stress (that is, the General Adaptation Syndrome). A diagram of his view is:

eustress [YOU-stress]
Positive or beneficial stress.

Stressor – – –> Stress (GAS) – – –> Healthy adaptation or illness

Later studies have found that stress is not a purely biological condition that can lead directly to illness. First, between the stressor and the stress is *the individual's evaluation of the event:* An event that is stressful for one person may be challenging for another and routinely boring for a third. Losing a job, traveling to China, or having "too much" work to do is stressful to some people and not to others. Second, between the stress and its consequences is *how the individual copes with the stress.* Not all individuals who are under stress behave in the same way. Not all get ill. Thus a revised diagram might look like this:

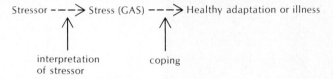

Because people differ in how they interpret events and in how they respond to them, many psychologists now prefer a definition of stress that takes into account aspects of the environment, aspects of the individual, and how the two interact. **Psychological stress** is the result of an exchange between the person and the environment, in which the person believes that the situation strains or overwhelms his or her resources and is endangering his or her well-being (Lazarus & Folkman, 1984).

Illness and immunology

Another approach to the psychological origins of illness came from the field of *psychosomatic medicine*, which developed in psychiatry at the turn of the century. **Psychosomatic** describes the interaction of mind (*psyche*) and body (*soma*). Freud was one of the main proponents of the idea that physical symptoms are often the result of unconscious conflicts. Other psychosomatic theorists maintained that many disorders—notably rheumatoid arthritis, asthma, ulcers, migraine headaches, and hypertension—are caused by neurotic personality patterns. Many of these early theories led to the mistaken view that a "psychosomatic illness" is "all in the mind," but they have not been supported by modern research. Today's field of psychosomatic medicine recognizes the complex nature of the mind-body relationship—not only how mind affects body, but also how body affects mind.

Some researchers, borrowing ideas from Selye and from psychosomatic medicine, are studying the effects of physical stress and psychological factors on the immune system. The immune system is designed to do two things: recognize foreign substances (antigens), such as flu viruses, bacteria, and tumor cells, and destroy or deactivate them. There are basically two types of white blood cells in the immune system: the *lymphocytes*, whose job is primarily to recognize and destroy foreign cells, and the *phagocytes*, whose job is to ingest and eliminate them.

To defend the body against foreign invaders, the immune system deploys different weapons (cells), sometimes together and sometimes alone, depending on the nature of the enemy. For example, *natural killer cells*, a type of lymphocyte, are important in tumor detection and rejection; *killer T cells* help destroy antigens that they have been exposed to previously. Prolonged or severe stress can suppress these cells and others that normally fight disease and infection.

The marriage of immunology and psychology has produced an offspring with the cumbersome name **psychoneuroimmunology**. This new field explores the connections among psychological processes (such as emotions, attitudes, and percep-

psychological stress *The result of a relationship between the person and the environment, in which the person believes the situation is overwhelming and threatens his or her ability to cope.*

psychosomatic *A term that describes the interaction between a physical illness or condition and psychological states; literally, mind (psyche) and body (soma).*

psychoneuroimmunology *[psycho/neuro/immu/nology] The field that studies the relationships among psychology, the nervous system, and the immune system.*

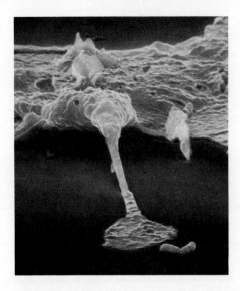

Like a fantastical Hollywood creature, a phagocyte reaches out with an extended "arm," called a pseudopod, to ensnare two unwitting bacteria.

tions), the nervous system, and immune functions. A basic assumption in this work is that *all* disease is the result of relationships among the endocrine, nervous, and immune systems; behavior; and emotions (G. Solomon, 1985). These relationships explain, for example, why of two people who are exposed to a flu virus, one is sick all winter and the other doesn't even get the sniffles (Kiecolt-Glaser & Glaser, 1989). In a study of medical students who had herpes virus, researchers found that herpes outbreaks were more likely to occur when the students were feeling loneliest or were under the pressure of exams. Loneliness and stress apparently suppressed the cells' immune capability, permitting the existing herpes virus to erupt (Kiecolt-Glaser et al., 1985a).

Some sources of stress

What are the stressors that might affect the immune system and thus lead to illness? Some psychologists study the significant events that disrupt our lives and take an emotional toll. Others count nuisances, the small straws that break the camel's back. Still others emphasize continuing pressures.

Life events. Years ago, Thomas Holmes and Richard Rahe (1967) identified 43 events that seemed to be especially stressful. By testing thousands of people, they were able to rank a series of "life-change events" in order of their disruptive impact. Holmes and Rahe then assigned each event a corresponding number of "life-change units" (LCUs). At the top was death of a spouse (100 LCUs), followed by divorce (73), imprisonment (63), and death of a close family member (63). Not all of the events were unpleasant. Marriage (50) was on the list, as were pregnancy (40), buying a house (31), and Christmas (12). Among people who had become ill, the large majority had had 300 LCUs or more in a single year.

Later studies found numerous flaws in the idea that *all* life events are stressful and lead to illness. First, many of the items on the Holmes-Rahe scale are the *result* of psychological problems or illness, not their cause (such as "problems at work" and "major changes in sleeping habits") (Hudgens, 1974). Second, some events become more stressful once a person is already depressed or ill (Dohrenwend,

1979). Third, as we saw in Chapter 14, many expected changes, such as retirement or having the children leave home, are not especially stressful for most people. Happy, positive events are not related (thank goodness) to illness or poor health (Taylor, 1986). Finally, simply counting "life-change units" is not enough: Having 17 things happen to you in one year is not necessarily stressful unless you feel overwhelmed by them (Cohen, Kamarck, & Mermelstein, 1983; Sarason, Johnson, & Siegel, 1978).

Bereavement and tragedy.   Some events, of course, are more shocking to the system, psychologically and physically, than others. The events at the top of the Holmes-Rahe list, death of a spouse and divorce, are powerful stressors that are linked to a subsequent decline in health. Widows and widowers are more susceptible to illness and physical ailments, and their mortality rate is higher than expected (Calabrese, Kling, & Gold, 1987). Divorce also often takes a long-term health toll. Divorced adults have higher rates of emotional disturbance, heart disease, pneumonia, and other diseases than comparable adults who are not divorced (Jacobson, 1983; Weiss, 1975).

Bereaved and divorced people may be vulnerable to illness because, feeling unhappy and lonely, they don't sleep well, they stop eating properly, and they consume more drugs and cigarettes. But animal and human studies suggest that separation *itself* creates changes in the cardiovascular system, a lowered white blood cell count, and other abnormal responses of the immune system (Laudenslager & Reite, 1984; Stein, Keller, & Schleifer, 1985). You may recall from Chapters 10 and 13 that attachment appears to be a basic biological need of the species, and broken attachments affect us at a basic cellular level. But the quality of the attachment is as important as its presence. Unhappily married individuals show the same decline in immune function as unhappy divorced people (Kiecolt-Glaser et al., 1987a).

Sadly, many people suffer shocking experiences that are not on the Holmes-Rahe list—experiences about which they feel so secret, and dirty, that the secret itself adds to the stress. (See "A Closer Look at Psychoneuroimmunology" for a fascinating case study of how this field's findings have yielded a therapeutic suggestion for recovery from trauma.)

Daily hassles.   Some psychologists argue that we handle most of the big problems of life relatively well; it's the daily grind that can get us down. "Hassles" are the irritations and frustrations of everyday routines, such as thoughtless roommates, traffic, bad weather, annoying arguments, broken plumbing, lost keys, and sick cats. Some research suggests that hassles are better predictors of psychological and physical symptoms than are life changes (DeLongis et al., 1982). In one study of 75 married couples, the frequency of daily hassles was related to later health problems such as flu, sore throats, headaches, and backaches (DeLongis, Folkman, & Lazarus, 1988).

Of course, a major event, such as divorce, often increases the number of hassles a person must contend with (new financial pressures, custody questions, moving) and might make a person more intolerant of small hassles. By and large, though, people's reports of being hassled are independent of life events. In a study of 210 police officers, the most stressful things they reported were not the dramatic dangers you see on television, but daily paperwork, annoyance with "distorted" accounts of the police in the press, and the snail-like pace of the judicial system (Grier, 1982).

How do you cope with headaches and hassles? These airplane passengers, frustrated about a canceled flight, show the many possible responses to life's annoyances: amused friendliness, sullen acceptance, efforts to get information, and just plain gloom.

Notice, though, that when people report that something is a hassle, they are really reporting their feelings about it. The activity itself might be neutral. A young mother who says that making meals every day is a hassle is revealing her attitudes and emotions about this chore. Perhaps because she has so many other things to do every day, preparing dinner feels to her like the last straw. Her husband might look forward to cooking as an enjoyable way to reduce tension. So the measure of "hassles," like that of "stressful events," may be confounded with existing symptoms of emotional distress (Dohrenwend & Shrout, 1985).

Continuing problems. Many stress researchers believe that people have a good ability to withstand acute (short-term) stress, even a massive blow. The real problem, they say, occurs when stress becomes interminable: working in a pressure-cooker occupation; living with a tyrannical parent; living with discrimination because of your color, religion, gender, or age; feeling trapped in a situation you can't escape.

Under conditions of chronic stress, many people do not show physical adaptation to the stressor. In a study of 34 people who were taking care of a relative with advanced Alzheimer's disease—a relentless source of stress if there ever was one—the caregivers had significantly lower percentages of T lymphocytes and helper T lymphocytes than the control group and showed other abnormalities of the immune system. Their immune systems were apparently not adapting to the chronic stress (Kiecolt-Glaser et al., 1987b).

Prolonged or repeated stress (from occupations such as air traffic controller or from circumstances such as unemployment) is associated with heart disease, hypertension, arthritis, and immune-related deficiencies (Taylor, 1986). Black men in America who live in stressful neighborhoods (characterized by poverty, high divorce and unemployment rates, crime, and drug use) are particularly vulnerable to hypertension and related diseases (Gentry, 1985; Harburg et al., 1973). Female clerical workers who feel they have no support from their bosses, who are stuck in low-paying jobs without hope of promotion, and who have financial problems at home are the women most at risk of heart disease (Haynes & Feinleib, 1980).

A Closer Look at Psychoneuroimmunology

Why Confession Is Good for the Soul — And the Body

Now pay attention: *Don't think of a white bear.* Are you not thinking of it? Anyone who has ever tried to banish an uninvited thought knows how hard it is to erase the mental tape of worries, unhappy memories, or unwished-for obsessions. In an actual study, people who were told not to think of a white bear mentioned it nine times in a five-minute stream-of-consciousness session (Wegner et al., 1987). The reason seems to be that when you are trying to avoid a thought, you are in fact processing the thought frequently—rehearsing it and making it more accessible to consciousness.

According to James Pennebaker and his associates, the prolonged inhibition of thoughts and emotions requires physical effort, which is stressful to the body (Pennebaker, Hughes, & O'Heeron, 1987). Yet many people do try to inhibit secret thoughts and feelings that make them ashamed or depressed. The inability or unwillingness to confide important or traumatic events places continuing stress on the system and can lead to long-term health problems. In study after study, such individuals prove to be at greater risk of illness than people who are able to talk about their tragedies, even though disclosures of traumatic events are often painful and unpleasant at first (Pennebaker, 1988).

This information poses a problem: If an event is stressful and trying to stop thinking about the event is stressful, what should you do? Research from *psychoneuroimmunology*, the growing field that bridges psychology and the immune system, suggests some answers.

In one study, college students were assigned to write about *either* personal, traumatic experiences *or* trivial topics for 20 minutes a day, four days in a row. Those who were asked to reveal "their deepest thoughts and feelings" about a traumatic event all had something to talk about. Many told stories of sexual abuse, physical beatings, emotional humiliation, and parental abandonment. Others described upsetting changes, such as coming to college and the loneliness associated with leaving home. Yet most had never discussed these feelings with anyone.

The researchers took blood samples to test for the immune activity of lymphocytes; they also measured the students' physical symptoms, emotions, and visits to the health center. On every measure, the students who wrote about traumatic experiences were better off than those who did not (Pennebaker, Kiecolt-Glaser, & Glaser, 1988). Some of them showed *short-term* increases in anger and depression; writing about an unpleasant experience was not fun. But as months passed, their physical and emotional well-being improved.

The researchers believe that "the failure to confront a trauma forces the person to live with it in an unresolved manner." Actively writing or talking about it apparently helps people assimilate the tragedy and come to a sense of completion about it. But confession must not turn to obsession. Confessing your "deepest thoughts and feelings" is not therapeutic if you keep rehearsing and confessing them endlessly to all who will listen. The key is physiological release *and* cognitive perspective.

For example, several students who wrote about the same experience day after day gradually gained insight and distance. One woman, who had been molested at the age of 9 by a boy a few years older, at first wrote about her feelings of embarrassment and guilt. By the third day, she was writing about how angry she felt at the boy. By the last day, she had begun to see the whole event differently; he was young too, after all. After the experiment, she said, "Before, when I thought about it, I'd lie to myself. . . . Now, I don't feel like I even have to think about it because I got it off my chest. I finally admitted that it happened."

To see if the research will benefit you, why not keep a diary this year? All you have to do is jot down, from time to time, your "deepest thoughts and feelings" about school, your past, your future, anything. Pennebaker predicts that you will have fewer colds, headaches, and trips to the medical clinic next year.

What is "stressful" about stress?

In general, health psychologists today believe that life changes *are* related to your state of health, although the relationship is weak (Cohen & Edwards, 1989). Something else is going on between the event and your response to it. One of those things, as by now you can guess, is your perception of how stressful an event, a "hassle," or an accumulation of events is. In turn, feeling overwhelmed by stress depends on whether or not you feel you can *control* it. What seems to be most debilitating about chronically stressful situations is the feeling of powerlessness, of having no control over what happens. People can tolerate years of difficulty if they feel they can *control* events or at least *predict* them (Laudenslager & Reite, 1984). These are not necessarily the same thing. You may not be able to control the stressful experience of an exam, but you can usually predict and prepare for it. When people know that they will be going through a hard time or living in a stressful environment, they can take steps to reduce stress. We will return to this important topic of control later.

QUICK ▪ QUIZ

We hope these questions are not sources of stress for you.

1. Steve is unexpectedly called on in class to discuss a question. He doesn't have the faintest idea of the answer, and he feels his heart start to pound and his palms to sweat. He is in the _____ phase of the GAS.
2. Which of the Holmes-Rahe "life-change events" has the strongest relationship to immune problems and illness? **(a)** marriage, **(b)** bereavement, **(c)** taking an exam, **(d)** moving, **(e)** hassles
3. Maria works in a fast-food shop. Which aspect of the job is likely to be *most* stressful for her? **(a)** the speed of the work, **(b)** the predictable routine, **(c)** feeling unable to make any changes in her job, **(d)** the daily demands from customers

Answers:
1. alarm 2. b 3. c

Coping with Stress

We have just discussed different, compelling sources of stress, yet the remarkable fact is that most people who are "under stress" do *not* become ill. Why not? What helps people manage endless hassles and recover from the most awful adversity? How, in short, do they cope? We define **coping** as the constantly changing cognitive and behavioral efforts to manage demands, in the environment or in oneself, that one feels or believes to be stressful (Lazarus & Folkman, 1984). Coping is not a single strategy to be applied at all times and in all circumstances. People cope differently with daily hassles, losses, dangers, or challenges (Feifel, 1985; McCrae, 1984).

Freud argued that the mind develops defenses to protect it from unpleasant

coping *Cognitive and behavioral efforts to manage demands in the environment or oneself that one feels to be stressful.*

How do you cope with inevitable events?

truths, experiences, or conflicts. Because he treated people with problems, his theory implied that defenses are usually unhealthy, maladaptive, and passive. Although clinical psychologists are still concerned with the defenses that keep people unhappy, most health psychologists prefer the term *coping* to reflect a more active, constructive, and sympathetic view of people's efforts to solve their problems.

The many successful ways of coping fall into three general categories: (1) attacking the problem, (2) rethinking the problem, and (3) accepting the problem but lessening the physical effects of its stress (Shaver & O'Connor, 1986). Notice that the first attacks the stressor, the second attacks your interpretation of the stressor, and the third attacks the physical effects of the stress.

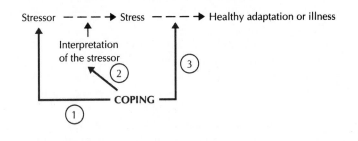

Attacking the problem

A woman we know, whom we will call Nancy, was struck by tragedy when she was 22. She and her new husband were driving home one evening when a car ran out of control and crashed into them. When Nancy awoke in a hospital room, she learned that her husband had been killed instantly. She herself had permanent spinal injury and would never walk again.

For many months, Nancy reacted with rage, despair, and grief. "Get it out of your system," her friends said. "You need to get in touch with your feelings." "But I *know* I'm miserable," Nancy lamented. "What do I *do*?"

What should Nancy do, indeed? Her predicament and her friends' advice point to the difference between *emotion-focused* and *problem-focused* coping (Lazarus & Folkman, 1984). Emotion-focused coping concentrates on changing or managing the emotions the problem has caused, whether anger, anxiety, or grief. Problem-focused coping attacks the problem itself.

The specific steps in problem-focused coping depend on the problem. (You may recall from Chapter 8 some of the stages of problem solving in general.) Sometimes the problem is clear (you lost your job). Sometimes it is uncertain (you suspect, but aren't sure, that you will lose your job). The problem may be a pressing but one-time decision; a continuing difficulty, such as living with a handicap; or an anticipated experience, such as the need to have an operation.

"Defining the problem" may sound easy: You're unhappy at work. But what does that mean? Is the problem your boss, your co-workers, your own attitude, or the work itself? How might your answer affect the way you cope with your unhappiness?

"Defining the problem" may seem obvious, especially when the Problem is standing there yelling at you. However, people often define a problem incorrectly and then set off down a wrong coping road. For example, unhappy couples often blame each other, or "incompatibility," for their misery. Sometimes, of course, they are right. But a study of several hundred couples found that marital unhappiness is often a result of misdiagnosis. A husband who is under great pressure at his office may decide that his problem is an unsupportive wife. A wife who is feeling too many conflicting demands may decide that her problem is her lazy husband. If this couple tries to cope with their unhappiness by attacking each other, they merely increase their misery. If they correctly diagnose the problem ("I'm worried about my job"; "I don't have enough leisure time to myself"), different coping solutions follow (A. Pines, 1986).

Once the problem is identified, the coper can learn as much as possible about it from professionals, friends, books, and others in the same boat. In Nancy's case, she can begin by learning more about her medical condition and prognosis. What can she do for herself? What kind of exercise will help her? How do other accident victims cope? Many people in stressful situations see no hope of escape. They divide their options into "stay here and suffer" versus "leave here and die" (Burns, 1980). What are Nancy's options? She could give up and feel sorry for herself. She could return home to live with her parents. She could learn to care for herself. She could go into the wheelchair business. She could. . . . (In fact, Nancy stayed in school, remarried, got a Ph.D. in psychology, and now does research and counseling with disabled people.)

Problem-focused coping has a large psychological benefit: It tends to increase a person's sense of self-esteem, control, and effectiveness (Pearlin & Schooler, 1978). Sometimes, though, emotions get in the way of assessing a problem accurately. When people are agonizing over a decision, they may, to relieve their anguish, make a fast, impulsive choice. They may say or do something in anger that worsens their predicament, or become so depressed that they cannot evaluate the situation carefully. That is why most people use a combination of emotion- and problem-focused coping (Folkman & Lazarus, 1980).

Rethinking the problem

Your first cognitive response to an event is a general evaluation, in which you decide whether the event is positive, neutral, or threatening and harmful. This global evaluation is followed by your judgment of whether you can handle the situation and, if so, how (Lazarus & Folkman, 1984). One way of coping with problems is to think about them in new ways, and there are several strategies for doing so. Shelley Taylor (1983, 1988), who has worked with cancer and cardiac patients, women who have been raped, and other victims of disaster or disease, finds that rethinking strategies have three goals:

▪ To find *meaning* in the experience: Why did this event happen to me? What does it mean for my life now?
▪ To regain *mastery* over the event and one's life: How can I keep this from happening again? What can I do about it now?
▪ To *restore self-esteem,* to feel good about oneself again in spite of the setback.

Among the many cognitive strategies that people use to reinterpret events, we will consider several of the most effective. (Again, keep in mind that their effectiveness may depend on the problem.)

Reappraisal: "It's not so bad."   When people cannot eliminate a stressor, they can choose to rethink its implications and consequences. Problems can be turned into challenges, losses into unexpected gains. You lost your job. Is that a disaster? Maybe it wasn't such a good job, but you were too afraid to quit to look for another. A study of 100 spinal-cord-injured people found that two-thirds of them felt the disability had had positive side effects (Schulz & Decker, 1985). Benefits included becoming "a better person," "seeing other people as more important," and having an "increased awareness of self" and a new appreciation of "brain, not brawn."

People also reappraise the motives behind the distressing behavior of others. Instead of becoming enraged at someone's actions, for example, the empathic per-

Would you be overwhelmed or challenged by having lots to do?

"My Mom says to come in and have a seat. She's on two lines and has three people on hold."

son tries to see the situation from the other person's standpoint in order to avoid misunderstandings and misperceptions (Miller & Eisenberg, 1988).

Social comparisons: "I'm better off than they are." In her study of women with breast cancer, Taylor (1983) found that successful copers compared themselves to others who were (they felt) less fortunate. This was true regardless of their age, marital status, or severity of the disease.

Thus women who had lumpectomies (removal of the lump itself) compared themselves to women who had the whole breast removed. One woman said, "I had a comparatively small amount of surgery. How awful it must be for women who have had a mastectomy." Yet women who had had mastectomies compared themselves to women whose cancer was far more serious. Said one, "It was not tragic. It's worked out okay. Now, if the thing had spread all over, I would have had a whole different story for you." Younger married women compared themselves to single women ("I can't imagine dating . . . and not knowing how to tell the man about it"), but no single woman felt it would have been easier for her if she had been married. The women who were worst off felt grateful that they were not dying and that they were not in pain. "The point, of course," concludes Taylor, "is that everyone is better off than someone as long as one picks the right dimension."

Avoidance: "It's not important; let's go to the movies." Is it ever a good idea to cope with a problem by ignoring it or running away from it? Suppose you are going to the hospital for routine surgery, such as for a hernia, gall bladder, or thyroid condition. Should you get as much information as you can about every detail and risk of the procedure, or, having decided to go ahead, should you avoid thinking about it?

In a study of this question, researchers divided 61 patients according to their style of coping with a forthcoming operation: "vigilance" or "avoidance" (Cohen & Lazarus, 1973). Avoiders showed a remarkable lack of interest in what was going to happen to them. They said such things as "All I know is that I have a hernia. It doesn't disturb me one bit." They didn't discuss the surgery in detail and said it was nothing to worry about. "Having an operation," said one avoider, "is like having a vacation."

In contrast, the vigilant types attended to every detail. They read articles about their condition and wanted to know everything about the surgery, including the type of incision that would be made and the anesthesia used. They learned about every risk, no matter how remote, and about possible postoperative complications. One patient said, "I have all the facts, my will is prepared . . . your heart could quit, you can have shock."

Some psychologists believe that vigilance is the best strategy, that "the work of worrying" prepares a person to cope with all possible results. In this situation, however, vigilance backfired. The avoiders fared much better. They needed fewer pain medications. They complained less about treatment. They had fewer minor complications such as nausea, headache, fever, or infection. They got out of the hospital sooner.

Many studies have now been done on the difference between people who are vigilant, who scan all information for evidence of threat to themselves, and those who avoid threatening information by distracting themselves (S. Miller, 1987, 1989). There are benefits and disadvantages to both styles of coping. Vigilant individuals, for example, are overly sensitive to their bodily symptoms, tend to exaggerate their importance, and take longer to recover from them (Miller, Brody, & Summerton, 1988). On the other hand, perhaps because they are so health con-

When should you try to leave your problems behind you . . .

When should you cope with a problem by attacking it head-on, and when should you ignore it? Under stress, is it better to be a tiger or an ostrich?

scious, they are more likely to look after themselves—say, by getting routine medical and dental exams.

Once you have all the necessary information to make a decision and that decision is out of your hands, avoidance—letting go of worry—is an excellent coping device. But vigilance is called for when action is possible and necessary. Sometimes both strategies can work together. In a hospital, for example, patients do best if they refuse to dwell on every little thing that could go wrong, if they distract themselves as much as possible. They also get well faster (and protect themselves) when they are vigilant about the care they are getting, when they protest incorrect or thoughtless treatment. The benefits of distraction do not mean you should lie there like a flounder and passively accept every decision made for you.

Of course, some people do more than ''distract'' themselves when they cope with a stressful situation; they deny it altogether. Is denial ever good for you? See ''Think About It.''

Humor: ''People are funny.'' ''A merry heart doeth good like a medicine,'' says Proverbs, and researchers are beginning to agree. Once thought too frivolous a topic for serious study, humor has made its way into the laboratory. Rod Martin and Herbert Lefcourt (1983) gave people tests to measure stress, mood, and sense of humor. ''Sense of humor'' includes the ability to respond with humor in real situations, to like humor and humorous people, and to use humor in coping with stress.

. . . and when should you laugh about them?

Martin and Lefcourt found that humor makes an excellent buffer between stress and negative moods. What's so funny about misery? ''He who laughs,'' thundered the German poet and dramatist Bertolt Brecht, ''has not heard the terrible news.'' But people who can transform the ''terrible news'' into a sense of the absurd or the whimsical, Martin and Lefcourt found, are less prone to depression, anger, tension, and fatigue than are people who give in to gloom. Supporting studies with more than 1000 college students found the same thing. Among students coping with unfortunate events, those who respond with humor feel fewer negative emotions and unhappiness later than do students who don't have a sense of humor or who instead succumb to moping and tears (Labott & Martin, 1986; Nezu, Nezu, & Blissett, 1988).

Some theories of laughter emphasize its ability to reduce tension and emotion. You have probably been in a tense group situation when someone suddenly made exactly the right crack to defuse the mood and make everyone laugh. Laughter seems to produce some beneficial biological responses, possibly stimulating the immune system or starting the flow of endorphins, the painkilling chemicals in the brain (Fry, 1986; J. Goldstein, 1987).

Other theories emphasize the cognitive components of humor. When you laugh at a problem, you are putting it in a new perspective—seeing its silly aspects—and gaining control over it (Dixon, 1980). Humor also allows you to express indirectly feelings that are hazardous to express directly, which is why it is so often the weapon of minorities. An old joke tells of a Jew who accidentally bumped into a Nazi on a street. ''Swine!'' bellowed the Nazi. ''And I'm Cohen,'' replied the Jew, ''pleased to meet you.''

Having a sense of humor, however, is not the same as smiling all the time or ''putting on a happy face.'' Many women, in particular, feel they have to smile, smile, smile, to put others at ease, but often this social smile masks feelings of insecurity and unhappiness (Frances, 1979). For humor to be effective in coping with stress, a person must actually use it during a stressful situation—seeing or inventing funny aspects of serious events and having the ability to laugh at them (Nezu, Nezu, & Blissett, 1988). Hostile humor therefore misses the point: Vicious,

Think About It

Are Illusions Healthy?

Denial is certainly a common response to stress: "This isn't happening to me"; "It is happening to me, but it isn't important"; "If I ignore it, the problem will go away." Since Freud, many psychologists have regarded denial as a primitive, dangerous defense mechanism that meant a person was out of touch with reality. And being out of touch with reality has long been assumed to be a hallmark of mental illness. Now some researchers are asking: When reality serves up a problem you can't do anything about, what's so bad about losing touch with it?

Emotionally healthy people supposedly are good at "reality testing" and do not need self-promoting illusions; they can face the truth about themselves. Today, the weight of evidence has shifted to the opposite view. After reviewing years of research, Shelley E. Taylor and Jonathon D. Brown (1988) conclude that well-being virtually depends on the illusions of "overly positive self-evaluations, exaggerated perceptions of control or mastery, and unrealistic optimism." These illusions, Taylor (1989) argues, are not only characteristic of normal human thought, but also necessary for the usual criteria of mental health: the ability to

care about others, the ability to be contented, and the ability to work productively. In fact, the people who score *highest* on tests of self-deception (for example, who deny threatening but universal feelings, such as ever having felt guilty) score the *lowest* on measures of psychopathology and depression!

Why should this be so? The mind is designed to filter all incoming information, say Taylor and Brown, distorting it in a positive direction to enhance self-esteem and ward off bad news. Positive illusions, they find, are especially useful under conditions of adversity—when people are threatened with illness, crisis, or attacks to their self-esteem. This strategy is adaptive and healthy, because if people judged their problems accurately, they might fold their tents and give up. In a situation in which your abilities are untested, as William James noted long ago, it is much more beneficial to try and possibly succeed than not to try at all.

On the other hand, health psychologists worry about the many self-destructive things that denial permits people to do: They drink too much, they smoke, they won't wear their seat belts, they don't take medication for chronic illness. When people

rude jokes at another person's expense are not stress reducers. They often create more tension and anger (Baron, 1977).

Living with the problem

In modern life, we often cannot escape life changes, ongoing conflicts, or the hassles of traffic, noise, or job or school pressure (see "Taking Psychology with You"). A third approach to coping concentrates on reducing the physical effects of stress itself.

Relaxation. The simplest way to reduce signs of stress, such as high blood pressure and rapid breathing, is to relax. Relaxation training—learning to alternately tense and relax certain muscles, to lie or sit quietly, to banish worries of the day—apparently has beneficial effects on the immune system. In a sample of 45 elderly people living in retirement homes, those who learned to reduce stress with relaxation techniques showed significant increases in natural killer (NK) cell activity and decreases in antibodies to herpes simplex virus, both signs of improved immune activity (Kiecolt-Glaser et al., 1985b).

make important decisions about themselves that are based on denial and self-flattering illusions, the results can be disastrous. It is dangerous when a woman ignores a lump in her breast, when a man having a heart attack says "it's only indigestion," when a diabetic fails to take needed medication.

Moreover, the illusion of invulnerability—"it will never happen to me"—can lead people to do all sorts of dangerous and stupid things. So strong is this illusion that it even affects people who should know better. The former Olympic diver Bruce Kimball, whose face and body were smashed in a car accident, recovered sufficiently to win a silver medal in the 1984 Olympics. But in 1988 he got blind drunk and careened his car into a group of teenagers, killing two and seriously injuring six.

Further, illusions are not necessarily beneficial if they keep people from recognizing their limitations. How long should you keep trying to join the major leagues if you just aren't a great ball player? People need to know when to quit, and what they can't do as well as what they can (Janoff-Bulman, 1988). People who overestimate their chances of success may spend excessive, wasteful years trying

to become something they are not (Baumeister & Scher, 1988). As W. C. Fields once observed, "If at first you don't succeed, try, try again. If you still don't succeed, quit. No use being a damn fool about it."

What happens when people must reconcile their former illusions with a traumatic event that cannot be ignored? The result is often, literally, dis-illusion (Janoff-Bulman, 1988). Some victims never return to their former illusions; they see the world as less benevolent and less meaningful than it had been and themselves as less worthy. Unable to create positive illusions, they often become depressed, anxious, and hopeless. Others do eventually reestablish a positive view of the world and themselves, finding new meaning in the tragedy (Collins, Taylor, & Skokan, in press).

What is the line between "healthy illusions"—those that maintain self-esteem and optimism—and self-destructive ones? How would you know which is which? Is it better to maintain illusions at all costs, if they protect your self-esteem, or to think critically about them and risk losing optimism? What do you think?

Some people learn to relax through systematic *meditation*, a practice aimed at focusing one's attention and eliminating all distracting thoughts. Short-term meditation does not produce a unique physiological or emotional state; studies find no difference between meditation and simple resting (D. Holmes, 1984; Holmes et al., 1983). In Eastern religions like Hinduism and Buddhism, however, meditation is much more than a relaxation or stress-reduction technique. The goal is not to unwind but to attain wisdom, acceptance of reality, emotional detachment, and transcendence of the self—states of mind not measurable on an EEG machine.

In a review of relaxation methods, two researchers found that methods that work for one person or one kind of problem may not be as successful with others (Woolfolk & Lehrer, 1984). For example, relaxation is helpful in reducing the pain of menstrual cramps if the pain is caused by muscle cramps and not fluid retention. Some people benefit from cognitive therapy or self-hypnosis, as well as relaxation, to learn to calm tense thoughts as well as tense muscles (see Chapter 17). And although biofeedback is often promoted as a stress-reducer, simple relaxation is just as effective, and a lot cheaper (Turner & Chapman, 1982a).

Exercise. Physical exercise, such as jogging, dancing, biking, and swimming, is very important in maintaining health and reducing stress (Hayden, 1984;

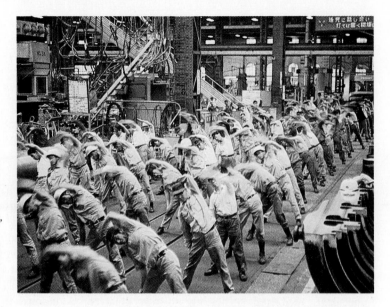

Exercise has many all-around health benefits, which is why some American companies are adopting the Japanese practice of scheduling exercise breaks for workers. Should exercise be a formal and required part of the work-day?

Taylor, 1986). An invigorating workout can leave you feeling refreshed and ener-getic—a nonhostile, nonaggressive workout, that is. People who think angry, com-petitive thoughts while they are exercising are, in effect, adding fuel to the fire (France, 1984).

Exercise is great, but is it a cure-all? When does it help you alleviate your problems, and when does it become an excuse to escape them?

Besides reducing tension, exercise combats anxiety, depression, and the blues. In one study of 43 college women, all moderately to severely depressed, researchers assigned the students to one of three groups. One group did aerobic exercise three times a week, another practiced relaxation and took leisurely walks four times a week, and a control group did neither. After five weeks and again after ten weeks, the women took tests of their aerobic capacity and level of depression. Those who exercised vigorously showed improved fitness and sharp declines in depression; the relaxation and control groups didn't reduce their depression levels (McCann & Holmes, 1984). Similarly, a study of 207 Denver workers found that the more these employees exercised, the fewer physical symptoms, colds, and stresses, and the less anxiety, depression, and irritability, they reported (Hendrix & Rodriguez, 1984).

Many popular books and magazines therefore advocate exercise as the all-purpose coping strategy. There is no doubt that regular exercise is an excellent all-around health tonic. But people who exercise in order to *avoid* their problems are not necessarily reducing their stress load, especially if they have to go back to the same old problem tomorrow. In one study of 230 working women, the strongest predictor of depression, anxiety, and physical stress was difficulty at work. The form of coping that helped best was dealing with the job problems directly (O'Neill & Zeichner, 1984). You can't, it seems, jog away from everything.

Looking outward

A psychologist who has worked with Holocaust survivors, prisoners of war, hos-tages, refugees, and other survivors of catastrophe believes that a key element in their recovery is compassion, ''healing through helping'' (Segal, 1986). People gain strength, he says, by giving it to others.

This observation echoes Alfred Adler's theory of *social interest* (see Chapter

11). To Adler (1938/1964), social interest has a cognitive component (the ability to understand others, to see the connectedness of humanity and the world), an emotional component (the ability to feel empathy and attachment), and a behavioral component (the willingness to cooperate with others for the common welfare). Although "social interest" is the opposite of selfishness, it is harmonious with self-interest. Adler believed that people who are involved with others, unlike those who are too self-involved, would be better able to cope with life's problems, have higher self-esteem, and be psychologically stronger (Ansbacher, 1968).

Adler's ideas have been supported. One large study used two measures of social interest: a scale of moral values and an index of cooperation in love, work, and friendship. People who were high in social interest, compared to others, had fewer stressful experiences and were better able to cope with the stressful episodes they did have. Among people low in social interest, stress was more likely to be associated with anxiety, depression, and hostility. Social interest seems to soften the effects of stress on psychological well-being (Crandall, 1984).

Why is social interest healthy? The ability to look outside of oneself, to be concerned with others, is related to virtually all of the successful coping mechanisms we have discussed so far. It tends to lead to solving problems instead of blaming others. It helps you reappraise a conflict, trying to see it as others do, instead of taking it personally. It allows you to get perspective on a problem instead of exaggerating its importance. Because of its elements of forgiveness, tolerance, and sense of connectedness, it helps you live with situations that are facts of life.

QUICK ▪ QUIZ

Can you cope with these refresher questions?

1. You accidentally broke your glasses. Which response is an example of cognitive reappraisal? **(a)** "I am such a stupid clumsy idiot!" **(b)** "I never do anything right." **(c)** "What a shame, but I've been wanting new frames anyway." **(d)** "I'll forget about it in aerobics class."
2. Finding out what your legal and financial resources are when you have been victimized by a crime is an example of **(a)** problem-focused coping, **(b)** emotion-focused coping, **(c)** distraction, **(d)** reappraisal.
3. Learning deep-breathing techniques to reduce anxiety in taking exams is an example of **(a)** problem-focused coping, **(b)** emotion-focused coping, **(c)** avoidance, **(d)** reappraisal.
4. "This class drives me crazy, but it's better than not being in school" is an example of **(a)** distraction, **(b)** social comparison, **(c)** denial, **(d)** empathy.
5. Your roommate has turned your room into a bomb crater, filled with rotten apple cores and unwashed clothes. Should you **(a)** nag, **(b)** start a quarrel, **(c)** resentfully clean the room yourself, **(d)** pile everything into a heap, put a flag on top, and add a sign: "Monument to the Battle of the Bilge"?

Answers:
1. c 2. a 3. b 4. b 5. d

The Individual Side of Health and Well-Being

Up to now, we have been discussing strategies that anyone can use in reducing the effects of stress. But people differ in how well they are able to cope and in what they do to protect their health. We now turn to four aspects of individual psychology that are related to health: negative emotions, "explanatory style," healthy habits, and locus of control.

Negative emotions

Efforts to document the relationship between emotion and disease go back many centuries, and today many people speak as if the connection were proven: Worriers get ulcers; irritable workaholics get heart attacks; asthmatics are emotionally repressed. Certainly it seems that some people manufacture their own misery. Send them to a beach far from civilization, and they bring along a bag of worries and irritations. But the connections between emotion and health are not simple.

An initial attempt to identify one of those connections focused on the *Type A behavior pattern*, a set of qualities that seemed to increase the risk of heart disease, the nation's leading cause of death (Friedman & Rosenman, 1974). Although Type A has been measured in different, often inconsistent ways, it basically refers to a constant struggle to achieve, a sense of time urgency, impatience at anyone or anything that gets in the way, irritability, and an intense effort to control the environment. Type B people are calmer and less intense. Researchers were excited about the Type A hypothesis, and so was the public. People began talking about what "type" they were and whether they could or should change it.

Today, however, the enthusiasm about Type A is a mere shadow of its former self. It turns out that different tasks and situations produce different physiological responses in the same people, and being highly reactive to stress and challenge is not in itself a risk factor in heart disease (Krantz & Manuck, 1984). Type A people *do* set themselves a fast work pace and a heavy work load, but many cope better than Type B people who have a lighter work load, and without a high physiological price (Frankenhaeuser, 1980). Further, people who are highly involved in their jobs, even if they work hard, have a low incidence of heart disease. "There'd be nothing wrong with us fast-moving Type A's," said a friend of ours, "if it weren't for all those slow-moving Type B's."

Nevertheless, something about Type A may be dangerous to one's health. Which aspects of the Type A pattern are unhealthy, and which are fine? One research team distinguished between two groups of ambitious, fast-moving people often called Type A: the "healthy charismatics," who are expressive, active, friendly, and relaxed, and the "hostile competitives," who are angry, tense, and defensive (Friedman, Hall, & Harris, 1985). As psychologists delved into the puzzle of Type A, they found that its hazardous ingredients are likely to be anger, anxiety, and depression (Friedman & Booth-Kewley, 1987a, 1987b). For example, men who are chronically angry and resentful and who have a hostile attitude toward others are *five times* as likely as nonhostile men to get coronary heart disease and other ailments, controlling for other risk factors such as smoking (Williams, 1989; Williams, Barefoot, & Shekelle, 1985).

Even then, not all kinds of hostility have turned out to be equally hazardous to

When you're under a lot of pressure, do you take it out on others?

health. *Neurotic hostility*, which describes people who are grumpy, complaining, and irritable, is *not* related to heart disease. (It seems to be part of the general personality trait of neuroticism, described in Chapter 11.) But *antagonistic hostility*, describing people who are aggressive, rude, confronting, cynical, and uncooperative, is, researchers find, the ''toxic'' hostility that is linked to heart disease (Dembroski & Costa, 1988). You can see, therefore, the importance of defining terms, such as ''anger'' and ''hostility,'' carefully.

Howard S. Friedman and Stephanie Booth-Kewley (1987a) took the next step, asking whether negative emotions are related to specific diseases. They selected several emotions or personality traits that have been implicated in illness (anger, hostility, depression, introversion, and anxiety) and five diseases believed to have psychological components (asthma, arthritis, ulcers, headaches, and heart disease). The researchers used a sophisticated statistical method to combine and summarize the results of 101 studies. To their surprise, they failed to find specific, disease-connected traits, such as the arthritic personality or the coronary-prone personality or the anger-suppressing ulcer patient. But the researchers did find evidence for a ''generic, disease-prone personality'' who is chronically depressed, angry and hostile, and anxious. Depression was most strongly implicated in four of the five diseases, excluding ulcers.

Before concluding that emotions or personality traits directly cause illness, Friedman and Booth-Kewley (1987b) observed that there are other possible links between personality and disease:

▪ *The disease causes the emotion*. Many psychotherapists and physicians see patients who are angry, depressed, or anxious because they are sick. It is an easy jump to the (wrong) conclusion that the anger, depression, or anxiety *caused* the sickness. In addition, some diseases or abnormalities, such as brain tumors or an oxygen deficiency, can directly cause mood change (see Chapter 16).

▪ *Unhealthy habits cause the disease*. Before you could conclude that ''an anxious personality style causes lung cancer,'' you would have to rule out the possibility that people who feel anxious are more likely to smoke or drink. Unfortunately, many studies that examine the links between personality and disease do not take health habits into account.

▪ *Something else entirely affects emotion* and *disease*. Another possibility is that some third factor is related both to an emotional style and a disease. For example, perhaps an overresponsive nervous system leads to the development of frequent anger and, independently, to the development of heart disease.

▪ *Personality leads to disease, which affects personality, which affects disease: the mind-body system*. A single personality trait or emotion rarely is ''the cause'' of disease. But chronic anxiety could lead to unhealthy practices, which could cause physical changes (influenced in turn by genetic makeup), which could make one's anxiety worse, which could keep one from taking care of oneself, which in turn. . . .

It is therefore one thing to say that emotions or personality factors are *involved* in illness. It is quite another to say that they *cause* illness. ''Personality may function like diet,'' the researchers concluded. ''Imbalances can predispose one to all sorts of diseases.'' Psychological disturbances affect the immune system *in general*, they observed. The occurrence of a *specific* illness depends on other factors, such as whether a person drinks excessively or smokes, the person's genetic vulnerabilities, and the biology of the disease itself.

If sick people are angrier than others, does that mean that anger caused their illnesses? Can you think of other explanations for a relationship between emotions and disease?

Studies suggest that explanatory style affects longevity. Zack Wheat, an outfielder for the Brooklyn Dodgers, had an optimistic explanatory style: "I'm a better hitter than I used to be because my strength has improved and my experience has improved." Wheat lived to be 83.

Explanatory style

Perhaps you remember from Chapter 9 the habits of thinking associated with depression. Depressed people tend to explain uncontrollable events as internal ("It's all my fault"), stable ("This misery is going to last forever"), and global ("It's going to affect everything I do"). Cheerful people regard the same events as external ("I couldn't have done anything about it"), unstable ("Things will improve"), and limited in impact ("Well, at least the rest of my life is OK").

Christopher Peterson and Martin Seligman (1984, 1987) call these characteristic ways of accounting for bad events *explanatory style*, and they observe that these two styles of thinking describe the difference between pessimists and optimists. Their research suggests that an optimistic explanatory style is related to self-esteem, achievement, and physical health and longevity (Peterson, 1988). Pessimists will probably complain that optimism is just a *result* of good health; it's easy to think positively when you feel good. But there is growing evidence that optimism may produce good health as well as reflect it.

In one imaginative study of baseball Hall-of-Famers who had played between 1900 and 1950, 30 players were rated according to their explanatory style. A pessimistic remark would be internal, stable, and global, such as "We didn't win because my arm is shot, it'll never get better, and it affects my performance every time." An optimistic version would be external, unstable, and specific: "We didn't win because we got a couple of lousy calls, just bad luck on this game, but we'll be great tomorrow." The optimists were significantly more likely to have lived well into old age than were the pessimists (Seligman, 1986).

What could be the link between pessimism and illness? One answer is that pessimism produces depression and stress, which in turn affect the immune system. High degrees of pessimism are independently associated with impaired immune activity (Rodin, 1988). This means that pessimists do not fall ill because they are sicker or more depressed to begin with. A longitudinal study of Harvard University graduates started out with young men who were in good health. But 35 years later,

Walter Johnson, a star pitcher for the Washington Senators, had a pessimistic explanatory style: "I can't depend on myself to pitch well. I'm growing old. I have had my day." Johnson died at the age of 59.

those who had had a pessimistic explanatory style were in significantly worse health than the optimists (Peterson, Seligman, & Vaillant, 1988).

A second explanation may have to do with how people cope with stress. Optimists tend to be problem-focused rather than emotion-focused. When faced with a problem, such as a risky operation or a serious continuing struggle with alcoholism, they focus on what they can *do* rather than on how they *feel*. They have a higher expectation of being successful, so they don't give up at the first sign of a setback (Carver & Scheier, 1987; Peterson & Barrett, 1987). Perhaps, then, pessimists are more likely to become ill because they stir up negative emotions rather than take constructive action.

Third, pessimists often fail to take care of themselves (on the belief, we suppose, that it won't do any good). When they develop colds or flu, for example, they are less likely than optimists to take the basic precautions: sleeping more, drinking fluids, not overdoing it. Perhaps this is why their colds and flu are more likely to return (Peterson & Seligman, 1987).

Can pessimism be "cured"? Optimists, naturally, think so. Cognitive therapy has been remarkably successful in teaching depressed people new explanatory styles (see Chapter 17). Psychologist Rachel Hare-Mustin told us how her mother cured her budding childhood pessimism—with humor. "Nobody likes me," Rachel lamented. "Don't say that," her mother said. "Everybody hasn't met you yet."

Healthy habits

We bet you $100 that you already know the basic rules for protecting your health: get enough sleep, get regular exercise, eat a nutritious diet, drink alcohol only in moderation, do not overeat, do not undereat (on starvation diets), and do not smoke cigarettes. A ten-year longitudinal study of nearly 7000 people in Alameda County, California, found that each of these practices was independently related to good health and lack of stress symptoms (Matarazzo, 1984; Wiley & Camacho, 1980).

The more of these practices people followed, the better their mental and physical health.

Well, why aren't you following all of them? Health psychologists study one of the perplexing riddles of human behavior: why, when people know what is good for them, they often don't do it. An important goal of health psychology is prevention: helping people eliminate the risk factors for illness before the illness has a chance to develop. One goal is to get people to change their unhealthy habits—to get them to quit smoking, say, or to cut down on junk food. Another goal is to keep people from developing the bad habits in the first place, for example, by demonstrating the dangers of smoking to preadolescent children. But health psychologists have found several obstacles in their pursuit of prevention (Taylor, 1986):

▪ Many health habits are entrenched in childhood, and parents play a powerful role in determining a child's health habits. For example, they determine what children learn about alcohol—whether to drink in moderation or go on "binges"—and what kind of food is best. It will be hard for you to give up a high-cholesterol diet if you associate it with home-cooked meals.

▪ People often have little incentive to change unhealthy habits. Smoking, drinking, eating junk food, and not exercising have no immediate consequences, and their effects might not become apparent for years. So many people in good health feel invulnerable.

▪ Health habits are largely independent of one another. Some people exercise every day and continue to smoke. Some people eat nutritious meals and take a lot of drugs.

▪ Health habits are unstable over time. Some people quit smoking for a year—and then take it up again. Others lose 50 pounds—and then gain 60.

In spite of these obstacles, health psychologists have identified many factors that influence your health habits. Some are in your social system: Do all your friends smoke and drink themselves into a stupor on weekends? Chances are that you will join them. Some are in your larger cultural environment: Does your culture think it is appropriate for women to exercise or for men to stop eating red meat? Some are in your access to health care services and information: Not everybody in this society has the affluence, insurance, or opportunity to consult doctors. Finally, some are in your basic attitudes and beliefs: Do you feel fatalistic about illness or in charge of your health?

The question of control: Fight or flow?

In Chapter 11 we described *internal and external* **locus of control**: People who feel that they are in charge of their lives (with an internal locus of control) often deal more effectively with problems and decisions than people who lack this sense of mastery (those with an external locus of control). "Internals" adjust their coping efforts to suit the problem, selecting the appropriate tactic from a range of possibilities (Parkes, 1984). People who feel powerless ("externals") tend to respond to stress with anger, depression, drug use, or physical symptoms (Langer, 1983). All of the factors we have discussed so far—negative emotions, pessimism, poor health habits, and an inability to cope—may in turn be related to this basic personality factor: feeling in control of one's life.

locus of control *A general expectation about whether the results of one's actions are under one's own control* (internal *locus) or beyond one's control* (external *locus).*

The benefits of control. Some years ago, a team of psychologists followed 259 business managers for five years, comparing those who developed illnesses with those who did not (Kobasa, 1979; Kobasa, Maddi, & Kahn, 1982). The healthy group turned out to have what the researchers called "hardy" personalities. "Hardiness" had three components: *commitment*, the feeling of attachment to one's activities and relationships; *challenge*, the willingness to accept new experiences, to see opportunities in change rather than losses; and *control*, the belief that one can influence most events and other people.

Like Type A, hardiness was a concept that almost immediately achieved great popular appeal. It sounded so right. However, the three components turn out to be largely independent of one another, and "challenge" is not directly related to health at all. Moreover, it is not the *presence* of commitment and control that lead to health; it is the *lack* of commitment and *lack* of control in specific situations that can be harmful (Funk & Houston, 1987; Hull, Van Treuren, & Virnelli, 1987). All things considered, the benefits of hardiness appear to be accounted for by the more general factor, locus of control (Cohen & Edwards, 1989).

The sense of being in control need not be enormous to be effective. When elderly residents of nursing homes are simply given more choices over their activities and environment and given more control over day-to-day events, the results are dramatic: They become more alert, more active, happier—and less likely to die (Langer, 1983; Langer et al., 1979).

Locus of control has many effects on mind and body. As we saw in Chapter 5, it is related to a person's appraisal that he or she can cope with pain (Litt, 1988). Control also influences how people experience and label their physical sensations: Is that twinge or cough a sign of something serious? In experiments that vary the amount of control people have over what happens to them, subjects given low or no control report more physical symptoms than those who feel more in control (Pennebaker, 1982). The sense of control also directly affects the neuroendocrine and immune systems. This fact may explain why an improved sense of control is so beneficial to old people, whose immune systems normally decline (Rodin, 1988).

Keep in mind, though, that the sense of control is not all in your head. It is also in your social circumstances, income, and status. Working-class people, for instance, have both less sense of control *and* worse health than more affluent people do. Moreover, the path between control and health runs in two directions. Control does affect health, but health also affects how much control you feel you have (Rodin, 1988).

Some problems with control. In general, a sense of control is a good thing. But believing that an event is controllable does not always lead to a reduction in stress, and believing that an event is uncontrollable does not always lead to an increase in stress (Folkman, 1984; S. Thompson, 1981). The question must always be asked: Control over what? If an unrealistically confident person tries to control the uncontrollable ("I'm going to be a movie star in 60 days!"), the resulting failure may lead to unrealistic helplessness (Fleming, Baum, & Singer, 1984). In one study of 45 adults, those who had the strongest internal locus of control were the most vulnerable to stressful events that were out of their control, as measured by their immune functioning (Kubitz, Peavey, & Moore, 1985).

It also doesn't help people to believe they have control over an event if they then feel unable to cope with it. Victims of abuse or other crimes, for example, often suffer because they blame themselves for having "provoked" their attackers, as if they could have controlled the criminal's behavior (Janoff-Bulman, 1988).

What, then, can we conclude about the importance of control to health? One answer comes from a psychologist we know, who once asked a Buddhist monk how to manage stress. The monk laughed. "The very question is the problem," he said. "Americans are always to trying to 'manage' and 'control' everything, as if one's

In general, it's good to feel in control of your life, but what does that mean exactly? Control over what? How much of your life? How do the events in your life affect your sense of control?

Sometimes life dishes up a disaster, as it has for many farm families who have lost their lands and livelihoods because of the changing economy. When is it helpful to believe we can control everything that happens to us, and when is it harmful?

feelings were unruly parts of nature that required taming.'' ''Management'' is a business term, he told our friend, and ''hardiness'' is a concept better suited to the pioneer life than to modern times. Buddhists believe that change and death are inevitable. Anyone who fails to recognize this truth, they say, cannot be healthy or at peace (Shaver & O'Connor, 1986).

Eastern and Western approaches both offer ways of feeling in control of one's life, but they are different ways and different kinds of control. In **primary control**, people try to influence existing reality by changing other people, circumstances, or events. In **secondary control**, people try to accommodate to external reality by changing their own perceptions, goals, or desires (Rothbaum, Weisz, & Snyder, 1982). By and large, the Western approach has been to aim for primary control: If you don't like something, change it, fix it, or fight it. The Eastern approach has been to emphasize secondary control: If you have a problem, learn to live with it or act in spite of it. In a comparison of the United States and Japan, one study found that these two perspectives influence practices in child rearing, socialization, religion, work, and psychotherapy (Weisz, Rothbaum, & Blackburn, 1984).

A Japanese psychologist offers some examples of Japanese proverbs that teach the benefits of yielding to the inevitable (Azuma, 1984): *To lose is to win* (giving in, to protect the harmony of a relationship, demonstrates the superior traits of tolerance, self-control, and generosity); *Willow trees do not get broken by piled up snow* (no matter how many problems pile up in your life, flexibility will allow you to survive them); and *The true tolerance is to tolerate the intolerable* (some ''intolerable'' situations are facts of life, and you do better to accept them than to protest uselessly). Perhaps you can imagine how long ''to lose is to win'' would survive on an American football field, or how long most Americans would be prepared to tolerate the intolerable!

The point is not that one form of control is better or healthier than the other, but rather that both have their place. The emphasis on primary control encourages self-expression, independence, and change, at a possible price of self-absorption and loneliness. The emphasis on secondary control leads to continuity, attachment, and serenity, at a possible price of self-denial and stagnation (Iga, 1986). Most problems require us to choose between trying to change what we can and accepting what we cannot. Perhaps a secret of healthy control lies in knowing the difference.

primary control *An effort to modify external reality by changing other people, the situation, or events; a ''fighting-back'' method of coping.*

secondary control *An effort to accept external reality by changing one's own attitudes, goals, or emotions; a ''learn to live with it'' method of coping.*

QUICK ▪ QUIZ

Do not interpret these questions as stressful:

1. Which of the following aspects of Type A behavior seem most hazardous to health? **(a)** working hard, **(b)** being in a hurry, **(c)** antagonistic hostility, **(d)** high physical reactivity, **(e)** neurotic hostility
2. "I'll never find anyone else to love because I'm not good-looking; that one romance was a fluke" illustrates a(n) _____ explanatory style.
3. Adapting yourself to the reality that you are getting older is an example of _____ control.
4. Joining a protest against sexual harassment on the job is an example of _____ control.

Answers:

1. c 2. pessimistic 3. secondary 4. primary

The Social Side of Health and Well-Being

Thus far we have been looking at individual factors involved in stress and illness. But health and well-being are not just up to you as an individual. They also depend on the people around you.

The Alameda County health study that we mentioned earlier (which followed nearly 7000 adults for a decade) also investigated the importance of social relationships to health. The researchers considered four kinds of social ties: marriage, contact with friends and relatives, church membership, and participation in other groups. The people who had few social networks were more likely to have died at the time of the ten-year follow-up than those who had many (Berkman & Syme, 1979).

Perhaps the people who died were sicker to begin with or had poorer health habits, which kept them from socializing? No. The importance of social networks was unrelated to physical health at the time the study began, to socioeconomic status, and to such risk factors as smoking.

Perhaps the people who died had some undiagnosed illness at the beginning of the study? This interpretation was possible because the study was based on the participants' self-reports. So the research was repeated with nearly 3000 people in Tecumseh, Michigan, and this time the investigators collected everyone's medical exams. Ten years later, those who had few social relationships were more likely to have died than the people who had many, even after age, health, and other risk factors were taken into account (House, 1986; House, Robbins, & Metzner, 1982).

As psychologists explored the benefits of friends and family, they noticed something else. Sometimes friends and family are themselves the source of hassles, headaches, and conflicts. There are two sides to the human need for social support.

When friends help you cope . . .

One psychologist calls friendship a form of "assisted coping": Friends help you deal with problems when you are too drained to budge (Thoits, 1984). By "friends" we mean family members, neighbors, co-workers, and anyone else in your social network.

Friends can be our greatest sources of warmth, support, and fun . . .

Friends do many "supportive" things. They provide *emotional support*, such as concern and affection. They offer *cognitive guidance*, helping you evaluate problems and plan a course of action. They offer *tangible support*, with resources and services such as loaning money or the car, or taking notes in class for you when you have to go to the doctor. They offer companionship (Rook, 1987). Perhaps most of all, they give you the feeling of attachment to others, of being part of a network that cares (Hobfoll & Stephens, in press; Sarason et al., 1987).

The effect of friends on your health depends on what the friends are doing for you and how much stress you are under. In studying a representative sample of more than 2000 adults, Karen Rook (1987) found that for people with *average*, everyday levels of stress, social support had no effect on health one way or the other. Among people who had *above*-average levels of stress, support from friends did help reduce their physical and emotional symptoms. But among people who had *below*-average levels of stress, such support was actually harmful. It was associated with more symptoms! Why might this be so? When people are going through a series of disasters, Rook believes, they need friends who can offer advice, assistance, and reassurance. But talking too much about daily, trivial nuisances may simply reward people's distress rather than helping them manage it.

Of course, individuals and cultures differ in how many friends and relations are needed for well-being. Mexican-Americans, for example, rely on their extended families for emotional support much more than Anglo-Americans do, and they show more anxiety when separated from them. Anglos have more casual networks—even listing co-workers among those they depend on—than do Mexican-Americans (Griffith, 1983).

Cultures also differ in the value they place on friends and family. Anglo-Americans value quick friendliness and sociability, a result perhaps of frequent moves and life changes, but in many other cultures friendship develops slowly. It takes a long time to flower, but then it blooms for life. The difference between Japanese and

. . . and also sources of exasperation, headaches, and pressure.

American culture shows clearly in the reactions to the proverb ''A rolling stone gathers no moss.'' To Americans, it means keep moving; don't let anything cling to you. To the Japanese, it means stay where you are; if you keep moving you will never acquire the beauty of stability (Syme, 1982).

. . . And coping with friends

Your neighbor tells you that your closest friend has betrayed your confidence. You ask a friend for help, and he says, ''Sorry—I'm too busy right now.'' You're in the middle of describing your most recent unhappy date, and your friend says, ''Oh, quit whining.'' You're in the hospital recovering from major surgery, and your closest friend never shows up for a visit.

As most of us learn, friends and relatives can be stress producing as well as stress reducing. They are often sources of hassles, quarrels, and conflicts (Kanner et al., 1981). When disaster or serious illness strikes, friends may blunder around, not knowing what to do or say. Cancer victims report that they are often upset and distressed by the well-meaning but unhelpful reassurances from their families and friends that ''all will be fine.'' They often feel better talking to other cancer patients (Dunkel-Schetter, 1984). Other stressful aspects of friendship include:

▪ *The contagion effect.* Helping a depressed or troubled friend may rub off, making you depressed and troubled too (Albrecht & Adelman, 1984). In serious situations, groups can create a ''pressure cooker effect.'' In one study of Israeli women whose husbands were away at war, talking with others and listening to rumors exaggerated their feelings of danger and helplessness (Hobfoll & London, 1986).

▪ *Network stress*. A friend's problems may become your problems and sources of stress. People are nearly as upset about events that happen to their friends and relatives as they are about things that happen to themselves (Eckenrode & Gore, 1981).

▪ *The burdens of care*. If too many people in your life require your energy and support, you can become stressed and exhausted.

Do the benefits of friendship outweigh the costs, or do they balance each other out? Do most people keep a sort of running balance sheet (''Well, Hildegard is a fussbudget, but she's very loyal'')? To find out, Karen Rook (1984a, 1984b) interviewed 120 older women, expecting to find that social support would balance social conflicts. She thought that the women would overlook their friends' misbehavior by remembering all their good deeds. Not a chance. Rook found that emotional well-being was affected more by having *problems* with friends than by having their *support*! Hassles, conflicts, and disappointments lowered the women's well-being more than the friends' good deeds elevated their well-being. It's not that stress makes you more critical of your friends, by the way. Friends who do the wrong thing are an independent source of aggravation and worry (Pagel, Erdly, & Becker, 1987).

A review of dozens of studies identified several factors that determine whether support helps or not (Shinn, Lehmann, & Wong, 1984):

1. *Amount of support*. Too much help and sympathy offered to someone in trouble can actually backfire, creating dependency and low self-esteem. For example, cancer patients who say they are receiving lots of support and that people are doing many things for them tend to have *lower* self-esteem and less sense of mastery than cancer patients who grumble about having to rely on themselves (Revenson, Wollman, & Felton, 1983).

2. *Timing of support*. After bereavement, divorce, or loss, a person needs lots of understanding. Friends who try to stem grief prematurely are not helping the sufferer. Later, however, they can prove helpful by trying to get the friend back into a social life.

3. *Source of support*. For a friend's advice and sympathy to be effective, the sufferer must feel that the friend understands and has been in the same boat. People who are under stress at work, for example, do better if they can talk their problems over with their employers or co-workers. Their spouses generally lack the experience to offer constructive advice (Kobasa & Puccetti, 1983).

4. *Density of support*. In dense social networks, friends all know one another. Dense networks are good for your sense of stability and identity, and in a crisis everybody in the network pitches in. But being in such a web can get sticky if you want to get out. Among women going back to school, those who were in a tightly knit group of friends showed worse adjustment, more physical symptoms, and lower self-esteem than women who were not in dense networks (Hirsch, 1981). ''Good old friends'' tend to want you to stay put. They can make you feel guilty for wanting to change.

Think for a moment about the future of friendship. Americans place great importance on their independence, yet studies suggest that the price they pay is widespread loneliness and anxiety. This dilemma—the choices between attachment and individualism, between tradition and change, between commitment to others and to oneself—is built into the very structure of American life (Bellah et al., 1985).

QUICK ▪ QUIZ

Identify which stressful aspect of friendship—contagion effect, conflicting demands, dense network, or badly timed support—is demonstrated by each of the following examples.

1. Your friends let you rage too long about an unfair experience.
2. You want to go away to graduate school, but your friends advise you to find a local job.
3. You start to feel your friend's unhappiness.
4. Two friends are having a quarrel and each wants you to take his or her side.

Answers:

1. badly timed support 2. dense network 3. contagion effect 4. conflicting demands

---

The Mind-Body Connection

Countless self-help books and workshops, based on a first wave of promising research, offer advice for coping with stress or for avoiding disease. (The more critical second wave of studies rarely makes the news.) Executives can take "hardiness" seminars. Type A workers can take workshops on "how to change your Type A personality." Some therapists offer "humordrama" groups to teach you how to find the humor in stressful situations.

Indeed, many people don't have problems any more; they have "stress," as if that explained something. If a friend says to you, "Gee, I've been under a lot of stress lately," you could say, "What a shame; have you tried relaxing, meditating, watching funny movies, or taking naps?" But if your friend says, "Gee, I have a problem; I'm about to be evicted because I can't come up with the rent," you wouldn't dream of advising only relaxation, because it would be wildly inappropriate.

We offer this anecdote because it draws attention to an important debate in health psychology: In studying the origins of health and illness, are we overestimating psychological factors (such as optimism, humor, and attitude) and underestimating economic and biological conditions (such as unemployment or disease)?

Without doubt, psychological factors are a link in a long chain that connects stress and illness, but researchers disagree about how strong that link is. At one extreme, some physicians think that psychology counts for almost nothing. Disease is a biological matter, they say, and personality cannot influence a germ or a tumor. An editorial in the *New England Journal of Medicine* lashed out against the "psychologizing" of illness. "At a time when patients are already burdened by disease," the editor wrote, "they should not be further burdened by having to accept the responsibility for the outcome" (Angell, 1985). At the other extreme, numerous popular books state or imply that health is largely mind over matter and that the worst diseases can be cured with jokes, papaya juice, and positive thinking.

What, then, are the most reasonable lessons to be drawn from health psychology? First, in terms of practical action, people ought to be following "good old-fashioned motherly advice" and practicing those *habits* associated with health, such as not smoking, not drinking excessively or in binges, and so on. Second, in terms

News reports often imply that health is mostly "mind over matter." What is the matter with overemphasizing the power of the mind— and, conversely, what's wrong with ignoring the mind's influence?

of psychological factors, the most consistent finding, as we have seen, is that the effects of stress are worsened when an individual feels helpless. Although many things happen that are out of our control—exams, accidents, a flu epidemic, natural disasters—we *do* have control over how we cope with them.

One way to restore a sense of control is to take responsibility for future actions, while not blaming ourselves for past ones. In the study of cancer copers, for instance, adjustment was related to a woman's belief that she was not to blame for getting sick but that she was in charge of taking care of herself from now on (Taylor, Lichtman, & Wood, 1984). "I felt that I had lost control of my body somehow," said a 45-year-old woman, "and the way for me to get back some control was to find out as much as I could." This way of thinking about illness allows a person to avoid guilt and self-blame while gaining mastery and control.

Moreover, once you are in a stressful situation, some ways of coping are better than others. If the situation requires action, problem-solving techniques are more helpful than wallowing around indecisively or simply venting your emotions. But if the situation is a fact of life, people who can use humor, hope, distraction, reappraisal, and social comparisons will be better off than those who are overcome by depression and pessimism.

Finally, one of the most important lessons from health psychology is that successful coping does not mean eliminating all stress. It does not mean constant happiness or a life without pain. The healthy person faces problems, "copes" with them, and gets beyond them, but the problems are necessary if the person is to acquire coping skills that endure. To wish for a life without stress would be like wishing for a life without friends. The result might be calm, but it would be joyless, and ultimately hazardous to your health. The stresses of life—the daily hassles and the occasional tragedies—force us to grow, and to grow up.

Taking Psychology with You

Noise, Crowds, and Weather: Living in a Stressful World

Writer Oscar Wilde once called the United States the noisiest nation that ever existed. That was in 1882. A century later, the din is even worse. Our ears are constantly assaulted by jackhammers, jet airplanes, motorcycles, lawn mowers, snowmobiles, chain saws, and blaring radios. To all that noise, add other nuisances, such as traffic jams, crowds, blizzards, and hot spells. What are the physical and psychological consequences of these environmental stressors?

Loud noise impairs intellectual performance on complex tasks, even when you think you have adjusted to it. Children in elementary schools that were beneath the flight path for Los Angeles International Airport were compared with children in quieter classrooms (Cohen et al., 1980). The two groups were matched in age, ethnicity, race, and social class. Children in the noisy schools had higher blood pressure, were more distractable, and had more difficulty with puzzles and math problems than children in quieter schools. Children raised in noisy environments also have trouble learning how to discriminate between irrelevant noise and the relevant task. They either tune out too much in the environment or cannot tune out enough (Cohen, Glass, & Phillips, 1979; Taylor, 1986).

Studies find that noise contributes to cardiovascular problems, ulcers, irritability, fatigue, and aggressiveness. All of these effects are probably due to overstimulation of the autonomic nervous system. Continuous noise also has a cumulative effect on hearing. At the University of Tennessee, 60 percent of 1410 freshmen had significant hearing loss in the high-frequency range. Their hearing resembled that of people more than twice their age (Lipscomb, 1972). Disc jockeys in discotheques, truck drivers, fire fighters, dentists, machinists, and shipbuilders all have a higher incidence of substandard hearing than the norm (Murphy, 1982).

The noise that is most stressful to people, however, is noise *they cannot control*. The rock song that you choose to listen to at jackhammer loudness may be pleasurable to you but intolerable to anyone who doesn't share your musical taste. The motorcycle without a muffler that makes you feel like Superman may make your neighbor feel like King Kong.

The same pattern of findings is true of crowding. At one time, environmental psychologists believed that crowding was a major source of most urban ills—crime, juvenile delinquency, infant mortality, family quarrels, and so on. This argument was not supported by subsequent research that controlled for income, class, and ethnicity (some cultures are used to high density; others are not). In Tokyo, where population density exceeds that of any U.S. city, crowding is not associated with crime.

Crowds themselves are not necessarily stressful. Sometimes they are even part of the fun, as on New Year's Eve or at baseball games. As with noise, crowds become stressful when they curtail your sense of freedom and control. They are stressful not when you *are* crowded but when you *feel* crowded (Y. Epstein, 1981). When people are able to work without interruptions in a densely packed room, they feel less crowded than if they work with interruptions in the same room with fewer people. Laboratory experiments and field studies find that the feeling of being trapped is more detrimental to health and intellectual performance than are most stressors themselves (Taylor, 1986). These negative effects can last long after the stressful event is over. Researchers therefore offer suggestions for asserting some control over environmental stressors and for living with those that are out of our control:

▪ If silence is golden, a little less noise will make us all a bit richer. So lower the volume of radios, TV sets, and stereos; don't turn stereos with earphones to full blast.

▪ If you work at a noisy job, be sure federal regulations are followed. To avoid permanent damage to the inner ear, constant noise levels for anyone working an eight-hour day may not exceed 90 decibels (dB).

▪ Stop shouting! If you are talking to someone, don't yell over the noise of the TV. Turn it down or shut it off. Then talk.

▪ Try to find a quiet place to study where you won't be interrupted by unpredictable noise, such as your brothers fighting over the car or your roommates wanting to play touch football.

▪ If you are trapped in a crowd over which you have no control (say, stalled in a traffic jam or in line at a busy store), relax. You can't do anything about it, and having a tantrum just raises your blood pressure and adds to the stress. Do some deep breathing, calm down, use the "extra" time to make lists or recite all the states in the union.

▪ If the weather is making you irritable—either because it snowed again for the ninety-fourth day or has been boiling hot for three weeks—well, join the group. Mark Twain tried to cheer up some New Englanders who were complaining about the unpredictable spring weather. "In the spring I have counted one hundred and thirty-six different kinds of weather," said Twain, "inside of twenty-four hours." As an editorial in the 1897 issue of the *Hartford Courant* lamented, "Everybody talks about the weather, but nobody does anything about it." You can't either. "Grin and bear it" is much less stressful than grumbling and being a bear.

KEY WORDS

health psychology 538
behavioral medicine 538
pathogenic 538
salutogenic 538
General Adaptation Syndrome (GAS) 539
alarm/resistance/exhaustion phases of GAS 539
eustress 540
psychological stress 541
psychosomatic 541
psychoneuroimmunology 541
life-change units 542
hassles 543
coping 546

emotion-focused coping 548
problem-focused coping 548
reappraisal 549
social comparisons 550
vigilance and avoidance 550
social interest 554
Type A behavior pattern 556
neurotic vs. antagonistic hostility 557
"disease-prone" personality 557
explanatory style 558
locus of control 560
hardiness 561
primary control 562
secondary control 562

SUMMARY

1. Hans Selye argued that environmental *stressors* (such as heat, pain, and toxins) cause the body to respond with fight-or-flee responses, as part of the *General Adaptation Syndrome*. If a stressor persists, it may overwhelm the body's ability to cope, and fatigue and illness may result. Current theories, however, emphasize the psychological factors that mediate between the stressor and the stress.

2. The immune system consists of several types of blood cells that are designed to recognize and destroy foreign substances, such as viruses. Researchers in the field of *psychoneuroimmunology* are studying how human behavior and emotion can affect the immune system.

3. Certain major events, such as the death of a loved one or divorce, are known to be extremely stressful. But some psychologists argue that daily hassles, such as traffic jams and interruptions, are more stressful than life-changing experiences, and that continuing situations are more stressful than one major event. Whatever the source, an important predictor of stress seems to be the inability to *control* and *predict* the environment.

4. Stress does not lead directly to illness. Two factors intervene: how the person interprets the event and how he or she copes with it. Coping involves a person's active and adaptive efforts to manage demands that he or she feels are stressful. Methods of coping include *attacking the problem*; *rethinking the problem* (finding meaning in the experience, comparing oneself to others who are worse off, seeing the humor in the situation, and, once a decision is made, not thinking or worrying about it); and *living with the problem* (reducing the physical effects of stress through relaxation, meditation, or exercise). Healthy coping also involves *social interest*, Adler's term for empathy, cooperation, and attachment to other people.

5. Individual factors that affect health and the ability to cope with stress include *negative emotions* (particularly anger, anxiety, and depression), *explanatory style* (optimism or pessimism), *health habits*, and *locus of control*. Although evidence for a Type A personality is mixed, studies indicate that antagonistic hostility in particular, and negative emotions that cluster together in general, can lead to a "disease-prone personality." However, there are many possible links between personality and disease: Disease may cause personality changes; some personality traits may cause unhealthy habits (such as smoking), which cause disease; a third factor may affect both personality and disease; and personality and illness may affect each other in a complex feedback loop.

6. An important goal of health psychology is prevention—getting people to eat nutritious meals, quit (or never start) smoking, not abuse drugs, and the like. Some problems in prevention are that health habits are often entrenched in childhood, people have little incentive to change their patterns, and health habits are independent of one another and are unstable.

7. *Locus of control* affects a person's neuroendocrine and immune systems, and the ability to live with stress and pain. However, control and health influence each other, and control is also affected by one's circumstances.

8. People can sometimes have too strong a sense of control over events. If something happens that is truly out of their power, they may not be able to cope. Health and well-being seem to depend on the right combination of *primary control* (trying to change the stressful situation) and *secondary control* (learning to accept the stressful situation). Cultures differ in the kind of control they emphasize.

9. Friendships, family, and acquaintances are important in maintaining physical health and emotional well-being. They provide emotional support, cognitive guidance, tangible support, companionship, and the sense of attachment. Friends can also be stressful—a source of hassles, conflicts, burdens, and betrayals. They sometimes provide the wrong kind of support or too much support or they offer support at the wrong time (too little too soon, too much too late). A *dense network*, in which many friends know each other, is good for stability and identity but can make change difficult if one member wants to break away.

10. Psychological factors are only one link in a long chain that connects stress and illness; illness is not "all in your mind" or easily cured with "the right attitude." Still, psychologists agree on the importance of learning good health habits and good coping skills. Coping with stress does not mean trying to live without pain, problems, or nuisances. It means learning how to live with them.

APPENDIX B

Sample Textbook Chapter

Homeostasis II: Temperature Regulation
(from Curtis, *Biology*)

CHAPTER 38

Homeostasis II: Temperature Regulation

For life forms, the seeming wastelands of the deserts and the poles represent great extremes of hot and cold. Yet, in fact, measured on a cosmic scale, the temperature differences between them are very slight. Life exists only within a very narrow temperature range. The upper and lower limits of this range are dictated by the nature of biochemical reactions, which sustain life and which are all extremely sensitive to temperature change.

Biochemical reactions take place almost entirely in water, the principal constituent of living things. The slightly salty water characteristic of living tissues freezes at −1 or −2°C. Molecules that are not immobilized in the ice crystals are left in such a highly concentrated form that their normal interactions are completely disrupted. In Chapter 8, we saw that, as temperature rises, the movement of molecules increases and the rate of biochemical reactions goes up rapidly. In fact, it is a convenient generalization that the rates of most biochemical reactions about double for every 10°C increase in temperature. The upper temperature limit for life is apparently set by the point at which proteins begin to lose their functional three-dimensional conformation (a process known as denaturation). Once denaturation occurs, enzymes and other proteins whose function depends on a specific shape are inactivated. As a consequence of this restriction to a very narrow tem-

38–1
Temperature regulation involves behavioral responses, as well as physiological and anatomical adaptations. Here a jackrabbit seeks shelter from the Arizona sun in the shade of a mesquite tree. Note the large ears, which are highly vascularized.

38-2

Life processes can take place only within a very narrow range of temperature. The temperature scale shown here is the Kelvin, or absolute, scale. Absolute zero (0 K) is equivalent to −273.1°C, or −459°F, and is the temperature at which all molecular motion ceases.

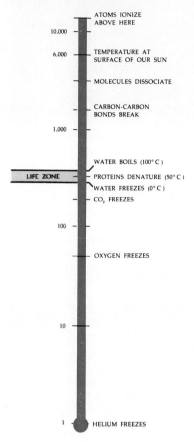

perature range, living organisms must either find external environments that range from just below freezing to between 45 and 50°C, or they must create suitable internal environments. (However, there are exceptions: cyanobacteria have been found in hot springs at 85°C, and recently bacteria have been discovered in the superheated waters of submarine vents, where heat escapes through fissures in the earth's crust. In the laboratory, these bacteria metabolize and multiply at temperatures of about 100°C. The special adaptations that make this possible are not yet known.)

The ways in which temperature requirements are met—and, in particular, the internal regulation of temperature, another example of homeostasis—are the subject of this chapter. Before going into the details of these processes, however, it is worth taking a moment to consider what excellent temperature regulators most mammals are. One of the simplest and most dramatic demonstrations of this capacity was given some 200 years ago by Dr. Charles Blagden, then secretary of the Royal Society of London. Dr. Blagden, taking with him a few friends, a small dog in a basket, and a steak, went into a room that had a temperature of 126°C (260°F).* The entire group remained there for 45 minutes. Dr. Blagden and his friends emerged unaffected. So did the dog. (The basket had kept its feet from being burned by the floor.) But the steak was cooked.

PRINCIPLES OF HEAT BALANCE

Water balance, as we saw in the preceding chapter, requires that the loss of water through urine, sweat, and respiration equal the water ingested. Similarly, maintaining a constant temperature depends on heat gains equaling heat losses. For living organisms there are two primary sources of heat gain: one is the radiant energy of the sun; the other is the heat generated by exothermic chemical reactions in an organism (Figure 38–3).

Heat Transfer

Heat is lost by transfer to a cooler body. If the two bodies are in direct contact, the movement of heat is called *conduction*. Conduction of heat consists of the direct transfer of the kinetic energy of molecular motion, and it always occurs from a region of higher temperature to a region of lower temperature. Some materials are better heat conductors than others. When you step out of bed barefoot on a cool morning, you probably prefer to step on a wool rug than on the bare floor. Although both are at the same temperature, the rug feels warmer. If you touch something metal, such as a brass doorknob, it will feel even cooler than the wood floor. These apparent differences in temperature are actually differences in the speed at which these different types of materials conduct heat away from your body. The doorknob, like all metals, is an excellent conductor, and wood is a better heat conductor than wool.

Water is a better conductor than air. You are quite comfortable in air at 21°C (70°F) but may be uncomfortable in water at the same temperature. Fat and air are poor conductors and so can serve as insulators. Animals that need to conserve heat are typically insulated with either fur or feathers, which trap air, or with fat or blubber.

---

* A Celsius to Fahrenheit temperature conversion scale can be found in Appendix B at the back of the book.

733   CHAPTER 38 *Homeostasis II: Temperature Regulation*

(a)

(b)

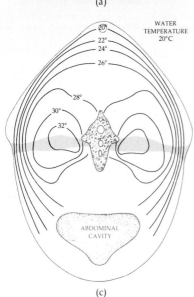

WATER
TEMPERATURE
20°C

20°
22°
24°
26°
28°
30°
32°

ABDOMINAL
CAVITY

(c)

38–3

Heat sources. (a) Within the wintering hive, bees maintain their temperature by clustering together in a dense ball; the lower the temperature, the denser the cluster. The clustered bees produce heat by constant muscular movements of their wings, legs, and abdomens. In very cold weather, the bees on the outside of the cluster keep moving toward the center, while those in the center move to the colder outside periphery. The entire cluster moves slowly about on the combs, eating the stored honey, which is their energy source. The photograph shows the upper half of an opened wintering hive. (b) Mound-building birds incubate their eggs in large compost heaps. The parent birds start by digging a pit, 3 meters wide and 1 meter deep, and raking plant litter into it. Following the spring rains, when the litter begins to decompose, the birds cover the fermenting heap with a layer of sand up to a meter in depth. The female lays her eggs in this mound, which is heated from beneath by the chemical reactions in the litter. The male regulates the temperature of the eggs by scraping away the sand around them to expose them to air or sun or piling up warm sand around them at night. The entire cycle from the beginning of mound building until the last egg hatches takes about a year. (c) Muscular activity and chemical ractions are also sources of internal heat. This diagram shows the temperatures in a cross section of a 70-kilogram big-eye tuna. The heat is produced by metabolism, particularly in the hard-working, red, myoglobin-containing muscle tissue, indicated in light color.

38–4

Heat exchanges between a mammal and its environment. The core body temperature of the man is 37°C. The air temperature is 30°C and there is no wind movement.

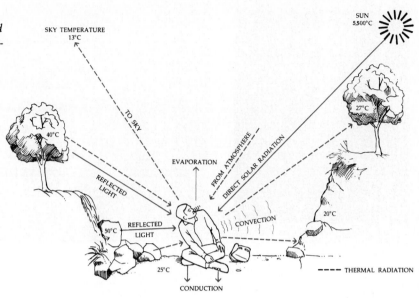

SKY TEMPERATURE
13°C

SUN
5,500°C

TO SKY

40°C

27°C

EVAPORATION

FROM ATMOSPHERE

DIRECT SOLAR RADIATION

REFLECTED LIGHT

REFLECTED LIGHT

50°C

CONVECTION

20°C

25°C

CONDUCTION

- - - - THERMAL RADIATION

CONDUCTION

Conduction in fluids (air or water) is always influenced by *convection*, the movement of air or water in currents. Because both air and water become lighter as they get warmer, they move away from a heat source and are replaced by colder air or water, which again moves away as it warms.

Radiation is the transfer of energy by electromagnetic waves in the absence of direct contact, as between the sun and an organism. The energy may be transferred as light or heat, depending on the wavelength of the radiation (see Figure 10–3 on page 212). Light energy falling on an object is either absorbed as heat or reflected. Dark objects absorb more than light-colored ones.

Another route of heat exchange is by evaporation. As we saw in Chapter 2, every time a gram of water changes from a liquid to a gas, it takes more than 500 calories away with it. Many organisms, including ourselves, have exploited this property of water as a means for rapid adjustment of the heat balance. These routes of heat transfer are summarized in Figure 38–4.

Size and Temperature

Heat is transferred into or out of any object, animate or inanimate, across the body surface, and transfer of heat, like diffusion of gases, is proportional to the surface area exposed. The smaller the object, as we saw in Chapter 5, the larger its surface-to-volume ratio. Ten pounds of ice, separated into individual ice cubes, will melt far faster than the equivalent volume in a solid block. For the same reason, it is much more difficult for a small animal to maintain a constant body temperature than it is for a large one.

735   CHAPTER 38 *Homeostasis II: Temperature Regulation*

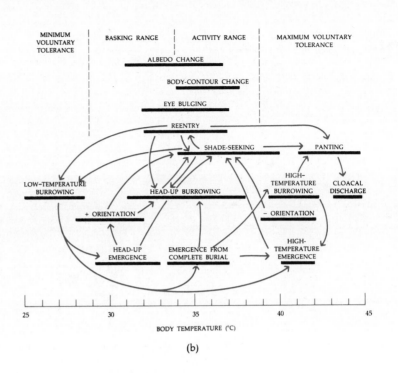

38–5

In laboratory studies, the internal temperature of reptiles was shown to be almost the same as the temperature of the surrounding air. It was not until observations were made of these animals in their own environment that it was found that they have behavioral means for temperature regulation. By absorbing solar energy, reptiles can raise their temperature well above that of the air around them. (a) Shown here is a horned lizard (often but not accurately known as a horned toad) that, having been overheated by the sun, has raised its body to allow cooling air currents to circulate across its belly. (b) This chart is based on field studies of the behavior of a horned lizard in response to temperature fluctuations. Changes in albedo (whiteness) are produced by pigment changes in the epithelial cells. Albedo changes affect the reflection versus absorption of light rays.

"Cold-blooded" and "Warm-blooded"

In common parlance, animals are often characterized as "cold-blooded" and "warm-blooded." This fits in with everyday experience: a snake is usually cold to the touch, and a living bird feels warm. Actually, however, a "cold-blooded" animal may create an internal temperature for itself that is warmer than that of a "warm-blooded" one. Another approach is to classify animals as ectotherms and endotherms. Ectotherms are warmed from the outside in, and endotherms are warmed from the inside out. These categories correspond approximately but not completely with "cold-blooded" and "warm-blooded." As we saw in Figure 38–3c, a large fish, such as a tuna, which is considered "cold-blooded," generates a considerable amount of metabolic heat. Finally, animals may be characterized as poikilotherms and homeotherms. A *poikilotherm* (from the Greek word *poikilos*, meaning "changeable") has a variable temperature, and a *homeotherm*, a constant one. These terms are generally used as synonymous with "cold-blooded" and "warm-blooded," though again the correspondence is not perfect. Fish that live deep in the sea, where the temperature of the water remains constant, have a body temperature far more constant than a bat or a hummingbird, whose temperatures, as we shall see, fluctuate widely depending on their state of activity. Nevertheless, poikilotherm and homeotherm are the most widely accepted terms and are those that we shall use in the rest of this discussion.

POIKILOTHERMS

Most aquatic animals are poikilotherms, with their temperatures varying with that of the surrounding water. Although the metabolic processes of such animals gen-

736   SECTION 6 BIOLOGY OF ANIMALS

erate heat, it is usually quickly dissipated, even in large animals. In most fish, for example, heat is rapidly carried from the core of the body by the bloodstream and is lost by conduction into the water. A large proportion of this body heat is lost from the gills. Exposure of a large, well-vascularized surface to the water is necessary in order to acquire enough oxygen, as you will recall from Chapter 35. This same process rapidly dissipates heat, so fish cannot maintain a body temperature significantly higher than that of the water. They also cannot maintain a temperature lower than that of the water, since they have no means of unloading heat.

In general, large bodies of water, for the reasons we discussed in Chapter 2, maintain a very stable temperature. At no place in the open ocean does the temperature vary more than 10°C in a year. (By contrast, temperatures on land may vary annually in a given area by as much as 60 to 70°C.) Because water expands as it freezes, ice floats on the surface of the water, insulating the water so that life continues beneath the surface of the ice. In shallower water, where greater temperature changes occur, fish seek an optimal temperature, presumably the one to which their metabolic processes are adapted. However, because they can do almost nothing to make their own temperature different from that of the surrounding water, they can be quickly victimized by any rapid, drastic changes in water temperature.

Terrestrial reptiles—snakes, lizards, and tortoises—are also poikilotherms, but they can often maintain remarkably stable body temperatures during their active hours, even though ambient temperatures vary. By careful selection of suitable sites, such as the slope of a hill facing the sun, and by orienting their bodies with a maximum surface exposed to sunlight, they can heat themselves rapidly (as rapidly as 1°C per minute), even on mornings when the air temperature, as on deserts or in the high mountains, may be close to 0°C. As soon as their body temperatures go above the preferred level, lizards move to face the sun, presenting less exposed surface, or they seek shade. By such behavioral responses, lizards are able to keep

38–6

Observed metabolic rates of mammals. Each division on the abscissa represents a tenfold increase in weight. The metabolic rate of very small mammals is much higher than that of larger mammals, owing principally to their greater surface-to-volume ratios.

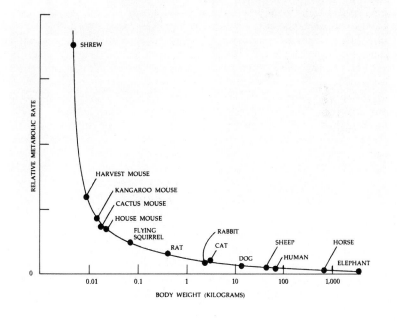

737 CHAPTER 38 *Homeostasis II: Temperature Regulation*

their temperatures oscillating within a quite narrow range. At night, when their body temperatures drop and they become sluggish, these animals seek the safety of their shelters. There they will not become immobilized in an exposed position, where they would be vulnerable to predators.

HOMEOTHERMS

Homeotherms are animals that maintain a constant body temperature despite fluctuations in their environment, and most maintain a body temperature well above that of their surroundings. Among modern organisms, only birds and mammals are true homeotherms. All homeotherms are endotherms, with the oxidation of glucose and other energy-yielding molecules within body cells as their primary source of heat. In terms of energy requirements, their cost of living is high: the metabolic rate of a homeotherm is about twice that of a poikilotherm of similar size at similar temperature. In short, homeotherms pay a high price for their independence. Also, the smaller the size, the higher the price. Small homeotherms have a proportionally larger heat budget than large ones, because of surface-to-volume ratios (see Figure 38–6).

Because it is heated from within, a warm-blooded mammal is warmer at the core of its body than at the periphery. (Our temperature usually does not reach 37°C, or 98.6°F, until some distance below the skin surface.) Heat is transported from the core to the periphery largely by the bloodstream. At the surface of the body, the heat is transferred to the air, as long as air temperature is less than body temperature. Temperature regulation involves increasing or decreasing heat production and increasing or decreasing heat loss at the body surface.

38–7
The size of the extremities in a particular type of animal can often be correlated with the climate in which it lives. (a) The fennec fox of the North African desert has large ears that help it to dissi-

pate body heat. (b) The red fox of the eastern United States has ears of intermediate size, and (c) the Arctic fox has relatively small ears. Like all mammals, these foxes are homeotherms, animals

that maintain a constant internal temperature despite variations in external temperature.

The Mammalian Thermostat

The remarkable constancy of temperature characteristic of humans, and many other animals as well, is maintained by an automatic system—a thermostat—in the hypothalamus. Like the thermostat that regulates your furnace, the thermostat in the hypothalamus receives information about the temperature, compares it to the set point of the thermostat, and, on the basis of this comparison, initiates appropriate responses. Unlike your furnace thermostat, however, the hypothalamic thermostat receives and integrates information from widely scattered temperature receptors. Also, rather than just controlling an on-off switch, the hypothalamic thermostat has a variety of responses at its command, as summarized in Figure 33–13 on page 669.

Under ordinary conditions, the skin receptors for hot and cold are probably the most important sources of information about temperature change. However, the hypothalamus itself contains receptor cells that monitor the temperature of the blood flowing through it. As some interesting experiments have demonstrated, information received by these hypothalamic receptors overrides that from other sources. For example, in a room in which the air is warmer than body temperature, if the blood circulating through a person's hypothalamus is cooled, he or she will stop perspiring, even though the skin temperature continues to rise.

The elevation of body temperature known as fever is due not to a malfunction of the hypothalamic thermostat but to its resetting. Thus, at the onset of fever, an individual typically feels cold and often has chills; although the body temperature is rising, it is still lower than the new thermostat setting. The substance primarily responsible for the resetting of the thermostat is a protein released by the white blood cells in response to a pathogen. The adaptive value of fever, if any—and we can only presume that there is one—is a subject of current research. One possibility, supported by some evidence, is that it creates an environment inhospitable to pathogens. Another is that it stimulates the release of a substance important in immunological reactions.

Regulating as Body Temperature Rises

In mammals, as the body temperature rises above its thermostat setting, the blood vessels near the skin surface are dilated, and the supply of blood to the skin increases. If the air is cooler than the body surface, heat can be transferred from the skin to the air. Heat can also be lost from the surface by the evaporation of saliva or perspiration. Some animals—dogs, for instance—pant, so that air passes rapidly over their large, moist tongues, evaporating saliva. Cats lick themselves all over as the temperature rises, and evaporation of their saliva cools their body surface. Horses and human beings sweat from all over their body surfaces. For animals that dissipate heat by water evaporation, temperature regulation at high temperatures necessarily involves water loss, which, in turn, stimulates thirst and water conservation by the kidneys. Dr. Blagden and his friends were probably very thirsty.

Regulating as Body Temperature Falls

When the temperature of the circulating blood begins to fall below the thermostat setting, blood vessels near the skin surface are constricted, limiting heat loss from the skin. Metabolic processes increase. Part of this increase is due to increased muscular activity, either voluntary (shifting from foot to foot) or involuntary (shivering). Part is due to direct stimulation of metabolism by the endocrine and

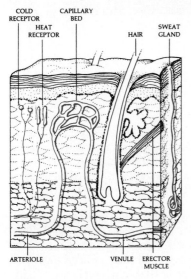

38–8

Cross section of human skin showing structures involved in temperature regulation. In cold, the arterioles constrict, reducing the flow of blood through the capillaries, and the hairs, each of which has a small erector muscle under nervous control, stand upright. Beneath the skin is a layer of subcutaneous fat that serves as insulation, retaining the heat in the underlying body tissues. With rising temperatures, the arterioles dilate and the sweat glands secrete a salty liquid. Evaporation of this liquid cools the skin surface, dissipating heat (approximately 540 calories for every gram of H_2O).

(a)

(b)

38–9

(a) Dogs unload heat by panting, which involves short, shallow breaths. When it is hot, a dog pants at a rate of about 300 to 400 times a minute, compared with a respiration rate of from 10 to 40 times a minute in cool surroundings. Evaporation of water from the tongue, unlike evaporation from the skin, does not result in the loss of salt or other important ions. (b) Elephants, lacking sweat glands, wet down their thick, dry skins with mud or water. They also unload heat by flapping their ears, which are highly vascularized.

nervous systems. Adrenaline stimulates the release and oxidation of glucose. Autonomic nerves to fat increase its metabolic breakdown. In some mammals, though apparently not in humans, the thyroid gland increases its release of thyroxine, the thyroid hormone. Thyroxine appears to exert its effects directly on the mitochondria.

Most mammals have a layer of subcutaneous fat that serves as insulation. Homeotherms also characteristically have hair or feathers that, as temperature falls, are pulled upright by erector muscles under the skin, trapping air, which insulates the surface. All we get, as our evolutionary legacy, are goose pimples.

Meeting Energy Costs

As we noted previously, maintaining a constant temperature adds significantly to an animal's energy budget. Birds, in particular, have high metabolic requirements. Although comparatively small, they maintain a higher body temperature—40 to 42°C—than most mammals. Also, unlike many other small homeotherms, they spend much of their time exposed. Flight compounds their problems. To fly, birds must keep their weight down, and so they cannot store large amounts of fuel. Because of this and the high energy requirements of their way of life, birds need to eat constantly. A bird eating high-protein foods, such as seeds and insects, commonly consumes as much as 30 percent of its body weight per day. Bird migrations are dictated not so much by a need to seek warmer weather as by a need for longer days with more daylight hours for feeding themselves and their young.

Cutting Energy Costs

Less energy is consumed by a sleeping animal than by an active one. Bears, for example, nap for most of the winter, living on fat reserves, permitting their temperature to drop several degrees, and keeping their energy requirements down.

Turning down the thermostat saves more fuel. Some small animals have different day and night settings. A hummingbird, for instance, has an extremely high rate of fuel consumption, even for a bird. Its body temperature drops every evening when it is resting, thereby decreasing its metabolic requirements and its fuel consumption.

740 SECTION 6 BIOLOGY OF ANIMALS

38-10

Heat conservation measures. (a) Hibernation saves energy by turning down the thermostat. This dormouse has prepared for hibernation by storing food reserves in body fat. (b) Note the heat-conserving reduction in surface-to-volume ratio in this hibernating chipmunk. (c) Many small animals, such as these penguin chicks, huddle together for warmth. Huddling decreases the effective surface-to-volume ratio. A few of the chicks have lifted their heads from the warmth of the huddle to observe the photographer at work.

Hibernation, which comes from *hiber*, the Latin word for "winter," is another means of adjusting energy expenditures to food supplies. Hibernating animals do not stop regulating their temperatures altogether—like the hummingbird, they turn down their thermostats. Hibernators are mostly small animals, including a few insectivores, hamsters, ground squirrels, some South American opossums, some bats, and a few birds, such as the poor-will of the southwestern United States. In these animals, the thermostat is set very low, often close to that of the surrounding air (if the air is above 0°C). The heartbeat slows; the heart of an active ground squirrel, for instance, beats 200 to 400 times a minute, whereas that of a hibernating one beats 7 to 10 times a minute. The metabolism, as measured by oxygen consumption, is reduced 20 to 100 times. Apparently, even aging stops; hibernators have much longer life spans than similar nonhibernators. However, despite these profound physiological changes, hibernators do not cease to monitor the external environment. If the animals are exposed to carbon dioxide, for example, they breathe more rapidly, and those of certain species wake up. Similarly, animals of many species wake up if the temperature in their burrows drops to a life-threatening low of 0°C. Hibernators of some species can be awakened by sound or by touch.

Arousal from hibernation can be rapid. In one experiment, bats kept in a refrigerator for 144 days without food were capable of sustained flight after 15 minutes at room temperature. As indicated, however, by the arousals at 0°C, the arousal is a process of self-warming rather than of collecting environmental heat. Breathing becomes more regular and then more rapid, increasing the amount of oxygen available for consumption; subsequently, the animal "burns" its stored food supplies as it returns to its normal temperature and the fast pace of a homeothermic existence.

(a)

(b)

(c)

741   **CHAPTER 38** *Homeostasis II: Temperature Regulation*

ADAPTATIONS TO EXTREME TEMPERATURES

We rely mainly on our technology, rather than our physiology, to allow us to live in extreme climates, but many animals are comfortable in climates that we consider inhospitable or, indeed, uninhabitable.

Adaptations to Extreme Cold

Animals adapt to extreme cold largely by increased amounts of insulation. Fur and feathers, both of which trap air, provide insulation for Arctic land animals. Fur and feathers are usually shed to some extent in the spring and regrow in the fall.

Aquatic homeotherms, such as whales, walruses, seals, and penguins, are insulated with fat (neither fur nor feathers serve as effective insulators when wet). In general, the rate of heat loss depends both on the amount of surface area exposed and on temperature differences between the body surface and the surroundings. These marine animals, which survive in extremely cold water, can tolerate a very great drop in their skin surface temperature; measurements of skin temperature have shown that it is only a degree or so above that of the surrounding water. By permitting the skin temperature to drop, these animals, which maintain an internal temperature as warm as that of a person, expend very little heat outside of their fat layer and so keep warm—like a diver in a wet suit.

Numerous animals similarly permit temperatures in the extremities to drop. By so doing, they conserve heat. The extremities of such animals are actually adapted to live at a different internal temperature from that of the rest of the animal. For example, the fat in the foot of an Arctic fox has a different thermal behavior from

38–11

Aquatic mammals, such as this bull fur seal, have a heavy layer of fat beneath the skin that acts, in effect, like a diver's wet suit, insulating them against heat loss. On land, they have a problem unloading heat. One way they do it is by keeping their fur moist; another is by sleeping, which, in some species, reduces heat production by almost 25 percent.

that of the fat in the rest of its body, so that its footpads are soft and resilient even at temperatures of −50°C. Also, for many of these animals, particularly those that stand on the ice, this capacity is essential for another reason. If, for example, the feet of an Arctic seabird were as warm as its body, they would melt the ice, which might then freeze over them, trapping the animal until the spring thaws set it free.

Countercurrent Exchange

In many Arctic animals, the arteries and veins leading to and from the extremities are juxtaposed in such a way that the chilled blood returning from the legs (or fins or tail) through the veins picks up heat from the blood entering the extremities through the arteries. The veins and arteries are closely apposed to give maximum surface for heat transfer. Thus the body heat carried by the blood is not wasted by

38–12
The principle of countercurrent heat exchange is illustrated by a hot-water pipe and a cold-water pipe placed side by side. In (a), the hot water and cold water flow in the same direction. Heat from the hot water warms the cold water until both temperatures equalize at 5. Thereafter, no further exchange takes place, and the outflowing water in both pipes is lukewarm. In (b), the flow is in opposite directions (that is, it is countercurrent), so that heat transfer continues for the length of the pipes. The result is that the hot water transfers most of its heat as it travels through the pipe, and the cold water is warmed to almost the initial temperature of the hot water at its source.

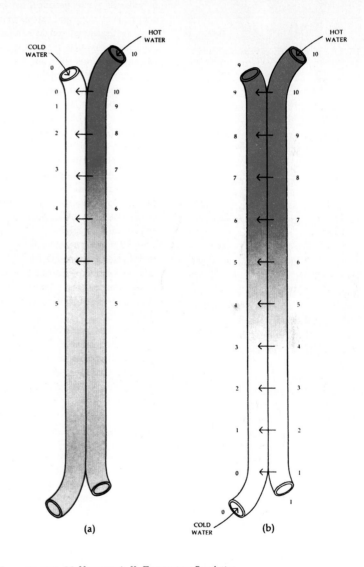

(a)   (b)

743   CHAPTER 38 *Homeostasis II: Temperature Regulation*

being dissipated to the cold air at the extremities. Instead it serves the useful function of warming the chilled blood that would otherwise put a thermal burden on the body. This arrangement, which serves to keep heat in the body and away from the extremities, is, of course, another example of countercurrent exchange.

Adaptations to Extreme Heat

We are efficient homeotherms at high external temperatures, as Dr. Blagden's experiment showed. Our chief limitation in this regard is that we must evaporate a great deal of water in order to unload body heat, and so our water consumption is high. The camel, the philosophical-looking "ship of the desert," has several advantages over human desert dwellers. For one thing, the camel excretes a much more concentrated urine; in other words, it does not need to use so much water to dissolve its waste products. In fact, we are very uneconomical with our water supply; even dogs and cats excrete a urine twice as concentrated as ours.

Also, the camel can lose more water proportionally than a person and still continue to function. If a human loses 10 percent of body weight in water, he or she becomes delirious, deaf, and insensitive to pain. If the loss is as much as 12 percent, the person will be unable to swallow and so cannot recover without assistance. Laboratory rats and many other common animals can tolerate dehydration of up to 12 to 14 percent of body weight. Camels can tolerate the loss of more than 25 percent of their body weight in water, going without drinking for as long as an entire week in the summer months, three weeks in the winter.

Finally, and probably most important, the camel can tolerate a fluctuation in internal temperature of 5 to 6°C. This tolerance means that it can store heat by letting its temperature rise during the daytime (which the human thermostat would never permit) and then release heat during the night. The camel begins the next day at below its normal temperature—storing up coolness, in effect. It is estimated that the camel saves as much as 5 liters of water a day as a result of these internal temperature fluctuations.

Camels' humps were once thought to be water-storage tanks, but actually they are localized fat deposits. Physiologists have suggested that the camel carries its fat in a dorsal hump, instead of distributed all over the body, because the hump, acting as an insulator, impedes heat flow into the body core. An all-over fat distribution, which is decidedly useful in Arctic animals, would not be in inhabitants of hot climates.

Small desert animals usually do not unload heat by sweating or panting; because of their relatively large surface areas, such mechanisms would be extravagant in terms of water loss. Rather, they regulate their temperature by avoiding direct heat. Most small desert animals are nocturnal, like the earliest mammals, from which they are descended.

SUMMARY

Life can exist only within a very narrow temperature range, from about 0°C to about 50°C, with few exceptions. Animals must either seek out environments with suitable temperatures or create suitable internal environments. Heat balance requires that the net heat loss from an organism equal the heat gain. The two primary sources of heat gain are the radiant energy of the sun and cellular metabolism. Heat

38–13

By facing the sun, a camel exposes as small an area of body surface as possible to the sun's radiation. Its body is insulated by fat on top, which minimizes heat gain by radiation. The underpart of its body, which has much less insulation, radiates heat out to the ground cooled by the animal's shadow. Note also the loose-fitting garments worn by the camel driver. When such garments are worn, sweat evaporates off the skin surface. With tight-fitting garments, the sweat evaporates from the surface of the garment instead, and much of the cooling effect is lost. The loose robes, which trap air, also serve to keep desert dwellers warm during the cold nights. Other adaptations of the camel to desert life include long eyelashes, which protect its eyes from the stinging sand, and flattened nostrils, which retard water loss.

is lost by conduction, the transfer of thermal energy from one object to another; by radiation via electromagnetic waves; and by evaporation.

Animals that take in energy primarily from the outside are known as ectotherms; animals that rely on internal energy production are known as endotherms. Most ectotherms are poikilotherms, animals whose internal temperature fluctuates with that of the external environment. Most endotherms are homeotherms, animals that maintain a constant internal temperature.

In mammals, temperature is regulated by a thermostat in the hypothalamus that senses temperature changes in the circulating blood and triggers appropriate responses. As body temperature rises, blood vessels in the skin dilate, increasing the blood flow to the surface of the body. Evaporation of water from any body surface increases heat loss.

As body temperature falls, energy production is increased by increased muscular activity (including shivering) and by nervous and hormonal stimulation of metabolism. Homeotherms in cold climates are usually insulated by subcutaneous fat and fur or feathers.

Energy can be conserved by setting the thermostat lower. Some small homeotherms, such as hummingbirds, have different day and night settings. Others, hibernators, make seasonal adjustments.

Adaptations to extreme cold principally involve (1) insulation by heavy layers of fat and fur or feathers, and (2) countercurrent mechanisms for conserving heat within the body. Adaptations to extreme heat are largely water conservation measures and also include many behavioral responses.

QUESTIONS

1. Distinguish among the following terms: endotherm, ectotherm, poikilotherm, and homeotherm.

2. Compare the surface-to-volume ratio of an Eskimo igloo with that of a California ranch house. In what way is the igloo well suited to the environment in which it is found?

3. Compare hibernation in animals with dormancy in plants. In what ways are they alike? In what ways are they different?

4. Plants, as well as animals, are warmed above air temperature by sunlight, and plants cannot actively seek shade. Why might the leaves in the sunlight at the top of an oak tree be smaller and more extensively lobed (more fingerlike) than the leaves in the shady areas lower on the tree?

5. In terms of temperature regulation, what is the advantage of having temperature monitors that are located externally, as on the outside of a building or in the skin? Why is it also important to monitor the internal temperature? Which should be the principal source of information for your thermostat?

6. Diagram a heat-conserving countercurrent mechanism in the leg of an Arctic animal.

Answer Key

Note: Answers are given for most items. A complete key appears in the *Instructor's Manual.* Answers are not included in this key for exercises that require lengthy or subjective response or the underlining or marking of passages.

PART ONE
Succeeding in College

Chapter 1
How to Succeed

EXERCISE 2
1. Identify and jot down areas (topics, periods) of weakness; look for patterns, such as types of questions missed; find out where questions were taken (text or lecture); use it as a review for final exam.
3. Review procedures before attending lab; underline key steps in lab manual.

EXERCISE 3
1. Talk with the instructor and ask for copies of any materials distributed; talk with classmates.
3. Organize materials in a loose-leaf notebook by chapter topic.

EXERCISE 5
1. Pressure and stress increase at the end of the quarter, possibly affecting her health.
3. The student should develop and follow a time schedule or routine to enable her to stay caught up on reading, to finish papers ahead of schedule, and to study for final exams. The student should pay extra attention to her health, including diet and exercise, when she feels pressured.

Chapter 2
Managing Your Time

EXERCISE 2
1. His choices include
   a. reducing work hours; seek financial aid if needed
   b. settling for less than a B average in some courses
   c. asking a family member to accept additional household responsibilities
   d. dropping one or more courses

3. Mark's plan has two faults. First, he should not leave the most difficult assignment requiring the greatest amount of concentration until last. Second, he should not schedule his study of subjects according to likes or dislikes but should instead allot his time according to the difficulty and type of assignment given.
5. Evaluate his study plan according to the suggestions given in the section "Building a Time Schedule." He should rearrange his schedule so as to follow the scheduling suggestions in Chapter 2.

Chapter 3
Becoming a More Successful Learner: Principles of Learning and Memory

EXERCISE 1
1. Approximately 23 percent.
3. Although taking the notes would serve as a form of rehearsal, without further review you should expect your recall to be fairly poor.

EXERCISE 2
1. Responses might include lighting, heating, color of walls, clock ticking, traffic in street, noise in corridor, feeling of watch on wrist.
3. Number Seven Theory: information is grouped.
5. It took longer than twenty seconds to reach the phone, or the person did not group the numbers together and could not remember each separately.

EXERCISE 3
1. Rote learning
3. Recoding
5. Recoding

EXERCISE 4
1. The group that paraphrased used recoding. Underlining is repetition (rote learning) of existing information. Rote learning alone is an inefficient learning strategy.
3. The film recodes and enables students to make elaborations.

EXERCISE 5
1. Retrieval
3. Encoding and storage
5. Retrieval

EXERCISE 6

1. a. She used only rote learning.
   b. She was not able to concentrate.
   c. She did not select what was important to learn.
3. The student did not selectively attend to the quiz announcement.
5. Selective attention.
7. He is providing for elaborative rehearsal.

EXERCISE 7

1. Categorization (group into political, economic, etc. aspects); association (associate with particular wars); elaboration.
3. Think of an instructor who exemplifies each feature.
5. Draw a graph that shows the relationship between price and quantity. Visualize stacks of dollar bills and piles of an item of variable demand.
7. Elaborate on each problem type by anticipating variations. Study similarities and differences among problem types. Determine and learn distinctive characteristics of each problem type.
9. Intent to remember: establish what is important to know about each stage. Categorization: organize information into a chart by stage and type of development. Elaboration: compare and contrast, think of examples at each stage.

PART TWO
Strategies for Active Learning

Chapter 4
Setting the Stage for Learning

EXERCISE 1

1. You already have associations built up for sleep and relaxation that will make studying more difficult.
3. Your attention will be divided; at least part of the time you will be listening to and thinking about the tape.
5. The snack bar is probably very busy during lunch hour and will be too distracting.
7. You are in an unfamiliar environment, and getting down to studying will be more difficult than in your own environment.

EXERCISE 6

1. This text takes a problem-solving approach and attempts to explain how social processes shape behavior.
3. This text is concerned with analysis of social issues and is research-oriented.

Chapter 5
Prereading and Predicting

EXERCISE 1

1. T	2. F
3. F	4. T
5. F	6. T
7. T	8. T
9. F	10. T

EXERCISE 2

1. The text contains a collection of articles written by different authors as well as reports of studies done on individuals.
3. The section is organized chronologically, or in order of occurrence in time.
5. b
7. The graph suggests that the relation of price to the production of various types of goods is an important topic in the chapter. The cartoon indicates that a key concept in economic systems is cost as it is influenced by consumer choice. The picture tells you that currency as a means of exchange of goods is considered in the chapter.

EXERCISE 4
Topics: 2, 5, 6, 8, 10

EXERCISE 5
Statements: 1, 2, 4, 6, 7

Chapter 6
Focusing and Monitoring Your Learning

EXERCISE 1

1. What are the aids that help merge files? How do they function?
3. How are electromagnetic waves produced?
5. What sociological factors are related to delinuency? How are they related?
7. What has been the influence of "experts" on child-rearing practices?
9. How are physical characteristics inherited?

EXERCISE 2

1. What are the three branches of philosophical analysis?
3. How has the treatment of conflict changed?
5. What do astronomers learn about the stars by studying light?
7. Why is latent heat important?
9. Why must the electrical terminals be insulated from the housing?

EXERCISE 5

1. Interpretation, close critical analysis, evaluation is required. Reread the poem several times, annotate, record your reactions and feelings.

EXERCISE 15

1. She threw away the exam paper instead of studying it to see which items were missed and why.
3. Answers will vary. May include:
   - monitor her comprehension during study time
   - use guide questions
   - make marginal notes
   - ask connection questions
   - review frequently

PART THREE
Comprehension Skills

Chapter 7
Understanding Sentences

EXERCISE 1

1. S
3. N
5. N
7. S
9. S

EXERCISE 2

	Subject	Verb	Object
1.	sister	took	car
2.	textbook	contains	exercises
5.	storage, processing retrieval	are	—
7.	companies	issue	warranties
9.	audit	is required	—

EXERCISE 3

1. C
3. C
5. C
7. S   the Cuban economy . . . sugar
9. S   they fall . . . air

EXERCISE 7

	Core parts	Crossed out
1.	industrialization—made	in the nineteenth century
3.	we—perceive	then
5.	graphite—is made	on the other hand; like sheets of paper

EXERCISE 8

1. steel—is
3. cause—cannot be determined
5. man—has been puzzled and exasperated; teaching—has been an attempt
7. human beings—have; they—amble, stride, jog, sprint
9. anthropologists—have accumulated

EXERCISE 9

1. Multiple personality is caused by stress.
3. Some individuals do not grieve because of personality factors or in particular situations.
5. The Soviet Union is more willing and able to deliver arms faster than the United States.

EXERCISE 11

1. French involvement, American involvement
3. Compute adjusted gross and taxable income; consult a tax table
5. Hearings are held; presidential review

EXERCISE 12

1. industry—displaced
3. Crimes—are
5. currency and things—are termed

EXERCISE 13

1. Brenner has done research linking mental illness to the state of the economy.
3. Women are moving toward economic equality with men owing to their growing importance in the work force.
5. Americans earn their living differently in the twentieth century than they did in earlier times.

Chapter 8
Understanding Paragraphs

EXERCISE 1

1. b
3. c
5. a
7. c
9. b

EXERCISE 2

1. Innovative solutions to energy conservation
3. Emotional responses and information processing
5. Pattern recognition
7. Limitation of computers or human instructions for computers
9. Automated or taped radio programs

EXERCISE 3

1. Second sentence
3. Third sentence
5. First sentence
7. Second sentence
9. Third sentence

EXERCISE 4

1. b, c, e
3. a, b, c, d
5. a, b, c, d, e
7. a, c, d, e
9. a, b, e

EXERCISE 5

1. Topic: Taste
   Main Idea: Taste is poorly developed in humans.
3. Topic: Theory
   Main Idea: A theory is at first an idea, than a hypothesis, and finally a verified explanation.
5. Topic: Formal organizations
   Main Idea: Formal organizations make it possible for members of a complex society to work together.
7. Topic: Government expenditures
   Main Idea: The two types of government expenditures are direct purchases and transfer payments.
9. Topic: Information explosion or revolution in communications
   Main Idea: The information explosion, along with cultural change, has produced a society in which young people influence adults and societal standards.

EXERCISE 6

1. Topic: Growth of Congress
   Main Idea: As the United States increased in population and admitted more states, Congress grew correspondingly.
3. Topic: Probability experiments
   Main Idea: Probability experiments involve trials and outcomes.
5. Topic: Conflict in speech making
   Main Idea: There are numerous ways to establish conflict in a speech.
7. Topic: Hearing loss or stimulation deafness
   Main Idea: Temporary hearing loss can occur from a single exposure to loud sounds, and permanent loss can occur from frequent exposure.
9. Topic: Growth of plant life
   Main Idea   Plant life on earth evolved slowly, over the course of a billion years.

Chapter 9
Following Thought Patterns in Textbooks

EXERCISE 4

1. Description
3. Description or fact/statistic
5. Fact/statistic
7. Example
9. Fact/statistic

EXERCISE 5

Class	Characteristic
1. period in human development	from between puberty and maturity

3. communication media — for transmitting TV signs through cables
5. spoken or written language — that attempts to sell

EXERCISE 6 (answers may vary)

1. as soon as, next, later, before
3. second, next, finally
5. first, second, finally

EXERCISE 7

	Content	Organization
1.	both	1, 2, or 3
3.	both	1, 2, or 3
5.	similarities	3

EXERCISE 8

1, 2, 5, 6

EXERCISE 9

1. sports, fashion, cooking
3. whales, dogs, cows
5. experience, education, career goal

EXERCISE 10

1. conservation of trees; both
3. fossil damage; solutions
5. unexpected question; both

EXERCISE 11

1. Cause-effect
3. Contrast
5. Enumeration

EXERCISE 12

1. Enumeration
3. Cause-effect
5. Cause-effect
7. Definition
9. Definition

PART FOUR
Learning From Texts

Chapter 10
Reading Graphics and Technical Material

EXERCISE 1

1. There is a direct relationship between labor unions and percentage of unemployed. (1940—27% in labor unions / 15% of labor force unemployed)
3. By 1950 more than half the women in the work force were married women and by 1970 they constituted 63% of female workers. Then there was a downward trend as more single women entered the work force. However, by 1986 mar-

ried women still composed more than half of
the female work force.

EXERCISE 2
Figure 10-9.
1. To show the growth of various areas of pub-
   lishing over a period of five years.
3. Religious
5. Greatest growth has occurred in trade and professional books. Sales are increasing in most
   areas.

Figure 10-10.
1. machinery
3. machinery

Figure 10-11.
1. Marital satisfaction of wives and husbands at
   various stages of their life together.
3. Negative.
5. The postparental years are the best years for
   marital satisfaction for both wives and husbands. Childrearing years tend to be less
   satisfying.

EXERCISE 3
Figure 10-15.
1. Coca-Cola classic
3. Yes. It is easier to see at a glance where each
   brand stands in the total market scene and in
   relationship to other brands.

Figure 10-16.
1. The specific tasks of a manager's job.
3. Directing

EXERCISE 4
1. To describe the process by which the constitution can be amended.
3. a. Proposed by a national constitutional con-
      vention requested by legislature of two-
      thirds of the states and ratified by legisla-
      tures of three-fourths of states.
   b. Proposed by a national constitutional con-
      vention requested by legislatures of two-
      thirds of the states and ratified by conven-
      tions called for the purpose in three-fourths
      of the states.

EXERCISE 5
1. Differences in the marriage ceremony in different cultures.
3. Cultural differences:
   U.S.—gaiety, informal, one with community
   Southeast Asia—solemn, formal, sense of regal
   dignity, aloofness

EXERCISE 6
1. photograph
3. table, line graph
5. table

7. diagram
9. map

Chapter 13
Study and Review Strategies

EXERCISE 1
1. At one time Morris spoke of the mystery of
   why men break the very laws in which they believe. A possible explanation is that instead of
   being absolutes these social norms seem to be
   merely signposts whose elasticity would include
   killing in time of war as well as providing ref-
   uge for the captured enemy. Likewise, in the
   event of a catastrophe it is deemed by many
   that the right to private property should be set
   aside so that eveyone may receive their proper
   share of available goods. The normative system
   of a society is charistisized by flexibility; i.e.,
   it is capable of responding and changing to new
   situations.
3. (1) All bills for raising revenue begin in the
       House of Representatives. The Senate may
       offer amendments.
   (2) Having passed the House of Representa-
       tives and the Senate, every bill must be pre-
       sented to the President of the United States
       before it becomes a law; if the President
       does not sign it, he returns the bill with his
       reasons for not accepting it to the house
       from whence it came to be reconsidered.
       Then, after each house again looks at the
       bill considering the objections raised by the
       President, the bill must be accepted by two-
       thirds of both houses in order to become a
       law. Both the affirmative and negative votes
       of members of both houses shall be re-
       corded. The bill is then returned to the
       President for his signature. In the event that
       a bill is not returned to the President within
       ten days after he has reviewed it, it will be-
       come a law without his signature unless the
       bill is detained by an adjournment of Con-
       gress; then it will not become a law.

EXERCISE 9
Psychology chapter: vocabulary review step, under-
   lining step
Biology chapter: record step or outline step

PART FIVE
Classroom Performance Skills

Chapter 14
Notetaking Techniques

EXERCISE 3
Recall clues: Freud's psychoanalytic theory, associa-

tion, repression, suppression, trauma, interpretation of dreams, three parts of personality.

Questions: What is free association? What is repression? What is suppression? What is trauma? How can dreams be interpreted? What are the three parts of the personality? What does each do?

Chapter 17
Taking Exams

EXERCISE 1
1. 1, 15, 5, 50, 4

EXERCISE 2
1. less	T
3. only	F
5. most	T
7. all	T
9. more	F

EXERCISE 3
	Topic	Limiting Word(s)	Key Word
1.	trend	long-term effects	discuss
3.	Industrial Revolution	one effect	explain
5.	War of 1812	events	describe
7.	textbook chapter	approach	describe
9.	lecturer	techniques	summarize

PART SIX
Vocabulary Development

Chapter 19
Expanding Your Vocabulary

VOCABULARY QUIZ
1. Answers will vary.
2. *Random House Collegiate Dictionary* lists 135 meanings.
3. A photographer in the retina of the eye.
4. Yes
5. No.
6. A social blunder or mistake.
7. Answers will vary. Example: My uncle is a credit to our family.
8. Lacking skill, lacking strength, lacking capacity.

EXERCISE 1
1. Obscure.
3. Answers will vary: *Webster's New World Dictionary* lists seventy.
5. Addenda.

7. Best, favorable, earliest part, highest quality.
9. Failing, weakness, foible, vice.

EXERCISE 2
1. Distressed, despondent, disheartened, sorrowful, grief-stricken.
3. Explaining, discussing, describing, arguing, debating, illustrating.
5. Excellent, praiseworthy, pleasing, superior, laudable.

EXERCISE 4
Biology chapter: conduction, convection, rediation, poikilotherm, homeotherm, countercurrent mechanisms, hibernators, endotherm, ectotherm . . .

Psychology chapter: Type A behavior pattern, stress, eustress, reappraisal, general adaptation syndrome, locus of control, psychosomatic, coping, psychoneuroimmunology . . .

Chapter 20
Effective Use of Context and Word Parts

EXERCISE 1
The underlined parts should be as follows:
1. a form of government in which the people effectively participate
3. an essentially fatty acid necessary for growth and skin integrity in infants
5. able to reach comfortably to the tips of all the other fingers

EXERCISE 2
1. Close, dependent
3. Negative emotional experience
5. Fears

EXERCISE 3
1. Strong, forceful
3. Delay, put off
5. Banished, excluded from a group

EXERCISE 4
1. Brought back into favor
3. Curses, expressions of abhorrence
5. Struck out, removed

EXERCISE 5
The underlined parts should be as follows (context clues are given in parentheses):
1. the principle that the powers of government should be separated and put in the care of different parts of government (definition)
3. amble, stride, job, and sprint (example/illustration)
5. ranging from treatment as innocents to being tolerated as fools to persecution as witches (example/illustration)

EXERCISE 6

1. a. Added to
    b. Authenticity, sense of reasonableness, or correctness
    c. Mentioning, referring to
    d. Not able to satisfy
    e. Eagerly
3. a. Provide a source of income
    b. Charitable gifts
    c. Distribute
    d. Expenses, costs

EXERCISE 7

1. Not normal, deviant
3. Not logical or reasonable
5. Unchangeable, not able to reverse

EXERCISE 8

1. Below standard, unacceptable
3. Communication over distance by radio, telephone, television, etc.
5. Taking effect at a specified date in the past
7. Not part of the required course of study
9. To transfer or introduce blood into a vein
11. Dishonest or incorrect use
13. Tiresome, lacking variety
15. Having several syllables

EXERCISE 9

1. Belief in only one God
3. Historical record, narrative
5. Process of carrying or removing goods from one country to another
7. Orderly process of reasoning about the unknown
9. Competent in many features, able to change or adapt.
11. The proportion of deaths per population or region
13. Loud, noisy
15. Belonging to a corporation

EXERCISE 10

1. Using force to intimidate or control
3. Belief in comfort and pleasure as highest goals or values

5. Not able to pass, blocked
7. Not touchable
9. Questioning, examining
11. Condition of being flustered (nervous, befuddled)
13. Out of regard or respect for
15. One who is nominated to an office

EXERCISE 11

1. Psychological development of an individual in relation to his social environment
3. Disordered or impaired functioning
5. Following injury or resulting from it
7. Looking forward in time
9. A new appraisal or evaluation

PART SEVEN
Reading Efficiency Techniques

Chapter 22
Skimming and Skanning

EXERCISE 1

1. c
3. a
5. b

EXERCISE 2

1. Doctors have a responsibility to be open and honest with their patients.
3. The article describes human factors psychology and lists the requirements of good product design: affordance, visibility, and mapping.

EXERCISE 3

1. Joules.
3. Manufacturing and services.
5. Costs are higher.
7. White.
9. Relief, recovery, and reform.

References

Warren K. Agee, Philip Ault, and Edwin Emery. *Introduction to Mass Communications*, 9th ed. New York: Harper & Row, 1988.

American Heritage Dictionary of the English Language. Boston: Houghton-Mifflin, 1978.

Tom Anselmo et al. *Thinking and Writing in College.* Boston: Little Brown, 1986.

Hugh D. Barlow. *Introduction to Criminology*, 3rd ed. Boston: Little, Brown, 1984.

Sylvan Barnet and Hugo Bedau. *Current Issues and Enduring Questions.* New York: St. Martin's Press, 1987.

Lois Berman and J. C. Evans. *Exploring the Cosmos.* Boston: Little, Brown, 1986.

Ralph T. Byrns and Gerald W. Stone. *Economics*, 4th ed. Glenview, IL: Scott, Foresman, 1989.

Bernard C. Campbell. *Humankind Emerging.* Glenview, IL: Foresman, 1985.

Roger Chisholm & Marilu McCarty. *Principles of Economics.* Glenview, IL: Scott, Foresman, 1981.

James Coleman et al. *Abnormal Psychology and Modern Life*, 7th ed. Glenview, IL: Scott, Foresman, 1984.

Andrew Crider, et al. *Psychology*, 3rd ed. Glenview, IL: Scott, Foresman, 1989.

Elliot Currie & Jerome H. Skolnick. *America's Problems: Social Issues and Public Policy.* Boston: Little, Brown, 1984.

Helena Curtis. *Biology*, 4th ed. New York: Worth Publishers, 1983.

Bowman O. Davis et al. *Conceptual Human Physiology.* Columbus, OH: Charles E. Merrill, 1985.

Randall C. Decker. *Patterns of Exposition 6.* Boston: Little, Brown and Company, 1978.

Raymond A. Dumont and John M. Lannon. *Business Comunications.* Boston: Little, Brown, 1985.

Randall B. Dunham and Jon L. Pierce. *Management.* Glenview, IL: Scott, Foresman, 1989.

Douglas Ehninger et al. *Principles and Types of Speech Communication.* Glenview, IL: Scott, Foresman, 1986.

Peter K. Eisinger et al. *American Politics: The People and the Policy.* Boston: Little, Brown, 1982.

Robert B. Ekelund and Robert D. Tollison. *Economics.* Boston: Little, Brown, 1986.

Encyclopedia Americana. Danbury, Conn: Grolier, 1991.

Ross J. Eshleman and Barbara G. Cashion. *Sociology: An Introduction*, 2nd ed. Boston: Little, Brown, 1985.

John H. Ferguson and Dean E. McHenry. *The American System of Government*, 12th ed. New York: McGraw-Hill, 1973.

Barbara Schneider Fuhrmann. *Adolescence, Adolescents.* Boston: Little, Brown, 1986.

Martin J. Gannon. *Management: An Organizational Perspective.* Boston: Little, Brown, 1977.

E. Thomas Garman et al. *Personal Finance.* Boston: Houghton Mifflin. 1985.

Peter Haggett. *Geography: A Modern Synthesis*, rev. 3rd ed. New York: HarperCollins, 1983.

Thomas Hardy. "The Darkling Thrush" in *The Norton Anthology of Modern Poetry.* Richard Ellmann and Robert O'Clair, eds. New York: Norton, 1973.

Paul B. Hewitt. *Conceptual Physics*, 5th ed. Boston: Little, Brown, 1985.

Michael C. Howard. *Contemporary Cultural Anthropology.* Boston: Little, Brown, 1986.

Sarah O. Jewett. "A White Heron" in *The American Tradition in Literature*, 6th ed. George Perkins, et al. eds. New York: Random House, 1985.

Walter S. Jones. *The Logic of International Relations.* Boston: Little, Brown, 1985.

Thomas C. Kinnear and Kenneth L. Bernhardt. *Principles of Marketing.* Glenview, IL: Scott, Foresman, 1986.

Watson M. Laetsch. *Plants: Basic Concepts in Botany.* Boston: Little, Brown, 1979.

Jack Levin and James L. Spates. *Starting Sociology*, 4th ed. New York: HarperCollins, 1990.

Robert L. Lineberry. *Government in America*, 3rd ed. Boston: Little, Brown, 1986.

Paul R. Lohnes and William W. Cooley. *Introduction to Statistical Procedures.* New York: John Wiley and Sons, 1968.

Marilu Hurt McCarty. *Dollars and Sense: An Introduction to Economics.* Glenview, IL: Scott, Foresman, 1985.

Donald L. Macmillan. *Mental Retardation in School and Society.* Boston: Little, Brown, 1982.

Charles D. Miller and Vern H. Heeren. *Mathematical Ideas.* Glenview, IL: Scott, Foresman, 1986.

Frederic S. Mishkin. *The Economics of Money, and Financial Markets.* Boston: Little, Brown, 1986.

Gary Nash et al. *American People*, 2nd ed. New York: HarperCollins, 1990.

Kenneth J. Neubeck. *Social Problems: A Critical Approach.* Glenview, IL: Scott, Foresman, 1979.

Sydney B. Newell. *Chemistry.* Boston: Little, Brown and Company, 1977.

Robert C. Nickerson. *Fundamentals of Structured Cobol.* Boston: Little, Brown, 1984.

John and Erna Perry. *Face to Face: The Individual and Social Problems.* Boston: Little, Brown, 1976.

Hal B. Pickle and Royce L. Abrahamson. *Introduction to Business.* Glenview, IL: Scott, Foresman, 1986.

Adele Pillitteri. *Maternal-Newborn Nursing.* Boston: Little, Brown, 1985.

Adele Pillitteri. *Nursing Care of the Growing Family.* Boston: Little, Brown and Company, 1976.

Henry L. Roediger III et al. *Psychology.* Boston: Little, Brown, 1987.

Frederick Ruso and Charles Kirkpatrick. *Marketing.* Boston: Little, Brown, 1982.

Norman Sigband and Arthur Bell. *Communication for Management and Business,* 5th ed. Glenview, IL: Scott, Foresman, 1989.

Gresham M. Sykes and David Matza. *American Sociological Review,* 22 (1957), pp. 666–670. In Delos H. Kelly, *Deviant Behavior,* 3rd ed. New York: St. Martin's Press, 1989.

Andrew D. Szilagyi, Jr. and Marc J. Wallace, Jr. *Organizational Behavior and Performance.* Glenview, IL: Scott, Foresman, 1987.

Barbara Upton with John Upton. *Photography* Boston: Little, Brown, 1985.

Carole Wade and Carol Tavris. *Psychology.* 2nd ed. New York: HarperCollins, 1990.

Robert A. Wallace. *Biology: The World of Life,* 5th ed. Glenview, IL: Scott, Foresman, 1987.

T. Walter Wallbank et al. *Civilization Past and Present.* Vol. 2. Glenview, IL: Scott, Foresman, 1987.

Gary Wasserman. *The Basics of American Politics.* Boston: Little, Brown, 1985.

Richard L. Weaver III. *Understanding Inter-Personal Communication.* Glenview, IL: Scott, Foresman, 1987.

O. G. Wilson and Roy C. McLaren. *Police Administration,* 3rd ed. New York: McGraw-Hill, 1972.

Burton Wright and John P. Weiss. *Social Problems.* Boston: Little, Brown, 1980.

Philip G. Zimbardo. *Psychology and Life,* 12th ed. Glenview, IL: Scott, Foresman, 1985.

Endnotes

CHAPTER 4

1. Levin and Spates, *Starting Sociology,* 4th ed., pp. 3–4.
2. Eshleman and Cashion, *Sociology—An Introduction,* p. vii.
3. Currie and Skolnick, *America's Problems,* 2nd ed., pp. iii–iv.

CHAPTER 7

1. Mishkin, *The Economics of Money, Banking, and Financial Markets,* p. 51.
2. Nickerson, *Fundamentals of Structured Cobol,* p. 8.

3. Perry and Perry, *Face to Face: The Individual and Social Problems,* p. 63.
4. Garmen et al., *Personal Finance,* p. 367.
5. Pillitteri, *Maternal-Newborn Nursing,* p. 312.
6. Campbell, *Humankind Emerging,* p. 45.
7. Campbell, p. 1.
8. MacMillan, *Mental Retardation in the School and Society,* p. 34.
9. Campbell, p. 45.
10. Campbell, p. 118.
11. Campbell, p. 119.
12. Campbell, p. 120.
13. Jones, *The Logic of International Relations,* p. 29.
14. Coleman and Butcher, *Abnormal Psychology and Normal Life,* p. 160.
15. Currie and Skolnick, *American's Problems; Social Issues and Public Policy,* p. 188.
16. Jones, p. 314.
17. Jones, p. 5.
18. Barlow, *Introduction to Criminology,* p. 422.
19. Chisholm and McCarty, *Principles of Economics,* p. 138.
20. Jones, p. 248.
21. Currie and Skolnick, p. 206.
22. Currie and Skolnick, p. 294.

CHAPTER 10

1. Wade and Tavris, p. 175.
2. Nash, et al., p. A–30.
3. Nash, et al., p. A–30.
4. Sigband and Bell, p. 353.
5. Byrns and Stone, p. 591.
6. Sigband and Bell, p. 349.
7. Crider, et al., p. 555.
8. Agee, Ault, and Emery, p. 184.
9. Dunham and Pierce, p. 185.
10. Crider, et al., p. 389.
11. Kinnear and Bernhardt, p. 634.
12. Szilagyi, p. 519.
13. Sigband and Bell, p. 353.
14. Sigband and Bell, Exhibit I.
15. Szilagyi, p. 6.
16. Wallace, p. 321.
17. Lineberry, p. 100.
18. Haggett, p. 130.
19. Levin, p. 229.
20. Jewett, p. 671.
21. Hardy, p. 50.
22. *Encyclopedia Americana.*
23. Wallace, pp. 237–238.

CHAPTER 20

1. Newell, *Chemistry,* p. 17.
2. Newell, p. 41.
3. Campbell, *Humankind Emerging,* p. 3.
4. Campbell, p. 107.
5. Wasserman, *The Basics of American Politics,* p. 25.
6. Wasserman, p. 8.
7. Newell, p. 43.

8. Pillitteri, *Nursing Care of the Growing Family*, p. 280.
9. Newell, p. 45.
10. Campbell, p. 21.
11. Gannon, *Management: An Organizational Perspective*, p. 20.
12. Decker, *Patterns of Exposition 6*, p. 9.
13. MacMillan, *Mental Retardation in the School and Society*, p. 5.

14. Campbell, p. 189.
15. Wasserman, p. 33.
16. Newell, p. 388.
17. Campbell, p. 16.
18. Wasserman, p. 87.
19. MacMillan, p. 11.

Credits

Warren K. Agee, Phillip H. Ault, and Edwin Emery, *Introduction to Mass Communications,* 9th ed. Copyright © 1988 by Harper & Row, Publishers, Inc. Reprinted by permission of HarperCollins Publishers.

Hugh D. Barlow, *Introduction to Criminology,* 3rd ed. Copyright © 1984 by Hugh D. Barlow. Published by HarperCollins Publishers.

Lois Berman and J. C. Evans, *Exploring the Cosmos.* Copyright © 1986 by J. C. Evans. Published by HarperCollins Publishers.

Sissela Bok, "To Lie or Not to Lie—The Doctor's Dilemma." Copyright © 1978 by The New York Times Company. Reprinted by permission.

Ralph T. Byrns and Gerald W. Stone, *Economics,* 4th ed. Copyright © 1989, 1987, 1984, 1981 by HarperCollins Publishers.

Bernard C. Campbell, *Humankind Emerging.* Copyright © 1985 by Bernard C. Campbell. Published by HarperCollins Publishers.

Roger Chisholm and Marilu McCarty, *Principles of Economics.* Copyright © 1987 by HarperCollins Publishers.

James C. Coleman, James N. Butcher, and Robert C. Carson, *Abnormal Psychology and Modern Life,* 7th ed. Copyright © 1984 by HarperCollins Publishers.

Elliott Currie and Jerome H. Skolnick, *America's Problems: Social Issues and Public Policy.* Copyright © 1984 by Elliott Currie and Jerome H. Skolnick. Published by HarperCollins Publishers.

Helena Curtis, *Biology,* 4th ed. New York: Worth Publishers, 1983. Reprinted by permission.

Bowman O. Davis et al., *Conceptual Human Physiology.* Columbus, OH: Charles E. Merrill, 1985.

Randall B. Dunham and Jon L. Pierce. Copyright © 1989 by Randall B. Dunham and Jon L. Pierce. Published by HarperCollins Publishers.

Douglas Ehninger et al., *Principles and Types of Speech Communication.* Copyright © 1986 by HarperCollins Publishers.

Robert B. Ekelund, Jr. and Robert D. Tollison, *Economics.* Copyright © 1986 by Robert B. Ekelund, Jr. and Robert D. Tollison. Published by HarperCollins Publishers.

Encyclopedia Americana. Danbury, Conn.: Grolier, 1991. Reprinted by permission.

Wolfram von Eschenbach, *Parzival.* Translated and with an introduction by Helen M. Mustard and Charles E. Passage. Copyright © 1961 by Helen M. Mustard and Charles E. Passage. Reprinted by permission of Vintage Books, a Division of Random House.

Ross Eshleman and Barbara G. Cashion, *Sociology: An Introduction,* 2nd ed. Copyright © 1985 by Ross Eshleman and Barbara G. Cashion. Published by HarperCollins Publishers.

James Geiwitz, *Looking at Ourselves: An Introduction to Psychology.* Copyright © 1976 by Little, Brown and Company. Reprinted by permission of the author.

Peter Haggett, *Geography: A Modern Synthesis,* rev. 3rd ed. Copyright © 1983 by Peter Haggett. Published by HarperCollins Publishers.

Thomas Hardy, "The Darkling Thrush" in *The Norton Anthology of Modern Poetry.* Richard Ellmann and Robert O'Clair, eds. New York: Norton, 1973. Reprinted by permission.

Paul B. Hewitt, *Conceptual Physics,* 5th ed. Copyright © 1985 by Paul B. Hewitt. Published by HarperCollins Publishers.

Michael C. Howard, *Contemporary Cultural Anthropology.* Copyright © 1986 by Michael C. Howard. Published by HarperCollins Publishers.

Sarah O. Jewitt, "A White Heron" in *The American Tradition in Literature,* 6th ed. George Perkins et al., eds. New York: Random House, 1985.

Walter S. Jones, *The Logic of International Relations.* Copyright © 1985 by Walter S. Jones. Published by HarperCollins Publishers.

Thomas C. Kinnear and Kenneth L. Bernhardt. *Principles of Marketing.* Copyright © 1986 by HarperCollins Publishers.

Jack Levin and James L. Spates, *Starting Sociology,* 4th ed. Copyright © 1990 by Jack Levin and James L. Spates. Reprinted by permission of HarperCollins Publishers.

Robert L. Lineberry, *Government in America,* 3rd ed. Copyright © 1990 by Robert L. Lineberry. Published by HarperCollins Publishers.

Marketing Division at Coca-Cola. Reprinted by permission of Coca-Cola USA.

Charles D. Miller and Vern H. Heeren, *Mathematical Ideas.* Copyright © 1986 by HarperCollins Publishers.

Maxwell M. Mozell et al., "Nasal chemoreception in flavor identification" in *Archives of Otolaryngology,* 90, p. 371. Copyright © 1969 by the American Medical Association. Reprinted by permission.

Gary B. Nash et al., *The American People: Creating a Nation and a Society,* 2nd ed., edited by Gary B. Nash. Copyright © 1990 by Harper & Row, Publishers. Reprinted by permission of HarperCollins Publishers.

Robert B. Nickerson, *Fundamentals of Structured Cobol.* Copyright © 1984 by Robert C. Nickerson. Published by HarperCollins Publishers.

Hal P. Pickle and Royce L. Abrahamson, *Introduction to Business.* Copyright © 1986 by HarperCollins Publishers.

Henry L. Roediger III et al., *Psychology.* Copyright © 1987 by Henry L. Roediger III, J. Philippe Rushton, Elizabeth D. Capaldi, and Scott G. Paris. Published by HarperCollins Publishers.

Roget's International Thesaurus, 4th ed., edited by Robert L. Chapman. Copyright © 1977 by Robert L. Chapman. Reprinted by permission of HarperCollins Publishers.

B. C. Rollins and H. Feldman, "Marital Satisfaction Over the Family Life Cycle" in *Journal of Marriage and the Family,* Vol. 32, No. 1, February 1970 by the National Council on Family Relations, 3989 Central Ave., Suite #550, Minneapolis, MN 55421. Reprinted by permission.

Norman B. Sigband and Arthur H. Bell, *Communication for Management and Business,* 5th ed. Copyright © 1989, 1986, 1982, 1976 by HarperCollins Publishers.

Gresham M. Sykes and David Matza, *American Sociological Review,* 22 (1957), pp. 666–670. In Delos H. Kelly, *Deviant Behavior,* 3rd ed. New York: St. Martins Press, 1989.

Andrew D. Szilagyi, Jr., *Management and Performance.* Copyright © 1988, 1984, 1981 by HarperCollins Publishers.

Andrew D. Szilagyi, Jr. and Marc J. Wallace, Jr., *Organizational Behavior and Performance.* Copyright © 1987 by HarperCollins Publishers.

"A Good Word for Bad Words" in *Time,* December 14, 1981. Copyright © 1981 by Time Warner Inc. All rights reserved. Reprinted by permission.

Mental Health, United States, ed. by Carl A. Taube and Sally A. Barrett. U.S. Department of Health and Human Services. DHHS Publication No. (ADM) 85-1378, 1985.

Carole Wade and Carol Tavris, *Psychology,* 2nd ed. Copyright © 1989 by Harper & Row, Publishers, Inc. Reprinted by permission of HarperCollins Publishers.

Robert A. Wallace, *Biology: The World of Life,* 5th ed. Copyright © 1990, 1987, 1981 by HarperCollins Publishers.

T. Walter Wallbank et al., *Civilization Past and Present,* Volume 2. Copyright © 1987 by HarperCollins Publishers.

Gary Wasserman, *The Basics of American Politics.* Copyright © 1985 by Gary Wasserman. Published by HarperCollins Publishers.

Richard L. Weaver III, *Understanding Interpersonal Communication.* Copyright © 1987 by HarperCollins Publishers.

Phillip G. Zimbardo, *Psychology and Life,* 12th ed. Copyright © 1988 by Phillip G. Zimbardo. Published by HarperCollins Publishers.

Photo Credits

Note: Some photos are slightly different from those originally appearing in Wade/Tavris, *Psychology,* and Curtis, *Biology.*

Page 421: © Tim Peters/Picture Group

Page 422: Wide World Photos

Page 424 (left): © Enrico Ferorelli; (right) © Allen Green/Photo Researchers

Page 426: Lennart Nilsson/Boehringer Ingelheim International

Page 428: © Paul Fusco/Magnum

Page 431: © George Zimbel/Monkmeyer Press

Page 433: Drawing by Koren, © 1984 The New Yorker Magazine Inc.

Pages 434, 435: Culver

Page 438: © Paolo Koch/Photo Researchers

Page 440: Focus on Sports

Pages 442, 443: National Baseball Library, Cooperstown, NY

Page 446: © Roy Roper/Picture Group

Page 448: Film Stills Archive, Museum of Modern Art

Page 449: Culver

Page 458: (a) Grant Heilman; (b) Jen and Des Bartlett/Photo Researchers; (c) after Gordon, *op. cit.*

Page 459: After Gordon, *op. cit.*

Page 460: (a) Jack Dermid

Page 461: After Schmidt-Nielsen, *op. cit.*

Page 462: (a) Ron Garrison, San Diego Zoo; (b) L. L. Rue III, Bruce Coleman; (c) L. L. Rue III, National Audubon Society Collection/PR

Page 464: (a) Spider, C. D. Marvin Winter; (b) George Daniell/Photo Researchers

Page 465: (a) Nicholas Mrosovsky; (b) L. L. Rue III, National Audubon Society Collection/PR; (c) Yvon Le Maho

Page 466: Phyllis McCutcheon Mithassel/Photo Researchers

Page 468: Dominique Reger, UNESCO

Index